Lecture Notes in Computer Science 5623

Commenced Publication in 1973
Founding and Former Series Editors:
Gerhard Goos, Juris Hartmanis, and Jan van Leeuwen

Editorial Board

Nuray Aykin (Ed.)

Internationalization, Design and Global Development

Third International Conference, IDGD 2009
Held as Part of HCI International 2009
San Diego, CA, USA, July 19-24, 2009
Proceedings

 Springer

Volume Editor

Nuray Aykin
Human Factors International, Inc.
Keyport, NJ 07735, USA
E-mail: naykin@att.net

Library of Congress Control Number: Applied for

CR Subject Classification (1998): H.5.2, H.5.3, H.3-5, C.2, K.4, D.2, K.6

LNCS Sublibrary: SL 3 – Information Systems and Application, incl. Internet/Web
and HCI

ISSN   0302-9743
ISBN-10   3-642-02766-0 Springer Berlin Heidelberg New York
ISBN-13   978-3-642-02766-6 Springer Berlin Heidelberg New York

springer.com

© Springer-Verlag Berlin Heidelberg 2009
Printed in Germany

Typesetting: Camera-ready by author, data conversion by Scientific Publishing Services, Chennai, India
Printed on acid-free paper   SPIN: 12708765   06/3180   5 4 3 2 1 0

Foreword

The 13th International Conference on Human–Computer Interaction, HCI International 2009, was held in San Diego, California, USA, July 19–24, 2009, jointly with the Symposium on Human Interface (Japan) 2009, the 8th International Conference on Engineering Psychology and Cognitive Ergonomics, the 5th International Conference on Universal Access in Human-Computer Interaction, the Third International Conference on Virtual and Mixed Reality, the Third International Conference on Internationalization, Design and Global Development, the Third International Conference on Online Communities and Social Computing, the 5th International Conference on Augmented Cognition, the Second International Conference on Digital Human Modeling, and the First International Conference on Human Centered Design.

A total of 4,348 individuals from academia, research institutes, industry and governmental agencies from 73 countries submitted contributions, and 1,397 papers that were judged to be of high scientific quality were included in the program. These papers address the latest research and development efforts and highlight the human aspects of the design and use of computing systems. The papers accepted for presentation thoroughly cover the entire field of human–computer interaction, addressing major advances in knowledge and effective use of computers in a variety of application areas.

This volume, edited by Nuray Aykin, contains papers in the thematic area of Internationalization, Design and Global Development, addressing the following major topics:

- Cross-cultural User Interface Design
- Culture, Community, Collaboration and Learning
- Internationalization and Usability
- ICT for Global Development
- Designing for eCommerce, eBusiness and eBanking

The remaining volumes of the HCI International 2009 proceedings are:

- Volume 1, LNCS 5610, Human–Computer Interaction—New Trends (Part I), edited by Julie A. Jacko
- Volume 2, LNCS 5611, Human–Computer Interaction—Novel Interaction Methods and Techniques (Part II), edited by Julie A. Jacko
- Volume 3, LNCS 5612, Human–Computer Interaction—Ambient, Ubiquitous and Intelligent Interaction (Part III), edited by Julie A. Jacko
- Volume 4, LNCS 5613, Human–Computer Interaction—Interacting in Various Application Domains (Part IV), edited by Julie A. Jacko
- Volume 5, LNCS 5614, Universal Access in Human–Computer Interaction—Addressing Diversity (Part I), edited by Constantine Stephanidis

- Volume 6, LNCS 5615, Universal Access in Human–Computer Interaction—Intelligent and Ubiquitous Interaction Environments (Part II), edited by Constantine Stephanidis
- Volume 7, LNCS 5616, Universal Access in Human–Computer Interaction—Applications and Services (Part III), edited by Constantine Stephanidis
- Volume 8, LNCS 5617, Human Interface and the Management of Information—Designing Information Environments (Part I), edited by Michael J. Smith and Gavriel Salvendy
- Volume 9, LNCS 5618, Human Interface and the Management of Information—Information and Interaction (Part II), edited by Gavriel Salvendy and Michael J. Smith
- Volume 10, LNCS 5619, Human Centered Design, edited by Masaaki Kurosu
- Volume 11, LNCS 5620, Digital Human Modeling, edited by Vincent G. Duffy
- Volume 12, LNCS 5621, Online Communities and Social Computing, edited by A. Ant Ozok and Panayiotis Zaphiris
- Volume 13, LNCS 5622, Virtual and Mixed Reality, edited by Randall Shumaker
- Volume 15, LNCS 5624, Ergonomics and Health Aspects of Work with Computers, edited by Ben-Tzion Karsh
- Volume 16, LNAI 5638, The Foundations of Augmented Cognition: Neuro-ergonomics and Operational Neuroscience, edited by Dylan Schmorrow, Ivy Estabrooke and Marc Grootjen
- Volume 17, LNAI 5639, Engineering Psychology and Cognitive Ergonomics, edited by Don Harris

I would like to thank the Program Chairs and the members of the Program Boards of all thematic areas, listed below, for their contribution to the highest scientific quality and the overall success of HCI International 2009 Conference.

Ergonomics and Health Aspects of Work with Computers

Program Chair: Ben-Tzion Karsh

Arne Aarås, Norway
Pascale Carayon, USA
Barbara G.F. Cohen, USA
Wolfgang Friesdorf, Germany
John Gosbee, USA
Martin Helander, Singapore
Ed Israelski, USA
Waldemar Karwowski, USA
Peter Kern, Germany
Danuta Koradecka, Poland
Kari Lindström, Finland

Holger Luczak, Germany
Aura C. Matias, Philippines
Kyung (Ken) Park, Korea
Michelle M. Robertson, USA
Michelle L. Rogers, USA
Steven L. Sauter, USA
Dominique L. Scapin, France
Naomi Swanson, USA
Peter Vink, The Netherlands
John Wilson, UK
Teresa Zayas-Cabán, USA

Human Interface and the Management of Information

Program Chair: Michael J. Smith

Gunilla Bradley, Sweden
Hans-Jörg Bullinger, Germany
Alan Chan, Hong Kong
Klaus-Peter Fähnrich, Germany
Michitaka Hirose, Japan
Jhilmil Jain, USA
Yasufumi Kume, Japan
Mark Lehto, USA
Fiona Fui-Hoon Nah, USA
Shogo Nishida, Japan
Robert Proctor, USA
Youngho Rhee, Korea

Anxo Cereijo Roibás, UK
Katsunori Shimohara, Japan
Dieter Spath, Germany
Tsutomu Tabe, Japan
Alvaro D. Taveira, USA
Kim-Phuong L. Vu, USA
Tomio Watanabe, Japan
Sakae Yamamoto, Japan
Hidekazu Yoshikawa, Japan
Li Zheng, P.R. China
Bernhard Zimolong, Germany

Human–Computer Interaction

Program Chair: Julie A. Jacko

Sebastiano Bagnara, Italy
Sherry Y. Chen, UK
Marvin J. Dainoff, USA
Jianming Dong, USA
John Eklund, Australia
Xiaowen Fang, USA
Ayse Gurses, USA
Vicki L. Hanson, UK
Sheue-Ling Hwang, Taiwan
Wonil Hwang, Korea
Yong Gu Ji, Korea
Steven Landry, USA

Gitte Lindgaard, Canada
Chen Ling, USA
Yan Liu, USA
Chang S. Nam, USA
Celestine A. Ntuen, USA
Philippe Palanque, France
P.L. Patrick Rau, P.R. China
Ling Rothrock, USA
Guangfeng Song, USA
Steffen Staab, Germany
Wan Chul Yoon, Korea
Wenli Zhu, P.R. China

Engineering Psychology and Cognitive Ergonomics

Program Chair: Don Harris

Guy A. Boy, USA
John Huddlestone, UK
Kenji Itoh, Japan
Hung-Sying Jing, Taiwan
Ron Laughery, USA
Wen-Chin Li, Taiwan
James T. Luxhøj, USA

Nicolas Marmaras, Greece
Sundaram Narayanan, USA
Mark A. Neerincx, The Netherlands
Jan M. Noyes, UK
Kjell Ohlsson, Sweden
Axel Schulte, Germany
Sarah C. Sharples, UK

Neville A. Stanton, UK
Xianghong Sun, P.R. China
Andrew Thatcher, South Africa

Matthew J.W. Thomas, Australia
Mark Young, UK

Universal Access in Human–Computer Interaction

Program Chair: Constantine Stephanidis

Julio Abascal, Spain
Ray Adams, UK
Elisabeth André, Germany
Margherita Antona, Greece
Chieko Asakawa, Japan
Christian Bühler, Germany
Noelle Carbonell, France
Jerzy Charytonowicz, Poland
Pier Luigi Emiliani, Italy
Michael Fairhurst, UK
Dimitris Grammenos, Greece
Andreas Holzinger, Austria
Arthur I. Karshmer, USA
Simeon Keates, Denmark
Georgios Kouroupetroglou, Greece
Sri Kurniawan, USA

Patrick M. Langdon, UK
Seongil Lee, Korea
Zhengjie Liu, P.R. China
Klaus Miesenberger, Austria
Helen Petrie, UK
Michael Pieper, Germany
Anthony Savidis, Greece
Andrew Sears, USA
Christian Stary, Austria
Hirotada Ueda, Japan
Jean Vanderdonckt, Belgium
Gregg C. Vanderheiden, USA
Gerhard Weber, Germany
Harald Weber, Germany
Toshiki Yamaoka, Japan
Panayiotis Zaphiris, UK

Virtual and Mixed Reality

Program Chair: Randall Shumaker

Pat Banerjee, USA
Mark Billinghurst, New Zealand
Charles E. Hughes, USA
David Kaber, USA
Hirokazu Kato, Japan
Robert S. Kennedy, USA
Young J. Kim, Korea
Ben Lawson, USA

Gordon M. Mair, UK
Miguel A. Otaduy, Switzerland
David Pratt, UK
Albert "Skip" Rizzo, USA
Lawrence Rosenblum, USA
Dieter Schmalstieg, Austria
Dylan Schmorrow, USA
Mark Wiederhold, USA

Internationalization, Design and Global Development

Program Chair: Nuray Aykin

Michael L. Best, USA
Ram Bishu, USA
Alan Chan, Hong Kong
Andy M. Dearden, UK

Susan M. Dray, USA
Vanessa Evers, The Netherlands
Paul Fu, USA
Emilie Gould, USA

Sung H. Han, Korea
Veikko Ikonen, Finland
Esin Kiris, USA
Masaaki Kurosu, Japan
Apala Lahiri Chavan, USA
James R. Lewis, USA
Ann Light, UK
James J.W. Lin, USA
Rungtai Lin, Taiwan
Zhengjie Liu, P.R. China
Aaron Marcus, USA
Allen E. Milewski, USA

Elizabeth D. Mynatt, USA
Oguzhan Ozcan, Turkey
Girish Prabhu, India
Kerstin Röse, Germany
Eunice Ratna Sari, Indonesia
Supriya Singh, Australia
Christian Sturm, Spain
Adi Tedjasaputra, Singapore
Kentaro Toyama, India
Alvin W. Yeo, Malaysia
Chen Zhao, P.R. China
Wei Zhou, P.R. China

Online Communities and Social Computing

Program Chairs: A. Ant Ozok, Panayiotis Zaphiris

Chadia N. Abras, USA
Chee Siang Ang, UK
Amy Bruckman, USA
Peter Day, UK
Fiorella De Cindio, Italy
Michael Gurstein, Canada
Tom Horan, USA
Anita Komlodi, USA
Piet A.M. Kommers, The Netherlands
Jonathan Lazar, USA
Stefanie Lindstaedt, Austria

Gabriele Meiselwitz, USA
Hideyuki Nakanishi, Japan
Anthony F. Norcio, USA
Jennifer Preece, USA
Elaine M. Raybourn, USA
Douglas Schuler, USA
Gilson Schwartz, Brazil
Sergei Stafeev, Russia
Charalambos Vrasidas, Cyprus
Cheng-Yen Wang, Taiwan

Augmented Cognition

Program Chair: Dylan D. Schmorrow

Andy Bellenkes, USA
Andrew Belyavin, UK
Joseph Cohn, USA
Martha E. Crosby, USA
Tjerk de Greef, The Netherlands
Blair Dickson, UK
Traci Downs, USA
Julie Drexler, USA
Ivy Estabrooke, USA
Cali Fidopiastis, USA
Chris Forsythe, USA
Wai Tat Fu, USA
Henry Girolamo, USA

Marc Grootjen, The Netherlands
Taro Kanno, Japan
Wilhelm E. Kincses, Germany
David Kobus, USA
Santosh Mathan, USA
Rob Matthews, Australia
Dennis McBride, USA
Robert McCann, USA
Jeff Morrison, USA
Eric Muth, USA
Mark A. Neerincx, The Netherlands
Denise Nicholson, USA
Glenn Osga, USA

Dennis Proffitt, USA
Leah Reeves, USA
Mike Russo, USA
Kay Stanney, USA
Roy Stripling, USA
Mike Swetnam, USA
Rob Taylor, UK

Maria L.Thomas, USA
Peter-Paul van Maanen, The Netherlands
Karl van Orden, USA
Roman Vilimek, Germany
Glenn Wilson, USA
Thorsten Zander, Germany

Digital Human Modeling

Program Chair: Vincent G. Duffy

Karim Abdel-Malek, USA
Thomas J. Armstrong, USA
Norm Badler, USA
Kathryn Cormican, Ireland
Afzal Godil, USA
Ravindra Goonetilleke, Hong Kong
Anand Gramopadhye, USA
Sung H. Han, Korea
Lars Hanson, Sweden
Pheng Ann Heng, Hong Kong
Tianzi Jiang, P.R. China

Kang Li, USA
Zhizhong Li, P.R. China
Timo J. Määttä, Finland
Woojin Park, USA
Matthew Parkinson, USA
Jim Potvin, Canada
Rajesh Subramanian, USA
Xuguang Wang, France
John F. Wiechel, USA
Jingzhou (James) Yang, USA
Xiu-gan Yuan, P.R. China

Human Centered Design

Program Chair: Masaaki Kurosu

Gerhard Fischer, USA
Tom Gross, Germany
Naotake Hirasawa, Japan
Yasuhiro Horibe, Japan
Minna Isomursu, Finland
Mitsuhiko Karashima, Japan
Tadashi Kobayashi, Japan

Kun-Pyo Lee, Korea
Loïc Martínez-Normand, Spain
Dominique L. Scapin, France
Haruhiko Urokohara, Japan
Gerrit C. van der Veer, The Netherlands
Kazuhiko Yamazaki, Japan

In addition to the members of the Program Boards above, I also wish to thank the following volunteer external reviewers: Gavin Lew from the USA, Daniel Su from the UK, and Ilia Adami, Ioannis Basdekis, Yannis Georgalis, Panagiotis Karampelas, Iosif Klironomos, Alexandros Mourouzis, and Stavroula Ntoa from Greece.

This conference could not have been possible without the continuous support and advice of the Conference Scientific Advisor, Prof. Gavriel Salvendy, as well as the dedicated work and outstanding efforts of the Communications Chair and Editor of HCI International News, Abbas Moallem.

I would also like to thank for their contribution toward the organization of the HCI International 2009 conference the members of the Human–Computer Interaction Laboratory of ICS-FORTH, and in particular Margherita Antona, George Paparoulis, Maria Pitsoulaki, Stavroula Ntoa, and Maria Bouhli.

Constantine Stephanidis

HCI International 2011

The 14th International Conference on Human–Computer Interaction, HCI International 2011, will be held jointly with the affiliated conferences in the summer of 2011. It will cover a broad spectrum of themes related to human–computer interaction, including theoretical issues, methods, tools, processes and case studies in HCI design, as well as novel interaction techniques, interfaces and applications. The proceedings will be published by Springer. More information about the topics, as well as the venue and dates of the conference, will be announced through the HCI International Conference series website: http://www.hci-international.org/

General Chair
Professor Constantine Stephanidis
University of Crete and ICS-FORTH
Heraklion, Crete, Greece
Email: cs@ics.forth.gr

Table of Contents

Part I: Cross-Cultural User Interface Design

Part II: Culture, Community, Collaboration and Learning

Part III: Internationalisation and Usability

Part IV: ICT for Global Development

Part V: Designing for E-Commerce, E-Business and E-Banking

Part I

Cross-Cultural User Interface Design

Identifying and Measuring Cultural Differences in Cross-Cultural User-Interface Design

Jasem M. Alostath[1], Sanaa Almoumen[2], and Ahmad B. Alostath[3]

[1,2] Department of Computer Science & Information Systems, Collage of Business Studies
jm.alostad@paaet.edu.kw, sh.almoumen@paaet.edu.kw
[3] Computer Department, The Telecommunication And Navigation Institute
PAAET, Kuwait, P.O. Box 23167, Safat, 13092, Kuwait
ab.alostath@paaet.edu.kw

Abstract. This paper is investigating the role of culture in cross-cultural user interface design, and particularly focused on e-banking user-interface design. The results of this research are presented in two phases. The first phase is focused on the development of a cultural model that has some HCI factors. The second phase introduces the Cross-Use experiment that aims to evaluate the mapping between website design elements and cultural attributes using a user-in-context evaluation approach. This is done by developing three User Interface designs, and applying them to 63 local participants from the case study cultures (Brazil, Kuwait, Egypt, and UK). The experiment was conducted using the developed prototypes was able to classify cultures differently, and highlighted those design markers that affects cultural differences in the design of e-banking websites. This is based on user preferences and usability.

Keywords: Culture, Usability, e-banking, user-in-context evaluation.

1 Introduction

The growth of internet-based software and services and the continued globalisation of businesses present new challenges for developing user-centred design. One of these challenges is how to understand and analyse cultural diversity between user groups and how to design user interfaces that accommodate this diversity. In this paper we are concerned with one particular aspect of this problem, which is how to support the design and development of usable systems across national cultures. Currently, designers are not equipped with tools that support culture-sensitive design [8, 21]. There are no guidelines yet published that guarantee international usability [10]. Many cross-cultural designs use existing websites designs in identifying cultural design differences. However, most of these designs are not supported with a cultural model, or adopt cultural models that are not design oriented for interpreting design based on culture [5, 6, 7, 8].

This paper is part of a research investigating into the role of culture in cross-cultural user interface design (Culture-Centred Design approach as an extension of user-centered design)[9], and focuses on e-banking user-interface design. The paper presents the results of a study that has been developed into two phases. The first phase

N. Aykin (Ed.): Internationalization, Design, LNCS 5623, pp. 3–12, 2009.

(see Section 3) involves the development of a cultural model that has some HCI factors based on 28 Cultural Attributes (CA) identified from cultural models literature. These attributes seems to show some relations to interface design that could present significance differences for the studied culture. The result of the first phase is in the form of design analysis that incorporates factors that play significance role in developing a cultural model for interactive interface.

In the second phase (see Section 4), the design analysis was used to design prototype websites for three countries these are Kuwait, Egypt and UK in e-banking domain. Usability studies in each of these countries were conducted, involving native users who empirically asses the level of the culture usability we have achieved. In this phase, a rigorous approach was adopted to determine whether these websites were in fact more usable or preferred by target users. We have also investigated whether websites designed for different cultures could lead to some usability problems or less preferences through the Cross-Cultural Usability experiment (phase 2).

2   Cross-Cultural Studies and Cultural Models

There are numerous approaches to the analysis of national cultural diversity from many disciplines such as psychology, sociology, and others [3]. There are also many approaches to the analysis of interface usability across cultures [5, 14]. These can be summarized as three strategic approaches. The first approach is the model-based approach that incorporates cultural models developed by other disciplines to understand the value systems, attitudes, experiences and expectations of the targeted national cultures. These models use survey and observation techniques to identify generic parameters, and determine where a particular national group is positioned in the space defined by this set of parameters (e.g., Hall [1]; Hofstede [4]; Victor [2]; and Trompenaars et al, [6]). The second approach is targeted specifically at interface design and employs inspection techniques designed for analysing interfaces that are used by particular national cultures in order to infer which interface components are particularly sensitive to cultural effects [5, 21]. The third approach is aimed at interface design and is based on user studies.

Cultural model is a set of cultural variables that is used to compare the similarities and differences between users' groups and/or cultures [3]. The cultural variable is a means of presenting the different categorizations that might cultural data contained. In this research the focus will be on national culture differences. This paper focuses on the four well-known cultural models as described by Hoft [3]. These are: Hofstede [4], Hall [1], Victor [2], and Trompennars [6]. Section 3 will show how to create a cultural model applying principles from HCI perspective.

3   Cross-Cultural Evaluation – Phase 1

As discussed earlier, most of the cultural models used within HCI research studies tend to understand and study culture based on non-HCI disciplines. In this study, we belief that in order to improve the study of culture in HCI, the creation of a model of culture that is HCI oriented is important. Therefore, this research aims to exploit these cultural models by exploring the effects of these models on UI design and usability.

3.1 Questionnaire Design and Data Collection

Questionnaire was used to collect the cultural data required to build up the cultural profile. The cultural attributes (CA) (28 CA's, see Table 1 in [9]) used in this questionnaire were derived from the cultural models founds in the literature [1-4, 6]. These specific CA's are the characteristics of CA are selected based on their suspected relation with the design of artifact UI. These CA are composed the three design dimensions model: Interaction information (I), Information or task processing (T) and Artifact-User relationship building (R) (Further details on 3-D model see [11]). The 28 (CA) are the dependent variables, while the independent variables are data such as nationality, sex, age, education, country, languages, and religion. The questionnaire was validated through a pilot study and three version on the questionnaire was developed (UK and Brazil questionnaires are in English, and Egypt and Kuwait questionnaires are in Arabic but different designs).

Table 1. Cultural Attributes

I1. Information Amount [1,2]	R1. Relationship type [1,4]
I2 Information Type [1,2]	R2. Rules expressing *and* Decision
I3. Information travelling [1,2]	making [1,3,4,5]
I6. Translation Language [2]	R3. Cultural awareness (or adaptation)
I9. Source of Information [3,4,5]	[1,2,3]
I10. Information Diffusion [3,5]	R5. User experience [5]
T1. Personal Space (Trust) [1,3,6]	R7. Communication medium [2,3,5]
T2. Task performance [1,3]	R8. New technology [2,3]
T7. Task organizational goal [3,4]	R10. Relationship symbols [2,3,4,5]
T8. Lack of expectation [1,4]	R11. Externalizing (expressing)
T10. Goal achievement speed [1,3,4]	R12. Security sensitivity [5]
T11. Task rules compliance [3,5]	R13. Credibility [1,2,3]
T12. Task medium preferred	R15. Work Quality [3,4,7,8]
T13. Information structure and navigation [3,4]	R16. Authoritativeness [2,3,4,5,7]
	R17. Gender Role [3,4,7]
	R19. Reputation [3,4,5]

Cultural profile is reporting the questionnaire data based on cultural differences. Cronbach's Alpha values shows that the questionnaire is high reliable ($\alpha = .75$, n = 709). The data collected involved 706 participants from diverse background, mainly in universities involving Kuwait (156, 22%), Egypt (303, 43%), UK (150, 21%), Brazil (97, 14%).

3.2 Results

3.2.1 Total Score for Cultural Profile

The data of participant's were entered into one-way ANOVA. The results show a significant difference among the nationalities in total score of cultural profile questionnaire ($F (3, 705) = 488.2$, $p = .000$). The result of Tukey HSD shows each nationality has significant difference with other nationalities in the total score of cultural profile questionnaire ($p > .001$). The differences among the nationalities in cultural

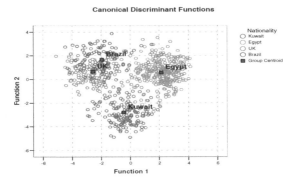

Fig. 1. Canonical Discriminant Functions plot: visualizing how two functions discriminate between groups by plotting the individual scores for the two discriminant functions.

profiles are clearly illustrated in a separate-group graph (see Fig. 1). The Discriminant Analysis (DA) Function classification result shows that it correctly classifies 89% of the cases. DA gets almost most of the Kuwaiti (94.2%), Egyptian (96.7%) and UK (86.7%) cases correctly classified. However, Brazil was less with 59.8% correctly classified and 42.2% misclassified and most of misclassified cases go with the UK (32%) and very less with other nationalities (Egypt 6.2% and Kuwait 2.1%). These results present a satisfactory DA.

3.2.2 Factor Analysis (FA) on Items of Interaction Information Dimension
The results of FA on items of interactive information shows there is just one factor in this part of cultural profiles questionnaire. All questions (I10, I2, I9, I3, and I1) of this part of the questionnaire have highly loading just in one factor. The results show there are significant difference in nationality (F (3, 706) = 56.484, p = .000) and religion (F (3, 706) = 1.456, p = .034) in mean of the factor. The Tukey HSD test shows there is no significant difference between Brazil and UK (p > .05), others are significant p =0.00.

3.2.3 Factor Analysis (FA) on Items of Information or task processing Dimension
The results of FA on items of Information processing (or task processing) shows there are three factors - *Task organizational goal, Information structure and navigation,* and *Personal Space (Trust).* The results show significant difference in nationality in factors of task processing: factor task clarity (F (3, 500) = 38.5, p = .000), task structure (F (3, 623) = 13.06, p = .000) and factor task sequence and trust (F (3, 935) = 5.31, p = .001). The Tukey HSD test for the *Task organizational goal* factor shows no significant difference between Brazil and Egypt (p > .05), while other interactions were significant (p = .000). The Tukey HSD test for the *Information structure and navigation* factor shows all nationality interactions are significant (p < .05). The Tukey HSD test for the third factor *Task Personal Space (Trust)* shows whereas there is a significant difference between Brazil and other nationalities (p < .05), other interactions were not significant (p > .05).

3.2.4 Factor Analysis on Items of Artifact-User Relationship building Dimension.

The results of FA of user-artifact UI relationship shows there are four factors in this part of cultural profiles questionnaire. These factors are: *Authoritativeness, Relationship symbols, Rules expressing and Decision making, Credibility.* The Tukey HSD test for the *Authoritativeness* factor shows whereas there is not a significant difference between Brazil and UK ($p > .05$), other interactions were statistically significant ($p = .000$). In the *Relationship and Symbols* factor, the results of Tukey HSD test show UK has significant differences with other nationalities ($p < .05$) but there are no differences among other nationalities ($p > .05$). The Tukey HSD test for the *Rules expressing and Decision making* shows there is no significant difference between Brazil and Egypt ($p > .05$). However, other interactions of nationalities were significant ($p = .000$). Finally, in the *Credibility* factor, the results of the Tukey HSD test shows whereas there is no significant difference between Brazil and UK ($p > .05$); other interactions were statistically significant ($p = .000$).

The factor analysis resulted in the identification of eight factors that play significant role in developing a cultural model for an interactive interface and these are: *Interaction information, Task organizational goal, Information structure and navigation,* and *Personal Space (Trust), Authoritativeness, Relationship symbols, Rules expressing and Decision making, Credibility.* These variables are used in the design analysis to develop a number of possible prototype websites. However, all these variables need to be culturally adapted to some degree. In order to decide between designs alternatives, a user testing approach was conducted (Phase 2).

4 Cross-Use: Cross-Cultural Usability User Evaluation – Phase 2

The design analysis results from the first phase are used to develop possible prototype websites that are culturally adapted for the Cross-Use experiment. The aim is to evaluate the mapping between website design elements and CAs using a user-in-context evaluation. The experiment design involves three national cultures, using three UIs for simple and complex tasks (3*3*2 mixed design). The prototype was developed based on the results of the design analysis. The 3 websites developed have one UI design for each culture that maximizes the cultural and genre attributes appropriate for that culture. 84 user variables are measured in this experiment (details in [9]. The experiments were conducted with 21 participants from each culture (Kuwait, UK, and Egypt) and they must be able to use the computer, internet, speak English

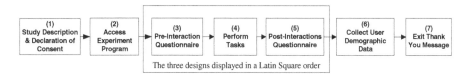

Fig. 2. Cross-Use experiment procedure

and were paid. The experiment has 7 stages (refer Fig. 2). In 1st stage, participants were given details about the three experiments. For the 2nd stage, they receives two 3-digit personal account codes and a password for them to run the experiment process and perform the online transactions. In the 3rd stage, a questionnaire was administered and during the 4th stage, participants perform 6 tasks, which are divided into 2 task groups. In the 5th stage, the participants were presented with several design layouts, and transactions processes, and were asked design questions to rank cultural design claims. Stage 6 ends the experiment. The experiment uses a laptop running (local webserver) with webcam Morae™ tasks recording tool.

The objective of the Cross-Use experiment is to substantiate the cultural design claims [9]. In order to test these objectives, several analysis methods were conducted, to examine the validity of the following hypotheses:

H1: Users will prefer the website designed for their own culture.

H2: Better usability results are achieved when websites designed for specific culture is tested by members of that culture.

H3: Using DA, it is possible to identify specific or aggregated DMs that are the main contributors to the observed user preferences and usability improvement.

The DA and Chi-Square statistical methods were used to analyse the data. DA shows the most important variables that discriminate the dependent variable or affect it, while the Chi-square is used to determine whether the groupings of cases on one variable are related to the groupings of cases on another variable.

4.1   Results

4.1.1   Cross-Cultural Design Preferences

Hypothesis (H1) predicted that when creating designs that are in accordance with cultural design claims [9], these designs are able to generate culturally sensitive designs. DA was performed with national culture as the dependent variable, and the DMs as independent variables. The results of this analysis confirmed hypothesis H1 (see Fig. 3 and Table 2). This indicates the ability of the website designs that adopted the cultural design claims to design for different cultures to capture users' preferences. The DMs that cause the cultural preference differences among specific national cultures resulting from the above DA test are shown in Table 2.

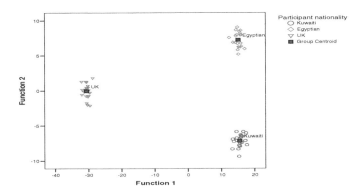

Fig. 3. Canonical Discriminant Functions plot: visualizing how the two functions discriminate between cultural groups by plotting the individual scores for the two functions

Table 2. Partial summary table for the user preferences DMs

CA	Claim	Design markers	KU	EG	UK	Related Question
R6, R7	C16	Religious Metaphors (Design A)	M	M	L	B2a (*)
T4	C21	Drop-down Menu (complex navigation)	H	M	H	A1a (*)
		Tree-view (complex navigation)	L	M	L	A1b

Legend
CA is refer to the cultural attribute code identified in the HCI-cultural model [see 10]
- Low (L): <2.49; Medium (M)=2.50..3.49; High (H): >3.49
- (*) DM identified to be significant (p<.001) based on both the DA with Univariate ANOVA tests

4.1.2 Cross-Cultural Design Usability
In this section, an investigation of a good representative score for the cultural usability factor is conducted. Then, two types of analysis are performed - Chi-square test, and DA. Chi-squared analysis shows that there is a significant relation between national culture and design usability (χ^2=19.08, df = 4, Sig. < 0.001). In Fig. 3, certain website designs are found to be more usable by certain national cultures is shown.

Discussions on validating hypothesis (H2) are based on Fig. 4, which shows a clear tendency for high usability by Kuwaiti participants in using their cultural design (design-A). But there is an exception to the hypothesis for Egypt and UK. Egyptian participants show high usability in using design-A, while UK participants have a usability score that is split between design-B and design-C. To further investigate the cause of this, in the following section, the DA is used to identify which specific variables were affecting usability scores for each of the cultures.

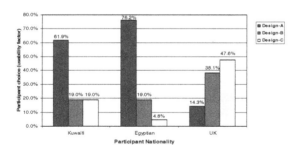

Fig. 4 The distribution graph for the usability scores according to culture and design

DA provides two types of result. The first is the classification of the three designs (A, B, and C) based on the usability factor for each case study culture (to determine the usability level on different designs). The second is in identifying the DMs, which cause usability improvements among specific national cultures as shown in Table 3. The DA results shows that the total validity of the proposed model is 100% for observations, which indicates that all cases were adequately categorized in all cultures. However, the design classification based on usability factor across cultures shows that design-A seems not to discriminate between Kuwaiti and Egyptian cultures. This confirms the results shown in Fig. 4, which stresses that at the cultural usability level, Kuwaiti and Egyptian participants show some similarities in usable DMs. This indicates that, based on usability, Kuwait and Egypt could share design-A and that the UK site (design-C) should be redesigned to have cultural DMs from design-B, in addition to design-C DMs. Thus, study hypothesis (H2) is partially confirmed for Kuwaiti culture.

Table 3. Partial summary table for cultural usability DMs

CA	Claim	Design marker	KU	EG	UK
		Relationship Metaphors			
R6, R7	C16	National Metaphors (Design B)		H†	
		Navigation tools			
T4	C21	Drop-down Menu (complex navigation)	H†		H†

Legend
† This symbol indicates that this DM affects usability for this particular culture (presenting a cultural-usability design). The result of this indicator is determined by performing DA.

The summary of DA results shown in Table 3 shows there is a clear tendency to identify specific DMs that are the main contributors to the observed participants' usability. Hence, H3 is confirmed for identifying the DMs for usability. This indicates the ability of the DA to identify the DMs that affect usability. These DMs are used as user-in-context based evidence in supporting or contradicting the cultural design claims. Reviewing the complete list of the usability DMs (see [9]) indicates that the shared DMs and cultures, based on the cultural usability factor shows that there are more shared cultural usability DMs between Kuwait and Egypt, followed with Kuwait and UK. However, between Egypt and UK, there are no shared DMs. This confirms the relation between Kuwaiti and Egyptian cultures discussed earlier.

5   Discussion and Conclusion

The general inspection of the two phases' results indicates that many CAs identified in the HCI-Cultural model affect usability, especially those attributes identified by the Factor Analysis in phase 1. The results show cultural differences when cultural attributes were transferred to design markers and tested by users from different cultures in phase 2.

The Cross-Use data analysis was presented through two models: (1) the cultural preferences model, which consists of the high level classification and DMs of cultural preferences, and (2) the cultural usability model, which consists of the high level classification and DMs of cultural usability. Both models have different concepts that require various analysis techniques, which produce diverse results and significance levels. The cultural preferences model concept was to identify whether the participants' preferences for using the three designs are different, where the experiment shows there are significant differences. This proves that the experiment designs were able to classify cultures based on participants' preferences for the DMs, which at one level substantiates the experiment design and on the other level shows that there are cultural design differences. In addition, this model shows that a high number of the identified DMs are culturally preferred, which indicates that most of the DMs can be differentiated based on participants' preferences.

The next challenge here was to see whether the usage of culturally preferred DMs in local designs improves local design usability. The cultural usability model was developed based on how the user performs the assigned six tasks. In this case the usability factor was developed to discriminate between the studied cultures. Based on this model, several issues were identified: there is a high relation between culture and design usability using the three designs. This indicates that the three designs were able to identify a relation between culture and usability, which shows that at the classification level culture preferences are able to make usable designs. However, based on the most usable design related to culture, the results show that the Egyptian culture reflects design-A as the most usable design compared to the earlier expectation, which is design-B. In addition, the UK participants shared both design-C and design-B as they are the most usable designs. Therefore, the cultural DMs based on usability are not the same as the cultural design claims. These findings motivate the investigation of cultural usability DM.

Earlier, design preferences and usability were discussed to determine their differences. Then, during the experiment evaluation, these two issues were tested using a process to evaluate users. The question here is whether the websites that have been designed based on user cultural preferences are necessarily presenting usable design. The answer to this question helps in recognizing the sensitivity of the approach in collecting data that provides results to help in delivering usable design. The study of Evers and Day [3] uses the culturally extended Technology Acceptance Model (TAM), which uses the usability variables such as usefulness, ease of use, and satisfaction to determine the UI acceptance. They use questionnaires to collect users' preferences. Their study indicates that design preferences affect interface acceptance across cultures. In the Cross-Use experiment, the general view of the design classification based on the usability factor for each culture shows higher differences on cultural preferences than usability (see [9]). This proves that participants prefer design differently, but when they use the design, it shows more differences in usability than originally expected. This highlights the complementary usage of the user-in-context evaluation in determining the usable cultural DMs.

Many website developers and evaluators use methods that assess user preferences aiming to create usable design. For example, the Cultural Markers [5], Website Audit [8], and user evaluation [10] using questionnaire based tools only are not sufficient in understanding and identifying the appropriate usability requirements. According to the results of Cross-Use experiment, as can be seen from Table 2, which presents user preferences CMs, and Table 3, which presents usability CMs, the comparison between the two markers indicates that the number of the identified markers in each type is different, and the identified markers based on preferences are not necessarily identified based on usability and vice-versa. The cultural usability model identifies fewer DMs than in the cultural preferences model. These prove that not all of the preferred DMs are necessarily usable DMs. Furthermore, the cultural usability DMs show that there are some DMs that are not shown to be preferred by the participants but are statistically proven to improve usability (e.g. Tree-view navigation DM in claim C21, as shown in Table 2 and Table 3). This suggests that research based on design preferences does not necessarily present the effects of usability as indicated by Constantine and Lockwood [4]. As a consequence, the results of such studies linking participants' preferences to design can be doubted, and this also affects the investigation of existing website design, as both adopt the same results. Therefore, the results obtained from users' preferences and usability should scale differently in supporting cultural design claims and in the later stages of the development of cultural design guidelines.

This conclusion strengthens the research results as they are obtained by evaluating both the cultural preferences and usability DMs. For the future research a detailed inspection method are expected to be used to analyse these results together with results of earlier research studies, which aims at developing evidence-based cultural design guidelines and recommendations.

References

1. MacKenzie, S.: Research Note: Within-subjects vs. Between-subjects Designs:Which to Use?. Toronto, Ontario, Canada (2002),
   http://www.yorku.ca/mack/RN-Counterbalancing.html
2. Pallant, J.: SPSS Survival manual. McGraw-Hill, New York (2005)
3. Evers, V., Day, D.: The Role of Culture in Interface Acceptance. In: Human-Computer Interaction, Interact 1997, London (1997)
4. Constantine, L., Lockwood, L.: Software for Use: A Practical Guide to the Models and Methods of Usage-Centred Design. Addison-Wesley, New York (1999)
5. Barber, W., Badre, A.: Culturability: The Merging of culture and usability. In: Proceedings of the 4th Conference of Human Factors and the Web (1998)
6. Marcus, A.: User Interface Design and Culture. In: Aykin, N. (ed.) Usability and Internationalization of Information Technology, Lawrence Erlbaum Associates, Mahwah, New Jersey (2005)
7. Bourges-Waldegg, P., Scrivener, S.A.R.: Applying and testing an approach to design for culturally diverse user groups. Interacting with computers 13, 111–126 (2000)
8. Smith, A., Dunckley, L., et al.: A process model for developing usable cross-cultural websites. Interacting with computers 16, 63–91 (2004)
9. Alostath, J.: Culture-Centred Design: Integrating Culture into Human-Computer Interaction. Doctoral Thesis, The University of York, UK (2006)
10. Evers, V.: Cultural Aspects of User Interface Understanding: An Empirical Evaluation of an E-Learning website by International User Groups. Doctoral Thesis, the Open University (2001)
11. Brace, N., Kemp, R., Rosemary, S.: SPSS for psychologists: A guide to data analysis using SPSS for Windows, vol. vii, p. 287. L. Erlbaum Associates, Mahwah (2003)
12. Rosson, M.B., Carroll, J.M.: Usability Engineering: Scenario-Based Developement of Human-Computer Interaction, USA (2002)
13. Alostath, J., Wright, P.: Integrating Cultural Models into Human-Interaction Design. In: Conference on Information Technology in Asia 2005 (CITA 2005), Kuching, Sarawak, Malaysia (2005)

Cross Cultural Computer Gaming

Joyram Chakraborty and Anthony F. Norcio

Department of Information Systems
University of Maryland, Baltimore County (UMBC)
Baltimore, MD 21250 USA
{chakraborty,norcio}@umbc.edu

Abstract. Computer game development is a rapidly growing global business. However, research in the understanding of the global user is lacking. This paper presents a survey of recent research on cross cultural game development. The paper proposes a cross cultural hybrid model to carry out user modeling to assist developers in understanding the cultural nuances of end users.

1 Introduction

Computer games are being played by an increasing global population. However, little research has been conducted to understand the cultural backgrounds of the end users. Software developers use creative programming techniques and tools to develop games with hopes of successful market penetration. It is the purpose of this study to discuss the effectiveness of hybrid cultural models in computer game development.

2 Background

Research has shown that user modeling studies can lead to effective software design [22]. The increasing appeal of computer games to a global audience dictates that user modeling must be carried out with an understanding of the targeted international culture. It is no longer sufficient to develop games in one culture and expect success in another environment. To account for this globalization process, software developers need to understand that simply accounting for language translation of their games for different countries and cultures in which they operate is not sufficient [3]. Developers must exhibit sensitivity for the nuances that exist in all cultures if their games are to be successful in gaining acceptance in the domestic markets. Indeed, today's developers must be charged with the task to think globally but act locally. The problem posed to researchers and developers alike is to identify a set of universally accepted design guidelines that are useful to developers in deigning games for a cross cultural audience [36, 28]. The importance of culturally appropriate interface design for gaming applications is emphasized by many researchers [15, 9, 20, 3, 27].

2.1 Culture

The majority of researchers in the cross cultural domain acknowledge the cultural model of Geert Hofstede [14] and use it to explain their findings. Hofstede's model of

N. Aykin (Ed.): Internationalization, Design, LNCS 5623, pp. 13–18, 2009.

cultural dimensions is derived from a factorial analysis of over 116,000 international personnel at IBM from 1967 - 1970. His questionnaire on work-related values related to universal aspects of social relationships collected data from subjects from 72 nationalities and in over 20 languages. As a result of this research he derived five different macro-cultural level cultural dimensions. They are Power distance, Uncertainty avoidance, Masculinity vs. Femininity, Individualism vs. Collectivism, and Time Orientation. Based on the results of the compiled data, Hofstede came up with a score for each nationality or culture. In each case, a high score refers to a higher value of that cultural dimension.

Using Hofstede's work as a template, researchers have analyzed cultural variables to help developers design culturally attuned products. Nielsen proposed a set of culturally relevant heuristics that are applicable in some product designs [23]. Marcus and Gould used Hofstede's cultural dimension model to propose a set of examples of website designs [21]. Other prominent works include those of Kaplan and Triandis. Kaplan researched the correlation between language and thought pattern and proposed several types of patterns, namely Linear, Semitic and Oriental [17]. Triandis carried out extensive research on Individualism and Collectivism and proposed a methodology to measure these cultural attributes [34].

The literature revealed extensive sets of cross-cultural studies where the researchers studied one or more cultural attributes using one or more different cultures. However, little research has been conducted on the use of hybrid cross-cultural models. Khaslavsky carried out one of the few hybrid studies. She selected cultural dimensions from the works of Halls, Hofstede and Trompenaars to come up with a model to study similarities and differences in the usability of interfaces between American and French users [13, 14, 18, 35].

This paper proposes an extension of the efforts of Khaslavsky by combining the most common variables studied by researchers into a hybrid model. The following variables have been found to be the most widely researched in the cross cultural domain: Color, Symbolism, Individuality, Knowledge Processing and Local Variables. Research into color and symbolism is quite extensive [16, 21, 25, 31]. Using this research, the color and symbolism choices were made. Marcus provides examples of images that are representative of individualism and collectivism [21]. Kaplan's research into Language and Thought patterns provides the framework for the selection of this factor [17]. The literature is abounding with examples of research into the necessity of understanding countless other local variables. Such is the diverse nature of local variables that the collection of an exhaustive list would prove very difficult given the number of global cultures [1, 2, 4, 8, 16, 20, 25, 30, 37]. However, the several local variables are repeated quite often. As a result, these variables were chosen as part of the preliminary study. These include: date and time format as well as local language.

3 Cultural User Modeling

To assist game developers in their understanding of culture, we propose the following cross cultural hybrid model

3.1 Symbolism

Through their respective studies, Cook [6], Fussell and Haaland [12], Marcus [19] and Piamontea et al. [24] have reported that not all messages mean the same thing in different cultures. Some cultures may not recognize or associate an image or symbol in interface design as the designers had intended. To enhance cross cultural sensitivity images or symbols must be carefully selected and designed with the target culture in mind. Designers must be educated and made aware of expected differences among cultures to recognize potentially sensitive images that are culturally specific and isolate them during the internationalization process [20]. It is recommended that designers work with international experts to determine whether images in a product are non offensive and universally recognized and understood [9]. If images are not likely to be recognized or may cause offense in the target culture, they must be isolated during the internationalization process.

3.2 Local Variables

One of the first steps in the preparation of entering a product into an international market is the issue of translation of all interface text into the local language. This can be a very complicated task as the translation must make accommodations for issues such as computer-human interaction [11]. This problem can be further accentuated if the interface developers are unaware of the language specifications of the target culture [33]. To avoid problems of this nature, developers and translators need to collaborate closely and familiarize themselves with the application domain. Having a working knowledge of human factors principles such as screen layout and the design of interactive behavior would be of further assistance [30]. The following checklist can be applied:

- Avoid Jargon
- Be careful of words that do not exist
- Carefully chose product names to avoid embarrassing translations
- Be mindful of text flow directions and character sets
- Use appropriate date, time and number notation formats

3.3 Individualism

Triandis [34] has carried out a very detailed study of Individualism and Collectivism. He defines Individualism "as a social pattern that consists of loosely linked individuals who view themselves as independent of collectives; are primarily motivated by their own preferences, needs, rights, and they contracts they have established with others; give priority to their personal goals over the goals of others; and emphasize the rational analysis of the advantages and disadvantages to associating with others" [34].

Triandis defines Collectivism as "a social pattern consisting of closely linked individuals who see themselves as parts of one or more collectives (family, co-worker, tribe, nation); are primarily motivated by the norms of, and duties imposed by, those collectives; are willing to give priority to the goals of these collectives over their personal goals; and emphasize their connectedness to the members of these collectives."

Individualism and Collectivism are difficult to measure as these terms are used by many people in different parts of the world and are given various meanings, they can be difficult to measure[34]. However, researchers such as Marcus [20] and Sheppard and Scholtz [26] have demonstrated the individualistic and collectivistic cultures through the use of cultural markers. Examples of these markers, found in cultures known to be individualistic or collectivistic according to Hofstede [14], were found in the design and layout of popular websites of these countries.

3.4 Color

What color represents and how it is interpreted varies greatly across cultures [31]. For example, Courtney [7] has found that while the color red is generally associated with danger in the U.S., it represents happiness in China. Similarly, the author reports that while the color yellow is generally used to refer to cowardice, it is viewed as a reflection of prosperity in Egypt.

3.5 Knowledge Processing

The works of Kaplan [17] have highlighted the differences in language and the thought pattern. Kaplan's study reports several types of thinking patterns namely linear, circular, parallel and random. Kaplan attributes the differences in these language styles to cultural variations. Differences in cognition and thinking styles have resulted in numerous misunderstandings. Understanding different culture's approach to cognition and problem solving can be challenging [36]. The complications in communication are furthered when hand gestures and non-verbal cues are taken into consideration [32].

4 Conclusions

The understanding and application of cultural variables can play a significant role in assisting software developers. By applying a culturally sensitive approach, game designers will no longer have to make assumptions of users. This paper proposes a new direction of research in the field of computer game design using a cross cultural hybrid model.

References

1. Apple Computer: Human Computer Interfaces Guidelines. Addison Wesley, Reading, Massachusetts (1992)
2. Aykin, N.: Usability and internationalization of information technology. Lawrence Erlbaum, Mahwah, NJ (2005)
3. Becker, S.A.: An Exploratory study on Web usability and the internationalization of US e-businesses. Journal of Electronic Commerce Research 3(4), 265–278 (2002)
4. Belge, M.: The next step in software internationalization. Interactions 2(1), 21–25 (1995)
5. Chakraborty, J., Norcio, A.F.: Preliminary Investigation into the Internationalization of User Interfaces. In: Proceedings of AEI 2008 – The Applied Human Factors and Ergonomics 2nd International Conference (2008)

Cross Cultural Computer Gaming 17

6. Cook, B.L.: Picture communication in Papua New Guinea. Educational Broadcasting International 13(2) (1980)
7. Courtney, A.J.: Chinese Population Stereotypes: Color Association. Human Factors 28(1) (1986)
8. Day, D., Evers, V.: Website Localisation, the good, the bad, and the ugly. In: International Workshop on Internationalisation of Products and Systems (IWIPS), Milton Keynes, UK (2001)
9. Del Galdo, E.M., Nielsen, J.: International user interfaces. Wiley Computer Publishing John Wiley & Sons, New York (1996)
10. Evers, V.: Human Computer Interfaces: Designing for Culture. Masters thesis, University of Amsterdam, Amsterdam (unpublished, 1997)
11. Evers, V.: Cultural differences in Understanding Human Computer Interfaces. Milton Keynes. The Institute of Educational Technology, the Open University, United Kingdom (1999)
12. Fussell, D., Haaland, A.: Communication with pictures in Nepal: results of practical study used in visual education. Educational Broadcasting International 11(1) (1978)
13. Hall, E., Hall, M.R.: Understanding Cultural Differences. Intercultural Press, Yarmouth, Maine (1990)
14. Hofstede, G.: Cultures and Organizations: Software of the Mind. McGraw-Hill, New York (1991)
15. Hornby, G., Goulding, P., Poon, S.: Perceptions of export barriers and cultural issues: the SME e-commerce experience. Journal of Electronic Commerce Research 3(4), 213–226 (2002)
16. Kano, N.: Developing International Software for Windows 95 and Windows NT. Microsoft Press, Redmond, Washington (1995)
17. Kaplan, R.B.: Cultural thought patterns in inter-cultural education. Language Learning 16(1) (1966)
18. Khaslavsky, J.: Integrating culture into interface design. In: Conference summary on Human factors in computing systems (CHI), Los Angeles, California (1998)
19. Marcus, A.: Icon and Symbol Design Issues for Graphical User Interfaces. In: Del Galdo, E.M., Nielsen, J. (eds.) International User Interfaces, pp. 257–270. John Wiley and Sons, Inc., New York (1996)
20. Marcus, A.: Cross-cultural web user-interface design. In: Human Computer Interface International (HCII), pp. 502–505. Lawrence Erlbaum Associates, New Orleans, Louisiana (2001)
21. Marcus, A., Gould, E.W.: Crosscurrents: cultural dimensions and global Web user-interface design. Interactions 7(4), 32–46 (2000)
22. Norcio, A.F., Stanley, J.: Adaptive Human–Computer Interfaces: A Literature Survey and Perspective. IEEE Transactions on Systems, Man, and Cybernetics SMC-19(2), 399–408 (1989)
23. Nielsen, J.: Designing for international use. Elsevier, Amsterdam (1990)
24. Piamontea, D.P.T., Abeysekera, J.D.A., Ohlssonb, K.: Understanding small graphical symbols: a cross-cultural study. International Journal of Industrial Ergonomics 27(6), 399–404 (2001)
25. Russo, P., Boor, S.: How fluent is your interface?: designing for international users. In: Conference on Human Factors in Computing Systems (CHI), Amsterdam, Netherlands (1993)
26. Sheppard, C., Scholtz, J.: The Effects of Cultural Markers on Web Site Use. In: 5th Conference on Human Factors and the Web, Gaithersburg, Maryland (1999)

27. Smith, A., Dunckley, L., French, T., Minocha, S., Chang, Y.: A process model for developing usable cross-cultural websites. Interacting with Computers 16(1), 63–91 (2004)
28. Stengers, H., De Troyer, O., Baetens, M., Boers, F., Mushtaha, A.N.: Localization of Web Sites: Is there still a need for it? In: International Workshop on Web Engineering Hypertext, Santa Cruz, California (2004)
29. Sun, H.: Building a Culturally-Competent Corporate Web Site: An Exploratory Study of Cultural Markers in Multilingual Web Design. In: 19th annual international conference on Computer documentation, Sante Fe, New Mexico (2001)
30. Sun Microsystems: Software Internationalization Guide. Internal Document. Sun Microsystems, Mountain View, California (1991)
31. Thorell, L.G., Smith, W.J.: Using Computer Color Effectively: An Illustrated Reference. Prentice-Hall, Inc., New Jersey (1990)
32. Ting-Toomey, S.: Communicating across cultures. Guilford Press, New York (1999)
33. Tractinsky, N.: A theoretical framework and empirical examination of the effects of foreign and translated interface language. Behavior and Technology (BIT) 19(1), 1–13 (2000)
34. Triandis, H.C., Bontempo, R., Villareal, M.J.: Individualism and collectivism: Cross-cultural perspectives on self-Ingroup relationships. Journal of Personality and Social Psychology 54(2), 323–338 (1988)
35. Trompenaars, F.: Riding the Waves of Culture: Understanding the Cultural Diversity in Business. Nicholas Brealey, London (1993)
36. Yeo, A.W.: Cultural User Interfaces. A Silver Lining in Cultural Diversity. ACM SIGCHI Bulletin 28(3), 4–7 (1996)
37. Zahedi, F., van Pelt, W.V., Song, J.: A Conceptual Framework for International Web Design. IEEE Transactions on professional communications 44(2), 83–103 (2001)

This Is Who I Am and This Is What I Do: Demystifying the Process of Designing Culturally Authentic Technology

Wanda Eugene[1], Leshell Hatley[2], Kyla McMullen[3], Quincy Brown[4], Yolanda Rankin[5], and Sheena Lewis[6]

[1] Department of Computer Science and Software Engineering, Auburn University, AL 36849
eugenwa@auburn.edu
[2] College of Information Studies, University of Maryland, College Park, MD 20742
leshell@umd.edu
[3] Computer Science Department, University of Michigan, Ann Arbor, MI 48109
kyla@umich.edu
[4] Department of Computer Science, Drexel University, Pa 19104
qb23@drexel.edu
[5] IBM Almaden Research Center, San Jose, CA 95120
yarankin@us.ibm.com
[6] Center of Technology and Social Behavior, Northwestern University, Evanston, Il 60208
sheena@u.northwestern.edu

Abstract. The goal of this paper is to bridge the gap between existing frameworks for the design of culturally relevant educational technology. Models and guidelines that provide potential frameworks for designing culturally authentic learning environment are explained and transposed into one comprehensive design framework, understanding that integrating culture into the design of educational technology promotes learning and a more authentic user experience. This framework establishes principles that promote a holistic approach to design.

Keywords: human-computer interaction, cultural relevance, educational technology, design.

1 Introduction

Over the years, the HCI community has established universal design practices, which enable designers to create technology to fulfill users' needs by leveraging attributes, commonly referred to as affordances. In the context of designing technology, Norman [27] defines affordances to be 'learned conventions' that intuitively inform the user about how to interact with technology [29]. The phrase 'learned conventions' correlates to socio-cultural norms or behaviors attributed to users who are members of one or more communities of practice [20, 27]. Traditional design practices allude to the importance of integrating culture into the design of technology. For example, Gaver et al. [9] introduced the concept of cultural probes, user interactions with objects (e.g. using a camera to take pictures of important items in the home) to identify socio-cultural

N. Aykin (Ed.): Internationalization, Design, LNCS 5623, pp. 19–28, 2009.
© Springer-Verlag Berlin Heidelberg 2009

norms of a particular population and subsequently inspire the design specifications of technology. Aykin [2] justifies developing products for international audiences (i.e. internationalization) based on understanding the specific needs of local users (i.e. localization). Bourges-Waldegg & Scrivener [7] emphasize shared context of meaning as a means of designing universal user interfaces that support culturally diverse groups of users. Grimes et al. [12] created a mobile phone application, designed to recognize the collectivist nature of African American communities, that allows users to record and share their eating routines as a method to encourage healthy dietary habits. As a result, these tools demonstrate a growing consensus in the HCI community that designing culturally-relevant technology is important. However, few guidelines exist that describe how to design technology that recognizes socio-cultural norms.

Today the demand for increased academic performance stipulates new and improved approaches to instruction delivery. Several education researchers have responded with calls for integrating culturally relevant pedagogy into classrooms as a method of student engagement, curricula development, knowledge construction, reflection, and applicability of skills learned. Therefore, the design of culturally relevant educational technology proves to be a timely and promising venue for the exploration and construction of a new framework that can used to substantively guide the design and development of technology.

Placed within the context of education and learning, this paper describes the work of prominent education researchers and their suggested models of culturally relevant pedagogy. These models are positioned along side those of culturally relevant educational software design principles in an attempt to create a more concise conceptual framework, *The Cultural Relevance Design Framework,* which is then introduced and explained. The goal of *The Cultural Relevance Design Framework* is to assist any design team with creating culturally authentic technology. This framework is designed to uncover the design team's beliefs and biases about their target audience, highlight aspects of about the target audience that might be unknown, and suggest cultural assets that can be investigated to provide building blocks for sound cultural representations. Overall, this framework informs decisions regarding cultural relevance at the onset of the design process as well as a method of evaluating the cultural relevance throughout production processes to help ensure goals.

2 Related Work

2.1 Socio-Cultural Learning Theory

Socio-cultural learning theory was first introduced and applied by L. S. Vygotsky [33] as he sought to explain cognitive development processes. This theory posits that all learning and cognitive development take place in a cultural context and are influenced by language and symbols. It asserts that culture and language play huge roles in the cognitive development of children [17, 33]. Vygotsky's socio-cultural learning theory suggests that new knowledge is developed, framed around, and reflected upon one's cultural knowledge and behavior. Therefore to maximize learning potential overall, this learning theory can and should be used to support the development of curricula and pedagogy to emphasize and mimic the assets of a learner's culture. *The Cultural*

Relevance Design Framework introduced here extends this learning theory to support the creation of educational technology to similarly emphasize and emulate the assets of a learner's culture. In this case, we propose that technology should be designed in such a way to build rapport with the user, thus becoming an educational artifact indicative of the socio-cultural norms attributed to the targeted group of users and situated within the user's culture.

2.2 Cultural Responsiveness in Learning Environments

Culturally-responsive teaching has become a mantra for many educators and scholars concerned with the learning and academic achievement of culturally and linguistically diverse students [1, 4, 10, 19, 22, 24]. These researchers and scholars have learned that students of different cultural backgrounds process information differently. For example, researchers have consistently found that African-American and European-American children differ in storytelling styles, knowledge of print conventions, oral language, and question asking style [2828]. Applying culturally responsive strategies to reading, science, and math instruction proves beneficial for students from several cultures learning to read, expanding their engagement in reading, as well as in science and math [5, 8, 19, 30, 32].

The collective research efforts mentioned above demonstrate the potential of culturally responsive learning environments which extends to the design of educational technology. Educational technology that integrates socio-cultural norms of the targeted group of users promotes enthusiastic engagement and interaction, academic development, and nurtures cultural competencies. The latter two are present in the Cultural Relevant Pedagogy, coined by Ladson-Billings [19] during her ethnographic study of cultural responsiveness fostered by eight exemplary teachers of African-American classrooms.

2.3 Design of Cultural Relevant Software

Thinking and learning are all related to the context in which they occur, thus contextualizing the learning experience in the cultural practices of the learner, impacts the learning experience [26]. Computer software design generally follows a systematic process that encompasses design decisions known to influence learning success [11]. Culture variables incorporated into the design process serve as a vehicle for enhancing engagement via computer software tools. As the practice of incorporating culture into design becomes more widespread there is a need for guidance and instruction for those wishing to engage in culturally relevant design [11]. Numerous tools have been developed and designed in response to this need.

The Instructional Design Framework, as discussed by Herrington and Oliver [16] applies a model of instructional design based on the theory of situated learning to the design of a multimedia-learning environment. Guided by nine situated learning design characteristics, a checklist of guidelines was created, that enables these characteristics to be operationalized to provide support for authors, researchers, and theorists. Their framework supports the acquisition for complex knowledge and the means for the creation of authentic learning environments based on situated learning theory.

The Culture Modeling Design Framework presented by Carol Lee offers a structure for the design of learning environments that explicitly accounts for culture [23].

Her framework targets the design of instruction in ways to leverage everyday knowledge to support specific learning enactment of curriculum. It aims to structure learning environments that primarily focus on the kinds of problems that are generative and help learners leverage prior knowledge in order to solve new problems.

Young's Culture Based Model presents an intercultural instructional design framework that guides designers through the management, design, development, and assessment process while taking into account explicit culture-based considerations [35]. Its design factors (again, list a few of the criteria) facilitate a broad examination of culture, instruction, learning and the application of these factors to cross-cultural audiences [35]. Young's model, asks high level questions to facilitate the big picture of the management of undertaking the design process. However, this model can become difficult to navigate for software designers in need of a direct guide to support the design and evaluation of a software artifact.

3 Proposed Comprehensive Framework

Despite the prominence of the models mentioned above, a gap still exists between the models proposed by educators and the guidelines used by technology designers and other members of the HCI community. More specifically, the above models are generally theoretical in nature and are used to guide the creation of curricula, teacher worldview, and the context of lesson plans. It is difficult, however, for designers to apply such theories to the research, specifications, and evaluation required in development of software. Therefore, *The Cultural Relevance Design Framework* attempts to bridge the gap between technology designers and the culturally responsiveness recommendations of educators and education researchers by providing questions that can influence the decisions as designers begin brainstorming the culturally relevant aspects of their intended products or by developers who would like to evaluate the culturally relevant aspects of a product already produced.

Designing culturally relevant tools can become a difficult endeavor to embark upon because of the varying definitions of 'culture,' and how to account for it in design practices. The essence of a culture is often described as how the members of a group interpret, use, and perceive artifacts, tools, or other tangible cultural elements; it is the values, symbols, interpretations, and perspectives that distinguishes the interpreted embodiments of symbols, artifacts, and behaviors of a group; consisting of patterns, explicit and implicit, of and for behavior acquired and transmitted by symbols, constituting the distinctive historically derived and selected ideas, repertoires of practice, and especially their attached values; measured by participation in communities of practice and considered as products of action, and as conditioning elements of further action [3, 14, 18]. Thus, the authors define culture along two dimensions: what we do and who we are. Yet, within these two dimensions a wide range of attributes can be complied to further capture and illustrate the concept of culture, as described above. To guide the design of culturally relevant tools we have chosen to depict these two dimensions within four themes: Practices, Ontology, Representation, and Tasks.

Practices. One of the best ways to develop an appreciation for the targeted group is to first identify and understand the cultural practices socio-cultural norms associated with the targeted group. This raises the question of what are the socio-cultural norms of the targeted group. Our framework requires the designer to first become acquainted with socio-cultural norms of the target culture and then appreciate unique aspects that characterize the targeted group of users. Wenger [34] defines practices to be the widespread agreed upon activities engaged in by members of a culture entity. Rogoff et al. [31] discuss the method of intent participation; members observe and eventually begin to partake in practices (e.g. watching how someone prepares a dish before attempting to cook that same dish). Brown et al. [6] describe the cognitive apprenticeship model in which novices work with an expert to master a particular skill set. We can extend the cognitive apprenticeship model to the manner in which members come to understand and practice the broad range of activities in a particular context. Why does the context matter? The context is what makes the particular activity authentic. For example, if the activity is playing dominoes, or *bones* as they are referred to within the African American community, while constantly insulting one's opponents; the context is a recreational activity where insults are traded in the spirit of fun with no serious repercussions. Though various theories explain how members of a culture entity enculturate these practices, designers may not necessarily share the same background or experiences as those of the targeted group of users. This theme provides explicit categories (e.g. religious ceremonies, holiday traditions, indoor/outdoor recreational activities, etc.) of practices, thus, enabling designers to consider the range of practices attributed to the targeted group of users and how some of these practices can be integrated into the learning tasks in the technology.

Ontology. Within every culture there is a shared ontology, an organizational structure of knowledge, rich with language and vocabulary that is understood by participants of that culture, representing knowledge and the organization of knowledge in a particular domain, for problem solving [25]. We believe that culturally relevant software should reflect the ontology of the culture it aims to teach to. For example, the instructions given should emulate the manner in which instruction is given within the target audience's culture. In the domain of football, if one were designing a piece of software for football players, the instructions would be very brief and concise, without the use of superfluous language, much like the interaction between a football coach and his players. Similarly, the manner in which feedback is given should be representative of the ways in which feedback is generally given within the culture of the targeted audience. It is also important that the learning technology makes use of the vocabulary common to the culture of its audience. Furthermore, the learning technology should use a familiar vocabulary when discussing the main ideas, abstract concepts, as well as activities found within the tool. Generally speaking, all spoken or written words within the context of the educational software should also utilize the language conventions practiced by the target audience.

Representation. Representation, the visual and physical manifestations commonly accepted within a culture, serves as the primary sensory mode for interpreting affordances and associations. These can often be included as part of the culture's conceptual model [29]. Thus a misrepresentation of culture elements can make it difficult or become a distracter for culture participants. For example, a participant in the culture of American football might associate certain representations affiliated with a football player. It is common for American football players to wear a helmet, facemask, shoulder pads, cleats. However a misrepresentation of this culture, i.e. a player wearing a tutu holding a tennis racket, can make it difficult for a participant to connect to the message being conveyed. Thus a designer engaging in culturally relevant design must ensure authentic representation (e.g. gestures, clothing, activities) of the targeted audience's perception of behaviors and visual cues of that culture. Designers are tasked with assuring their artifacts are respectful of targeted audience's cultures. The imagery, attitude or perspective, and graphical images, should reflect the target audiences' culture(s) (colors, background and foreground, clothing, etc.) and culture norms. In addition, the elements of sound/music of the targeted culture must also be accounted for within the design. The design must also ensure that the following aspects of appearance are culturally representative of the targeted audience: body, face, shape, ethnicity, age, clothes, gestures, and eye contact [13].

Table 1. *The Cultural Relevance Design Framework*

	Definition	Investigative Question	Criteria
Practices	Shared socio-cultural conventions that emerge and evolve when people who have common goals interact as they strive towards those goals	Does the technology emulate the practices and "ways of thinking" of the targeted culture?	Gender, Family & Community Roles Religious & Other Holidays Family Gatherings and Rituals Music and Dance Interaction with Community, Elders, Peers Play activities Food
Ontology	The shared or understood vocabulary of a culture or community of practice	Does the language demonstrated in the technology reflect the language of the targeted audience?	Native language Idiomatic expressions Slang and other Vernacular characteristics Sentence Composition Style of writing
Representation	The way in which the visual cues and symbolic thought reflect the patterns, values, knowledge and beliefs of a group	Does the technology reflect the appearance of the targeted audience?	Aspects of appearance: (body, face, shape, ethnicity, age, eye contact)
Tasks	The set of actions or functions prescribed to accomplish a goal or objective	Does the technology reflect who would typically do this task(s) in the targeted culture?	young vs. old male vs. female expert vs. novice maternal society vs. paternal society

Tasks. Tasks include the familiar actions and goals associated with a culture. With respect to the technology being designed our framework views tasks as the activities that users engage in while completing the overall goals of the technology. For example, the tasks can be the basic actions within a treasure hunt game such, as characters walking, climbing, or reading while trying to find the treasure. We suggest that an understanding of tasks common to the target audience's culture can lead to the design of technology that is consistent with the end users cultural tasks. We view the tasks with respect to who the target audience is by considering the tasks typically associated with users' age, gender, etc. as well as what they do (e.g. teacher, student, parent, child). We believe that the nature of the tasks exhibited in the technology should reflect the culture of the end users. For example, does the person doing the task in the technology (e.g. a mother or father, a young or older person) mirror who is doing the task in the technology? In addition to understanding who engages in these tasks, the actions users engage in should allow users to apply skills and information from their culture to their interactions with technology.

These four themes form *The Cultural Relevance Design Framework* to engage designers in the practice of culturally relevant design. The framework is organized such that each of the themes are presented in Table 1 with a definition, an investigative question, and suggested criteria to help the designer explore and better understand the culture of the target audience.

4   Proposed Application of Framework

Recommended steps towards applying The Cultural Relevance Design Framework to any design effort are described here and illustrated in Figure 1. Once the target audience(s) of a design effort has been determined, the design team should:

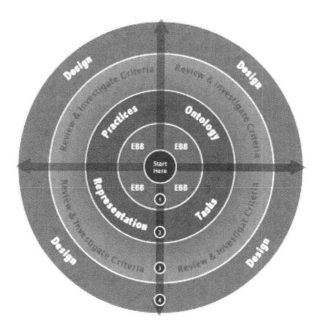

Fig. 1. Illustration of steps towards applying The Cultural Relevance Design Framework

Step One: Examine beliefs and biases about the targeted culture(s). These overall beliefs and biases may fall within the themes presented here as well as throughout other aspects of the targeted culture. This step may also uncover cultural aspects of the target audience that are unknown or that may need further investigation.

Step Two: Determine the themes within the framework (Practices, Ontology, Representation, Tasks) that are applicable to the design effort and review suggested criteria. The criteria presented here are intended to serve as suggestions and do not represent an exhaustive list. Other appropriate and meaningful criteria can be added.

Step Three: Use the suggested criteria to identify authentic socio-cultural norms of the target audience and devise strategies for the acquisition of additional information as needed.

Step Four: Incorporate what has been learned into the design effort, continuing to use the framework as an evaluation tool throughout the entire production process to ensure successful accomplishment of cultural relevance goals.

5 Conclusion

The aim of this paper is to introduce a software design framework that facilitates the creation of culturally authentic technology, providing designers of educational technology with concrete criteria that correlate to the socio-cultural norms of the targeted group of users. Based upon pre-existing yet disjointed culturally responsive models situated within multiple disciplines such as education, computer science, psychology, and anthropology, we present The Cultural Relevance Design Framework, a cohesive framework for integrating the practices, ontology, representation and tasks of potential users into the design of educational technology. The Cultural Relevance Design Framework initiates discussion and reflection among designers, but from the perspective of potential users. Future work includes using the Cultural Relevance Design Framework to design, implement and evaluate educational technology for its cultural authenticity.

References

1. Adams, N.G.: What Does It Mean?: Exploring the Myths of Multimedia Education. Urban Education 30, 27–39 (1995)
2. Aykin, N.: Usability and Internationalization of Information Technology. Lawence Erlbaum Associates, Mahwah (2005)
3. Banks, J.A., McGee, C.A.: Multicultural Education. Allyn & Bacon, Needham Heights (1989)
4. Barba, R.: Multicultural Infusion: A Strategy For Science Teacher Preparation. In: National Association for Research in Science Teaching Atlanta (1993)
5. Boykin, A.: Harvesting Talent and Culture: African American Children and Educational Reform. In: Rossi, R.J. (ed.) Schools and Students at Risk: Context and Framework for Positive Change, pp. 116–138. Teachers College Press, New York (1994)
6. Brown, J., Collins, A., Duguid, P.: Situated Cognition and the Culture of Learning. Educational Researcher 18, 32–41 (1989)

7. Bourges-Waldegg, P., Scrivener, S.A.R.: Applying and Testing an Approach to Design for Culturally Diverse User Groups. Interacting with Computers 13, 111–123 (2000)
8. Feger, M.: "I Want to Read": How Culturally Relevant Texts Increase Student Engagement in Reading. Multicultural Education 13(3), 18–19 (2006)
9. Gaver, B., Dunne, T., Pacenti, E.: Cultural Probes. ACM Interactions Magazine 1, 21–29 (1999)
10. Gay, G.: Culturally Responsive Teaching. Teachers College Press, New York (2000)
11. Green, J.W., Holmes, G., Sherman, T.A.: Culture as a Decision Variable for Designing Computer Software. Journal of Educational Technology Systems 26, 3–18 (1997)
12. Grimes, A., Bednar, M., Bolter, J.D., Grinter, R.E.: EatWell: Sharing Nutrition-Related Memories in a Low-Income Community. In: Computer Supported Cooperative Work 2008, San Diego, CA (2008)
13. Gulz, A., Haake, M.: Virtual pedagogical agents - design guidelines regarding visual appearance and pedagogical roles, Current Developments in Technology-Assisted Education, pp. 1848–1852 (2006)
14. Gutierrez, K., Rogoff, B.: Culture Ways of Learning: Individual Traits and or Repertoires of Practice. Educational Researcher 32, 19–25 (2003)
15. Heath, S.B.: Ways with words: Language, life, and work in communities and classrooms. Cambridge University Press, Cambridge (1983)
16. Herrington, J., Oliver, R.: An Instructional Design Framework For Authentic Learning Environments. Educational Technology Research and Development 48, 23–48 (2000)
17. John-Steiner, V., Mahn, H.: Sociocultural approaches to learning and development: A Vygotskian framework. Educational Psychologist 31 (1996)
18. Kroeber, A.L., Kluckhohn, C.: Culture: A critical review of concepts and definitions. Harvard University Peabody Museum of American Archeology and Ethnology Papers 47 (1952)
19. Ladson-Billings, G.: Toward a theory of culturally relevant pedagogy. American Educational Research Journal 32(3), 465–491 (1995)
20. Lave, J.: Situating learning in communities of practice. In: Resnick, L., Levine, S., Teasley, L. (eds.) Perspectives of socially shared cognition, Leithwood, K., Begley, P.T., Cousins, J., pp. 63–82. American Psychological Association, Washington (1988)
21. Lee, C.D.: Bridging home and school literacies: Models for culturally responsive teaching, a case for African American English in Heath. In: Brice, S., Lapp, D. (eds.) A Handbook for Literacy Educators: Research on Teaching the Communicative and Visual Arts, Macmillan Publishing Co., New York (1997)
22. Lee, C.D.: Toward A Framework for Culturally Responsive Design in Multimedia Computer Environments: Cultural Modeling as a Case. Mind, Culture, and Activity 10(1), 42–61 (2003)
23. Lee, C.D.: Culture, Literacy, and Learning Taking: Taking Bloom in the Midst of the Whirlwind. Teachers College, New York (2008)
24. Leonard, J., Davis, J.: Cultural Relevance and Computer-Assisted Instruction. Journal of Research on Technology in Education 37(3) (Spring, 2005)
25. Merrill, M.D.: Instructional transaction theory (ITT): instructional design based on knowledge objects. In: Reigeluth, C.M. (ed.) Instructional Design Theory and Models: A New Paradigm of Instructional Theory, vol. II, Lawrence Erlbaum Associates, Hillsdale (1999)
26. Nasir, N.: Points ain't everything": Emergent goals and average and percent understandings in the play of basketball among African American students. Anthropology and Education 31(1), 283–305 (2000)

27. Norman, D.: Affordances, conventions and design. ACM Interactions Magazine, 38–42 (May/June 1999)
28. Pinkard, N.: Lyric Reader: Creating Intrinsically Motivating and Culturally Responsive Reading Environments. CIERA Report. CIERA/University of Michigan (2001), http://www.ciera.org
29. Preece, Y., Rogers, H.S.: Interaction Design: beyond human-computer interaction. John Wiley & Sons, Inc., New York (2002)
30. Reis, N.M., Kay, S.: Incorporating Culturally Relevant Pedagogy into the Teaching of Science: The Role of the Principal. Electronic Journal of Literacy Through Science 6(1), 54–57 (2007)
31. Rogoff, B., Paradise, R., Arauz, R.M., Correa-Chavez, M., Angelillo, C.: Firsthand learning through intent participation. Annual Review of Psychology 54, 175–203 (2003)
32. Tharp, R.G.: Culturally compatible education: A formula for designing effective classrooms. In: Trueba, H.T., Spindler, G., Spindler, L. (eds.) What do anthropologists have to say about drop outs?, pp. 51–66. Falmer Press, NY (1989)
33. Vygotsky, L.S.: Mind in Society: Development of Higher Psychological Processes, 14th edn. Harvard University Press (1978)
34. Wenger, E.: Communities of Practice: Learning, Meaning, and Identity. Cambridge University Press, Cambridge (1998)
35. Young, P.A.: The Culture Based Model: Constructing a Model of Culture. Educational Technology & Society 11(2), 107–118 (2008)

Cultural Dimensions in User Preferences and Behaviors of Mobile Phones and Interpretation of National Cultural Differences

JuHyun Eune[1] and Kun-Pyo Lee[2]

[1] Seoul National University, Faculty of Design, Intermedia Lab, Seoul, Republic of Korea
[2] KAIST ,HCIDL Lab, Daejon, Republic of Korea
jheune@snu.ac.kr, KPlee@Kaist.ac.kr

Abstract. The purpose of this study is to identify the differences in user behaviors and cultural tendencies which will develop a cultural evaluation frame work for mobile phone design among countries in the mobile telecommunication market. Cultural taxonomy helps the understanding of cultural differences. To help understand the Asian market more clearly, a brief overview of Geert Hofstede's findings (Individualism, Uncertainty avoidance, Power distance, Masculinity, and Long-term orientation) and the K.P. Lee's Cultural Variables (Way of Task Handling, Temporal Perception, Conception of Nature, Adherence to rules, Relationship with Human, Nature of Human Activity, Message Contexting, and Expression of Emotion) for the index of different cultures was used in this study. This research is based on an online survey in three countries (Korea, China and Japan), summarizing the responses of questionnaire about user preferences, and behavioral perceptions of UI Design of mobile phones. The result of this research identified the differences and similarities among countries clearly, reorganized the cultural variables. After comparing values of author's value from online survey and two other variables, this study found that Hofstede's and KP Lee's are very meaningful to identify cultural-based national characteristics. This verifies that differences of usage behavior and preference for mobile phone reflect cultural perspectives. This cultural research is the key to understanding these needs and to providing the companies with advanced market positioning. This study should not stop at a simple cross-national comparison but be a cultural comparison framework for giving companies a clear future direction for globalization-based design development.

Keywords: Mobile Phone, Interaction Design, Cultural Comparison, Behavior, Preference, User Questionnaire.

1 Introduction

1.1 Background and Purpose

Many cognitive psychologists have studied differences in cognitive styles between Easterners and Westerners. Nisbett [10] compared Asians' and Westerns' points of view in his book. He proposed that the thought patterns of East Asians and Westerners

N. Aykin (Ed.): Internationalization, Design, LNCS 5623, pp. 29–38, 2009.

differ greatly and classified these differences as holistic and analytic. Holistically-minded people have a tendency to perceive a scene globally and to perceive the context and the field as a whole. They also tend to focus on the relationships between objects and the field. On the contrary, analytically-minded people such as Westerners have a tendency to perceive an object separately from the scene and tend to assign objects into categories. Therefore, analytically-minded people are more field-independent.

The research said that Westerners assume Asians' behaviors are similar because they, geographically, live close together and look similar and vice versa. However, Hofstede observed that Korea's value did not fit well with the Asian averages. Instead, South Korea displays similar to Latin American countries in Geert Hofstede Dimensions. [1] Like this, no people can be separated by only one line.

Cultural variables can be too abstract to explain the behaviors of mobile phone users which make the variables difficult to use directly in design practice. So, transformation from cultural variable to design specification is needed. The survey questions and responses will provide good guidelines to understand different cultural markets. Therefore, the purpose of this study is to determine the distinctive cultural inclinations of each country in user behaviors related to mobile phones. This study will help to provide companies with the necessary knowledge and framework in advance of their product launch abroad.

1.2 Method and Scope

This is part of a cross-national cultural research project. Previous research [7] from online surveys has been performed in Korea, China and Japan. Those were survey [5]. Many questions were asked. Only 22 questions were used in this study to be analyzed, however, because only they were relevant to cultural perspectives such as habitual behavior, and perception (See Table 4).

The survey was done on male and female internet users between 15-39 years of age with experience in mobile phone use. Age ratio of those surveyed was 2:4:4 (age of 15-19:20-29:30-39). Purposive Quota Random Sampling was used. The Online Surveys from three countries (Korea, China, and Japan) were collected through e-mail, combined and analyzed through full packaging software application. After researching various cultural variables, one standard cultural index was developed. Using this index, other research results and cultural dimensions were compared.

Table 1. Survey Scheme

Target for Survey	Korea	China	Japan
Number of sampling	1040	644	527
Sampling method	Purposive Quota random Sampling		
Survey Institute	Metrix Inc	Infoplant	Marcom-China
Method and Duration	Online survey through email for 2 weeks		

---

[1] South Korea's Index values are: PDI=60 IDV=18 MAS=39 UAI=85. South Korea's closest correlation to another country in the Hofstede survey is to El Salvador's values of PDI=66 IDV=19 MAS=40 UAI=94.

As a foundation for this research which is the comparison of mobile phone cultures in China, Japan and Korea, earlier research [7] focused on general usage patterns and user perceptions by placing greater emphasis on depth in marketing view. Thus, as part of an effort to develop a methodology and process promoting the application of cultural factors in design, cultural comparisons and interpretations were conducted to establish a framework for research in the area of mobile interface design. These identified a relationship between cultural characteristics and mobile handset usage and confirmed cultural discrepancies reflected in the usage of mobile phones. In this research, Cultural Dimension by Hofstede Geert and K.P. Lee's Cultural Variable have been the main focus. The reason why this research chose Hofstede's Cultural Dimension, it is widely accepted and used for cross-national research in organizational and managerial settings. KP Lee's Cultural Variables [8] used the research for cross-cultural comparison on microwaves usage in Korea and Japan. One of the procedures of my research will be to verify and compare the results of these two studies.

2   Cultural Models

2.1   Cultural Dimension by Hofstede

Geert Hofstede states that Culture is more often a source of conflict than of synergy. In addition, cultural differences are a nuisance at best and often a disaster for marketing pitfall. His research gives us insights into other cultures so that we can be more effective when interacting with people in other countries. If understood and applied properly, this information should reduce the level of frustration, anxiety, and concern. Cultural research will provide the 'edge of understanding' which translates to more successful results for marketing. Hofstede's Cultural Dimensions are explained as follows.

Table 2. Hofstede's Cultural Dimensions

Power Distance Index (PDI)	focuses on the degree of equality, or inequality, between people in the country's society. A High Power Distance ranking indicates that inequalities of power and wealth have been allowed to grow within the society. It is the extent to which the less powerful members of organizations and institutions (like the family) accept and expect that power is distributed unequally.
Individualism (IDV)	focuses on the degree the society reinforces individual or collective achievement and interpersonal relationships. A High Individualism ranking indicates that individuality and individual rights are paramount within the society.
Masculinity (MAS)	focuses on the degree the society reinforces, or does not reinforce, the traditional masculine work role model of male achievement, control, and power. A High Masculinity ranking indicates the country experiences a high degree of gender differentiation.
Uncertainty Avoidance Index (UAI)	focuses on the level of tolerance for uncertainty and ambiguity within the society for unstructured situations; it ultimately refers to man's search for Truth. A High Uncertainty Avoidance ranking indicates the country has a low tolerance for uncertainty and ambiguity.
Long-Term Orientation (LTO)	focuses on the degree the society embraces, or does not embrace long-term devotion to traditional, forward thinking values. High Long-Term Orientation ranking indicates the country prescribes to the values of long-term commitments and respect for tradition.

2.2   KP Lee's Cultural Variables

KP Lee [8] researched this dimension when he compared microwave usage between Koreans and Japanese. In order to conduct to develop a research framework for a cultural user interface study, the cross-cultural comparative study evaluated the usage pattern of microwave ovens. KP Lee's Cultural variables were used for cross-cultural research. This Cultural dimension was the modification with Trompenarrs's and Parson's. Each pair of dimensions and their descriptions are as follows.

Table 3. KP Lee's Cultural Variables and Description

Cultural Variables	Dimension	Description
1. Way of Task Handling:	Sequential vs. Synchronous	The temporal preference in performing tasks; Do only one thing at a time: Do many things at once
2. Temporal Perception	Past vs. Future oriented	People's perception toward priority in time
3. Conception of Nature	Subjugate vs. Control	The extent of mastering environment; Follows nature : masters environment
4. Adhere to rule	Universalism vs. Particularism	The extent of keeping standards; Adhere to standards : Adhere to focus on the exceptional nature of present circumstances
5. Relationship with Human	Individualism vs. Collectivism	The relationship between people; put more values in individual responsibility : regard group consensus more important
6. Nature of Human Activity	Ascription vs. Achievement	Achievement oriented cultures accord status to people on the basis of their achievement: Ascription cultures ascribe it to them by virtue of age, class, gender, education and so on
7. Message Contexting	Specific vs. Diffuse	The degree to which people engage others in specific areas of life; diffusely in multiple areas of our lives: at several levels of personality at the same time
8. Expression of Emotion	Affective vs. Neutral	The degree of Control people's feeling and express one's feeling

3   Interpretation of National-Cutural Differences

First of all, the basis for the cross-cultural comparative study was established by defining the essence of culture and theoretical framework. In doing so, it was attempted to interpret the interrelationships among characteristics of usage patterns, subjective preference, and cultural values of users.

3.1   Interpretation of National-Cutural Differences by Hofsted's Cultural Dimension

Here are the cultural implications by nation based on Cultural Dimension for Hofstede's view. Following are the results when the three individual nations (Korea, China, and Japan) are separated for comparison purposes. This should facilitate an understanding of the differences among them and compared with the Asian and World averages.

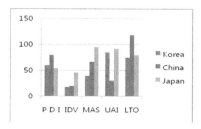

Fig. 1. Hofsteopde's Value Graph[2]

Table 4. Questions and Results

Cultural	Variables	Questions
Way of Task Handling	Sequential-Synchronous **Japan<China<Korea**	-Do you prefer to use a menu' vs. 'Do you prefer to use hot keys'? -Do you want to make calls while walking? -Do you keep the phone at hand or keep in pocket while it's not being used? -Are most of your calls out of necessity (not to chat or enjoy conversation)?
Temporal Perception	Past-Future ***Japan<China<Korea***	-Do you prefer additional functions besides current functions? - Do you prefer sleek and futuristic design styles?
Conception of Nature	Subjugate-Control **Korea<China<Japan**	-Do you use service outlets shop rather than to trouble shoot yourself? - What do you do when the call doesn't go through? Rather than just giving up, I would leave a voice message or use SMS.
Nature of Human Activity	Achievement-Ascription Japan<=China< Korea	-Is Function more important than the size of the phone? -Would you keep your current phone as long as it doesn't break down?
Adhere to Rule	Universal-Particular Japan<Korea<China	-Do you like to use your mobile service to keep your appointment times flexible? -Do you use functions besides phone calls & SMS very often? -Level of use of alarm function; Do you use the alarm function to awaken you up in the morning?
Relation-ship with Human	Collectivism-Individualism Korea <China<Japan	-Do you try to keep your voice down when using the phone in public places? -Do you turn off your mobile phone when you do not want to be bothered? -Do you Prefer standard design styles to Fashionable Design Styles?
Message Contexting	Specific-Diffuse China<Korea <Japan	-Do you use your home telephone when it is cheaper in cost at home instead of the mobile phone? -Do you lock your mobile phone with a secret code so that only you can access the phone? -Are you interested in mobile phone related sales events and discount benefits?
Expression of Emotion	Affective-Neutral China<Korea <Japan	-Do you keep conversations short without chatting? -Do you decorate your phone with stickers and accessories? -Do you prefer dynamic animated screens over static screens?

---

[2] www.geert-hofstede.com/ Using each Hofstede's value of nation, the values for Korea, China, and Japan are selected and re-arranged for the purpose of this study.

(1) Korea[3]. South Korea's highest Hofstede Dimension is Uncertainty Avoidance (UAI) at 85, indicating the society's low level of tolerance for uncertainty. In an effort to minimize or reduce this level of uncertainty, strict rules, laws, policies, and regulations are adopted and implemented. The ultimate goal of this population is to control everything in order to eliminate or avoid the unexpected. As a result of this high Uncertainty Avoidance characteristic, the society does not readily accept change and is very risk-adverse. South Korea has a low Individualism (IDV) rank of 18.

(2) China[4]. Geert Hofstede analysis for China has Long-term Orientation (LTO) the highest-ranking factor (118), which is true for all Asian cultures. This Dimension indicates a society's time perspective and an attitude of persevering; that is, overcoming obstacles with time, if not with will and strength. The Chinese rank lower than any other Asian country in the Individualism (IDV) ranking, at 20 compared to an average of 24. This may be attributed, in part, to the high level of emphasis on a Collectivist society by the Communist rule, as compared to one of Individualism.

(3) Japan[5]. The Buddhist-Shinto societies also have an additional Dimension, that of Long Term Orientation (LTO). Geert Hofstede added this Dimension after the original study, and it was applied to twenty-three of the fifty original countries in his study. The Buddhist/Shinto Countries of Taiwan and Japan have LTO as the most closely correlating Dimension.

3.2 Interpretation of National-Cultural Differences by Hofsted's Cultural Dimension

Relevant questions were extracted from more than 40 existing questions in online surveys. Fifteen people categorized the 22 questions into 8 cultural variables. Two or three questions were allocated to category of each cultural variable. Concept of Cultural dimension was used as a comparison tool of different cultures.

Each dimension has several questions for surveys related to these subjects. Questions were asked to three nations. Following are result of the comparisons

- **Way of Task Handling: Sequential vs. Synchronous.** Koreans have the most Synchronous ability in terms of the temporal simultaneously in performing tasks. Koreans do many things at once or do only one thing at a time such as carrying their cell phones close to them and are fanatical about them using them most frequently and in the greatest variety of ways. Most Japan users keep their handsets in carry bags or purses and use them mostly when a need arises. Meanwhile, they appear to be the most considerate of others: most people make phone calls from home rather than the workplace or school for reasons of privacy.
- **Temporal Perception: Past vs. Future oriented.** Koreans always pursuit the future as people's perceptions has priority in time. They like new and innovative functions and designs. Koreans prefer phones with a luxurious, advanced and high-tech image, which appears to be closely tied to the new product policies of phone manufacturers, which emphasize new technologies. Japanese have relatively low demand for additional features such as games, audio or video recording due to prevalence of diverse electronic devices on the market.

---

[3] http://www.geert-hofstede.com/hofstede_south_korea.shtml
[4] http://www.geert-hofstede.com/hofstede_china.shtml
[5] http://www.geert-hofstede.com/hofstede_japan.shtml

- **Conception of Nature: Subjugate vs. Control.** Japanese has strong will to control environment. For example Japanese tend to fix problem by themselves and most of them tried not to give up but to leave a voice message. Korea and China are very similar characteristics of this concept of nature. Most of Korean tends to go to service outlet to get be fixed.

- **Adhere to rule: Universalism vs. Particularism.** For Chinese, flexibility is important: the replacement cycle is the shortest, brands and advertising are key factors influencing purchase decisions, and contract periods are flexible. On the contrary, Japanese reluctantly change meeting times and usually use main functions on mobile phones. Characteristics of Koreans are middle of one of Chinese and Japanese. Even though Korean seems to flexible, they most keep the alarm clock and is also familiar to additional mobile phone function

- **Relationship with Human: Individualism vs. Collectivism.** Koreans try to strictly keep their voice down when they use a mobile phone in public places according to survey. And Koreans tend to always connect to others. They also prefer moderate design because Koreans have a consciousness about others. Koreans like to be a member of their group. However, Chinese tend to go for familiarity and aesthetic designs: they appreciate variety in the colors of phones, such as pink, blue, red and green, and design is a larger factor than brand when it comes to purchase decisions. Japanese turn off my mobile phone when they do not want to be bothered and respect their privacy. They like both moderate and distinct and fashionable design.

- **Nature of Human Activity: Ascription vs. Achievement.** Koreans judge things by achievement, according to survey. Koreans tend to pursue stability rather than change, contradictory to the bias. Korean mobile phone users agreed on the importance of the size and thickness of handsets compared to function. Chinese are in the middle. Chinese think of function as more important than the size of phone. Chinese have the strongest willingness to buy premium phones, prefer a unique design image, and are easily influenced by peers or family members. In Japan, there is a broad range of brands consumers can choose from. Mobile phone users prefer a brand image that is best suited to their own lifestyle. They suit trend of mobile phone and willingly to change phones. They are concerned over the size of their mobile phones.

- **Message Contexting: Specific vs. Diffuse.** Japanese are most diffuse and Chinese are most specific. Japanese have low rate of preference to icon based screen. Japanese use practically cheap wired phone at home instead of mobile phone. Japanese consumers tend to choose what they personally prefer rather than following the opinions of others. Koreans have preferable icon based display to text based display. Koreans frequently use mobile phone for convenience and privacy despite of high cost. However, they rarely set up password to call. They are focused on benefit and event of Point of sale. There are some contradictory. Chinese prefer icon based GUI screen. Chinese keep privacy using password lock and frequently use mobile phone at home. They are not interested in sale event.

- **Expression of Emotion: Affective vs. Neutral.** Japanese are so neutral and logical in terms of the degree of Control people's feeling and express one's feeling. They showed noticeably low rate of call for killing time and chatting. They also prefer phones with simple designs that are likely to be enduring, and text-oriented, static designs for backgrounds. Koreans' characteristics are between the Chinese and

Japanese. They call for chatting with their acquaintances. They like simple and modern design without decoration. China also demonstrate a clear preference for dynamic background screens, enjoy chatting on mobile phones and sending text messages, and access wireless Internet content such as online chatting/ dating/ communities relatively frequently. All in all, the Chinese wireless population appears to place emphasis on dynamic and pleasurable features.

4   Results and Discussion

Thus, as part of an effort to develop a methodology and process promoting the application of cultural factors in design, this research was conducted establishing a framework for cultural research in the area of mobile interface design, identifying a relationship between cultural characteristics and mobile phone usage, and distinguishing cultural discrepancies reflected in the usage of mobile phones in the target market. As a foundation for this research into and comparison of mobile phone cultures in Korea, China, Japan. This study focused on general usage pattern and user perception by placing greater emphasis on cultural view. Common characteristics as well as discrepancies among the three neighboring countries will not only prove to be useful data in attempting to understand each nation, but also valuable for businesses making inroads into one of these countries. The questionnaire helped to give us an overview of mobile phone usage patterns, design preferences, awareness of next-generation mobile phones, and cultural characteristics reflected in the usage of mobile phones in Korea, China and Japan. It led us to reach the following conclusions.

Table 5. Results by cultural variables

	1 Way of Task Handling:	2. Temporal Perception	3. Conception of Nature	5. Relationship with Human	6. Nature of Human Activity	4. Adhere to Rule	7. Message Contexting	8. Expression of Emotion
Korea	Synchronous	Future	Subjugate	Collectivism	Achievement			
China						Particular	Specific	Affective
Japan	Sequential	Past	Control	Individualism	Ascription	Universal	Diffuse	Neutral

These cultural value systems affect human thinking, feeling, and acting, and the behavior of using mobile phones in predictable ways. Common characteristics as well as discrepancies among the three neighboring countries will not only prove to be useful data in attempting to understand each nation, but also valuable for businesses making inroads into one of these countries. The findings could be more significant if they were to be applied in formulating new technology-related design development strategies, moving beyond a simple comparison of cultures. Meanwhile, designers need to be involved in creating products with well-grounded cultural knowledge and a systematic methodology. I.S. Lee [6] has provided knowledge about cross-country and cross-product cultural characteristics that will enhance our understanding of the intricate interaction between the culture and the user experience, a small but important step toward the development of culture-centered systems.

Table 6. Framework of Cultural Comparison for mobile phone UI design

Categories	Cultural Variables	Questions
Attitude of Time	1 .Way of Task Handling 5. Long-Term Orientation (LTO)	-Do you prefer to use a menu' vs. 'Do you prefer to use hot keys'? -Do you want to make calls while walking? -Do you keep the phone at hand or keep in pocket while it's not being used? -Are most of your calls out of necessity (not to chat or enjoy conversation)?
	2. Temporal Perception 5.Long-Term Orientation (LTO)	- Do you prefer additional functions besides current functions? - Do you prefer sleek and futuristic design styles?
Nature of Motivation	3. Conception of Nature 3.Masculinity (MAS)	-Do you use service outlets shop rather than to trouble shoot yourself? - What do you do when the call doesn't go through? Rather than just giving up, I would leave a voice message or use SMS.
	6. Nature of Human Activity 1.Power Distance Index (PDI)	-Is Function more important than the size of the phone? -Would you keep your current phone as long as it doesn't break down?
Related to Human	4. Adhere to Rule 2. Individualism (IDV)	-Do you like to use your mobile service to keep your appointment times flexible? -Do you use functions besides phone calls & SMS very often? -Level of use of alarm function; Do you use the alarm function to awaken you up in the morning?
	5. Relationship with Human 2. Individualism (IDV)	-Do you try to keep your voice down when using the phone in public places? -Do you turn off your mobile phone when you do not want to be bothered? -Do you Prefer standard design styles to Fashionable Design Styles?
Communica tion matters	7. Message Contexting 4.Uncertainty Avoidance Index (UAI)	-Do you use your home telephone when it is cheaper in cost at home instead of the mobile phone? -Do you lock your mobile phone with a secret code so that only you can access the phone? -Are you interested in mobile phone related sales events and discount benefits?
	8. Expression of Emotion 4.UncertaintyAvoidance Index(UAI)	-Do you keep conversations short without chatting? -Do you decorate your phone with stickers and accessories? -Do you prefer dynamic animated screens over static screens?

Therefore, Cultural variables are useful to compare because it is possible to formulate a parameter, a good index measurement. Three parameters between author's value, and Hofstede's were not 1:1 matched. However, grouping these values provided a meaningful analysis of user behaviors and preferences.

References

1. Anbari, F.T., Umpleby, S.A.: Cross Cultural Differences and Their Implications for Managing International Projects (2003)
2. Trompenaars, F.: Riding the Waves of Culture: Understanding Diversity in Global Business. Economist (1993)
3. Geert HofstedeTM Cultural Dimensions (April 11,2008),
   http://www.geert-hofstede.com
4. Hall, E.T.: Beyond Culture. Anchor Doubleday Press, Garden City (1976)
5. Cho, I.S., et al.: Reports on surveys of mobile phone users of Korea, China, and Japan, Matrix Inc. (2004)
6. Lee, I.S., Kim, J.W., et al.: Cultural Dimensions for User Experience: Cross-Country and Cross-Product Analysis of Users' Cultural Characteristics, the British Computer Society (2008)

7. Eune, J., et al.: A Design Direction for Mobile phones between Comparison of Users from Korea, China and Japan, KSDS (2007)
8. Lee, K.P.: Culture and Its Effects on Human Interaction with Design with the Emphasis on Cross-Cultural Perspectives between Korea and Japan, Doctorial Thesis, Journal of University of Tsukuba, Japan (2001)
9. Penn, M., Kinney Zalesne, E.: Microtrends: The Small Forces Behind Tomorrow's Big Changes (2007)
10. Nisbett, R.E.: The Geography of Thought: How Asians and Westerners Think Differently and Why. The Free Press, NY, USA (2003)
11. Lee, S.J., Eune, J., et al.: Report on Analysis of Design trend and User culture by the comparison of mobile phones of Korea, China and Japan, Korean Design Research Institute (2004)

Culture and Co-experience: Cultural Variation of User Experience in Social Interaction and Its Implications for Interaction Design

Jung-Joo Lee

[1] University of Art and Design Helsinki,
Hämeentie 135 C, 00560 Helsinki, Finland
Jung-joo.lee@taik.fi

Abstract. The notion of how multi-users experience technology as a group has opened important vistas in interaction design. Even though literature in cultural anthropology and cognitive psychology implies cultural influence on user experience in social interaction, a cross-cultural notion has, however, been overlooked in this area. This paper aims at exploring relationship between culture and a social aspect of user experience, in a catchier term, "co-experience," drawing on the concept of "role-takings" by following the framework in symbolic interactionism. Based on literature review, we build the conceptual framework of how role-takings vary in different cultures and how the variations can shape different co-experience. In order to illustrate how this framework can be applied in a real design case, a novel interactive system called "Visual-talk table" is introduced. In so doing, we argue how the framework and the design experiment with this technology can serve as a tool to facilitate cultural aspect of social interaction in designing especially tangible and ubiquitous interaction.

Keywords: culture, co-experience, social interaction, interaction design.

1 Introduction

Over the last decade HCI community has played a leading role in propagating importance of user's cultural background knowledge in interaction design. In previous conferences and publications of the HCI community, thematic areas such as "Internalization and localization," "Cross-cultural user interface design," and "Universal access in human-computer interaction," have opened a key forum for this notion [12]. The studies on cultural interface design have varied from addressing linguistic and semiotic perspectives [6], creating new user experience [16], and comparing human cognitive styles [8][15].

Meanwhile, several approaches are engaged in establishing design knowledge about users' social interaction within or in parallel to HCI, as the development of information communication technologies and consumer products support users as social actors in various ways [1][17]. Such fields, namely CSCW and Social Computing, criticize that existing interaction design frameworks have mostly been used in an individualistic way, by placing the individual into the center of thinking. This notion

N. Aykin (Ed.): Internationalization, Design, LNCS 5623, pp. 39–48, 2009.
© Springer-Verlag Berlin Heidelberg 2009

shifted a focus of interaction design from relationship between a single user and a system to that among multi-users. With the regards to cultural variations in communication strategies and attribution styles, proven robust in recent studies from cultural anthropology, cognitive psychology, as well as communication study [8][11][20][22], this shift allows us to infer the way people shape social actions around technology and the meaning making process can depend on users' cultural backgrounds.

Very recently some studies address this issue by investigating influence of culture on technology use in intercultural collaborations. Diamant et al. [7] showed the interactive effect of culture and technology on member's attribution of performance by comparative experiments with Chinese and Americans. These studies, however, have their focus on user's technology evaluation and team performance and do not address the role of culture in shaping actions, emotions and meanings, which are notable factors in a current paradigm of interaction design [1][10][24]. To address the latter issue may lead us to new dimensions of putting users' socio-cultural aspects into designing interactive systems.

This paper aims at exploring what role users' cultural backgrounds play in organizing social actions and making meanings towards technology, which constitute user experience. We build the conceptual framework by reviewing literature in symbolic interactionism, user experience and cultural anthropology as a tool for further empirical exploration. Then we discuss implications of the framework by introducing an example of a design experiment with new technology.

2   User Experience in Social Interaction: "Co-experience"

This section delineates current notions of multi-users' social interaction in user experience research and interaction design with the perspective of their relation to culture. We especially introduce the concept of "co-experience," as a key concept to explain what constitutes lines of actions and emotions in social situations, which formulates a conceptual framework in this study.

2.1   Co-experience

User experience has been one of the cornerstone concepts in HCI and design research over the last decade. The frameworks in user experience design have evolved as the advances in consumer products and available technologies bring new possibilities for product related experiences [1]. "Co-experience" was introduced by Battarbee [1] to address limitation in user experience literature that was missing social aspects in organization of user experience. In his book on "designing for social interaction," Ludvigsen [17] advocates Battarbee's notion:

> With a notion of experience design beyond the single user, Battarbee argues that it is limiting to see the user in the context of interactive technology as standing alone and be a passive consumer of whatever the designer has designed for them. Instead, users hack and rearrange their technology to fit with the activities at hand and especially in order to support social interaction and activities, and the construction of social spaces.

The central idea of co-experience is to explain how people become engaged in a social situation and, once engaged, how they interpret the situation and shape actions towards it [1]. To explain this initiation and reciprocation, she followed the framework of symbolic interactionism formulated by Blumer [3]. Symbolic interactionism is a theory of social interaction that sees meaning as something created by people interacting with others in the world. In the following, this theory is explained in more detail with the cultural perspective.

2.2 Role-Taking

According to Blumer, the framework of symbolic interactionism is based on three main principles:

1. people act upon and towards things according to the meanings they have for them.
2. these meanings arise from interaction with other people and then
3. these meanings are handled in and modified by people in an interpretive process [3].

What people see as a proper way of acting in any situation depends on how they position themselves and others into it. In particular, what interactionists call "role-taking" plays a crucial role: identities and roles are key resources when people construe lines of actions for any situation [18].

What is interesting in the concept of "role-taking" is that how people perceive their roles and shape actions towards perceived roles can be different in different societies. For example, Blumer's view of symbolic interactionism whose origin is in Chicago of the 1930s, a city of restlessness with high immigration and social disorder, understands acting as a labile process, reducing role-taking almost to situational improvisation [3][1]. However, once these meanings are learned, they remain relatively stable, and even in restless environments, people strive for stability and respectability of conduct [9]. In more stable and tradition respecting societies, structural role-identities such as age, social status, or gender can play a more crucial role in shaping actions in a social situation. This linking between role-taking and culture provides a robust basis to deduce what role culture will play in creation of co-experience.

2.3 The Role of Interactive Technology in Co-experience

Interactive technology plays also an important role in organization of co-experience, as well as the role-taking process. Above all, it is evident that interactive technology opens a social situation in the first place by working as a communication means or drawing people's attention: for example interactive installation in children's science museum can engage group of children or a new hand-held device with innovative touch screen interface can draw surroundings' attention. Moreover, it also participates in shaping properties and lines of actions in the process of social interaction. For instance, when sending a photo by MMS (mobile multimedia service) and IM (instant message), lines of actions and emotions created are different despite the same purpose. Through these social interactions, people come to make meanings to technology. All this meaning making process finally organizes co-experience, which implies that how given technology intervenes in role-takings, whether support or interrupt them, can result in different co-experiences.

3   Co-experience in Cultural Terms

Based on previous discussion of what constitute co-experience, this section has a sharper look at what aspects of culture affect role-takings and how this affect can shape different co-experience. Then we formulate a framework of relationship between co-experience and culture.

3.1   Cultural Differences in Communication Styles

What is considered appropriate is different in different cultures. This different value attribution results in different role-takings and different communication strategies. Ting-Toomey [22] formulated the framework on cultural differences in communication styles by adapting a politeness theory in which a central notion is human desire to maintain their "face." Cultural variations in terms of the facework and communication styles are distinguishable particularly in the dimension of *high-context* culture versus *low-context* culture, the well-known framework formulated by Edward T. Hall [11].

In the field of cognitive psychology, Ross and Nisbett [21] and Choi et al. [5] found robust evidence that a person's cultural background affects the way he or she interpret others and situations. According to them, people of *low-context* culture, such as that of the United States, value personal initiative and independence in group work. In contrast, people of *high-context* culture, such as that of China or South Korea, value group solidarity and tend to rely on member's nonverbal behaviors when collaboratively solving a problem. Based on these studies, cultural differences in communication styles can be presented as Table 1.

Table 1. Comparison of communication styles in *high-context* versus *low-context* culture

Elements	High-context culture (e.g. East Asia)	Low-context culture (e.g. U.S.A., Western Europe)
Identity	Emphasis on "We" identity	Emphasis on "I" Identity
Supra-Strategy	'Face-giving', supporting others' needs for appreciation	'Face-restore', protecting own freedom and space
Style	Obliging, avoiding, affective-oriented style	Controlling, confrontational, solution-oriented style
Nonverbal acts	Contextualistic (role-oriented) acts, indirect emotional expressions	Individualistic acts, direct emotional expressions
Value when solving a problem	Group solidarity	Personal initiative and independence

3.2   Cultural Differences in Role-taking and Co-experience

The preceding discussions on co-experience, role-takings and cultural differences enable us to formulate the conceptual model of relationship between culture and co-experience as Figure 1.

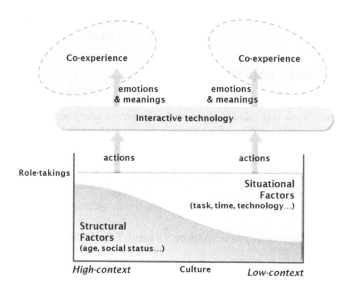

Fig. 1. The process of organization of co-experience in different cultures: When people perceive their roles in a group, structural factors (age, social status or gender) and situational factors (task, time or technology) affect in role-takings. In this process, structural factors become more salient in *high-context* culture, while situational factors become more influencing in *low-context* culture. Then people shape their actions according to the perceived roles, and interact with technology as well as other members. Emotions and meanings to the situation and technology arise and transform in this interaction. This process constitutes user experience in social interaction, i.e. co-experience.

Based on this framework, we can give a sociological interpretation for how cultural identities play out in certain situations as follows:

- In *high-context* cultures such as China and Korea one has to act not only in terms of situational identities, but also on structural identities by for example giving priority to more senior and higher stats people. Technology should also follow the direction coming from social organization: if it intrudes with social order, it can insult seniors.
- On the other hand, urban California is an example of a *low-context* culture in which people play down issues like honorifics and status, encouraging people to go with the flow. Interactive technologies can be built for maximal efficiency without recourse to how it functions in social organization.
- Similarly, some of the claims of Hofstede's [13] study can lead to technology-related hypotheses. For example, in countries with *high power distance*, action is organized through status hierarchy, while in countries with *high uncertainty avoidance* scores, it is up to the highest status people to voice complains about ambiguity and take lead in reducing it.
- Furthermore, with social change, these patterns change. According to Inglehart [14], as societies get wealthier, over the course of a few generations, they drift from traditionalist through materialist to post-materialist values. In his study, Scandinavia is the world leader in terms of post-materialistic values, while Korea is more materialistic. However in a study of social change in Korea, Na and Cha [19] have shown

that young metropolitan Koreans are far more post-materialistic than their order and rural countrymen, who lean towards materialistic and traditional values.

4 Towards Design Experiments

The next step is to feed the conceptual framework with empirical data. In order to validate the framework and yield design implications, we take the approach of design experiment, following the notion of *exemplary design research* [2]. As a design intervention to explore the research question, i.e. *how people in different cultures organize co-experience with interactive technology, intervened by role-taking process*, we designed a new technology called "Visual-Talk Table." In this section, we depict how the framework of culture and co-experience led to design of "Visual-Talk Table" and how this technology can serve as a tool for testing the framework and hypotheses.

4.1 Visualize the Degree of Participation. "Visual-Talk Table"

In the context of team work, the development of group dynamics and the degree of participant's involvement cannot be isolated from cultural context [23]. The development of group dynamics in group discussion is a good example of how role-taking functions in social situation. We came up with the idea that intervening group dynamics in group discussion situations can be a design experiment setting for observing influence of role-takings on co-experience. The design idea was how people will react to technology when the technology visualizes each member's participation pattern. How will their role-takings shape actions responding to this visualization?

"Visual-Talk table" was designed to explore these questions, visualizing each member's verbal participation by lights on the tabletop (Figure 2). Typically the combination of a table and chairs can invite a group of people and create social interaction in nature, for example, tea time, a brainstorming meeting or a group game.

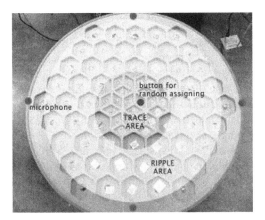

Fig. 2. Design of "Visual-Talk table": For displaying patterns on the table, we designed a honeycomb pattern which consists of 75 hexagons containing microprocessor units with dual LEDs in each because a honeycomb pattern is capable of displaying various kinds of patterns on it and associated with patterns of tablecloths. Four directional microphones are embedded on the edges of four different sectors so that they can sense a voice from each participant.

On the table, light areas are divided into two; one is the ripple area displaying participants' ongoing talking and another is the trace area collecting the amount of each participant's speaking and remaining traces of their verbal social interaction. The main functions of the table are as follows:

Visualizing the amount of speech and its flow. When a microphone senses the voice from an assigned sector, LEDs mounted on the tabletop are turned on from the side of a person currently speaking. As speaking continues, the light ripples with yellow color spread. They go off when speaking stopped. When a person speaks long enough for ripples to reach the trace area in the middle of the table, one of blue LEDs in the person's sector is turned on. The light ripples and traces enable members to recognize who talked the most and the least as well as interaction flows by the shape of traces.

Visualizing intersections and random turn-taking. When ripples form different sides are intersected, lights show higher intensity so that it can represent intensive interaction or even interference between two persons. When nobody speaks, participants can press the button which can randomly point out one person in order to instigate speech. When the button is pressed, lights of one sector are randomly turned on, meaning a person in the sector should speak.

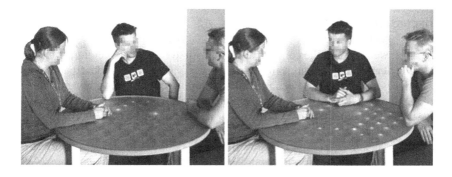

Fig. 3. "Visual-Talk table" in use denoting members' talking by lights

4.2   Experiment Design

In order to explore the relationship among role-takings, culture and co-experience, we can put this new design in the real world and observe how people use, interpret and appropriate given technology. Building case-specific hypotheses can provide us with more focused indicators for observation and analysis.

Experimental hypotheses. The way Visual-talk table visualizes group members' participation and verbal social interaction is not necessarily compatible with their role identities. Social position gives power to the highest-status person; the table denotes who talks most. It can infringe with the demands of social position. In high-context culture like China or South Korea people can be more sensitive to these infringements than in low-context culture like U.S.A. or the Netherlands; high-status people can get annoyed if their role is challenged by technology and low-status people will get embarrassed because they feel high-status people lose their face.

In addition, who defines the line of actions related to technology, for example, drawing attentions from ongoing discussion to the technology and deciding what to do with it, can show variations according to cultures. In *high-context* culture, high-status people may get these turns more while these are distributed more evenly in *low-context* culture. Judgments concerning the table's behaviors can be also more voiced by higher status people in *high-context* culture, while this process will be more equal in *low-context* culture.

Experiment procedure. The design experiment with Visual-talk table should be carried out in a real context where group activities are organized, such as a meeting room or a coffee room in the office for two weeks. When people gather around the table, a video camera set in the room starts to record. After the events, people are interviewed in order to identify participants in mixed status groups.

Analysis will be first qualitative. From what people do around the table, we will identify instances in which it enters talk as a topic of its own and how this happens, and how people attribute changes in interaction and experience to the table. This analysis will be summarized with simple quantitative measures following quasi-experimental logic [4]. These measures will be also probed in interviews.

5 Discussion and Further Work

In this paper, we first built the conceptual framework to explain how cultural variations in role-taking can entail variations in "co-experience." Then we introduced an example of a design case to illustrate how the conceptual framework can move towards empirical study. Because this paper is from ongoing study of the design experiment with "Visual-talk table," comparative observations and result analysis should be the next step.

Despite promising observation data for further work, the paper brings important implications for interaction design in two aspects: "cultural aspect of co-experience" as a sensitizing concept for new design and an evaluation tool for cultural fitness. More specifically users' role-taking of experiencing interactive system can provide a new dimension in interaction design. In this study, we designed a novel interactive technology called "Visual-talk table," inspired by the concept of role-taking. Observation on ways people create experience with this technology, which designers might not even expect, will produce more implications for both the framework and the design. A new design can be an interactive system better supporting role-takings in certain cultural domains. A system can also be designed to manipulate role-takings in order to create new user experience.

Moreover, the experiment design of Visual-talk table implies how the conceptual framework can be specified into indicators to evaluate cultural adaptability of interactive systems. Especially since few studies on cultural aspects in tangible and ubiquitous interaction are found, this approach can make convincing contributions in such areas.

References

1. Battarbee, K.: Co-Experience: Understanding User Experiences in Social Interaction. UIAH Press, Helsinki (2004)
2. Binder, T., Redstrom, J.: Exemplary Design Research. In: Design Research Society Wonderground International Conference 2006, Lisbon (2006)
3. Blumer, H.: Symbolic Interactionism. Perspective and Method. University of California Press, Berkeley (1968)
4. Cook, T.D., Donald, T.C.: Quasi-Experimentation. Design and Analytic Issues for Field Settings. Rand McNally, Chicago (1979)
5. Choi, I., Nisbett, R.E., Norenzayan, A.: Causal Attribution across Cultures: Variation and Universality. Psychological Bulletin 125, 47–63 (1999)
6. de Souza, C.S., Laffon, R., Leitão, C.F.: Communicability in Multicultural Contexts: A study with the International Children's Digital Library. In: 1st IFIP Human-Computer Interaction Symposium HCIS 2008, pp. 129–142. Springer, Boston (2008)
7. Diamant, E.I., Fussell, S.R., Lo, F.: Where Did We Turn Wrong? Unpacking the Effects of Culture and Technology on Attributions of Team Performance. In: Proceedings of CSCW 2008, pp. 17–26. ACM publications, New York (2008)
8. Dong, Y., Lee, K.: A Cross-Cultural Comparative Study of Users' Perceptions of a Webpage: With a Focus on the Cognitive Styles of Chinese, Koreans and Americans. International Journal of Design 2(2), 19–30 (2008)
9. Duneier, M.: Slim's Table: Race, Respectability, and Masculinity. University of Chicago Press, Chicago (1992)
10. Forlizzi, J., Ford, S.: The Building Blocks of Experience. An Early Framework for Interaction Designers. In: Proceedings of DIS 2000, pp. 419–423. ACM publications, New York (2000)
11. Hall, E.T.: Beyond Culture. Doubleday & Company, Inc., New York (1981)
12. HCI International, http://www.hci-international.org/
13. Hofstede, G.: Cultures and Organizations: Software of the Mind. McGraw-Hill, New York (1991)
14. Inglehart, R.: Mordernization and Postmodernization. Princeton University Press, Princeton (1997)
15. Kim, J., Lee, K., You, I.: Correlation between Cognitive Style and Structure and Flow in Mobile Phone Interface: Comparing Performance and Preference of Korean and Dutch Users. In: Aykin, N. (ed.) HCII 2007. LNCS, vol. 4559, pp. 531–540. Springer, Heidelberg (2007)
16. Konkka, K.: Indian Needs: Cultural End-User Research in Mombai. In: Lindholm, C., Keinonne, T., Kiljander, H. (eds.) Mobile Usability: how Nokia changed the face of the mobile phone, pp. 97–112. McGraw-Hill, New York (2003)
17. Ludvigsen, M.: Designing for Social Interaction: Physical, Co-located Social Computing. Aarhus School of Architecture Press, Aarhus (2006)
18. McCall, G.J., Simmons, J.L.: Identities and Interactions. Free Press, New York (1978)
19. Na, E., Cha, C.: Changes in Values and Generation Gap During the Past Tow Decades (1979-1998) in Korea. In: Han, K., Lim, J., Sasse, W. (eds.) Korean Anthropology: Contemporary Korean Culture in Flux, Hollym, Elizabeth, NJ, Seoul (2003)
20. Nisbett, R.E.: The Geography of Thought: How Asians and Westerners think differently– And why. Free Press, New York (2003)
21. Ross, L., Nisbett, R.E.: The Person and the Situation: Perspectives of Social Psychology. McGraw Hill, New York (1991)

22. Ting-Toomey, S.: Intercultural Conflicts Styles. A Face-negotiation Theory. In: Kim, Y.Y., Gudykunst, W.B. (eds.) Theories in Intercultural Communication, pp. 213–235. Sage, Newbury Park (1998)
23. Toseland, R.W., Jones, L.V., Gellis, Z.D.: Group dynamics. In: Garvin, C.D., Gutierrez, L.M., Galinsky, M.J. (eds.) Handbook of Social Work with Groups, pp. 13–31. Guilford Publications, New York (2004)
24. Wright, P., McCarthy, J., Meekison, L.: Making Sense of Experience. In: Blythe, M.A., Overbeeke, K., Monk, A.F., Wright, P.C. (eds.) Funology – From Usability to Enjoyment, Kluwer Academic Publishers, Dordrecht (2003)

Cultural Aspect of Interaction Design beyond Human-Computer Interaction

Rungtai Lin[1], Po-Hsien Lin[1], Wen-Shin Shiao[1], and Su-Huei Lin[2]

[1] Crafts and Design Department, National Taiwan University of Art
Ban Ciao City, Taipei 22058, Taiwan
rtlin@mail.ntua.edu.tw
[2] Department of Fashion Imaging, Mingdao University
Peetow, Changhua 52345, Taiwan
eric@mdu.edu.tw

Abstract. Over the past several decades, we have made many efforts to understand Human-Computer Interaction (HCI). But beyond HCI, we need a better understanding of Human-Culture Interaction not just for taking part in the cultural context, but also for developing the interactive experience of users. Therefore we propose a general framework for cultural product experience that applies to the mental models of designer and user and which can be experienced in Human-Culture Interaction. Then, based on the interactive experience of users with an aboriginal cultural object, the Linnak (a twin drinking cup), a modern Linnak was proposed to demonstrate how to design a successful cultural product using the human-culture interaction framework. The intended purpose of this paper is to provide a framework for examining the way designers interact across cultures and the interactive experience of users in the design process.

Keywords: Interaction Design, User Experience, Cultural Product Design.

1 Introduction

The growth of interest in human-computer interaction (HCI) over the past decades has been extraordinary, and it is one of the most rapidly developing subjects in the field of computer science and human factors. HCI became a fascinating research subject and is now recognized as a vital component of successful computer applications [4, 17]. Over the past several decades, researchers made great efforts to understand HCI. Based on scientific research and development, we know a great deal about creating successful human - computer interaction. The influence of HCI science in interaction design plays an important role in product design and development, especially for information technology products. The multidisciplinary development of HCI has advanced many research and design models. In designing products with embedded information technologies, the role of HCI is a basic, fundamental consideration. As such, the challenge exists of regarding the development of mature HCI research and its impact on design and investigating what dimensions beyond HCI will be exploited in increasingly transforming our lives at home and at work [4, 18, 19].

N. Aykin (Ed.): Internationalization, Design, LNCS 5623, pp. 49–58, 2009.
© Springer-Verlag Berlin Heidelberg 2009

Recently, Kansei engineering has gained popularity and broad application in human product interaction design. Kansei engineering is a design method developed to construct relationships between user experiences and product properties in order to use these properties to design products that fulfill a user's desired experiences [1, 20]. Desmet & Hekkert [2] had mentioned that experience is not a property of the product but the outcome of human-product interaction and the results depend on what temporal characteristics and product experiences the user brings into the interaction. Therefore, this study intends to combine Kansei engineering and affective design to explore the Human-Culture Interaction beyond HCI.

Interaction design has switched focus from usability and cognitive ergonomics to the affective and interactive experience of users. Culture plays an important role in products with embedded information technologies, and designing culture into products will become a design trend in interactive design. Beyond HCI then, we need a better understanding of Human-Culture Interaction not just for taking part in the cultural context, but also for developing the interactive experience of users. With technical advances, HCI has also advanced phenomenally over the last ten years [17]. In addition, HCI has extended our understanding of interaction with information technology products and how to put this understanding to practical use in the design and evaluation of daily used products. The concept is supported by Shneiderman [21] who noted that we are now in the second transformation of computing, in which the shift from machine-centered automation to user-centered services and tools, is enabling users to be more creative. The HCI design process asserts that the architecture of system and interface components should be directed by a holistic understanding of "use and user needs through a process of intelligent and conscious design." [7, 3].

Norman [15] argued that affect and emotion are not as well understood as cognition, but are both considered part of the information processing system with different functions and operating parameters. Therefore, we propose a general framework for cultural product experience that applies to the mental model of designer and user and which can be experienced in Human-Culture Interaction. Then, based on the interactive experience of users with the aboriginal cultural object, Linnak (a twin drinking cup), a modern Linnak was proposed to demonstrate how to design a successful cultural product using the human-culture interaction framework. The intended purpose of this paper is to provide a framework for examining the way designers interact across cultures and the interactive experience of users in the design process.

2   Cultural Product Design Model – Linnak as the Example

Using Cultural features to add extra value to a product can benefit not only economic growth, but also promote unique local culture in the global market. Therefore, because transferring cultural features into a cultural product becomes a critical issue, a cultural product design model including three main parts: conceptual model, research method, and design process, was proposed for combining culture levels, layers, and design features which facilitate understanding cultural product design [11,12].

In Lin's paper [11], the "Linnak", a twin-cup, was chosen as the cultural object to transfer its cultural features into a modern product. After its appearance, usability, and cultural meaning were studied, the usage behavior and meaning of "sharing with each other" was identified. The "Eternity", a modern twin-cup shown in Figure 1, was proposed to show the culture meaning of "sharing with each other" from the original cultural object – the Linnak. The "Eternity" is a symmetrical pair of cups connected together inversely to show the close relationship of the drinkers as a couple. This design won the gold award at the "2006 5th Bombay Sapphire Designer Glass Competition Taiwan," and was chosen to enter the global competition that takes place each April in Milan, Italy, during the Salone del Mobile, the world's biggest design fair.

The "Eternity" was designed as an interactive modern product to be used for example in a night club. In the use scenario shown in Figure 2 [11], a man wanting to develop a relationship with a lady, treats her with wine in the drinking cup. The design concept constituted the communication with man to woman and the drinking behavior became the mid-level relation. In the inner level of the Linnak, "sharing with each other" is transformed to communication with each other. It was romance that used the cultural object for modern social behavior.

Fig. 1. The Eternity – a modern twin cup

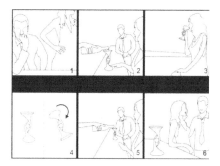

Fig. 2. The scenario of Eternity

3   Framework for Human – Culture Interaction

Taking the "Eternity" as an example, the "Linnak" is a typical cultural object which can be transformed into a contemporary design for the current consumer market. There are social meanings, ergonomic concerns and functional achievement associated with this cultural object. To provide an ideal drinking cup for the modern market, both the social and operational interfaces of the "Linnak" need to be well-designed. However, the contemporary consumer market may need a new form of the "Linnak" suitable for the modern environment. Thus, how to communicate with the "Linnak" and extract the idea of "sharing with each other" in the design of the "Eternity" are valuable for enhancing usage in our daily life [11]. Based on the previous studies and Norman's conceptual models [15], a framework of Human-Culture Interaction (Figure 3) was proposed for examining the way designers communicate across cultures as well as the cultural aspect of interaction and user experience in the design process.

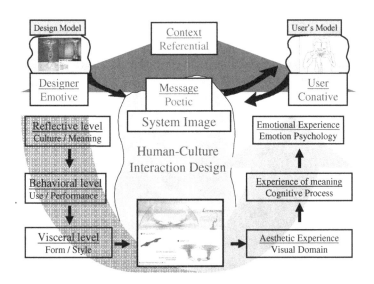

Fig. 3. The Human-Culture Interaction Model

For the design model, the designer focuses on the analysis of cultural meaning, operational interface, and the scenario in which the cultural object was used. System image results from the cultural features that have been redefined in order to design a cultural and aesthetical product. The user's model is the mental model developed through interaction with the cultural product. Based on the cultural context, the designer expects the user's model to be identical to the design model through the culture aspect of interaction design.

For the designer's conceptual model, there are three levels of processing including: visceral, behavioral, and reflective design. Using the "Eternity" as an example, the design features of "Linnak" has been identified with three levels of cultural features: (1) reflective design (inner-level) focuses on the cultural meaning of "making friendship", "working together", and "sharing with each other."; (2) behavioral design (mid-level) focuses on the consumer behavior and the scenario in which people will use the "Linnak" on various occasions; and (3) visceral design (outer-level) focuses on the "Linnak" form factors which are associated with material, colors, texture, and pattern [9,10,11,15].

For the user's model, the user communicates directly with the cultural product. If the cultural product does not make the culture meaning clear and attractive, then use will end with the wrong message during the human-product interaction. There are also three levels of human-product interaction: aesthetic experience, experience of meaning, and emotional experience. The aesthetic experience involves a cultural product's form, color, texture etc., to delight the user's sensory modalities. The experience of meaning involves the user's ability including operation, safety etc., to assign the design features and assess user pleasure with the cultural product. The emotional experience involves user emotion including self-image, personal satisfaction, memories etc., which are elicited by the cultural objects and designed into the cultural product.

Based on communication theory, according to Jackson's model [6], a designer sends a message to a user via the cultural product. The designer recognizes that this cultural product must refer to something other than itself which is called the culture context. The emotive function is to communicate the designer's emotions which extract from a cultural object all those elements that make its meaning unique. The other end of the process is the conative function which refers to the affection produced in the user by the cultural product. The referential function is the most important part of human-product interaction in culture meaning of the cultural product. The framework indicates how to extract the cultural features for designing a cultural product. These features underlie the different conceptual models of cultural product experiences which are used to explain the process and culture meaning of human-culture interaction.

4 Ergonomic Considerations for Human Product Interaction

The most important ergonomic consideration for designing daily-life products is "designing for human use", especially when addressing the issue of applying anthropometric data. In ergonomic considerations, the requirement in anthropometric design is to determine a value for some design parameter in terms of a percentile cutoff for an anthropometric value in order to meet a target percentage for a population of interest. The anthropometric database is used as a design reference for daily used products. However, the most effective application of such data in product design is another important issue [13, 14].

The "Linnak" ranges in length from 43cm (low percentile) to 91cm (high percentile). Its average length is about 74.4cm (50 percentile). In addition , the average width and height of the twin cup are 11cm, and 7.3cm respectively. The distance between the center of two cups varies from 29 to 42cm, and the capacity is about 600 c.c.. These dimensions have indicated the way in which this cultural object was used and these distances indicated an invisible space between two people. From a usability point of view, the diamond shape cup illustrates that an angular mouth was used for ease of drinking wine. Furthermore, the drinking process has emphasis the meaning of "working together" and "sharing with each other."

After reviewing the literature and studying the drinking situation, two kinds of drinking situations were found to be most common with the aborigine twin cup. When it is used in special situations (e.g. wedding ceremony), the couple or the intimacy will be as shown in the top of Figure 4. That was the close face-to-face mode showing an intimate close relationship. When the twin cups are used in the normal situation, people drink the wine together to demonstrate their friendship, and the drinking situation will be shoulder to shoulder as shown in the bottom of Figure 4.

Fig. 4. Drinking in the close relationships

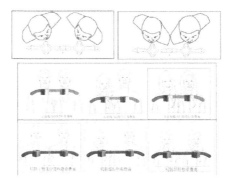

Fig. 5. The simulation of drinking situations

When applying anthropometric data, three anthropometric design principles must be considered: extreme individuals, an adjustable range, and the average. For example, using the average size twin cups, the results showed that the users' heads would not be touched to each other while they are drinking but their shoulders would. In this situation, they will not feel uncomfortable about their body. Figure 5 shows the simulation of drinking postures under different situations.

5   Testing Interactive Experience of a Cultural Product

Using anthropometric data in design involves art as well as science. However, in the use of such data for designing daily-life products, there are generally two aspects: 1) determine what anthropometric design principle should be applied, and 2) achieve the anthropometric considerations in the most cost effective manner. Based on these principles, the recommendations of ergonomic dimensions for the ideal twin cup were studied. Therefore, this study focused on the application of anthropometric data by collecting the suitable dimensions of twin cups. Then the minimum, the average, and the maximum sizes were chosen as the examples and three kinds of model were built and used as samples to test the operation of a "Linnak." as shown in the Figure 6.

Fig. 6. Three kinds of wooden models as test samples

Fig. 7. The Experimental Situation

Using the wooden Linnak models, an experiment was conducted to explore the operation of user experience. In the experiment, the two cups can be moved by the participants to form the most agreeable situation (Figure 7). 40 students who are 20 couples of intimacy served as the subjects. Subjects were told the purpose of the study. A PowerPoint presentation was prepared to introduce the cultural meaning and use scenario of the Linnak to the participants. Then they were asked to used the Linnak model for simulating the drinking situation and exploring the preference gesture in drinking. Finally, they were asked to answer a subjective questionnaire about their user experience.

Using user experience information, the communication between a cultural object and its users has been studied. For designers following the "Cultural Product Design Model", the important consideration of the design elements had been extracted from the culture meaning. Thus the user experience related to the cultural object followed the human-culture interaction model [11].

6   Designing "Friendships" into the "Eternity"

In Lin's study [11], the "Eternity" demonstrates the value of Aboriginal culture in design. After the paper was published, some comments came from many readers arguing the loss of the culture meaning of "sharing with each other". In Figure 2, the use scenario of "Eternity" in the night club indicated that the "Eternity" lost the culture meaning of close relationships when two people are not drinking at the same time. For example, Norman's personal communication stated that:

> *"I still very much like the Linnak cup in which the two people drink at the very same time, side by side. I am afraid that this behavior has been lost with the "Eternity": With Eternity, the two people have to drink one at a time – this is very different. I wonder if your students would explore this difference?"*

These comments emphasize the cultural aspect of human-culture interaction design, therefore, designing the culture meaning of "sharing with each other" into the "Eternity" became an important issue in the cultural product design process. Following the scenario of using "Eternity" at a night club (Figure 2), in which the man wants to develop a relationship with a lady using just the standard form of "Eternity", subjects communicated developing a relationship with their friends. When the "Eternity" bridges close relationships, then the next step is to use the ball (in the middle of two cups) as pivot and turn the bottom cup to a traditional Linnak as shown in figure 8. At this time, the couple can drink together at the same time, side by side, shoulder by shoulder, or even face to face to show how intimate they are!

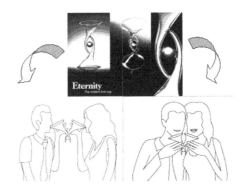

Fig. 8. The concept of drinking together using "Eternity"

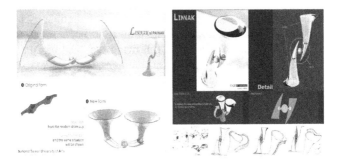

Fig. 9. The redesign of "Eternity" in case A and B

Based on the structure of the "Eternity" and the user experience and comfort considerations, the refined version of designing "close relationships" into "Eternity" was developed. The design case A is shown in the left of Figure 9. A special joint device was designed for transforming three usage forms—the standard form of cups up and down; the turning form via the rolling ball; and the two cups side by side. In testing user experience, the users stated that "positive relationship with the partner will make them take the two cups closely." According to user response, a metal device joining the glass-body of cups was proposed to transform the cup form and fit the different relationships and drinking situations. Figure 9 (right) shows design case B. The rolling ball device for transforming to fit different drinking situations was retained. For usability considerations, design case B added the new handle part at the side of the cup edge, and made the edge of cup thick and solid to become the holder.

7 Conclusion

"Culture" plays an important role in the interaction design field and has been considered a key design evaluation point for the future. Designing "culture" into products will be a design trend in the global market. The importance of studying culture in human product interaction design is shown repeatedly in several studies in all areas of technology design. In addition, HCI considerations in system design continues to progress, and in the field of interaction design between human and product especially, the cultural aspect of interaction design and affective interactive experience of users will be more broadly used. Therefore, this paper proposed a framework of human culture interaction that shows how the cultural aspect of interaction design would be developed in the field of human interactive design beyond the human-computer interaction process.

The culture of drinking wine is a very common social event in human society around the world, and it presents the emotional communication of user experiences. With the primitive behavior of human beings, the social events of drinking wine culture proceeded constantly and wine related products became popular daily products in the design fields. The "Eternity" presented in this study provides a good example of applying cultural features to interaction design while still retaining a meaningful cultural value. Taking "Eternity" as an example, this paper demonstrated the cultural features of "Linnak" found in three culture levels and how to transform those cultural features of interactive experiences into a new cultural product design which can fit into the contemporary market.

The framework of human-culture interaction that was proposed in this paper provides a different way of thinking about interactive experiences with acculturation. The acculturation process is the exchange of features that are composed of the traditional culture, cultural features, cultural objects, interface design, interaction experience, user emotion, and user response [8]. The most important part of this process is the user experience added in the cultural product design process and involved Kansei engineering considerations . The framework is of value for designers because it can help to design "culture features" into interaction design, as well as provide users with a valuable reference for understanding interactive experience.

For future studies, we need a better understanding of the acculturation process not only for the designer's model, but also for that of the user's. While cultural features become important issues in the interactive experiences of users, the acculturation process between human and culture becomes a key issue in the cultural product design and are worthy of further in-depth study.

Acknowledgments. The authors gratefully acknowledges the support for this research provided by the National Science Council under Grants No. NSC-96-2221-E-144-001. The author also wishes to thank the various students who designed the products presented in this paper, especially, C. H. Hsu, H. Cheng, M. X. Sun, and E. T., Kuo, and colleagues who have contributed to this study over the years, especially, Dr. J. G. Kreifeldt.

References

1. Chang, W.C., Wu, T.Y.: Exploring types and characteristics of product forms. International Journal of Design 1(1), 3–14 (2007)
2. Desmet, P.M.A., Hekkert, P.: Framework of product experience. International Journal of Design 1(1), 57–66 (2007)
3. Edgar, A., Sedgwick, P.: Key Concepts in Cultural Theory. Routldge, NY (1999)
4. Faiola, A.: The Design Enterprise: Rethinking the HCI Education Paradigm. Design Issues 23(3), 30–45 (2007)
5. Handa, R.: Against arbitrariness: Architectural signification in the age of globalization. Design Studies 20(4), 363–380 (1999)
6. Jakobson, R.: Closing Statement: linguistics and poetic. In: Sebeok, T. (ed.) Style and Language, MIT Press, Cambridge (1960)
7. Kapor, M.: A Software Design Manifesto. In: Winograd, T., Bennett, J., DeYoung, L., Hartfield, B. (eds.) Bringing Design to Software, Addison Wesley, New York (1996)
8. Kottak, C.P.: Windows on Humanity. McGraw Hill, New York (2005)
9. Lee, K.P.: Design methods for a cross-cultural collaborative design project. In: Redmond, J., Durling, D., de Bono, A. (eds.) Proceedings of Design Research Society International Conference – Futureground. Paper No.135, Monash University, Melbourne (2004)
10. Leong, D., Clark, H.: Culture-based knowledge towards new design thinking and practice - A dialogue. Design Issues 19(3), 48–58 (2003)
11. Lin, R.T.: Transforming Taiwan Aboriginal Cultural Features Into Modern Product Design Case Study of Cross Cultural Product Design Model. International Journal of Design 1(2), 45–53 (2007)
12. Lin, R., Cheng, R., Sun, M.-X.: Digital Archive Database for Cultural Product Design. In: Aykin, N. (ed.) HCII 2007. LNCS, vol. 4559, pp. 154–163. Springer, Heidelberg (2007)
13. Lin, R., Yang, S.-W., Siao, W.-S., Lin, H.-y., Kang, Y.-Y.: Designing "Height" into daily used products - A case study of universal design. In: Stephanidis, C. (ed.) HCI 2007. LNCS, vol. 4554, pp. 207–216. Springer, Heidelberg (2007)
14. Lin, R.T., Kreifeldt, J.G.: Ergonomics in Wearable Computer. International Journal of Industrial Ergonomics, Special Issue: Ergonomics in Product Design 27, 259–269 (2001)
15. Norman, D.A.: The Psychology of Everyday Things. Basic Books, New York (1988)
16. Norman, D.A.: Emotional Design. Basic Books, New York (2004)
17. Preece, J., Rogers, Y., Sharp, H., Benyon, D., Holland, S., Carey, T.: Human-computer interaction. Addison Wesley, New York (1994)
18. Roberts, M.: Border crossing – The role of design research. International Product Development in AIGA Journal of Interaction Design Education 3(2), 29–39 (2001)
19. Schein, M.: The corporate culture survival guide. Bass Jossey, San Francisco (1999)
20. Schütte, R.: Developing an Expert Program Software for Kansei Engineering. Linköping University, Sweden (2006)
21. Shneiderman, B.: Leonardo's Laptop: Human Needs and the New Computing Technologies. MIT Press, Cambridge, MA (2002)

Cross-Cultural Analysis of Social Network Services in Japan, Korea, and the USA

Aaron Marcus and Niranjan Krishnamurthi

Aaron Marcus and Associates, Inc.,
1196 Euclid Avenue, Suite 1F, Berkeley, CA, 94708 USA
Aaron.Marcus@AMandA.com, Niranjan.Krishnamurthi@AMandA.com

Abstract. The techniques of cross-cultural analysis of Websites based on culture models are used to examine user-interface components (the metaphors, mental models, navigation, interaction, and appearance) of social networking sites in three countries. The authors note and evaluate patterns of similarity and difference in the Website designs that seem to link social networking sites by culture dimensions.

Keywords: appearance, China, culture, culture model, design, interaction, interface, Japan, Korea, language, mental model, metaphor, navigation, network,social, user.

1 Introduction

Social networking services (SNSs) are online communities that focus on bringing together people with similar interests or who are interested in exploring the interests and activities of others. SNSs have come a long way since the initial efforts of computer-mediated social networking such as USENET, LISTSERV and Bulletin Board Services. Today, there are numerous SNSs that cater to audiences around the globe and they are fast becoming a staple of online consumer activity. What is interesting to note, however, is that none of these sites are equally popular across cultures. The fact that MySpace is very popular in the USA, with about 74% of the market share 3 despite its famously cluttered layout but only captures 2.9% of the Japanese market share 14 could be attributed to differences in American and Japanese culture. There may be MySpace features that are so appealing to Americans as to forgive its bad design while the same may not hold true for Japanese users.

Using previous work by one of the authors as a guide, 9 and 8, this paper seeks to analyze differences and similarities of user-interface (UI) design for SNSs from Japan, South Korea, and the USA in order to understand to what extent the designs seem to exhibit patterns of difference and similarities that relate to corresponding cultural differences and similarities.

A fundamental basis of this paper and several others cited is Geert Hofstede's model of five cultural dimensions 4, in which culture is exhibited by behaviors, heroes/heroines, signs, and values, and each country is assumed to have a dominant culture. See Figure 1 for a comparison of the cultures/countries studied in this paper. Another important aspect considered in this paper is the concept of user-interface components 10, which are metaphors, mental models, navigation, interaction and appearance.

N. Aykin (Ed.): Internationalization, Design, LNCS 5623, pp. 59–68, 2009.

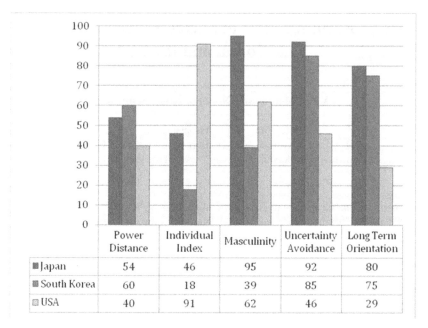

	Power Distance	Individual Index	Masculinity	Uncertainty Avoidance	Long Term Orientation
■ Japan	54	46	95	92	80
■ South Korea	60	18	39	85	75
▢ USA	40	91	62	46	29

Fig. 1. Comparison of 5 typical cultural dimensions as explained by Geert Hofstede 4. Each dimension derives from a study of participants in 74 countries.

Combining Hofstede's cultural dimensions with the five user-interface components, a paper by Marcus and Baumgartner 8 analyzed 25 possible areas to evaluate how a company's corporate Website seems localized to a specific culture and found several observable patterns that were typical to certain cultures. Another work with the same principles as 8 is a tutorial presentation by the authors' firm 7, which analyzed the cultural differences between mobile platforms developed for Western cultures such as the United States and Europe and those developed for Eastern cultures such as Japan, South Korea and Taiwan.

This initial analysis attempts to use the methods proposed by Marcus and Baumgartner 8 to observe and analyze patterns that may be distinguished by culture.

2   Methodology

To analyze the cultural differences in SNSs, the authors' firm compiled a list of 39 seemingly well-known SNSs from Japan, South Korea, and the USA (one project assistant collecting sample sites was from Japan, and one was from South Korea). The team divided the SNSs into four categories based on the site's apparent main objective: fostering business relationships, sharing music and videos, sharing photos, and appealing to a youth market. In order to keep to the modest effort and time available for this project, the team considered only a select number of pages to visit for each SNS:

- First Page: Typically an introduction to the services provided to members and non-members by the SNS. On some sites, the first page is also where the user signs into his or her account.
- Sign-up Page: The sign-up page allows a user to join the SNS. Usually, the user enters some amount of private information and creates a unique identification (ID) that will be used to identify him/herself on the site. This page is also where the user creates a personal password to ensure that access to his/her membership remains secure.
- Sign-in Page: On SNSs that do not integrate the sign-in dialogue into the first page, there is a unique page that allows users to enter his/her site ID and password to enter the members-only area of the SNS.
- Home Page: The homepage is the first page the user sees after signing in. On the home page, the user can access all the main elements of the SNS such as chat, messaging, blogging, photo sharing, search, etc.

Table 1. Summary of features analyzed on selected SNS pages. Note: CAPTCHA test cited in the table stands for "Completely Automated Public Turing test to tell Computers and Humans Apart".

First Page	Home Page	Sign-up Page	Sign-in Page
Cuteness in design	Cuteness in design	Display of site benefits	Location of sign-in link/box on first page
Number of advertisements	Number of advertisements	User identity authentication	Prominent sign-in link/box on first page
Symmetrical layout	Symmetrical layout	CAPTCHA test 2	Use of separate page for sign-in
Simplicity in design	Simplicity in design	Type of privacy statement	Use of icons
Use of icons	Use of icons	Use of icons	
Public display of private member photos	Display of other members		
Public display of member directory	Display of friends		
Number of links	Number of links		
Type of colors used	Type of colors used		
Slogan uncertainty	Customization		
Selling explanation	Personalization		

The details examined on each page were restricted to items that were readily observable. As Table 1 indicates, not all features apply to every page. For example, the use of identity verification is only applicable during the sign-up process. Many of the features are quantified as simple yes/no questions. Some other features, such as the number of advertisements on the home page are numerically quantified. Finally, there are other elements, such as the display of a privacy statement on the sign-up page, where there were numerous options. In this case, the privacy statement could be a link to another page, a check-box that needs to be checked before the user may continue, or a full display of the privacy statement on the sign-up page.

Table 2. Matrix of design components vs. cultural dimensions.

Components / Dimensions	Power Distance	Individuality Index	Masculinity vs. Femininity	Uncertainty Avoidance	Long Term Orientation
Metaphor					
Mental Model					
Navigation					
Interaction					
Appearance					

Combining the five cultural dimensions as discussed by Hofstede with the five design components results in a 5-by-5 matrix as shown below in Table 2. For each component in the matrix, SNSs from several different countries were compared and contrasted to evaluate the possible influence of culture on their designs. The observations are discussed in the next section.

3   Analysis of Cultural Dimensions and UI Components

The following sections discuss Hofstede's cultural dimensions and the user-interface components within them. Examples cite specific SNSs. To clarify some descriptions, visual examples appear from the sites being compared. All cultural dimension and corresponding values mentioned in this section can be referred to in Figure 1.

3.1   Power Distance: High vs. Low

3.1.1   Navigation: User-Identity Authentication
Following Hofstede's definition of Power Distance, we assume that low power-distance countries prefer open access, multiple options, and sharable paths. On the other hand, high power-distance countries have a higher use of authentication and passwords, and they prefer prescribed routes and restricted choices. A clear example of this difference can be seen in the sign-up pages of Cyworld, a youth orientated SNS, in the USA and South Korea. The power distance value for the USA (40) is lower than that of South Korea (60). To register on Cyworld USA, one only needs to enter basic credentials and create a password. None of the information entered is

verified, so it is easy for one to impersonate someone else. On the other hand, Cyworld South Korea verifies identity using a credit card and then requests for authorization by sending a text message to the user's cell phone. Unless both of these steps are completed, an account cannot be created.

3.2   Collectivism vs. Individualism

3.2.1   Metaphors: Public Display of Members' Private Pictures

Applying Hofstede's theory, we assume metaphors used in collectivist countries might be relationship-oriented and content-oriented, whereas those in individualist countries might be action- or tool-oriented. Given this understanding, it is reasonable to see members' pictures viewable by non-members on the first page of MySpace in the USA (individualist, with a individuality index of 91), because the members typically want to have as many friends as possible on their "friends list". Contrasting this action-oriented objective with that of Mixi in Japan (collectivist, with an individuality index of 46), one can see that no member information is accessible by non-members. An example of the display of members' pictures on MySpace appears in Figure 2, in which the members are labeled as "Cool New People".

Fig. 2. Display of members' pictures on the front page of MySpace in the USA

3.2.2   Appearance: Use of Cartoons to Replace Member Pictures

People from individualistic countries are typically more independent and strive to be unique individuals. In contrast, people from collectivistic countries prefer not to stand out and are more discreet. This difference is apparent when comparing user-profile pictures in Cyworld USA (individuality index of 91) with those of Cyworld Japan (individuality index of 46), as in Figure 3. As can be seen, the user-profile pictures from the USA are of the individuals themselves. However, this treatment is different for Cyworld Japan, in which pictures of animals, toys, or even celebrities are used in a user's profile in place of her/his photo.

Fig. 3. User profile pictures in Cyworld USA (left) and in Cyworld Japan (right)

3.3 Femininity vs. Masculinity

3.3.1 Navigation: Limited vs. Variable Choices

Hofstede's theory on femininity vs. masculinity asserts that more feminine countries would prefer multiple-choices, multi-tasking and polychronic approaches, whereas more masculine countries would prefer limited choices and synchronic approaches. We compare Mixi from Japan (high masculinity rating, with a value of 95) with MySpace from the USA (lower masculinity rating, with a value of 62). Mixi provides its users with a limited amount of options and customizability. The user's homepage features, layout and colors are not changeable. MySpace takes a different approach, where almost every aspect of the user's homepage is customizable. As determined by the user, features such as music, YouTube clips, photos and others can be added or removed from the homepage.

3.4 Uncertainty Avoidance

3.4.1 Metaphors: Use of Icons

Applying Hofstede's theory about uncertainty, we assume cultures with lower uncertainty avoidance would not shun, and might even prefer, novel, unusual, vague, or abstract references, whereas cultures with a higher amount of uncertainty avoidance might prefer familiar, stable, and clear references to daily life and be more comfortable with representation instead of abstraction. We compare the use of icons by Mixi in Japan (higher uncertainty avoidance, with a value of 92) with that of Fotolog in the USA (lower uncertainty avoidance, with a value of 46) as shown in Figure 4. Notice that Mixi has an icon for every link, whereas Fotolog has none.

Fig. 4. Use of icons in Mixi (Japan) and Fotolog (USA)

3.4.2 Mental Model: Display of strangers

Considering the mental model, we expect tolerance for ambiguousness in countries with low uncertainty avoidance. Conversely, we expect simple, explicit, clear articulation in countries with high uncertainty avoidance. Therefore, it is not surprising to see a pane in the user's home page in Facebook (USA, low in uncertainty avoidance) dedicated to "People You May Know" as in Figure 5. Such a feature creates uncertainty as one begins to wonder if they actually know the members featured on this pane. To the authors' knowledge, no Japanese or South Korean SNS implements a similar feature.

Fig. 5. "People You May Know" feature in Facebook (USA)

3.4.3 Navigation: Unique Sign-In Page

Countries with higher uncertainty avoidance tend to prefer clear, explicit articulation and limited choices; whereas countries with lower uncertainty avoidance are more tolerant of implicit structures and complexity. A simple example of this distinction can be seen by comparing the sign-in pages of two business SNSs, Ning in the USA (lower uncertainty avoidance, with a value of 46) and Linknow in South Korea (higher uncertainty avoidance, with a value of 85), as shown in Figure 6. On the first page of Ning, the user is directed to another page to sign in. This link is text-based, small, and on the upper-right-hand corner of the screen. On the other hand, there is a prominent sign-in box on Linknow's first page, a design that clearly reduces ambiguity of navigation.

Fig. 6. Sign-in link on Ning (USA) and sign-in box on Linknow (South Korea)

3.4.4 Appearance: Symmetrical Design

Countries with high uncertainty avoidance may prefer simple, clear, and consistent UI layout when compared to countries with low uncertainty avoidance. A simple way to analyze this factor is by comparing the layouts of different SNSs. Figure 7 shows the top of the homepage of Linknow in South Korea (higher uncertainty avoidance) with that of Linkedin in the USA (lower uncertainty avoidance). We observe that Linknow

Fig. 7. Symmetrical (Linknow, South Korea) vs. asymmetrical (LinkedIn, USA) design

has a more structured, symmetrical design with the page header set as tabs. Also, the header is aligned with the main content of the page. In contrast, LinkedIn has a less symmetrical look, as the page header does not align with the main content. Besides that, the components of the page in LinkedIn appear to float in the main content area.

3.5 Long-Term Time Orientation

3.5.1 Mental Model: Purpose / Age Divide

Hofstede's theory seems to imply that long-term time-oriented countries would more actively pursue the long-term perspective. Given this theory, we can assume that SNSs from long-term time-orientated countries such as Japan and South Korea would cater towards more longer-term relationship building when compared to SNSs from short-term time-orientated countries such as the USA where target audiences are less loyal to a brand. Numerous SNSs from South Korea, a country with high long-term time-orientation, such as Cyworld, IDtail and PlayTalk are promoted to a general audience in which users can establish longer-term relations. In contrast, there is a distinct age divide for SNSs in the United States, a country with relatively lower long-term time-orientation. Disney XD is an SNS designed for preteens, MySpace for teenagers and youths, Facebook for young adults, and Eons for baby boomers. Users can be expected to enter and leave these as their ages, interests, social connections, and preferences change. Also, there are many SNSs that are designed around certain special interests, such as LibraryThing for books lovers. Some of these differences arise from the strong individualist orientation as well as the shorter time perspective of American culture.

Note that a new Chinese SNS site FaceKoo has had some success appealing only to a youth market 1. This contradiction is explained by the growing shift of culture values in some segments of Chinese society, especially the wealthier, more modernized, more individualistic eastern regions most affected by technology change.

4 Discussion

From the analysis above, it becomes obvious that there are numerous cultural artifacts that integrate with the design of SNSs. However, it is important to not over-generalize, and assume that all design elements successful in one of these countries is guaranteed to provide the same results in other countries ranking similarly on Hofstede's cultural dimensions. Katayama 5 gives an example of how Cyworld Japan has failed to take-off especially when compared to Cyworld's huge success in its home country of South Korea. In the article, the Public Relations Manager for Cyworld Japan states "The Japanese tend not to talk about personal topics online." Therefore, Cyworld Japan created friend grouping functions and the option of censoring who can see certain information about the user. Related to the uniqueness of Japanese culture is the success of Mixi in Japan. Mixi is the most popular SNS in Japan with 84.8% of the market share. Toto of TechCrunch 12 states that one of the important features of Mixi allows Japanese users to maintain a high level of anonymity. This feature, so-called ashi-ato (Japanese for footprint) allows the user to retrace every visitor on his or her profile page, thus improving the feeling of personal security.

Other examples of SNSs venturing into cultures different from their originating country include Facebook's foray into Asian countries as well as Cyworld's expansion into the United States. An example of Facebook's failure to understand local Japanese culture is apparent when, while in Tokyo, Mark Zuckerberg, the founder and CEO of Facebook mentioned that one of the unique selling points of Facebook is the usage of real names and photos in profiles 13. However, this selling point may be exactly what the Japanese users are trying to avoid, as reasoned in Section 3.2.2. Cyworld USA implements features that may be better suited for South Korean culture than American culture. Its use of acorns to represent money 6 may be more confusing to users in the United States who may not understand the relationship between acorns and money, as they are more task-orientated.

While this paper provides some insights into apparent cultural differences in SNSs, more research needs to be done to obtain a clearer picture of the cultural artifacts involved in the different SNS sites. One way to move forward in obtaining more information is to complete more cells in the 5 by 5 matrix shown in Table 2. The inclusion of Europe into the study would also help give a clearer picture of how cultural differences affect patterns observed on SNS sites across the world. Europe was not included in this paper due to a lack of time and funding. Different types of more focused comparisons can be made as well. For example, the differences and similarities between the different Cyworld sites (South Korea, Japan and the United States) can be analyzed to see if any patterns emerge. Another option would be to narrow the focus of the research to one particular category of SNSs such as youth, photo sharing, or music and videos. Finally, a more through option to consider is to use the best-of-breed cultural dimensions as proposed by Marcus and Baumgartner 11 to replace Hoftstede's cultural dimensions. The best-of-breed dimensions are context, technology, uncertainty avoidance, time perception, and authority conception, in that order. However, more data needs to be obtained from South Korea and Japan if these dimensions are to be used.

Acknowledgements

The authors acknowledge the assistance of previous Designer/Analysts at the authors' firm, who carried out the original gathering of SNS Website samples and initial analysis of design characteristics: David Chang, Kaoru Kimura, and Hye-min Kim.

References

1. Gage, D.: Western Ideas, Tailored to East. The San Francisco Chronicle, Technology, January 12, 2009, D1 (2008)
2. Grossman, L.: Computer Literacy Tests: Are You Human? TIME, June 5 (2008),
   http://www.time.com/time/magazine/article/
   0,9171,1812084,00.html
3. Hitwise: MySpace Received 74 Percent of U.S Social Networking Visits for April 2008 (May 6, 2008),
   http://www.hitwise.com/press-center/hitwiseHS2004/
   social-networking-visits-april.php

4. Hofstede, G., Hofstede, G.J.: Cultures and Organizations – Software of the Mind. McGraw-Hill, New York (2005)
5. Katayama, L.: Japanese Facebook takes Model T approach. The Japan Times Online, June 25 (2008),
   http://search.japantimes.co.jp/cgi-bin/nc20080625a1.html
6. Kirkpatrick, M.: Massive Korean Social Network Cyworld Launches in US. TechCrunch, July 27 (2006),
   http://www.techcrunch.com/2006/07/27/
   this-is-nuts-cyworld-us-opens-for-use/
7. Marcus, A.: Cross-Cultural User-Interface Design Patterns for Mobile Products in Japan, Taiwan, and the USA. Aaron Marcus and Associates, Inc. (2007)
8. Marcus, A., Baumgartner, V.J.: Culture vs. Corporate Global Web UI Design. Aaron Marcus and Associates, Inc. (2004)
9. Marcus, A., Gould, E.W.: Cultural Dimensions and Global Web User-Interface Design: What? So What? Now What? In: Proc. 6th Conference on Human Factors and the Web, University of Texas, Austin, TX, June 19 (2000),
   http://www.tri.sbc.com/hfweb
10. Marcus, A.: Graphical User-Interfaces. In: Helander, M., Landauer, T.K., Prabhu, P.V. (eds.) Handbook of Human-Computer Interaction, ch. 19, pp. 423–444. Elsevier, Amsterdam (1997)
11. Marcus, A., Baumgartner, V.-J.: A practical set of culture dimensions for global user-interface development. In: Masoodian, M., Jones, S., Rogers, B. (eds.) APCHI 2004. LNCS, vol. 3101, pp. 252–261. Springer, Heidelberg (2004)
12. Toto, S.: Japan's Mixi: A Social Network As A Purely Local Phenomenon. TechCrunch, July 20 (2008),
   http://www.techcrunch.com/2008/07/20/
   japans-mixi-a-social-network-as-a-purely-local-phenomenon/
13. Toto, S.: Taking social networks abroad – Why MySpace and Facebook are failing in Japan. TechCrunch, August 3, 2008 (2008),
   http://www.techcrunch.com/2008/08/03/taking-social-networks-
   abroad-why-myspace-and-facebook-are-failing-in-japan/
14. Web Marketing Guide: Survey on utilization and current situation of SNS (translated). Web Marketing Guide, June 8 (2008),
   http://www.e-research.biz/profile/003437.html

Cross-Culture and Website Design: Cultural Movements and Settled Cultural Variables

Abdalghani Mushtaha and Olga De Troyer

Vrije Universiteit Brussel, Department of Computer Science
Research Group WISE, Pleinlaan 2, 1050 Brussels, Belgium
{abdalghani.mushtaha,Olga.DeTroyer}@vub.ac.be

Abstract. This paper reports on research carried out to determine the settled as well as other types of cultural markers including interface design elements and cultural dimensions that are appropriate to be used for cultural-centered website design and localization. For this, research discussed in this paper builds upon the existing body of research in website design and anthropologists' cultural dimensions. The research was performed in two phases: a first study was carried out to re-evaluate some pre-researched websites, and the second study was performed to evaluate and rank anthropologist's cultural dimensions. The findings of both research studies were evaluated and compared against earlier research results in order to provide insight into the evolution of the use of cultural markers. The results, a grouping of the cultural markers into 5 levels can be used for designing cultural-centered websites.

Keywords: Website localization, Cultural markers, Cross-cultural usability.

1 Introduction

The huge growth of Internet and particularly the Web has increase the emphasis on making a website usable for users and to localize it for a specific website audience. A lot of research studies have been done on the topic of localization and cross-cultural interface adaptation [9][13][17]. Most of these research studies investigated how to make a website more usable for users by localizing it for a special group of users: for a particular country, culture, or market.

Previous studies in the area of cross-cultural and website design usability [9][11][16], mostly concluded that the cultural background of a website visitor indeed has an impact on understanding and accepting a website. Moreover, many of these cross-cultural and website design studies proposed a cultural localization model based on anthropologists' cultural values.

At the Web & Information System Engineering (WISE) Laboratory, we have also done some studies aiming at verifying the relationship between websites and anthropologists' cultural dimensions [14][17]. The purpose of these studies was to determine the extent to which local web sites reflected the anthropologists' score assigned to their country for different cultural dimensions. Our research results looked inconsistent with the research findings of the other research studies. Nevertheless, our research findings highlighted some cultural values which do have an impact on the user's perception

N. Aykin (Ed.): Internationalization, Design, LNCS 5623, pp. 69–78, 2009.
© Springer-Verlag Berlin Heidelberg 2009

towards understanding and accepting a website. Therefore, we decided to identify the settled as well as different types of cultural variables that are applicable for cultural-centered website design and localization.

2 Purpose of Research

A number of researchers have attempted to define a cross-culture usability model for websites through empirical research; most of the researches have based their evaluation on testing some websites [3][6][9]. Because of that, some research results are quite different from other research results, as our last research studies proved [14][17]. For this, presently, there are few settled cultural variables and there is no clear cross-culture usability model agreed upon by all researchers. This research intended to fill this gap by exploring settled as well as the different types of cultural markers, including interface design elements and cultural dimensions that are appropriate to be used for cultural-centered website design and localization.

2.1 Research Approach

In order to achieve our goal, a multi-method approach was used. We have divided the research into two main studies: cultural markers evaluation and cultural dimensions verification study.

A first study, the cultural makers evaluation, was carried out to re-evaluate some pre-researched websites. In this study, we reviewed some well-known examined websites and tried to evaluate them again against the old research results. Comparing current and earlier versions of the same website can give valuable information on cultural movements and settled cultural variables.

In a second research study, the cultural dimension verification study, nineteen (Website developer, localization, translation and internationalization experts) were asked to evaluate 16 cultural dimensions, which were investigated by anthropologists and systems designers. The aim of this study was to find out which cultural dimensions are really important for cultural-centered website design and localization, and to compare them with earlier research results.

3 Cultural Markers Evaluation

This study seeks to compare cultural markers in current and earlier versions of the same website on the Web. The websites, which were involved in this study, were websites that were involved in previous research studies [3][4][12][13][21].

3.1 Methodology for the Cultural Markers Evaluation

People from Malaysia, Greece, United Kingdom, Nederland, United States and Japan were asked to join this study to evaluate the two versions of 22 websites. We selected people from different countries because local people are better able to evaluate their local websites. Moreover, they know their own habits, cultures and are best placed to evaluate if an object is linked to their own culture or not.

Evaluation and comparison were focused on five main design components; (1) Text density, size, orientation, style and type (2) Page layout, (3) Colors, (4) Pictures, graphic elements and sound and (5) Interaction and navigation. The selection of these design elements components to be evaluated was based on previous research in cross-cultural and website design.

A scale of 1 to 5 was used in rating the extent to which a new website version was related to an old version. Here the rating scale was: 1 = not perceptible: "no difference between the two versions of the website", 2 = hardly perceptible, 3 = perceptible to some extent, 4 = clearly perceptible and 5 = strongly perceptible: "total difference between the two versions of the website".

3.2 Findings

This section summarizes our key findings emerging from this study. The findings from this exploratory study indicate that there is a variation in some cultural markers between current and earlier versions of the same website.

- Text on websites:
Current websites containing more text than previous website versions, with an average score of 3.3, while text availability in older website version was 2.4 (on a 1 to 5 scale).

- Page layout:
The results showed that current websites focus on design the content by means of "blocks of data". Moreover, the data presented in current websites were in the centre of the screen and not restricted to left-aligned fixed-width layouts. Layout of the current website versions was clearly perceptible with a score of 3.7, while layout of earlier website versions was perceptible to some extent with a score of 3 (on a 1 to 5 scale). This study found that, current websites layout is totally different from the earlier website versions and the layout differences between both versions were clearly perceptible, with a score of 4.

- Colors:
Current website versions seem to use less colors to decorate the website. Using colors in current website versions were perceptible to some extent with an average score of 3.1 and 3.3 for earlier website versions (on a 1 to 5 scale).
The results show significant differences perceptible to some extent between the two categories with an average score of 3.2 (on a 1 to 5 scale).

- Pictures, graphic elements and sound:
The research found that, current website versions contain many attractive elements, and a lot of small icons to attract the visitor's attention with an average score of 3.8, while in earlier website versions, there were only a few websites with an average score of 3.1 (on a 1 to 5 scale).
There exists a perceptible sensory difference and also a similarity between samples of two websites groups; therefore, the differences between the two website versions were perceptible to some extent. The average score given for the general perceptibility rating of the extent to which new website versions related to old versions was 3.3.

- Interaction and navigation:
The average score given for general perceptibility was 4 for current websites homepages and 3.1 for earlier websites (on a 1 to 5 scale). While, the differences between two websites versions were perceptible with an average score of 3.4.

Overall, from the data and analyses presented above, it is clear that current website versions used website design component perceptible better than earlier website versions with an average score of 3.6, while earlier website versions had an average score of 3 (on a 1 to 5 scale). Moreover, the differences between the two groups of website versions were perceptible, with an average score of 3.4.

We also noticed that some cultural markers disappear and some are new, while others are still used. Therefore, we distinguish three types of cultural markers. The first type are the old cultural markers and some website design technologies, which appeared before in the old website versions disappeared in the current versions. The second type are the new cultural markers; this group contains cultural markers and website design technologies which appears in current websites and did not appear before. And the third type are the shared cultural markers; these are the stable cultural markers and website design technologies which appeared before and are still used. (The full details available with the authors)

Color is an example of a shared cultural marker. It is still a cultural oriented marker, and is still used in current website versions, while pictures are slightly more used in current website versions. It is also important to note that most of the websites have the following cultural markers: few graphic elements and more text, and the text plays a vital part in the current website versions.

Empirical research carried out by Gould [6] has shown that the website of the Universiti Utara Malaysia (www.uum.edu.my) presented and focused on authority figures and contained power symbols. In their investigation they found that, the Malaysian website contained links on the home page to website administration, pictures and symbols focusing on the country itself rather than featuring photographs of individuals. Moreover, black background, monumental buildings, top level menu selection focused on symbolism and information about the leaders of the University, which correlates well with Malaysian cultural background. By contrast, the current version of the Malaysian university website focuses on individuals. The website now contains pictures of students and teachers, the black background has disappeared, no pictures of monumental buildings anymore and the website's menu is more focused on students. But still there are some cultural markers available in the current website version. Colors, logos, social activities are some cultural markers that still appear. As an example, the current website contains a picture in the home page of a girl wearing a scarf, which is a symbol for Muslims girls.

4 Verifying Cultural Dimensions

The theoretical frameworks that have been used to guide this study are the cultural dimensions of the following anthropologists and systems designers: Nancy J. Adler [1], Edward T. Hall [10], Geert Hofstede [11], Fons Trompenaars [13], David A. Victor [19] and Quincy Wright [16]. The following cultural dimensions are used:

Human Nature Orientation [12], *Individualism vs. Collectivism* [1][10][19], *Internal vs. External Control* [1][13][19], *Time Orientation* [12], *Authority Conception* [20], *Context* [14][17][20], *Gender Roles* [10], *Power Distance* [10][17], *Uncertainty Avoidance* [10], *Universalism vs. Particularism* [19], *Achievement vs. Ascription* [19], *Affective vs. Neutral* [19], *Specific vs. Diffuse* [19], *Experience of Technology* [20], *Face-Saving* [13][20], *and International Trade and Communication* [15].

4.1 Methodology of the Study

Questionnaires were sent out to 50 experts with different backgrounds, such as: Website developer; localization, internationalization and translation experts. Responses were received from nineteen experts, who were then requested to further participate in the study. Experts who participate in this study had more than 6 years of experience in the field of user-interface design, localization or translation. The experts had different cultural backgrounds: Belgium, United Kingdom, Luxembourg, France, United States of America, Palestine, Egypt, United Arab Emirates and Jordan.

Sixteen cultural dimensions of the anthropologists and systems were presented by means of statements and cases. Every cultural dimension was explained in terms of its effects on website design. The participants were asked to indicate how much she or he agreed with the importance of the dimension as cultural dimension. The responses to these questions reflect how the participant sees the importance and the influence of every cultural dimension on cultural-centered website design and localization.

Participants were asked to read each cultural dimension details separately and then to rate it from 1 to 5, according to its importance for cultural-centered website design and localization. The rating scale was as follows: 5 = most important, 4 = important, 3 = important to some extent, 2 = not sure and 1 = not important.

4.2 Findings

Overall, the study revealed that participants were showing a clear interest in the research. Some participants agreed on the importance of some cultural dimensions in designing cultural-Centered website. Table 1 shows the ranking scores for each cultural dimension based on the marks given by experts. The column Average shows the average score given by the experts, while the columns Minimum and Maximum shows the lowest and highest score given by the participants.

The feedbacks we have gotten from this study showed that seven cultural dimensions are important and play a role when designing websites for cross-cultural audiences. They have an average score of more than 3.5 (on a 1 to 5 scale).

1. Experience of Technology
The cultural dimension "Experience of Technology" has got the highest score in this study from the experts. It refers to the attitude of certain society members towards technology. Participants were given comments such as: "It is always a challenge to make a product suitable for a specific society", "The first thing I have to think about is what is the level of technology experience the target audience has, because it is important to understand if a target audience society is willing to use a new technology to explore new things, or use a product without complaining."

Table 1. Cultural dimensions evaluation average rating

Dimension No.	Dimension Name	Cultural dimension ranking		
		Average	Minimum	Maximum
1	Experience of Technology	4.8	3	5
2	Context	4.7	3.5	5
3	International Trade and Communication	4.5	3	5
4	Gender Roles	4.3	2	5
5	Uncertainty Avoidance	4	2.5	4.5
6	Human Nature Orientation.	3.9	1.5	4.5
7	Power Distance	3.8	1	5
8	Time Orientation	3.4	2	4
9	Individualism vs. Collectivism	3.3	1	5
10	Authority Conception	3	1	5
11	Achievement vs. Ascription	2.8	1	4.5
12	Face-Saving	2.6	1	5
13	Specific vs. Diffuse	2.6	1.5	4
14	Affective vs. Neutral	2.4	1	5
15	Internal vs. External Control	1.8	1	4
16	Universalism vs. Particularism	1.7	1	4.5

2. Context

This cultural dimension seems to be the most important cultural dimension. All the participants agreed on the fact that amount of text, formality of website content, meaning of pictures and icons, information formality, explicit meaning or implicit information meaning of all those elements are cultural sensitive, and this cultural dimension affects website design.

3. International Trade and Communication

International Trade and Communication is a universal law rather than a cultural value. Study results showed that some countries are well aware of international standards and national trade and others do not care. For example, one of the participants noted: "The type of online payment, the level of trust and the procedure of payment should meets international standards, at the same time be compatible with user's culture background".

4. Gender Roles

Experts believe that women and men have different needs and interests in life in general, and this could affect their behaviour and interests in Websites.

5. Uncertainty Avoidance

Overall, experts recognized that it is worthwhile to understand how the target audience deals with uncertain and unexpected situations, such as: what is the reaction of the target people if the website navigation or any of design elements are not familiar to them?; Are the target audience afraid of strange and unexpected information or actions?

6. Human Nature Orientation

Study participants found that, human nature orientation gives a good indication for website localisers if the target society is able to change or not, and the degree of accepting changes. In other words, if people are accepting things which were not accepted in their own culture such as pictures, symbols, mental models, text...

7. Power Distance

Most of the participants agreed that website structure, type of messages, instructions and navigational structure are different among nations. One of the participants believes this cultural dimension is the most important one, he noted: "This is about the relationship between website owners and website visitors. For example, for this cultural dimension is important to know if website visitors are allowed to give comments or feedback on website content or not".

- Comparing our research results against earlier research results

In 2004, Aaron Marcus and his team at the AM+A studied the most practical set of culture dimensions for user interface design [12]. The following table (table 2) shows the comparison between the AM+A research results and our own research results.

Table 2. Comparing research results of the top seven important cultural dimensions

	Aaron Marcus (old research results)	Current research results
1	Context	Experience of Technology
2	Technological development	Context
3	Uncertainty avoidance	International Trade and Communication
4	Time perception	Gender Roles
5	Authority conception	Uncertainty Avoidance
6	Affective vs. neutral	Human Nature Orientation.
7	Face-saving	Power Distance

As can be seen in table 2, both research studies found that Context and Experience of Technology are the most important cultural dimensions for cultural-centered website design, followed by Uncertainty Avoidance and Power Distance. The cultural dimensions Time Perception, Affective vs. Neutral and Face-saving seem to be less important nowadays since those cultural dimensions do not appear in the current research results. Furthermore, current research results found that some cultural dimensions are now important for cultural-centered website design while they were not in the past: International Trade and Communication, Gender roles and Human Nature Orientation.

5 Discussion and Conclusion

The two research studies that we conducted have proven that some cultural markers are important for cultural-centered website design. Therefore, Web developers should be careful when a cultural-centered website design need to be developed.

— Website content, type of communication, colors and pictures are the website design elements that are mostly affected by the culture of peoples (cultural sensitive elements)

The research results emphasize the importance of the previous mentioned design elements in the design of cultural-centered websites.

5.1 Cultural Movements

It is a fact that most of the websites are changing from time to time and that is because the Web is a very dynamic environment. Nevertheless, our research found that some culture markers are still noticeable in new website versions but appear in different ways than in the past. The results of the cultural markers evaluation study showed that cultures markers are still notable in all websites examined and that the cultural differences between societies shift and change together. All people change together and therefore cultural differences remain between societies, and these differences are still perceptible in websites. Furthermore, we can state that:

• Rapid website development influence cultural shifts in websites

Due to the rapid development of web technologies and websites, there is a kind of competition between website owners to develop and keep track of new technology to highlight the content of a website in better and more appealing way and to make the website more usable. This development acceleration has induced the disappearance of some cultural markers from the past. In spite of this rapid development and its effects on website changes, some local cultural markers still appear in local websites but in another way. Another observation is:

• A culture that emerged from the use of the Web, and the local culture dominate the design of websites

Our research results of the cultural markers evaluation study and the verification of the cultural markers study found that the Web has decreased the cultural gap between Internet users. This new multicultural network creates an intercultural communication between people. Therefore, new cultural values appear and people who use the Web understand them:

• New cultural dimensions and markers became important for cultural-centered website design

Our research results show that some new cultural dimensions and cultural markers are important for cultural-centered website design. Perhaps the explanation for this is that, in the last four years, social networking sites, Wiki's, and communication tools became important and are used frequently. Furthermore, the Web transformed from a so-called "Read-only Web" to a "Read-Write Web" [5], in which content is created, shared, remixed, repurposed, and passed along. After a four year time period between the old and new research, research results still emphasize the importance and influence of anthropologists' cultural models. Our research shows a strong relation between culture and website design. All experts who participate in the second study, strongly advised to use anthropologist models for website design:

• Anthropologist cultural dimensions are still applicable for designing cultural-centered websites.

5.2 Five Levels of Cross-Cultural Markers for Cultural-Centered Website Design

It was found that, not all websites in a society fit its own cultural pattern exactly. Therefore, it is difficult to establish absolute criteria for what is important and which cultural makers are applicable for cultural-centered website design. Therefore, we have divided the cross-cultural markers that are suitable for designing cultural-centered website and localization into five levels:

1. **Context-dependent cultural markers** (e-culture): This research study reported that some cultural markers are shared between users who use the same website category. For example, people who use news website frequently have some shared semantic meaning for website elements related to news website.
2. **Settled cultural markers:** These are the website design elements and cultural dimensions which were confirmed by current and earlier research studies.
3. **Broad cultural markers:** These are the new cultural dimensions and markers that were discovered in this research study.
4. **Variable cultural markers:** These are the cultural markers and dimensions that were discovered in previous research and did not appear in this current research.
5. **Vista cultural markers:** These are all the other cultural dimensions. This type of cultural markers is identified and characterized at the national level.

Each level represents a group of related cultural markers and anthropologists' cultural dimensions, having its own sensitivity and level of importance for website localization. The first level (called the e-culture) has the highest priority level in website localization, the second priority is level 2 (the settled ones), and so on, while the least priority is the Vista level with the most cultural oriented group of markers. In this way, website developers can choose between the five levels, depending on the cultural adaptation needs formulated for the website.

The variations between the use of cultural markers in websites for the same nation are usually the result of differences in the type of website. For example university websites use cultural elements different from those used by e-commerce websites or news websites. Each website has its own identity, context, and target audience. And for that, the level of cultural adaptation may differ between websites for the same nation. Thus, the five levels identified can be used to build cultural-centered websites depending on the type of website. The relation between these five levels of cultural markers and the type of website will be explained in more details in the near future.

References

1. Adler, N.-J.: International dimensions of organizational behavior Cincinnati. South-Western/Thomson Learning, Ohio (2002)
2. Alexakis, P.: Cross-Cultural Issues in Web Development. University of Southampton (2001)
3. Aykin, N.: Usability and Internationalization of Information Technology, p. 392. Lawrence Erlbaum, New York (2005)
4. Barber, W., Badre, A.: Culturability: The Merging of Culture and Usability. In: 4th Conference on Human Factors and the Web, Basking Ridge NJ (1998)

5. Best of ReadWriteWeb, http://www.readwriteweb.com/bestof.php
6. Gould, E., Zakaria, N., Yusof, S.A.M.: Applying culture to website design: a comparison of Malaysian and US websites. In: 18th ACM International Conference on Computer documentation: technology & teamwork, Cambridge, Massachusetts, pp. 161–171 (2000)
7. Huang, K.H., Deng, Y.S.: Social interaction design in cultural context: A case study of a traditional social activity. International Journal of Design 2(2), 81–96 (2008)
8. Hofstede, G.: Cultures and Organizations: Software of the Mind. McGraw-Hill, London (1991)
9. Instone, I., Czerwinski, M., Mountford, S.J., Nielsen, J., Tognazzini, B.: Web Interfaces Live: What's Hot, What's Not? In: Proceedings of ACM-CHI, pp. 103–104 (1997)
10. Marcus, A., Baumgartner, V.: Visible Language, Special Issue Cultural Dimensions of Communication Design. Part 2 ISSN 0022-2224, pp. 252–261 (2004)
11. Marcus, A., Gould, E.W.: Cultural Dimensions and Global Web User-Interface Design: What? So What? Now What? In: 6th Conference on Human Factors and the Web in Austin. Texas (2000)
12. Mushtaha, A., De Troyer, O.: Cross-cultural understanding of content and interface in the context of E-learning systems. In: Aykin, N. (ed.) HCII 2007. LNCS, vol. 4559, pp. 164–173. Springer, Heidelberg (2007)
13. Quincy, W.: The Study of International Relations. Appleton-Century-Crofts, New York (1955)
14. Smith, A., Dunckley, L., French, T., Minocha, S., Chang, Y.: A process model for developing usable cross- cultural websites. Interacting with Computers. Interacting with Computers 16(1), 63–90 (2004)
15. Stengers, H., De Troyer, O., Baetens, M., Boers, F., Mushtaha, A.: Localization of Web Sites: Is there still a need for it? In: International Workshop on Web Engineering (HyperText 2004 Conference), Santa Cruz, USA (2004)
16. Sun, H.: Building a Culturally Competent Corporate Web Site: An Exploratory Study of Cultural Markers in Multilingual Web Design. In: Proceedings of SIGDOC, pp. 95–102. ACM Press, New York (2001)
17. Trompenaars, F.: Riding the waves of culture, Understanding Cultural Diversity in Business. Brealey London (1995)
18. Victor, A.: International Business Communication. Prentice Hall, New York (1997)
19. de Wit, F., Diehl, J.C., Arts, F.A.: How to design cultural appropriate web sites for knowledge transfer: understanding preferences. In: IWIPS 2005: designing for global markets 7. S.l.: P&SI, pp. 143–149 (2005)
20. Yammiyavar, P., Clemmensen, T., Kumar, J.: Influence of cultural background on nonverbal communication in a usability testing situation. International Journal of Design 2(2), 31–40 (2008)

Cross-Cultural Design and Evaluation of the Apple iPhone

Michael A. Oren, Utkarsh Seth, Fei Huang, and Sunghyun Kang

Springer-Verlag, Computer Science Editorial, Tiergartenstr. 17,
69121 Heidelberg, Germany
{moren,useth,feihuang,shrkang}@iastate.edu

Abstract. In this paper, we report the design and results of a study to improve the usability of the iPhone for a global audience, particularly in India and China. With extensive research in cultures of three countries China, India, and the United States, the iPhone interface was redesigned with an eye to culturally universal (for the three cultures of interest to this study) and ease of access of functions most used by mobile phone users in these cultures. Both the iPhone and the new prototype interfaces were tested to measure their usability and results are reported here.

Keywords: Global Design, Usability, iPhone, Mobile Interfaces.

1 Introduction

In an ever shrinking world and increasing globalization, cross cultural studies while designing products is proving to be a valuable tool for its effectiveness. From Switzerland to Singapore, from Boston to Bombay, the latest electronic designs are familiar icons of modern technology & culture. Despite this globalization, it is detrimental to the selling value of the product if it is not designed keeping the culture in mind where the product is going to be used in. Previous work on mobile device redesign has been conducted by Lee, et al who looked into cultural issues with menu hierarchies of mobile devices [1].

The product in question, the iPhone, was launched in June 2007 by Apple Inc. The phone, hailed for its revolutionary technology, indeed had lots of design problems. There were functions that were present in the phone but the user had no clue how to access them. The visual cues, which could tell the user what a function or icon does, provided to the user were also not very intuitive or logical. Some of the most common features that a user wished to access in a minimum number of steps were embedded down in the hierarchy of menus. The phone also lacked consistency among the screens where it performed different actions on the same inputs (such as tapping a name found in recent calls resulting in calling the person, whereas tapping a name in contact would take the user to more details about the contact). And most important of all, the phone was not designed to cater to the needs of various cultures where the mobile phone market is surging.

The current iPhone has several flaws which makes it unsuitable for different cultures. For example the icon of the "Maps" is not very intuitive when we talk about

N. Aykin (Ed.): Internationalization, Design, LNCS 5623, pp. 79–88, 2009.

various cultures. The icon displays an interstate Logo which is indeed very common to the people living in the USA. But when we talk about people from India and China there is no concept of an "interstate" there so if this version of the iPhone is launched in these countries people there might be clueless about what the icon represents.

To explore similar type of problems and solve them eventually we need to interview people from different countries and ask them about their inhibitions with the iPhone. We will have them do specific tasks and will ask for their input on the product. This way we will get a clear idea as to what people from different cultures like India and China expect from the product.

There were also general usability problems that were found in the iPhone. Those were inconsistency problems with the interface that are discussed in detail in the design goals. There were also opportunities to maximize the use of the multi-touch functionality in the iPhone. We came up with several efficient designs that would provide more uses for the touch functions beyond simply just tapping the screen.

Our study of the iPhone took place from January through May 2008 using version 1.14 of the iPhone OS.

2 Early Evaluation

Before redesigning the iPhone, we conducted exploratory research to determine the most used features of mobile phones among the three cultures. We also conducted a study of the current iPhone icons to determine how easily identifiable users found the icons to determine which icons required a redesign.

2.1 General Cell Phone Study

One of the early evaluation tools we used was a short survey to poll potential users regarding what features they most commonly use on their cell phones and the steps they have to take to use those features. One of the most striking things we learned from this survey was that although the majority of respondents indicated that the alarm clock was one of the most common features they use, only one person (out of 5 who listed alarm as a critical feature) listed fewer than seven steps in order to set an alarm. One person even had to take twenty steps on his LG cell phone. The iPhone also suffered from superfluous steps in order to set the alarm, so we decided that this would be one of the key tasks for users to complete. As part of this survey, we asked non-iPhone users what features they most desired to see from the iPhone and the response was overwhelmingly data based features such as the web browser and Google Maps. Current iPhone users often stated that they feature they wanted improved the most were missing features, such as copy & paste rather than requesting changes to the current design. However, this might be early adopter bias not willing to admit Apple makes design mistakes.

2.2 Icon Evaluation

Sixteen participants (six Chinese, five Indian, and five American) participants completed a survey of the thirty-two icons used by the iPhone in version 1.14 of the OS. With the exception of icons appearing within menus, such as the clock under phone, no contextual information was given about the icons on the survey. Participants were given the survey with blank lines beneath the icons and told to write down what mobile phone functions they thought the icon represented.

Table 1 presents the number of participants (out of 16) that correctly determined what each icon in the original interface represented.

Table 1. The number of users (of 16) properly identifying the icon

Map	Calendar	Notepad	Weather	Stocks	Clock	YouTube	iTunes Download
13	16	4	16	7	16	3	4
Calculator	Settings	Photos	Camera	SMS/Text	Phone	Mail	iPod/Music
15	7	12	8	9	14	8	14
Mute	Keypad	Speaker Phone	Add to Conversation	Hold	Contacts	Recent Calls	Browser
11	6	2	3	13	3	0	2
Contacts	Keypad	Voicemail	Favorites	World Clock	Alarm	Stopwatch	Timer
4	3	4	9	7	14	11	4

Sixteen of thirty-two icons performed very poorly, with fewer than eight people properly recognizing the icons. In order from "least recognized" to "most recognized", the icons receiving fewer than three correct identifications were: recent calls (0); speaker phone (2); Internet browser (2); YouTube (3—the response "video" was accepted); add to conversation (3); contacts—under Phone (3); keypad—in a call (3); contacts—while in a call (4); timer (4); voicemail (4); iTunes Download (4—the response "download" was accepted); notepad (4); keypad—under phone (6); stocks (7-both American and Chinese participants had over 50% recognition, but none of the Indian participants recognized this icon); settings (7); world clock (7). In addition, the mail icon had 50% recognition rate (8 participants recognized it), but it was skewed because all five American participants recognized it while only two of six Chinese participants and one of five Indian participants properly identified it.

3 Methods

All studies took place in an isolated office or room. The original iPhone interface was tested using a 4 GB iPhone running the latest version of the iPhone OS (1.14) and participants hands were recorded via a mini-DV camcorder mounted on a tripod placed behind the participant's shoulder. A Windows XP laptop was used to run the prototype of the new interface, which used Camtasia to record the screen and the participant's voice.

Participants were randomly assigned to start with either the original iPhone interface or the prototype interface and after completing all tasks they would switch to the other version. There were seven tasks users were asked to complete, which were evaluated based on completion time and the number of clicks it took them to complete the tasks. The seven tasks users were asked to complete were

1. Turn phone on
2. Set the alarm to recur every weekday at 4:45 AM (time varied)

3. Call the contact Google411 and place the call on speaker phone
4. Add a recent call as a new contact named "Joe Smith"
5. Rearrange the home-screen
6. Silence the phone
7. Turn phone off

These tasks were randomly assigned to participants, with the notable exception of turning the phone on and turning the phone off, which relied on the current state of the phone to determine whether the participant would be able to complete the task.

Participant performance was measured by the amount of time taken (measured in seconds) to complete each task as well as by the number of clicks the user took to complete tasks. Correct clicks when typing in a name were not counted, nor were clicks (or the time taken) that led to portions of the interface that had not been implemented in the prototype but would have normally worked (clicks that led to unimplemented areas that would not have led to successful completion of the task were counted). Significance level was calculated with 95% confidence using a Student's t-test.

3.1 Participants

We recruited five (3 males, 2 females) American participants, five (1 male, 4 female) Indian participants, and six (3 male, 3 female) Chinese participants, primarily through a word-of-mouth recruitment strategy. One American participant owned an iPhone, while the remaining American participants owned other phones (two Motorola—one was a smart phone, two Sony Ericcson). Three Indian participants owned a Samsung phone, one a Sony phone, and the last a Motorola—not of the phones were smart phones. Likewise, none of the Chinese participants had a smart phone as their primary phone—four had an LG brand phone and two had Motorola brand phones. Three American participants fit into the primary target age range of 20-30; however, one participant was over the age of 50 and one was under 20. The participant under 20 was not yet a college graduate. All other participants had completed high school or higher. Other than the participant over the age of 50 rating the intuitiveness of many of the original interface functions lower than the other participants, there was no notable difference between the users that fit into our target demographic and the outliers. All five participants in the Indian group were between the ages of 20-30. Five of the six participants in the Chinese group were between the ages of 20-30, the sixth was between 30-40 years of age. Unlike the American outlier, however, the Chinese participant in the age range of 30-40 did show significant performance differences when compared to the other Chinese participants—taking a significantly longer amount of time spent on several tasks (they were removed from the analysis of those tasks noted below).

4 Results

Only three tasks resulted in a statistically significant improvement for the American group with a 95% confidence level between the original design and the new design: calling a contact on speakerphone, adding a recent contact, and turning the phone off. This improvement was both in the time needed to complete the task as well as the number of times participants clicked on elements of the interface (both results were significant). Marginal significance (p <= 0.10) was also found for the tasks of silencing the phone and rearranging the home-screen, but this marginal significance was only an indication of reduced number of clicks in the new interface as compared to the old interface not in the amount of time used to complete tasks.

All but one task (setting the alarm) resulted in statistically significant improvement in terms of number of clicks for participants in the Indian group with a 95% confidence level. The task of setting an alarm did result in marginally significant improvement for Indian participants. Likewise, five of seven tasks resulted in statistically significant improvements in the time spent to complete the tasks on the new prototype for Indian participants, only the times for adding a recent call and turning the phone off did not show significant improvement.

Chinese participants saw four of seven tasks show a significant improvement in the time to complete the task with a 95% confidence level, with the task of placing a call on speakerphone showing marginally significant improvement. The tasks of turning the phone on and setting the alarm did not show significant improvement for completion time, and neither of these tasks showed a statistically significant improvement in terms of number of clicks required to complete tasks. Four tasks showed statistically significant improvement for the number of clicks required to complete tasks, and silencing the phone showed marginally significant improvement for the number of clicks required.

While on most tasks the American participants still performed better than the Indian and Chinese participants, the difference between the number of extra clicks and time needed for Indian and Chinese participants as compared to the American participants was reduced (this was not a statistically significant improvement for the majority of tasks).

4.1 Survey Results

For all tasks, nine out of the sixteen participants indicated that the new interface made the task more intuitive. For the task of silencing the phone, three of the five participants preferred the new interface. Only one American participant preferred the new interface for the task of setting the alarm (all six Chinese participants preferred the new interface and three Indian participants preferred it for the alarm task), but one of the American participant indicated this response had more to do with the style of the sliders, which we were unable to duplicate for this study. While five participants each in both the American and Chinese groups preferred the new interface for silencing the phone, only two of five participants in the Indian group preferred the new interface. It was unclear why the Indian participants felt this way, quantitatively the participants did significantly better using the new silence function (p < .003) for both clicks and time required to silence the phone.

All but four (2 Chinese and 2 Indian—all 4 of whom had heard of it) participants indicated that they knew about the iPhone beyond its name, three (2 American and 1 Chinese) had used one before but did not own one, and one American participant owned an iPhone. Two (1 American and 1 Chinese—the Chinese participant also used Windows) participants used OS X on their primary computer; one American participant used OSX, Linux, and Windows on a daily basis; one American participant used

Windows XP and Linux on a daily basis; all remaining participants (5 Indian, 3 American, and 5 Chinese) participants used Windows XP exclusively.

Participants were asked to rate the intuitiveness of each task on each interface based on a 5-point scale (1-Not at all intuitive; 5-Very intuitive).

On the original interface, three tasks had mean scores that were below three for the American group: turning the phone on (2.6); turning the phone off (2.8); and rearranging the home-screen (2.8). The Chinese group only scored one task below 3 (rearranging the home-screen with a mean score of 2.3) and silencing the phone had a mean score of exactly 3 points for the Chinese group. The Indian group was by far the most favorable of the original interface with no task receiving a mean score of less than 3.4. When all 16 participants were combined, only the task of rearranging the home-screen had a mean score less than three (only 6 of 16 participants scored it 4 or higher—all other tasks had at least 50% of participants scoring it 4 or higher). The fact that turning the phone on scored lowest for the American participants, despite taking most participants fewer clicks and less time than either of the other two tasks seems strange, but may indicate that participants feel this is an important task to keep as simple as possible. Furthermore, only two tasks scored above a mean score of 4 on the original interface (when all participants were combined): setting the alarm (4.3 and 14 of 16 participants scoring it 4 or higher) and making a call on speaker phone (4.3—with 13 of 16 participants giving it a score of 4 or higher).

In contrast, all but one task (turning the phone off—3.8 for the American group but over 4 for Indian and Chinese groups) had a mean score above 4 in each respective group when participants rated the intuitiveness of completing tasks on the new interface. When combining all participants, all tasks scored at least a 4.2 for the new interface and had at least 13 of 16 participants rating it a 4 or higher on intuitiveness. Furthermore, while 8 of 16 users ranked rearranging the home-screen as the most difficult task on the original interface, there was no clear "worst" task on the new interface.

It should be noted that the original interface scored an overall intuitive mean score of 3.6 (Chinese 3.83; American 4; Indian 3.6) whereas the new interface received a just barely better score of 3.8 (Chinese 3.7—worse than original; American 3.6—worse than original; Indian 4.2—only better than original). However, one American user rated the overall intuitiveness of the new interface a '5' on all but one task (rearranging the home-screen—4) and indicated that they preferred the new interface for all tasks (and overall), but scored the overall intuitiveness of the new interface a '1'. This seems to be a mistake by the participant that has skewed this particular result significantly due to the small sample size. A similar mistake appeared to have occurred with one Chinese participant (who also rated the new interface a '1' and the old interface a '4' despite very high marks for the new interface as compared to the old and listing preferences for the new interface for all tasks other than silencing the phone)—this participant also noted that the original interface definitely needs to be improved.

At least 9 of 16 participants preferred the new interface on all tasks (turning the phone off—9 participants; and setting the alarm—10 participants had the fewest people prefer them). Overall, 14 of 16 (all but 1 American and all but 1 Indian) users indicated that they preferred the new interface to the old interface. For the alarm task, it is our belief, based on feedback from participants that the old interface was preferred only due to the fact that we were unable to mock up the iPhone-style sliders on the computer. In general though, this indicates a remarkable success for our new design within the American, Chinese, and Indian marketplaces.

5 Design

Most of the tasks showed considerable improvements in terms of fixing general usability issues and bringing all three cultural groups to a roughly equal level of performance on tasks they were completing for the first time. However, a large performance gap was still very apparent in adding a recent call as a new contact between the Chinese group and the other two cultural groups. Furthermore, 16 of the 32 icons on the iPhone were identified correctly by fewer than half of the participants. Using these findings we undertook efforts to redesign the remaining elements of the iPhone.

While all tasks showed statistically significant improvement overall from the original design to the first prototype and each individual group always showed improvement (although not always significant) from the first prototype to the new prototype on all tasks, adding a recent call as a new contact appeared to have a cultural gap between the Chinese group and the other two cultural groups (see figure 1).

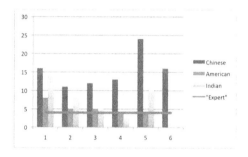

Fig. 1. A graph showing the number of clicks each participant took to complete the task

As this chart clearly shows, Chinese participants used 10 or more clicks than the average American participant. In reviewing the recording of the participants, these excessive clicks appeared to be due to participants in this group not noticing either the green plus or blue arrow that they needed to click in order to complete this task. Whether this was due to the buttons not being salient enough or whether it had to do with the button functionality not being obvious enough was unclear. As such, we chose to go about a redesign that would attempt to address both of these potential problems (see figure 2).

In order to address the issue of what the button does, we added the contact icon (address book) to the icon to make it clear that the "+" meant "add to contacts". While undergoing this redesign, we also decided to make it more obvious what the blue arrow on the right-hand side of each contact represented, which we achieved by grouping the time/day of the call with the blue arrow, which suggests that clicking that button will lead the user to additional information about the call. As an added bonus, this redesign also increases the surface area where the user can press in order

Fig. 2. The redesigned recent calls screen

to add a call as a new contact or get additional information since one of the problems we found with this task was that the blue arrow was simply too small for most users to easily click.

In order to address the problem of saliency (e.g. the button going unnoticed), we increased the size of the button (partially as a natural function of adding the icon). We also chose a shade of green that stood out more from the blue of the rest of the interface. In addition, we made the contact icon brown as an additional method of catching the users eye as the combination of green, white, and brown on an otherwise consistent color palette draws the eye's attention to the button and ensures that users are able to notice its presence.

As we were unable to conduct a second study, we are unable to verify this claim. In addition, it is possible that the redesign creates an interface that distracts users from their primary goal on the recent calls page in order to promote a (possibly) rarely used feature. These are both considerations that would need to be addressed in a future study but are beyond the scope of this current project.

With half of the icons currently on the iPhone failing our low expectations of at least 50% user recognition, we knew that serious problems existed. To be fair, many of the icons that users failed to identify with 50% accuracy are ones that are fairly common on phones in the US (such as voicemail) so it is understandable why Apple may have chosen them; however, in order for Apple to succeed in the international marketplace they must consider icon designs that are easily recognizable to a wider audience. Out of these icons, we chose to redesign 15. We chose not to redesign the 'recent calls' icon (despite 0 of 16 users recognizing it) due to the fact that none of the users had trouble finding/going to recent calls when asked to complete that task so we felt that was simply an issue of the survey not providing enough context for that icon. In addition, we chose not to redesign the settings ('gears') icon as our group was unable to decide on a universal design for it. Many of our redesigns used the concept

Table 2. Original icons and the redesigned versions

Function	Original	New
Keypad		
YouTube		
Maps		
Music Store		
E-mail		
Contacts		
Notepad		
Internet Browser		
World Clock		
Timer		
Voicemail		
Speakerphone		
Add Caller		

of combining two common, easily recognizable icons in order to create one icon that was easy for all three cultures to recognize and interpret. The redesigned icons can be seen in Table 2.

6 Conclusion

We managed to identify key cultural design flaws and general usability problems present in the iPhone and successfully redesign it to reduce (although not completely eliminate) these problems. With the information presented here, Apple and other cell phone manufacturers should be able to guide their design in order to ensure that the widest possible world population can use it. The three cultures that were the focus of this study represent roughly half of the world's population as well as some of the largest, fastest growing mobile markets.

As noted earlier, these design solutions do not completely solve the cultural bias of the original iPhone and further iterative testing and redesign would help to further reduce the level of culturally based performance differences. Given more time, it might also be possible to infer more general cultural usability design guidelines based on these findings; however, such a goal was beyond the focus of this study. If our team had more time, it would have been ideal to run another study to confirm that the final redesign successfully addressed the most glaring remaining issues. However, overall, we feel that this was an extremely successful redesign that will help prevent calls to Apple's help desk when the iPhone is officially released in India, China, and other world markets.

Reference

1. Lee, Y., Ryu, Y., Smith-Jackson, T., Shin, D., Nussbaum, M., Tomioka, K.: Usability Testing with Cultural Groups in Developing a Cell Phone Nevigation System. In: The Proceedings of Human-Computer Interaction International (2005)

Cross-Cultural Understanding of the Dual Structure of Metaphorical Icons: An Explorative Study with French and Turkish Users on an E-Learning Site

Kerem Rızvanoğlu[1], and Özgürol Öztürk

Galatasaray University, Faculty of Communication,
Ciragan Cad. No:36 Ortakoy 34357 Istanbul, Turkey
{krizvanoglu,ozozturk}@gsu.edu.tr

Abstract. Research on the cross-cultural understanding of different interface aspects is an area of growing interest in human-computer interaction discipline. This paper mainly investigates the influence of culture on understanding metaphors in graphical user interfaces. Considering the dual coded structure of compound metaphorical icons which is composed of two major units: image and label, this study evaluates the main hypothesis that understanding of graphical and textual elements of the metaphors differs due to the real world and language experiences of the users. An empirical study on a French e-learning site - based on a spatial "Campus" metaphor- was conducted with 68 Turkish and French students. The study applied a multi-method approach including data collection instruments like questionnaires for understanding of metaphorical icons and interview. Findings do suggest differences in understanding across the two cultural groups and provide an in-depth analysis on the process of cross-cultural understanding of metaphors by focusing on the metaphorical inconsistencies

Keywords: Metaphor, icon, culture, understanding, user interfaces.

1 Introduction

Metaphors are the core idioms of the contemporary graphical user interfaces (GUI) and have an important role in helping users interact with computer systems, since they carry the experiences of the real world to the interactive media. However, every culture shares different experiences and values [1]. On Internet their members may not share the knowledge of the contexts in which the intended meanings of metaphors are rooted and this can produce difficulties in understanding during system interaction. Users may easily be frustrated by a culturally inappropriate metaphorical interface, because it would not represent their view of the real world. This lack of familiarity would easily lead to frustration and finally, rejection of the interface.

Previous studies showed that the experience with the physical world around users and experience with language are both rooted in culture and may affect the individual's understanding [2, 3]. However, there is not much empirical study investigating

---

[1] This study has been realized under the coordination of Assist. Prof. Elgiz Yılmaz with the support of Galatasaray University Scientific Research Fund.

N. Aykin (Ed.): Internationalization, Design, LNCS 5623, pp. 89–98, 2009.

the cross-cultural understanding of the metaphors. In this context, our study aims to evaluate the hypothesis that the understanding of graphical and textual elements of the metaphors differ due to the real world and language experiences of the users. The study also aims to provide an insight on the process of cross-cultural understanding of metaphors for the researchers and practitioners who work on cross-cultural issues in the area of human-computer interaction (HCI) by focusing on the possible inconsistencies. The remainder of this paper consists of a review of relevant literature. Afterwards, the methodology of the study will be explained followed by a discussion of the results and conclusion

2   Theoretical Background

2.1   Metaphors and Cross-Cultural Research on Metaphors in HCI

Lakoff and Johnson asserted that the metaphors are used to define our relationship with the physical environment and create a context of communication [1]. A metaphor utilizes familiar concepts or attributes from a source domain to provide insights about a target domain by an interpretation on similarities and differences between the source concepts and the target. Kittay [4] pointed out to the interaction of these similarities and differences and claimed that this interaction creates internal tension, which seems important in understanding metaphors. Lakoff and Johnson [1] called this interaction as the "recursive refinement process" and suggested that this interactive process plays a major role in reshaping an individual's understanding of the metaphor. Through this interaction, Kittay [4] categorized properties of target as having either affinity or contrast. Properties of the target, which are appropriate to intent and context, display affinity, while properties that do not appear to match intent and context display contrast [5]. An optimal interaction should exhibit high degrees of affinity, which are consonant with the experiences of our users or acceptable levels of contrast that encourages users to reinterpret and reconstruct [6] their understanding of the intended function. Over-estimation of this interaction results in the frustration of the users in two ways. "Alty and Knott identify two major kinds of confounding metaphors: metaphorical inconsistencies, where the interface function is not consistent with the metaphor and conceptual baggage, where the user is led by the metaphor's presence to believe he or she can do something that the product cannot accomplish" [5]. Cates [5] divide metaphors in technology-based learning products into two classes: underlying (or primary) metaphors and auxiliary (or secondary) metaphors. An underlying metaphor is the principal or first metaphor employed whereas an auxiliary metaphor is a subsequent metaphor employed by the product. Cates [5] stated that such an interaction also occurs between underlying and auxiliary metaphors.

Metaphor is a very popular but also a debated issue in the area of HCI. Though the fundamental role of metaphor in communication, interaction, learning, teaching and cognition is acknowledged by many studies [7], there are also other researchers, who reject the metaphor-based design approach in interfaces by referring to their limitations [8]. There are several studies, which aimed to develop guidelines for selecting and implementing metaphors for user interfaces [5, 9] whereas some other researches tried to extend the desktop metaphor into new prototypes [10]. Despite the vast literature on interface metaphors, there are only a few studies in the literature, which investigated the cross-cultural understanding and use of interface metaphors [2][11]. These researches pointed out to the complexity of intercultural understanding process and emphasized the need for further empirical research with diverse cultural groups on the perception and understanding of interfaces and metaphors. Focusing mainly on the understanding of metaphorical icons at both the levels of graphics and text, this study attempts to provide contributing findings for cross-cultural usability and design by presenting an analysis of the metaphorical inconsistencies caused by cultural differences.

2.2   Language and the Dual Structure of Metaphorical Icon: Image vs. Text

"Paivio [12] argued that much of our cognitive "knowledge" is actually dual coded" [5]. He claimed that this knowledge exists in related forms in both the semantic and imaginal systems and any representational theory must accommodate this dual functionality. These systems can operate both separately and cooperatively. As the properties of source and target are considered in the recursive refinement process, spread of activation occurs in both systems. Pavio [13] claimed that metaphor might be a particularly effective way of stimulating interaction between the semantic and imaginal systems. The dual structure of metaphorical icons with image and label seems to stimulate this interaction. In this context, Cates [5] highlighted the importance of dual coding: "If dual coding plays a major role in the operation of our cognitive processes, users cannot easily separate the image from the related verbal label, nor can they isolate themselves from the associated spread of activation that occurs naturally when they are exposed to either verbal labels or images."

There have been several studies investigating the effects of images versus text on understanding and learning [14]. Paivio [15] has claimed that text and graphics together may be more elective than pure graphics. Blackwell [16] claimed that connecting any concrete image with text information can increase recall through dual coding. Kacmar and Carey [17] have shown that text and graphics together improve performance. The studies showed that image and label items of the icons may be both effective on understanding. Therefore, it is probable that language experience and perfection level may influence metaphor understanding. Evers [18] describes metaphors as good examples of the inter-relationship between language and culture in interface design. Evers [2] also argued that the cross-cultural understanding of the textual design items in interfaces are influenced by the experience of the users with the language used in the interface. Kukulska-Hulme [3] also pointed out to the importance of language in understanding the metaphor as a whole. She claimed that recognition of the graphical element of a metaphorical icon might not be enough to lead the user to an explicit meaning. The user should be familiar with the language used in the label and with the context the label roots in.

3   Research Methodology

"Culture is always a collective phenomenon, because it is at least partly shared with people who live or lived within the same social environment, which is where it is learned" [19]. It is difficult to measure culture and its effects, but 'cultural variables' such as those developed by Hofstede [19] can be used to classify and evaluate different cultural groups.

In this study, Hofstede's definition of culture is adopted. Evers' study [2] has showed that users' understanding of icons was influenced by their understanding of what a graphic was associated with or what a label meant to them. In order to analyze the participants' understanding of these metaphorical icons in detail, it was considered advantageous to decompose the icons and investigate the graphical and textual items separately. Below are the two research questions:

Research question 1: Do users' physical experience within the real world influence their understanding of graphical elements of metaphorical icons?

Research question 2: Does the experience of users with the official language of a website and other languages affect their understanding of textual elements of metaphorical icons?

This qualitative study with ethnographic aspects is based on a multi-method approach, which consists of questionnaires for the understanding of metaphorical icons and a semi-structured debriefing interview. The open-ended questionnaires were adapted and developed from the questionnaires used in the study of Evers [2] and provided feedback on the cross-cultural understanding of the graphical and textual elements of the metaphorical icons separately. Final structured debriefing interview provided complementary findings. Cross-cultural findings were mainly evaluated qualitatively with simple complementary quantitative data.

The national cultures included in this research were French and Turkish. Cultural value orientations for two cultural groups proposed by Hofstede [19] indicate that there is a significant difference between the two groups especially at the "individualism/collectivism" variable. Turkish culture reveals collectivist aspects whereas French culture reveals individualist aspects. "Individualism and collectivism variable" describes the way in which cultures perceive the role of the individual in a group. In this study, it is expected that the findings should reflect this difference. The lack of cross-cultural usability research on Turkish and French culture was also one of the important reasons for the choice of this group. Each group consisted of 17 men and 17 women, aged between 21-24, who were students in the communication faculties in France and Turkey at the 3rd or 4th grade with an average computer and Internet experience. All the Turkish participants could speak advanced level of French certified by DALF language qualification of the French government.

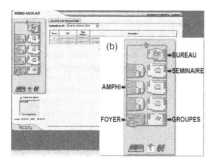

Fig. 1. (a) ACOLAD Homepage (b) Navigation bar (c) "Foyer" page

An e-learning site was chosen for the study, because educational institutions, which offer distance learning to students globally, are mostly faced with challenge of cultural diversity. Our research site was "Apprentisage COLlaboratif A Distance" (ACOLAD) which was the official e-learning site of Louis Pasteur University in Strasbourg, France. By referring to the metaphor taxonomy of Cates [5] ACOLAD was based on an underlying spatial "Campus" metaphor including auxiliary metaphors like "Bureau", "Foyer", "Amphitheatre", "Groupes", "Seminaire". Mostly valuing the student initiative, ACOLAD enabled collaborative group study as well as synchronous and asynchronous communication. The study was focused mainly on the homepage (Figure 1a) and "Foyer" page (Figure 1c) of the ACOLAD web site.

4 Results

4.1 Understanding the Underlying "Campus" Metaphor

In the first questionnaire, the main page of the ACOLAD was shown to the participants and they were asked to answer the questions by mainly focusing on the main navigation bar, which included different metaphorical icons that provided access to the sub pages. Each icon in the navigation bar (Figure 1b) was in the form of architectural plans of different spaces in the virtual campus like "Bureau" and "Amphitheatre", which were also auxiliary metaphors of the system. The questions first asked the participants what ACOLAD reminded them of and what they thought they might be able to do in such a place. "Bureau", "Seminaire", "Amphitheatre", "Foyer" and "Groupes" icons were marked with numbers and the users were asked to make potential associations by considering the possible functions of the marked icons. All the associations were aggregated into categories by the researchers by referring to the content of the information manual proposed by the developers of ACOLAD. The findings showed that users understand the underlying spatial "Campus" metaphor of ACOLAD by associating it to the places that they are familiar and to their experiences within those places. Having their education in similar buildings, both groups were able to understand the "Campus" metaphor presented in ACOLAD. Cultural differences were mostly found in the understanding of auxiliary metaphors like "Seminaire", "Groupes" and "Foyer". It was found that French participants could easily understand these metaphors. Moreover, French participants could suggest detailed functions for these metaphors. In the interview, they also stated that these interfaces seemed very similar with the spaces in their universities and this familiarity was evaluated as one of the best aspects of the website. These findings showed that the auxiliary metaphors employed within the "Campus" metaphor were really consistent with the French culture. However, the findings on the understanding of Turkish group revealed some metaphorical inconsistencies. It was found that the Turkish participants had some difficulties in understanding the intended meaning proposed by these metaphors. Turkish participants had problems in associating the icons like "Groupes" and "Foyer" with their real world counterparts, as they were not very familiar with such education methods and such spaces in their universities.

Similar inconsistencies were found between the underlying "Campus" metaphor and one of the auxiliary metaphors: "Bureau". "Bureau" was designed as a private feature that enabled the students in ACOLAD to organize their schedules, projects, seminaries, etc. However, neither the Turkish group nor the French group had private rooms in their universities. Therefore, "Bureau" metaphor did not overlap with the experience of the real world and resulted in inconsistency. Both groups associated the interface with 'administration offices' as the decoration of the "Bureau" in the interface resembled so. Even though, the idea of a "private study room" in the context of e-learning seemed functional, the proposed "Bureau" metaphor displayed excess amount of contrasts that caused misunderstanding.

4.2   Understanding the Underlying "Campus" Metaphor with labels

After having completed the first questionnaire, the participants were enabled to examine the labels of the icons in the navigation bar (which were active on roll-over) and they were again asked to answer the same questions in order to investigate the influence of text on understanding. It was found that the information in textual form in the labels either consolidated the meaning users got through the graphical elements of the metaphors or caused frustration. It was obvious that most of the users could recognize the icons easier with labels, which overlapped with the related literature. However, it was found that the textual content of the icons were more effective on the understanding of the French group. Having seen that the labels confirmed the functions they proposed at the evaluation of the graphical elements, they proposed more detailed functions about ACOLAD. At this point, it is thought that the French participants benefited from the fact that the official language of the site was their native language. This statement was supported with the findings of Turkish participants, which showed that the Turkish group placed more importance on graphics in trying to understand a compound metaphorical icon. The frequency of the answers given was found to diminish when they failed to understand the labels of the icons. In such cases of failure, it was observed that Turkish participants started to interrogate their experience with French language and subsequently loose their self-confidence about their expertise on French. Moreover, in the debriefing interview some of the Turkish participants expressed the need for different language options for the site.

The experience of the users with other languages was also considered as a reason that influences the interest of the users towards the textual elements. The findings from the background questionnaire showed that French participants could speak more languages than the Turkish participants.

4.3   Understanding the Auxiliary "Foyer" Metaphor

In the third questionnaire, the "Foyer" page (Figure 1c) including diverse metaphorical icons without the labels was shown to the participants and they were asked what "Foyer" reminded them of and what they thought they might be able to do in such a place. What the "Foyer" page reminded participants without the labels seemed to overlap with the findings of the evaluation in the previous stages. Both the Turkish group and the French group associated the interface with 'extra-curricular activities'. Besides, Turkish participants also made associations with the familiar spaces in their universities like 'canteen or cafeteria'. The proposed activities displayed significant differences across two groups. Turkish participants evaluated the interface as a free and relaxing place in which users can 'chat and have fun'. However, by referring to the exact experiences in a typical foyer in French universities, French participants proposed functions like 'discussion' and 'relaxing'. It was evident that the "Foyer" metaphor was culturally appropriate for the French group with aspects reflecting the daily university life in French universities.

4.4 Understanding the Auxiliary "Foyer" Metaphor with Labels

The last questionnaire was a replicate of the third one, but this time the participants were enabled to examine the labels in the "Foyer" page that were active on roll-over. When the replies were analyzed, it was found that the findings overlapped with the ones from the evaluation of the graphical elements. The findings on the understanding of the compound metaphorical icons (combined with graphics and text) in the "Foyer" interface provided us the possibility to discuss the potential metaphorical inconsistencies that can occur in cross-cultural interfaces. "Foyer" was directly associated with social activities and a university canteen by the Turkish group and this led to expectations of familiar activities. However, the insistent accent by several icons on the function of "discussion" in "Foyer" caused frustration and rejection of the interface. Features in the "Foyer" like "Bar" was not also much familiar for the Turkish group and this unfamiliarity was found to be another reason for the rejection. In the interview, Turkish group evaluated ACOLAD as a web site, which is really for away from satisfying the expectations for a real university. This metaphorical inconsistency was caused because of the excessive tension created between the source function (which is synchronous and asynchronous communication in an e-learning website) and the target (which is the "Foyer" interface) employed to convey that meaning (Figure 2).

On the other hand, it was found that too much affinity with the metaphors could influence understanding negatively and result in conceptual baggage for the users. At the graphical level, the "Foyer" metaphor was observed to be very familiar for the French group. However, when they were asked to state possible activities that can be realized in this place, it was interesting to see that some of the participants proposed activities like 'smoking, having a cup of coffee and eating', which seemed to overestimate the metaphor. The excessive affinity of the metaphor with its counterpart in the real world caused such an interpretation. The weak tension between the source function "e-learning" and the target "Foyer" caused conceptual baggage for the participants and led them by the metaphor's presence to expect that they could do something that the interface cannot accomplish. Though in theory, "Foyer" metaphor seemed very suitable for the French group, it was found to be confounding in practice.

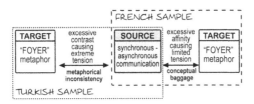

Fig. 2. How "Foyer" metaphor can be confounding for both cultural groups

Findings also revealed that the interaction between the graphical and textual elements of a metaphorical icon had an impact on cross-cultural understanding. For example the interaction between "round table and chairs" icon in the "Foyer" and its label "discussion" can be evaluated as consistent and reasonable. However, this interaction led to different cross-cultural interpretations. This interaction was culturally consistent for the French group, as French culture highly valued the free individualistic expression of opinions in discussions, but for the Turkish group, which prioritizes collectivism rather than individualistic initiative, it was found to be inconsistent and confounding. Therefore, if the image had a label like "chat" which is culturally familiar for the Turkish group, this would lead to the reinterpretation and reconstruction of the understanding of the intended function, but the label "discussion" increases the tension between the source and target by displaying excessive contrasts, which resulted in the inconsistency of the metaphor (Figure 3). The preference of the label "discussion" for the Target 1 instead of the label "chat" in Target 2 impedes the accurate understanding for the Turkish group.

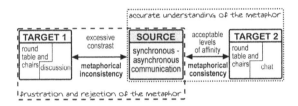

Fig. 3. The influence of the interaction between the image and text components of "discussion" icon in "Foyer" on the understanding of Turkish group

5 Conclusion

Findings of this study do suggest differences in understanding of the metaphors across the two cultural groups involved. It was found that users' physical experience with the real world influence their understanding of graphical elements of metaphorical icons and hence, of the overall interface. Users understand the visual spatial metaphors by associating them to the places that they are familiar and to their experiences within those places. Findings also showed that the experience of users with the language used in a website and other languages affect their understanding of textual elements of metaphorical icons. This finding points out to the importance of cultural localization at both graphical and textual levels of interface design.

The results also enabled an in-depth analysis on understanding of the compound metaphorical icons (combined with graphics and text) and provided us the possibility to explore the potential metaphorical inconsistencies that can occur in cross-cultural interfaces. Findings on metaphorical inconsistencies led to following implications for the selection of suitable metaphors for cross-cultural user interfaces:

Designers should develop suitable metaphors, which can present acceptable levels of affinity and contrast and thus can create an optimal interaction or tension between the source function and target.

Culturally appropriate interface metaphors match the real world experience of the culture and produce acceptable levels of affinity between the source and target, which causes a creative tension. These consistent metaphors enable the reconstruction of the meaning and lead to an accurate cultural understanding of the intended function.

Interface metaphors that do not fit to the real world experience of the users produce excessive contrasts between the source function and the target, which causes an extreme tension. These metaphorical inconsistencies impede accurate understanding and may bring out the rejection of the interface and user frustration as well.

Excessive familiarity with the metaphor can easily result in conceptual baggage for the users. The excessive affinity of the metaphor with its counterpart in the real world can lead the users to take metaphor too literally, which mostly causes misconceptions. The weak tension between the source function and target can make the users by the metaphor's presence to expect that they could do something that the interface cannot accomplish. Such metaphors tend to limit the functionality of the interface to that of the physical analog and thus impede maximum utilization of the capabilities of the system.

The recognition of the graphical element of a metaphorical icon is not enough for the user to develop an overall understanding. Metaphorical icons are dual coded in structure and the interaction between the graphical and textual elements of a metaphorical icon has also an impact on cross-cultural understanding. Being a major part of the target of the metaphor, labels have different connotations due to the cultural contexts in which they are rooted and therefore convey varying meaning. The user should be familiar with the language of the label and with the context the label roots in. Textual content of the icons enhance the understanding of the users who are native speakers of the official language of the web site used. Those users can grasp the indented meaning and develop deeper analysis on the functionality of the system easily. In a metaphorical icon, the target should be composed by the image and label in such a way that they should work cooperatively to stimulate the creative tension inbetween and convey the intended meaning.

Similarly, an optimal interaction should also be created between the underlying metaphor and auxiliary metaphors used within a cross-cultural interface. The auxiliary metaphors employed under a culturally appropriate underlying metaphor should be consonant enough to avoid drawbacks that can cause mismatches and misunderstanding.

Considering the lack of cross-cultural usability research on Turkish and French culture, this study also contributed to the relevant literature by providing findings on these cultural profiles. In order to establish new culture-specific patterns in interface and metaphor understanding, further empirical studies with larger user groups from diverse cultures should be conducted.

References

1. Lakoff, G., Johnson, M.: Metaphors We Live By, pp. 210–211 (1980)
2. Evers, V.: Cross-Cultural Aspects of the Human Computer Interface. PhD thesis, Open University (1999),
   http://staff.science.uva.nl/~evers/publications.html

3. Kukulska-Hulme, A.M.: Language And Communication: Essential Concepts For User Interface And Documentation Design. Oxford University Press, Oxford (1999)
4. Kittay, E.F.: Metaphor: Its Cognitive Force and Linguistic Structure. Oxford (1987)
5. Cates, W.M.: Systematic Selection and Implementation of Graphical User Interface Metaphors. Computers and Education 38, 385–397 (2002)
6. Miller, G.: Images and Models, Similes and Metaphors. In: Ortony, A. (ed.) Metaphor and Thought, pp. 202–250. Cambridge University Press, Cambridge (1979)
7. Carroll, J.M., Mack, R.L.: Metaphor, Computing Systems, and Active Learning. International Journal of Human-Computer Studies 51, 385–403 (1999)
8. Halazs, F., Moran, T.P.: Analogy Considered Harmful. In: Conference on Human Factors in Computer Systems, pp. 383–386. ACM Press, New York (1982)
9. Marcus, A.: Metaphor Design in User Interfaces. Journal of Computer Documentation 22(2), 43–57 (1998)
10. Agarawala, A., Balakrishnan, R.: Keepin' It Real: Pushing the Desktop Metaphor with Physics, Piles and the Pen. In: CHI 2006, pp. 1283–1292. ACM Press, New York (2006)
11. Duncker, E.: Cross Cultural Usability of the Library Metaphor. In: 2nd ACM/IEEE-CS, pp. 223–230 (2002)
12. Paivio, A.: Mental Representations: A Dual Coding Approach. Oxford University Press, Oxford (1986)
13. Paivio, A.: Psychological Processes in Comprehension of Metaphor. In: Ortony, A. (ed.) Metaphor and Thought, pp. 150–171. Cambridge University Press, Cambridge (1979)
14. Hsu, Y.: The Effects of Visual Versus Verbal Metaphors on Novice and Expert Learners' Performance. In: Human-Computer International 2007, pp. 264–269 (2007)
15. Paivio, A.: Imagery and Verbal Processes. Holt, Reinhart and Winston (1971)
16. Blackwell, A.F.: Pictorial Representation And Metaphor In Visual Language Design. Journal of Visual Languages and Computing 12, 223–252 (2001)
17. Kacmar, C.J., Carey, J.M.: Assessing the Usability of Icons in User Interfaces. Behaviour and Information Technology 10, 443–457 (1991)
18. Evers, V.: Cross-Cultural Understanding of Metaphors in Interface Design. In: CATAC 1998 (1998)
19. Hofstede, G.: Cultures and Organisation: Software of the Mind, p. 2. McGraw-Hill, New York (1991)

Cultural Representation for
Multi-culture Interaction Design

Javed Anjum Sheikh, Bob Fields, and Elke Duncker

Interaction Design Centre, School of Engineering & Information Sciences,
Middlesex University, London, UK
{j.anjum,b.fields,e.duncker}@mdx.ac.uk

Abstract. This research works towards the integration of cultural factors in global information systems like the Web or digital libraries to enhance global access to information and services. In this context, we study cultural differences in categorization and classification by means of card sorting experiments in combination with observations and interviews. An initial analysis of data collected in Pakistan and UK reveals a number of differences between Pakistani and British participants as to how they classify every-day objects. The differences found suggest a number of design solutions for cultural inclusion.

Keywords: Cross-cultural design, cross-cultural classification, classification systems, human–computer interaction, globalisation, localisation, cultural inclusion.

1 Introduction

The potential of the internet as a tool for global access to knowledge, goods services is undisputed. However, this globalisation potential cannot be fully realised, as long as information and services of one culture are less accessible to other cultural groups. Problems do not only arise from obvious matters such as language translation, currency translation, formats of numbers and dates, etc. but from deeply rooted cultural differences that can cause non-understanding and misinterpretation of user interfaces and information given.

A question of recurrent interest is how easily certain groups of users can retrieve information from web-based information sources. A wide range of online classification schemes can be found, of which some seem to have a wider applicability and acceptance than others. For example, UK online stores do not only sell different products compared to similar German online stores, they often classify their products differently[1]. Similar things can be said for classification systems in libraries. The Dewy decimal system is used world-wide and yet, it classifies books differently to the German library classification systems in general and in particular to specialty related classification systems [6][12]. This means that not only the content but also the way this content is organised and classified reflects the values and interpretive practices of the culture in which it was produced. Therefore, problems can arise, when content

---

[1] For a comparison see for instance the Galeria-Kaufhof website and the Debenhams website.

N. Aykin (Ed.): Internationalization, Design, LNCS 5623, pp. 99–107, 2009.

designed, organised and classified by members of one culture is used by members of another culture. Typically, web content, its organisation and its classification reflect values and interpretations of western cultures rendering it less appropriate to non-western cultural user groups.

As part of a larger study, this research focuses on cross-cultural classification practices. It examines

- the way how people classify representations of every-day objects
- the differences in classification practices and classifications
- the cause for these differences

In what follows, we review related works on culture and design in section two. In section three we describe our research methods. Section four presents the results of our study and the analysis thereof. Following a discussion of links to interaction design in section five, our conclusions and directions for future work are presented in the last section.

2 Background

Globalisation faces major challenges, when it comes to localising the organisation and classification of globally available information. Cultural aspects of classification play an important role in these difficulties. Some scholars have studied the influence of culture on classification systems [2], but many questions remain unanswered, particularly with regards to online information systems that are not digital libraries.

Researchers and designers sometimes unintentionally apply their own cultural values when designing and developing computer applications. Although Microsoft and other development organisations consider cultural issues, they mostly involve language translation and visual aspects of the interface instead of the underlying structure of the application. Therefore, users who are culturally different from the researchers and designers face difficulty in using computer applications [6][17]. Cross-cultural research is time-consuming and expensive, relatively few studies have looked at cultural differences in computing systems.

However, most studies focus on language translation [14] and attitudes towards and acceptance of technology [8] and various cultural issues for example of nationalism, language, social context, time, currency, units of measure, cultural values, body positions, symbols and aesthetics [3]. Cultural models (for example, see [7][18] are widely studied but it has been argued that such models are used inappropriately [11] and do not have enough potential to fulfil the requirements of every culture [19]. Consequently, the above research is not well suited for computer scientists. Therefore, it is essential to consider designing for different cultural groups [20].

Culture-specific study is an important tool in research, but computer scientists have sometimes tended to downplay the importance of the user in general, and of their culture in particular [3][15]. The rapid growth of computing raises issues of cultural representation. As there is inadequate representation of non-western culture, user from these cultures is deprived of the true benefit of computing. Several studies [10][16] show a strong inclination of users to use their own language and cultural environment. Other studies show developers face difficulties in the successful integration of culture into interface design [4][14].

3 Methods

In order to investigate the question of how different cultures organise their knowledge differently, we employ a research method based on card sorting. In a card sorting experiments participants are asked to arrange cards into groups. On these cards one finds pictures or the names of objects. Card-sorting experiments can reveal different ways in which participants organise their understanding of the world.

The approach is widely used for initial exploration, in the field of knowledge acquisition [13]. It helps to develop and identify concepts, models, attitudes, trends, patterns and values for capturing information from the mental model of the participants. This mental model suggests possible taxonomies.

Card sorting is widely used in the field of Human Computer Interaction, psychology, and knowledge engineering for knowledge elicitation. It helps to evoke participants' domain knowledge [14], distinguish the level of the problem [1], and reflects ideas about knowledge [20]. Furthermore, card sorting is often used to gather data about personal constructs, for instance menu structure specifications and to understand users' perceptions of relationships among items.

This research uses card sorting as a method to identify categories of food items. In contrast to the above card sorting experiments, which always use one layer of grouping cards, we allow the participants to use as many layers as they find adequate, so that groups can be subdivided into lower level groups.

This layered approach is closer to people's every day use of classification, but also poses quite a challenge for the analysis, particularly for large data sets. For this reason we automated part of the analysis, i.e. the measuring of the difference between two classifications as edit distance. Other differences were observed and analysed manually, such as the width and the depth of the classification. Furthermore, we employed cluster analysis (K-means) to determine, whether the cultural backgrounds of participants are a potential explanation for the observed differences.

3.1 The Study

The card sorting experiment was conducted in this way: Thirty-nine cards with names of a variety of food items were used. Participants were asked to group these cards. Subsequently, they were asked to label each group. Then they were asked for each group of cards, if they would like to subdivide the group. The participants labelled the subgroups as well. The process was repeated until participants no longer wanted to subdivide any groups. While the participants were grouping cards and labelling the groups the researcher recorded the emerging tree structures. As the study was a cross-cultural one, the food items were translated into the participant's first language.

The data collection generated hierarchical tree structures representing the classifications that the participants revealed by grouping the cards. The analysis of the data revolves around the discovery of similarities and differences between the hierarchies, and whether those similarities and differences are aligned with cultural identity. The investigation proceeded informally at first, looking for patterns in the data that were suggestive of culturally aligned classificatory practices (see Section 4.1). The initial analysis pointed the way for a more systematic analysis that lent itself to automated support (see Section 4.2).

3.2 Participants

A total of 160 (PK n=80 and UK n=80) subjects participated in this study and were selected based on the ethnicity. They were literate, over 18 years of age and were familiar with all the items on the cards. Pakistani participants are from Karachi, Lahore, Islamabad, and Bahawal Pur. UK participants live in London and their grandparents are also UK born.

4 Findings

4.1 Observations

The initially observations were conducted informally and manually, with a search for patterns of similarity and difference between the hierarchies produced by members of the different groups. Figure 1a and 1b shows, that Pakistani participant's categorisation is relatively flat, where as the UK participant added an extra layer of categorisation.

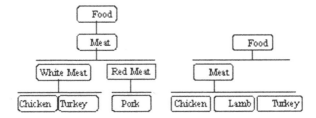

Fig. 1a & 1b. The UK and Pakistani categorisation

The observations showed that Pakistani and British participants differed in their categorisation judgments. However, they shared a common representation structure in some categories. The differences are also noticed within each culture. Observations suggest clear differences between the categorisations produced by Pakistani participants and those produced by their British counterparts. For instance, fragments of typical categorisations produced by a Pakistani and British participant are shown in Figures 2a, and 2b respectively.

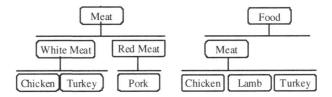

Fig. 2a & 2b. Sample categorisations produced by members of different cultures

However, Figure 3 shows a fragment of the categorisation that was generated often, being common to many participants, irrespective of their cultural background.

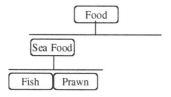

Fig. 3. Sample categorisation produced by members of different cultures

In other cases, participants produced structurally identical classifications, but used different terminology to refer to parts of the classification tree, as illustrated in Figure 4a and 4b.

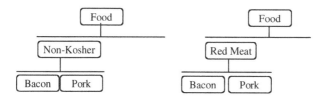

Fig. 4a & 4b. Sample categorisations produced by members of same cultures

The study gave valuable insights regarding food classification with relation to different cultures (Pakistani and British), suggesting that members of different cultures systematically organise and categorise items differently. Additionally, the informal analysis was sufficient to suggest that a more systematic analysis of similarity and difference would be a profitable line of inquiry.

4.2   A Systematic Approach to Analysis

The initial analysis of the study indicates a cultural difference in food categorisation among people belonging to different cultures that appears to be greater than the differences between people within the same culture. The studies suggest that both the 'national culture' and the 'belief system' of a participant shape the way they categorise items. By 'belief system' here, we refer roughly to religious background as this is a highly significant factor in the way people understand food and the various domestic practices that surround it. It seems likely that other elements of culture, such as professional cultures or membership of communities of practice would gain greater significance.

4.3   Hypotheses

Based on our findings, we can more confidently assert that categorisation is influenced by culture and belief, and several open questions exist as to the nature of this influence.

A first step towards conducting analysis in a more rigorous manner was to formalize the complimentary notions of 'similarity' and 'difference' that are at work. A number of possible formulations are possible, but the one that proved to be most promising was the notion of 'edit distance': the difference or distance between two tree structured hierarchies is considered to be the number of editing steps necessary to transform one tree into the other. This measurement of distance was implemented in software based on a freely available framework called SimPack.[2]

The algorithm for computing the 'edit distance' between trees facilitated the construction of a 'distance matrix' that encodes the edit distance between the hierarchies produced between all pairs of study subjects, and the discovery of structure in the population of subjects entails an exploration of this distance matrix.

Two approaches to this exploratory task were employed. A more traditional statistically-based approach was implemented using a variant of the k-means cluster analysis algorithm to discover clusters of subjects who were 'close together' in that they produced similar hierarchies. This formal style of analysis was complemented with a more exploratory tool that produces a visualization of the distance matrix, based around the physical analogy of data points joined by a collection of springs whose length is determined by the edit distances[3]. A simulation of such a system yields a dynamic network that tends to settle in a 'low energy' configuration. The latter technique provides a useful visual way of seeing how a structure emerges from the confusion, as similarly similar trees tend to gravitate towards one another.

The results obtained from the cluster analysis algorithm are, informally, at least, in accord with the graphical simulation. Figure 5 illustrates this by showing the graphical display in which subjects are shown as numbered nodes in the graph. The physical distance between nodes in the figure is a reflection of the network of edit distance relationships. Overlaid on the figure are the four clusters found by a run of the cluster analysis algorithm.

5 Towards Interaction Design

A starting assumption for this research was that no scheme for organising information is likely to be equally effective for a range of cultural groups. The current research aims to make a contribution in this area, not by finding a universal way of classifying information, but by providing a method for investigating classification in a locale in order to generate localised interface designs. The expected solution will be based on local user access needs and capability of the local users.

The analysis so far has given a way of identifying clusters of related structurings of a set of objects. A number of strategies exist to take this forward into interaction design. An obvious approach is to provide a localized user interface for each cluster, choosing a representative element from a cluster (for example, using the edit distance metric to find the most central element in a cluster) to guide the structure of navigation elements on an interface.

---

[2] SimPack is an open source collection of software tools for investigating the similarity between 'ontologies'. Available from http://www.ifi.uzh.ch/ddis/simpack.html

[3] The tool is based on the Graph demonstration program that is part of the Java Software Development Kit available fromjhttp://ava.sun.com

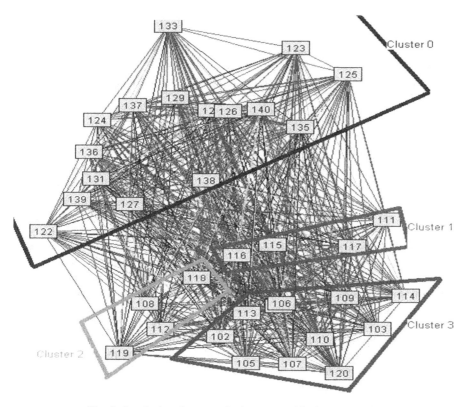

Fig. 5. Overlaying cluster analysis on a graphical representation

6   Conclusion and Future Work

The contribution of this research is to introduce a new analysis technique based on SimPack's modified classes to discover/measure similarity and edit distance. This method will help to understand how different cultures view similar concepts.

We propose a cultural based interface obtained from local knowledge. Our interface will show a common concept which is result of hierarchical clustering analysis of multi cultural representation. It will allow user to explore effectively in comparison to a non-cultural based interface.

The interface is user perspective, which will help the user to interact effectively and close to human to human interaction. When the users visit the main page the interface user will find cultural based navigations/classifications close to the particular culture. If the user clicks on a particular culture for example Pakistan, the user will get additional options from four cities. We hope this will enable the reader to understand the problem and its solution will give them better overview of this research. The aim of this research is to propose a design for all cultures to increase usability enhancement and interaction patterns in categorising that lead to browser design. The result and analysis we presented in this paper is intended to guide design of cross-cultural inter-face. We used mixed methods to interpret the result. Our studies explored cultural difference by card sorting and result analysis through cluster analysis to compare both cultures. Significant differences were found in term of categorisation. The result increase usability enhancement and interaction patterns in categorising that lead to interface design

The paper presents a concept of cultural representation for interaction design. The important features of interaction design here are

- Sorting of cultural concepts
- Integration of concepts into categorization
- Interaction design for cultural representation.

This research leads towards culturally-based design and shows how user concepts can be organised. At present, a large scale study has been completed in Pakistan, and in the UK. Our immediate aim is to design a more detailed method for cultural representation and apply it for development of multi culture interaction design. An attempt to validate the approach will address one of the open questions surrounding this approach: does organising a user interface around the cluster of categorizations produced by members of a particular culture yield a more usable or effective interface or a more rewarding user experience? Another collection of challenging questions remain open in the area of scalability. For instance, while it may be possible to use the results of a card sort experiment with a few tens of items to provide localised organization of those very same items, is it possible to scale-up the results of a small study to provide design guidance when faced with a large number of items? Such questions are likely to be of relevance for the design of online stores where the organization of many thousands of items must be based on a more tractable and economically justifiable study.

References

1. Barrett, A.R., Edwards, J.S.: Knowledge Elicitation and Knowledge Representation in a Large Domain with Multiple Experts. Expert Systems with Applications 8, 169–176 (1996)
2. Caidi, N., Komlodi, A.: Digital Libraries across Cultures: Design and Usability Issues. SIGIR Forum 37(2), 62–64 (2003)
3. Fernandes, T.: Global interface design: A guide to designing international user interfaces. AP Professional, Boston, MA (1996)
4. Hannerz, U.: Cultural Complexity; Studies in the social organisation of meaning. Columbia University Press, New York (1992)
5. Heiner-Freiling, M.: DDB und DDC – Die Deutsche Bibliothek und die Dewey-Dezimalklassifikation (in Dutch) Perspektiven, Befuerchtungen, Hoffnungen in Bibliotheksdienst, Heft 12 (1998)
6. Hofstede, G.H.: Cultures and Organizations: Software of the Mind. McGraw-Hill, London (1991)
7. Igbaria, M., Zviran, M.: Comparison of end-user computing characteristics in the U.S. Israel and Taiwan. Information and Management 30, 1–13 (1996)
8. Lopez, A., Atyran, S., Coley, J.D., Medin, D.L., Smith, E.E.: The tree of life: universal and cultural features of folk biological taxonomies and inductions. Cognitive Psychology 32, 261–296 (1997)

9. Luna, D., Peracchio, L.A., de Juan, M.D.: Cross-cultural and cognitive aspects of Web site navigation. Journal of the Academy of Marketing Science 30(4), 397–410 (2002)
10. Lynch, P.D., Kent, R.J., Srinivasan, S.S.: The global Internet shopper: Evidence from shopping tasls in twelve countries. Journal of Advertising Research, 16–23 (May/June 2001)
11. Marcus, A., Gould, E.W.: Cultural dimensions and global web user-interface design: What? So What? Now What (2000), http://www.amanda.com (September 06, 2007)
12. Romaine, S.: Language in Society. Oxford University Press, Oxford (1994)
13. Russo, P., Boor, S.: How fluent is your interface? Designing for international users. In: Human Factors and Computer Systems. Conference Proceedings of the conference on Human factors in computing systems, pp. 342–347. Addison-Wesley Longman Publishing, Boston (1993)
14. Sackmary, B., Scalia, L.M.: Cultural patterns of World Wide Web business sites: A comparison of Mexican and U.S. companies. In: The 7th Cross-Cultural Consumer and Business Studies Research Conference, Cancun, Mexico (1999)
15. Simon, S.J.: The impact of culture and gender on web sites: An empirical study. ACM SIGMIS Database 32(1), 18–37 (2001)
16. Thippaya, C.: Cultural Differences and End-User Computing. In: IEEE Symposium on Visual Languages & Human-Centric Computing, pp. 326–326 (2006)
17. Trompenaars, F.: Riding the waves of culture: understanding cultural diversity in business. Nicholas Brealey, London (1993)
18. Yeo, A.W.: Global-software development lifecycle: An exploratory study. In: Human Factors and Computer Systems. Proceedings of the SIGCHI conference on Human factors in computing systems, pp. 104–111. ACM Press, New York (2001)
19. Zakaria, N., Stanton, J.M., Sarkar-Barney, S.T.M.: Designing and implementing culturally sensitive IT applications. Journal of Information Technology and People 16, 49–76 (2003)
20. Zimmerman, D.E., Akerelrea, C.: A Group Card Sorting Methodology for Developing Informational Web Sites. In: The Proceedings of International Professional Communication Conference, IPCC (2002)

Designing for a Dialogic View of Interpretation in Cross-Cultural IT Design

Huatong Sun

English Department, Miami University, Oxford, OH 45056, USA
huatongs@gmail.com

Abstract. To search for ways of better communicating the intended meanings to culturally diverse users, this paper uses Bakhtin's concept of dialogicality and its application to examine how interpretation functions in cross-cultural design. It argues for a dialogical view of interpretation based on the genre notion with its features of situatedness and dynamism. This view of interpretation connects action and meaning in cross-cultural IT design and makes a design appealing to a local context without stereotyping the local culture in an essentialist fashion.

Keywords: interpretation, genre, dialogicality, cross-cultural design.

1 Introduction

Interpretation is a central issue in HCI design ([21]), particularly in the area of cross-cultural design. As Bourges-Waldegg & Scrivener ([6]) points out, designing for culturally diverse users is "a problem of communicating the intended meaning of representations" (p.299). The completion of design goals depends on whether local users are able to interpret meanings mediated by a technology in their own contexts as intended. However, current cross-cultural IT design practices face two problems of interpretations.

First, there is a conflict between a preferred interpretation based on one mental model from the development phase and multiple interpretations derived at the localization phase. In a common cross-cultural IT development cycle, designers develop core functionalities based on a mental model which comes either from user studies or from designer's imagination, and then localization professionals customize interface features for targeted users in various locales. However, top-level interface features are closely connected to the user model and its derived functionalities on the bottom level. Since sociocultural contexts tend to be overlooked in IT design practices, low-level tasks distilled from sociocultural contexts are usually modeled in design rather than high-order processes and more meaningful activities embedded in the local context ([17]); design generally aims toward one preferred interpretation ([20], [21]) based on one mental model representing those low-level tasks, wherever the user is situated. Thus it is doubtful how effectively all the interface alternations, coming from the same— possibly problematic— mental model, could lead to multiple interpretations.

Second, the models of cultural dimensions are usually applied to the localization process in a narrow way, and designing for a local culture might fall into a pitfall of

N. Aykin (Ed.): Internationalization, Design, LNCS 5623, pp. 108–116, 2009.

stereotyping the culture. As a popular design approach, cultural dimensions are employed to guide processes of internationalization and localization. These cultural dimensions are built on well-developed intercultural communication theories from scholars such as Hofstede, Hall, and Victor. While they help designers to focus on "the regularities between cultures" by reducing "cultural differences to a manageable number" ([11]), they usually only represent dominant values in a national culture and ignore other subcultural factors. Furthermore, most of these variables are value-oriented, and they do not attend to concrete cultural realities, including the messiness and complexities of local contexts or concrete user activities.

Both problems indicate a disconnect between interaction and interpretation that hurt design outcomes. It causes poor user experience, culturally. The reality is that miscommunication would occur on various levels, ranging from a small icon which brings about unexpected interpretations, to a simple task that might not make sense at all to users who do not share the mental model. This paper tackles this problem by examining the dimension of interpretation in cross-cultural IT design. It argues for a dialogical view of interpretation based on the genre notion. This view of interpretation connects action and meaning in cross-cultural IT design and makes a design appealing to a local context without stereotyping the local culture in an essentialist fashion.

2 Disconnect between Interaction and Interpretation

Though being envisioned as a central issue in IT design, the mediation of meaning has been a weak area in practices. IT design tends to prioritize interaction over interpretation, and thus designing for the mediation of action usually precedes designing for the mediation of meaning in practices. This often leads to use breakdowns when only tasks are modeled in design without considering other social and cultural factors in user contexts. When users and designers share a similar sociocultural context, this problem does not appear obvious since users are able to interpret implicitly the artifact, deeply rooted in local cultural practices, where designers are situated, and use it even though meaning might not be adequately considered in design. However, users do not have this luck when they are distant from designer's culture. If meaning and cultural factors are not carefully studied and attended to in design, serious breakdowns will occur.

Due to the tendency of representing low-level tasks in IT design ([1], [16], [24]), generally low-level tasks from a particular cultural context (typically an American culture) are represented and modeled in cross-cultural design. This causes the following problems: The designed technology only supports low-level actions rather than high-order activity; low-level actions that are packaged in cultural metaphors originating from the cultural context of designers are confusing or even unrecognizable to users from another culture who are unfamiliar with the cultural practices associated with metaphors. The low-level actions usually represent the cultural ways of doing certain daily tasks in one cultural context, and these everyday practices might be vastly different from users in other cultural contexts. For example, research shows that American people prefer to see things or phenomena in parts rather than in wholes, whereas Chinese would prefer to do the reverse ([26]). In the case of a simple application such as an address book, though it is very common and natural for American users to group contacts in categories of work vs. family vs. friends, some Chinese users might find it uncomfortable to classify their contacts in this way. Their contacts usually form a big and complex *guanxi,* or network, and it is hard to separate contacts into family, work, and friends. Similarly, while the yellow file folder icon of the Windows system is explicit for American users who use manila folders to organize files in their daily lives, it causes confusion for users in another culture who have not used or seen a manila folder before, for example, some European and Japanese users ([13]).

The disconnect between action and meaning on low-level tasks can be compared to the example of structural differences across cultures in a writing genre such as business letters. Though aiming for the same goal of reaching a potential customer, an American business letter would go to the topic right away while a letter from Japan would establish long-term relationship first and then refer to the business opportunity towards the end. If we believe that an effective business letter to a Japanese customer should follow the rhetorical moves of Japanese business letters and think in a Japanese way, why do designers keep designing technologies for users in another culture by following the rhetorical moves of their own culture?

Two types of breakdowns occur in this situation. First, there is an incompatibility between user expectation of the high-order activity and low-level actions represented by functions. Dunker ([9]) discusses how the seemingly universal and simple library classification systems originated from Western cultures are incomprehensible to Maori users in New Zealand. The collectivist Maori culture values shared knowledge among group members and approaches information and knowledge in its unity. When Western library classification systems divided the high-order activity of learning about a Maori tribe genealogy by searching for a related book into the low-level actions of locating the book's subject heading, publication format, volume, and issue number, Maori users got lost in a digital library. Second, there is a conflict between the meaning conveyed through low-level program functions and the local meaning. In the case of file folder icon, a yellow file folder icon does not suggest the filing practice to a European user but appears only as a yellow rectangle. This user would expect to see a cardboard box he uses to hold files. Furthermore, the "local" here does not stop at the nation/state level, depending on target users. In some cases, the local would go to the community and even the individual level for a sub-culture. However, many times local meanings are plagued by discourse hegemony that lacks respect for individual subjectivity, which makes the breakdown of local meaning even worse.

For fixing use breakdowns, some might argue that it will not be difficult to replace an American file folder icon with a European cardboard box, a Chinese file envelope, or another cultural metaphor meaningful to a local culture, but how about making task representations transparent and meaningful to local users, in the case of Maori digital library users? Action and meaning is more intertwined in cross-cultural design, and we need to look for better ways of fusing the material and the discursive, as well as integrating implementation and interpretation in local uses.

3 Dialogicality

To search for ways of better communicating the intended meanings to culturally diverse users, I use Bakhtin's concept of dialogicality and its application in technology design, cultural psychology, and rhetorical genre theory to examine how interpretation functions in cross-cultural design. This section introduces the dialogical worldview first, then discusses how a dialogical approach connects actions and meaning, and cognition and meaning in technology design, and explores technological artifacts as instantiations of genres informed by this dialogical methodology.

Dialogicality and dialogic interactions is the cornerstone of Baktin's philosophy ([3], [4]). Built on his studies in speech genres and social language, Bakhtin believes that nothing is isolated in the world, and any unity is accomplished dialogically. McCarthy and Wright ([14]) state that Bakhtin's dialogical worldview and his exploration of everyday meaning-making experience of individuals is valuable to user experience design because this dialogical worldview connects action and meaning through "intoning": "[Bakhtin's] approach to activity is to focus on how individuals intone acts of living and knowing. By 'intone' he means how individuals make acts their own, how they make them unique, personal experiences through the particularities of interpreting, feeling, and making value judgments and distinctions that are ethically worthwhile" (p.56). Informed by this dialogical methodology, they argue for a holistic approach of experience that is "lived, felt experience as prosaic, open, and unfinalizable, situated in the creativity of action and the dialogicality of meaning making, engaged in the potential of each moment at the same time as being responsive to the personal stories of self and others, sensual, emergent, and answerable" (p. 184). In this regard, users are part of the design process, and there is a more robust interaction between designers and users. The dialogical view of technology design is both material and interpretive, and actions and meaning are treated in a holistic way.

Cultural psychologist Wertsch ([25]) interprets Bakhtin's dialogical approach of meaning is "an active process rather than a static entity" (p. 52). He found Bakhtin's dialoglicality is instrumental to integrate meaning and cognition: "human communicative & psychological processes are characterized by a dialogicality of voices" (p. 13). In his studies of language use in the schooling practices, he appropriates Baktin's social language and speech genres to illustrate how the influences from the sociocultural setting shape the development of individual psychological process. He is interested in exploring "why certain forms of speaking and thinking (voices) rather than others are invoked on particular occasions" (p. 14), more specifically, "why a particular voice... is 'privileged' in a particular setting"(ibid). Here "being privileged" suggests "being more appropriate and efficacious than others" (p. 124). Though Wertsch did not examine technology as meditational means in his studies, his findings are insightful for the HCI field. User modeling based on cognition has been a driving force in HCI design, but it is not well connected with the interpretative aspect of actions. Usually the two aspects have been treated as two parallel factors that overdetermine a design. On the other hand, as universalistic approaches of cognitive models overshadowed other cognitive approaches in HCI designs for a long time, particularly during the 90s, the sociocultural situatedness of cognition was ignored. Accordingly, user models based on a universal and individualist design philosophy have caused many problems to cross-cultural IT design, as discussed in the previous section. So when Wertsch illustrates the sociocultural situatedness of mediated action (i.e., user tasks accomplished with an IT) in a convincing argument with Baktin's notion of dialogicality, it shows us possible ways of connecting user modeling to the interpretation on the top level. Furthermore, his interest in studying "why a particular voice […] is 'privileged' in a particular setting" (p.14) shares with one of the central goals of rhetorical genre theory.

Rhetorical genre theory attends to textual and contextual regularities, repeated actions, and technological influences, both across texts and across practices by examining social exigencies of genres ([8]). Erickson ([10]) has a concise summary of genre as below:

> *"A genre is a patterning of communication created by a combination of the individual (cognitive), social, and technical forces implicit in a recurring communicative situation. A genre structures communication by creating shared expectations about the form and content of the interaction, thus easing the burden of production and interpretation."*

Though genres are usually classified by their distinctive textual features, genre theory is more interested in genres' functions and in the interactions between functions and texts. Social practices represented by generic features are what attract researchers to study genres. In IT research, the definition of genres is expanded from textual ones to artifact categories (e.g., [7], [22], [27]). As genre theory brings a peculiar lens to typified human activities through the mediated artifacts, it has been widely adopted in the fields of HCI, information studies, and technical communication. For example, Anderson ([2]) claims that "user studies [in library and information studies] would be genre studies" (p. 342).

Genres are the outcome of typified human activities. According to Spinuzzi ([22]), genres imply a worldview, an understanding of a certain human activity and what it values. As patterns of typified human activities, genres are always associated with surrounding situations. The situation here should not be narrowly interpreted as a task context, but instead, it is a local context layered with multiple sociocultural factors. Spinuzzi stresses that genre's role as tradition in technology design. Drawing on Baktin's dialogic worldview, he states, "genres are the result of an ongoing dialogue among speakers in a particular sphere of activity, and the past dialogue of those speakers imposes itself on present speakers in ways that they might not even recognize" (p.43). In this view, genres are value-laden artifacts situated in a particular sociocultural setting: They are "traditions of producing, using, and interpreting artifacts" and "traditions that make their way into the artifact as a 'form-shaping ideology'" (p.41). And an individual artifact is "an instantiation" of a genre or multiple genres. In his study of traffic workers' textual mediation practices in a state transportation department, Spinuzzi scrutinizes traditional paper forms and web forms as different artifacts instantiated for the same genre, more accurately, for the same activity of logging traffic accidents.

At the same time, as the outcome of "an ongoing dialogue," genres are never stable. Genres change as activities change. Berkenkotter and Huckin ([5]) describe genres as "sites of contention between stability and change. They are inherently dynamic, constantly (if gradually) changing over time in response to the sociocognitive needs of individual users" (p.6).

Here, the genre notion with its features of situatedness and dynamism helps us to see, in the arena of cross-cultural design, why certain instantiations of genres, certain voices, and certain interpretations are privileged (i.e., accepted) in a local context, and why other forms are rejected.

4   A Dialogic View of Interpretation

A dialogic view of interpretation based on a genre notion provides an essential clue in understanding the use of technological artifacts in a sociocultural context and in investigating how the connection of design and use is dynamically settled in different interface features by inquiring about rules and habits related to genres in cross-cultural design ([7], [22], [27]). For example, a structured layout on a German website and vibrant colors on a Brazilian website reveal different local reading habits and visual preferences through their different generic features.

The dynamic nature of genres shows the possibility of fusing action and meaning through a structuration process that occurring around genres. Influenced by Gidden's structuration theory, Miller ([15]) suggests genres are capable of reproducing social structures with their recurrent nature in situated communication. Orlikowski ([18]) further describes that social structures are not embodied in technology genres, but are "only instantiated in practice" (p. 406). Recurrent interaction with a technology "produces and reproduces a particular structure of technology use" (p. 407). She names this as technology *enactment*. The process of enactment asserts that technology use is socially and culturally determined, and thus generic features of a technology carry meanings and enhance culturally situated actions and local practices. Laundry practices vary greatly across the globe, for example, how to take care of 18-foot-long saris made in fine cotton or silk is a big concern for Indian housewives while Brazilian housewives believe a pre-soaking is important to achieve a clean wash. Thus a popular washing machine in India has a specially designed agitator that does not tangle saris, and a Brazilian model includes a soak cycle to accommodate local preferences [12].

A genre view connects various levels of contexts in one artifact as the structuration process impacts on different levels: from individual through community then through the society level. A decision of adopting and using a technological genre is not only an individual decision based on the user's identity, lifestyle, subjective experience, and other individual factors, but also related to a discourse community where people share similar interpretive conventions about a particular genre and a particular communication activity. Moreover, the values of that society will be reinforced in this adoption process. Spinuzzi describes genre as "an integrated-scope of unit of analysis" ([22]): On the macroscopic level, genres are "shaping and being shaped by its sociocultural milieu as social memory" (p. 44); on the mesoscopic level, genres function as a tool-in-use, "typically taken to be instantiated in an artifact" (p.46); on the microscopic level, genres represent "a coherent collection of habits" and "a set of operationalized actions" (p. 46).

In the case of business letters, the practice of business letter writing is disciplinary and culturally oriented. As an important component of global trade, it is deeply related to various ways of how people do business in local culture on the macroscopic level. On the mesoscopic level, different technological artifacts serve as various instantiations depending on local needs, for example, they can be traditional letters, faxes, and email messages. In this case, a genre view makes us be aware of what voice is "privileged" in a community as Wertsch suggests. On the microscopic level, a typical American letter has the following generic features including letterhead, date, inside address, salutation, body message, complimentary closing, and signature blocks. These features serve as a formula and direct a proficient writer to complete routinized actions in a task context.

With this cross-scope flexibility, a dialogic view of interpretation in cross-cultural design would not just stay at the level of national values, but would dig further into rich contextual factors through the community level to the individual level. It will look at these issues ranging from "How should I accomplish this task with this technology?" to "What does this use activity mean to me in my social group or in my professional community?" to "What role does this technology play in shaping my personal life and my social identity?"

Regarding generic features as affordances, this dialogical view demonstrates how technology affordance comes from the milieu of the artifact, user, and activity. During the structuration process, structuring forces and social habits (i.e., rules) are clustered and instantiated in a technological genre (i.e., tool), solidified as generic features. A genre view of technological artifacts is crucial to technology affordances because it helps interpret an artifact's use in context by providing socially constructed interpretive conventions. These generic features are affordances, which unfold in this praxis of use and develop as a result of the interplay of habituated uses and sociocultural factors. In this case, a Korean refrigerator does not only refrigerate or freeze food, but also ferment kimchee, a pickled cabbage serving as a daily staple on Korean's dining tables.

Users play an important role during the heterogeneous co-constitution of technology across a transnational stage. As part of a dialogical structuration process, a technology-in-use is a response to local conditions. Indeed, the practice of technology use is a dialogue between the user and the technology, the technology and local conditions, and the present and the past. Generic features emerge dynamically due to the enactment. Therefore, design is to start and initiate a dialogue, and it is user's task to respond and complete the dialogue. The success of Twitter does not only belong to designers but also to users. After designers noticed Twitter users would refer to fellow Twitterers by name like this: @TwitterID, they incorporated it in design. The same case applies to user convention such as "RT" (retweet) [19].

The characteristic of dialogicality also sheds light on how cultural dimensions affect a particular IT design and use. The emergent feature of affordance manifests in cross-cultural design. The same technology could enact different technologies-in-use in different local contexts in the process of articulating multiple interpretations, and thus we need to design corresponding affordances for them. For example, when mobile text messaging is found to be used to conduct long conversations in one culture and for small talk in another culture ([23]), we would want to design different interface features to support these different user tasks.

Understanding the dynamism of the technology enactment process shows the possibility of avoiding the pitfall of stereotyping local culture in cross-cultural design. If cultural patterns are utilized in a dynamic fashion to explore the enactment process, then we will be able to stay away from reducing concrete culture into static patterns and negotiate diverse interests from different parties and communities into one artifact. To design a technology is to immerse oneself in a local context and understand the socially and historically developed, typified activities related to that technology.

5 Conclusion

My goal in this paper is to argue for a dialogic view of interpretation that connects action and meaning in cross-cultural IT design and makes a design appealing to a local context without stereotyping the local culture in an essentialist fashion. After showing how a dialogical view of interpretation functions in cross-cultural IT design, the issue here is how we could develop a dialogical rhetoric to facilitate conversation between the local and the global and between designers and users, and to initiate and sustain multiple interpretations. Further questions need to be explored in this area. For example, it is possible that certain genre is simply not fit in a certain sociocultural context which does not have that situatedness, or there is an inherent conflict between local structure and the new structure introduced by a technology. And even there seems a fit, designers need to be aware of whether the design has enhanced or altered local structure. For those emerging technologies, it is always important to locate previous instantiations of the genre for the shared activity.

References

1. Albrechtsen, H., Andersen, H.H.K., Bødker, S., Pejtersen, A.M.: Affordances in Activity Theory and Cognitive Systems Engineering. Riso National Laboratory, Roskilde (2001)
2. Andersen, J.: The concept of genre in information studies. Annual Review of Information Science and Technology 42, 339–367 (2008)
3. Bakhtin, M.M.: The Dialogic Imagination Four Essays. University of Texas Press, Austin (1981)
4. Bakhtin, M.M.: Speech Genres and Other Late Essays. University of Texas Press, Austin (1984)
5. Berkenkotter, C., Huckin, T.N.: Genre Knowledge in Disciplinary Communication. Lawrence Erlbaum Associates, Mahwah, NJ (1995)
6. Bourges-Waldegg, P., Scrivener, S.: Meaning, the central issue in cross-cultural HCI design. Interacting with Computers 9(3), 287–309 (1998)
7. Brown, J., Duguid, P.: Borderline issues: Social and material aspects of design. Human-Computer Interaction. Special Issue on Context in Design 9(1), 4–36 (1994)
8. Dias, P., Freedman, A., Medway, P., Pare, A.: Situating writing. In: Worlds apart: Acting and writing in academic and workplace contexts, ch. 2, pp. 17–46. Lawrence Erlbaum Associates, Mahwah, NJ (1999)
9. Dunker, E.: Cross-Cultural Usability of the Library Metaphor. In: Proceedings of Joint Conferences on Digital Libraries 2002, pp. 223–230 (2002)
10. Erickson, T.: Rhyme and punishment: The creation and enforcement of conventions in an on-line participatory limerick genre. In: Proceedings of the 32nd Hawaii International Conference on System Sciences, HICSS 1999 (1999)
11. Gould, E.: Synthesizing the literature on cultural values. In: Aykin, N. (ed.) Usability and internationalization of information technology, pp. 79–122. Lawrence Erlbaum Associates, Mahwah, New Jersey (2004)
12. Heskett, J.: Design: A very short introduction. Oxford University Press, Oxford (2002)
13. Marcus, A.: Icon and Symbol Design Issues for Graphical User Interfaces. In: Del Galdo E, Nielsen J. International User Interfaces, pp. 257–270. John Wiley and Sons, New York (1996)
14. McCarthy, J., Wright, P.: Technology as Experience. MIT Press, Cambridge, MA (2004)
15. Miller, C.R.: Rhetorical community: the cultural basis of genre. In: Freedman, A., Medway, P. (eds.) Genre and the new rhetoric, pp. 67–78. Taylor & Francis, London (1994)
16. Mirel, B.: Advancing a vision of usability. In: Mirel, B., Spilka, R. (eds.) Reshaping Technical Communication, pp. 165–188. Lawrence Earlbaum Associates, Mahwah, NJ (2002)

17. Mirel, B.: Interaction Design for Complex Problem Solving – Developing Useful and Usable Software. Morgan Kaufmann, San Francisco, CA (2004)
18. Orlikowski, W.J.: Using Technology and Constituting Structures: A Practice Lens for Studying Technology in Organizations. Organization Science 11(4), 404–428 (2000)
19. Pogue, D.: Twitters? It's What You Make It, New York Times (February 11, 2009), http://www.nytimes.com/2009/02/12/technology/personaltech/12pogue.html?_r=1
20. Sengers, P., Gaver, W.: Designing for Interpretation. In: Proceedings of the 11th International conference on Human-Computer Interaction, Lawrence Erlbaum Associates, Mahwah (2005)
21. Sengers, P., Gaver, W.: Staying open to interpretation: engaging multiple meanings in design and evaluation. In: Proceedings of the 6th conference on Designing Interactive systems, pp. 99–108. ACM Press, New York (2006)
22. Spinuzzi, C.: Tracing Genres through Organizations: A Sociocultural Approach to Information Design. The MIT Press, Cambridge, MA (2003)
23. Sun, H.: The triumph of users: Achieving cultural usability goals with user localization. Technical Communication Quarterly 15(4), 457–481 (2006)
24. Virkkunen, J., Engestrom, Y.: Usability and the changing producer-user relationship (2001), http://mlab.uiah.fi/culturalusability/papers/Virkkunen_Engestrom.pdf
25. Wertsch, J.V.: Voices of the Mind. Harvard University Press (1991)
26. Yang, K.S.: Chinese personality and its change. In: Bond, M.H. (ed.) The psychology of the Chinese people, pp. 106–170. Oxford University Press, New York (1986)
27. Yates, J., Orlikowski, W.J.: Genres of Organizational Communication: A Structurational Approach to Studying Communication and Media. The Academy of Management Review 17(2), 299–326 (1992)

Exploring Cultural Context Using the Contextual Scenario Framework

Eric Swanson, Keiichi Sato, and Judith Gregory

Institute of Design at the Illinois Institute of Technology, 350 N. LaSalle
Chicago, IL 60610
{erics,sato,judithg}@id.iit.edu

Abstract. In applications where individuals in different contexts interact with a technology system, cultural issues present complex challenges for developers attempting to understand context of use. Three features of culture stand out: individuals embody overlapping cultural memberships; cultures and roles interact; and individuals make erroneous assumptions of others' cultural membership. This paper illustrates how the *Contextual Scenario Framework (CSF)* can address these cultural challenges. The CSF is a tool that supports scenario-based design by structuring, organizing and automatically recalling contextual information. The mechanisms of the CSF enable exploration of human activity in context, linking characters within scenarios to contextual influences discovered in primary field research and secondary analysis.

Keywords: Culture, Context, Scenario, Scenario-Based Design, Information Systems Design, Human-Computer Interface.

1 Introduction

As technology becomes more ubiquitous and more mobile, assumptions about a user's cultural surrounding that could be made in the past are becoming less viable. According to Agre [2], *Institutions* – persistent structures of human relationships – are losing their ties to *Architecture* – the built environment.

Complex systems, particularly for cooperative work, are likely to be multi-actor environments, and so embody multiple viewpoints. In such systems, "differences among actors' views cannot be conceived as affecting only narrowly circumscribed domains... but involve actors' whole cultural order" [Mantovani [10], p. 257].

This paper will describe the *Contextual Scenario Framework* (CSF) and how it addresses three challenges with exploring contextual influences related to culture. The CSF is a scenario-based tool for the structuring, organization and automatic recall of contextually-relevant information during systems design. It takes advantage of the existing ability of scenario-based design to support iterative and experimental design practices [5], but adds structured connections between scenario characters and contextual factors identified in primary field research and secondary analysis.

This paper uses data from a semester-length qualitative study conducted in the Fall of 2007. The study, "The Lived Experience of Sandwiched Caregiver Families"

N. Aykin (Ed.): Internationalization, Design, LNCS 5623, pp. 117–126, 2009.
© Springer-Verlag Berlin Heidelberg 2009

(www.id.iit.edu/833/), gained deep appreciation of the experience of a small number of participants through ethnographic observation and a participatory design-based workshop. The pilot study was of "sandwiched" caregivers, defined as adults who provide parental care to their own dependent children or stepchildren, while simultaneously caring for a dependent elder relative living with a chronic condition. In the following analysis, the data are used for illustration purposes only.

The CSF is part of our ongoing goal of developing contextually-rich research and design methodology for complex information systems.

2   Three Complexities in the Contextual Influence of Culture

Individual Embodiment of Multiple Cultures. Individuals do not participate in just one social world at a time; they belong to multiple social worlds simultaneously [8]. Such social contexts not only surround an individual, but also lie within [e.g. 10]. As a result, individuals can be made up of a metaphoric cacophony of voices [11].

The term "cacophony" highlights the complexity that simultaneous membership entails. Just as noises interact in a cacophony, an individual's multiple social worlds can interact and even clash. A tool for supporting multiple cultures must permit two things: the ability of human actors to embody multiple social worlds simultaneously, and a means to see interactions among factors arising from those social worlds.

Interaction Between Roles and Cultures. Knowing that an individual is a member of a culture is not enough to understand their culture. Individuals can embody different roles within a culture, and those roles can entail very different perceptions and actions. "[R]oles and the taking and making of roles are seen as fundamental to the process by which social groupings become more than mere aggregates of people" [7, p. 231]. A tool that addresses this must be able to differentiate roles within a culture, and must allow for differing combinations of roles and cultures.

Erroneous Cultural Assumptions. In real situations, individuals have only imperfect information about the worlds of others with whom they interact. People can easily operate under a false assumption about the cultural background of another, after misinterpreting some culture cue. In distance work, for example, global team members improperly interpret conventions about dress as personality cues: "Mexican engineers in khaki shirts and sunglasses looked suspicious to the shirt-and-tie U.S. engineers. Silicon Valley engineers in t-shirts and blue jeans and Big Five consultants in their formal corporate wear made incorrect attributions about each other" [12, 170].

Here, point of view matters. In a realistic model, a false ascription of culture from one person's point of view (e.g. a "shirt-and-tie U.S. engineer") would not be negated by the cultural reality of the person in focus. The "error" must be preserved.

3   Existing Methods for Reusing Situated Data

Complete Methodologies. These systems development methodologies have been designed explicitly to incorporate contextual understanding at all stages of design. Their *raison d'être* is to develop contextually-centered systems.

Contextual Design was developed to maintain customer-centered focus throughout the front end of systems design [6]. It starts with Contextual Inquiry and Work Modeling stages to understand current work of the customer. Consolidation follows creating a map of the customer population and to show the underlying structure of their work. Work Redesign integrates ideas, while User Environment Design and Mockup and Test with Customers create the system.

Soft Systems Methodology (SSM) addresses "real-world problems in which known-to-be-desirable ends cannot be taken as given" [7, p. 318]. Phenomenological in stance, SSM concerns itself with human activity systems. It builds a rich model of "the situation in which there is perceived to be a problem" [7, p. 163], leading to a concise description of the human activity system (from a particular point of view).

Contextual Design and SSM share the goal of creating systems around holistic models of their contexts of implementation. The two methodologies differ in scope: Contextual Design on specific technology systems; SSM on human activity systems, in scales up to an entire society. These methodologies could be complemented by tools that enable moment-to-moment exploration of context by accumulation of detail.

Scenario and Use Case Modeling Tools. These focus on integrating an understanding of work practices as activities into the software development processes.

Coherence is an integrated approach to social and object-oriented analysis [15]. It uses multiple forms of modeling to represent the learnings of ethnographic methods regarding work processes. Coherence uses standard industry approaches (use cases and UML) as the means to integrate the social modeling with industry standard models, as well as a Viewpoints model that elaborates concerns in descriptive prose.

Scenario-Based Requirements Engineering (SBRE) [14] contains both a method and a software tool for scenario-based requirements engineering. It integrates with use case approaches to object-oriented development. It models a use case with a structured language, enabling the use of abstract libraries to discover generic requirements. Exception types (including extensive varieties of human error) are applied to normal event sequences to suggest possible abnormal events. Scenario paths are automatically generated and validated using rule-based frames.

Both models formalize contextual data, with SBRE being the more strictly formal. While formalization makes integrating material with systems design processes easier, even modest formalization bears the risk of stripping contextual data of its interpretive qualities. There is opportunity to re-introduce the interpretive by pairing the systematically-created scenarios of SBRE or the semi-formal UML Use Cases of Coherence with a mechanism for adding contextual content to scenarios.

4   A Scenario-Based Framework for Reusing Contextual Data

The CSF is a mechanism for the structuring, management, and utilization of contextual data in support of scenario-based design, including the iterative design of human-computer interaction. It is designed to address complex situations, such as those in which multiple people interact with a technology (e.g. CSCW).

Previous literature suggests several challenges in working with contextual data in human activity. For example, both the sources of contextual effect and the effects themselves often remain hidden from direct observation. Much of what is contextual arises, in part, from elements internal to the experience of the individual [9, 4]. Such "internal" contextual effects are not necessarily causes in themselves, but are brought out based on the individuals' *relationship* with elements in the "external" world [1]. Additionally, the effects of context are dynamic and self-interactive [9]. Even within the context of a scenario, changes in the situation can result in changes to the context, which then further change the situation [10]. Finally, domain research which generates contextual understanding (e.g. ethnomethodology) is often interpretive, rather than quantitative, which does not lend itself to formalization [3].

4.1 Structuring Contextual Data for Reuse

The CSF takes advantage of the scenario author's third-person omniscient perspective to explore contextual data. With this perspective, the scenario author has the power to declare that a human actor embodies some combination of contextually relevant features, *even if those features could not be directly observed*. A contextual feature that took careful observation and analysis to comprehend in the source data can be, subsequently, reused in a scenario merely by declaring that a character embodies it.

The CSF uses structured natural language to preserve some of the interpretive quality of the source contextual material. All contextual data in the CSF is structured into a single, standard data type: natural language sentences, called *Contextual Factors* (Fig. 1). Each Contextual Factor reflects a link between some potential element of context (indexed to its *Triggering Situation*) and some potential effect identified from real data through research and analysis (its *Contextual Influence*).

Contextual Factors. A Contextual Factor joins a simplified situation, applicable to an individual human actor, to Contextual Influences arising from it. A Contextual Factor has two parts: (1) zero to many Contextual Influences, (Fig. 1, lower box) and (2) one *Triggering Situation* indicating when they apply (Fig. 1, upper box).

Contextual Influence. A Contextual Influence is a contextual attribute of a human actor derived from domain research. It describes an alteration in (or setting of) the way an individual thinks, feels, perceives or chooses to act, in the form of a sentence with the implied subject, "A human actor in a similar situation" (Fig. 1, lower box).

Triggering Situations. A *Triggering Situation* is the set of conditions that elicit, for a specific character within a scenario, the Contextual Influence for a Contextual Factor (Fig. 1, lower box). Each *Triggering Situation* consists of one *Primitive Situation (PS)* or more than one PS connected with AND or NOT (Fig. 2). Triggering Situations act as indexes, linking each character in a scenario to his or her relevant contextual data.

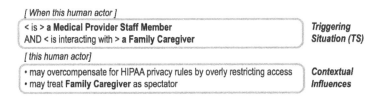

Fig. 1. A Contextual Factor and its Elements

[When this human actor]
< is > **a Medical Provider Staff Member**   *Primitive Situation*
AND < is interacting with > **a Family Caregiver**   *Primitive Situation*
Actor-Element Relation   Scenario Element Primitive

Fig. 2. A Triggering Situation and its Elements

Primitive Situations. A Primitive Situation is a very simple situation–a relationship between a single human actor and one element of a scenario. It consists of one *Scenario Element Primitive* (SEP) and one *Actor-Element Relationship*. (Fig. 2).

Table 1. Categorization of Scenario Element Primitives and Actor-Element Relationships

Scenario Element Primitive category	Actor-Element Relationships	Primitive Situation (PS) examples
Individual Role / Condition	< is > < is in the presence of > < is interacting with > < is subject / client of >	[This Human Actor] **is** a Family Caregiver: Sandwiched [HA] **is in the presence of** a Mood-Impared Care Recipient [HA] **is interacting with** a Bureaucratic Representative [HA] **is the client of** a Medical Professional: Geriatric
Activity / Action / Event	< is a subject of > < is engaged in > < is in the presence of > < is performing >	[HA] **is a subject of** Caregiving False Emergency [HA] **is engaged in** Planning Long-Term Care [HA] **is in the presence of** Medical Emergency [HA] **is performing** Verifying Caregiving Role to Officialdom
Physical Surrounding	< is within >	[HA] **is within** A Sandwiched Caregiving Household
Social / Cultural Surrounding	< is a member of > < is interacting w/member of > < is amongst >	[HA] **is a member of** a Sandwiched Caregiving Household [HA] **is interacting w/member of** Cancer Support Group [HA] **is amongst** Emergency Room Waiting Area Family
Tangible Object / Tool / System	< is in the presence of > < is operating > < is sharing operation of > < is interacting w/operator of > < is utilizing > [system] < is manipulating >	[HA] **is in the presence of** an Amplified Telephone Ringer [HA] **is operating** an Electronic Calendar [HA] **is sharing operation of** On-Line Medical Record [HA] **is interacting w/operator of** Paper-based Record System [HA] **is utilizing** a Family-Assembled Medical Record Binder [HA] **is manipulating** a Paper-based Individual Medical Record

SEPs represent a single aspect of an entity or state within a scenario, in the form of a noun. A Scenario Element may have more than one SEP. A smart phone, for example, may be a "Mobile Phone," an "Electronic Calendar" and a "Techno-Status Symbol."

SEPs fall into categories based on the type of scenario element they represent. Each category has a defined list of relationships a human actor might hold with them - their Actor-Element Relationships (Table 1, middle). SEPs act as the predicates of sentences with "this human actor" as the implied subject (Fig. 2; Table 1, right).

4.2   Creating Scenarios with Contextual Data

The CSF connects scenarios with contextual data from the research by generating lists of contextual influences for each scenario character. This occurs in three phases.

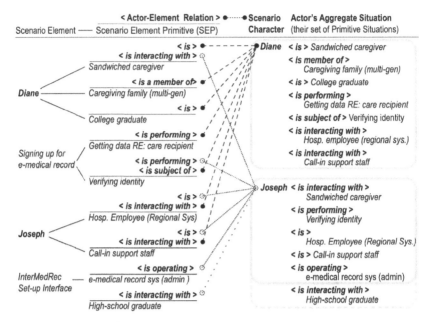

Fig. 3. Creation of a Character's Aggregate Situation

Phase 1: The Scenario Author Assembles Scenario Elements. The author begins by creating the scenario by identifying the *Scenic Elements* - elements of the scenario with real-world equivalents, be they observable or internal, that are present at the start (Fig. 3, column 1). Next, the author identifies an appropriate set of Scenario Element Primitives (SEPs) for each Scenario Element (Fig. 3, 2nd column, italic text).

With the SEPs in place, the author now builds each character's *Aggregate Situation*. The Aggregate Situation is the set of Primitive Situations applicable to a character at a specific event in the scenario (Fig. 3, boxes). To create this, the scenario author determines the relationship (if any) between each character and each SEP, assigning them Primitive Situations describing that relationship (Fig. 3, dashed lines).

Phase 2: CSF Aggregates Influence Lists from Primitive Situations. At this point, one Aggregate Situation has been created for each character (Fig. 4, left boxes). The CSF compares this list of Primitive Situations with the Triggering Situations (Fig. 4, middle column) in the database of Contextual Factors (Fig. 4, two rightmost columns). When the Triggering Situation of a Contextual Factor matches some combination of a character's Primitive Situations, that Factor applies to that character. The CSF appends its Contextual Influence to a list for that character (Fig. 4, right boxes), aggregating contextual influences from that character's point of view.

Phase 3: The Scenario Author iterates through a Scenario. Dynamic contextual change can be discovered by stepping through a scenario event-by-event and altering the actions of its characters based on their accumulated contextual influences. Event-to-event changes occur in three ways: adding or removing a Scenario Element (and its associated SEPs); adding or removing an SEP (and its associated Primitive Situations); and changing the assignment of Primitive Situations to Scenario Characters (Fig. 5).

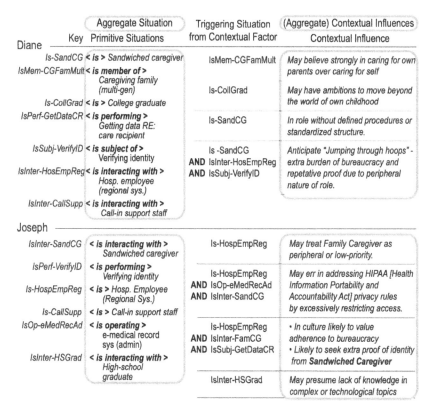

Fig. 4. Aggregate Contextual Influences, as Generated by Aggregate Situations

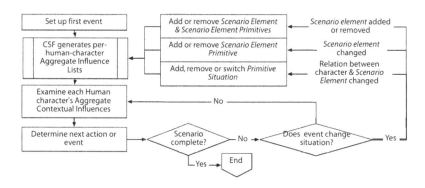

Fig. 5. Iterating through a Scenario

Changes within a scenario can cause the author to add or remove a Scenario Element, such as when an actor enters or exits the situation, when a tool is no longer in use or when the physical location of the scene changes. A Scenario Element Primitive can be added or subtracted to reflect a change within a Scenario Element, such as when there is a change in conditions, such as a character's mood, the weather, or a person's role.

Finally, a character can change his or her relationship to a Scenario Element, which the analyst reflects by selecting a Primitive Situation with a different Actor-Element Relation between the actor and the SEP.

5 Application Case

Throughout this article, we have been using data relating to our application case: a two person over-the-phone interaction regarding setting up an online medical record. The scenario of use (Fig. 6) involves a form of remote cooperative work not commonly considered Computer Supported Cooperative Work: phone support for an activity done online.

The CSF and overlapping cultures. Two features are necessary to address the overlapping of cultures within an individual: the ability of characters within a scenario to simultaneously embody multiple social worlds, and a means for users of the tool to see interactions among factors arising from those social worlds.

Within the CSF, no structures limit the membership of a character to a single social world. In Fig. 3, Diane is linked to two social worlds simultaneously: *Caregiving family (multi-gen)* and *College graduate.* This reveals potentially interacting Contextual Influences: "May believe strongly in caring for own parents over caring for self" and "May have ambitions to move beyond world of own childhood." The author explores this interaction in the scenarios' next-to-last sentence (Fig. 6), where an already troubled interaction is worsened as Diane experiences the frustration of conflict between her role in family culture and her ambition as an educated adult.

Diane's Aggregate Contextual Influences

May treat Family Caregiver as peripheral or low-priority

May err in addressing HIPAA [Health Information Portability and Accountability Act] privacy rules by excessively restricting access

• *In culture likely to value adherence to bureaucracy*
• *Likely to seek extra proof of identity from* **Sandwiched Caregiver**

May presume lack of knowledge in complex or technological topics

On her last visit to St. Mary's with her mother, Diane, a college-educated sandwiched caregiver, received a flyer for a new on-line medical record. She called the number and found herself talking to Joseph, from the call-in support staff. The conversation did not go well. Joseph was cautious -even cagey - about potentially giving away any information regarding Diane's mother. Eventually, he settled on having Diane read information from her latest medical receipts to confirm that she was actually the daughter of and caregiver to her mother.
Satisfied of her identity, Joseph moves on to guiding her through the on-line set-up. Noting from her file that Diane lives in a working-class neighborhood and she lists her occupation as a stay-at-home parent, Joseph presumes that she has a high-school education or less. Joseph selects the "novice user" script, while Diane has already logged into the system. As Joseph steps her through the script, Diane rolls her eyes. She knows she is honor-bound to put up with frustrations like this, yet she is again reminded of how her obligations restrict her world. The conversation has gone poorly indeed.

Joseph's Aggregate Contextual Influences

Anticipate "Jumping through hoops" - extra burden of bureaucracy and repetitive proof due to peripheral nature of role

May believe strongly in caring for own parents over caring for self

May have ambitions to move beyond world of own childhood

In role without defined procedures or standardized structure

Fig. 6. Scenario Created by Iterating through Aggregate Lists of Contextual Influences

CSF and the relation between roles and cultures. The ability to differentiate among roles within a culture is necessary to address the complexity of culture.

In the application case, Joseph embodies both a culture, *Hospital employee (region system)* and a role, *Call-in support staff* (Fig. 3, lower right). When Joseph interacts with a sandwiched caregiver; the combination of Primitive Situations matches the Triggering Situation for the Contextual Influence "*In a culture likely to value adherence to bureaucracy*". Change Joseph's role to *Medical Practitioner*, though, and that influence disappears – reflecting, perhaps, a surgeon's ambivalence to bureaucracy.

CSF and erroneous cultural assumption. Embodying individual points of view is necessary for handling errors in cultural assumption. During the course of the scenario, Joseph comes to embody an erroneous assumption about Diane – that she is only a *High-school graduate*. (This dynamic mid-scenario change is represented in Fig. 3 and Fig. 6 by dashed-line boxes). Joseph's error has no effect on the Scenic Elements linked to Diane, just as, in real life, someone else's mistake does not automatically cause another person to change. Conversely, the reality of Diane's Scenic Element link of *College graduate* has no effect on Joseph's error. Joseph's error leads him to an improper choice in using the e-medical record administrative interface tool – using a 'novice' instruction script when an 'internet savvy' script might have been more appropriate. This worsens an already awkward situation.

6 Discussion

The contributions we have described in this paper are twofold: the ability of the Contextual Scenario Framework to act as a mechanism for dynamic reuse of contextual information and the ability of the structures within CSF to handle complexities raised by issues of culture. The latter demonstrates the flexibility of the CSF to work with data generated using interpretive research methodologies.

Still to be determined, however, is the degree to which the structured information formats capture and reproduce contextual information accurately, appropriately and efficiently. Can Contextual Factors capture a broad range of categories of contextual information? Would data in a large CSF database prove to be accessible and useful as a project, or an organization, evolves? And what are the trade-offs in time and effort?

In further work, we would like to integrate the CSF with existing systems development methodologies and tools. We would like to extend the scope of research to large-scale systems development projects, to explore its scalability.

Acknowledgements. This research was made possible by Rethinking Health initiative (www.id.iit.edu/828/), launched August 2007, thanks to a generous gift from Robert Pew, Chairman of the Board of Steelcase and Chair of ID's Board of Overseers.

References

1. Agre, P.: Changing Places: Contexts of Awareness in Computing. Human-Computer Interaction 16(2/4), 177–192 (2001)
2. Agre, P.E.: The Dynamic Structure of Everyday Life (PhD Dissertation), UMI Order Number: AITR-1085, Massachusetts Institute of Technology (1988)

3. Akman, V.: Rethinking Context as a Social Construct. Journal of Pragmatics 32, 743–759 (2000)
4. Bainbridge, L.: The Change in Concepts Needed to Account for Human Behavior in Complex Dynamic Tasks. IEEE Transactions on Systems, Man, and Cybernetics 27, 351–359 (1997)
5. Bardram, J.: Scenario-Based Design of Cooperative Systems: Re-Designing a Hospital Information System in Denmark. Group decision and negotiation 9, 237–250 (2000)
6. Beyer, H., Holtzblatt, K.: Contextual Design. Academic Press, San Diego (1998)
7. Checkland, P.: Systems Thinking, Systems Practice. John Wiley & Sons, New York (1984); reprint with 30-year retrospective (1999)
8. Fitzpatrick, G., Mansfield, T., Kaplan, S.M.: Locales Framework: Exploring Foundations for Collaboration Support. In: OzCHI 1996, p. 34-4 (1996)
9. Greenberg, S.: Context as a Dynamic Construct. Human-Computer Interaction 16, 257–268 (2001)
10. Mantovani, G.: Social Context in HCI: A New Framework for Mental Models, Cooperation, and Communication. Cognitive Science 20, 237–269 (1996)
11. Nielsen, L.: From User to Character – An Investigation Into User-Descriptions in Scenarios. In: Proc. DIS 2002, pp. 99–104 (2002)
12. Olson, G.M., Olson, J.S.: Distance Matters. Human-Computer Interaction 15(2-3), 139–178 (2000)
13. Sato, K.: Context-Sensitive Approach for Interactive Systems Design: Modular Scenario-Based Methods for Context Representation. J. Physiol. Anthropol., Appl. Human Sci. 23(6), 277–281 (2004)
14. Sutcliffe, A.G., Maiden, N.A.M., Minocha, S., Manuel, D.: Supporting Scenario-Based Requirements Engineering. IEEE Transactions on Software Engineering 24(12), 1072–1088 (1998)
15. Viller, S., Sommerville, I.: Ethnographically Informed Analysis for Software Engineers. International Journal of Human-Computer Studies 54, 169–196 (2000)

Attention to Effects of Different Cross-Cultural Levels in User Research Method's Interface: Discipline or Nationality – Which Has Stronger Force?

Trang Thu Tran[1] and Kun-Pyo Lee[2]

Department of Industrial Design, KAIST, 335 Gwahangno, Yuseong-gu, Daejeon, 305-701, South Korea
its2trang@gmail.com, kplee@kaist.ac.kr

Abstract. In the recent years, design research have developed a long way in investigating about the users and their contexts. It was aimed to challenge the way 'cross-culture influence' has been considered in design research field: should there be better way than profiling users solely based on nationality in multinational research project for product specification. Major findings through this research included (1) Nationality factor influenced remarkably on user performance but not much on user attitude. In contrast, discipline factor influenced significantly on every elements of user participation. (2) The gaps of user attitude and performance with nationality as the function maintained same levels while the effects from discipline factor intensified upon the increase of task complexity and change of ask characteristic. Overall, Discipline factor dominated Nationality factor, insisting on the importance of considering different levels of participants' cultures in designing the interface of user experience research methods.

Keywords: design research methodology, generative session, cross culture.

1 Introduction

Generative Session technique is a form of participatory design. It was first introduced by Elizabeth B-N Sanders in 1992 and was later described by the author as "these techniques can reveal tacit knowledge and expose latent needs". This technique is very different to the prior invented methods such as *usability tests* (in which users "do" something) and *questionnaire* or *interview* (in which users "say" something). In *Generative sessions,* users are the creators, who "make" designerly artefacts to express aspects of their situation, life, worries, and joys, etc. [1]

The method was inspired by the designers' ideation and communication activities. Furthermore it was based on the belief that "all people can project and express their needs, wants and aspirations through the use and interpretation of ambiguous visual stimuli.". These two points were considered as the key points and core innovativeness of the method.

---

[1] The concept of users "say-do-make" is mentioned by Sanders (1999) in her model: UX method and level of user experience knowledge.

N. Aykin (Ed.): Internationalization, Design, LNCS 5623, pp. 127–134, 2009.

2   Cultural Effects on User Research and Cross-Culture

2.1   Cultural Effects on User Research

Based on the study on "culture and layers of influence on design research", Tran (2008) suggested the model of *stimuli to cognitive programming* as following.

There have been much attention paid to the cross-cultural effects in interface design and UX research in the recent years, in which researchers have been focusing on the effects of the middle layer: socio-cultural stimuli. Though *socio-culture* can be defined in multiple levels of groups (eg. Nationality, local area, career discipline, hobby, age, social class, etc.), most of the studies only have focused on the *national culture* level. There has been little study on the effects of *sub-culture* level. This initiated my question: further than *national culture*, can there be other level of *socio-culture* that makes stronger effects on user participation?

2.2   Cross-Socio Cultural Factors on User Research

According to psychologists, behaviours and cognition can be differentiated by occupations - a mind formation and changing process. Such process is done and amplified through education and daily practice (Gardner, 2006). As mention in previous section, the key "interface" of Generative session technique include holistic thinking,

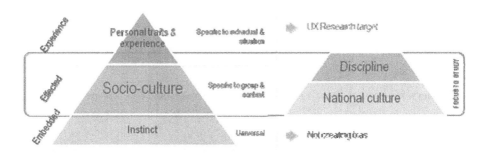

Fig. 1.

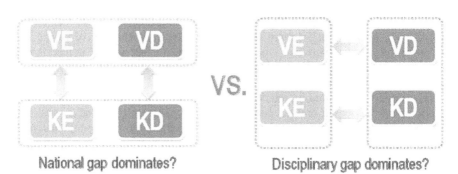

Fig. 2.

ambiguous terms, and richly visual interaction, question can be raised for this method: how this method is affected by the responses of participants from different groups of disciplines, which have different levels of intensiveness in daily practice with ambiguity and rich visual materials.

The experiment was carried out to answer the question: Among the two (major) factors (NAT and DIS), which one does generate more significant differences?

3 Methods

3.1 Participants

A proportionate, stratified, random sample was employed. Totally there were 60 participants recruited and divided into four groups of 15.

All the Korean participants were students in various departments of Korea Advanced Institute of Science and Technology, South Korea. The Vietnamese-Designer participants were recruited from one design consultant company and the University of Architecture and Design of Ho Chi Minh City, Vietnam. The Vietnamese-Engineer participants were randomly recruited from the Institute of Environmental Technology located in Ho Chi Minh City, Vietnam.

The basic criteria for all participants were within the age range 20-30 and have at least 3 years experience in the career discipline. The latter condition was to ensure all participants had at least completed the basic skill training period in each discipline, so that the effects of discipline factor is significant to observe. There was a fairly equal distribution of genders in each group (7 or 8 among 15 participants belonged to one gender).

3.2 Experiments

The participants were asked to perform two tasks in *Generative session* designed following the experiment done by Sanders and Stappers in 2003[2]. In the first task, the participants were provided 120 trigger images and 90 words and were requested to

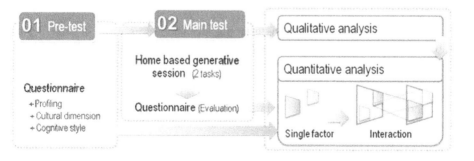

Fig. 3. Experiment scheme

---

[2] The experiment was conducted by the method inventors to test several combinations of elements in *Generative sessions* and to give the guideline to tune the method.

collage that representing their experience in taking photos. In the second task, they were requested to choose an image that best represents their ideal experience of taking photos as the starting point. From the starting point, they were to expand it into a *brainstorming map*. Both tasks were expected to be done in a poster format.

The double task application was to check the effects in different levels of task complexity. Task 1 was claimed as the basic level among generative session techniques. Task 2 was stated as more difficult because the participants were not aided with triggers and they had to generate the map/poster basically from nothing. In addition, the characteristic of task 2 is not as 'free-style' as task 1, i.e. requiring more analytical thinking.

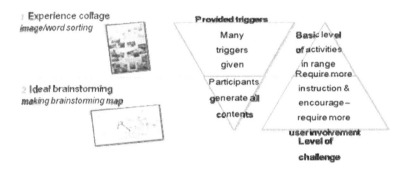

Fig. 4. Structure of task difficulties

Studies on user involvement in psychology and information system proved that there is a strong correlation between user attitude and user involvement, which is in turn correlated with the results. Moreover, it is possible to measure the involvement with questionnaires about user attitude and perception of how much the task relevant to their life experience. The latter notion however is not suitable in UX research as it is the main target of study[3].

To predict the biased effects in *user participation*, we measured the user's *attitude* towards the task, based on the user evaluation, and their *performance*, based on the researcher's evaluation of participant generated results. *User attitude* includes three elements: *time perception* – does the user consider this task is waste of time or not, *enjoyment perception* – how much does the participant enjoy the task, and *difficulty perception* – how much difficult (s)he thinks the task is. The *user performance* was evaluated based on four elements: *task completion time, imagery expressiveness* – level of expressiveness through imagery elements (from triggers and outsources), *textual expressiveness* – level of expressiveness through texts, and *expression relevancy* – how much relevant and specific user's expression of their experience is.

The participant generated posters were qualitatively analysis, using content analysis protocols. Their performance was translated into score in scale of 5 (1 for the lowest and 5 for the highest). The scales of score were the same in both *attitude* and *performance*. Finally, multiple fatorial ANOVA analyses were used to compare the user participation between two groups.

3.3 Analyzing Framework

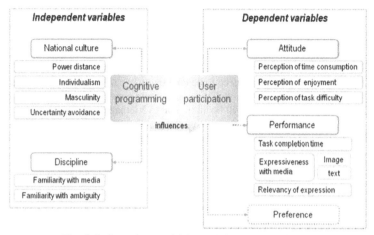

Fig. 5. Independent variables and dependent variables

4 Results

Major findings through this research included (1) *Nationality* factor influenced remarkably on user *performance* but not much on user *attitude*. In contrast, *discipline* factor influenced significantly on *every elements* of user participation. (2) The gaps of user *attitude* and *performance* with *nationality* as the function maintained same levels while the effects from *discipline* factor intensified upon the increase of task complexity and change of ask characteristic. Overall, *Discipline* factor dominated *nationality* factor, hypothesis [H0] was supported[3], insisting on the importance of considering users' disciplines in designing 'Generative session' and ULX research.

A closer look into each element also revealed some complex influencing interactions: (1) the alternation of 'freshness' factor (research activity is different to daily practice thus interesting for participants) towards engineering groups' results but not on design groups, (2) the suspect of influence from nationality factor is not solely due to cultural dimension difference but rather socio-economic-education factors, and (3) among all user participation elements, 'perception of enjoyment' and 'task completion time' had odd pattern of influence which was caused by the interaction of NAT*DIS factors, this effects required more investigation.

Based on the findings and insights, guideline for method enhancement was suggested. Main recommendation focused on noting on what works with which group and suggesting different ways of presenting instruction and material provision for different groups of participants.

The guideline was divided in three parts: on *cross national dimension*, on *cross disciplinary dimension*, and for *compound national-disciplinary profiling* (case study of Korean-Vietnamese and Design-Engineering compounding matrix).

The following guidelines will be presented in table format. The left columns display the reference tags (of that particular guideline) that link back to findings from proceeding section.

---

[3] Details are provided in Table 2. Summary of hypotheses confirmation (section 5.5, page 69).

On cross national dimension

Ref. tag	Guideline and discussion
A1	Both Korean and Vietnamese participants do not complain about their encountered difficulties with researchers so it is up to the researchers to check over the participants periodically and give aid when needed. Korean participants need to be encouraged by the beginning of the test. After that they can manage to complete the task on their own. Vietnamese participants prefer direct contact and need to be continuously encouraged and checked during their task conducting period. Therefore remote generative session is possible for Korean participants but will be inefficient to Vietnamese.
P1	For Vietnamese users to be able to express themselves efficiently, more sensitizing should be provided to understand the topic and to get used to expressing techniques. Pilot generative sessions with eventual increasing in complexity before real session are suggested.
P2	Similar issue as previous point [P1]. Additional point is the national difference in performance also is influence by socio-national circumstances. Since they are inevitable, before designing research method, secondary research stage should include study of national education system and style, general media contents, etc. to gain understand of how people obtain and express opinions.

On cross disciplinary dimension

Ref. tag	Guideline and discussion
A2, A3, and A4	There is a strong relation between enjoyment and perception of time consumption. In order to gain user enjoyment, two approaches are available: Carefully brief and psychologically prepare the participants, especially engineers, about the process and that it may take long time. Showing examples of pre-done similar works with notion of time can be helpful. Exploit the 'freshness' factor by integrate many beautiful visual elements in research package. However, pattern of how much visual elements and level of cuteness to be used should be studied further.
A5	Consideration of participant's career discipline and expressing ability should be integrated in early stage of experimental design. With the same question, it is recommended to be delivered in different formats and manners to designers and engineers: designers will have more freestyle expressing task while engineers will have well-refined, structured task.
P3 (linked to A2)	The extra time spending by participants when they are involved deeply to the task should be predicted and informed to participants in advance so it will not turn a pleasurable experience (of task conducting) to negative emotion (time concerning).
P4	There should be consideration for profiling regarding users' skill and ability of expression when applying the generative session techniques. Consequently they should not be analyzed on the same base of assumption. Since UX researchers usually have design background, it probably will be hard for them to be completely objective while analyzing mixed designer and non-designer results. Therefore setting up separated criteria and assessment framework for each group of participants is suggested.
P5	Although ambiguous stimuli are essential part of Generative session techniques, explicit level in task instruction and hints should be negotiated to a comprehensible level for engineers as ambiguous expession is unfamiliar to them. More study to determine the suitable level is advisable.

For compound national-disciplinary profiling (Korean-Vietnamese and Design-Engineering case)

Korean design group appeared to have the best performance among the four groups overall. Their generated results were also the closest to researchers' normal expectation of collected data. Vietnamese engineering group had the lowest performance yet with very good attitude. Vietnamese designers did not perform as well as Korean designers but much better than the two engineering groups.

Ref. tag	Guideline and discussion
E1	Affluent visual element support to Korean designers is important to keep them interest. (Note that the experiment in this study provided around 140 images, which was already more than a standard package used in US or the Netherlands, yet it was not enough.)
E2	If the task is conducted offline, bring in the convenience: provide pre-cut images and in sticker forms. However, there is a down side of cost and effort for preparing such package, thus an online generative session will solve this two matters. The trade off for online version is the technology barrier for some participants. Furthermore, it is believe that people tend to be more creative with hand-on tasks than computerized tasks.
A6	Vietnamese designers had strong art based training so well structured expression (such as making process diagrams or maps) is not preferable to them.
P6	Both engineering groups require much more sensitization than the method already provides. Current method focuses on familiarize participants with the topic. However, for non-designer users to be able to express themselves efficiently, more sensitizing is needed for them to understand and be used to expressing methods. Pilot generative sessions with eventual increasing in complexity before real session are suggested. In addition, researchers can include animated or interactive step-by-step instruction of the expressing method and topic to educate the participants how-to-express-your-experience.
A7, P6	Except for Korean designers, all other groups had problem (in different levels) with interpreting the request in task 2. For countries with high uncertainty avoidance, an abstractive request such as 'talk about your ideal experience of xyz' as in original method is not suitable and bring in unpleasant. A considerable way to rephrase the question is to provide them more information of the circumstance. The procedure is like: (1) provide the participants the descriptions of a certain ideal circumstance or an ideal scenario, then (2) ask for their response upon that scenario: "Have you ever experience this situation/experience? If yes, tell us more detail of that time. If no, what would you consider and do if you were in that case? Imagine your case and tell us."

5 Application and Discussion

The final accomplishment of this research was giving a guideline to enhance the method, showing practical experience and proven information to other researchers who intend to conduct related studies. It also raised some issues for further study of method enhancing.

Through this research, the upper level of mental programming stimuli (sub-culture discipline) was found to override the lower level (national culture). This result, firstly, was against the conventional belief in anthropology field that lower level always dominates upper level of the mental programming stimuli pyramid. It implied the change in human being's values and break of models within this ever-developing world. It further contributed to the dilemma in contemporary product development and business: globalization or localization, and to which level.

However, this study contained some limitations. Firstly, the results only apply for this specific case. More study needed for generalization of the theories as well as determine the pattern of influence. Secondly, the recruited participants were not equal in condition, such as the design participants were from different departments of design which may have different training programs and focus, as the same case as engineering participants. The impacts of compound variables are believed to exist.

Since this research only focused on one case study, with a two dimension matrix, it should be treated as pilot study and case study. The further work after this is suggested to be investigation of different combination of nations and disciplines, as well as different level of method complexity.

References

1. Sadler-Smith, E., Riding, R.J.: Cognitive style and instructional preferences. Instructional Science 27, 355–371 (1997)
2. Sanders, E.B.-N.: Postdesign and Participatory Culture. In: Proceeding in Useful and Critical: The Position of Research in Design, University of Art and Design Helsinki (UIAH), Tuusula, Finland (1999)
3. Barki, H., Hartwick, J.: Rethinking the Concept of User Involvement. MIS Quarterly 13, 53–63 (1989)
4. Gardner, H.: Changing Minds: the Art and Science of Changing Our Own and Other People's Minds. Harvard Business School Press, Boston (2006)
5. Rijn, H., Bahk, Y., Stappers, P., Lee, K.P.: Three Factors for Contextmapping in East Asia: Trust, Control and Nunchi. CoDesign 2, 157–177 (2006)
6. Stappers, P.J., Sanders, E.B.-N.: Generative Tools for Context Mapping: Tuning the Tools. In: Proceeding in Third International Conference on Design & Emotion, Taylor & Francis, Loughborough (2003)
7. Stappers, P.J., Sanders, E.B.-N.: Tools for designers, Products for Users? The Role of creative Design Techniques in a Aqueezed-in Design Process (2003)
8. Jordan, P.W.: Designing Pleasurable Products – An Introduction to the new Human Factors. Taylor & Francis Group, London (2002)
9. Schuler, Namioka: Participatory design. Lawrence Erlbaum, Mahwah (1993)

A Cross-Cultural Study on the Perception of Sociability within Human-Computer Interaction

Fang-Wu Tung[1], Keiichi Sato[2], Yi-Shin Deng[3], and Tsai-Yi Lin[4]

[1] Dept of Industrial Design, National United University, 1, Lienda, Miaoli, 36003 Taiwan
[2] Institute of Design, Illinois Institute of Technology,
350 North La Salle St. 4th Floor, Chicago, Illinois 60654 USA
[3] Institute of Applied Arts, National Chiao Tung University
1001 University Road, Hsinchu, 30080 Taiwan
[4] Department of Fashion Imaging, MingDao University
369, Wen Hwa Road, Pee-Tow , Chang-Hwa, 52345 Taiwan
fwtung@gmail.com, sato@id.iit.edu, ydest@faculty.nctu.edu.tw,
lintsaiyi99@yahoo.com.tw

Abstract. This study tries to use speech and dynamic emoticons as social cues to create a more sociable human-computer interaction. A cross-cultural study was conducted to investigate the influence of cultural backgrounds (Taiwan and America) on children's perceptions of sociability within human-computer interaction and explore how the management of social cues affects their engagement in e-learning environments. A 2x2 (Taiwan/America, speech/dynamic emoticon) quasi experiment was conducted to investigate the effects of the independent variables on children's perception of social presence and intrinsic motivation. Cultural differences in the perception of social presence are observed. American children reported higher perceived social presence than Taiwanese children did. No differences of effects of speech and dynamic emoticons on children's feelings of social presence and motivation are found. It suggests that children's social responses and learning motivations are triggered equally strongly by the two social cues. These findings suggest that designers of educational technology could use speech or dynamic emoticons to build more sociable interfaces that could boost children's motivation in learning.

Keywords: Cultural difference, Sociability, Interaction design, Speech, Dynamic Emoticon, Children.

1   Introduction

1.1   The Social-Emotional Interaction between Human and Computer

People are emotional and social. The role of human emotions is an influential factor in the way people deal with and relate to objects and artifacts [22]. Given this, human emotional needs and social desires have to be taken into consideration in developing products for people. Research also reveals that human-computer interaction is on both a social and emotional level. In light of the findings, new theories that enable or augment socio-emotional interaction between people and computers are explored [18, 24].

N. Aykin (Ed.): Internationalization, Design, LNCS 5623, pp. 135–144, 2009.
© Springer-Verlag Berlin Heidelberg 2009

Indeed, technologists have aspired to make computer interfaces more human-like and sociable because it is suggested that more humanized interfaces convey a sense of comfort and ease to the user [15, 27]. Besides the use of sophisticated computing technology or artificial intelligence, utilizing social cues in user interface may offer an uncomplicated and inexpensive way to achieve the goal of humanized interface.

Moving beyond theory, several experimental studies have demonstrated that people do not respond to a computer merely as a tool. Instead, a wide range of social rules and learned behaviors lead humans to interact with and attitudes toward computers [23, 26]. The finding that people appear to have social relationships with computers raised attention for its potential to promote the interaction between humans and computers. Computers could act as social partners of humans. From this perspective, Nass et al. [20] have empirically proven that people socially interact with computers and claim that "Computers are social actors (CASA)". CASA claims that computers that exhibit social cues can convey a sense of sociability and intimacy and thereby induce social responses from people, which lead people to treat computers in the way as they treat other people. Just as mentioned by Norman [22], people have evolved to interpret even the most subtle of indicators and are predisposed to anthropomorphize, and so to project human emotions into everything. Thus, anthropomorphic responses can bring great delight and pleasure to the user of a product due to human tendency to interpret and anthropomorphize things.

1.2 Enhancing Social Presence in Computer-Mediated Learning Environments

CASA paradigm is based on a concept of social presence, and involves the social responses of people not to other entities within a medium, but to cues provided by the medium itself [16]. The degree of social presence supported by the media used in learning environments can also affect learning. Gunawardena [6] agues that social presence is necessary to enhance and improve effective instruction in both traditional and technology-based classroom. Studies have suggested that enhancing social presence in an e-learning environment can instill the learner with an impression of a quality learning experience [21, 29, 34]. As claimed by CASA paradigm, computers are social actors. It suggests that a learner can perceive the social presence created by the computer itself. Thus, computers may be perceived on social dimension to improve motivation while a single learner participates in a computer learning activity with no instructor involved. Such experiences may enable an individual to perceive that another social being exists and is interacting with them.

Studies have tried to study the affective and emotional dimension of people's interactions with computers in the hope of proposing a new direction for educational software design [1, 177, 30, 31]. The results suggest that designers may consider developing products that deliberately elicit social responses from learners. Employing social cues derived from social psychology and sociology to interface design can enable users to sense a high degree of social presence from the medium itself and a sense of intimacy accordingly. Given this, human-computer interactions can be improved by incorporating a set of social cues into user interface design by replicating human-human interaction. The current study attempts to use two important social cues in interpersonal communication, speech and facial expressions, as social cues in e-learning environments and examine the effects of the two social cues on children's perceived social presence and learning motivation.

1.3 Speech vs. Dynamic Emoticons

Just as the brain processes voices differently than all other sounds, it processes faces differently than all other objects [19]. To compare the two social cues, dynamic emoticons and speech, involves further issues of nonverbal communication versus verbal communication as well as visual modality versus audio modality. Posner et al. [255] argued that visual stimuli are less likely to automatically engage attention than auditory stimuli, and people have to learn to direct their attention to visual information. Compared with texts and symbols in the visual channel, speech in the auditory channel is less cognitively demanding [73]. Besides, speech is a dynamic process which can trigger people to focus on the content and keep the audience in awareness during its creation [1], leading to exerting a high degree of social presence.

Judging from above, speech seems to be superior to emoticons. The sound of speech is effective in gaining users' attention; nevertheless, Zaidel and Mehrabian [36] claimed that faces are more important than voices in interpersonal interaction. As mentioned above, dynamic emoticons being visual cues may not draw as much attention as speech in terms of sensory aspects. However, the dynamic emoticon as a representation of the facial expression which is most powerful channel of nonverbal communication and expresses more explicit emotions fitting in the situation than speech does. Speech may transmit emotional messages by changing pitch, tempo as well as loudness, but research revealed information about emotions transmitted by the facial expression is more precise than speech [3]. Burns and Beier [1] also pointed out that visual cues are also more influential and accurate than vocal cues in the designation of a mood state. Moreover, Ekman [3] indicated that happiness is an easily recognizable facial expression, while it is more difficult to identify in the voice. These strengths may enable dynamic emoticons to receive more attention and as such yield higher social presence. Thus, it is interesting to investigate whether dynamic emoticons used in computer interfaces have the same effect on children's feeling of social presence as speech does. The two social cues, speech and dynamic emoticons, used to enhance the level of social presence in e-learning environments are derived from interpersonal communication. As communication is involved in the issue, it is inevitable to consider the factor of the cultural differences because the communication process is different in individualistic and collectivistic cultures or in terms of low-context and high-context communication.

1.4 Cultural Differences in the Perception of Social Cues

To understand cultural differences, Hofstede's International cultural dimensions and Hall's high-context and low-context culture provide useful frameworks to approach the issue [7, 9]. Hofstede proposed four international dimensions including power distance, uncertainty avoidance, Individualism, and Masculinity. Although the concept of culture is multidimensional proposed by Hofstede, individualism-collectivism has been empirically developed and is found to have the strongest variation across cultures.

The individualism-collectivism dimension is the preference to act as individuals rather than as a member of a group [1010, 28]. It refers to the tendency to focus on the needs of self as opposed to community and society. Cultures high on the individualism dimension promote individual identity while collectivistic cultures are more group oriented. In terms of communication, collective cultures depend more on high context messages, while individualistic cultures depend ore on low context messages [11]. Thus, members in collectivistic culture value a more subtle form of communication. In other words, they would be more negatively affected by the less social cues when going from human-human interaction to human-computer interaction in comparison to individualistic ones. As a result, the study expects that children from Taiwan perceive a lower level of social presence in e-learning environments than children from the US do.

Another lens to view cultural differences in communication is Hall's concept of high-context and low-context communications. Hall [8] points out that a high-context individual as someone who engages feelings in a relationship. It suggests that low-context cultures don't differentiate as much as high-context cultures between in- and out-groups. Thus, high-context communication involves emotions and closer relationships while low-context communication relies on logical part of the brain and is less personal. Individuals in high-context culture learn to understand others through nonverbal responses while ones in low-context culture rely on verbal communication more. Also, research suggests that information in the verbal content of East Asian language is relatively low so nonverbal cues provide the missing link in the communication process [1212]. According to the difference in the usage of nonverbal communication, the study assumes that speech and dynamic-emoticons feedbacks have different impacts on the level of social presence perceived by children from different cultural backgrounds.

Concluded from above, the current study attempts to employ speech and dynamic emoticons as social cues in e-learning environments and to compare their effects on children's perceived social presence and motivation. Further, cultural differences in the research issue are examined by recruiting participants from Taiwan and America. Three questions are addressed in this paper. First, do the social cues of speech and dynamic emoticons yield the same impacts on children's perceived social presence and learning motivation? Second, do different cultural backgrounds influence perceived social presence and learning motivation? Third, what is the relationship between perceived social presence and learning motivation?

2 Hypotheses and Research Questions

Concluded from the individualism-collectivism dimension and low-context and high-context communication in terms of cultural differences, it leads to the following hypotheses:

H1. The effects of speech and dynamic-emoticon feedbacks on Taiwanese and American participants' perceived social presence are different.

H2. American participants perceived higher level of social presence in e-learning environments than Taiwanese participants do.

The effects of speech and emoticons on children's motivation in e-learning environments are examined and the correlation between perceived social presence and their motivation is investigated in the study. Three research questions are as follow.

R1. Do the two social cues, speech and dynamic emoticons, have same impacts on children's motivation in e-learning environments?

R2. Do different cultural backgrounds influence children's motivation differently while participating in e-learning activities?

R3. Does the social presence perceived from the medium itself correlate with learners' motivation?

3 Method

Participants. Seventy-seven subjects participated at the study. Forty 5th and 6th graders (21 girls and 24 boys) were recruited from an elementary school in Hsinchu, Taiwan. Thirty-two 5th and 6th graders (15 girls and 17 boys) were recruited from 2 elementary schools in Chicago, America.

Experiment design. A mixed factorial design of experiment was employed to investigate the effect of two factors. The first factor, cultural background, is a between-subject factor of Taiwan and America. The second factor, social cue, is a within-subject factor of speech or dynamic emoticons. It is a two by two mixed factorial design. The dependent variables were the children's perceived social presence and their intrinsic motivation.

Experiment material. The instructional material was prepared as a math problem-solving practice program designed in Macromedia Flash. The instructional program had seven math problems. The degree of level of the questions was discussed with teachers of the selected schools. The feedbacks provided by the program including presenting a text-based greeting at the beginning, showing the "right" symbol as feedback and automatically guide the participant to the next question when a participant answers correctly, or showing the "wrong" symbol and text-based message which suggested the participant to press "again" or "next" icon for proceeding when a participant fails to answer correctly, presenting the counts of correct and positive comments after all questions have been attempted.

The program then developed into two versions to present the two manipulated conditions by providing speech outputs and dynamic emoticons in the above-mentioned feedbacks. The emotion of speech and facial expression suitable for each feedback were determined by the focus group, which was formed by two teachers and four students. Speech used in the instructional program was created from recordings made by two young ladies; one is from Taiwan and the other one is from America. Dynamic emoticons start with a neutral face, which then continuously evolves into full expression. The speed of the dynamic display is 12 frames per second.

Measurement tools. The dependent variables of social presence and intrinsic motivation were measured using a set of paper-and-pencil questionnaires.
1. The first set questions adopted the four items proposed by Short, Williams, and Christie (1976) to measure social presence, sociable/unsociable, personal/impersonal, sensitive/insensitive, and warm/cold, and applied a semantic differential technique. (Cronbach's $\alpha = 0.86$)
2. The second set of questions was adapted from the Activity-Feeling Scales (AFS) developed by Reeve and Sickenius (1994) and used to measure the subjects' intrinsic motivation. The 12-item measure made up of separate 3-item scales to assess

self-determination, competence, relatedness, and tension. The name and individual items for each index are as follows: self-determination-- offered choice what to do, I want to answer the questions, and my participation is voluntary; competence-- capable, competent, and achieving; relatedness-- intimate, involved with friends, part of a team; Tension-- pressured, uptight, and easy (reverse). (Cronbach's $\alpha = 0.74$)

Procedure. The study took place in the computer labs of the selected schools during one of their computer class session or recess. Each participant was assigned to one computer in the lab. The two conditions of speech and dynamic emoticon are counterbalance. The experiment took around 100 minutes. Upon completing the experiment, the subjects were debriefed and thanked with a toy.

4   Results

Social presence. Fig 1. shows the results of the perceived social presence. The analysis of variance of within-subjects effects indicated that the effect of speech and dynamic emoticons on perceived social presence is not significant ($F(1,75)=0.05$, $p=0.83$, 2 tails). No significant interaction effect is found ($F(1, 75)=2.01$, $p=0.16$, 2 tails). The H1 is not supported. The American participants reported stronger feelings of social presence 6.85 (sd 1.47) than Taiwanese participants did 6.42 (sd 1.09). The analysis of variance of between-subjects effects indicates that the American participants perceived significant higher social presence than Taiwanese participants did ($F(1, 75)=2.89$, $p<0.05$, 1 tail). The H2 is supported.

Intrinsic motivation. Fig 2. shows the results of the intrinsic motivation. The analysis of variance of within-subject effects indicated that the effect of social cues on intrinsic motivation is not significant ($F(1, 75)=1.13$, $p=0.26$, 2 tails). No significant interaction effect is found ($F(1, 75)=0.88$, $p=0.35$, 2 tails). The analysis of variance of between-subject effects indicates that the effect of cultural backgrounds on intrinsic motivation is not significant ($F(1, 75)=0.50$, $p=0.48$, 2 tails). No cultural differences are found in participants' intrinsic motivation. Also, it is observed that no significant difference in effects of social cues on intrinsic motivation.

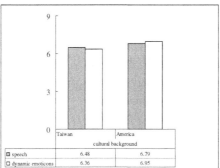   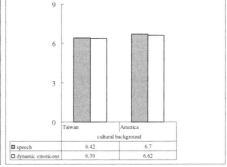

Fig. 1. Results of perceived social presence   **Fig. 2.** Results of intrinsic motivation

Correlation between social presence and intrinsic motivation. The mean of American participants' social presence and intrinsic motivation is 6.87 (SD. 1.20) and 6.66 (SD. 1.32), respectively. A highly positive correlation (Pearson r =0.75, p<0.001) is found between the two variables. The mean of Taiwanese participants' social presence and intrinsic motivation is 6.42 (SD. 1.09) and 6.40 (SD. 1.28), respectively. A positive correlation (Pearson r =0.69, p<0.001) is also found between the two variables. The results indicate that feelings of social presence from a computer itself can mediate children's intrinsic motivation.

5 Discussion

The cultural differences in the perception of social presence are observed in the study. The results support that American children perceived a higher degree of social presence than Taiwanese children did during interaction with computers. As mentioned above, collectivistic cultures depend more on high context messages while individualistic cultures depend more on low context messages. Given this, members in individualistic cultures would still feel comfortable with less social cues in human-computer context compared to the real context. As predicted in H2, the finding shows that American children feel stronger social presence than Taiwanese children do. Wegerif [35] has proposed the concept of social threshold. The social dimension of learning networks depended upon the extent to which learners were able to cross a threshold from feeling like outsiders to feeling like insiders. It means that a leaner would feel computer on social dimension while crossing the threshold. Regarding the concept of social threshold, it has been observed that members in low-context cultures like American don't differentiate as much as high-context cultures between in- and out-groups. The current study echoes the social threshold idea proposed by Wegerif.

No cultural differences in children's intrinsic motivation in e-learning environments are found in the study. In other words, cultural backgrounds do not affect children's motivation while participating in e-learning activities. That children both from America and Taiwan are exposed to various digital media and educational technology nowadays as computers are wildly used may account for the results.

As for the effects of speech and dynamic emoticons, the results do not support the expectation that effects of social cues on Taiwanese and American participants' feelings of social presence were different. The nonverbal usage in communication is different between in low-context and high-context cultures. The findings, however, are not consistent with cultural differences in low- vs. high-context communication. It indicates that speech and dynamic emoticons could yield the same level social presence for children regardless of cultural backgrounds. Besides, the effects of speech and dynamic-emoticon feedbacks on children's motivation in e-learning environments are not different either. Therefore, the e-learning environments with the application of speech or dynamic emoticons could equally motivate children to practice learning activities.

The development of a sociable interface has never meant the direct embedding of social cues without prudential consideration. Rather, it is required to investigate users' attitudes and perceptions more closely. Comparing speech with dynamic-emoticon feedbacks, the former is a channel of verbal communication and an audio modality while the latter is one of nonverbal communication and a visual modality. The research provides evidence that dynamic emoticons and speech almost have the same impacts on inducing social responses from children and engaging them in e-learning environments. The results may provide designers with research based guidelines in consideration of speech or emoticon techniques to design sociable interactions for children.

The study supports that the social presence perceived from the medium itself positively correlate with learners' motivation. It suggests that the social presence provided by a computer itself also can improve children's motivation in computerized learning with no instructor or other colleagues involved. Some research in educational technology has considered computers as being neutral cognitive tools and has emphasized the cognitive and information processing aspects of learning [14]. Turkle[32] described the computer as Rorschach to present the computer as a relatively neutral screen onto which people were able to express their thoughts and feelings. Nevertheless, Turkle [333] indicates that the computational object is no longer effectively neutral. People perceive computers on a social dimension and attribute personality and emotion to them. Thus, the findings suggest that designers of educational technology may move beyond an emphasis on merely cognitive aspects of learning with computers and pay attention to the effects of social traits of computers.

6 Conclusion

People appear to form affective attachments to and affective relationships with objects. Our anthropomorphic perceptions may reflect the social nature of humans. Computers are responsive and interact with people in more engaging ways, with which people might expect to have a social relationship. From this perspective, this study aims at incorporating social cues adopted from human-human interaction into human-computer interaction to intensify the sense of social presence in child-computer interaction and hence motivate them in learning activities. With technology advancing rapidly, computer-mediated learning may come in a variety of applications such as educational products, systems, interactive toys, or even robots. Creating a social interface for those applications can help counterbalance the feeling of isolation when children interact with them individually. In a world that is becoming increasing globalized, a cross-cultural study helps us to obtain a comprehensive understanding of the issue and the findings may benefit design and development for related products.

Acknowledgments. This material is based upon work supported by the National Science Council of the Republic of China under grant NSC 95-2411-H-158-003 and 096-2917-I-009-005. We thank Yumao Feng for help developing the instructional programs. We thank David Groves, Gabrielle Parra, Hua-Min Chang, Jun-Zhi Chen, Nikki Krieger, and Yung-Yuan Liu for their assistance and helpful input in the study.

References

1. Burns, K., Beier, E.: Significance of vocal and visual channels in the decoding of emotional meaning. Journal of Communication 23, 118–130 (1973)
2. Chalfonte, B.L., Fish, R.S., Kraut, R.E.: Expressive Richness: A Comparison of Speech and Text as Media for Revision. In: Robertson, S.P., Olson, G.M., Olson, J.S. (eds.) Proceedings of the ACM CHI 1991 Human Factors in Computing Systems Conference, New Orleans, Louisiana, pp. 21–26 (1991)

3. Ekman, P.: The nature of emotion: fundamental questions. Oxford University Press, New York (1994)
4. Ekman, P., Friesen, W.V.: Unmasking the face. A guide to recognizing emotions from facial clues. Prentice-Hall, Englewood Cliffs, New Jersey (1975)
5. Ferdig, R., Mishra, P.: Emotional Responses to Computers: Experiences in Unfairness, Anger, and Spite. Journal of Educational Multimedia and Hypermedia 13(2), 143–161 (2004)
6. Gunawardena, C.N.: Social presence theory and implications for interaction and collaborative learning in computer conferences. International Journal of Educational Telecommunications 1(2/3), 147–166 (1995)
7. Hall, E.T.: Beyond Culture. Anchor Books Editions (1989)
8. Hall, E.T.: The power of hidden differences. In: Bennett, M. (ed.) Basic concepts in intercultural communication, pp. 53–67. Intercultural Press, Inc., Maine (1998)
9. Hofstede, G.: Dimensions of National Cultures in Fifty Countries and Three Regions. In: Deregowski, J.B., Dziurawiec, S., Annis, R.C. (eds.) Expiscations in Cross-Cultural Psychology, Lisse NL, Swets and Zeitlinger, pp. 335–355 (1983)
10. Hofstede, G.: Cultural Differences in Teaching and Learning. International Journal of Intercultural Relations 10(3), 301–320 (1986)
11. Hofstede, G.: Culture and Organizations: Software of the Mind. McGraw-Hill International, New York (1991)
12. Kitayama, S., Ishii, K.: Word and voice: Spontaneous attention to emotional utterances in two languages. Cognition & Emotion 16, 29–59 (2002)
13. Kroll, B.M.: Cognitive egocentrism and the problem of audience awareness in written discourse. Research in the Teaching of English 12, 269–281 (1978)
14. Lajoie, S.P., Derry, S.J.: Computers as cognitive tools. Erlbaum, Hillsdale, NJ (1993)
15. Laurel, B.: Interface Agents: Metaphors with Character. In: Laurel, B. (ed.) The Art of Human-Computer Interface Design, pp. 355–365. Addison-Wesley, Reading (1990)
16. Lombard, M., Ditton, T.B.: At the heart of it all: The concept of presence. Journal of Computer-Mediated-Communication 3(2) (1997), http://www.ascusc.org/jcmc/vol3/issue2/lombard.html
17. Mishra, P.: Affective Feedback from Computers and its Effect on Perceived Ability and Affect: A Test of the Computers as Social Actor Hypothesis. Journal of Educational Multimedia and Hypermedia 15(1), 107–131 (2006)
18. Muller, M.: Multiple paradigms in affective computing. Interacting with Computers 16(4), 759–768 (2004)
19. Nass, C., Brave, S.: Wired for speech: How voice activates and advances the human-computer relationship. MIT Press, Cambridge, MA (2005)
20. Nass, C., Steuer, J., Tauber, E.: Computers are social actors. In: Proceedings of the SIGCHI conference on Human factors in computing systems: celebrating interdependence, Boston, Massachusetts (1994)
21. Newberry, B.: Raising student social presence in online classes. In: Fowler, W., Hasebrook, J. (eds.) Proceedings of WebNet 2001 World Conference on the WWW and the Internet, pp. 905–910. Association for the Advancement of Computing in Education, Orlando, FL, Norfolk, VA (2001)
22. Norman, D.: Emotional Design: Why we love (or hate) everyday things. Basic Books, NY (2004)
23. Picard, R.: Affective Computing. The MIT Press, Cambridge, Saarni and Harris (1997)
24. Picard, R., Wexelblat, A., Nass, C.: Future interfaces: social and emotional. In: CHI 2002 extended abstracts on Human factors in computer systems, Minneapolis, Minnesota (2002)

25. Posner, M.I., Nissen, M.J., Klein, R.M.: Visual dominance: An information-processing account of its origins and significance. Psychological Review 83, 157–171 (1976)
26. Reeves, B., Nass, C.: Media equation: how people treat computer, television, and new media like real people and places. Cambridge University Press, New York (1996)
27. Sproull, L., Subramani, M., Kiesler, S., Walker, J.H., Waters, K.: When the interface is a face. Human-Computer Interaction 11, 97–124 (1996)
28. Triandis, H.C.: The self and behavior in different cultural contexts. Psychological Review 96, 506–520 (1989)
29. Tu, C.H.: How Chinese perceive social presence: An examination of interaction in an online learning environment. Educational Media International 38(1), 45–60 (2001)
30. Tung, F.W., Deng, Y.S.: Designing social presence in e-learning environments: Testing the effect of interactivity on children. Interactive learning environments 14(3), 251–264 (2006)
31. Tung, F.W., Deng, Y.S.: Increasing Social Presence of Social Actors in E-learning environments: Effects of Dynamic and Static Emoticons on Children. Displays 28(4-5), 174–180 (2007)
32. Turkle, S.: Computer as Rorschach. Society 17(2), 15–24 (1980)
33. Turkle, S.: Sociable Technologies: Enhancing Human Performance when the computer is not a tool but a companion. In: Roco, M.C., Bainbridge, W.S. (eds.) Converging Technologies for Improving Human Performance, pp. 151–158. Kluwer Academic Publishers, Netherlands (2003)
34. Walther, J.B.: Interpersonal effects in computer-mediated interaction: A relational perspective. Communication Research 19, 52–90 (1992)
35. Wegerif, R.: The social dimension of asynchronous learning networks. Journal of Asynchronous Learning Networks 2(1), 34–49 (1998)
36. Zaidel, S.F., Mehrabian, A.: The ability to communicate and infer positive and negative attitudes facially and vocally. Journal of Experimental Research in Personality 3, 233–241 (1969)

Part II

Culture, Community, Collaboration and Learning

The Use of Hypertext as a Vocabulary Acquisition Strategy for English as Second Language Learners

Devshikha Bose and Dotty Sammons

Department of Educational Leadership and Instructional Design
Idaho State University (ISU),Pocatello, ID 83209 USA
{bosedevs,sammdott}@isu.edu

Abstract. This paper has two parts. The first part is a literature review which discusses vocabulary acquisition in ESL learners in context of 1) vocabulary acquisition strategies used by ESL learners 2) efficacy of Computer Aided Language Learning (CALL) in ESL vocabulary acquisition, 3) the use of hypertexts to aid vocabulary acquisition among ESL learners, 4) hypertext use strategies, and 5) hypertext design considerations. The second part of the paper is a proposed study on the use of a website evaluation rubric to evaluate the effectiveness of selected websites based on best practices of teaching-learning ESL.

Keywords: Hypertext, ESL, Vocabulary Acquisition Strategies, CALL, CAI, Rubric.

1 Introduction

Observations have revealed that major groups of middle school English as Second Language (ESL) students show severe English usage limitations despite residence in the United States since elementary school [16]. English Language Learners (ELLs) who go through the ESL curriculum often appear to lack the metacognitive skills necessary for choosing appropriate strategies for dealing with academic texts. ESL learners have often been found to be processing small sections of a printed text in a disconnected, linear fashion which makes it difficult for them to make sense at a discourse level. Vocabulary is one of the building blocks in language learning [10]. Vocabulary learning strategies are part of language learning strategies which are included in general learning strategies.

2 Vocabulary Acquisition Strategies Used by ESL Learners

There is more to vocabulary learning than acquiring knowledge of meaning [26]. The teaching-learning of vocabulary requires attention to aspects of meaning, use, formation, and grammar. Results of a study by Lai [19] on the vocabulary and English as Foreign Language (EFL) reading comprehension strategies of Taiwanese college students indicated that rote memorization and other cognitively less demanding strategies were often used by students rather than the use of study aids, social learning activities, and monolingual dictionaries. Proficient learners were found to use more

N. Aykin (Ed.): Internationalization, Design, LNCS 5623, pp. 147–155, 2009.
© Springer-Verlag Berlin Heidelberg 2009

metacognitive and context-related strategies while the less proficient learners used more mechanical ones. Though rote learning strategies can easily be the preferred mode for many learners, contextually based strategies have been found to bring about gains in terms of improved test scores [23].

New words may be remembered if they are incorporated into language that is already known [23]. Learning and retention can be improved if learners are encouraged to use and interact with new words [26]. Learners often prefer to learn sentence patterns by applying them to complete communication tasks [7]. Deep, rich semantic processing such as creating a mental image of a word's meaning, judging the formality of the word, or grouping the word with other conceptually similar words may enhance learning more than mere rote repetition [26]. Results of a study by Collins [9] indicated that for ESL pre school learners, vocabulary learning was enhanced through adult support in the form of rich explanations, cognitively challenging discussion questions, and home reading which helped learners in vocabulary acquisition and comprehension. The teaching-learning of words which are similar in meaning and pronunciation should be avoided at the same time as it may confuse the learner [26]. Learners can use various strategies like guessing the meaning of the word in context, using a glossary, or the dictionary to self-teach vocabulary though there appears to be some disagreement on the efficacy of the use of translation and bilingual dictionaries [18].

Learners who take advantage of both their inner means and the outer resources available to them in the Second Language (L2) society seem to succeed [6]. A combination of situational factors like L2 input, individual differences, learning strategies, awareness of inner and outer resources, and the will to make use of these resources seem to lead to language and vocabulary gains.

3   Efficacy of Computer Aided Language Learning (CALL) in ESL Vocabulary Acquisition

Language learners can develop second language literacy skills and intercultural understanding by reading authentic texts on the internet and in multimedia computer-assisted language learning environments [2]. Students have been found to make significant learning gains when they were able to use technology supported scaffolds that were congruent to their preferred learning strategies than they did in non-technology supported learning conditions [22]. Learners using a CALL program were seen to have better retention of vocabulary items and attain better pronunciation skills than learners who used the ordinary desktop dictionary method of learning ([14], [32]).

Computer aided learning through blogging - a canon for which best practices are still emerging - holds promise for young writers because of its potential for providing an authentic and interactive medium where writing, reading, and thinking can be learned and taught [27]. Students in computer - assisted writing classes using Learning Management Systems (LMS) like WebCT reported that the use of computers facilitated acquisition of writing skills [15]. The students found instructor feedback and peer responses to be valuable. Students also found that using computers made writing tasks easier and faster to complete than was possible through traditional means. Ghandoura [15] mentioned that students' attitudes toward the use of WebCT were related to their grades in class.

A study conducted in India, which has the largest number of out-of-school children, to compare the effects of computer-aided-instruction (CAI) and traditional teacher-based instruction revealed that learning took place at a faster pace with CAI than in the traditional method [17]. The results of this study support the use of CAI among the marginalized sections of society in a developing country like India.

4 Use of Hypertexts to Aid Vocabulary Acquisition among ESL Learners

An educational system is often a unique combination of pedagogy, social interaction, and technology [31]. The pedagogical design of instruction should aim toward scaffolding students from different backgrounds to meet their different needs and learning intentions. Interactivity is a major characteristic of any learning environment. A technology based interactive learning environment involves mainly three types of interaction: learner-content, learner-instructor, and learner-interface. Therefore interface design is an important component while designing the learning environment because it is the medium through which interaction with the content and with learners take place.

Results of a study which compared the use of traditional glossaries to the use of hypermedia annotations showed that learners who made use of hypermedia annotations out performed their counterparts who used the glossary at the end of the text [1]. Learning theories based on constructivism which focus on learner-centered education appears to favor the use of hypertexts in digital environments which enable non-hierarchical, non-chronological, and multi-layered acquisition of knowledge [5]. According to the Cognitive Flexibility Theory, learners can benefit from an information retrieval that is a 'landscape-criss-crossing' rather than a linear knowledge acquisition process [33]. Hypertexts can help learners go beyond given information and to revisit certain facts at different times and contexts. Knowledge provided in its full complexity enhances transfer by providing learner's the opportunity for thematic criss-crossing.

Other studies indicate that readers find learning through hypertext use more difficult than through traditional print [24]. Strategies that work for reading passages on printed text often do not work in a hypertext environment where texts can link to other texts and readers have the freedom to choose their own paths [25]. Teenagers have been seen to perform poorly on online reading tasks when compared to adults and many students have been found to have been distracted or confused. The use of hypertexts may be more cognitively demanding and require a higher degree of relational processing than that is required for traditional text use. It can prove to be an impediment rather than an aid especially when user technological and intellectual skill level is low. Theories of mental models suggest that global coherence is generally established by reference to related mental models [33]. If the learner does not have a mental model or schema with which new information can be integrated, the non-linear hypertext media can prove to be disadvantageous.

However complexity of the learning material or the text type needs also to be considered when comparing hypertext with regular text [33]. Certain types of texts like fairy tales or other script-based texts are traditionally linear in structure and appear to be unsuitable for non-linear presentation. On the other hand traditionally non-linear texts like encyclopedias are suitable for hypertext presentation because there may be a natural lack of coherence between single chapters.

According to Calisir and Gurel, hypertextual structures may increase the comprehension of more advanced learners while less advanced learners may be more comfortable in a linear text structure (as cited in [5]). Langley (1996) mentioned how humans have incremental information systems where sequences can dramatically affect learning, especially reading comprehension (as cited in [33]). However, well structured hypertexts, as compared to less structured ones, have been found to be more helpful for less proficient readers [4]. A well structured hypertext system can be a tool that can encourage deeper thinking by illustrating connections between ideas and concepts [5]. The additional cognitive load caused by hypertext use does not necessarily lead to poor learning outcomes [33]. Learning through hypertexts requires a more through reflection on available information than is needed for learning through linear texts. This additional processing can lead to increased learning.

Hypertext reading environments are different from traditional paper-based ones in terms of textual boundaries, mobility, and navigation [28]. Readers use different strategies while reading using hypertexts. Hypertext selection was found to be affected by three factors – coherence, personal interest, and location. The mobility and flexibility provided by the hypertext environment where the users follow their own investigation path can itself be challenging because it entails taking decisions as the user selectively browses through the material [29]. However linear texts may not prove to be advantageous in terms of learning outcomes when compared to hypertexts [33].

Zumbach [33] mentioned that there are no crucial differences, in the reading comprehension skill requirements between hypertext and regular print reading. The cognitive and metacognitive skills involved in the reading comprehension process, the knowledge building process related to the selection of information, and navigation planning appear to be similar. Reading a textbook requires the reader to make connections between paragraphs within the book and with other opinions outside the book in the same way as a reader of hypertexts would do. Being lost in hyperspace is not a problem unique to hypertext or hypermedia. It is equally possible to be lost while using a print text book as in a non-linear hypertext situation. Disorientation in hyperspace is a result of bad hypertext design just as lack of reading comprehension may be a result of a poorly structured book.

5 Hypertext Use Strategies

A hypertext learning environment differs from other systems like Computer Aided Instruction (CAI) or Computer Assisted Learning (CAL) in that it is user controlled [11]. Learners who made use hypermedia annotations out performed their counterparts who used the glossary at the end of the text [1].

Zumbach [33] suggested that in order to enhance contextual authenticity and transfer, learning goals should be integrated within scenarios. Hypertexts should be used to access and support information seeking during problem solving tasks. In this way hypertext learning is placed within a meaningful framework and increases learner motivation by decreasing oversimplified learning scenarios and providing content or domain complex learning scenarios.

6 Hypertext Design Considerations

The structure and presentation of a text has an effect on how well information is retained [20]. Hypertext use provides opportunities for flexible information access [13]. However as Jonassen, Peck and Wilson pointed out, hypermedia should be seen as an environment where personal knowledge is constructed. Learners learn with the interaction rather than from instruction (as cited in [13]). Hypertext is more about construction of meaning when the learner interacts with the instructional material than about transfer of message.

A student's prior knowledge played a vital role in influencing learning achievement through the use of hypertexts [8]. Learners with a high spatial ability were found to be more efficient hypertext users than otherwise [3]. A lack of prior knowledge can increase the cognitive load of a text [33]. Hypertexts designed using instructional strategies proposed by Reigeluth's Elaboration Theory were found to be superior to the use of linear hypertexts in enhancing the achievement of factual and conceptual knowledge [8].

The design of hypertext nodes is important while determining its educational functionality in the sense of whether they are locally coherent or require additional information delivered through other nodes in order to be understood [33]. The link structure provided by the authors may be problematic. The links should be exhaustive rather than confusing and unnecessary. Text linearity verses nonlinearity is not the only factor that requires attention while deciding whether learning outcomes have been reached. There are other variables which also require consideration.

The problem of disorientation or being 'Lost-in-Hyperspace' can occur in non-linear as well as linear text [33]. Disorientation is a result of an unstructured text containing features like missing paragraphs, headings, or texts containing complex sentence structures. Faulty instructional decisions at this micro level can increase the cognitive load and affect instructional design decisions at the macro level. Disorientation can also occur at a macro design level when the narration format does not match the presentation format leading to increase in extraneous cognitive load. For example, presenting a fairy tale which traditionally has a linear format, when presented in a non-linear format can be unnecessarily confusing.

Most experiments which have shown hypertexts to be unfeasible, appears to have been conducted using linear texts which are meant to be read in a linear fashion but were converted into hypertexts for the sake of the experiment [11]. Therefore conclusions drawn from such experiments may be biased.

Creating hypertext environments with additional navigational aids like a suggested path may be helpful for learners with different learning preferences [11]. Individual learning styles and the use of an additional path in the document may not have a global influence on how much students can learn from hypertext use; however students with a sequential learning style have been shown to perform better with hypertexts which contain structural aids. Learners with a sequential learning style appear to depend on linear structures to build up their understanding of a topic and my find it difficult to understand the information even if they are able to learn the facts, when they do not find a structural aid. Therefore using structural aids may not be disadvantageous to global learners but may be beneficial to sequential learners.

Structure and organization are very important parts of hypertext design because users have to allocate part of their attention to the process of navigation [12]. The structure of a hypertext document is different from a traditional document. Hypertext displayed through the limited screen size of a computer can display only part of the content at a time as compared to a traditional text like the newspaper, where the reader has access to a larger amount of information at a glance.

Hypertexts usually lack sensory-motor, spatio-visual cues, typographic, and structural standards [12]. Therefore hypertext users have to use their navigation skills more actively than readers of traditional texts. Dillon mentions that readers of hypertext documents have to see the broad structure or shape of the information scenario. In order to reduce the cognitive load of navigating through a non-linear hypertext system, adaptive navigation support needs to be provided [30]. Students must be provided with scaffolds which can help them understand the structure of a hypertext system.

Fastrez [12] proposes four principles for structuring a hypertext – rationality versus functionality and simplicity and usability versus deliberate complexity. Notions of simplicity and usability imply that the structure of the hypertext has to be simple for the user to grasp it. The document structure as well as the browsing path should be easy to identify and reconstruct. A simple and usable structure should allow the user to concentrate on the content or information provided by the text rather than on navigational tasks. Norman suggested that a user-centered design should make it easy for the user to determine the possible navigation actions at any given moment (as cited in [12]). All elements should be easily visible, including the conceptual model of the system. The design should follow the natural mappings between user intentions and the required actions to make those intentions effective. The interface design should ensure that the users do not waste any time figuring out how a hypertext document is organized and should not require any external instruction.

Cognitive Flexibility theorists support the notions of deliberate complexity in hypertext design [12]. Accordingly, hypertexts provide an excellent medium to introduce learners to complexity as early as possible by highlighting the multiple links that exist between concepts. Making such connections seem to contribute toward the acquisition of complex and ill-structured knowledge.

The concepts of functionality in hypertext design is dependent on two notions – on the one hand functional structure is a type of structure which is specific to the organization of knowledge in memory; on the other hand functional knowledge also describes knowledge activated by an individual in a specific context [12]. Individuals often activate the same concepts in different ways depending on the context of use. It is therefore difficult to design a hypertext system which can accommodate an infinite number of structures for the same information. Therefore a good instructional hypertext should be structured rationally. Such a structure is categorized logically or hierarchically with chunks of information belonging to sections and subsections.

Text formats can affect a reader's recall and feeling of disorientation especially when we take into consideration an individual's limited working memory capacity and prior level of experience in hypertext use [21]. Results of a study by Lee and Tedder [21] indicate that both different styles of information presentation as well as the working memory capacities of different individuals influence how well information presented is recognized. This study also indicates that the time an individual spends on reading, rather than cognitive load or disorientation influences how much information is learned. Different types of information presentation styles appear to influence the amount of time spent reading which in turn affects learning and retention. For those with low prior hypertext experience, Paged Hypertexts were found to be most disorienting while the expanding ones were found to be the least disorienting. Participants high on hypertext experience found Paged Hypertexts to be the least disorienting while they found the Scrolling Hypertext to be the most disorienting.

7 Proposed Study

The researcher proposes to develop a rubric based on ESL best practices derived from a review of literature in the field. The rubric may contain elements on user interaction with new words, incorporation of new words into prior language knowledge, text type, complexity of learning material, level of user control, learner spatial ability, access to support information, interface design and structural, considerations, The elements of the rubric will be validated using the Delphi method.

7.1 Proposed Method

The proposed rubric will be piloted with advanced students in ESL teaching programs who will evaluate a series of websites selected by the researcher. Inter-rater reliability will be established, and the rubric expanded and revised as appropriate. When the rubric has been validated and determined reliable, it will be used to evaluate ESL websites.

7.2 Significance

The development of the of the rubric will provide a way of developing a reliable and validated means of determining whether E-learning applications like the use of hypertexts in ESL websites meet best teaching-learning practices. Results of the proposed study may help further research on whether best principles of hypertext design as applied to the teaching-learning of ESL may be used for any electronic L2 acquisition.

8 Conclusion

The literature review indicated that though the use of hypertext may be successful in providing the learner with a lot of potentially useful information, there are chances of the user getting lost in hyperspace. Hypertext design and structural considerations are important wherein instructional hypertext should be structured rationally with information categorized logically or hierarchically in sections and sub-sections. The proposed rubric may be useful in providing a reliable and valid way of evaluating websites in terms of how their hypertext facility can be effectively used as a strategy in vocabulary acquisition.

References

1. AbuSeileek, A.: Hypermedia annotation presentation: Learners' preferences and effect on EFL reading comprehension and vocabulary acquisition. CALICO Journal 25(2), 260–275 (2008)
2. Abraham, L.: Computer-mediated glosses in second language reading comprehension and vocabulary learning: A meta-analysis. Computer Assisted Language Learning 21(3), 199–226 (2008)
3. Ahmed, I., Blustein, J.: Influence of spatial ability in navigation: Using look-ahead breadcrumbs on the web. International Journal of Web Based Communities 2(2), 183–196 (2006)
4. Al-Seghayer, K.: The role of organizational devices in ESL readers' construction of mental representations of hypertext content. CALICO Journal 24(3), 531–559 (2007)
5. Brandes, G., Boskic, N.: Eportfolios: From description to analysis. International Review of Research in Open and Distance Learning 9(2), 1–17 (2008)
6. Cervatiuc, A.: Highly proficient adult non-native English speakers' perceptions of their second language vocabulary learning process. Ph.D. dissertation, University of Calgary, Canada (2007); retrieved from Dissertations & Theses: A&I database (Publication No. AAT NR33791) (November 26, 2008)
7. Chang, D.: Comparing the effects of traditional vs. non-traditional reading instruction on level of reading comprehension, and use of metacognitive strategies in EFL learners in Taiwan. Ed.D. dissertation, La Sierra University, United States – California (2006); retrieved from Dissertations & Theses: A&I database (Publication No. AAT 3227046) (November 26, 2008)
8. Chen, W., Dwyer, F.: Effect of varied elaborated hypertext strategies in facilitating students' achievement of different learning objectives. International Journal of Instructional Media 33(2), 165 (2006)
9. Collins, M.F.: ESL preschoolers' English vocabulary acquisition and story comprehension from storybook reading. Ed.D. dissertation, Boston University, United States – Massachusetts (2004); retrieved from Dissertations & Theses: A&I database (Publication No. AAT 3124816) (November 26, 2008)
10. David, A.: Vocabulary breadth in French L2 learners. Language Learning Journal 36(2), 167–180 (2008)
11. Dunser, A., Jirasko, M.: Interaction of hypertext forms and global versus sequential learning styles. Journal of Educational Computing Research 32(1), 79–91 (2005)
12. Fastrez, P.: Navigation entailments as design principles for structuring hypertext. Education, Communication & Information 2(1), 7–22 (2002)
13. Gall, J.: Orienting tasks and their impact on learning and attitudes in the use of hypertext. Journal of Educational Multimedia and Hypermedia 15(1), 5–29 (2006)
14. Ghabanchi, Z., Anbarestani, M.: The effects of call program on expanding lexical knowledge of EFL Iranian intermediate learners. Reading Matrix: An International Online Journal 8(2), 1–10 (2008)
15. Ghandoura, W.A.: College ESL students' attitudes and beliefs about computer-assisted writing classes. Ph.D. dissertation, Indiana University of Pennsylvania, United States – Pennsylvania (2006), Retrieved from Dissertations & Theses: A&I database (Publication No. AAT 3215779) (November 26, 2008)
16. Hazelrigg, A.: Second language reading research: A Critical Review. Online Submission, (ERIC Document Reproduction Service No. ED502487) (2008); Retrieved from ERIC database (November 19, 2008)

17. Karnati, R.: Computer aided instruction for out-of-school children in India: An impact study in Andhra Pradesh. Ph.D. dissertation, University of Pennsylvania, United States – Pennsylvania (2008); Retrieved from Dissertations & Theses: A&I database (Publication No. AAT 3309451) (November 26, 2008)

18. Kim, E.: Beliefs and experiences of Korean pre-service and in-service English teachers about English vocabulary acquisition strategies. Ph.D. dissertation, New York University, United States – New York (2008); Retrieved from Dissertations & Theses: A&I database (Publication No. AAT 3308302) (November 26, 2008)

19. Lai, S.: The vocabulary knowledge, vocabulary strategies and EFL reading comprehension of Taiwanese college students. Ph.D. dissertation, Indiana University of Pennsylvania, United States – Pennsylvania (2007); Retrieved from Dissertations & Theses: A&I database (Publication No. AAT 3257966) (November 26, 2008)

20. Lee, M., Tedder, M.: The effects of three different computer texts on readers' recall: based on working memory capacity. Computers in Human Behavior 19(6), 767–783 (2003)

21. Lee, M., Tedder, M.: Introducing expanding hypertext based on working memory capacity and the feeling of disorientation: tailored communication through effective hypertext design. Journal of Educational Computing Research 30(3), 171–195 (2004)

22. Li, J.: Orientations to English academic language learning among Chinese high school students in a technology-supported learning environment in Canada. Ph.D. dissertation, University of Toronto (Canada), Canada (2007); Retrieved from Dissertations & Theses: A&I database (Publication No. AAT NR27927) (November 26, 2008)

23. Mast, D.W.: The effects of learning and reading strategies upon Spanish vocabulary acquisition amongst middle school students. Ph.D. dissertation, Temple University, United States – Pennsylvania (2008); Retrieved from Dissertations & Theses: A&I database (Publication No. AAT 3319976) (November 26, 2008)

24. McEneaney, J.E.: Does hypertext disadvantage less able readers? Journal of Educational Computing Research 29(1), 1–12 (2003)

25. McNabb, M.: Navigating the maze of hypertext. Educational Leadership 63(4), 76–79 (2006)

26. Mei-fang, L.: Teachers' role in vocabulary teaching: Strategies for vocabulary teaching. Sino-US English Teaching 5(8), 1–6 (2008)

27. Olander, M.V.: Painting the voice: Weblogs and writing instruction in the high school classroom. Ph.D. dissertation, Nova Southeastern University, United States – Florida (2007); Retrieved from Dissertations & Theses: A&I database (Publication No. AAT 3283949) (November 26, 2008)

28. Protopsaltis, A.: Reading strategies in hypertexts and factors influencing hyperlink selection. Journal of Educational Multimedia and Hypermedia 17(2), 191–213 (2008)

29. Puntambekar, S., Goldstein, J.: Effect of visual representation of the conceptual structure of the domain on science learning and navigation in a hypertext environment. Journal of Educational Multimedia and Hypermedia 16(4), 429–459 (2007)

30. Puntambekar, S., Stylianou, A.: Designing metacognitive support for learning from hypertext: What factors come into play? In: Proceedings of the 11th Conference on Artificial Intelligence in Education, Sydney, Australia (2003)

31. Wang, Q.: A generic model for guiding the integration of ICT into teaching and learning. Innovations in Education and training International 45(4), 411–419 (2008)

32. Yoshii, M., Flaitz, J.: Second language incidental vocabulary retention: The effect of text and picture annotation types. CALICO Journal 20(1), 33–58 (2002)

33. Zumbach, J.: Cognitive overload in hypertext learning reexamined: Overcoming the myths. Journal of Educational Multimedia and Hypermedia 15(4), 411–432 (2006)

A Systematic Review of Technologies Designed to Improve and Assist Cognitive Decline for Both the Current and Future Aging Populations

Kelley Gurley and Anthony F. Norcio

Department of Information Systems
University of Maryland Baltimore County (UMBC)
Baltimore, MD 21250 USA
{kgurley1,norcio}@umbc.edu

Abstract. This paper serves as a literature review focused on understanding the technologies available for all aging populations. It also presents some limitations involved in providing alternative health care and discusses some considerations to designing technologies for future aging populations.

Keywords: Cognitive Decline, Aging Population, Assistive Technologies, Robotics, Telehealth.

1 Introduction

Information and communication technologies have become ubiquitous in today's everyday life [41]. A few years ago it was almost inconceivable that most of yesterday's human to human interactions would be replaced with the use of some form of human to computer interaction. Most of the generation x population i.e. people born between 1965 and 1980, use technology to assist in accomplishing tasks and to provide some form of communication and entertainment in their everyday use. According to future projections, many people from this future population would have attained higher levels of education than previous generations and would also have more computer skills than the previous generations. Trend projections explain that more than 32 million of older adults have a computer at home and 26% are internet users. This is in contrast to 62 million people between 35- 54 years old having a computer and 80% of people age 30 – 49 years old using the internet. This information demonstrates the shift of technology users and their comfort levels with devices, technology, gadgets etc. [12]. This may demonstrate an easier transition to depend on technology and limit some of the concerns with the adoption of technology that is faced by the current aging generation [31].

As we age, there are also many medical ailments that we may encounter, regardless of educational background or socioeconomic status. Some of these include chronic diseases like heart conditions, diabetes mellitus, arthritis, neurological conditions, cognitive impairment, along with decreased hearing and vision [32]. Special accommodations of equipment or software due to age-associated cognitive or perceptual changes may also be required for all aging populations [22, 24].

N. Aykin (Ed.): Internationalization, Design, LNCS 5623, pp. 156–163, 2009.

It is important to indicate that this review is focused on technologies designed to support normal decline associated with aging and not decline from Alzheimer's disease. This is an incurable progressive and fatal brain disease [2] and requires medical investigations, treatments and intervention. We will review what the current literature suggest about the familiarity to technology and how it can assist, prevent, slow down or reverse cognitive decline [37, 45]. Though the current literature provides methodologies to produce efficient technologies and interfaces for the current aging population [11,15,40,46], there is still a gap in providing solutions for a population that will be much more advanced, more technologically savvy and much more knowledgeable in what they consider to be good end products and good usable design [7, 47]. There are also many studies that discuss the aging adult and cognitive decline on the current population [4, 41, 44], but no significant literature that focuses on the future aging population who has been projected to have a higher standard of expectations for how things should be done and who will aggressively seek a well designed product [10, 12, 43].

2 Background

Currently, there are less than 10% of aged individuals in the society. Predictions have been made that by the year 2050; more than 20% of the population will be older than 80 years of age [35]. As the aging population becomes a more significant part of the overall US population, it is important to consider how one could retain current cognitive vitality. Cognitive decline, memory loss, decline in processing speed and the slowing of basic cognitive process to some degree are almost expected in normal aging and are frequently studied [42]. There are several research studies that have documented the effects of either training interventions that involve some type of memory training or discuss how the older adult depends on environmental support for memory retrieval operations [4, 5, 37, 48]. There is also documentation that shows significant improvement in cognition when participating in different types of physical activities and exercise, (riding a bicycle, reading, climbing stairs etc) by finding patterns which can show significant ways for improving cognitive decline to some degree [9]. Good user design also considers cognitive load, memory and spatial design factors for their end user [10, 48].

3 Technologies

Technologies have been able to provide medical assistance for many years. From, Wilhelm Conrad Röntgen in 1895 [29], who discovered the medical use of x-rays, to the recent home health device by Intel that supports telemedicine, humans have been using technology to assist with medical diagnosis, treatments and support for many years. Though, many diseases have been eradicated through the forecasting and diagnostic use of technology [36] and many health conditions, impairments and disabilities alleviated through the supportive use of technology, decline in cognitive performance is still a major threat and a review of some existing technologies is necessary.

3.1 Tele-health

Tele-health involves the communication of images, voice, and data between two or more sites using telecommunications [39]. This provides health services such as clinical advice, consultation, education, and training services [23]. This form of tele-medicine has been used in many countries for the delivery of mental health care, particularly psychiatric services, but there is not much documented data that demonstrates the effectiveness of this approach to this form of health services delivery. A big advancement in this field is the new monitoring device by Intel [17]. This device captures patient vital signs (blood pressure, weight, blood glucose etc) and sends this electronically to the primary care provider who can contact the patient direct through the video conferencing functionality.

Another form of telemedicine is robotic surgery. This involves the surgeon and a robot to work in a master-slave capacity while performing some form of surgery. However, at present they have only been approved for limited clinical use [3]. A main barrier to the development of these types of systems is the rigorous licensure requirements and the difficult process to get "buy in" from each state for a physician to practice telemedicine [28]. A common barrier to physicians is the non-existent reimbursement process for providing telemedicine. The high cost of telecommunications has also affected the growth of this aspect of health care.

3.2 Adaptive Technologies

Adaptive technologies refer to technologies, devices etc. that can adapt to the current user [30]. This will be important for adults that develop disabilities or limitations in using particular devices and generally for the older adult who responds more slowly to simple stimuli and take longer to learn new material [14]. An example of an adaptive technology which can be worn by the user would be a pair of eyeglasses that can enhance the peripheral field of vision of the user [18]. Another type called a microelectromechanical system, can be placed in regular objects, an example would be a sensor, which can be placed into a cane (used by the blind or people with low vision) that provides information about nearby structures [16]. A third type is one that a user will normal interact with like the display on the dashboard while driving [14].

3.3 Assistive Technologies

Assistive technologies can assist a user with specific deficits in their abilities; find an alternative way of performing a task, an action or an activity [22]. These have been studied in detail for the rehabilitation treatment of cognitive disorders along with compensation for specific impairment and assessing the user's cognitive status [1]. These assistive technologies comprise of three main forms: Assurance, Compensation and Assessment systems [35].

Assurance Systems assist in ensuring safety and well-being. Sensors are a type of assurance system that can convert a physical signal into an electrical signal that may be manipulated symbolically on a computer. These can also be placed around a home to depict whether a stove top has been forgotten on and turn it off, etc or contact the caregiver [13, 21]. Transmittal of information to caregivers in real time is also helpful [33]. This can help monitor activities and help reduce the man power that is required to manage home health care. It also assists with the aging in place initiatives which can be used to help an older adult live independently for longer periods [19, 26]. Interfaces that can be personalized by the user are currently being researched as cognitive decline occurs gradually in most cases. One example is that of a person forgetting to take their medications and the system tracking this continued pattern and initiate reminders through the television between the commercials or use of other familiar technology like a verbal reminder over the telephone [13].

However, these systems may give them a false sense of security as care-giver notification can be sent automatically and if malfunctions occur with failed delivery or receipt, alternative plans of action may not have been considered. For example, if a patient or elderly person falls, technologies exist that can notify emergency services. Also, if vital signs go below a specific threshold a notification can be sent to a caregiver to assist this person. However, if the caregiver does not respond at what point will emergency services be contacted? Additional questions that may be raised regarding this scenario may include: After how much time will an action occur? Can the user override the decision made by the system? Who will be responsible if the situation is not resolved in a timely manner? There are many more legal and ethical questions that could be raised and should be considered before full adoption and reliance of such systems.

Compensation systems help guide the user to complete daily activities. When a system monitors a user and determines that assistance is needed to help complete a task, a second set of systems is designed to help compensate for the cognitive impairment that the individual has encountered. They also encompass navigational support systems that help older adults navigate around their environment.

Assessment systems gather information to provide some sort of evaluation to determine how a person is doing. It can help monitor their cognitive functioning and work with other assistive technologies and adaptive technologies to assist the user in accomplishing a task. These are frequently studied and can encompass recording of vital signs, detecting user location etc. There are many benefits to such systems in independent care living and retirement communities as it can be informative to the caregiver and also help detect a user at risk for a fall or other events. Robots and other forms of artificial intelligence can also assist older adults, as memory deficits can lead to forgetting tasks; for example forgetting to take medications. A Personalized Robotic Assistant can remind the user that it is time to take the medications [35]. It can track whether an individual who has cognitive decline and incontinence has used the bathroom in the last 30 minutes and offer reminders when necessary. This also facilitates the idea of older persons managing their own health care and being able to better communicate with their health care providers [25].

4 Cognitive Orthotics

Cognitive orthotics or cognitive prosthetics are another form of assistance that are frequently studied and was developed for specific types of cognitive decline due to some type of trauma, disability, impairment or decline. Similar to how a prosthetic limb can help the user perform regular activities that would be difficult and sometimes impossible to perform, so can computer-based assistive technology work to benefit the user with the special need, in this case an aging adult with some form of cognitive decline [8, 34]. It has been discussed that frequent cognitive training may reverse cognitive decline but there are still many questions that surround this reversal [42]. However, reversal has been successfully documented in several experiments that demonstrate the ability of cognitive training with the use of technology. A specific case was one of a medical doctor who began to show signs of significant memory deficits to a point where he was unable to remember any new information after 30 minutes. After using a scheduler system to help initiate an action, over a period of 6 months, he began to show improvement in his functional memory [8].

5 Technology Abandonment

It has been reported, that approximately one third of all assistive technologies are abandoned within one year of use especially within the first three months. Abandonment rates are from 8% for life-support devices to 75% for hearing aids depending on the device [38]. This failure of adoption rate can be explained in terms of the user, the environment surrounding the user and the device [19]. Many devices are designed to match a user with a specific need instead of matching the user to a device that will meet their needs. Sometimes the designers of these devices do not always know all of the situations surrounding the use of the device or the user's real needs. The constraints of time and money have led to many devices being tested on persons for whom they were not designed [6] which has lead to devices that do not meet the user's specific needs. Many devices are designed without proper considerations of human factors during the design of the device which can lead to an un-usable or inefficient device. In attempting to develop devices that are useful and usable, the designers and developers must involve the users of the products and when necessary their caregivers to encourage sustainability of the end product [20].

6 Conclusion

There are many limitations that are faced by the aging population today. These vary from their comfort levels of learning new technology, to using devices or interfaces that do not consider the older user in its design process. These can make it difficult to use and therefore difficult to adopt on a daily basis [27, 49]. There is also a need to research technologies that not only focus on assisting mild cognitive decline but also focus its reduction or reversal. Most of the literature focuses on physical impairments and cognitive decline of the aging population and explains how technology is being used to assist them. However, there is much needed information on how the current population will age and interact with existing and new technologies. This leads us to several theoretical questions about this future aging population and the use of technology. Would the "future aging population" really use technology more readily and more efficiently than the current older population? How do we test for this prediction as most of the technology that will be used has not yet been invented? Do we hypothesize on the current use of technology in specific cohorts and use this information to predict future patterns? How do we test accuracy on these predictions? What type of methodology may be used to test these theories? There is significant ground work that needs to be completed and focus should be given to facilitating initiatives that involve studying this paradigm and developing methodologies towards the human-computer interaction for the future aging adult.

References

1. Agree, E.M., Freedman, V.A.: Incorporating Assistive Devices into Community-Based Long-Term Care: An Analysis of the Potential for Substitution and Supplementation. Journal of Aging and Health 12, 426–450 (2000)
2. Alzheimer's Association website, http://www.alz.org
3. Ballantyne, G.H.: Robotic surgery, telerobotic surgery, telepresence and telemonitoring. Surgical Endosc 16, 1389–1402 (2002)
4. Ball, K., Berch, D.B., Helmers, K.F., Jobe, J.B., Leveck, M.D., Marsiske, M., Morris, J.N., Rebok, G.W., Smith, D.M., Tennstedt, S.L., Unverzagt, F.W., Willis, S.L.: Advanced Cognitive Training for Independent and Vital Elderly Study Group. Effects of cognitive training intervention with older adults: A randomized controlled trial. JAMA 288(18), 2271–2281 (2002)
5. Birren, J.E., Schaie, K.W.E.: Handbook of the Psychology of Aging. Academic Press, San Diego (1996)
6. Boyd-Graber, J., Nikolova, S., Moffatt, K., Kin, K., Lee, J., Mackey, L., Tremaine, M., Klawe, M.: Participatory Design with Proxies: Developing a Desktop-PDA System to Support People with Aphasia. In: CHI 2006 Proceedings, pp. 151–160 (2006)
7. Carroll, J., Howard, S., Vetere, F., Peck, J., Murphy, J.: Just what do the youth of today want?. In: Proceedings of Hawaiian International Conference on Systems Sciences (2002)
8. Cole, E., Dehdashti, P.: Computer-based cognitive prosthetics: Assistive technology for the treatment of cognitive disabilities. In: Proceedings of the Third International ACM Conference on Assistive Technologies (ACM SIGCAPH - Computers and the Physically Handicapped), Marina del Rey, CA (1998)
9. Colcombe, S., Kramer, A.F.: Fitness effects on the cognitive function of older adults: A Meta-analytic study. Psychological Science 14(2), 125–130 (2003)
10. Czaja, S.J., Charness, N., Fisk, A.D., Hertzog, C., Nair, S.N., Rogers, W.A., Sharit, J.: Factors predicting the use of technology: Findings from the Center for Research and Education on Aging and Technology Enhancement (CREATE). Psychology and Aging. Psychol Aging. 21(2), 333–352 (2006)
11. Czaja, S.: Human Factors Research needs for an aging population. National Academic Press, Washington DC (1990)
12. Czaja, S., Lee, C.C.: Information Technology and older adults. In: Sears, Jacko, J. (eds.) The Human-Computer Interaction Handbook, 2nd edn., pp. 777–792. Lawrence Erlbaum and Associates, Mahwah, NJ (2007)
13. Dishman, E., Matthews, J., Dunbar-Jacob, J.: Everyday Health: Technology for Adaptive Aging. In: Pew, R.W., Van Hemel, S.B. (eds.) Technology for adaptive aging, pp. 179–208. The National Academies Press, Washington (2004),
http://www.geron.uga.edu/pdfs/BooksOnAging/AdaptiveAging.pdf
14. Fisher, D.L.: Cognitive aging and adaptive technologies. In: Stern, P.C., Carstensen, L. (eds.) Committee on Future Directions for Cognitive Research on Aging. The Aging Mind: Opportunities in Cognitive Research, pp. 166–188. National Academy Press, Washington (2000)

15. Fisk, A., Roger, W., Charness, N., Czaja, S., Sharit, J.: Design for Older Adults: Principles and Creative Human Factors Approaches. CRC Press, Boca Raton, FL (2004)
16. Gao, R., Cai, X.: A wireless ranging system as an embedded sensor module for the long cane. In: IEEE instrumentation and Measurement Technology Conference, pp. 547–552 (1998)
17. Intel (2008),
    http://www.intel.com/pressroom/archive/releases/
    20080710corp_b.htm
18. Jebara, T., Eyster, C., Weaver, J., Starner, T., Pentland, A.: Stochasticks: Augmenting the Billiards Experience with Probabilistic Vision and Wearable Computers. In: IEEE Intl. Symposium on Wearable Computers, Cambridge, October 23-24 (1997)
19. King, T.W.: Why AT fails: A human factors perspective. In: King, T. (ed.) Assistive technology, essential human factors, pp. 231–255. Allyn and Bacon, Boston (1999)
20. Kintsch, A., DePaula, R.: A Framework for the Adoption of Assistive Technology SWAAAC: Supporting Learning through Assistive Technology, pp. E3 1–10. (2002)
21. Korhonen, I., Parkka, J., Van Gils, M.: Health monitoring in the home of the future. IEEE Eng. Med. Biol. Mag. 22, 66–73 (2003)
22. LaPlante, M.P., Hendershot, G.E., Moss, A.J.: Assistive Technology Devices and Home Accessibility Features: Prevalence, Payment, Need, and Trends. Advance Data: Centers for disease control - National Center for Health Statistics (1992)
23. Loh, P.K., Maher, S., Goldswain, P., et al.: Diagnostic Accuracy of Telehealth Community Dementia Assessments. J. of American Geriatric Society 53, 2043–2044 (2005)
24. McGee, J.S., Van der Zaag, C., Buckwalter, J.G., Thiebaux, M., Van Rooyen, A., Neuman, U., Sisemore, D., Rizzo, A.A.: Issues for the Assessment of Visuospatial Skills in Older Adults Using Virtual Environment Technology. Cyber Psychology & Behavior 3(3), 469–482 (2000)
25. Morrell, R.: Older Adults, Health Information and the World Wide Web. Lawrence Erlbaum Associates, Mahwah (2002)
26. Mynatt, E., Essa, I., Rogers, W.: Increasing the opportunities for aging in place. In: Proceedings from the conference on Universal Usability, pp. 65–71. ACM Press, Arlington, Virginia (2000)
27. Neilsen Norman Group Report, http://www.nngroup.com/reports/seniors/
28. Nickelson, D.: Telehealth and the Evolving Health Care System: Strategic Opportunities for Professional Psychology. Professional Psychology: Research and Practice 29(6), 527–535 (1998)
29. Nobel Prize,
    http://nobelprize.org/nobel_prizes/physics/laureates/1901/
    rontgen-bio.html
30. Norcio, A.F., Stanley, J.: Adaptive human-computer interfaces: A literature survey and perspective. IEEE Transactions on Systems, Man, and Cybernetics SMC-19(2), 399–408 (1989)
31. Oblinger, D.G., Oblinger, J.L. (eds.): Educating the net generation. Boulder, CO: EDUCAUSE (2005),
    http://www.educause.edu/educatingthenetgen/5989
32. Ormel, J., Kempen, G., Phenninx, B., Brilman, E., Beekman, A., Van Sonderen, E.: Chronic medical conditions and mental health in older people: disability and psychosocial resources mediate specific mental health effects. Psychological Medicine 27(5), 1065–1077 (1997)

33. Pineau, J., Montemerlo, M., Pollack, M., Roy, N., Thrun, S.: Towards robotic assistants in nursing homes: Challenges and results. Robotics and Autonomous Systems 42, 271–281 (2003)
34. Pollack, M.E.: Planning technology for intelligent cognitive orthotics. In: 6th International Conference on Automated Planning and Scheduling, pp. 322–331. AAAI Press, Menlo Park (2002)
35. Pollack, M.E.: Intelligent Technology for an Aging Population: The Use of AI to assist Elders with Cognitive Impairment. AI Magazine 26(2), 9–24 (2005)
36. Rabinovich, R.N., McInnes, P., Klein, D., Hall, F.: Vaccine Technologies: View to the Future. Science, New Series 265(5177), 1401–1404 (1994)
37. Schaie, K.W., Willis, S.L.: Can decline in adult intellectual functioning be reversed? Developmental Psychology 22, 223–232 (1986)
38. Scherer, M.J., Galvin, J.C.: An outcome perspective of quality pathways to most appropriate technology. In: Galvin, J.C., Scherer, M.J. (eds.) Evaluating, selecting and using appropriate assistive technology, pp. 1–26. Aspen Publication, Gaithersburg (1996)
39. Schopp, L., Johnstone, B., Merrell, D.: Telehealth and neuropsychological assessment: new opportunities for psychologists. Prof Psychology Research and Practice 31, 179–183 (2000)
40. Sears, A., Young, M., Feng, J.: Physical Disabilities and Computing Technologies: An Analysis of Impairments. In: Sears, A., Jacko, J. (eds.) The Human-Computer Interaction Handbook, 2nd edn., pp. 829–852. Lawrence Erlbaum and Associates, Mahwah (2007)
41. Selwyn, N., Gorard, S., Furlong, J., Madden, L.: Older adults' use of information and communications technology in everyday life. Ageing and Society 23, 561–582 (2003)
42. Stine-Morrow, E.A.L., Miller, L.M.S.: Basic cognitive processes. In: Cavanaugh, J.C., Whitbourne, S.K. (eds.) Gerontology: An interdisciplinary perspective, pp. 186–212. Oxford University Press, New York (1999)
43. Tapscott, D.: Growing up Digital. The Rise of the Net Generation. McGraw Hill, New York (1998)
44. Valentijn, S.A., Van Hooren, S.A., Bosma, H., Touw, D.M., Jolles, J., Van Boxtel, M.P., et al.: The effect of two types of memory training on subjective and objective memory performance in healthy individual aged 55 years and older: a randomized controlled trial. Patient Education and Counseling 57(1), 106–114 (2005)
45. White, J., Weatherall, A.: A grounded theory analysis of older adults and information technology. Educational Gerontology 26, 371–386 (2000)
46. Willis, S.: Technology and learning in current and future older cohorts. In: Pew, R.W., Van Hemel, S.B. (eds.) Technology for adaptive aging, pp. 209–229. The National Academies Press, Washington (2004),
http://www.geron.uga.edu/pdfs/BooksOnAging/AdaptiveAging.pdf
47. Willis, S.L.: Technology and learning in current and future generations of elders. Generations, Summer, pp. 44–48 (2006)
48. Willis, S.L., Schaie, K.W.: Training the elderly on the ability factors of spatial orientation and inductive reasoning. Psychology of Aging 1, 239–247 (1986)
49. Zimmer, Z., Chappell, N.: Receptivity to new technology among older adults. Disability and Rehabilitation 21(5-6), 222–230 (1999)

Developers and Moderators: Observations in the Co-development of an Online Social Space

David Gurzick and Kevin F. White

University of Maryland, Baltimore County
Dept. of Information Systems
1000 Hilltop Circle
Baltimore, MD 21250 USA
{gurzick1,kwhite2}@umbc.edu

Abstract. Online social spaces have emerged at the confluence of three notable trends: an increasing amount of interaction occurring over digital channels, an awareness of the range of technical and social affordances such spaces provide, and a growing participatory culture that fosters member involvement in the creation and maintenance of digital locales. At the same time, these trends offer both great promise and significant challenges to the creation and maintenance of online social spaces. This paper unpacks the observations from the creation of one such online social space developed with involvement from the moderators tasked with facilitating its operation. Observations run the gamut from the technical (modifying system features to meet described work practices) to the social (fostering a joint ownership in the success of the social space) and set the stage for a broad research agenda for discovering best practice in constructing social spaces online.

Keywords: Online Communities, Sociotechnical Systems, Adolescents, Moderation, Design, Tools.

1 Introduction

There is a buzz around participatory, collaborative development. Shown to foster increased efficiency in the development process and improved satisfaction of the final product [1, 2], organizations have adopted collaborative development approaches to design software [3-5], deliver course material [6], and enhance organizational processes [7]. Just as collaborative approaches to development have been embraced by organizations, they have also become an accepted practice in the creation and maintenance of online communities. As with YouTube's reliance on user-generated media and the army of writers and editors needed to sustain Wikipedia, many online communities have grown reliant on members to handle the critical tasks of creating and maintaining the online social spaces for these communities. Yet more than just serving as managers of existing community artifacts, these members are now filling another role by helping to guide the ongoing development of these spaces.

Designers have long lauded the incorporation of feedback loops into the design of online social spaces as a means for providing a legitimate channel for members to

N. Aykin (Ed.): Internationalization, Design, LNCS 5623, pp. 164–172, 2009.

communicate concerns or voice opinions [8-10]. However three unique trends are changing the nature of the conversation that these channels can support. These trends include:

A substantial (and increasing) amount of interaction is now occurring over digital channels. With a growing number of users connecting and participating in online communities [11], involvement in online social spaces has become a norm for those accustomed to the Internet and digital life. They have become adept at communication devoid of non-verbal cues, limiting the amount of discussion needed to ascertain meaning.

Users have an awareness of the range of technical and social affordances such spaces provide. The popularity of online communication has given rise to a variety of different formats, styles, and processes for handling this discourse. As such it is common for users to have experience using a number of different online communication systems and it is natural for users bring their knowledge of interaction within other social spaces to bear on the plethora of communities they frequent.

There is a growing participatory culture that fosters member involvement in the creation and maintenance of digital locales. It has become the norm to request members to help maintain and improve the shared resources of the community. As of December 2006, it was reported that over a quarter of Internet users had tagged photos, rated content, or posted reviews [12]. Moreover, many large-scale online social spaces rely on member participation for daily operations, as with the submission and scoring of news stories at Digg.com [13] and the moderation and meta-moderation of comments at Slashdot [14].

Together, these trends point toward a new dialogue that is related not just to the purpose of the communities hosted within an online space, but to the very way these spaces are functionally constructed to support the community. But the widespread involvement of members in the co-development of the spaces hosting their communities is still a relatively new practice and community managers are still in need of effective ways to leverage this new paradigm. This paper expands on the growing body of literature that investigates this emerging field. We do so by looking at the unique interchange that accompanied and informed the development of the social space created to support the moderators of the nascent online community "Fieldtrip".

2   The Fieldtrip Online Community

Fieldtrip is an online community launched as part of a research project that sought to explore whether the growing use of information and communication technologies by adolescents could be leveraged to help them rethink their ideas about learning and education. Nearly eighty adolescents enrolled to take part in a month-long pilot of the community that was run during the Spring of 2007. Joining the adolescents in this community were seventeen moderators, college undergraduates that were primarily tasked with ensuring that the discourse in the community remained civil and on topic[1]. To assist in these tasks, the moderators were given access to a special administrative

---

[1] Institutional board requirements mandated that the community be staffed by at least one moderator during each hour of its operation (from 6AM – 2AM EST daily).

portion of the website distinct from the main community. A number of communication tools were provided in this administrative site, including a threaded discussion forum (fig. 1) and a utility to record and display field notes (fig. 2).

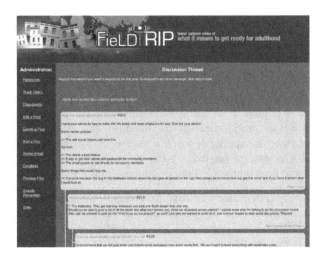

Fig. 1. This figure shows one of the threads of discussion in the moderator/developer "back channel" that was available in the administrative page of the Fieldtrip online community

Fig. 2. This figure shows the field notes page in the administrative section of the Fieldtrip online community. Each moderator was asked to write a field note at the conclusion of his/her shift (normally lasting 1-2 hours). Over 400 field notes were recorded during the pilot.

The moderators, versed in the goals of the community, quickly began discussions surrounding unique ways of using the moderation tools in the administrative site. These included an activity-tracking tool, which allowed moderators to examine the actions in the site at the individual user level. This functionality, it was thought, would enable the moderators to quickly respond to a disruptive member by locating all of the places in the website where the member had previously posted and allow the moderators to establish a context for determining the severity of claims made by a participant [15]. Secondly, moderators were provided a facility to edit and delete messages in the main community forums. Finally, an email utility provided moderators opportunity to contact adolescents directly to correct behavior should the necessity arise.

Discussions between moderators quickly developed to include advice on workarounds to limitations imposed by the tools and desires for modifications to the site. The moderators were not alone in the administrative website; access was also given to members of the Fieldtrip development team. Through the field notes and discussion forum an interchange quickly arose between the developers and moderators concerning the construction of the online social space itself.

3 Method

The findings presented within this paper were extracted from a grounded theory analysis of the digitally recorded and archived points of interaction between the developers and moderators. These included the posts made to the administrative discussion forum, as well as a collection of field notes which moderators were required to submit at the end of their assigned shift. Field notes were visible to all members of the moderator community as well as site developers, but could not be accessed by the adolescents.

Textual data was first coded for interactions relevant to the design, construction, or maintenance of the community. These codes were then grouped into related concepts on the co-development of the online social space. It is the concepts that emerged from this process that are elaborated below.

3.1 Promoting a Formative Dialogue between Developers and Moderators

The first step to co-development is the cultivation of awareness around the use and expectations for the online social space. In the case of the moderators and developers of Fieldtrip, this step involved learning by both parties; the developers learned how the moderators went about performing their tasks, including how they used the tools available to them to meet their needs; the moderators learned how the developers envisioned the moderation tools to be used and the rationale behind their selection and construction.

This discussion was led by the moderators, who recounted their use of the tools while performing their daily tasks

> *[Today I kept] refreshing the track page...nothing, no one looking around, absolute zero activity. I watched the new videos and updated on reading the comments like always.*

And I noticed that it is handy to have a document open anyway to note things of interest while modding.

I watched the two new videos and then, kept refreshing the discussion page.

Not much activity around this time, so I spent most of my time reviewing new posts and videos. I also added a new suggestion for the site in the admin discussion page.

Such comments by the moderators were often accompanied by remarks on problems or difficulties encountered with the administrative tools.

The fieldnotes. They get [jarbled] whenever you post one that's longer than one line.

Is it by any chance possible to have everything on the community site accessible directly from the admin site? i mean it's really not a big deal to switch back and forth - especially if you just keep two windows open - but I just figure if it can be done then why not? just wondering;)

Hearing of these problems prompted the developers to become involved, at times acknowledging the problems with the tools, "Thanks, I'm posting the first update to the admin site tonight. It should fix the fieldnote problem", and at other times adding their insight into the why particular aspects of the system operated as they did:

Moderator - *I noticed that there are 2 pages for the last discussions...would it be possible to keep it on one page or could the first page show the most recent posts? It just gets annoying to going back and forth to make sure all the posts are read.*

Developer - *This was actually a design decision to ensure that the topics and films are only permitted 10 entries on the main page (to ensure the topics doesnt get all filled up and take over the other areas).*

Occasionally the developers would step in with advice and suggestions for using the tools, *"One suggestions is to sort by last comment to avoid that hassle."* This practice was quickly joined by the moderators:

I responded to an older video ... because I wanted to leave the newer videos for students to comment on, and bring up older videos to see if we can get some fresh opinions ... I think that's going to be my strategy from now on - every shift I'll pick an old thread to bump back up to the top

The only way to know this is (a) are they doing activity? if so, you can see this in track users, (b) are they logged in? plenty of people don't log out of a site just because they aren't looking at it, so this data would be nigh-useless.

3.2 Modifying System Features to Meet Work Practices

Once an understanding was established between the moderators and developers around the use and expectations for the online social space they shared, the discussion moved towards an exploration of the ways that the tools provided to the moderators could be reconfigured to bring them into alignment with their work practices. Much of the discussion centered on functionality the moderators deemed missing from the current tools. This interchange was bidirectional, as the developers enlisted the moderators to test/debug changed features and reported their progress to the group. An example of this is seen in the exchange between the moderators and developers regarding the problem of handling duplicate posts:

Moderator - *How do I edit or delete [duplicate posts]?*

Developer - *I have a way of handling this through merging of records in the database (I'd make a tool for everyone, but by the time I was done the project would be over). If you send me an email ... with the red ID #s of the duplicate posts I will merge them together. I should add that this is only within a single thread of discussion.*

Moderator - *They were duplicates, but I don't have the ability to delete them so I just put up (*duplicate post*). Deleting would've been much easier*

Developer -*I need someone to help me test this feature - any takers, and when are you on?*

Moderator - *I wouldn't mind testing it out...My shifts are usually 4-6pm but I'm on here and there throughout the day. Let me know if I can help.*

Developer - *Thanks ... it looks to be working ok so far.*

Developer - *Hi there [delete has been added] - you can use this message thread as your testing area. Just enter in the number of the post you want to delete (ie 546) and the click "load this post". All the messages that will be deleted will show up in the area below. If these are acceptable, then click the submit button at the bottom right of the screen to delete them. Let me know if you still have problems.*

Moderator - *Delete function works as of 2:55!! :o)*

After witnessing the co-development activities that remedied a missing piece of essential functionality in the space, the moderators shifted to suggest modifications to existing tools that, while not considered essential, were perceived as aiding moderators in performing their assigned tasks. Once these ideas were presented, they gathered support from other moderators.

It would be great and helpful for us to be able to see who is logged on in the administration site. I know we can track movement, but it would be great if there was a list of current users on the site when we're monitoring - just to give us a feel for how active the site is when we're on.

Nah I agree, this would be a good addition

...it would give us an idea of whos on at one time. I've looked around and a lot of other forums and facebook have this option, so i think it can still be useful.

3.3 Fostering a Joint Ownership in the Success of the Social Space

The shared experience of creating and implementing modifications to the underlying online social space engendered a progressive consideration for how the space might be further augmented. In this new discourse, moderators took the role of introducing suggestions for new features not only to the developers, but also to their fellow moderators.

I was thinking that if there's time and if it isn't too much trouble we could look at adding a "tag" feature on this site. A lot of other sites have this, but basically you would just tag a video/post with the topic that it is discussing. For example, on ... Lauren's new Altercation video we could tag it with "fighting" and etc. ... This would really help organized the videos/posts to categories for viewers to easily find their topic of interest; just not sure the logistic of implementing it though.

I was thinking about this yesterday, it would be great if we could initiate a "pop-up" message that said something like "don't forget to tell us what you think about the film to get the second half of your iTunes!" so the person watching the film could see it. It's not something that should pop up automatically, because we don't want to annoy those who do comment, but if we notice a person is just watching the clips but not commenting, we could remind them. I'm saying this because I've noticed that even if I apply the most intriguing question :), chances are I won't get an immediate reply. Just a thought.

In some cases, the moderators were cognizant to the location of data that might lead to the inception of new features, even if they were unaware of what those features might be. To illustrate, one moderator described how an archive of tracking data, visible to the moderators through the activity-tracking tool, might be used in aggregate to suggest ways of dealing with a problem of scheduling moderators:

No activity at all. I can't even figure out a pattern to user activity except for weekends nothing generally happens, and on holidays nothing happens period. I'm sure with the saved time tracking data you can find out something interesting but I can't see it.

4 Toward a Broader Research Agenda in the Co-development of Social Spaces

This study investigated an online social space co-developed through the shared labors of its developers and moderators. As this study was limited in scope, the reported observations should be construed not as generalizable findings, but rather as background to the creation of questions to guide more in-depth, empirical research. To start this process, we conclude this paper by offering a trio of questions that arose during our analysis:

Q1: With a preponderance of new programming tools and packaged services, the lines between developer and moderator are blurring. This draws the questions of whether these roles should be distinct and what might be the pros and cons of separating the role of development from the role of moderation?

Q2: As online communities move to occupy many social spaces simultaneously, it seems inevitable that these spaces will become more intertwined. How will the activities of co-development present in this new environment? What new tools and practices will be needed to support this change?

Q3: Lastly, in this paper, we explored the co-development of an online social space that housed a community with a relatively limited geographic dispersion (mostly concentrated in one state in the US mid-Atlantic, with no international members). Do these concerns apply when considering a larger, international audience? How do cultural differences confound the roles of developers and moderators and impact the processes of co-development?

Acknowledgments. Support for this project was provided by the NIH Grant #1 R41 RR024089-01 the Robert W. Deutsch Foundation, and NOKIA. Special thanks to the developers and moderators of the Fieldtrip project.

References

1. Muller, M., Kuhn, S.: Participatory design. Communications of the ACM 36(6), 24–28 (1993)
2. Neale, M., Corkindale, D.: Co-developing products: Involving customers earlier and more deeply. Long Range Planning 31(3), 418–425 (1998)
3. Ault, C., et al.: Collaborative learning via 3-D game development. In: ACM SIGGRAPH Educators program, Massachusetts, ACM, New York (2006)
4. Domino, M.A., et al.: Conflict in collaborative software development. In: SIGMIS conference on Computer personnel research: Freedom in Philadelphia–leveraging differences and diversity in the IT workforce, Philadelphia, Pennsylvania, ACM, New York (2003)
5. Xiao, W., Chi, C., Yang, M.: On-line collaborative software development via wiki. In: International symposium on Wikis, Montreal, Quebec, Canada, ACM, New York (2007)
6. Talbott, D., Gibson, M., Skublics, S.: A collaborative methodology for the rapid development and delivery of online courses. In: 20th annual international conference on Computer documentation, Toronto, Ontario, Canada, ACM, New York (2002)
7. Fraser, P., Farrukh, C., Gregory, M.: Managing product development collaborations—a process maturity approach. Proceedings of the Institution of Mechanical Engineers, Part B: Journal of Engineering Manufacture 217(11), 1499–1519 (2003)
8. Kim, A.J.: Community Building on the Web: Secret Strategies for Successful Online Communities. Peachpit Press, Berkeley, CA (2000)
9. Powazek, D.M.: Design for Community: The Art of Connecting Real People in Virtual Places. New Riders (2002)
10. Preece, J.: Online Communities: Designing Usability and Supporting Sociability. John Wiley & Sons, Inc., New York (2000)
11. Lenhart, A.: Adults and social network websites. Pew Internet & American Life Project, Washington (2009)
12. Rainie, L.: 28% of Online Americans Have Used the Internet to Tag Content. Pew Internet & American Life Project, Washington (2007)

13. Lerman, K.: User Participation in Social Media: Digg Study. In: IEEE/WIC/ACM International Conferences on Web Intelligence and Intelligent Agent Technology, IEEE Computer Society Press, Los Alamitos (2007)
14. Lampe, C., Resnick, P.: Slash(dot) and burn: distributed moderation in a large online conversation space. In: Proceedings of the SIGCHI conference on Human factors in computing systems, Vienna, Austria, pp. 543–550. ACM Press, New York (2004)
15. Gurzick, D., et al.: Examining moderator use of activity-tracking in a nascent online community for adolescents. In: Annual meeting of the Institute for Operations Research and the Management Sciences (INFORMS), Washington (2008)

Anthropomorphic Systems:
An Approach for Categorization

Kathryn Howe

Department of Information Systems
University of Maryland Baltimore County (UMBC)
Baltimore, MD 21250 USA
khowe@umbc.edu

Abstract. Are systems that incorporate anthropomorphic attributes better at interactivity with a user than systems that do not use such attributes? Do these systems allow a user to interact with the system in a natural way; or can the system cause more frustration then aid? It is a fact that many systems nowadays are attempting to make their interfaces more natural to use. Some systems attempt to do so by the advance of various input systems, such as touch screens, screen readers, etc. Other systems attempt to create user interfaces that a user can easily relate to. They can take on various anthropomorphic attributes such as emotion, speech, cognition and learning abilities. These systems vary dramatically in how they incorporate the attributes as well. Some systems use an interface of cartoon characters that allow a user to believe that the character can speak and learn like the user, while still keeping a separation of the virtual and real world by its physical form. Others attempt to effect human attributes so much that it could be difficult to distinguish between the two.

1 Introduction

In this paper, various levels of anthropomorphism are explored and evaluated as to its usability. Within each level, real world applications will be discussed to show both benefits and constraints. The final section will review the findings and attempt to determine whether the use of anthropomorphism is beneficial or a hindrance, and to what level its use should be limited to.

2 Background

Systems that provide anthropomorphic attributes can be classified into four levels. These levels differentiate by the sophistication and similarity to true human to human interaction. Level I discuss systems that show intelligence in learning how to operate a task. These systems demonstrate this ability through some sort of primitive anthropomorphic interface.

Level II holds the systems that have the same level of intelligence but also can reflect personality, behaviors and social etiquette while interacting with the user and other agents. The GUI used in level II agents could use the same type of physical interface as level I or can create a more human like interface.

N. Aykin (Ed.): Internationalization, Design, LNCS 5623, pp. 173–179, 2009.
© Springer-Verlag Berlin Heidelberg 2009

Level III houses the systems that show the same intelligence as level II, but also has the capabilities of showing emotion and behaviors with the use of more sophisticated physical embodiment; such as muscular distinctions in the agent's face and body posture. Level III agents are often very human like in the physical model, allowing for a very believable, human to human interface. Not only can level III agents interact with each other and display body language, but these agents are also capable of reading, reacting to and understanding the same body language given off by the users.

Level IV, the highest level in the categorization, has all of the attributes of the lower three levels, but also has the ability to self replicate and to essentially "live" both inside and outside of a virtual environment.

3 Discussion

As previously discussed, level I anthropomorphic systems are among the least realistic systems. These systems are relatively simple in graphics; often only being displayed as a line drawing or cartoon character. These systems are used often times as assistive agents to help the user by offering suggestions or to take on current tasks. These agents have the ability to think independently and to learn the processes of the user.

Examples of such systems can include email agents [6]. In this particular scenario, the agent was a simple drawing of a human face. This face had a few variations. The first variation was an inquisitive look to show the user that it was attempting to learn what the user was doing, and for what purpose. If the agent was learning about what the user was trying to accomplish, and had a suggestion, a light bulb would appear above the figures' head. Another was a look of concentration on an object. This face allowed the user to see that the agent was currently busy working on a task.

Many benefits come from the use of a level I agent. These agents lessen the workload of the user, allowing that user to become more efficient. Prendinger and Ying Zi found that level I interface can also help users concentrate on specific objects and understand the agent's goals by examining the use of an animated real estate agent named "Kosa Ku". When users looked at a virtual tour of a home that was "shown" by Kosa Ku, users often watched the agent until she pointed to the area of interest; and then, after looking at the pointed area, focused attention once again to Kosa Ku. This allowed for the type of interaction expected in human to human interaction. When using other application types, such as text screens along with voice readers, users had to spend more effort and time reading the text; less time was spent looking at the actual tour of the home [11].

As with any system, there are cons that come with level I anthropomorphic systems. Often times, such agents can be viewed as irritating or redundant by experienced users who do not need suggestions. Other systems that takeover tasks for the users benefit must also have a certain level of trust from the user in order for that user to be comfortable with a task takeover. One of the biggest concerns that should be reviewed, especially with animated agents, is the concern of to what level of "cuteness" should be instilled to the agent. Agents that are too cute can quickly loose credibility by users who could most benefit from them.

4 Classifications

Anthropomorphic agents classified in the second level are those agents that have all the features discussed in level I agents, but also are able to display characteristics of personality, behavior and interaction with other agents. The addition of etiquette is also often incorporated into level II agents. Behavioral and emotional additions are important when attempting to create an agent that is believable to the user. Level II agents often times use the physical shape of a human and can include not only the face, but a body as well to show simple body gestures as a supplemental means of communication. They may also take on the shapes of other animated objects such as cartoon animals. Without the use of some basic emotion though, agents lack the believability of "living", which is an essential part in making an agent believable.

Personality is very important for agents who display behavioral actions. An agent's personality will determine differences and uniqueness in physical actions among agents. An agent with a friendly personality may display behaviors such as smiling and winking; where as agents with unfriendly personalities might display behaviors such as frowning or sulking. These personalities will also determine how agents may interact with one another. An agent with an unfriendly personality will often be rude or angry towards other agents, while friendly personalities might be more amicable and patient.

Beyond the use of behavior and personalities in an agent, social role awareness, or etiquette, is also an integral part in creating a believable, anthropomorphic agent. The awareness of social roles and adherence to such roles allows an agent to not only be believable as human like, but also allows the agent to become a peer to the user or other agents. Social role awareness dictates in what manner the user, or the agent, acts.

A study by Prendinger and Ishizuka demonstrates how the use of social role awareness enhances believability of an agent. In this particular study, multiple agents are able to interact with each other in a coffee house setting. Each agent is programmed to alter their behaviors based on the role of the agent that they are interacting with. For example, a customer interacts with a waiter by asking for a beer. The waiter, who has an unfriendly personality, easily gets irritated by the customer asking for a beer in a coffee shop and speaks rudely to the customer. When that same unfriendly waiter asks the manager for some time off, the friendly manager politely says no. The waiter is irritated by the manager's response, but reacts calmly and accepts the answer because the manager's social role is higher than the waiter's; requiring respect by the waiter [10].

The use of social role awareness is also useful when an agent must interact with a user. Agents that adhere to behavioral & social standards are simpler to communicate with because a user knows what to expect while interacting with the agent. Such social standards help to dictate conversational rules and the use of (or lack of use of) language type, speech speed, volume and exclamation, all based on the environment and context of the conversation.

5 Applications

The discussions on level II agents show many benefits when these agents are used. By far the use of behavior, based on personality, and the restrictions of these behaviors because of social roles, allows an agent to become much more lifelike then those agents in level I. The use of personalities also allow for agents to become unique among others, also bringing a level of acceptance by the users. There are, of course, downsides to the use of level II agents. Every day applications currently lack the need for agents that truly act in a human like manner. Most applications that use level II agents reside in the entertainment and gaming industry. Aside from the current limit of use, another major setback with level II agents is the higher level of user expectations. As agents become more anthropomorphic, user's expectations for the abilities of agent comprehension and response also rise. The fact is, however, that an agent is still a computer system and is bound to the parameters set by their designers. If an agent is not fast enough to respond, or able to interact naturally, frustration by the user can often become an issue.

Level III agents are very similar to level II agents in that they are able to display behaviors and personality traits that are often constrained by social roles and environmental parameters. Level III, however takes these features and limits them by their physical features. These limitations include the limitation to speech or the ability to manipulate their environment based on the limitations of the "body" that these agents inhabit.

Level III systems can show more control over facial features which allow them to communicate to the user what the agent is doing or thinking. Facial displays in communication can offer non verbal cues to each participant of the interaction. The raising of an eyebrow, or the avoidance of eye contact; even the slight downturn of the lips can allow the user to subconsciously display confusion, understanding, or provide an emphasis on what is said or being understood. These types of features can also allow the system to spend time "thinking"; while offering a user a means to understand that it is thinking, suggesting they be more patient to the potentially perceived slower response rate.

If a computer system can take advantage of human facial displays and body language as an input as well as output, the system can determine on its own if the user is confused and stop itself and ask if the user needs clarification. This allows for a more natural means of communication between user and system. A good example of such an interface is the REA agent developed by Bickmore and Yan. REA is a virtual real estate agent that is able to interact with other agents and objects within her own environment. REA is also able to fully communicate with users, as if they were in her environment as well. REA, and her world, is displayed in life like proportions upon a blank wall. A user comes into the room where REA is located and she can detect, not only when someone has entered, but also where they are in the room. REA then focuses on the user and introduces herself. If REA is speaking, and the user motions to her as if they wanted to speak, REA is able to detect such actions and stop herself, to allow the user to speak. If the user's facial displays show signs of confusion, REA can react by asking if they need any clarification. While a user speaks, REA's facial displays give cues of attentiveness and comprehension. If REA is asked a question that requires "thought", she can give cues such as looking up and away while saying "umm", telling the user that she is thinking about how to answer the question and that they should allow her time to think. This sort of non verbal communication was once only available between humans.

Level III agents are able to avoid potential frustration by the user because they are able to react to action from the user and offer cues when "thinking" or when an agent needs to pause. As agents become more believable as anthropomorphic agents, users trust in them will undoubtedly also rise. Although this rise in trust and reliance on a system is ultimately what designers are striving to achieve, the issue of ethical limitations become more essential. Without ethical and moral regulations, such a system could easily be used to exploit the user and take advantage of them.

Level IV agents achieve, currently, the highest level of anthropomorphism. These systems embody the true meaning of artificial live, virtual realities and can also transcend into our virtual plane. Systems categorized within level IV are agents that own all qualities discussed in previous sections but are also able to evolve, adapt and replicate themselves. Level IV agents truly "live" within their own world; for lack of a better term. Other kinds of level IV agents are removed from their own virtual world and become members of the physical world in the form of robots; and are therefore distinct from their lower level anthropomorphic counterparts.

Agents who live in their own virtual reality are able to not only interact logically with their environment, but can actually sense what is there and react accordingly to the situation as it occurs. Not only can these agents react to other agents or objects within their world, but they can change their surroundings, change the behaviors of other agents and influence other's personalities. Agents can adapt to normal styles and evolve when conflicts occur without the requirement of outside influences. These agents can choose their own actions, no longer bound by the initial parameters set by their designers. These agents, and the world in which they live, is the equivalent to our own reality, including all of the positives and negatives that goes with it.

Bruce Blumburg, of MIT Media Lab, has created a system that reflects a level IV type agent. His system, called Artificial Life Interactive Virtual Environment, or ALIVE, is an entire interactive program in which users and characters within the virtual world can fully interact in a real time environment with each other. Although characters in level IV systems may or may not always embody a human form (where in contrast, level III systems are mostly in some level of human form), these characters are so lifelike in the world that they live, the boundary of human shape is not always necessary; though the use of human form would most certainly add to the believability of their true existence.

The other types of level IV agents, robots, are similar to their virtual reality counterparts. Robots are able to sense their surroundings and adapt themselves to their surroundings. Robots are able to communicate with other robots, computer systems, and human users. Applications often associated with robots are categorized as commercial, fictional and research. The more fictional robots are, the more anthropomorphic they can become. Robots are still in their infancy and require much more work and evolution to truly embody the human physical form and be able to do the things that humans are capable of doing. Even with these anthropomorphic limitations, robots are still categorized as level IV agents because they are the only agents that have been removed from a virtual environment and have transcended to the physical world.

One of the biggest constraints to level IV agents is the theory that an agent can become too realistic and that they can become counter productive. This theory, called the "uncanny valley" was created by Mashiro Mori and it specifies that, as robots increase their anthropomorphic attributes, user's comfort level with them begin to diminish.

Mori provides an example: "if you shake an artificial hand (that you perceive to be real) you may not be able to help jumping with a scream, having received a horrible, cold, and spongy grasp". The point of this theory is that, at least in terms of computer agents that transcend to the physical world, there may be a cap to which these agents can evolve. Not in terms of whether anthropomorphic advances can happen, but whether or not humans will accept them.

6 Findings and Conclusions

This paper attempts to categorize various anthropomorphic systems into four levels of evolution. Each level adds more human like attributes to the systems housed in them. Level I being the lowest and most primitive in terms of physical and mental anthropomorphism. Level II adding the use of emotion, behavior and etiquette to their systems. Level III incorporates a more refined physical structure allowing for physical constraints to the agents, which help with more natural, non verbal communication; as well as the ability to read such cues from the users. Level IV is the creation of a truly independent, self sufficient virtual world in which agents "live". Systems that have entered the physical world in the form of robots also are considered level IV agents. Each level has real life applications that show both benefits and downfalls attributed to them.

When it comes to an anthropomorphic system's usability, the requirements needed for a system should determine to what level of anthropomorphism is needed, if indeed, any is needed at all. Without a doubt, the use of these systems allow for ease of use for a novice user, or those users who might be uncomfortable with the idea of learning new and complex systems. The area of systems training could benefit greatly from the use of more human like interfaces and are already being adapted into such systems today. In the future, more systems will likely adopt the use of anthropomorphism in their designs. As the use of these systems rise, it is likely that the level of anthropomorphism within those systems will also rise.

References

1. Bates, J.: The role of emotion in believable agents. Communications of the ACM 37(7), 122–125 (1994)
2. Boling, E., Sousa, G.A.: Interface design issues in the future of business training. Business Horizons 36, 50–54 (1993)
3. Cassell, J., Bickmore, T., Vilhjalmsson, H., Yan, H.: More Than Just a Pretty Face: Affordances of Embodiment, pp. 52–59. ACM, New York (2000)
4. DiSalvo, C., Gemperle, F., Forlizzi, J., Kiesler, S.: All Robots are Not Created Equal: The Design and Perception of Humanoid Robot Heads. In: ACM DIS 2002, pp. 321–326 (2002)
5. Kirlik, A.: Modeling strategic behavior in human-automation interaction: Why an "aid" can (and should) go unused. Human Factors 35(2), 221–242 (1993)
6. Maes, P.: Agents that reduce work and information overload. Communications of the ACM 37(7), 30–40 (1994)
7. Marcus, A.: The Cult of Cute: The Challenge of User Experience Design. Interactions, 29–34 (November/December 2002)

8. Millier, C.: Human-Computer Etiquette: Managing Expectations with Intentional Agents. Communications of the ACM 47(4), 31–34 (2004)
9. Norman, D.A.: How might people interact with agents. Communications of the ACM 37(7), 68–71 (1994)
10. Prendinger, H., Ishizuka, M.: Social Role Awareness in Animated Agents, pp. 270–277. ACM, New York (2001)
11. Prendinger, H., Ma, C., Yingzi, J.: Understanding the Effect of Life-Like Interface Agents Through User's Eye Movements, pp. 108–115. ACM, New York (2005)
12. Takeuchi, A., Nagao, K.: Communicative Facial Displays as a New Conversational Modality, pp. 187–193. ACM, New York (1993)
13. Terzopoulos, D.: Artificial life for computer graphics. Communications of the ACM 42(8), 32–35 (1999)

Cyber Society and Cooperative Cyber Defence

Peeter Lorents[1], Rain Ottis[1], and Raul Rikk[2]

[1] Cooperative Cyber Defence Centre of Excellence, Filtri 12, 10132 Tallinn, Estonia
[2] General Staff of Estonian Defence Forces, Juhkentali 28, 15007 Tallinn, Estonia
{Peeter.Lorents,Rain.Ottis}@ccdcoe.org,
Raul.Rikk@mil.ee

Abstract. Emergence of cyber societies places new emphasis on the protection of information and information services. The paper provides a definition for the concept of information that is based on the concept of knowledge and a definition for cyber society, which encompasses the relationship between a society of humans and a network of computers. Estonia and the cyber attacks of spring 2007 are briefly examined as an example of an early cyber society under cyber attack. Finally, the role and principles of the Cooperative Cyber Defence Centre of Excellence are explained.

Keywords: Knowledge, information, cyber society, cyber attacks, cooperative cyber defence, CCD COE.

1 Introduction

When talking about cyber society and all that it implies (including vulnerability, threats, defense etc.) it is important to clearly define *cyber society*, a term that differs from information society, IT-society, e-society etc. Without diluting our focus by comparing all the various opinions on the subject (although, see [1] for some key points) we identify aspects that describe what could be called a cyber society:

- information's importance is equivalent to traditionally valued concepts, such as energy, money etc.
- information is transmitted, processed, stored etc. on mostly computer-based systems (including universal, specialized, miniature computers etc.)
- computers are used to govern the society.

Based on the above we get to the following definition:

Definition 1. A cyber society is a society where computerized information transfer and information processing is (near) ubiquitous and where the normal functioning of this society is severely degraded or altogether impossible if the computerized systems no longer function correctly.

Following this definition, cyber society is an advanced form of human-computer interaction. This relationship (human-computer interaction) involves not just a single human and a single computer, but encompasses the relationship between a society of humans and a network of computers.

N. Aykin (Ed.): Internationalization, Design, LNCS 5623, pp. 180–186, 2009.

In order to fully understand a cyber society, including its strengths and weaknesses, we must first understand the concept of information. We will begin by defining information and other necessary concepts. Then we focus on the Republic of Estonia as an example of an early cyber society. We will also provide a short overview of the cyber attacks against Estonia that took place in the spring of 2007 and provide some lessons learned from this experience. Finally, we will discuss the principles, structure and areas of activity of the Cooperative Cyber Defence Centre of Excellence, which received its NATO accreditation in 2008.

2 Information and Information Corruption

One of the instruments for understanding various objects and processes in the world is "finding" and formally describing the relationships between them. Unfortunately, relationships come in two categories:

- Relationships that can be defined (including definitions using other relationships)
- Relationships that cannot be defined

The last types of relationships are called *fundamental relationships*.

Example. In set theory (see [2] and [3]) the concept of *being an element of* is a fundamental relationship, which is designated with a stylized "e" or the symbol "∈". On the other hand, the concept of *being a subset of* (designated with the symbol "⊆") is not a fundamental relationship, since it can be defined with the concept of *being an element of,* among other things (one set is a subset of another set, if every element of the first set is also an element of the second set).

In this paper we rely on the fundamental relationship of notation-denotation (see [4]), which is designated by a stylized letter "s" or the symbol "∫". If some objects A and B have this relationship, then A is the notation for B and B is the denotation for A. Let us agree that if we have formed an *ordered pair* of A and B, where A is the first element and B is the second element then we write this down as ⟨A,B⟩.

Definition 2. We call an ordered pair ⟨A,B⟩ *knowledge*, if A is the notation (symbol) for B and B is the denotation (meaning) for A. [4]

Note. A and B constitute knowledge, if they have the notation-denotation relationship "∫" or if A∫B.

Often knowledge is represented in text form, but not always.

Example 1. ⟨π, ratio of a circle's circumference to its diameter⟩ is knowledge, because π∫ *ratio of a circle's circumference to its diameter.*

Example 2. ⟨the diagonal of a square, a straight line joining the opposite corners of a square⟩ is knowledge, because *the diagonal of a square ∫ a straight line joining the opposite corners of a square.*

Example 3. A red traffic light is the notation for a prohibition for moving forward. This piece of knowledge (where the color of the traffic light is the notation and the corresponding meaning is the denotation) is necessary for anyone navigating city streets.

Example 4. Hoisting the flag upside down signals distress. Unfortunately, not many are aware of this piece of knowledge, where the "wrong position" of the flag is the notation and the emergency is the denotation.

Definition 3. D is data, if there is such an A, where ⟨A,D⟩ is knowledge, or if there is such a B, where ⟨D,B⟩ is knowledge. [5]

Example. The question – what is the air temperature in the coming days – is answered by a list of numbers. Therefore, the numbers constitute data that is the *denotation* (meaning) of the words "air temperature in the coming days". The question – what do you call the country that shares a land border with only Latvia and Russia – can be answered as "Estonia", "Eesti", "Viro" etc. Therefore, in this case all these words are a *notation* (symbol) for the same country.

Note. In order to have data it is necessary to have the corresponding knowledge. If, for some X nobody knows, has known and will never know, what is the notation or denotation of X, then X *is not* data!

Definition 4. *Information*, or more shortly *info*, is either knowledge or data.

According to the definition, only one that has knowledge or data also has information. If someone holds some X, which is not knowledge or at least part of knowledge (an object in the form of a notation or a denotation), then X is not information. Following the definition the information can be corrupted by using one or more of the three main options:

- corrupt the notation;
- corrupt the denotation;
- corrupt the relationship between notation and denotation.

Depending what operations are done with the information (see [5]) – for example, transmission, storage, manipulation, systematization, destruction etc. - a suitable method can be found to corrupt the operation (which can bring about, but does not require, the corruption of the information itself). For example, enough extra information can be "pumped into" the information transmission channels that the *transmission speed* of the necessary information becomes intolerably slow. In order to corrupt a database or knowledge base it is enough to corrupt the *system*, which can be realized by deleting the data within. A more sophisticated way to corrupt a system would employ moving the data or changing the relationships between data objects etc.

3   Estonia as an Example of an Early Cyber Society

According to the definition in the introduction, a cyber society is based on ubiquitous computing and that a loss of these computer services directly affects the normal existence of this society. Computing deals with manipulating information (knowledge and data) for the benefit of the user. For example, the concept of money no longer requires a physical entity (coins, bills) that can be passed between transaction parties (from one wallet to another). Instead, the passage of wealth can be represented with a simple change of numbers in the related accounts (stored in computer systems). Therefore, money is accompanied with the knowledge about the ownership of namely this specific wealth. In operations with money, old knowledge changes to new knowledge.

The financial sector in Estonia (which is equivalent to the blood circulation in the human body) is almost fully computerized. The following facts are a good illustration of this claim:

- 98% of all bank transactions are completed via electronic means (on-line payments, credit card use, signing up for new bank services on-line etc). [6]
- 88% of all income tax declarations were entered on-line in 2008 and 17% of those on the first day of the declaration period. In 2009, the number of first day declarations rose 43%. [7]

The exchange of information is also largely facilitated by computer systems:

- major newspapers are represented on-line
- some key information forums are only available on-line
- medical records available to doctors via a national information system
- school grades, homework assignments and messages to and from parents are implemented in an e-school system
- Estonian police and courts use an e-case system, which allows for easy sharing of information about criminals

Leadership and management of the society is strongly reliant on computer systems:

- government holds paperless e-cabinet meetings
- local and state elections offer both manual and an electronic vote option

NB! This is not merely using „electronic gadgets" but information transmitting, processing, storing etc. with computers in order to ensure the running of critical processes at the national level! Therefore, many (if not all) of these services should be considered critical information infrastructure and any attacks against them should be viewed in the context of national security. In most cases, attacks against these systems have a tangible effect on ordinary citizens, who can no longer get access to the services they need. This illustrates the dangers of over-dependence between human society and computer networks.

4 An Overview of the 2007 Spring Cyber Attacks Against Estonia

In the spring of 2007 many Estonian government and private information systems came under a wide scale cyber attack campaign that lasted for 22 days, from April 27th to May 18th. The attacks were a response to the Estonian Government's decision to relocate a Soviet WWII monument to a military cemetery. The decision met with much criticism by the Russian authorities, as well as the ethnic Russian minority in Estonia. Following two nights of looting and rioting in Tallinn, a campaign of cyber attacks was launched by presumably ethnic Russian activists, located in Russia, Estonia and elsewhere. To this day no official connection has been made to the Russian government. [8]

Majority of the attacks were relatively simple and robust, using well known methods and vectors. Most prominent were the distributed denial of service attacks (SYN flood, PING flood, mass e-mail etc.) which were launched both manually and via botnets. However, the size and length of the attack was unexpected for most targets and therefore various services were either degraded or disabled throughout the conflict. The most prominent target categories were: government web and e-mail servers, on-line banking services, on-line news services, as well as the network infrastructure (DNS servers and network routers) at ISP level. [8]

It is important to note that this was a purely political attack – there is no information about financial motivation among the attackers. And yet, many "civilian" systems were purposefully targeted, including commercial banks and private news companies. This would indicate that the attackers were interested in damaging the Estonian cyber society in all the relevant categories identified in the introduction:

- targeting the banking infrastructure has serious economic consequences if services remain out of operation for more than a few hours or days
- attacks against news services bring about an (partial) information blockade both nationally and internationally (fortunately alternative media channels were not affected by this attack)
- attacks against government systems diminish the government's ability to properly govern the state.

In this light, the attackers were aiming at critical sectors of the Estonian cyber society, but were fortunately unable to cause serious harm. However, attacks like this are becoming more commonplace and should be addressed at a national level for any country that is in the process of transforming into a cyber society.

5   On Cooperation

An important lesson from these attacks is that the Internet has empowered the people not only by giving them access to information and nearly free communication around the globe, but also by letting people attack any connected target no matter the physical location. While this is usually not a problem, it can become one quickly enough if a critical mass of attackers converges on a target. Simplest denial of service attacks require no training or specialized software, so it is just a matter of finding enough committed attackers and coordinating their effort.

As a result of this relative ease we witness cyber attacks becoming more popular as a tool for political activism. Politically motivated cyber attacks have become commonplace. It is no longer surprising if a military conflict in Israel coincides with hacking on both sides, or if a political row between Russia and its neighbors also escalates into cyber space. In essence, cyber militias are developing in many countries around the world, some of them undoubtedly with the (passive?) support of the interested government. [9]

Since these cyber conflicts lack a clear legal status they usually boil down to technical countermeasures at the service provider and target level. Usually the attacks cross international boundaries, which means that the service providers and incident handlers (computer emergency response teams) need international cooperation in order to stem the tide of the attacks.

6 The Cooperative Cyber Defence Centre of Excellence

Understanding the importance of cooperation in cyber defence, in 2004 Estonia offered to establish and host a multi-national organization focused on developing this aspect within NATO. The Alliance supported this idea and after thorough preparation the Cooperative Cyber Defence Centre of Excellence (CCD COE) was formally established in the spring of 2008 and accredited as an International Military Organization in the fall of 2008. In addition to Estonia, it currently includes six more sponsoring nations: Germany, Italy, Latvia, Lithuania, Slovak Republic and Spain, with a few more in the process of joining the Centre.

The nature of the CCD COE is to develop new concepts, methods, tools, training materials, as well as analytical products. It is by no means intended or equipped as an operations organization, such as the various computer incident response teams etc. Instead, it is designed as a vessel for assisting NATO's transformation process, especially in the matters of cyber defence.

Organizationally the CCD COE is divided into three branches: administrative, research and development, training and doctrine. However, much of the work is done using a virtual matrix structure that "ignores" the official organization chart and uses the necessary manpower as ad-hoc project teams, regardless of the position of the personnel. This allows for a much more flexible approach when tackling complex problems.

7 Summary

As information technology becomes ever more integrated into our daily life, we transform into a cyber society. We have discussed that cyber society is, in fact, an advanced form of human-computer interaction, which encompasses the relationship between a society of humans and a network of computers.

In the preceding sections we have briefly covered the definition of information that is based on the concept of knowledge and main principles to corrupting it. We defined the concept of cyber society, identified Estonia as an early cyber society and examined the cyber attacks that brought this into focus in 2007. Finally, we discussed the principles behind the establishment and running of the Cooperative Cyber Defence Centre of Excellence.

References

1. Wiener, N.: The human use of human beings. Cybernetics and society. Doubleday Anchor Books, Doubleday&Company, Inc., Garden City, New York (1956)
2. Fraenkel, A.A., Bar-Hillel, Y.: Foundations of Set Theory. North-Holland Publishing Company, Amsterdam (1958)
3. Potter, M.: Set Theory and its Philosophy. Oxford University Press, Inc., New York (2004)
4. Lorents, P.: Formalization of data and knowledge based on the fundamental notation-denotation relation. In: Proceedings of the International Conference on Artificial Intelligence, IC-AI 2001, Las Vegas, USA. USA, vol. III, pp. 1297–1301. CSREA Press (2001)

5. Lorents, P.: Knowledge and Taxonomy of Intellect. In: Proceedings of the International Conference on Artificial Intelligence, IC-AI 2008, Las Vegas, USA, July 25-28, vol. II, pp. 484–489. CSREA Press (2008)
6. Hiie, I.: Sulgkerged teenuste halduse protsessid. In: ITSMF 2007 conference, Tallinn, Estonia, November 22 (2007),
   `http://www.itsmf.ee/itsmf2007/`
   `itsmf_estonia_2007_sulgkerged_protsessid.pdf` (last accessed March 16, 2009)
7. Estonian Tax and Customs Board: Press Release (February 16, 2009),
   `http://www.emta.ee/?id=25369&tpl=1026` (last accessed March 15, 2009)
8. Ottis, R.: Analysis of the 2007 Cyber Attacks Against Estonia From the Information Warfare Perspective. In: Proceedings of the 7th European Conference on Information Warfare and Security, Plymouth, UK, June 30-July 1, pp. 163–168. Academic Publishing Limited, Reading (2008)
9. Ottis, R.: Theoretical Model for Creating a Nation-State Level Offensive Cyber Capability. In: Proceedings of the 8th European Conference on Information Warfare and Security, Lisbon, Portugal, July 6-7, 2009 (accepted for publication)

Constructing a Model of Internet-Based Career Information System for Industrial Design Students in Universities

Ming-Ying Yang[1], Manlai You[2], Ya-Lin Tu[3], and Yung-Ping Chou[1]

[1] Dept. of Industrial Design, National United University
1, Lienda, Miaoli, Taiwan 36003
ymy@nuu.edu.tw
[2] Dept. of Industrial Design, National Yunlin University of Science and Technology
123 University Road, Section 3, Douliu, Yunlin, Taiwan 64002
youm@yuntech.edu.tw
[3] Dept. of Industrial Design, Huafan Unversity
1 Huafan Rd., Shihding Township, Taiwan 22301
tuooid@cc.hfu.edu.tw

Abstract. This study aims to propose a model of Industrial Design Career Information System (IDCIS) to help ID students plan their career. The study was divided into three stages. The content analysis of nine relevant websites framed a basic structure of IDCIS. Next, four focus groups with a total of twenty-four ID students were interviewed to find out what career information they would like to know. Finally, a web-based model of IDCIS was simulated and eight ID students were invited to provide their feedback. The outcome would provide an integrated base to help students be aware of the ID profession and plan their career in advance during the school years. Also, the process of constructing a model of IDCIS adopted by this study could be a reference for other fields.

Keywords: Industrial Design, Career Information System, Design Education, Career Guidance.

1 Introduction

Studies show that college students demand more for the career guidance than for the academics and life guidance, especially for vocational choices and career planning [1-2]. When students make their career decisions, they need to know the information about occupations, educational institutions, training programs, potential employers, industries, family, leisure, and so on. The functions of career information acquisition include: 1) to narrow the options; 2) to help individuals to know what occupations match their values, interests, skills, family conditions, and needs for training and educational programs; 3) to understand what training plans and educational institutions are helpful to individuals before entering occupations; 4) to understand what the job objectives, industries, and employers can match individual's values, interests and skills; 5) to help individuals to prepare job interviews [3].

N. Aykin (Ed.): Internationalization, Design, LNCS 5623, pp. 187–196, 2009.

Following technological development, Internet-aided career guidance has been popular recently, and it can satisfy the preliminary, preventive, and repetitive career guidance needs of students in universities without time and space constraints [4]. It also would alleviate the shortage of guidance personnel in universities [5]. College students can collect online and updated career information via Internet. They also can connect to other career resources within and out of campus, which facilitate their interactions and communications with others. In addition, students do not have to go to career centers in person within the office hours for receiving career information. Therefore, students do not have to seek help face-to-face, and the cost of printed career booklets can be significantly reduced. Although the Internet may provide abundant online career information, sometimes the information comes in excessive amounts and unorganized; without effect guidance, students may waste much time on digesting the information [6-7]. Moreover, career information currently provided by most of career service websites covers as many programs and occupations as possible. Since it is necessary to consider the characteristics and specialty for individual professionals when providing career information, a career information system capable of automatically customizing career guidance for information requesters becomes important. The current study is aimed to develop such a system for ID students.

The ID profession covers various specialties, and indeed there are diverse employment opportunities in the job market for the ID graduates. However, the above information about the ID profession is not complete and presented systematically yet. The development of ID education in Taiwan has a history spanning more than forty years. Students in Taiwan spend most of their time in studying and surviving examinations, and consequently their career exploration tasks at each stage are not well developed [8]. A study shows 58% of ID students in Taiwan are acquainted with contents and future development of the ID profession when they decided to study ID [9]. In addition, ID programs in universities nowadays recruit students through different channels with various backgrounds. As a consequence, ID students may vary considerably in their abilities, aptitudes, and career goals, and they are in an urgent need of appropriate career guidance [10]. The authors have conducted a series of studies about the career guidance needs and aim to construct guidance models of ID students in universities of Taiwan. The needs of career guidance for ID students include: 1) exploration of their own aptitudes and interests; 2) a better understanding of the ID profession; 3) understanding the connections between their course work and the job requirements; 4) understanding of the match between themselves and jobs; 5) assistance in finding internship and employment; 6) knowing about advanced studies and exams; 7) learning about career planning and career decision making; and 8) providing career consultation and role models [10]. This paper is aimed to propose a model of Industrial Design Career Information System (IDCIS) for satisfying ID students' needs on career information. The outcome of this study is significant to both design education and profession. It would help students to be aware of the ID profession and plan their career in advance during the school years.

2   Research Design

The study was conducted in three stages: 1) content analysis of relevant websites; 2) focus group interviews; and 3) constructing, simulating and evaluating a model of

IDCIS. Firstly, the authors used keywords, "career guidance" and "career center", on the Google search engine to collect and browse websites of career guidance organizations and career centers in universities. Also, in order to consider the specialty for design domain, the authors referred the contents and structures about career information provided by some official websites of ID, creative industries, and architecture communities and organizations. In other words, the authors adopted the purposive sampling method to include three types of websites: career guidance organizations, career centers in universities, and design related professions providing the concept of career development. The top 150 websites were browsed, and three of the most complete websites were selected for each category respectively.

In the final stage, the authors analyzed the contents of nine websites: 1) career guidance organizations - CareerInfoNet [11], iseek [12], Prospects.ac.uk [13]; 2) career centers in universities - FSU Career Center [14], Stanford University Career Development Center [15], NC State University Career Center [16] ; 3) design related professions - IDSA [17], Architecture.com [18], Your Creative Future [19]. With regard to the process of content analysis for websites, the authors selected the websites, listed the contents for each category and item one by one, drew the framework for each website, compared the frequency for each item. Then, the authors summarized the contents and features to be included within the career information system as a basic framework for the IDCIS.

Next, four focus groups (composed by freshmen, sophomores, juniors, and seniors respectively) with a total of twenty-four ID students (11 males and 13 females) were interviewed to find out what information about ID career they would like to know. The participants were sampled for each focus group to consider the variety of gender, the entry channel to university, and backgrounds in the senior high schools. The instruments included a semi-structured outline, a tape recorder, and finally a transcript of each interview for analysis.

Then, based on analyzing the students' opinions, the authors proposed a model of IDCIS. A web-based model of IDCIS was simulated and presented, and eight ID students (four males and four females) were invited to provide their feedback to the simulated model.

3   Content Analysis of Relevant Websites

The contents and categories of each of the websites were analyzed and thereby reduced to essential function items a career information system should have. The deduced function items were further classified into five gross categories: career overview, education and training, seeking a job, resource links, and personalized functions. Table 1 shows the comparison in frequencies over the function items appearing in the websites. The functions of occupation description, information for further studies, preparing for job finding, corporate information, career planning resources, and consultation & help are most frequent. On the other hand, the information of professional training, certificate, professional activity and competition, beginning an undertaking, and international employment and education opportunities in other countries were less frequently demanded. Despite the low frequency, the demand is still significant. Because of the diversity of the nine selected websites and the variations in types of available information, all the reduced function items were held till further filtering evaluation was done.

Table 1. Comparison in frequencies over the function items in relevant websites

Type of websites / Category & function items	Career guidance organizations			Career center in university			Design related professions			frequency
	a1	a2	a3	b1	b2	b3	c1	c2	c3	
Career overview										
Occupation description	•	•		•	•	•	•	•	•	8
Employment trends			•		•					2
Related occupations	•	•	•							3
Sharing of career experiences			•		•				•	3
Self-evaluation tools				•	•	•				3
Education & training										
Career development stages in university				•	•	•		•		4
Information for further studies	•	•		•	•	•	•	•		7
Career training information			•							1
Certificate information	•									1
Professional activity and competition information							•	•		2
Scholarships or other financial subsidies	•				•		•	•		4
Seeking a job										
Preparation for job finding	•		•	•	•	•		•		6
Job vacancy information		•	•	•	•					4
Corporate information	•	•	•	•	•	•		•		7
Industry information	•	•			•					3
Regional manpower information	•	•						•		3
Information for beginning an undertaking		•						•		2
Resource links										
Other professional resources				•			•	•	•	4
International employment and education information			•							1
Career planning resources	•	•	•		•	•				5
Personalized functions										
Personal skill profile	•		•	•						3
Personal career portfolio			•	•	•					3
Career chat-room			•							1
Consultation & help			•	•	•	•	•			5
Discussion forum			•				•	•		3
Job shadowing					•					1

a1: CareerInfoNet; a2: iseek; a3: Prospects.ac.uk; b1: FSU Career Center; b2: Stanford University Career Center Student Service; b3: NC State University Career Center; c1: IDSA; c2: Architecture.com; c3: Your Creative Future

The respective contents of each function items in each of the categories are described as follows. The category of *career overview* provides the students with information about various occupations as well as a mapping to a student's aptitude and available skills. The descriptive information of an occupation includes job description, graduate employment rate, related occupations, career experiences sharing, and tools for self-evaluation. The category of *education and training* provides the students with information about education opportunities provided by various channels, on- and off-campus, from the university entrance to post graduation, which includes career development tasks in the university years, graduate school information, vocational training information, professional certificate information, professional activity and competition information announcements, scholarships and other subsidies. The category of *seeking a job* provides the students with information about job selection, which includes information of preparing job hunting, job vacancies, company situations, industry situation, labor data in various regions, and the know-how of starting an enterprise. The category of *resource links* provides the students with information about professional knowledge, employment and education in other countries, and career planning. The category of *personalized functions* provides the students with information about personal skill analysis, career portfolio, career chat room, asking for consultation, discussion forum and job shadowing.

4 Constructing a Model of IDCIS

4.1 Focus Group Interviews

The main points of the results of the focus interviewing are described as follows. A total of twenty-four students in four focus groups heard about ID from different information channels. Most of the interviewed students knew little about the career opportunities in ID, or some of them had misconception of the career when entering universities, which caused significant confusion during the subsequent school years. Some interviewees later became familiar with future job orientation via experiences sharing from senior students or teachers. Some of the interviewees extrapolated possible future job opportunities mainly from what they have been learning in the department. Very few of the interviewees got to know the actual workplaces in the ID domain through attending cooperative programs with the industry or internship. What the interviewed students wanted to know the most about future jobs are the know-how of starting their own business, job contents, salary, employee qualification, and career anchor. Beside information related to future jobs, the interviewees' information needs polarize toward further studies and resources of realistic design examples.

With regard to career consultation service, the current websites already provide such service via the Internet; however, the persons who provide counseling are either teachers or career counselors. The interviewees showed a strong demand of peer consultation. Therefore, the future career information system will incorporate senior students in providing career consultation. It is also found that the interviewees hold a positive attitude toward tools of aptitude test, but the result of such tests has little influence on their career decisions. Thus, the test tools are viewed as additional resources and will not be a category.

In a nutshell, the initial contents and structure for the IDCIS, as derived from content analysis of the nine selected websites, can meet most of the needs raised by the interviewed ID students. However, the needs of learning resources and peer consultation and help cannot be satisfied by currently available websites. The authors therefore included these two services respectively in the categories of links to resources and personalized functions. The authors integrated the results from the content analysis of the websites and the focus group interviews and then proposed a preliminary structure for IDCIS, which consists of 27 function items, as shown in Figure 1.

4.2   Proposing a Model of IDCIS

In order to understand what the ID students thought about the appropriate structure of a career information system, the authors built a set of web pages simulating and expressing the initial design idea for the students to provide their feedback. The web pages were made by Dreamweaver and Photoshop software. The contents expressed within the web pages that simulating the preliminary system were retrieved by: 1) relevant information in Chinese found by the Google search engine from government, enterprise, ID related, and personal websites; and 2) information taken from the nine selected websites and translated into Chinese.

Table 2 shows the respective contents of items in each of the categories. Figure 2 is an example of the arrangement of the web pages. The content items on the second level under a category are listed on the left-hand side of the page. For this example, the category is occupation description, and therefore the items shown on the left are job description, graduate employment rate, related occupations, career experiences sharing, and tools for self-evaluation. If the job description is selected, the central portion of the page will show an introduction to an industrial designer. When another content item is selected, the information will be shown in a same fashion.

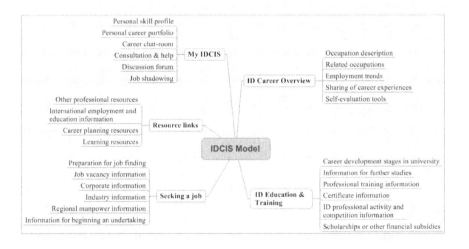

Fig.1. A structure for the model of IDCIS

4.3 Students' Feedback

The authors invited eight students, two from each grade, to provide their feedback about the model of IDCIS. Their opinions were classified into three categories: positive opinions, negative opinions, and questions/suggestions for future operation of the system.

Generally speaking, the students affirmatively supported the design concept of the IDCIS. They agreed with the idea of integrating the otherwise distributed resources of career information within a single website, which makes planning career development easy for the ID students. This is exactly what the students need with regard to their respective career planning. The function of "personal skill profile" was highly praised because the students felt it would be an effective reference for making career decisions. However, the scale meter therein was too lengthy to answer. It was also mentioned by the evaluating students that the information appeared on the web page contained too many texts, easily causing a loss of patience. This study is focused on the evaluation of items and categories of career information that meet ID students' needs. Thus, the issues of web usability and esthetics will be considered in a later stage of the system development.

Fig. 2. An example of the arrangement of the web pages

It is also found that there exist significant differences in needs of information among student groups of different grades. Therefore, in a future version of the information system, students of different grades could be provided with different categories of information. Alternatively, a hierarchy of information can be designed for displaying introductory and easily comprehensible information on the first layer; simultaneously, links to more advanced information could be displayed. Also, language translation could be an obstacle to the students with regard to reading comprehension and therefore

Table 2. The content of items in the model of IDCIS

ID Career Overview	
Occupation description	Describing ID occupation in terms of its occupation activities, job situations, work environments, aptitudes of the workers, occupation prospects, associated preparations for entering ID, in the forms of text or video.
Employment trends	Detailing employment trends of graduates, such as: employment rate, job titles, and percentage of graduates pursuing further studies.
Related occupations	Introducing other possible related occupations and their descriptions for graduates
Sharing of career experiences	Sharing of career experiences and role models by professionals.
Self-evaluation tools	Providing introduction to useful self-evaluation tools for measuring skill, interest, personality, and value systems; Providing many-to-one connection to a personal skill profile.
ID Education & Training	
Career development stages in university	Providing mechanism for organizing a statement of career development tasks of each year in the university.
Information for further studies	Providing information for further studies in domestic or foreign universities, such as information about schools, departments, admission and entrance examinations.
Professional training information	Providing course and contact information about institutions of job training programs.
Certificate information	Providing information related to certificates and licenses, such as issuing institutions, qualifications, and examination dates.
Professional activity and competition information	Posting information about professional activities and competitions.
Scholarships or other financial subsidies	Providing the application information of scholarships and other financial subsidies.
Seeking a job	
Preparation for job finding	Facilitating the preparation of curriculum vitae, job application letters, recommendation letters, portfolios, job interviews, and the construction of personal networks.
Job vacancy information	Providing access to a built-in databank of vacancies for full-time, part-time, and internships jobs, and links to web-pages of job banks and public/private organizations' recruits.
Corporate information	Providing information about employers, such as company names, persons in charge, business types, business sizes, recruiting channels, positions, job contents, recruiting qualifications, job training programs, contact information, company website links.
Industry information	Providing industry overview, strength/weakness analysis, main role in economy, job description and suggestions, employment trend, and growth rate.
Regional manpower information	Providing data of labor population, unemployment rate, average household income, per capital income, job ranking, average education, and major employers.
Information for beginning an undertaking	Providing information about available resources, regulations and legal issues, trade norm of fees, and contract specifications.
Resource links	
Other professional resources	Introducing the publication information about professional magazines and books. Providing links of professional organizations and corporate websites.
International employment and education information	Providing links to websites about general information, education, emigration, and job vacancies.
Career planning resources	Providing contact information of career service organizations, evaluation tools, and employment and education information in other countries.
Learning resources	Providing information about trends, innovative ideas, materials, technology, design tools, shops, etc. to inspire ID students.
My IDCIS	
Personal skill profile	Providing a skill measurement form for analyzing the fitness of personal skills to the job requirements of an occupation.
Personal career portfolio	Organizing personal profile, skill learning portfolio, curriculum vitae, portfolio, references and recommendation files; setting of access restriction for viewing the personal career portfolio.
Career chat-room	Providing students with instant message service for discussing with corporate staff representatives or guidance professionals about career related questions.
Consultation & help	With various practitioners, councilors, instructors, or senior students serving as career guidance volunteers, student users seek help from a selected volunteer via sending him/her an email with career questions for consultation.
Discussion forum	Providing a user-friendly platform for discussing job-related issues with text asynchronously.
Job shadowing	Applying for job projection activities and online viewing video files.

a problem that influenced the web content evaluation. Further, since there exists no professional certificate for industrial design in Taiwan yet, some interviewees suggested that the item of "certificate information" be removed.

The interviewees highly expected the actualization of the career information system in the near future; but they are also concerned with issues like: "Who will lead and maintain the development for the system?" and "Who will participate in and facilitate the project?"

5 Conclusion

ID students are looking forward to information about professional skills, design workplaces, practical training and job opportunities, advanced study, and design affairs that motivate learning; they further need a platform for consultation by professionals on issues of career planning. Neither current websites aimed at career planning guidance nor others related to ID profession can satisfy students' needs for career development. This study proposes the idea of integrating career information of various categories in the field of industrial design at a single website, which includes occupation descriptions, further studies, job opportunities, career planning, and design resources. Moreover, the platform includes novel functions of "personal skill profile" and "personal career portfolio" for assisting the students in evaluating own professional skills and recording various skill learning processes.

This study is mainly a conceptual development of such a career information system. In the concept, the career information in the field of ID will be delivered via the Internet by ID promotional units or professional organizations to ID students in universities and senior high school students who are interested in the field. This study is focused on understanding what students think about the model of IDCIS. The students generally supported the design concept of the IDCIS. Meanwhile, they offered suggestions for improvements in web interface usability, webpage esthetics, hierarchy of information based on comprehensibility, what kind of persons should facilitate the operation of the system, and so on. Because career information covers a wide range, huge amounts of manpower and resources should be invested in the construction phase of the system. Before the operation, complete career information in the field of industrial design has to be collected, and norms necessary for self skill evaluation must be built to form a huge database. Furthermore, the function of career consultation cannot be done without the support of the professional community of industrial design. The results from the current study can be regarded as a basic system structure for assisting the ID students in their career planning. On the other hand, the research process that includes the steps of website content analysis, focus group interviews, reduction to function items and the associated user evaluation of the system may have some reference value for building career information systems in other professional fields.

Acknowledgements. This research was partly supported by the National Science Council of the Republic of China under Project No. NSC93-2213-E-224-003.

References

1. Jin, S.R., Lin, C.S., Tian, S.L.: The Career Development of Chinese College Students in Taiwan (in Chinese). Bulletin of Educational Psychology 22, 167–190 (1989)
2. Sie, S.W., Liao, J.M., Lin, W.S., Cai, P.J.: Choices-Seniors' Feelings about Their Career Decisions (in Chinese). Journal of Social Science 9, 153–182 (2001)
3. America's Career InfoNet (2006/03/11), http://www.acinet.org/acinet/exp_info.asp
4. Huang, D.S., You, S.J.: Career Guidance for Teenagers in E Generation. The Guidance Information of High School in Taiwan 63, 31–37 (2000)
5. Sampson Jr., J.P.: Enhancing the Use of Career Information with Computer-Assisted Career Guidance Systems. In: The Present and Future of Computer Assisted Career Guidance Systems in Japan. Symposium conducted at the meeting of The Japan Institute of Labor, Tokyo, Japan (1997)
6. Kirk, J.J.: Web-Assisted Career Counseling. Journal of Employment Counseling 37, 146–159 (2000)
7. McCarthy, C.J., Moller, N., Beard, L.M.: Suggestions for Training Students in Using the Internet for Career Counseling. The Career Development Quarterly 51(4), 368–382 (2003)
8. Ministry of Education Student Affairs Committee, Planning of Career Guidance for Undergraduate (in Chinese). Student Guidance 30, 58–69 (1994)
9. Yang, M.Y.: A Study on the Construction of Internet-Aided Career Guidance Model for Industrial Design Students in Universities (in Chinese), Unpublished Dissertation, Institute of Design at National Yunlin University of Science & Technology (2005)
10. Yang, M.Y., You, M., Chen, F.C.: A Study on the Difficulties and Career Guidance Needs of Industrial Design Students: Implications for Design Education (in Chinese). Design Journal 10(2), 57–76 (2005)
11. CareerInfoNet (2005/02/01), http://www.acinet.org/acinet/default.asp
12. iseek (2005/02/05), http://www.iseek.org
13. Prospects.ac.uk (2005/02/10), http://www.prospects.ac.uk/
14. FSU Career Center (2004/02/22), http://www.career.fsu.edu/
15. Stanford University Career Development Center (2005/02/24), http://cardinalcareers.stanford.edu/students/
16. NC State University Career Center (2005/02/24), http://www.ncsu.edu/career
17. IDSA (Industrial Designers Society of America) (2005/03/07),http://www.idsa.org
18. Architecture.com (2005/02/25), http://www.architecture.com/go/Architecture/Home.html
19. Your Creative Future, http://www.yourcreativefuture.org.uk

Factors Affecting Online Game Players' Loyalty

Fan Zhao and Xiaowen Fang

Lutgert College of Business, Florida Gulf Coast University
School of Computing, College of Computing and Digital Media, DePaul University
fzhao@fgcu.edu, xfang@cdm.depaul.edu

Abstract. In the past decade, online games have become an important electronic commerce application. A good understanding of customer online game
behaviors is critical for both researchers and practitioners, such as game vendors and game developers. Many researchers focus their studies on the consumers' intention to play online games. However, the industry becomes more and
more interested in the key factors to retain customers. To tackle the retention
problem, this paper proposes a research framework of online game play loyalty.
Based on this framework, thirteen hypotheses were developed and tested
through a survey in U.S. universities. Overall, the results indicate the following:
1) Online game technology factors, such as the game story, game graphics,
game length, game control and online game services, have significant impact on
players' game enjoyment; 2) Game enjoyment and social norms have positive
effects on intention to play; 3) Social norms, quality of online game community
and intention to play are important predictors of online game loyalty.

Keywords: online games, loyalty, intention, enjoyment.

1 Introduction

In recent years, online games have gained popularity around the world. According to
the new Online Game Market Forecasts report by DFC Intelligence [10], PC online
game revenue alone passed $7 billion in 2007 (not including video online games).
Online games are computer controlled games, including both PC games and video
games, played by consumers over network technology, especially through the Internet. Online games can be categorized into multiplayer and single-player games. At
present, multiplayer games, especially massively multiplayer online games (MMOG)
are most successful among all online games. World of Warcraft, one of the famous
MMOG, surpasses 11 million monthly subscribers this year.

The rapid growth of online games has caught the attention of the gaming industry.
Investigation of consumers' online behavior becomes critical. According to Lo and
Chen [18], the profitable life cycle of an online game goes down to 8 months to a year
from 18 months to 3 years in average in the past. This means majority online game
players switch their games every 8-18 months. Typical customers only focus on one
or two online games at a certain time and customers are demanding on all aspects of
the online games, including game stories, game graphics, game services, and so
on [26]. Therefore, it is increasingly important to study the key factors for retaining

N. Aykin (Ed.): Internationalization, Design, LNCS 5623, pp. 197–206, 2009.

customers in the game. As suggested by Semeijin et al. [22], maintaining customer loyalty not only lowers the cost of acquiring new customer, but also brings in substantial revenues. Typically, the longer time players play the online games, the more money they will spend on the game, and this will bring more revenue to the game vendors or developers. Few empirical research has been conducted on how to extend current customers' playing time or how to increase online game players' loyalty. The purpose of this study is to exam what factors affect online game adoption and how to extend online game playing time.

2   Theoretical Background and Research Framework

Based on the technology acceptance model (TAM) [9] and previous studies, we propose a conceptual online game loyalty model as depicted in Figure 1. This model integrates the motivational perspective into the original TAM. Discussions of this model are presented in the following sections.

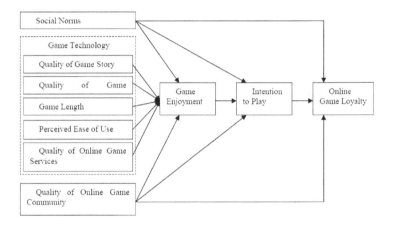

Fig. 1. Conceptual Online Game Loyalty Model

2.1   Social Norms

Social factors profoundly impact on user behavior. The theory of reasoned action (TRA) [1] suggests that a person's behavioral intentions are influenced by subjective norms as well as attitude. Hsu and Lu [15] indicate that social influences, including perceived critical mass and social norms, significantly and directly, but separately, affect player attitude and intention of playing online games. Choi and Kim [8] also note the importance of social interactions on continuing to play online games. Additionally, Chang, Lee, & Kim [5] emphasize the impact of perceived popularity on online game adoption and continuance among South Korea college students. Thus, we propose that social norms impact on game enjoyment, intention to play and online game loyalty:

H1. There is a positive relationship between social norms and online game enjoyment.

H2. There is a positive relationship between social norms and intention to play.

H3. There is a positive relationship between social norms and online game loyalty.

2.2 Game Technology

Product quality is one of the crucial factors influencing customers' consumption [6]. For online products, since most purchasing and service activities are completed over the Internet, both product quality and service quality are important determinants of customers' behavioral intentions [3]. As online products, online games' quality is important. It includes but not limited to game story, game graphics, game length, and game operations.

Game Story. Most online games create virtual environments in the game. Game stories are often used to immerse game players in the virtual world. A good story attracts players' attention and increases players' curiosity to explore the virtual world. The story makes the game more enjoyable and fulfilling. These attractive tasks, like projects in real life, keep players continuously returning to the game whenever they have time to play [23]. A good story offers a wonderful growing space for the actors created in the game. From the beginning of the story, game players "watch" and "feel" the growth of their actors along the story phases. The good story environment let the players create the history using their actors in the virtual world. The players will cherish the stories they created in the game and this will bring them enormous enjoyment in the game and let them forget all the unpleasant things in their real lives [26]. Thus, we proposed that quality of game story impacts on game enjoyment:

H4. There is a positive relationship between quality of game story and online game enjoyment.

Game Graphics. Graphic attractiveness is a key element in creating an enjoyable user experience in online games [26]. Graphic designs for online games consist of static graphics, movement graphics and special graphics. Static graphics refer to the non-movement items in the game environment. A better design of static graphics makes players feel more real in the virtual world. Movement graphics includes all the movement design in the game, such as running, fighting, etc. A better movement graphics construct more precise and nuanced characters and creatures in the game. Special graphics are animations and special actions or poses for the characters in the game. Animations will increase enjoyment in the game and special actions or poses will represent reality. Graphics play a central role in how people perceive and enjoy the game experience [12]. It gives the player a whole new level of feel, excitement and atmosphere. Therefore, the better the graphics, the more enjoyment [7]. We propose that quality of game graphics impacts on game enjoyment:

H5. There is a positive relationship between quality of game graphics and online game enjoyment.

Game Length. The game length refers to the average time game players complete the online games by reaching the highest level of the actors, winning the final game items, or completing all the core game tasks. There is no best number to target regarding online game length because each online game is unique with special story and special game settings. However, there could be an ideal length uniquely for each game [28]. For a certain game, players will not have enough time to enjoy the story and all the graphic designs in the game if the game is too short. On the other hand, if the length of the online game is extended too long, players may be exhausted and eventually quit if they can hardly see the end of the road. Additionally, since game players enter the same online games in different times, some players may find 'unfair' situations if they enter the game very late. An appropriate game length will lead to an enjoyable experience. Thus, we propose that game length impacts on game enjoyment:

H6. There is a positive relationship between appropriate game length and online game enjoyment.

Perceived Ease of Use. The technology acceptance model (TAM) [9] is one of the most widely used models for IT adoption. According to TAM, an individual's IT adoption is influenced by perceived usefulness and perceived ease of use. Perceived ease of use (PEOU) refers to the degree to which a person believes that using a particular system would be free of effort. In a gaming context, perceived usefulness is no longer applicable and therefore not an appropriate measure of extrinsic motivation [24]. Perceived ease of use focuses on the use of the interface of the online games. We propose that perceived ease of use impacts on game enjoyment:

H7. There is a positive relationship between perceived ease of use and online game enjoyment.

Quality of Online Game Services. Service quality is one of the key factors in e-commerce success [25]. The quality of online game services are evaluated directly by game players according to the response promptness, problem solving ability, problem solving time, information richness of the game, attention to particular player needs, promise-keeping, game master (instant helper in the game) service behavior, and so on. Online players will perceive the services and make their judgments to determine the service quality. Their judgments significantly impact on their enjoyment of the game playing [14]. Thus, we propose that quality of online game services impacts on game enjoyment:

H8. There is a positive relationship between quality of online game services and online game enjoyment.

2.3 Online Game Community

An online community is defined as social groups of people who communicate with each other via network technology, such as Internet. Through the online game community, players share their game information, seek helps from the community for game activities, and even build their social network beyond the game. This community network encourages player intention to play the game and eventually increase their loyalty to the game [15]. Thus, we propose that quality of online game services impacts on game enjoyment, intention to play and online game loyalty:

H9. There is a positive relationship between quality of online game community and online game enjoyment.

H10. There is a positive relationship between quality of online game community and intention to play.

H11. There is a positive relationship between quality of online game community and online game loyalty.

2.4 Game Enjoyment

Strong empirical evidence indicates that the motivational basis of human activity relies on two rather independent systems: a so-called approach system and an avoidance system [11]. Activation of the approach system results in pleasure, whereas activation of the avoidance system leads to pain [2]. Research in psychology and neuroscience most often uses the term pleasure to describe agreeable reactions to experiences in general. Most communication researchers have used the term enjoyment to describe and explain such positive reactions toward the media and its contents. Our framework uses enjoyment to describe and explain positive reactions derived from game play. According to previous studies [14, 17, 24], perceived enjoyment significantly impacts on customers' intention to use online services or systems. Thus, we propose that game enjoyment impacts on intention to play:

H12. There is a positive relationship between game enjoyment and intention to play.

2.5 Intention to Play and Online Game Loyalty

Intention to play is the positive attitude or preference to play online games. Most studies adopting the theory of reasoned action (TRA) focus on intention to use certain information systems [17, 24]... However, intention to play only means that the customers have positive attitude or preference to play the game [19]. They may not continue to play the games in the future if there are new games available. However, customer loyalty has become one of the important issues in e-commerce. Loyal customers will keep a longer relationship with the business and use the services for a longer time [21]. Loyalty is the intention to keep using certain services or systems. In this article, we define online game loyalty as the degree to which game players believe that they will continue to play the game. Thus, we propose that intention to play has an impact on online game loyalty:

H13. There is a positive relationship between intention to play and online game loyalty.

3 Methodology

3.1 Data Collection

A survey was conducted in two U.S. universities. A total of 315 usable questionnaires were collected. Among the respondents, 173 were male and 142 were female. All of the accepted participants have experience of playing online games (average playing time is 7.2 hours/week).

3.2 Measures

The measures of this study were adapted from previous studies with modifications to fit the specific context of the online game playing. All the measurements were phrased on a seven-point Likert scale, from 1=strongly disagree to 7=strongly agree. Table 1 shows the instrument references for the survey questionnaires.

Table 1. Instrument References

Construct	References
Social Norms	[27]
Quality of Game Story	[26]
Quality of Game Graphics	[26]
Game Length	[26]
Perceived Ease of use	[15]
Quality of Online game services	[14]
Quality of Online game community	[14]
Game enjoyment	[27]
Intention to play	[5]
Online game loyalty	[19]

4 Results

In the data analysis, we first validated the reliability and validity of the measurements and then conducted a structural modeling analysis.

4.1 The Measurement Model

Reliability. As Fornell [13] and Nunnally [20] suggest, a composite reliability of 0.70 or above and an average variance extracted of more than 0.50 are deemed acceptable. Table 2 shows the composite reliabilities range from 0.76 to 0.91 and the average variance extracted ranges from 0.53 to 0.76 for all the measures.

Validity. Table 3 shows that the square root of average variance extracted for each construct is greater than the correlations between the constructs and all other constructs. This implies that constructs are empirically distinct. The results suggest an adequate discriminate validity of the measurements.

Table 2. Reliability Measures

Construct	Item	Loading	Composite reliability	Average variance extracted
Social Norms	SN1	0.65	0.77	0.58
	SN2	0.78		
	SN3	0.85		
Quality of Game Story	GS1	0.82	0.85	0.65
	GS2	0.74		
	GS3	0.88		
Quality of Game Graphics	GG1	0.85	0.83	0.62
	GG2	0.81		
	GG3	0.79		
Game Length	GL1	0.77	0.79	0.56
	GL2	0.85		
	GL3	0.74		
Perceived Ease of use	PE1	0.88	0.86	0.69
	PE2	0.84		
	PE3	0.79		
Quality of Online game services	QS1	0.81	0.87	0.68
	QS2	0.90		
	QS3	0.84		
Quality of Online game community	QC1	0.77	0.86	0.67
	QC2	0.89		
	QC3	0.85		
Game enjoyment	GE1	0.82	0.88	0.67
	GE2	0.81		
	GE3	0.91		
Intention to play	I1	0.90	0.89	0.68
	I2	0.86		
	I3	0.88		
Online game loyalty	L1	0.93	0.90	0.75
	L2	0.85		
	L3	0.87		
	L4	0.91		

4.2 The Structural Model

We adopted maximum likelihood method to estimate the framework. According to Browne & Cudeck [4] and Joreskeg & Sorbom [16], an acceptable fit exists where AFGI>0.80 and RMSEA<0.10. The fit statistics indicate that the research model provides a good fit to the data (AGFI=0.89; RMSEA=0.07). Figure 2 shows the results of structural modeling analysis. The findings indicated that game technology, including quality of game story, quality of game graphics, game length, perceived ease of use, and quality of online game services) posited a significant effect on game enjoyment. Social Norms did not have any significant impact on game enjoyment. However, it had significant direct effects on both intention to play and online game loyalty. Quality of online game community exhibited significant impact on online game loyalty, but the data did not support quality of online game community as a predictor to both game enjoyment and intention to play. In summary, the results supported hypothesis 2, 3, 4, 5, 6, 7, 8, 11, 12 and 13, respectively.

Table 3. Correlation Matrix of the Constructs

	SN	GS	GG	GL	PE	QS	QC	GE	I	L
Social Norms (SN)	0.67									
Quality of Game Story (GS)	0.18	0.75								
Quality of Game Graphics (GG)	0.11	0.15	0.65							
Game Length (GL)	0.21	0.12	0.16	0.70						
Perceived Ease of use (PE)	0.17	0.24	0.19	0.21	0.62					
Quality of Online game services (QS)	0.13	0.19	0.23	0.16	0.22	0.78				
Quality of Online game community (QC)	0.22	0.12	0.11	0.10	0.18	0.27	0.82			
Game enjoyment (GE)	0.27	0.20	0.19	0.23	0.26	0.17	0.21	0.70		
Intention to play (I)	0.18	0.17	0.20	0.15	0.18	0.25	0.27	0.42	0.76	
Online game loyalty (L)	0.10	0.14	0.16	0.17	0.11	0.22	0.36	0.38	0.52	0.79

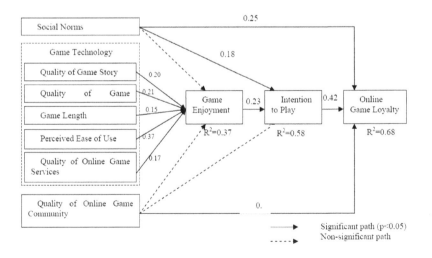

Fig. 2. Results of Structural Modeling Analysis

5 Conclusions

The purpose of this study was to exam the key factors affecting customers' online game loyalty. The measurement model was confirmed with adequate convergent and discriminant validity. The structural model provided a good fit to the data. Seven of the ten paths were found statistically significant and the remaining three paths (from Social Norms to game enjoyment, from quality of online game community to both game enjoyment and intention to play) were not significant. The results showed that technology factors of an online game, such as the game story, game graphics, game length, ease of use of the game and online game services, played an important role in players' game enjoyment. Social norms were found an important predictor to both intention to play and online game loyalty, but not to game enjoyment. Interestingly, quality of online game community influenced online game loyalty, but it did not posit a significant impact on both game enjoyment and intention to play. Online game community provides game related information for players. It may not directly impact players' perspectives about playing the game. In other words, players can gather useful information about online games from the community, but they may not feel enjoyable by collecting the information from the website. Similarly, visiting community may not directly stimulate customers' intention to play the game. We therefore believe that quality of online game community is not a crucial factor in explaining both game enjoyment and intention to play. Furthermore, the data revealed that game enjoyment played a critical role in determining intention to play and the latter has significant impact on online game loyalty. This research makes several contributions to our larger understanding of online game adoptions and customer loyalty. First, we identify attributes that may contribute to customer online game loyalty. In addition, as one of the few attempts to investigate online game loyalty, our study provides a conceptual model that will help researchers clarify critical issues of online game playing, such as how and why customers may be a loyal online game player. These constructs are extremely important to online game research and they will contribute significantly to the study of customer behaviors in online game playing. Our findings also provide practitioners (game vendors, game developer, and so on) important guidelines on the design and implementation of the online game innovations. According to our study, to increase game players' loyalty, practitioners should try to focus on their game technologies, such as a good game story, great graphic design, appropriate length of the game, easy game control, and good game services. They also should pay attention to their online game community to ensure customers have positive perspectives to the community.

References

1. Ajzen, I., Fishbein, M.: Understanding attitudes and predicting social behavior. Prentice-Hall, Englewood Cliffs (1980)
2. Berridge, K.C.: Pleasures of the brain. Brain & Cognition 52, 106–128 (2003)
3. Boyer, K., Hult, G.: Customer behavioral intentions for online purchases: An examination of fulfillment method and customer experience level. Journal of Operations Management 24, 124–147 (2006)

4. Browne, M., Cudeck, R.: Alternative ways of assessing model fit. In: Bollen, K., Long, J. (eds.) Testing Structural Models, pp. 136–162. Sage Publications, Newbury (1993)
5. Chang, B., Lee, S., Kim, B.: Exploring factors affecting the adoption and continuance of online games among college students in South Korea. New Media & Society 8(2), 295–319 (2006)
6. Chinen, K., Jun, M., Hampton, G.: Product quality, market presence, and buying behavior: Aggregate impages of foreign products in the U.S. Multinational Business Review 8(1), 29–38 (2000)
7. Choi, S., Chang, H., Kim, K.: Development of Force-Feedback Device for PC-Game using vibration. In: ACE 2004, Singapore (2004)
8. Choi, D., Kim, J.: Why people continue to play online games: in search of critical design factors to increase customer loyalty to online contents. Cyberpsychology & Behavior 7(1), 11–24 (2004)
9. Davis, F.D.: Perceived usefulness, perceived ease of use, and user acceptance of information technology. MIS Quarterly 13(3), 319–339 (1989)
10. DFC Intelligence (2008), http://www.dfcint.com/wp/?p=222 (October 2008)
11. Elliot, A.J., Thrash, T.M.: Approach-avoidance motivation in personality: Approach and avoidance temperament and goals. Journal of Personality and Social Psychology 82, 804–818 (2002)
12. Feldman, A.: Designing Arcade Computer Game Graphics. Wordware Publishing (2001)
13. Fornell, C.: A second generation of multivariate analysis methods. Praeger Special Studies, New York (1982)
14. Holsapple, C., Wu, J.: Building effective online game websites with knowledge-based trust. Information Systems Front 10, 47–60 (2008)
15. Hsu, C., Lu, H.: Consumer behavior in online game communities: A motivational factor perspective. Computers in Human Behavior 23, 1642–1659 (2007)
16. Joreskeg, K., Sorbom, D.: LISREL7: A guide to the program applications. SPSS, Inc., Chicago (1989)
17. Koufaris, M.: Applying the technology acceptance model and flow theory to online consumer behavior. Information Systems Research 13(2), 205–223 (2002)
18. Lo, N., Chen, S.: A study of anti-robot agent mechanisms and process on online games. In: IEEE International Conference on Intelligence and Security Informatics, pp. 203–205 (2008)
19. Lu, H., Wang, S.: The role of Internet addiction in online game loyalty: an exploratory study. Internet Research 18(5), 499–519 (2008)
20. Nunnally, J.: Psychometric Theory. McGraw-Hill, New York (1967)
21. Otim, S., Grover, V.: An empirical study on web-based services and customer loyalty. European Journal of Information Systems 15, 527–541 (2006)
22. Semeijn, J., Riel, A., Birgelen, M., Steukens, S.: E-services and offline fulfillment: how e-loyalty is crated. Managing Service Quality 15(2), 182–194 (2005)
23. Sweetser, P., Wyeth, P.: GameFlow: A Model for Evaluating Player Enjoyment in Games. ACM Computers in Entertainment 3(3), 3–24 (2005)
24. Van der Heijden, H.: User acceptance of hedonic information systems. MIS Quarterly 28(4), 695–704 (2004)
25. Wang, Y.: Assessing e-commerce systems success: a respecification and validation of the DeLone and McLean model of IS success. Information Systems Journal 18(5), 529 (2008)
26. Wu, J., Li, P., Rao, S.: Why they enjoy virtual game words? An empirical investigation. Journal of Electronic Commerce Research 9(3), 219–230 (2008)
27. Wu, J., Liu, D.: The effects of trust and enjoyment on intention to play online games. Journal of Electronic Commerce Research 8(2), 128–140 (2008)
28. Zeschuk, G., Muzyka, R.: Why don't people finish games? (2004), http://www.gamestar.com/12_04/features/fea_finish_jadeempire.shtml (October 2008)

Exploring the Influences of Individualism-Collectivism on Individual's Perceived Participation Equality in Virtual Learning Teams

Yingqin Zhong, Na Liu, and John Lim

Department of Information Systems, School of Computing, National University of
Singapore, Lower Kent Ridge Road Building "SOC1", 117543, Singapore
{zhongyin,liuna,jlim}@comp.nus.edu.sg

Abstract. This study aims to investigate the effects of equal participation on individual member's self assessment in terms of self-reported learning, self-perceived value of contribution, group identity and process satisfaction. Further, we examine how these effects of equal participation on individual learners are moderated by learners' cultural orientation in terms of individualism-collectivism. Data were collected from 65 virtual learning teams involving 195 undergraduates in a college in south China. MANOVA tests were performed to test the hypotheses. Findings revealed supportive results to most of posited main effects as well as moderating effects.

Keywords: Computer Supported Collaborative Learning (CSCL); e-Learning; Individualism-Collectivism; participation; learning outcomes.

1 Introduction

Thanks to the current advancement in the Information and Communication Technologies, e-learning has been found effective to support teaching and learning in today's information age [1]. The design and usage issues of e-learning are receiving unprecedented attention from not only computer scientists, but also educational psychologists, organization theorists and Information Systems (IS) professionals. In particular, institutions and educators are increasingly turning to a new paradigm emphasizing the use of e-learning to support computer supported collaborative learning (CSCL), in which a group of learners achieve meaningful learning through task completion and shared reflection in technology mediated environments [2]. Moreover, the emerging Web 2.0 turns out to be an enabling framework for institutions to support CSCL in virtual learning teams – the experience could better prepare learners to meet the contemporary demands towards globalization [3].

The notion of collective intelligence – which refers to the group decisions that tend to better than those prediscussion decisions of individual members – highlights the importance of the communication process and the collective knowledge building among learners in CSCL. Based on Social Interdependence Theory, the interaction among learners is crucial for the collaborative learning activities to be effective [4]. It has been found that computer mediated environments help to bring about greater

N. Aykin (Ed.): Internationalization, Design, LNCS 5623, pp. 207–216, 2009.
© Springer-Verlag Berlin Heidelberg 2009

equality of participation of learners, but the learning outcomes vary with the characteristics of the individuals and groups [5]. In this regards, more research efforts are called for to understand the interlocking effects between equal participation and other group level and individual level characteristics. This study aims to investigate the effects of equal participation on individual member's self assessment in terms of self-reported learning [6], self-perceived value of contribution [7], group identity [8] and process satisfaction [9]. Further, we examine how these effects of equal participation on individual learners are moderated by learners' cultural orientation.

Users' culture orientation is a pertinent and salient concern in CSCL research, as it influences individual's cognitive process [10]. Study of individualism- collectivism (I-C) at the individual level is concerned with psychological and individual differences. Interaction effects between I-C and equal participation in group learning have been highlighted [11]. In this study, we focus on the I-C dimension, a cultural dimension that captures the relative importance people accord to personal interests and to share pursuits [10].

In this paper, sections 2 and 3 briefly review related theories and studies, derive a research model, and formulate research hypotheses. The research method is discussed in section 4. Sections 5 address data analysis. Discussion of results and implications are drawn in Section 6.

2   Theoretical Foundation

Contributed greatly by information and communication technologies (ICTs), the twentieth century dramatically changes the use of team structures by moving from centralized, collocated teams to virtual teams which bring together members across geographical boundaries [12]. Virtual teams rely primarily on ICTs to communication and collaborate. Research on the medium effects in CSCL has found that ICT tools enhance openness of opinion-sharing and help to bring about greater equality in participation by offering collective memory and structuring features [13, 14]. Cognitive activities among group members require access to collective memory and coordinate consensus building; the system features facilitate the interactions among group members to accomplish the assigned tasks. However, being dependent on technology with limited communication cues for coordination, virtual teams commonly face challenges in achieving collaboration effectiveness and member commitments. In addition to the technology features, characteristics of users and groups have been acknowledged to be associative notably with variations in interaction process as well as collaboration outcomes within the context of e-collaboration [15]. Particularly, antecedents affecting team members' commitment within virtual teams have little exploration in recent research [12]. The collaboration process is the heart of CSCL [16]. It has been highlighted by previous studies that the effect of collaboration learning should be more specific about the effects of particular activities involved in a learner's participation so as to gain better understanding of the underlying mechanisms [17]. Participation and contribution of group members are found to be pertinent predictors of group process success. The effects of equality in participation on group development and learning activities can be demonstrated by looking at interaction process [14, 18].

Individuals' behaviors and satisfactions in team contexts are joint manifestations of their cultural backgrounds and their evaluation about other members' contribution [19]. culture orientation referring to the basic beliefs, preferences or tendencies rather than to exhibited behaviors [20], are found to affect the way individuals make predictions about the interaction and subsequently the communication in the initial contacts [21]. Collectivism is defined as "a social pattern consisting of closely linked individuals who see themselves as parts of one or more collectives", while individualism is "a social pattern that consists of loosely linked individuals who view themselves as independent of collectives" [10]. In addition to explaining cross-culture difference, I-C also shows within-cultural variability and can be used in explaining individual differences pertaining to communication and collaboration [10, 22]. The cultural dimension, I-C, has been widely studied at the individual level to investigate the cultural orientation impacts on participants' perceptions prior to actual usage [20, 23, 24]; and these perceptions determine the intention to use a technology. Individual belief about their dependency with others (independent or interdependent) has been the key issues in these studies of individualism-collectivism [10, 25].

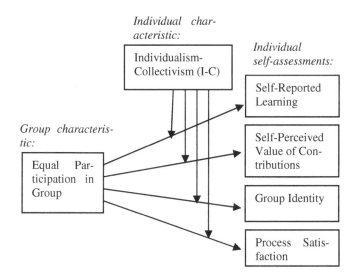

Fig. 1. The Research Model

3   Research Model and Hypotheses

Figure 1 depicts the research model. Socio-cultural theory, socio-constructivist theory and shared cognition theory are theories that establish the theoretical platform for collaborative learning [17]. These theories bring to light the two dominating aspects of outcome measures, affective and cognitive, which coincide with a learner's social-emotional and task-oriented activities respectively during the participation in the group learning process [26]. In other words, a learner's motivations, attitudes and feelings are directly affected by the interaction process [27]. In this study, equality of members' participation is of interest to investigate the effects of the interaction process on members' learning outcomes. Dependent variables self-reported learning and self-perceived value of contribution are indicators of cognitive outcomes; on the other hand, group identity and process satisfactions are affective outcomes.

The most widely studied outcome measures are self-reported learning and satisfaction with the process [16, 28]. Self-reported learning (SRL) measures the extent to which students believe they have learnt in the course. Process satisfaction (PS) reflects both relational and procedural aspects of the group collaboration, and thus has been found to be affected by member contribution as well as participation [18]. Self-perceived value of contributions (SPVC) measures the degree to which participant feel that his/her input was valued by and influential to other group members [7]. Group identity (GI) refers to an individual's self-concept which derives from the emotional significance attached to a particular group membership [29], which refers to the membership of a virtual learning team in this study. The hypothesized relationships in the research model are derived in the remaining of the section.

3.1 Main Effects of Equality of Participation in Group

Group performance would benefit from the resources contributed by members; individual member's learning can be enhanced by considering the multiple perspectives shared in the group [4]. Members learn in their attempted questions and answers, as well as the evaluation of others' input during the collaborative process. Both the social-cultural theory and the social-constructivist theory have highlighted the importance of these forms of discourses in individual's cognitive development and learning outcomes. In other words, when the exchange of ideas is active among members by dynamically asking questions or expressing opinions, members tend to be engaged in both knowledge co-construction and socialization processes effectively [30]. The positive effects of active interactions among members on collaborative learning connote the importance of equality in group participation. Arguably, inequality in group participation hampers member's learning process. If members' participation is not equal (i.e., having someone dominate or free-ride the discussion), members are likely to miss out the chances in either clarify their doubts by asking questions or improve their ideas by receiving and replying to feedbacks from others. Therefore, equal participation is expected to result in higher self-reported learning. Similarly, thanks to the two way communications among members in groups with equal participation, individual member tend to perceive that their opinions are well received by others and incorporated into the group decision. Thus, equal participation tends to result in higher self-perceived value of contributions by individual members.

> H1a: Members in groups with equal participation result in higher *self-reported learning* than those in groups with unequal participation.
>
> H2a: Members in groups with equal participation result in higher *self-perceived value of contributions* than those in groups with unequal participation.

Also, equal participation has been found to lead members to feel emotionally fulfilled [9]. Based on equity theory [31], individual member tends to believe that other members' activities will reflect their degree of commitment towards the team, and this perceived relationship are equitably applicable to all members. If an individual believes other team members' effort are sufficient and predictable, then trust, commitment and attachment can emerge within the team [12]. It is thus posited that equal participation would lead to higher group identity.

In CSCL, learner's process satisfaction is affected by how members work together, such as whether everyone does his/her part of the work, whether members remain on the task, and whether there is a good working atmosphere in the group [9]. Therefore, we hypnotize as following:

H3a: Members in groups with equal participation result in higher *group identity* than those in groups with unequal participation.

H4a: Members in groups with equal participation result in higher *process satisfaction* than those in groups with unequal participation.

3.2 Moderating Effects of I-C

Generally speaking, the attitude-behavior links are relatively weaker among collectivists than individualists [32]. The basic motive structure of individualists reflects their internal needs, rights, and capacities, while collectivists show a relatively high need for abasement, socially oriented achievement, and endurance. The effect of equal participation on self-reported learning is expected to be more significant among individualists than collectivists; equality is compatible with productivity, competition, and self-gain, hence it fits the values of individualists. Moreover, it is noted that collectivists tend to over-evaluate partner's performance and under-evaluate themselves [10]. Thus, the effect of equal participation on self-perceived value of contribution is less significant among collectivists.

H1b: The effect of equal participation on *self-reported learning* is expected to be more significant among individualists than collectivists.

H2b: The effect of equal participation on *self-perceived value of contributions* is expected to be more significant among individualists than collectivists.

Identity among collectivists is defined by relationship and group memberships; individualists define identity on what they own and their experiences. The emotions of collectivists tend to be other-focused and of short duration (i.e., they last as long as the collectivists are in a situation). Further, motivation is socially oriented among collectivists, and equality is associated with harmony and cohesion. Subordination of group goals to personal goals is the attribute distinguishing individualists from collectivists, and collectivists tend to accept unequal participation in group to a greater extend than individualists [11]. Hence, the effects of equal participation on group identity and process satisfaction are expected to be less significant among collectivists.

H3b: The effect of equal participation on *group identity* is expected to be more significant among individualists than collectivists.

H4b: The effect of equal participation on *process satisfaction* is expected to be more significant among individualists than collectivists.

4 Research Method

A lab experiment was conducted in this study, as it is appropriate for testing causal relationships among variables. Data were collected from undergraduate students enrolled in a college in south China. 195 subjects were assigned and allocated to 65 virtual learning teams (size=3); group members in each team did not know one another prior to the experiment. Subjects' average age was 20.6 years (s.d.=2.8); 101 were male. They are students from different faculties across the college. All teams were required to perform a group learning task about a lesson in identifying mushrooms [33].

A web-based CSCL system was developed and used in this study; it consisted of three components, reading materials, online quiz (i.e., the group task), and communication tools. Instructions were integrated and displayed in the system to guide subjects in completing the experiment according to the designed procedures. The experimental task required each learning group to hold discussions toward answering a quiz closely related to the reading materials. Each team was asked to submit a group report to answer the quiz questions. All communication and collaboration among members were requested to conduct in the system provided.

Prior to the experimental session, the subject completed a questionnaire aimed at ensuring no pre-experimental differences in terms of computer experience [34] and collaborative learning [35]. I-C was measured through questionnaires prior to the learning task and other dependent variables were measured by post-questionnaire. Next, the subject studied the materials provided by the system in an individual capacity, and then discussed with the other members to work in the quiz questions. To motivate their involvement, the top 20% among the groups will receive prices. Participation was captured by communication log, and equality of group participation was measured by a peer-review approach [24]. Finally, the subject completed a questionnaire on the dependent variables; the measurements were adapted from previous validated scales.

Equal perception in group was measured by a peer assessment, in which subject were asked to allocate 100 points among all group members including themselves. They were asked to allocate the points in a manner reflecting the degree of effort contributed by each member in the discussion process. For each subject, their perception about equal participation in group is measured by the standard deviation of the three scores from 33 – the average score of a three person group. Higher deviation values indicated higher degree of *inequality* in group participation perceived by an individual. Moreover, it was noted that agreement about each individual's rating was quite high within groups, as indicated by a reliability estimate of 0.88 [24]. Based on the results, the 65 groups were classified into two categories: equal vs. unequal participation.

Based on the pre-experimental measurement about subject's I-C values (ranging from 2 to 7, s.d.= 1.36), subjects were categorized into two types: Individualists and Collectivists (matching method based on comparing against the mean value 4.68). After the categorization, MANOVA and ANOVA tests were conducted to test the research model.

5 Data Analysis and Results

Prior to the model testing, the measurement scales were examined in terms of the convergent validity and discriminant validity. The average variances extracted were above 0.50 for all constructs. Given that all constructs had items with loading above 0.60, and composite reliability scores as well as Cronbach's alpha above 0.7, we deemed the measurement items possessed adequate reliability. These results indicated that the convergent validity of the measurement model was fair. To ensure the discriminant validity, the squared correlations between constructs were found smaller than the average variance extracted for a construct.

MANOVA and ANOVA were performed to test the hypotheses. Table 1 summarizes the descriptive statistics on the dependent variables. Table 2 and 3 reports the MANOVA and the ANOVA results respectively. Revealed from the MANOVA and ANOVA results, hypotheses H1a, H2a and H3a are supported. Members perceived equal participation among members tended to report higher self-reported learning, self-perceived value of contribution, and group identity, as compared to those perceived unequal participation in their groups.

Table 1. Outcome variables: Mean (standard deviation)

	I-C	SRL	SPVC	GI	PS
Unequal	I (n=31)	4.94 (.62)	5.13 (.80)	4.72 (.78)	5.05 (1.05)
Participation	C (n=68)	5.70 (.77)	5.87 (.74)	5.43 (1.03)	5.55 (.90)
	Total	5.46 (.81)	5.64 (.83)	5.21 (1.01)	5.40 (.97)
Equal Par-	I (n=60)	5.85 (.75)	5.98 (.64)	5.85 (.62)	5.88 (.72)
ticipation	C (n=36)	5.96 (.58)	6.05 (.59)	5.81 (.72)	5.70 (.82)
	Total	5.89 (.69)	6.00 (.62)	5.83 (.66)	5.80 (.76)
Total	I (n=91)	5.53 (.83)	5.69 (.80)	5.47 (.86)	5.60 (.93)
	C (n=104)	5.79 (.72)	5.93 (.70)	5.56 (.95)	5.60 (.87)
	Total	5.70 (.78)	5.82 (.76)	5.51 (.91)	5.60 (.90)

Table 2. MANOVA test

Source	SRL		SPVC		GI		PS	
	MS	F	MS	F	MS	F	MS	F
EP	15.07	29.82**	11.44	23.53**	24.90	36.60**	10.18	13.78**
I-C	8.32	16.45**	7.21	14.84**	4.79	7.04**	1.10	1.49
EP*I-C	4.58	9.06**	4.98	10.26**	6.16	9.06**	5.11	6.92**

$** p<0.01$ $* p<0.05$

Table 3. ANOVA tests

Source	SRL		SPVC		GI		PS	
	MS	F	MS	F	MS	F	MS	F
EP	7.50	14.77**	6.10	13.31**	8.21	11.92**	1.18	1.63
IC	.88	1.73*	.84	1.83*	.86	1.25	.82	1.13
EP*I-C	.50	.98	.84	1.84*	1.13	1.65*	1.20	1.65*

$** p<0.01$ $* p<0.05$

The ANOVA results implied joining effects of equal participation and members' I-C value, so further analysis was conducted to understand the moderating effects of members' I-C on the link between equal participation in group and the two dependent variables, namely self-reported value of contribution and group identity (i.e., H2b and H3b). Results supported H2b as the main effect of equal participation on self-reported value of contribution was found significant only among individualists (F=30.16, p<0.01) but not collectivists. Main effects of equal participation on group identity were found significant among individualists (F=56.60, p<0.01) and collectivists (F=3.88, P<0.05); H3b was supported.

6   Discussion and Concluding Remarks

Findings revealed supportive results to most of posited relationship, both main effects of equality participation and moderating effects of I-C. For both individualists and collectivist, members who evaluate the participation among all members as equal tend to result in higher self-reported learning than those evaluate the participation as unequal. This highlights the importance of cultivating a group norm of equal participation in virtual learning team; learners can enhance learning in the interaction process. Moreover, learners' cultural orientation has found to affect their self-evaluation and attachment to the virtual learning teams. The effects of equal participation in group have revealed to be more imperative on self-perceived value of contribution and group identity among individualists than collectivists. This connotes more or different contextual factors should be concerned in virtual learning teams formed by collectivists.

This study has several limitations. Subjects were recruited to work in a assigned team for a single session; future work should employ a longitudinal design to study the participation process. The use of subjects from the same country leaves room for future works. Lastly, this study focus on a single dimension of culture, comparative efforts shall involve related as well as other cultural dimensions in future studies.

This study adds insights to the current understating of CSCL and virtual learning teams. We have proposed and investigated a pertinent process variable, namely equal participation in group. This variable has been found influential to both cognitive and affective outcomes in CSCL. Moreover, this study can serve as a benchmark to inform cross-culture research in future. Besides theoretical implications, finding is also expected to provide practical insights. The lessons drawn would inform system designers and educators how to employ virtual learning teams in CSCL activities.

References

1. Beekman, G., Quinn, M.: Tomorrow's Technology and You, 8th edn. Prentice-Hall, Upper Saddle River (2007)
2. Francescato, D., Porcelli, R., Mebane, M., Cuddetta, M., Klobas, J., Renzi, P.: Evaluation of the efficacy of collaborative learning in face-to-face and computer-supported university contexts. Computers in Human Behaviors 22(2), 163–176 (2006)
3. Overbaugh, R.C., Casiello, A.R.: Distributed collaborative problem-based graduate-level learning: Students' perspectives on communication tool and efficacy. Computers in Human Behavior 24, 497–515 (2008)

4. Johnson, D., Johnson, R.T.: New developments in social interdependence theory. Genetic, Social, and General Psychology Monographs 131(4), 285–358 (2005)
5. Lipponen, L., Rahikainen, M., Hakkarainen, K., Palonen, T.: Effective participation and discourse through a computer network: investigating elementary students' computer supported interaction. J. of Educational Computing Res. 27(4), 355–384 (2003)
6. Alavi, M.: Computer-mediated collaborative learning: an empirical evaluation. MIS Quarterly 18(2), 159–174 (1994)
7. Karakowsky, L., McBey, K.: Do my contributions matter? The influence of imputed expertise on member involvement and self-evaluations in the work group. Group & Org. Management 26(1), 70–92 (2001)
8. Terry, D.J., Hogg, M.A., White, K.M.: The theory of planned behaviour: self-identity, social identity and group norms. British J. of Social Psychology 38, 225–244 (1999)
9. Gunawardena, C.N., Nolla, A.C., Wilson, P.L., Lopez-Islas, J.R., Ramirez-Angel, N., Megchun-Alpizar, R.M.: A cross-cultural study of group process and development in online conferences. Distance Education 22(1), 122–136 (2001)
10. Triandis, H.C.: Individualism and Collectivism. Westview, Boulder, CO (1995)
11. Oetzel, J.G.: Self-construals, communication processes, and group outcomes in homogeneous and heterogeneous groups. Small Group Res. 32(1), 19–54 (2001)
12. Powell, A., Galvin, J., Piccoli, G.: Antecedents to team member commitment from near and far. Inform. Tech. and People 19(4), 299–322 (2006)
13. Orlikowski, W.J.: Using Technology and Constituting Structures: A Practice Lens for Studying Technology in Organizations. Org. Sci. 11(4), 404–428 (2000)
14. Daily, B.F., Teich, J.E.: Perceptions of contribution in multi-cultural groups in non-GDSS and GDSS environments. European J. of Operational Res. 134, 70–83 (2001)
15. Pissarra, J., Jesuino, J.C.: Idea generation through computer-mediated communication. Journal of Managerial Psychology 20, 275–291 (2005)
16. Dewiyanti, S., Brand-Gruwel, S., Jochems, W., Broers, N.J.: Students' experiences with collaborative learning in asynchronous Computer-Supported Collaborative Learning environments. Computers in Human Behavior 23, 496–514 (2007)
17. Dillenbourg, P., Baker, M., Blaye, A., O'Malley, C.: The Evolution of Research on Collaborative Learning. In: Reimann, P., Spada, H. (eds.) Learning in human and machines. Towards an interdisciplinary learning science, pp. 189–211. Pergamon, London (1995)
18. Burke, K., Aytes, K., Chidambaram, L.: Media effects on the development of cohesion and process satisfaction in computer-supported workgroups - An analysis of results from two longitudinal studies. Information Technology & People 14, 122–141 (2001)
19. Mohammed, S., Dumville, B.: Team mental models in a team knowledge framework: Expending theory and measurement across disciplinary boundaries. J. of Organizational Behavior 22, 89–106 (2001)
20. Alavi, S.B., McCormick, J.: Theoretical and measurement issues for studies of collective orientation in team contexts. Small Group Res. 35, 111–127 (2004)
21. Ji, L.J., Zhang, Z., Nisbett, R.E.: Is it culture or is it language? Examination of language effects in cross-cultural research on categorization. Journal of Personality and Social Psychology 87(1), 57–65 (2004)
22. Kagitcibasi, C.: Autonomy and relatedness in cultural context: Implications for self and family. J. of Cross-Cultural Psy. 36, 403–422 (2005)
23. Marcus, A., Gould, E.W.: Crosscurrents: cultural dimensions and global Web user-interface design. Interactions 7(4), 32–46 (2000)
24. Wagner III, J.A.: Studies of individualism-collectivism: Effects on cooperation in groups. Academy of Management Journal 38, 152–172 (1995)

25. Triandis, H.C., Gelfand, M.J.: Converging measurement of horizontal and vertical individualism and collectivism. J. of personality and social psy. 74, 118–128 (1998)
26. Jones, A., Issroff, K.: Learning technologies: Affective and social issues in computer-supported collaborative learning. Comp. & Edu. 44(4), 395–408 (2005)
27. Lepper, M.R., Woolverton, M., Mumme, D., Gurtner, J.: Motivational techniques of expert human tutors: Lessons for the design of computer-based tutors. In: Proceedings of the 32nd HICSS. IEEE Press, Los Alamitos (1993)
28. BenbunanFich, R., Arbaugn, J.B.: Separating the effects of knowledge construction and group collaboration in learning outcomes of web-based courses. Information & Management 43(6), 778–793 (2006)
29. Tajfel, H.: Social identity and intergroup relations. Cambridge University Press, New York (1982)
30. Williams, E.A., Duray, R., Reddy, V.: Teamwork orientation, group cohesiveness, and student learning: a study of the use of teams in online distance education. J of Management Edu. 30(4), 592–614 (2006)
31. Adams, J.S.: Inequity in social exchange. Adv. Exp. Soc. Psychol. 62, 335–343 (1965)
32. Kashima, Y., Siegel, M., Tanaka, K., Kashima, E.S.: Do people believe behaviors are consistent with attitudes? Toward a cultural psychology of attribution processes. British J. of Social Psy. 33(1), 111–124 (1992)
33. Lim, J., Zhong, Y.: The interaction and effects of perceived cultural diversity, group size, leadership, and collaborative learning systems: an experimental study. Information Resources Management Journal 19(4), 56–71 (2006)
34. Hilmer, K.M., Dennis, A.R.: Stimulating thinking in group decision making. In: Proceedings of the 33rd HICSS. IEEE Press, Los Alamitos (2000)
35. Ross, J.A.: The influence of computer communication skills on participation in a computer conferencing course. J. of Educational Computing Res. 15(1), 37–52 (1996)

Part III

Internationalisation and Usability

Application of the Labeled Magnitude Scale in Kansei Research

Chun Yueh Chen[1] and Kuohsiang Chen[2]

[1] University Rd., Tainan City 701, Taiwan (R.O.C.)
karmaforza@gmail.com, kchen@mail.ncku.edu.tw

Abstract. This study intended to construct a labeled magnitude scale based on Kansei researches so that data with ratio-level can be retrieved easily and further extensive analysis can be conducted. In this study, scale derivation was generated based on the research of Green et al.[8] 32 subjects, include 23 male and 9 female, average age of 24.6 yrs with design education background, participated in the experiment. 19 car samples and 5 Kansei phrases were used in the experiment. Results showed that the intensity indicators were significantly different in the experiment ($F_{1,137}$=.122,p=.727). But subjects in the experiment gave rating in different ways to each Kansei phrases (Kansei phrases * intensity indicators, $F_{20,2952}$=3.55,p=.00). This may due to the status quo bias of subjects. Comparisons with OPUS (Oral Pleasantness /Unpleasant scale) [9] and CALM (Comfort Affective Labeled Magnitude) [5] showed similar orders of intersity indicators but different maximum magnitude in each scales.

Keywords: Kansei research, labeled magnitude scale (LMS), scale method, sensory evaluation.

1 Introduction

Kansei engineering has been proved a powerful tool in product development. With the increasing successful cases in Kansei engineering, the engineering methods in Kansei engineering have evolved for specific usages. But the basic principle of Kansei engineering still the same: to know what the customers' feelings are and to measure how strong the feeling (Kansei) is.

Conventional Kansei questionnaires use Likert scale or semantic differential scale as the scaling method. Both of these two methods belong to category scale. And category scale has its own nature limitation. Category scales yield ordinal-level data, sometimes interval level data. And the deficit limits the further statistical analysis of retrieved data.

With the study of Green et al. [8], a line scale with uneven-placed intensity labels was derived and the result from the scale is proved comparable with the result retrieved by magnitude estimation. The advance of the scale compared to line scale with even-placed labels was proved. That is the labeled magnitude scale, or the LMS in the study.

This study will construct a Kansei labeled magnitude scale based on the methodology of Green et al. [8] Comparison to labeled magnitude scales in other fields will be conducted.

N. Aykin (Ed.): Internationalization, Design, LNCS 5623, pp. 219–227, 2009.

2 Literature Review

2.1 Kansei Engineering

2.1.1 The Definition of Kansei Engineering

This term, 'Kansei engineering ', or Kansei ergonomics, was first introduced by Dr. Nagamachi in Hiroshima University in about 30 years ago [14]. And the most general definition of Kansei is "*A field that deals Kansei with engineering techniques, and to analyze Kansei by engineering means for the development of product. Therefore products with fulfillment and delight can be introduced.*"

Nagamachi has divided Kansei engineering/ergonomics into three subsections. They are :

- Kansei engineering type I is a method of category classification. The method is to break down the Kansei categories elicited by classification and systemize the categories into hierarchical structures.
- Kansei engineering type II is an expert system that translates consumers' feelings and images into design details of related products.
- Kansei Engineering type III is also called KEM, Kansei Engineering Modeling. The technique is to establish a mathematic, rule-based model to get ergonomic results from inputted Kansei phrases. [13]

2.1.2 Applications of Kansei Engineering

Kansei engineering has been accepted broadly and applied in many fields for product developments. For example, Mitsubishi, Mazda, Toyota, Honda, Ford, Hyundai, Delphi Automotive Systems in automobile industries, Sharp, Sanyo, Matsushita, Matsushita Electric Works, LG, Samsung in consumer electronics business, Matsushita Electric Works, YKK Design, Tateyama Aluminum, Kansai Electric Power Plant in house construction corporations, [14] and even Asahi beer in food industries, have carried out Kansei engineering methods as means of new product design, development and information mining from customers.

2.2 Sensory Evaluation

As the first human being using his or her own sensation to tell the quality of food, water, cloth or anything can be used or consumed, the history of sensory testing had begun. Human, as the only measuring instrument used in sensory evaluation, is not perfect, or prone to go wrong. Testers in a sensory evaluation are quite variable over time, variable between themselves, and apt to be biased. So scientists have developed formalized, structured, codified methodology for better assessing humans' sensory. A formal sensory study consists of at least seven stages. They are determining the project objectives, determining the test objectives, screening the samples, designing the test, conducting the test, analyzing the data and interpreting/reporting results.

2.2.1 Scaling Methods in Sensory Evaluation

There are four kinds of methods used in sensory evaluation. They are classification, grading, ranking, and scaling. [12] The method discussed further here belongs to scaling methods.

Category scale:
The earliest category scale were devised by the Greek Astronomer Hipparchus (190~120 B.C.) to assess the brightness of star. In category scale, subjects are asked to rate the intensity of preferred attributes by assigning values on a limited, often numerical, scale. The data from category scale is usually considered to be at least ordinal-level data, sometimes interval-level data.

Line scale
Line scale is a kind of scale considered to yield interval-level data. Subjects in line scale rate the intensity of a given stimulus by having a mark on a horizontal line that represents the amount of the perceived intensity. The line used in line scale has intensity marks, or anchors in both ends. In general, the left end of the line corresponds to "none" or zero and the right end of the line are a very large amount of stimulus. The line scale could be uni-polar or bipolar.

Magnitude estimation
Magnitude estimation is a scale method based on Stevens' power law [12].

$$\text{Steven's power law: } R=KC^n$$

The first sample a subject receives is assigned a free-chosen number (the number can be assigned by the experimenters or the subject him/herself). Subjects are then asked to assign all following-up ratings for the following-up samples in proportion to the first sample rating. If a sensation of a sample is three times strong of the first sample, then the rating of the sample should be assigned three times of the first rating. Subjects are reminded to keep the rating in proportion to the ratios among sensations.

Magnitude matching
Magnitude matching is a scale method that yields ratio-level data. In this technique, subjects match the intensity of one attribute to another attribute. If the perceived magnitude and the physical intensity follow the Stevens' power function, the attribute used to compare with would obtain the ratio property of the original attribute. Another benefit is that there is no number assigned in the technique, so people who used to use number differently will not interfere with the results.

2.2.2 Green's Labeled Magnitude Scale (LMS)

Labeled Magnitude Scale is a line scale with uneven-positioned intensity labeled. The intensity indicators on the scale are placed according to the retrieved magnitude estimates [4]. Green and his colleagues verified the scale by holding experiments comparing the LMS with magnitude estimation and ordinary line scale with evenly-spaced intensity labels. The comparisons shown that the LMS yielded ratio-level data as magnitude estimation did and was better than ordinary even-label-placed line scale.

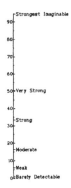

Fig. 1. The Labeled Magnitude Scale derived from Green et al.

2.2.3 Bartoshuk's General Labeled Magnitude Scale (gLMS)

In her researches, Bartoshuk and her colleagues found genetic variation may alter human oral sensations of PROP (Propylthiouracil) [3]. And prior pain experiences may also distort or change the inner pain scale for those who had suffered extremely painful events [7]. The alternation of inner sensation scale is called '*elastic ruler*'.

Bartoshuk and her colleagues introduced the general Labeled Magnitude Scale based on the LMS [8] to avoid the elastic ruler conundrum, and the semantic intensity labels have been altered for better fitting cross-modality usages.

Compared with the results of magnitude matching, that of the gLMS were found to provid valid cross-group comparison as Magnitude Matching did, but invalid comparison could occur when the maximum magnitude is correlated with preference of sensation.

Although with found limitation of usage, the gLMS showed 'the paradigmatic advance' in across-group comparisons. Further researches and implement in various fields were suggested.

2.3 The Application of Labeled Magnitude Scale in Kansei Research

Kansei researches suffer from the issues of invalid cross-group comparison with conventional categories scales. For example, gender difference may cause the 'elastic ruler' conundrum and direct comparisons become impossible. With the application of the LMS, direct comparisons between different groups with varied sensations are possible. And the data yielded from the LMS is ratio-level that creates more freedom for statistical analysis.

With the advantages in cross-group comparison and statistical analysis, the application of LMS to Kansei researches is beneficial.

3 Experiments

3.1 Scale Generation

The experiment employed the method of LMS with adjustments based on gLMS [2] to fit the usage of Kansei evaluation. In the experiment of scale generation, the subjects were asked to make modulus-free magnitude estimates for a series of intensity indicators (semantic labels) of five Kansei phrases adopted from previous study. The six descriptors used were 'barely detectable', 'weak', 'moderate', 'strong', 'very strong', and 'strongest imaginable of any kind' for all 5 Kansei phrases. A set of car photos were sampled to represent the whole car category.

According to the study of Ma [11], five pairs of Kansei phrases were selected by experts of car styling for Kansei evaluations. The five chosen pairs of Kansei phrases were 'streamlined–geometric', 'staid-light', 'rounded-sharp', 'complex-simple', and 'speedy-dilatory'. In this study, one out of each pair of Kansei phrase was selected and used for Likert scaling in the experiment. The chosen Kansei phrases were 'streamlined', 'light', 'sharp', 'simple' and 'speedy'.

Consumer Report magazine classifies passenger cars into twenty four categories. Each category of passenger cars had one model chosen as experimental samples. Model photos were collected via internet from manufacturers' official websites or press resources. In order to equalize the general images delivered by samples photos, all car models were in similar posing angles in photos.

All sample photos were processed to remove the background of car models. Brand marks and model labels of each sample were also removed. All sample photos were in monochrome for avoiding color biases. [15]

Twenty-three males and nine females with average age 24.9 yrs (range from 20~46) participated in this experiment. All subjects had at least 3 years training or education in industrial design and styling.

The subjects were told to have an experiment about Kansei engineering and all they had to do was to give ratings to the samples. No prior information about the process of experiment and samples were given during the recruitment.

3.2 Procedure

Before the experiment sessions getting started, subjects were instructed about the process of the experiment and what they were expected to do in the experiment sessions. A set of sample image cards was provided for reference. The experiment had three sessions. In session 1, subjects were asked to assign an intensity indicator displayed one by one in random order on the screen to each Kansei phrase for 19 samples. Subjects were asked to press the confirm button when an appropriate intensity descriptor shown. In session 2, subjects were asked to rate the intensity magnitude for each Kansei phrase. Session 3 was the matching stage. The intensity indicator assigned in the first stage and the values given in the second stage were exhibited side by side for subjects to review and verify their ratings.

Fig. 2. The experimental interface in sessions 1, 2, and 3

In all three stages, the presenting orders of samples and Kansei phrases were randomized. And all values or intensity indicators subjects gave could be reviewed and corrected by the subjects anytime during the experiment.

4   Results

All experiments were held within one week. The data collected from the experiment were first treated with modulus equalization. After that, results of the linear mixed-model analysis indicated that gender difference in the subjects didn't alter the rating results ($F_{1,137}$=.122,p=.727), and intensity indicators did differ from each other ($F_{5,207}$=43.82,p=.00). So the meaning of each descriptor should be well accepted and understood by the subjects. But the results in linear mixed-model analysis with Kansei phrases * Intensity shown that subjects in the experiment gave rating in different ways to each Kansei phrases (Kansei phrases * intensity indicators, $F_{20,2952}$=3.55,p=.00).

Pairwise tests also shown that all intensity indicators were well differentiated (p<.05) but exception still existed. In the case of Kansei phrase 'streamlined', the descriptor pair 'very strong - strongest imaginable of any kind' was not well differentiated. In the phrase 'simple', three descriptor pairs 'barely detectable - weak', 'strong - very strong', and 'very strong - strongest imaginable of any kind' were not significantly different. In the phrase 'speedy', the descriptor pairs 'barely detectable - weak' and 'very strong - strongest imaginable of any kind' were not significantly different. For the phrase 'light', 'barely detectable - weak', 'strong - very strong', and 'very strong - strongest imaginable of any kind' were not significantly differentiated. In the pairwise test for 'sharp', between the intensity indicators 'barely detectable - weak' and 'very strong - strongest imaginable of any kind' were not significantly different.

The geometric means and standard deviation of each intensity descriptor were calculated based on the research of Alf and Grossberg [1]. Values of geometric means and standard deviation are shown in table 1.

Table 1. Geometric means and the standard deviations of magnitude estimates (n = 32) given to six different intensity indicators in each category of Kansei phrase

Intensity indicators	Stream-lined	simple	light	Sharp	Speedy	Over all
Barely detectable	2.70 (0.18)	3.37 (0.34)	3.74 (0.21)	3.75 (0.11)	3.39 (0.26)	3.44 (0.12)
Weak	4.96 (0.27)	5.57 (0.22)	6.29 (0.33)	6.13 (0.54)	4.85 (0.31)	5.58 (0.16)
Moderate	8.36 (0.22)	6.05 (0.24)	10.45 (0.41)	8.41 (0.37)	8.02 (0.27)	8.44 (0.14)
Strong	12.57 (0.47)	10.27 (0.28)	15.87 (0.88)	13.61 (1.03)	10.94 (0.35)	12.09 (0.27)
Very strong	16.80 (1.39)	14.33 (0.97)	19.53 (2.06)	17.66 (2.97)	16.53 (1.25)	16.53 (0.74)
Strongest imaginable of any kind	19.44 (1.33)	16.26 (2.04)	22.85 (2.62)	26.68 (6.05)	17.84 (1.88)	19.63 (1.04)

Standard deviation in parentheses (Alf & Grossberg, 1979)

5 Discussions

Results from thirty-two subjects showed that there were significant differences between the ratings of intensity indicators of five Kansei phrases. But subjects also rated each Kansei phrase in significantly different way. So do the results suggest that a universal labeled magnitude scale of Kansei doesn't exist, or the experiments were influenced by some unexpected factors?

5.1 Generality of the Scales

Results indicated that subjects did give ratings in different ways for different Kansei phrases. And significant differences between Kansei phrases were only found in the middle segment of intensity indicators, such as 'moderate', 'strong', 'very strong'. There are several questions laid among the findings. It may be caused by magnitude equalization which was used to equalize the range of data and keep the structure inside. Since the range of the data was about the same, the anti log magnitude estimation value of the first two intensity indicators and the last one would be about the same. The difference of data would appear in the middle section of intensity indicators.

5.2 Status Quo Bias in Kansei

As previous mentioned, Kansei is the general images or attributes aroused by sensory stimuli of certain objects or events. Since Kansei phrases represent the attributes of general images, Kansei phrases may be assigned a default value by the subjects. The default value in Kansei phrases, may cause status quo bias [10] because there is always a status quo of specific sample used as the standard or reference no matter the referential sample is assigned or not. If a reference is not assigned in a Kansei evaluation, the panelists in the evaluation still compare all the samples with their own prior experiences.

5.3 Compare with Existing Scales

This research is the first try to adopt labeled magnitude scales into Kansei researches. And the comparison to the labeled magnitude scales from other fields reveals agreements and differences.

The currently developed LMS can be divided into the sensory scale and the affective scale. In the work of Guest and his colleagues [9], they suggested that there is a general dichotomy between affective and intensive sensations. The following is how they discriminate sensory scale and affective scale.

"For example, Gracely et al.(1978a) found that the most intense general sensory descriptor in a set of 15 was rated as 85 times more intense than the weakest descriptor, i.e., the sensory range was 85:1. Similarly, the ratio between most and least intense descriptors in Green et al.'s LMS is 69:1. In contrast, for classes of affective intensity indicators, the sensory range has consistently been found to be much smaller, varying from 9:1 for positive affect in Schutz and Cardello's LAM, through 10:1 (Gracely et al., 1978a) to 15:1 for our OPUS" [9]

According the definition by Dr. Nagamachi, Kansei is more likely to be an affective sensation than a sensory sensation. And the result of experiments in this study agrees with Dr. Nagamachi's words. Therefore, the LMS of each Kansei phrase will be compared with the oral sensation scale for comparison here is OPUS, oral pleasantness /unpleasant scale and the tactile sensation scale for comparison is CALM, Comfort Affective Labeled Magnitude scale [5].

Figure 7 is the comparison of five Kansei phrases scale with OPUS and CALM. OPUS was conducted by Cardello and Shuntz [6] with an adverb intensity descriptor system, and is different from the LMS [8]. As the figure shows, the order of intensity indicators in OPUS is similar to the scales of five Kansei phrases. The most difference occurs in the maximum magnitude. The mean of the maximum magnitude of five Kansei phrases is 19.63, with a standard deviation of 1.04. However, the maximum magnitude of OPUS is about two times larger than the maximum value in Kansei scales. The maximum pleasant magnitude is 51.90 (1.67), and the maximum unpleasant magnitude is 54.44 (1.72). The same circumstance is also found in CALM. The most comfort magnitude originally retrieved in the experiments of CALM is 366.72 (0.10), and the most uncomfortable magnitude in CALM is 350.67 (0.10).

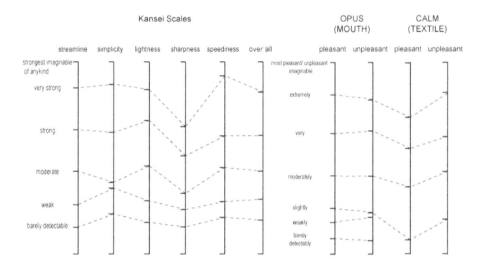

Fig. 3. The comparison of the scales of five Kansei phrases with OPUS and CALM

6   Conclusions

With this study, a Kansei labeled magnitude scales have been devised based on the method suggested by Green et al. [8]. An experiment comparing intensity indicators with magnitude estimation has been carried out. Kansei phrases used in this experiment are acquired in the study of Ma [11] and the intensity indicators in the experiment are from the study of Bartoshuk and his colleague [2]. In the experiments, corresponding geometric means of each intensity indicators have been retrieved and these values are used for deriving the labeled magnitude scale for these Kansei phrases.

In the experiments, significant difference between intensity indicators was found. But analysis also showed that there was significant difference between the five Kansei phrases. This phenomenon may due to the effect of loss aversion. Comparison between the labeled magnitude scales in other sensations shown great difference in the maximum intensity magnitude.

Acknowledgement. Prof. Chin-Fang Sheu and Prof. Kuohsiang Chen helped a lot to foster the idea, and the support from my family and friends. Thanks to all of them.

References

1. Alf, E.F., Grossberg, J.M.: The geometric mean: Confidence limits and significant tests. Perception & Psychophysics 5(26), 419–421 (1979)
2. Bartoshuk, L.M., Duffy, V.B., Green, B.G., Hoffman, H.J., Ko, C.-W., Lucchina, L.A.: Valid across-group comparisons with labeled scales: The gLMS versus magnitude matching. Physiology & Behavior 82, 109–114 (2004)
3. Bartoshuka, L.M., Duffy, V.B., Fast, K., Green, B.G., Prutkin, J., Snyder, D.J.: Labeled scales (e.g., category, Likert, VAS) and invalid across-group comparisons: what we have learned from genetic variation in taste. Food Quality and Preference 22, 125–138 (2002)
4. Butler, G., Poste, L.M., Wolynetz, M.S., Agar, V.E., Larmond, E.: Alternative analyses of magnitude estimation data. Journal of Sensory Studies 2, 243–257 (1987)
5. Cardello, A.V., Winterhalter, C., Shuntz, H.G.: Predicting the handle and comfort of military clothing fabrics from sensory and instrumental data: development and application of new psychophysical methods. Textile Research Journal, 221–237 (2003)
6. Cardello, A.V., Schutz, H.G.: Research note: Numerical scale-point locations for constructing the LAM (labeled affective magnitude) scale. Journal of Sensory Studies 19(4), 341–346 (2004)
7. Dionne, R.A., Bartoshuk, L., Mogil, J., Witter, J.: Individual responder analyses for pain:does one pain scale fit all? TRENDS in Pharmacological Sciences 26(3), 125–130 (2005)
8. Green, B.G., Shaffer, G.S., Gilmore, M.M.: Derivation and evaluation of a semantic scale of oral. Chemical Senses 18(6), 683–702 (1993)
9. Guest, S., Essick, G., Patel, A., Prajapati, R., McGlone, F.: Labeled magnitude scales for oral sensations of wetness, dryness, pleasantness and unpleasantness. Food Quality and Preference 18, 342–352 (2007)
10. Kahneman, D., Knetsch, J.L., Thaler, R.H.: Anomalies: The Endowment Effect, Loss Aversion, and Status Quo bias. Journal of Economic Perspective 5(1), 193–206 (1991)
11. Ma, C.-C., Shieh, M.-D.: Using Neural Networks in Automobile Shape Feature Design. Tainan: NCKU, Master Thesis (in Chinese) (2005)
12. Meilgaard, M.C., Civille, G.V., Thomas Carr, B.: Sensory evaluation techniques, 4th edn. CRC Press, Taylor &Francis Group, Boca Raton (2007)
13. Nagamachi, M.: Kansei Engineering: A new ergonomic consumer-oriented technology for product development. International Journal of Industrial Ergonomics, 3–11 (1995)
14. Nagamachi, M.: Technical note:Kansei engineering as a powerful consumer-oriented technology for product development. Applied Ergonomics 33, 289–294 (2002)
15. Wong, J.-S., Chen, L.-L.: A Study on the Relationship of Automobile Shape Morphing to Affective and Aesthetic Responses. Taipei: NTUST, Master thesis (in Chinese) (2004)

Internationalizing Mainframe Applications through Screen Scraping

Chris Durand

Chief Technology Officer, Bridge360
1016 La Posada Drive, Suite 120, Austin, TX 78752, USA
chris_durand@bridge360.com

Abstract. This paper is a case study describing the internationalization of a mainframe application without changing mainframe code. By utilizing screen scraping techniques, the project team created Chinese and Korean versions of mainframe application screens and reports. The paper describes specific issues encountered on the project, the solutions considered, and the strengths and weaknesses of the selected solution. It also describes an algorithm used to perform efficient translation of system messages with embedded variables.

1 Introduction

This project involved enabling a mainframe supply chain management application to work in Chinese and Korean. The application included nearly 400 application screens and over 100 reports. Due to time and budget constraints, it was not possible to take a traditional internationalization approach of modifying the original application to support Chinese and Korean. Instead, the project leveraged off-the-shelf "screen scraping" tools and techniques alongside custom development to meet the project requirements in the necessary timeframe.

2 What Is Screen Scraping?

Screen scraping is a method where one program utilizes a human interface of a second application to interact with the second application. A simple example would be writing a program to extract stock prices from a web application's HTML output. By utilizing the interface intended for human users, the first program is able to interface with the web application without requiring changes to the web application.

Screen scraping is often used to create an HTML, browser-based user interface to an existing mainframe application ("re-facing") without changing the underlying application. The browser-based interface allows for a richer user experience than can be achieved through a typical 3270 "green-screen" interface via graphics, interactive JavaScript, and other modern browser technologies.

There are a number of commercial off-the-shelf (COTS) tools available to facilitate mainframe-to-web screen-scraping solutions. The tool used on the project utilized the architecture illustrated in Figure 1.

N. Aykin (Ed.): Internationalization, Design, LNCS 5623, pp. 228–235, 2009.
© Springer-Verlag Berlin Heidelberg 2009

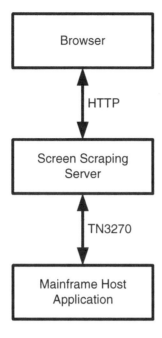

Fig. 1. Screen Scraping Architecture

Roughly speaking, the process works as follows. Using a browser, a user navigates to the web application running on the screen-scraping server ("server") via HTTP. The server connects to the host application ("host") via a 3270-based protocol such as TN3270 and retrieves the initial host application screen, typically a login screen. The server converts the host screen into an HTML page that is returned to the user's browser. The user enters his or her username and password and submits the web page back to the server. The server extracts the username and password from the browser's request, simulates the filling out of the host screen form and submits the host screen back to the host. The host processes the login request and sends the next screen back to the server, and the process continues. All the while, the host application is unaware that it is in fact communicating with another program instead of a human operator using a 3270 terminal emulator.

3 Screen Translation

Creating translatable screens formed the bulk of project. The application included nearly 400 screens. Typical screens included forms users could fill out, menus, and tables of data returned from the application's data store. From a translation perspective, application text could be divided into three basic categories: static text, dynamic text, and application data.

3.1 Static Text

Static text refers to field labels and other text on the screen that never changes, such as "Street:" as part of an address form. The screen scraping tool enabled designers to build web pages corresponding to each mainframe application screen. This enabled designers to make any UI adjustments necessary to accommodate translations that were longer than the original English text. Text could also be marked as translatable in the design tool and the resulting server application would load translations from an external file, similar to a Java .properties file. Since static text never changes it was trivial to translate this text for the web pages via human translators, and the application looked up the translation for the current language at runtime. Translating static text in this manner is well documented elsewhere [1].

3.2 Dynamic Text

Dynamic text refers to text that can vary at runtime. Dynamic text includes application messages that are displayed periodically, or labels for fields that are only visible under certain conditions. For example, a screen allowing users to enter shipping information may have different fields depending on whether or not the shipment was performed by rail (e.g. a railcar number) or airplane (e.g. an airbill number).

Dynamic text can be further subdivided into two categories: dynamic text without variables and dynamic text with variables. Dynamic text without variables is similar to static text, except the application has to determine at runtime whether or not to display the text on the screen. For example, an error message stating "A1234: Invalid date" would only be displayed when an invalid date value was entered, but when such a message is displayed it is always the same. This sort of text can be translated in a similar manner to static text.

Dynamic text with variables presents a more difficult challenge. For example, an error message stating "B5678: Shipping code XYZ is invalid" will vary depending on the invalid shipping code ("XYZ") entered by the user. To translate this message, the original English message must be parsed at runtime to extract the variable portions of the message, and the variable portions must be inserted into the appropriate locations in the translation. Since there are a known, fixed number of messages, translations can be created by human translators with placeholders for the variable portions of the text.

While methods for substituting variables into translations are well documented [2], in a screen scraping application there is the additional challenge of recognizing the English message so the application can locate the appropriate translation. Locating a translation for static text merely requires a lookup into a table of translations based on a binary comparison of the English text to the table's keys. However, variables in dynamic text render a simple binary comparison ineffective. To overcome this, the project created regular expressions to recognize each English message with dynamic text. For messages with variables, the regular expressions automatically extracted each variable portion of the English message that was later inserted into the translation.

Since there were approximately 10,000 dynamic messages, it was important to efficiently identify the matching regular expression and the associated translation. A brute-force approach of trying each regular expression in sequence would require on average 5,000 attempts before a match would be found and could have exceeded target system response time as the number of concurrent users of the system increased.

An elegant solution to rapidly find the correct regular expression would be to build a specialized lexical analysis tool similar to the open-source *flex* lexical analyzer generator typically used to generate lexical analyzers for compilers [3]. Such a tool would take regular expressions for all 10,000 dynamic messages and build an efficient deterministic finite automaton to quickly parse text according to the supplied regular expressions. Such a tool would be a modest extension to *flex*. However, since most software developers are not familiar with algorithmically-complex applications such as *flex*, long-term maintenance of this approach would have been difficult due to staff turnover over time.

Ultimately, the project took another approach by exploiting the fact that nearly all dynamic messages started with an alphanumeric code (e.g. "A1234"). This led to the algorithm shown in Figure 2. Essentially, the screen scraping server first checks to see if the English message begins with a message number. If so, the regular expression for that message number is looked up via a hash table. If the regular expression matches the message, the translation can then be performed. If the regular expression does not match, or the English message does not appear to start with an alphanumeric code, the application resorts to a brute-force search. Message codes were mostly unique, but the algorithm is still capable of finding the correct regular expression even in the case of duplicate message codes. If the regular expression looked up via the message number hash table does not match, the brute-force search would find regular expressions for any additional instances of a particular message number. Ultimately this algorithm was implemented quickly and provided acceptable performance.

3.3 Application Data

While application data, such as product descriptions in a customer's order, is similar to dynamic text described earlier in many ways, there are several key differences from a translation perspective. Dynamic text is bounded (i.e. all text that needs to be translated is known), whereas application data is created by users and therefore all possible values are not known beforehand. Therefore pre-translation by human translators is not an effective solution. Further, dynamic text rarely changes (such as when a new screen is added or business logic is updated), but application data changes frequently (such as every time a new product is added to the system).

Storing user-entered application data also posed a challenge in this project as the mainframe application only supported storage of user-entered data in the EBCDIC-US encoding (IBM code page 037).

Adding the capability to store Chinese and Korean characters (i.e. Unicode support) would have required significant modifications to the application's IMS database, or introduction of a separate database capable of storing these characters. Screen scraping alone could not address this issue.

While the initial project requirements included application data translation and storage of non-English characters, during the design phase the project team concluded that meeting these requirements would add significant risk to the project budget and schedule, as well as complicate the system architecture substantially. Therefore these requirements were deferred. Since the vast majority of the application data was non-translatable (e.g. alphanumeric codes), dropping these requirements had only a modest impact on system usability.

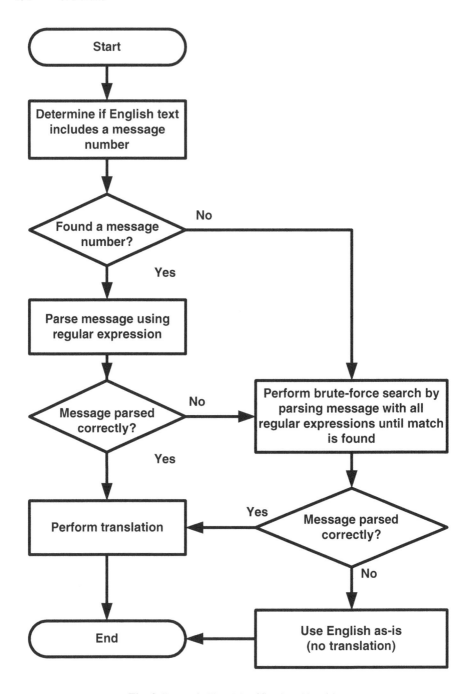

Fig. 2. Dynamic Text Identification Algorithm

Had the project been required to support data translation, there were several approaches briefly considered. Machine translation might have been a viable approach given the relatively narrow scope of the application. Accuracy was not paramount since the system was for internal company use only. Another approach would be to create a human-centric process whereby the application tracked when new translatable text was added and would automatically notify a human translator that new data had been added.

3.4 Other Considerations

There are many aspects to a fully-internationalized application besides translation, such as locale-sensitive formatting of dates, times, and currency. As an application for internal use only, this project had no requirements beyond translation. However, a screen scraping process could have easily made the necessary conversions to and from U.S. locale conventions as text and data was passed between the host application and the user's browser.

Locale-sensitive collation, however, cannot be well handled via screen scraping. When displaying a list, the host application can only show a single screen of data at a time, which is all the screen scraping application has access to. It is possible for the screen scraping application to scan multiple screens of data on the host, cache the results, sort them in the user's desired locale-sensitive sort order, and display the complete list to the user. However this is only feasible for small data sets. In general, collations must be dealt with in the host application.

3.5 Results

The screen-scraping approach used by the project for screen translation provided good results in a short amount of time despite the shortcomings noted. Even if the project team had the option to change mainframe program code, it is unlikely all necessary code changes could have been performed in the available timeframe without a large implementation team and excessive risk to the project budget and schedule. While all screen scraping implementations increase the maintenance burden relative to making changes in the original application (since the screen-scraped version of an application screen usually must be updated when its corresponding host screen changes), screen scraping merits consideration for future mainframe projects that require internationalizing application screens.

4   Report Translation

While application screens were accessible via a 3270 interface, mainframe reports were generated in English by mainframe batch programs and made available to the project in text files formatted for mainframe printers. The project required that these reports be displayed to users in Chinese or Korean. Similar to mainframe screens, project requirements forbade changes to the report generation programs. Mainframe users utilized an off-the-shelf report archiving solution for working with English-language reports. Reports generated by the batch programs were automatically loaded into the report archiving system for users to view, search, or print.

Creating translated reports required solutions to two overall problems: converting English reports into Chinese or Korean, and allowing users to access reports for viewing, printing and other operations.

4.1 Conversion of English Reports

The project considered two basic approaches to this problem. First, the data of the report could be extracted (into an XML file, perhaps) and then a new report program could convert the extracted data into a report in the target language. This solution would provide a tremendous amount of flexibility as only the data from the original report would be used, while the formatting and presentation of the translated report could be created as necessary. While elegant, this solution would require new report programs to duplicate much of the logic in the original mainframe report programs such as layout, paging, and the calculation of subtotals.

The project instead implemented a second solution, which was to identify translatable text in the English report and replace the text in-place with translations. This approach is simpler than the first approach as it does not attempt to duplicate the layout, paging and totaling capabilities of the mainframe report program. However, translated reports are constrained by the layouts of the English reports. For example, if a column header only allotted three-characters for the English header (often an abbreviation) it was often difficult for translators to create a reasonable translation that would fit in three characters. In many cases the original English was retained for the translated report due to lack of space for adequate translations.

To translate text in-place, the translatable text first had to be identified. Identification of translatable text in reports is more difficult than in screens. While screen text essentially appears in the same position each time a screen is displayed, reports are a stream of data. Different runs of the same report often produce different results, such as a varying number of pages for each report run due to the specific report parameters selected by the user or changes in data over time.

The solution implemented by the project included a general-purpose report conversion engine and report conversion rules for each report stored in XML files. To convert a report, the conversion engine identified the report based on report header pages and applied the conversion rules in the appropriate XML rule file.

The XML rule files consisted of two types of entries: "search" rules and "replace" rules. "Search" rules were used to identify a particular line in the report, and were based on regular expressions. Each "search" rule had one or more "replace" rules associated with it. Once the conversion engine used a "search" rule to identify a particular line in a report (e.g. a line containing column headers), the engine would apply each associated "replace" rule. Each "replace" rule included the start column of the text to be replaced, the number of characters to be replaced, and the translation to be used in place of the replaced text. "Replace" rules were also capable of spanning multiple rows.

As an English report was processed the translated version was written out in HTML format.

4.2 Report Access, Display, and Printing

Once a report was converted, it was necessary to enable users to select reports for viewing or printing. Given that the host application already relied upon an existing report system to display English reports (along with the numerous auxiliary functions required to do this, such as user authentication and authorization), the project opted to screen scrape the relevant report selection application screens and convert them into Chinese and Korean instead of implementing report system functions in a new application.

Once users selected the desired reports, the screen scraping server transferred control to a separate custom web application that displayed the selected report in a new browser window. Users used their web browsers to navigate and print reports like any web page.

Unfortunately, the solution had some shortcomings when printing reports. Reports are typically generated using fixed-width fonts to maintain columnar layouts. However, Chinese character glyphs are wider than normal Latin character glyphs so when the report conversion engine replaced standard Latin glyphs with the wider glyphs included in Chinese fonts, this caused translated reports to become much wider than the original English reports. Font sizes on printed reports had to be reduced to avoid splitting report rows across multiple pages which made them difficult to read when printed. Ultimately users tended to use the translated versions for on-screen use but used the untranslated English versions when printed reports were necessary.

4.3 Results

Overall the project's report conversion solution worked well for producing translated reports for on-screen viewing and was implemented in a short timeframe. Projects with a heavy reliance on printable reports may prefer to extract data from English reports and create re-formatted translated reports, as was initially considered for this project.

5 Conclusion

Screen scraping proved to be a viable approach for translating mainframe screens and reports into Chinese and Korean without changing mainframe code. The project's screen-scraping solution had several shortcomings, most importantly the lack of a reasonable solution for storing non-EBCDIC application data created by users and the inability to support locale-specific collation without code changes to the mainframe application. Printed reports could also be improved. Despite these limitations, screen scraping allows organizations to derive additional value from their mainframe application investments by making host applications available in multiple languages in a cost-effective manner.

References

1. Dr. International: Developing International Software, 2nd edn. Microsoft Press, USA (2003)
2. MessageFormat (Java 2 Platform SE v1.4.2),
   http://java.sun.com/j2se/1.4.2/docs/api/java/text/
   MessageFormat.html
3. Flex: The Fast Lexical Analyzer, http://flex.sourceforge.net/

A Case Study in Community-Driven Translation of a Fast-Changing Website

David Ellis

Facebook
dellis@facebook.com

Abstract. Facebook's translation tool allows users (translators) to click on a phrase as they browse the site, and inline see the original native string, vote on translations suggested by their peers or offer their own. We offer an innovative approach to web site internationalization that leverages a unique infrastructure and a dedicated user community to keep our interface up-to-date in translation

1 Introduction

Facebook's translation tool allows users (translators) to click on a phrase as they browse the site, and inline see the original native string, vote on translations suggested by their peers or offer their own. We offer an innovative approach to web site internationalization [1] that leverages a unique infrastructure and a dedicated user community to keep our interface up-to-date in translation. Each language community starts by translating glossary terms to encourage consistency across the site. Once phrases are translated (inline and/or in bulk mode), we hire professional linguists to ensure quality in the most commonly viewed strings.

2 Motivation

A variety of factors motivated the design of our translations process and application, but chief among them are speed, quality, cost and reach.

2.1 Speed

It is essential for our translations to keep up with new features and other changes to the interface. The traditional model is both costly and unscalable. Crowdsourcing allows us to take advantage of the size and motivation of our user community (more than 25,000 Turkish users added the translations application), often completing translations in days or weeks (as opposed to months required by professionals).

Our user base keeps growing, and with each person who signs up for Facebook but can't view it in their language, we have another potentially motivated translator. Using collaborative translations, Spanish and German were translated in

N. Aykin (Ed.): Internationalization, Design, LNCS 5623, pp. 236–244, 2009.
© Springer-Verlag Berlin Heidelberg 2009

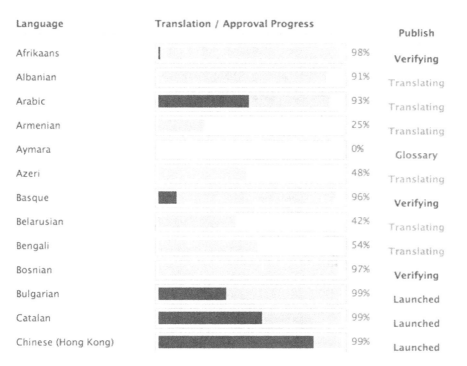

Language	Translation / Approval Progress		Publish
Afrikaans		98%	Verifying
Albanian		91%	Translating
Arabic		93%	Translating
Armenian		25%	Translating
Aymara		0%	Glossary
Azeri		48%	Translating
Basque		96%	Verifying
Belarusian		42%	Translating
Bengali		54%	Translating
Bosnian		97%	Verifying
Bulgarian		99%	Launched
Catalan		99%	Launched
Chinese (Hong Kong)		99%	Launched

Fig. 1. Progress of a few languages, along with publication status

one week, a draft of French (ready for review) was completed in 24 hours, and we have launched over 40 languages within the first year of our localization effort. For statistics on progress of languages from A to Ch, see Fig. 1.

2.2   Quality

A translation is of high quality if it does all of the following:

1. Accurately conveys the original meaning of its source.
2. Does not sound like a translation, but a native phrase or document.
3. Results in clear and unambiguous text.

A method to achieve quality entails employing the right combination of people, process and technology. Selected people must be linguistically competent and must be experts in the relevant industry. The process should facilitate speed and quality. The best technology is one that allows the implementation of process with the least friction, which we are actively working to iteratively improve.

We also have a style guide and glossary for each language, and in-tool warnings for inconsistent punctuation (e.g., translating "Click here:" as "¡Haga clic aquí!"), for leaving out glossary terms (e.g., translating "A friend's profile has the following components..." without using the translated glossary term "amie" for friend), and for submitting identical translations.

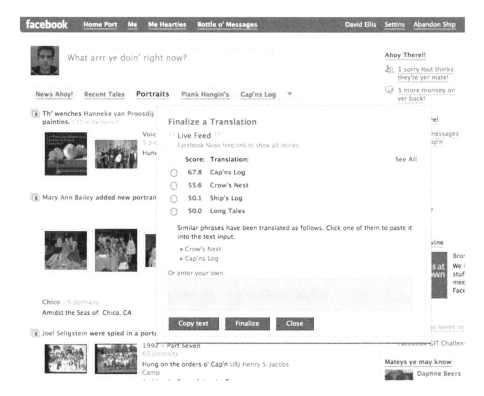

Fig. 2. Inline approval mode, in the English (Pirate) locale

2.3   Cost

Investment in crowd-sourcing technology offers some of the savings associated with "free" translations. However, much of that is spent because the majority of community translations undergo extensive quality assurance effort by professional agencies. Our cost advantages are achieved through unsupported languages, process automation and the ability to prioritize text.

Unsupported Languages. Welsh is our first unsupported language (chosen largely due to the relatively low visibility and small adoption), but there are many more in the long tail that will go without professional quality assurance. We also offer translation into "English (Pirate)", which has launched in beta through the efforts of over 20,000 volunteer translators who have submitted and voted on nearly 40,000 translations.

Automation. The automation extends even to the quality assurance, which takes place in our tool. See a screenshot of its welcome page in the Estonian locale in Fig. 3. We have begun to hire full-time, onsite language managers for popular languages (including French, Spanish, Chinese, Japanese, and German).

Prioritization. Rather than compile a word-processing document or spreadsheet containing a batch of new phrases to be translated, we ask translators

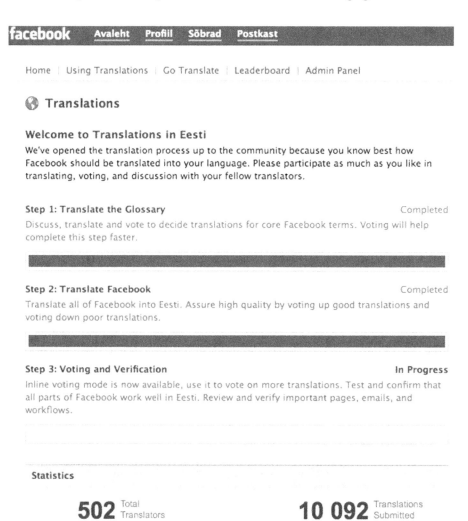

Fig. 3. The translations application, in the Estonian locale

(normal users and contracted professionals) to browse the site, a process which will naturally surface high-visibility untranslated strings. But most users rarely see some parts of the site: for instance, the sign-up flow. Since these are critical to growth and new user experience, we prioritize them in the bulk interface (as in Fig. 4).

2.4   Reach

Our crowd-sourced translations process allows us to extend the reach of Facebook to all internet users, including speakers of commonly ignored languages. We also give application developers access to the same technology and process as used

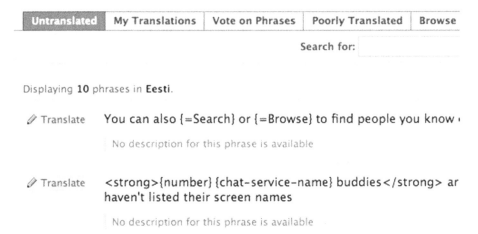

Fig. 4. The bulk translation interface, which allows translators to translate or vote on strings, filtering by a specific page or group of pages

on the rest of our site [3]. Note that with Facebook Connect, those applications don't even need to be on Facebook, and can allow a user to carry his identity, friends and locale (language preferences) to any domain, where the translated interface is generated using our process.

3   Framework

We offer a rich interface with simple but powerful controls, an example of which can be seen in Fig. 5. Many phrases on the site necessarily involve tokens like "{name}" that are replaced with values that depend on the context in which they appear (e.g., which user is logged in). Translating tokenized phrases is problematic because the values (words) need to be inflected in some languages. We have two systems in place to enable correct translations, requiring minimal effort from translators.

3.1   Dynamic Explosion

This technique allows us to split strings on language-specific variations based on translator feedback. For example, a Hebrew translator indicates that in the phrase "name wrote on your wall", the verb conjugation depends on the gender of the subject. Translators can then submit (and vote on) translations for each case: where the actor is male, female, or unspecified.

In Arabic, there are different inflections for singular, dual and plural, so in the phrase "number hours ago", the value of the number affects the translation.

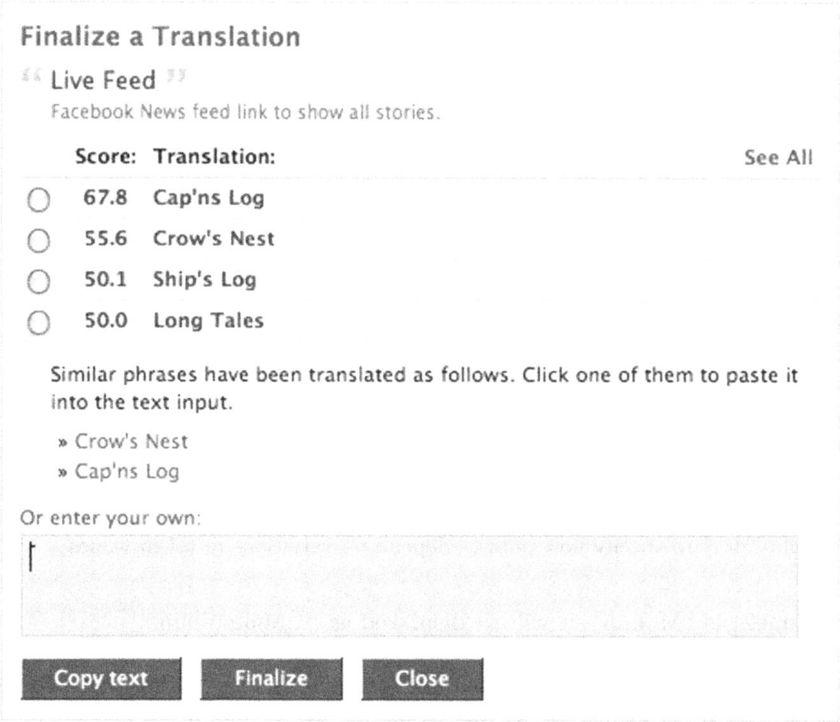

Finalize a Translation

" Live Feed "

Facebook News feed link to show all stories.

	Score:	Translation:	See All
○	67.8	Cap'ns Log	
○	55.6	Crow's Nest	
○	50.1	Ship's Log	
○	50.0	Long Tales	

Similar phrases have been translated as follows. Click one of them to paste it into the text input.

» Crow's Nest
» Cap'ns Log

Or enter your own:

[Copy text]   [Finalize]   [Close]

Fig. 5. A close-up of the inline translation dialog (from Fig. 2) that includes results of voting on existing translations, and reveals similar-phrase translations (to ease translators' burden and encourage consistency)

Translators can easily see and modify each of these translations (as in Fig. 6), and the appropriate variant is shown to Arabic users (in this case, in their newsfeeds).

3.2 Phonological Rules

Orthographic or phonological rules [4] can affect the spelling of words, and are applied automatically when tokens are substituted with their values. For example, Turkish inflection rules affect any token in possessive, dative or accusative case, such that there are 12 different forms for each. We allow translators to use a proto-form that will be adjusted to match the token when displayed.

Specifically,

"{name1} wrote on {name2}'s wall"

is translated as follows:

"{name1} {name2}'(n)in duvarına yazdı"

Fig. 6. This interface, for separation (explosion) of a native string into related strings, allows translators to specify how phrases depend on variations in token values

If {name2} is "Malmö", it will be displayed as "...Malmö'nün..."

But if {name2} is "Barış", it will be displayed as "...Barış'ın..."

Without this framework for handling dynamic content in a linguistically sound manner, many users would see the site as having worse than a 3-year-old's comprehension of their language.

4 Conclusion

Over 90 languages are in active translation using our tool. We have recently launched (in beta) languages with right-to-left scripts, like Hebrew and Arabic, where the layout must match the directionality of the text (see 7). Since we began this effort, our international growth has skyrocketed [5], and user experience (as measured by activity) per locale has improved with the quality of translations. Application developers on Facebook Platform can take advantage of the same tight integration and feedback loop to get their interface translated by interested users [2].

4.1 Challenges

We have to keep the community interested and engaged throughout the initial translation and maintenance phases. It is also important that we have enough available contributors to complete the translation, especially when working with "unsupported" languages. Ensuring acceptable quality in all languages is very important and difficult.

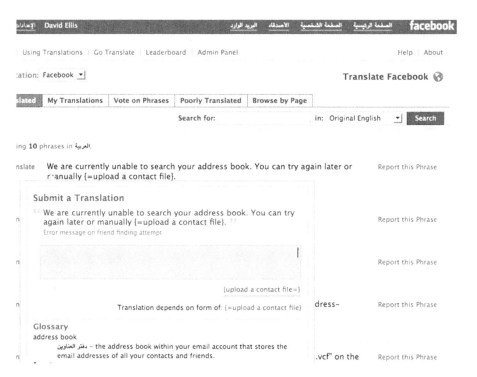

Fig. 7. Bulk translation interface in Arabic, where layout is appropriately shifted (e.g., our logo is on the right of the header)

Language re-use could be useful, particularly in cases of related languages or dialects (e.g., Spanish from Spain versus Latin America, Catalá, Portuguese (Brazil and Portugal)), but how can we allow them to share translations, and streamline the process of finer-grained localization? We have experimented with shallow machine translation in these cases, but the quality isn't yet good enough.

From an engineer's perspective, technical issues, including access, scalability, control, and security are also essential for the tool to be useful. From a linguist's perspective, the highly dynamic nature of our text, along with the complexity of some languages, must be properly handled to ensure high quality.

Acknowledgments

This technology has been developed with support from i18n team (engineers, language managers and others) at Facebook, and all our international users.

References

1. Aykin, N.M.: Internationalization and localization of the web sites. In: Bullinger, H.-J., Ziegler, J. (eds.) HCI (1), pp. 1218–1222. Lawrence Erlbaum, Mahwah (1999)
2. Bunyan, K.: Tutorial: Translating your applications using Facebooks crowd-sourced translation service (2008)

3. Facebook. Translating platform applications: Facebook developers wiki. Website (2009),
   `http://wiki.developers.facebook.com/index.php/Translating_Platform_`
   `Applications`
4. Kaplan, R.M., Martin Kay, T.: Regular models of phonological rule systems. Computational Linguistics 20, 331–378 (1994)
5. Sargent, B.B.: Community translation lifts facebook to top of social networking world (2008)

Rescaling Non-metric Data to Metric Data Using Multi-Dimensional Scaling

Kelley M. Engle and Guisseppi A. Forgionne

Department of Information Systems
University of Maryland Baltimore County (UMBC)
Baltimore, MD 21250 USA
{kelley.engle,forgionn}@umbc.edu

Abstract. Rescaling of nominal- and ordinal-scaled data to interval-scaled data is an important preparatory step prior to applying parametric statistical tests. Without rescaling, the analyst typically must resort to non-parametric tests that are less robust statistically than the metric counterparts. Multi-dimensional scaling (MDS) is a procedure that can be used to perform the desired rescaling. This paper utilizes MDS to transform nonmetric data from the IAN (Interactive Autism Network) and illustrates the application of the results to autism. Two simulated distributions were created from the MDS procedure to determine the best transformation. The tests reveal that either a normal or uniform distribution is acceptable with the uniform distribution performing marginally better than the normal.

Keywords: rescaling techniques, MDS (Multi-dimensional scaling), parametric test requirements, autism, data mining.

1 Introduction

Mining techniques can detect important patterns in voluminous data. To explain the patterns, however, it is often necessary to employ statistical methods that rely on metric measurements. Rescaling of nominal- and ordinal-scaled data to interval-scaled data can facilitate the needed statistical analysis. The study of autism offers a pertinent illustration.

Autism is a significant medical disorder affecting many children, their parents, and society. Data on the disorder is available from the IAN (Interactive Autism Network) project[1] [1] and consists of 7,269 children between the ages of 0-18 that have been diagnosed with some form of autism or related disorder (i.e., PDD-NOS also referred to as Pervasive Developmental Disorder – Not Otherwise Specified). Understanding the factors involved in the disorder and the potential interrelationships between these factors can help medical professionals design appropriate preventative and rehabilitative programs to reduce the consequences of the disorder.

---

[1] Data used in the preparation of this article were obtained from the Interactive Autism Network (IAN) Research Database at the Kennedy Krieger Institute and Johns Hopkins Medicine – Baltimore, sponsored by the Autism Speaks Foundation, version dated 2.0.2. For up-to-date information see www.ianproject.org

N. Aykin (Ed.): Internationalization, Design, LNCS 5623, pp. 245–253, 2009.
© Springer-Verlag Berlin Heidelberg 2009

A number of statistical tools can be used to facilitate understanding. The most robust tools, such as ANOVA and multiple regression, depend on interval-scaled data to properly perform the analyses [2]. Yet, much of the IAN data are ordinal and nominal (non-metric) in nature. There is value, then, in rescaling the ordinal/nominal data to interval-scaled data prior to applying any statistical analyses.

There are a number of different methods that can be used for the rescaling of ordinal/nominal data including IRT (Item Response Theory) [3], MDS (Multi-dimensional scaling), Thurstone's Case V method [4], and Osgood's semantic differential [4], among others. A preliminary correlation analysis with the available IAN data revealed that many of the variables were inter-correlated. Consequently, using a method, such as IRT (Item Response Test), was deemed inappropriate since it assumes variable independence. Instead, MDS was used to scale the data because of the variable inter-correlations. The research question was to determine which, among competing distributions, provided the best metrically scaled IAN data for analytical purposes.

2 Background

Scale construction refers to the process of developing an instrument designed to elicit information from a user group. This instrument should be designed in a way that preserves internal and external validity [5, 6, 7]. Numerous methods have been proposed for scale development, including Thurstone's psychophysics methods [8, 9, 10]. Rasch's model is also commonly used in item scaling [11, 12, 13].

The IRT (Item Response Test) [3] is an individual item analysis that was designed to address weaknesses in CTT (Classical Test Theory). These weaknesses included the CTT model's inability to accommodate nominal or ordinal data [14]. CTT is considered a group assessment model and consequently is deemed by some to be weak because the assumptions required by the theory are easily met [15]. Others, such as Harwell and Gatti [16], believe that CTT's deficiencies include "its inability to produce an interval scale for test scores and its failure to take the characteristics of items into account or to provide information about the reliability of estimated scores or proficiencies."

The are four basic steps involved in rescaling ordinal (or nominal) data to interval data using IRT: (1) Identifying an appropriate IRT model; (2) Estimate item parameters; (3) Estimate proficiency parameters and; (4) Assess model-data fit [16]. The model chosen will be determined by the type of item response data and the kinds of item parameters. For instance, one of the simplest models to use is the one-parameter Rasch model [13] [16]. IRT, depending on the model chosen, has specific requirements that must be met. Tests, such as the chi-square goodness-of-fit test for individual items, will determine if the IRT model chosen is a good fit for the data [16].

MDS (Multidimensional scaling) is a scaling technique which is primarily used to find hidden patterns among data by projecting the data into a 2 – or 3-dimensional space [17]. A simple analogy given by Kruskal and Wish [17] explains the basic concept quite well:

> *"Suppose you are given a map showing the locations of several cities in the United States and are asked to construct a table of distances between these cities. It is simple matter to fill in any entry in the table by measuring the distance between the cities with a ruler, and converting the ruler distance into the real distance by using the scale of the map (e.g., one cm. = 30 kilometers). Now consider the reverse problem, where you are given the table of distances between the cities, and are asked to produce the map. In essence, MDS is a method for solving this reverse problem."*

MDS incorporates a proximity parameter which measures the distances between points. Depending on the type of MDS model, these measurements can be for metric or non-metric data Metric MDS is closely related to factor analysis and calculates the distance based on the Euclidean formula. Non-metric data assume an ordinal relationship among the points, and non-metric MDS analyzes only the rank order of the items [17]. Shepard [18] made evident that is was possible to derive metric results from ordinal data and developed the first computer program to conduct this "nonmetric" multidimensional scaling.

A central concept in MDS is defining the objective function, or as defined by Kruskal, the stress measure (a more detailed account of the stress function can be found in [19]). The stress function measures the badness-of-fit for the MDS results and is essentially a "residual sum of squares" which determines whether or not a perfect monotonic relationship exists between the dissimilarities and the distances [19].

In typical applications of MDS, methods for obtaining the proximities generally include asking respondents to judge the distance between two items (i.e., asking respondents to judge how closely Coke and Pepsi taste) [17]. To utilize MDS as a rescaling technique for secondary data, an ideal distribution of the ordinal data is required to determine the proximity or distance between the ideal and the actual data values. This distribution should match the population distribution (i.e., uniform, normal distribution), if known.

Preliminary data analysis suggested that MDS would be an appropriate rescaling technique for the IAN data. This conclusion was reached because of the nonmetric nature of the data and the interrelationships that existed between the variables.

4 Data Collection and Analysis

There were a number of data cleansing activities required to prepare the sample dataset for the MDS testing. These activities included determining the inclusion criteria; for example, we only included autistic children who had corresponding treatment data as well as SCQ (Social Communication Questionnaire) scores. As a result of these criteria, out of the 7,269 autistic children, only 3,926 were included. It was considered critical to have treatment data for each child since for future data mining/statistical analysis activities, linking treatment to outcomes, is a primary consideration. Table 1 lists all the 10 attributes that were selected from the IAN dataset as well as a scale nature and description.

Table 1. Data Description

ATTRIBUTE	SCALE	DESCRIPTION
First ASD Diagnosis	Nominal	Captures the first ASD diagnosis such as ASD (Autism Spectrum Disorder), CDD (Childhood Disintegrative Disorder), PDD-NOS (Pervasive Development Disorder – Not Otherwise Specified).
Influenced Decision	Nominal	Lists the professional(s) that most influenced the parent's decision to begin treatment (i.e., pediatrician, psychiatrist, teacher etc.).
Who Prescribed	Nominal	If a treatment required a prescription this attribute contains the information on the prescriber (i.e., Primary care pediatrician, clinical psychologist, speech pathologist etc.).
Funding Source	Nominal	If a treatment is covered under a funding source such as the public school system, state early childhood program or other source of public funding (excluding Medicaid), then this attribute will list the funding source.
Work up Satisfaction	Nominal	Rates parent's satisfaction with an evaluation or work-up prior to commencing treatment Consists of a Yes/No/Not Applicable response.
Expected Improvement	Ordinal	A 5-pt Likert scale response rating the parent's expectations for this treatment (prior to starting).
Potential Risk	Ordinal	A 5-pt Likert scale response rating the parent's perception of potential risks associated with a treatment.
Expected Burden	Ordinal	A 5-pt Likert scale response rating the parent's expectations for this treatment (prior to starting).
Insurance Coverage	Nominal	Determines if any of the cost associated with the treatment is being covered either by private health insurance or by Medicaid.
9 point Likert Scale Treatment Efficacy	Ordinal	This is a combination of three different attributes from the original dataset which captures the parent's assessment of the efficacy of the particular treatment.

Due to some anomalies in the data, a number of records were further excluded from the dataset. These anomalies included conflicting data values for the treatment efficacy or where the parent refused to rate the efficacy of a treatment. After completing all data cleansing tasks, there were 3,283 autistic children with a total of 14,351 corresponding treatment records – on average, each child is currently receiving 4.37 treatments.

Once all data cleansing was complete, the dataset was then randomly split into two separate samples – this was performed within SAS [20] using the surveyselect procedure. The creation of two separate samples was performed to avoid the Bonferroni correction [21] which states that for every 20 hypothesis tests, there will be one result, purely by chance, that has significant results (i.e., an alpha value = .05). Therefore, to account for the fact that chance may create statistical significance; two tests were run to confirm all results.

4.1 Results for Spearman's Chi-Square Test

Because of the nonmetric nature of the data, a chi-square test was performed to determine if there existed any correlation among the variables. This step was necessary to determine if IRT (Item Response Test) could be used for rescaling. The results of the test indicated that there were multiple correlations between the variables in both samples and therefore IRT was deemed not a good fit for this dataset.

4.2 MDS

Due to the correlations discovered in the chi-square test, multidimensional scaling (MDS) was chosen as the rescaling method in lieu of IRT (which requires independent variables). MDS does not have this limitation regarding variable independence.

Two simulated data files were created in SAS – one with a uniform distribution and one with a normal distribution. These files will become the ideal measure that the original dataset will be compared to during the MDS procedure.

Our research question was to determine which of the two ideal measures – uniform or normal – generated the best data fit for the MDS procedure. Best fit is further defined as the badness-of-fit criterion [19], which will be reported for each test. The following lists the null and alternative hypotheses:

Null and Alternative Hypotheses

> H_0: There is no difference in the results between the normal and uniform distribution when using the MDS procedure.

> H_A: There is a difference in results between the normal and uniform distribution when using the MDS procedure.

The hypotheses were tested through the following MDS comparisons:

1. MDS – Sample1 and uniform data
2. MDS – Sample1 and normal data
3. MDS – Sample2 and uniform data
4. MDS – Sample2 and normal data

For each MDS procedure, the data from each sample were combined with the distribution data and a new variable called subject was added to the dataset. The purpose of adding the subject attribute was to allow the MDS procedure to compare the two groups. The definition for subject is user-defined – for our purposes we called the sample data S and the distribution data either U for uniform or N for normal. MDS requires the number of records to be a multiple of the number of variables; consequently, the total records in each of the combined datasets was 14,350 (a multiple of 10).

Dimensionality Issue. Choosing the number of dimensions for the MDS procedure required a more detailed investigation. Dimensions refer to the number of coordinate axes, or as described in [17] "the number of coordinate values used to locate a point in the space." Typically, MDS is used with either 2- or 3-dimensions with little regard to the true dimensionality of the data. This typical use is due to an ease of use factor that considers result interpretation. The MDS procedure will produce plots of the transformed data and therefore, when using more than 2-dimensions, the ability to visualize the plotted data is obscured. This obscuring effect is particularly true for the plot of configuration and plot of dimension coefficients for each subject that is generated within SAS.

For the goal of rescaling non-metric data, the final outcome for this procedure was the actual transformed data – not the plots themselves. Therefore, we were more interested in determining the correct dimensionality for this group of variables then we were in preserving the "ease of interpretability [17]." To determine the true dimensionality, there is a "good statistical method" that is discussed in more detail in Kruskal and Wish [17].

The simplest method to determine dimensionality was to assume that each variable corresponds to one axis, or dimension. However, as stated by Kruskal et al. in [17], "Although a dimensional interpretation frequently involves one interpretation for each dimension of the space, the dimensionality is not necessarily the number of relevant characteristics involved." One or more variables may not greatly affect the MDS configuration due to correlation with other variables or because these variables only affect a small subset of the data.

Table 2. Dimensionality Test

Number of Dimensions	Badness-of-fit Criterion
2	24.24%
3	18.41%
4	14.32%
5	11.91%
6	9.25%
7	8.12%
8	6.24%
9	4.46%

Stress, also called the badness-of-fit criterion (or goodness-of-fit criterion in earlier literature), is crucial in determining the number of dimensions to choose. All other constants held equal and assuming complete convergence, increasing the number of dimensions should decrease the badness-of-fit measure. To verify this effect, multiple experiments were conducted utilizing the MDS procedure while varying the dimensions from two to nine. The data for this test were a combination of the data from sample 1 and the simulated uniform distribution. As can be seen from the results in Table 2, for every dimension added to the MDS procedure the stress level, or badness-of-fit criterion, decreases. With the maximum number of dimensions chosen (9),

Table 3. Kruskal's Stress Heuristics

Stress	Badness-of-fit
20%	Poor
10%	Fair
5%	Good
0%	Perfect

the stress level is at approximately 4.5%, which is considered good according to Kruskal [19]. As a result of these findings, the four MDS experiments were conducted using the maximum nine dimensions.

4.3 MDS Results

The results for each of the experiments are shown below in Table 4. The uniform distribution performed slightly better than the normal distribution in determining the badness-of-fit criterion. Due to the cross-comparisons by variable, the transformed data set consisted of 129,150 records. These data were outputted to the RES dataset and can be found in the TRANDATA column (See appendix for the MDS procedure code).

Table 4. Overall Results – Badness-of-fit Criterion

Sample	Uniform	Normal
Sample 1	5%	5%
Sample 2	5%	6%

5 Findings

After evaluating the badness-of-fit criterion for the four MDS experiments, there is notably very little difference between the uniform and normal distributions. The uniform distribution had slightly better results but not enough to definitely reject the null hypothesis. Therefore, for these experiments, the null hypothesis is accepted and for all practical purposes either distribution can be used to transform the data. These findings are limited to only the sample used; for future releases of the IAN data these results may or may not hold true. The experiments then should be recreated to confirm or refute these results.

Another issue to consider with the transformed data is the sheer number of records created. The IAN project is expected to register up to 100,000 autistic children. Given a larger sample size as is projected for the IAN project, the number of transformed records will grow exponentially. Statistical programs, such as SAS and SPSS, are typically not used for extremely large datasets. One such solution would be to randomly sample the transformed data prior to performing statistical analyses.

Alternatively, a random sample of the original data can be obtained prior to the transformation in order to decrease the total number of transformed records.

6 Conclusion

MDS (Multi-dimensional scaling) is a technique that is predominantly used for detecting patterns along a multi-dimensional space. However, MDS can be used to transform nonmetric scaled data to a metric scale. The details of this process have been described in this paper as a practical aide to implementation. Prior to actually executing the MDS procedure in SAS some preprocessing is necessary. This includes: (1) Data prep and cleansing and; (2) Creating a simulated file using either a uniform or normal distribution to match the original data. Ideally, the number of dimensions should be the number of variables included in the dataset (n) – 1 in order to assure the best fit. After executing the MDS procedure, the badness-of-fit criterion should be analyzed for sufficiency according to Kruskal's heuristics.

The overall purpose of this paper was to present a viable method for rescaling nominal and ordinal data to interval-scaled data in the presence of significant interrelationships among the studied variables. By rescaling the data, more powerful parametric statistical tests can be performed on the transformed data. The rescaling method used was MDS (Multi-dimensional scaling) and was carried out on the IAN (Interactive Autism Network) data, which is dataset of approximately 5 000 autistic children from across the United States. A number of variables were extracted from this dataset and rescaled using the MDS procedure. The research question was to determine whether to use a normal or uniform distribution for the ideal measure in MDS. The experiments indicate that there is no significant difference in the badness-of-fit criterion for these two distributions. Therefore, researchers requiring metric data for their analyses could use either the normal or uniform distribution with the MDS procedure to transform the IAN data.

References

1. IAN (Interactive Autism Network) (homepage on the Internet), Kennedy Krieger Institute, Baltimore (2007-2008), http://www.ianproject.org (cited November 13, 2008)
2. Cooper, D.R., Schindler, P.S.: Business Research Methods, 9th edn. Mc-Graw Hill Irwin, New York (2006)
3. DeVellis, R.F.: Scale Development Theory and Applications, 2nd edn. Sage Publications, Thousand Oaks (2003)
4. Green, P.E., Tull, D.S.: Research for Marketing Decisions, 4th edn. Prentice-Hall, Inc., Englewood Cliffs (1978)
5. Dawis, R.V.: Scale Construction. Journal of Counseling Psychology 34(4), 481–489 (1987)
6. Edwards, A.L.: Techniques of Attitude Scale Construction. Appleton-Century-Crofts, Inc., New York (1957)
7. Dunn-Rankin, P.: Scaling Methods. Lawrence Erlbaum Associates Publishers, Hillsdale (1983)
8. Thurstone, L.L.: A law of comparative judgment. Psychological Review 34, 273–286 (1927)

9. Thurstone, L.L.: The method of paired comparisons for social values. Journal of Abnormal and Social Psychology 21, 384–400 (1927)
10. Thurstone, L.L.: Psychophysical analysis. American Journal of Psychology 38(3), 368–389 (1927)
11. Andrich, D., Luo, G.: A hyperbolic cosine latent trait model for unfolding dichotomous single-stimulus responses. Applied Psychological Measurement 17(3), 253–276 (1993)
12. Andrich, D.: Relationships between the Thurstone and Rasch approaches to item scaling. Applied Psychological Measurement 2(3), 449–460 (1978)
13. Wright, B.D., Masters, G.N.: Rating Scale Analysis. Mesa Press, Chicago (1982)
14. McCartney, K., Burchinal, M.R., Bub, K.L.: Best Practices in Quantitative Methods for Developmentalists. Blackwell Publishing, Boston (2006)
15. Sapp, M.: Basic Psychological Measurement, Research Designs, and Statistics without Math. Charles C. Thomas Publisher, Ltd., Springfield (2006)
16. Harwell, M.R., Gatti, G.G.: Rescaling ordinal data to interval data in educational research. Review of Educational Research 71(1), 105–131
17. Kruskal, J.B., Wish, M.: Multidimensional Scaling. Sage Publications, Beverly Hills (1978)
18. Shepard, R.N.: The analysis of proximities: multidimensional scaling with an unknown distance function. Psychometrika 27, 125–140, 219–246 (1962)
19. Kruskal, J.B.: Multidimensional scaling by optimizing goodness of fit to a nonmetric hypothesis. Psychometrika 29(1), 1–27 (1964)
20. SAS Software (homepage on the Internet). Business Intelligence Software and Predictive Analytics, Cary, NC (2008), http://www.sas.com (cited November 13, 2008)
21. Abdi, H.: Bonferroni and Sidak corrections for multiple comparisons. In: Salkind (ed.) Encyclopedia of Measurement and Statistics, Sage, Thousand Oaks (2007)

Intercultural Usability Surveys:
Do People Always Tell "The Truth"?

Emilie W. Gould

Adjunct Professor, Center for Distance Learning, SUNY Empire State College
111 West Avenue, Saratoga Springs, NY, USA 12866
goulde@alum.rpi.edu

Abstract. Researchers have identified many ways that culture affects usability methods – interviews, moderated tests, think-aloud protocols, and card sorts. This paper reviews some of that literature and discusses a project investigating the effect of culture on usability surveys.

Keywords: culture, cultural usability, survey methodology.

1 Introduction

Developing reliable, valid surveys for usability research is not easy. People may use words differently; apply different end-points (and middle-points) to scales; and situate answers in different social realities. By following principles of survey design, we can generally achieve statistical reliability. However, closer inspection of subsamples sometimes shows patterns of skipped questions and spoiled surveys – or a decreased or skewed range of answers.

Similarly, during pilot tests, interview guides for requirements gathering and usability reviews often change substantially. Researchers discover the questions that elicit abundant feedback and eliminate those that are redundant. Connotations emerge and words turn out to have different meanings in context.

However, we muddle on – assessing usability through processes that rely heavily on survey. We base our methods on assumptions that are part of the "culture of usability evaluation" [1].

Traditionally, we have assumed two things:

- we should ask all users the same questions to make it possible to compare feedback
- users will answer our questions truthfully

Within our own cultures, these assumptions may be more or less true. Unfortunately, when we begin to collect data in vastly different cultures, our assumptions are probably false.

2 What Kind of Methodology Problems Have People Already Found in Intercultural Evaluations?

Since the mid-1990s, people have been reporting problems with interviews, moderated tests, think-aloud protocols, and other methodologies used in international usability evaluations.

N. Aykin (Ed.): Internationalization, Design, LNCS 5623, pp. 254–258, 2009.

At CHI98, Alvin Yeo (then a student) discussed a usability study he had done to localize a spreadsheet. His evaluators were Malaysian staff at his university – higher and lower in status to himself. Despite bad experiences with the software, only those who were higher in status rated the software negatively; those with equal or lower status were more positive. Similarly, high-status evaluators made more negative comments and were "harsher" in the way they phrased them; low-status evaluators were more polite and "subtle." Yeo [2, 3] concluded that such self-censorship was based on the relationship of the evaluators to the test moderator. Malaysia is classified as a high power-distance, moderately high collectivist society by Hofstede [4]. In general, Yeo believed people sought to preserve harmony and save face – his own as well as their own – by refusing to be negative. By contrast, the high-status evaluator felt her problems had made her look incompetent so she criticized the software. Yeo suggested that Western usability assessment techniques should only be used with people who were already experienced users, familiar with the experimenter, and higher in status than the experimenter.

Needless to say, these recommendations pose some problems for our traditional focus on inexperienced users. In addition, they unbalance the experimental design of most usability assessments.

Apala Chavan [5] found similar "relational problems" in her research in India. Gender, youth, and class all affected the willingness of evaluators to talk about products. Women would often speak only with women; younger researchers had more success than older, more senior people. Unlike Yeo, Chavan attributed the difference to stronger social affiliations based on liking for people similar to one's self.

Clemmensen, Shi, Kumar, Li, Sun, and Yammiyavar [6] found support for both explanations in a study comparing the role of test moderators in usability assessments in India, China, and Denmark. Indian moderators had to deal with self-censorship, based on gender and age, among traditional end users in India. Male researchers needed to include a male relative in interviews with rural women, and older researchers "frightened" younger rural evaluators. In China, they found female moderators seemed to do better with male evaluators, an apparent reversal of power distance. However, in Denmark, usability tests ran most smoothly when the researchers and evaluators were the same gender, age, and shared the same level of job experience.

Clemmensen et al. suggested that intercultural usability tests need to:

- include "hidden user groups" (those less comfortable with foreigners or more traditional)
- estimate the "evaluator effect" and select researchers appropriate to those groups
- review the detection rate to see if these groups identify different types of problems
- modify the test protocols to localize scenarios, use more direct probes, or ask different questions

One suggestion for localizing test protocols adopts a technique developed by Chavan [5, 7]. She notes that Indian evaluators are often unwilling to criticize under any circumstance and recommends using dramatistic techniques rooted in Bollywood and traditional Indian theatre. For instance, Bollywood scenarios free people from the constraints of the "real world" and allow them to speculate about emotion and effects that belong to an idealized product or situation.

However, there could be some difficulty in applying this recommendation due to the aesthetic divergence between these traditions. Both began as sacred drama but the Western tradition focuses on using poetics (a counterpart to logic and rhetoric) to find concrete "truths," while the Indian tradition looks for release and transcendence.

> The compulsions of the Indian theory of anukarana or imitation are different from the Greek ones. The success of anukarana is not judged in terms of its ability to represent the world but by its capacity to create a new world.
>
> The method of abhinaya ... is not a mimesis of things but of bhavas (moods) which are ever changing in significance....
>
> One drama exploits free will, the other, destiny; one exploits tension, the other conspires to eliminate it. (Chavan [7] quoting Gupt [8])

Although Chavan suggests art can be used as a medium to contextualize usability, there seem to be practical problems at the level of asking questions and interpreting answers.

Finally, usability researchers have examined the effect of culture on think-aloud protocols. Yeo [2] noted that most of his evaluators had difficulty sustaining a commentary on their actions. Clemmensen et al. [6] found that moderators running tests in China needed to use many more direct probes since evaluators would not identify their actions unless prompted. However, after a period of silence, many often provided a retrospective think-aloud analysis of their choices.

Shi [9], reviewing usability tests in Beijing, also found that Chinese people needed regular prompting. He attributed their silence to the holistic thinking style and interpersonal needs of East Asians. His explanation draws on Nisbett's [10] description of Asian and Western cognitive styles – the first derived from the five Confucian relationships and the second from Greek philosophy. Nisbett believes Asian thought focuses on relations among people and events, social harmony, and the acceptance of natural processes and change; Western thought is more attentive to objects, formal logic, categories, control, and stable theories of explanation. When faced with contradiction, Asian people tend to look for a middle way; Western people insist on correctness and "truth." Nawaz, Plocher, Clemmensen, Qu, and Sun [11] found support for holistic thinking among Chinese evaluators in a card-sorting exercise designed to test information structure.

All these studies – and there are many more now available in research journals and proceedings from the ACM, HCI International, and IWIPS – demonstrate that our usability methods are not as "methodical" as we once believed. Culture seems to affect interviews, moderated tests, think-aloud protocols, and card-sorts. Explanations can be found in theories of cultural dimensions, sociology, and cognitive differences. Recommendations include limiting (or expanding) types of evaluators, selecting test moderators and researchers on the basis of their similarity (or dissimilarity) to the evaluators, localizing scenarios, applying theories from drama to contextualize tests, and modifying probes.

Such diversity should not be unexpected; usability research began adopting qualitative methods in the 1980s and lack of generalizability is one of the key features of such research. Ethnographic methods provide rich data but that data must be "grounded" and interpreted to make it useful for product development. We have begun to understand some of the ways culture affects tests and interviews. My current research looks at ways survey data may be skewed in intercultural usability assessments.

3   Does Bias Affect Surveys Used in Intercultural Research?

While working on my PhD thesis, I developed surveys for Malaysia and the United States [11]. Colleagues translated my terminology into Bahasa Malaysia but I am the first to recognize that some of the differences that I saw in my return rate may have reflected incomplete localization. However, I also found higher rates of deliberately spoiled surveys, plus skipped questions and skewed scales from Malaysian respondents. These seemed to reflect conscious choices based on attitudes, not accidents.

Such differences pose the following questions for research:

- Are there underlying cultural attitudes to survey research that lead to such behavior?
- Is the problem simply that surveys are less common in some countries?
- Do people in some countries actively resist data collection by survey? Does such resistance depend on who developed the survey or where the survey originated?
- Do people feel compelled to reveal everything in surveys? Is it ever okay to lie?
- Do survey scales match people's confidence in their answers?
- Do people prefer anonymity or situations where they have a relationship with the researcher?
- Are people more positive about participating in interviews than in surveys?
- How do these attitudes relate to multinational companies doing usability research?

I am currently collecting and analyzing data to answer these questions using focus groups with international students in the United States and Canada. Because such students have experienced two cultures, they are in a position to compare and contrast their experiences in dealing with surveys. However, this same experience also makes these students an atypical minority within their own countries. As a result, international colleagues are also conducting a limited number of focus groups to validate my results. Full results will be presented at HCII 2009.

References

1. Wallerstein, I.: The heritage of sociology, the promise of social science (1998), http://www.binghamton.edu/fbc/iwprad1.htm
2. Yeo, A.: Cultural effects in usability assessment. In: CHI 1998, pp. 74–75. ACM Press, New York (1998)
3. Yeo, A.: Are usability assessment techniques reliable in non-Western countries? Elec. J. on Info Sys in Dev Countries 3(1), 1–21 (2000)
4. Hofstede, G.: Cultures and organizations: Software of the mind. McGraw-Hill, New York (1997)
5. Chavan, A.: Usability in India, is it different? In: HCII 2005, Lawrence Erlbaum, Mahwah (2006)
6. Clemmensen, T., Shi, Q., Kumar, J., Li, H., Sun, X., Yammiyavar, P.: Cultural usability tests – how usability tests are not the same all over the world. In: Aykin, N. (ed.) HCII 2007 LNCS, vol. 4559, pp. 281–290. Springer, Heidelberg (2007)

7. Chavan, A.: What about a 'local' wrapper around an 'universal' core? In: CHI 2008, pp. 2605–2607. ACM Press, New York (2008)
8. Gupt, B.: Dramatic concepts, Greek and Indian: A study of Poetics and Natyasastra. D.K. Printworld, New Delhi (1994)
9. Shi, Q.: A field study of the relationship and communication between Chinese evaluators and users in thinking aloud usability tests. In: NordiCHI 2008, pp. 344–352. ACM Press, New York (2008)
10. Nisbett, R.: The geography of thought: How Asians and Westerners think differently and why. Free Press, New York (2003)
11. Nawaz, A., Plocher, T., Clemmensen, T., Qu, W., Sun, X.: Cultural differences in the structure of categories in Denmark and China. Working paper 03-2007, Department of Informatics, Copenhagen Business School (2007)
12. Gould, E.W.: Applying cultural dimensions to website design: A case study from Malaysia and the United States. Doctoral dissertation, Rensselaer Polytechnic Institute, 2004. In: Dissertation Abstracts International (2004)

Cultural Interface Design Advisor Tool: Research Methodology and Practical Development Efforts

Irina Kondratova and Ilia Goldfarb

National Research Council Canada Institute for Information Technology
46 Dineen Drive, Fredericton, NB, Canada E3B 9W4
{Irina.Kondratova,Ilia.Goldfarb}@nrc-cnrc.gc.ca

Abstract. Within the cultural user interface design research and development project we address the need in culturally appropriate user interface design that is brought up by globalization. Globalization is affecting most computer-mediated communication and, in particular, user interface design for the Internet applications. To address this need, we are building a cultural "look and feel" advisor tool that is based on the research study utilizing cultural analysis of a large number of websites for a particular locale. This paper addresses the research methodology we employed in manual evaluation of specific cultural markers on a large set of country-specific websites and reports on several important aspects of transferring our research results into the practical implementation of the cultural design advisor tool.

Keywords: Cultural preferences, color theory, cultural user interface, usability.

1 Introduction

Cultural appropriateness of user interface design directly impacts on the user's perception of credibility, trustworthiness and user acceptance of websites. "Global businesses are losing market share worth as much as $1.6 billion per year, or $4.7 billion over three years, by failing to localize product information" (Forrester Consulting, 2008). Our background research shows that there is a lack of software development tools to support culturally sensitive user interface design. Availability of such tools will aid in broadening global business opportunities for small and medium size business enterprises (SME)s and help governments to inclusively provide electronic services to all segments of population including ethnic communities and recent immigrants.

In our research project we address the need in culturally appropriate user interface design that is brought up by globalization and is affecting most computer-mediated communication and, in particular, user interface design for the Internet, including e-business, eHealth and web-based advanced training and collaboration applications.

In our background research, in the onset of the project, we discovered that, in spite of the wealth of information available regarding the issues related to design of international user interfaces, it is not easy for Web designers and developers to acquire a deep cross-cultural understanding of user interface design. There is a number of existing cultural models and theories, which can be used to develop a set of broad cross-cultural

N. Aykin (Ed.): Internationalization, Design, LNCS 5623, pp. 259–265, 2009.

guidelines, similar to ones developed by Marcus and Gould [6]. However, this approach results in a mostly theoretical model of cross-cultural design, while the practical website development approach requires effective prototyping.

In our research we utilize a new approach to cultural user interface development. We are building a cultural "look and feel" prototyping tool that is based on the broad-based research study utilizing semi-automated analysis of a large number of websites for a particular locale. This tool is envisioned as an advisor tool that can aid software development teams in the quick production of the first draft of the cultural "look and feel" design. Data collection for the study was conducted using both automated and manual approach. The methodology and results of our automated data collection that involved around 36, 000 websites for 36 countries were described in detail in [4].This paper addresses the research methodology we employed in manual evaluation of specific cultural markers on a large set of country-specific websites and reports on several important aspects of transferring our research results into the practical implementation of the cultural design advisor tool.

2   Manual Evaluation: Methodology

We conducted two research studies to investigate color and imagery selection and design trends on websites from around the globe. We studied the usage of specific cultural markers for website design using both automated cultural web mining tools and visual observations by human observers. The first study was completed in 2007 and utilized automated evaluation tools, such as a Cultural Web Spider tool (CWS) and color analysis and visualization tools [4]. The visual cultural markers we investigated in this study were colors, font usage, number of images, and layout of the webpage. Clearly, not all cultural markers could be automatically collected. By their nature, some cultural markers, especially those related to images, such as icons, flags, symbols, pictures related to geography, shape and architecture require involvement of human evaluators. This was accomplished in the design of the second study. The second study (currently in progress) utilizes novel evaluation methodology and a survey tool to further research design trends observed on a large number of website from different countries such as use of images, graphics, typography, as well as color.

2.1   Data Collection Methodology

For this research study, we chose the following design elements that would be analyzed by human evaluators: typography, graphics and layout, in combination with color. A survey tool was developed using these elements in general, as well as any relevant sub-category of each of the elements, adding up to twenty five different variables to be observed by human evaluators for each website (represented in Table 1). A sample of 100 out of 1000 websites, specific to a particular country, was examined in close detail by at least two human evaluators using this cultural visual design survey tool. Any indication of reoccurring trends was recorded. The trends observed were confirmed by researchers' observations on the rest (around 900) of websites for a specific country. Based on the results of this evaluation work, some general and country-specific recommendations for culturally appropriate design were developed. These recommendations, along with research results from the first study and the results of the literature review, form a part of the content within the cultural design advisor tool.

Table 1. Survey tool categories

Colors	International 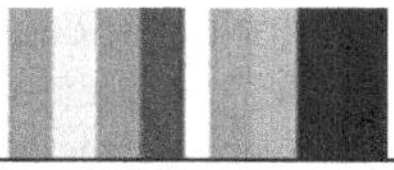
	Country specific colors 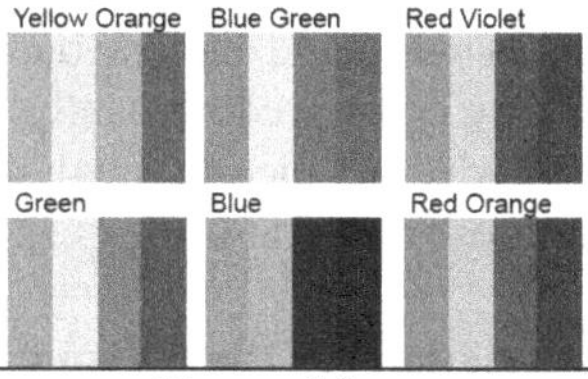 Yellow Orange Blue Green Red Violet Green Blue Red Orange
Typography	Type of fonts
	Colored fonts
Graphics	Number
	Types
Layout	Banners
	Menu location
	Use of white space
	Justification
	Number of columns
Culture	Holfstede's dimensions

2.2 Examination of Color Usage in Web Design

Color usage in web design was examined using country-specific color swatches identified by researchers based on the results from our initial web color usage study [6] and the application of the color theory [3]. In particular, the country-specific color preferences for a particular country were identified by removing the color hues that belonged to the "international" color palette (depicted in Figure 2) from data on total color usage obtained in our research study for a particular country, as shown in Figure 2 for Brazil.

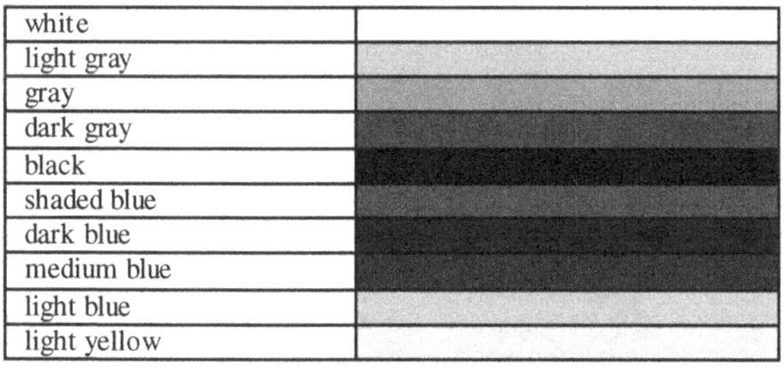
white
light gray
gray
dark gray
black
shaded blue
dark blue
medium blue
light blue
light yellow

Fig. 1. "International" color palette

To obtain country-preferred color combinations, two top ranked country-specific colors were selected from the resulting color usage pie chart (Figure 3) and combined with their opposing or neighboring colors on the color wheel. The resulting choice of color preferences for a particular country was cross-referenced with the results of the ethnographic studies conducted by Cabarga [1]. Two color palettes (international and country-specific) were defined for each country and used by researchers in our manual evaluation to survey color usage in web design to a deeper level. It is important to note, that, as we found though our visual observations, in some countries designers are using blue color predominantly in their domestic design palette (e.g. UK, Australia), this is why we incorporated shades of blue within the country - specific color palette for these countries.

2.3   Examination of Other Visual Cultural Markers

Of equal importance to the design of culturally appropriate web sites is the use of imagery in combination with layout.   In our research, imagery included graphics, photographs of people or things, cartoons, maps, graphs, even banners that display

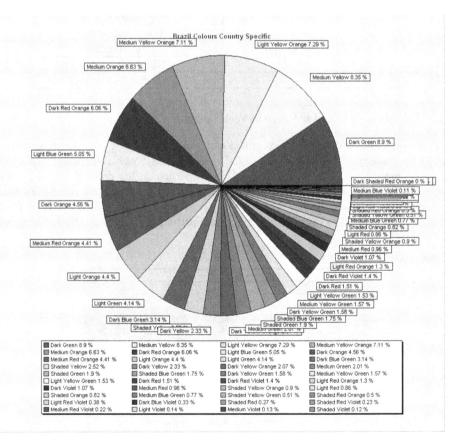

Fig. 2. Brazil country-specific colors pie chart

stylized fonts. In our survey tool we identified certain country-specific imagery preferences that can be attributed to cultural dimensions or attributes specific to the country. Within the imagery, we were looking for preferences in using images of people, people's close-ups, or images of "things" (e.g. buildings, landscapes, equipment, etc.).

In our manual evaluation process through visual observations of a representative set out of 900-1000 website per country, we also recorded visual design features based on Hofstede's cultural factor model [2], in particular on cultural factors such as Power distance; Uncertainty avoidance; and Masculinity vs. Femininity as reflected in the visual interface design. As per research done by Marcus [5], we measured power distance by site's focus on logos/seals or focus on people. When evaluating tendency towards femininity/masculinity dimension in visual design, we were looking for women's editions of popular websites. To estimate tendency to uncertainty avoidance factor, we were looking for navigation and the amount of links on the menu.

Predominant typography features on web pages for a particular country were examined as well. In particular, we paid attention to the usage of elaborate heading fonts, and recorded the usage of color in typography.

3   Implementation of Findings within the Advisor Tool

We are designing an advisor tool that could be used by Web developers and SMEs to aid in their production of the first draft of the cultural "look and feel" design for a particular locale. We want it to be used by the companies to help them in collaboration with clients in defining appropriate user interface and in balancing client preferences for product interface design with culturally appropriate design features. We believe that our tool would be especially useful for SMEs that want to develop software applications for international markets, but frequently do not have in-house internationalization/localization expertise or the budget to hire a professional localization company. This focus on SMEs defines the features of the tool.

Our advisor tool contains a step-by-step design guide, a set of cultural templates, as well as useful information on local culture, and results of our studies, including our findings on usage of color, imagery, fonts, and other observations. We envision that the tool could be used in the following fashion by potential users.

3.1   Usage of the Advisor Tool by Non-expert Designers

We see the advisor tool being used by non-expert designers (e.g. novice website developers or SMEs) in the following fashion. The designer can choose a region or a particular country directly from the menu. After this, the designer will follow the step-by-step design process, starting from the choice of design style, followed by the choice of color palette and typography. At the end of the process the designer will have a choice of a ready-to-go, culturally appropriate web template for a particular country, which is based on the choices made. The user can also skip the design process altogether and go directly to the set of templates prepared for a country and choose from them. These templates are created by a designer/researcher within the team and are deeply inspired by the results of the manual evaluation. Within the tool, there is also plenty of supplementary information on our research findings for the country and on research results from others, this information can aid greatly in the decision process.

3.2 Usage of the Advisor Tool by Experienced Web Designers

We believe the advisor tool could be also useful for expert designers who are not familiar with cultural user preferences for a particular country. This especially relates to the choice of culturally appropriate color palettes. Since all our research results, including information on country specific color usage and preferred color palettes is incorporated within the tool, experienced designers will have all valuable data in their hands to support design decisions, including statistical results on color usage per country (Figure 2), average number of images per page, preference towards colored fonts, usage of white (empty) space, justification, menu placing preferences, image preferences.

4   Conclusions

The cultural interface design study investigates the usage of specific cultural markers for website design in a number of countries, in order to incorporate the results into a cultural interface design advisor tool. In particular, along with other visual markers, such as fonts, layout, number of images, we investigated usage of color for website design in different countries and developed recommendations for country-specific color palettes which are culturally appropriate. In our research, we utilized automated web data mining tools and complemented results with a manual evaluation of a representative number of the website per country. This methodology allowed us to: confirm results of automated evaluation; complement automated cultural data mining results with observations of researchers, and to develop a set of cultural web templates that are inspired by country-specific web design preferences.

An additional outcome of this research study is that we developed a suite of tools and research methodologies that could be used by researchers for conducting ethnographic and cultural studies on the Internet, by marketing and advertising companies to identify cultural trends for advertising and marketing purposes, and by web designers to design culturally appropriate web user interfaces.

Acknowledgements. The authors would like to acknowledge the support for this research project provided by the National Research Council Canada.

References

1. Cabarga, L.: The Designer's Guide to Global Color Combinations. Designer's Guide to Color Combinations - 500 Historic and Modern Color Formulas in CMYK. Northern Lights Books (1999)
2. Hofstede, G.: Cultures and Organizations: Software of the Mind. McGraw-Hill, New York (1991)

3. Itten, J.: The Art of Color: The Subjective Experience and Objective Rationale of Color. John Wiley and Sons, Chichester (1974)
4. Kondratova, I., Goldfarb, I.: Color Your Website: Use of Colors on the Web. In: Aykin, N. (ed.) HCII 2007. LNCS, vol. 4560, pp. 123–132. Springer, Heidelberg (2007)
5. Marcus, A.: Cross-Cultural Web User-Interface Design. In: Proc. Human-Computer Interaction (INTERACT 2001), pp. 832–834 (2001)
6. Marcus, A., Gould, E.W.: Cultural Dimensions and Global Web User Interface Design: What? So What? Now What? In: Proc. 16th Conference on Human Factors and the Web, Austin, Texas (2000)

An Investigation of the Relationship between Digit Ratio and Spatial Ability

Hanyu Lin[1], Moli Yeh[2], and Yenyu Kang[1]

[1] Industrial Design Department, National Kaohsiung Normal University
No.62, Shenjhong Rd., Yanchao, Kaohsiung, Taiwan
[2] Fashion Imaging Department, Ming Dao University
No.369, Wenhwa Rd., Peetow, Changhwa, Taiwan

Abstract. Spatial ability plays a key role in many types of reasoning and communication, and is important in domains such as design. Digit ratio is related to a range of cognitive abilities, including spatial ability. In digit ratio studies, most studies were limited by using only one test for spatial ability. The purpose of present study was to investigate which sub-factors of spatial ability are related to digit ratio. We analyzed sex differences and the relationship between digit ratio and three sub-factors of spatial ability. Our results found that right hand digit ratio was significantly lower in males than in females, no significant differences were found between males and females on the left hand ratio. For female samples, both hands digit ratio were significantly negative correlated with perceptual speed factor of spatial ability. There was no association between digit ratio and spatial visualization factor and spatial relation factor.

Keywords: digit ratio, spatial ability, perceptual speed.

1 Introduction

Spatial ability plays a key role in many types of reasoning and communication, and is important in domains such as design, mathematics, natural sciences, and engineering. Researches have demonstrated that spatial ability is a predictor of success in an engineering graphics design class [2] [15]. For example, tests of spatial abilities are the best predictors of success in engineering courses, particularly engineering drawing [13].

Industrial design is based not only on technical expertise but also on creative thinking. Creative thinking involves mental transformation, mental combination, and mental synthesis [10]. According to Roth [30], creative thinking, conceptual problem solving, and concept generation are associated with spatial ability. Thus, spatial ability would seem to be important to designers.

What is spatial ability? Spatial ability may be defined as the ability to generate, retain, retrieve, and transform well-structured visual images [18]. Halpern [12] states that the term "visual-spatial abilities" it is not an easy term to define, because it is not a unitary concept. According to Carroll [5], the sub-factors of spatial ability include: spatial visualization, spatial relation, closure speed, closure flexibility and perceptual speed. Spatial visualization, spatial relation and perceptual speed are frequently mentioned sub-factors.

N. Aykin (Ed.): Internationalization, Design, LNCS 5623, pp. 266–273, 2009.

The most extensively studied factor is the spatial visualization factor [17], and tests that load on this factor involve "processes of apprehending, encoding, and mentally manipulating spatial forms" (as cited in [26]). Spatial relation factor is similar to spatial visualization. It also requires mental transformations but differ in that it involves manipulations of two-dimensional objects that can be completed in a single step, and in that it tends to emphasize speed. Perceptual speed involves no spatial transformations, and primarily requires rapid matching of visual pattern. Psychometric tests that load on this factor assess individual differences in the speed or efficiency with which one can make relatively simple perceptual judgments [5]. These three factors are moderately correlated with one another. In fact, depending on the tasks included in the analysis, some factor analysis studies have failed to find a clear distinction between the Spatial Visualization and Spatial Relations factors [5] [18] (cited in [26]).

Some evidences suggest a positive correlation between testosterone and spatial ability [6] [16] [34]. Studies also suggest that changes testosterone level in adulthood cause differences in spatial ability. Study of Janowsky, Oviatt and Orwoll [16] indicates that higher levels of testosterone contribute to superior performance on spatial tests, but do not facilitate performance on verbal ability tests. Moffat, Zonderman, Metter, Blackman, Harman and Resnick [28] found that an increased testosterone index was associated with improved scores on visual memory and visuospatial function. In other studies, Shute, Pellegrino, Hubert and Reynolds [33] have found an inverted U-shape relationship between testosterone levels and spatial ability; lower levels of testosterone had low spatial ability scores, whereas intermediate levels of testosterone were associated with better performance.

Literature on the relationship between testosterone levels and performance on spatial task is less consistent. Some studies report negative relationship [11] [27], but some found no relationship [1] [24]. For example, Keever and Deyo [25] failed to find any relationship between testosterone levels and spatial visualization tests in both men and female students. Hooven, Chabris, Ellison and Kosslyn [14] explained the inconsistent results in the following three factors: (1) methods of measuring testosterone levels; (2) subject samples; (3) measures of spatial ability. Hooven et al. [14] focus on the relationship of testosterone to response time, and error rate on a test of spatial ability. They found that high testosterone levels are associated with lower error rates and faster response. Brosnan [3] suggested that high testosterone levels enhance the development of the right side of the brain, resulting in enhanced spatial thinking.

The ratio of the length between the index finger (second digit, 2D) and the ring finger (fourth digit, 4D) acts as a marker of the levels of testosterone. It is thought to be an indirect measure of testosterone. Evidence suggests that the 2D:4D ratio is a negative correlate of prenatal and adult testosterone [21].

Higher levels of testosterone result in a lower digit ratio [19] [20] [21]. The ratio reliably differs by sex, with females typically having a higher ratio (2D:4D) than males [21]. Digit ratio is also known to be stable over lifetime[20].

Digit ratios have been found to predict job performance, such as athlete, musician and trader. Manning and Taylor [22] reported that, among men, 2D:4D ratio was negatively associated with sports attainment. Sluming and Manning [35] found a significant relationship between 2D:4D ratio and rankings of musical ability of male musicians within a symphony orchestra, low 2D:4D was associated with high rank within the orchestra. Coates, Gurnell and Rustichini [7] found that traders with a lower 2D:4D make greater long-term profits and remain in the business for a longer period of time.

There is evidence that digit ratio does correlate with cognitive performance. Sanders, Sjodin and Chastelaine [32] found a negative correlation between digit ratio and spatial ability. Manning and Tayler [22] and McFadden and Shubel [23] found that men with low digit ratio have higher scores on the mental rotation. Bull and Benson [4] reported that participants with lower digit ratio on the right hand showed a stronger SNARC (Spatial Numerical Association of Response Codes) effect. But these relationships have not been replicated in other studies. For example, Coolican and Peters [8] found that none of the correlations between 2D:4D ratio and mental rotation performance were significant. However, because the used of large samples (237 males) in their study, large sample size had good statistical power. So they concluded that a relationship between 2D:4D ratio and mental rotation performance in males was not established.

Spatial ability does not show a reliable correlation between task performance and digit ratio. Bull and Benson [4] pointed out that spatial tasks are typically fairly complex in nature requiring not only spatial ability, but also attention and cognitive skills, such as short-term memory and working memory. It may also be possible to use verbally mediated strategies to aid performance on such tasks. Differences in the contribution of such additional variables to performance may partially account for the lack of consistent findings in previous studies.

In 2D:4D ratio studies, most studies used only one test for spatial ability. A small number of studies included two or three spatial tests. For example, Poulin, O'Connell and Freeman [29] used mental rotation test, free recall test and placement recall test. In order to find out which sub-factors of spatial ability are related to 2D:4D ratio, we examined the relationship between 2D:4D ratio and three sub-factors of spatial ability, namely: spatial visualization factor, spatial relation factor, and perceptual speed factor.

2   Method

2.1   Participants

A total of 40 undergraduate students (14 male, 26 female) were recruited from a Design Methods class at the National Kaohsiung Normal University. Participants who reported injuries to their 2nd and/or 4th digits were excluded from the present study. Data from two male participants were subsequently discarded due to a high error rate on the tasks. Thus, their data were not included in analysis.

2.2   Measurement of 2D:4D

Participants were requested to place their hands palm down in a relaxed position on the surface of a scanning device, and one scanning per hand was made. The scanned images were processed in Adobe Photoshop. Two raters measured the index and ring finger. A vertical line was drawn from the midpoint of the basal crease of the finger to the midpoint of the fingertip. The 2D:4D ratio was computed by dividing the length of the index finger by the length of the ring finger. By the two raters, reliabilities (Cronbach's alpha) for the 2D:4D ratio were: left ratio .98, right ratio .98. So the ratios from each observer were averaged to obtain the final 2D:4D ratio for each participant.

2.3 Material

Three spatial ability tests were used in this study. Spatial visualization factor was evaluated using paper folding test; spatial relation factor was evaluated using card rotation test, as well as perceptual speed factor was evaluated using hidden patterns test [9].

Paper folding test: This test consists of two parts, each of which has 10 items. Participants required to mentally folding a piece of paper and punching a hole in it. Participants were asked to determine the position of the hole when the paper is unfolded. Each part was given 2.5 minutes to complete. The score was the result of the total number of correct answers minus the number of incorrect answers.

Card rotation test: A 2D mental rotation test where participants were required to decide whether rotated figures were identical to the original figure or were a mirror image. This test consists of two parts, each of which has 10 rows of eight test figures. Each part was given 2 minutes to complete. The score was the result of the total number of correct answers minus the number of incorrect answers.

Hidden patterns test: This test also consists of two parts; each part contains 200 figures composed of line drawing. Participants must identify whether the model pattern was embedded in each test figure. Each part was given 1.5 minutes to complete. Participants were asked to respond as quickly and as accurately as possible. The test was scored for the total number of correct answers minus the number of incorrect answers.

2.4 Procedure

Participants were tested in a group setting in a large lecture room and were asked to perform three spatial tests. They were given group instructions and were told the time limit for each test. In each test, after being shown two example tests, they were instructed to perform the task. Participants were first administered the paper folding test, followed by the card rotation test, and finally the hidden patterns test. Measurement of three spatial tests took about 20 minutes. At the end of three spatial tests, scans were taken from left and right hands of each participant.

3 Results

A comparison of sex differences in three spatial tests and 2D:4D ratio on the right and on the left hand was tested by t-tests for independent sample. Pearson correlations were computed between three spatial tests and 2D:4D ratio of left and right hands within each sex group.

3.1 Sex Differences

The results of two-tailed independent sample t-tests were shown in Table 1. 2D:4D ratio was significantly lower in males than in females on the right hand ($t(38)=-2.699$, $p< 05$)

But 2D:4D ratio was not significantly different between males and females on the left hand (t(38)=-.983, p=.332). Males scored significantly higher than females on hidden patterns test (t(38)=2.217, p<.05). Male-female differences in paper folding test and card rotation test scores were not found.

Table 1. Sex differences in 2D:4D ratio and spatial abilities

	Male(n=14) Mean(SD)	Female(n=26) Mean(SD)	t	P
Right 2D:4D ratio	.946(.028)	.969(.023)	-2.69	.010*
Left 2D:4D ratio	.957(.023)	.967(.031)	-.983	.332
Paper folding test	13.64(5.55)	12.34(3.13)	.948	.349
Card rotation test	102.78(30.33)	93.65(23.16)	1.066	.293
Hidden pattern test	160.14(22.83)	141.88(25.82)	2.217	.033*

SD = standard deviation; *p < .05.

3.2 Correlations of 2D:4D Ratio with Spatial Tests

Table 2. shows the correlation between 2D:4D ratio and three spatial tests. For the female samples, both right hand and left hand 2D:4D ratio were significantly negative correlated with the hidden pattern test (left hand, r=-.555; right hand, r=-.408). This means that female participants with high 2D:4D ratio had lower score on hidden pattern test. No similar correlation of 2D:4D ratio with hidden pattern test was found in male (left hand, r=.025; right hand, r=-.293). In right hand and left hand for male and female participants, none of the correlations between 2D:4D ratio and paper folding test and card rotation test performance were significant.

Table 2. Correlation between 2D:4D ratio and three spatial tests

	Paper folding test	Card rotation test	Hidden pattern test
Male R hand	.157	-.038	-.293
Male L hand	.246	.230	.025
Female R hand	-.138	-.138	-.408*
Female L hand	-.076	-.013	-.555**

R=right; L=left; *p<.05, **p<.001

4 Discussion

The purpose of present study was to investigate which sub-factors of spatial ability were related to 2D:4D ratio. We focused on spatial visualization factor, spatial relation factor, and perceptual speed factor. For females, both right hand and left hand 2D:4D ratio were significantly negative correlated with perceptual speed factor. Perceptual speed factor task (e.g. hidden pattern test) assessed individual differences in speed or efficiency judgment. Female with low 2D:4D ratio had high speed perceptual judgment in figures. The conclusion of this study was that only one perceptual speed factor of spatial ability correlated with digit ratio in female.

Our data did not found a relationship between 2D:4D ratio and mental rotation. Our results are consistent with other published reports. For example, Coolican and Peters [8] and Poulin, O'Connell and Freeman [29] found no relationship between 2D:4D ratio and mental rotation. But in other studies, a negative relationship between 2D:4D ratio and mental rotation ability was found for either females or males. Sanders, Bereczkei, Csatho and Manning [31] found that 2D:4D ratio is negatively correlated with mental rotation test score in men but not women. So, the relationships between 2D:4D ratio and mental rotation were not conclusive, and this issue needs more research in the future.

We found that males displayed significantly lower 2D:4D ratio than females in right hand, consistent with findings of other studies (e.g. [29]). This result was also consistent with East Asian samples. Yang, Gray, Zhang and Pope [36] investigated Chinese adult samples; they found that males displayed significantly lower 2D:4D ratios than females. We found a significant difference in 2D:4D ratio between Taiwanese males and females, and this finding gives further support to the validity of this measure across ethnic groups. We are also interested in comparing different ethnic groups in the 2D:4D ratio. For UK samples, the female digit ratio=1.00, male=0.98 [3], for Chinese samples, male right hand ratio = .951, male left hand ratio = .955, female right hand ratio = .972, female left hand ratio = .972 [36]. Our Taiwanese samples data: male right hand ratio = .946, male left hand ratio = .957, female right hand ratio = .969, female left hand ratio = .967. According to these 2D:4D ratio data, we found that digit ratios are similar between the Taiwanese samples and the Chinese samples, but the Taiwanese samples have lower digit ratios than the UK samples.

References

1. Alexander, G.M., Swerdloff, R.S., Wang, C., Davidson, T., McDonald, V., Steiner, B., Hines, M.: Androgen-behavior correlations in hypogonadal men and eugonadal men. II. Cognitive abilities. Hormones and Behavior 33, 85–94 (1998)
2. Besterfield-Sacre, M., Atman, C.J., Shuman, L.J.: Characteristics of freshman engineering students: models for determining student attrition in engineering. Journal of Engineering Education 86(2), 139–149 (1997)
3. Brosnan, M.: Digit ratio and Faculty membership: implications for the relationship between prenatal testosterone and academic ability. British Journal of Psychology 97(4), 455–466 (2006)
4. Bull, R., Benson, P.J.: Digit ratio (2D:4D) and the spatial representation of magnitude. Hormones and Behavior 50, 194–199 (2006)
5. Carroll, J.B.: Human cognitive abilities: A survey of factor-analytic studies. Cambridge University Press, New York (1993)
6. Christiansen, K., Knussmann, R.: Sex hormones and cognitive functioning in men. Neuropsychobiology 18, 27–36 (1987)
7. Coates, J.M., Gurnell, M., Rustichini, A.: Second-to-fourth digit ratio predicts success among high-frequency financial traders. Proceedings of the National Academy of Sciences 106(2), 623–628 (2009)
8. Coolican, J., Peters, M.: Sexual dimorphism in the 2D/4D ratio and its relation to mental rotation performance. Evolution and Human Behavior 24, 179–183 (2003)

9. Ekstrom, R.B., French, J.W., Harman, H.H., Dermen, D.: Manual for Kit of Factor-Referenced Cognitive Tests. Princeton, New Jersey, Educational Testing Service (1976)
10. Finke, R.A.: Principles of mental imagery. MIT Press, Cambridge (1989)
11. Gouchie, C., Kimura, D.: The relationship between testosterone levels and cognitive ability patterns. Psychoneuroendocrinology 16, 2323–2334 (1991)
12. Halpern, D.F.: Sex differences in cognitive abilities. Lawrence Erlbaum Associates, Hilsdale (1986)
13. Holliday, F.: The relations between psychological test scores and subsequent proficiency of apprentices in the engineering industry. Occupational Psychology 17, 168–185 (1943)
14. Hooven, C.K., Chabris, C.F., Ellison, P.T., Kosslyn, S.M.: The relationship of male testosterone to components of mental rotation. Neuropsychologia 42, 782–790 (2004)
15. Hsi, S., Linn, M.C., Bell, J.: The role of spatial reasoning in engineering and the design of spatial instruction. Journal of Engineering Education 86(2), 151–158 (1997)
16. Janowski, J.S., Oviatt, S.K., Orwoll, E.S.: Testosterone influences spatial cognition in older men. Behavioral Neuroscience 108, 325–332 (1994)
17. Just, M.A., Carpenter, P.A.: Cognitive coordinate system: accounts of mental rotation and individual differences in spatial ability. Psychological Review 92, 137–172 (1986)
18. Lohman, D.F.: Spatial abilities as traits, processes and knowledge. In: Sternberg, R.J. (ed.) Advances in the psychology of human intelligence, Erlbaum, Hillsdale (1988)
19. Lutchmaya, S., Baron-Cohen, S., Raggatt, P., Knickmeyer, R., Manning, J.T.: 2nd to 4th digit ratios, fetal testosterone and estradiol. Early Human Development 77, 23–28 (2004)
20. Manning, J.T.: Digit Ratio: A Pointer to Fertility, Behavior, and Health. Rutgers University Press, New Brunswick (2002)
21. Manning, J.T., Scutt, D., Wilson, J., Lewis-Jones, D.I.: The ratio of 2nd to 4th digit length: a predictor of sperm numbers and concentrations of testosterone, luteinizing hormone and oestrogen. Human Reproduction 13, 3000–3004 (1998)
22. Manning, J.T., Taylor, R.P.: Second to fourth digit ratio and male ability in sport: implications for sexual selection in humans. Evolution and Human Behavior 22, 61–69 (2001)
23. McFadden, D., Shubel, E.: The relationships between otoacoustic emissions and relative lengths of fingers and toes in humans. Hormones and Behavior 43, 421–429 (2003)
24. McKeever, W.F., Rich, D.A., Deyo, R.A., Conner, R.L.: Androgens and spatial ability: failure to find a relationship between testosterone and ability measures. Bulletin of the Psychonomic Society 25, 438–440 (1987)
25. McKeever, W.F., Deyo, R.A.: Testosterone, dihydrotestosterone, and spatial task performances of males. Bulletin of the Psychonomic Society 28, 305–308 (1990)
26. Miyake, A., Friedman, N.P., Rettinger, D.A., Shah, P., Hegarty, M.: How are visuospatial working memory, executive functioning, and spatial abilities related? A latent-variable analysis. Journal of Experimental Psychology: General 130, 621–640 (2001)
27. Moffat, S.D., Hampson, E.: A curvilinear relationship between testosterone and spatial cognition in humans: Possible influence of hand preference. sychoneuroendocrinology 21(3), 323–337 (1996)
28. Moffat, S.D., Metter, E.J., Blackman, M.R., Harman, S.M., Resnick, S.M.: Longitudinal assessment of endogenous bioavailable testosterone predicts memory performance and cognitive status in elderly men. Journal of Clinical Endocrinology and Metabolism 87(11), 5001–5007 (2002)
29. Poulin, M., O'Connell, R.L., Freeman, L.M.: Picture recall skills correlate with 2D:4D ratio in women but not in men. Evolution and Human Behavior 25, 174–181 (2004)

30. Roth, S.: Visualization in science and the arts. In: Art, science & visual literacy: Selected readings from the 24th Annual Conference of the International Visual Literacy Association, Pittsburg, pp. 81–85 (1993)
31. Sanders, G., Bereczkei, T., Csatho, A., Manning, J.: The ratio of the 2nd to 4th finger length predicts spatial ability in men but not women. Cortex 41, 789–795 (2005)
32. Sanders, G., Sjodin, M., de Chastelaine, M.: On the elusive nature of sex differences in cognition: Hormonal influences contributing to within-sex variation. Archives of Sexual Behavior 31, 145–152 (2002)
33. Shute, V.J., Pellegrino, J.W., Hubert, L., Reynolds, R.W.: The relationship between androgen levels and human spatial abilities. Bulletin of the Psychonomic Society 21(6), 465–468 (1983)
34. Silverman, I., Kastuk, D., Choi, J., Phillips, K.: Testostcrone levels and spatial ability in men. Psychoneuroendocrinology 24, 813–822 (1999)
35. Sluming, V.A., Manning, J.T.: Second to fourth digit ratio in elite musicians: evidence for musical ability as an honest signal of male fitness. Evolution and Human Behavior 21, 1–9 (2000)
36. Yang, C.J., Gray, P.B., Zhang, J., Pope Jr., H.G.: Second to fourth digit ratios, sex differences, and behavior in Chinese men and women. Social Neuroscience 4, 49–59 (2008)

"Whose Rule Is It Anyway?" – A Case Study in the Internationalization of User-Configurable Business Rules

Morgan McCollough

Bridge360
1016 La Posada Dr, Suite 120
Austin, TX 78752
morgan_mccollough@bridge360.com

Abstract. This paper consists of a case study concerning the internationalization of an electronic invoice management web application and its central rules engine. It examines the challenges faced in introducing internationalization changes at the level of a custom scripting language processor and the problems inherent in maintaining compatibility with existing deployments. The paper outlines the specific solution and the ways in which the key concepts of locale context and lazy initialization may be applied to other similar internationalization problems.

1 Introduction

In early 2007 Bridge360 was challenged with the internationalization (i18n) of a client's flagship web application. The client was taking the first steps into the European market and had limited experience with global software. The application in question was a web-based, ASP.NET system developed for large organizations to automate the process of managing electronic invoices. The system was originally an outgrowth of an effort to establish standards for certain types of electronic invoices and tools to handle them. The invoice management system created value for large organizations by requiring the electronic submission of all invoices using a specific standard and serving as a conduit for invoice approval workflows and integration with accounts payable.

The particular challenge concerning this case study is not the internationalization of the invoice management application in general, but rather one of its core components, the rules engine. The rules engine is a custom scripting language that provides a framework for customers to develop and add their own business processes, rules, and workflows to an existing system. For example, a billing management system might be customized through the use of a rules engine to automatically apply a certain percentage discount for all clients in a particular region. In the context of electronic invoices, rules could be developed to automatically apply rate adjustments to invoices arriving from particular vendors, to raise errors when an invoice is submitted against a project not approved for payment, or to insert warnings directly into an invoice when the total amount billed for a particular project climbs over a certain threshold. In general the strength of a rules engine lies in the ability to customize the behavior of a software system for any particular client in the field.

N. Aykin (Ed.): Internationalization, Design, LNCS 5623, pp. 274–282, 2009.

The rules engine in this specific application was implemented using a custom scripting language processor, which allowed for a great deal of flexibility in customization for customer deployments due to its expressive power. However, this flexibility also presented complications in the area of internationalization. This case study will focus on the challenges encountered when implementing a solution capable of supporting global environments. The difficulties in the project centered on two central issues. First, the server had to run in one language environment but service users in different languages. Second, the locale under which the rule was initially executed did not necessarily match the locale under which its results were viewed. The final solution will also be described, along with the core concepts of locale context and lazy initialization, which may be applied to other similar internationalization problems.

2 The Project

The first step in the project was an internationalization assessment of the automated invoice management system. This is a useful technique to gain an overall picture of an application's code base and discern its internationalization shortcomings. Despite the fact that the server application was written in C#.NET, a language with a large amount of internationalization support built-in, the assessment revealed a number of potential problems. This was largely because the system was never architected to support multiple languages and hence included a number of U.S.-specific assumptions as well as places where the built-in i18n support of C# was not utilized. The application also employed a number of 3rd party components that were incapable of performing correctly in an international environment.

2.1 Rules Engine

The rules engine in the client's invoice management system was implemented as a custom scripting language processor. In other words, the client created a completely new, custom scripting language, solely for the purpose of defining business rules to modify the behavior of the system. The rules engine consisted of a single process which ran the language interpreter to parse, compile, and execute the various rules scripts defined in the engine's configuration file. As invoices were posted into the system, rules were executed in the context of each invoice as a whole or for each individual line item in an invoice.

The scripting language was straightforward but highly configurable. It was never intended to be a fully-expressive programming language and therefore consisted mainly of conditional statements, a few basic mathematical operations, and a small set of actions or functions that could be performed on an invoice. Each defined rule consisted of a context definition (invoice or line item), a conditional expression to examine the incoming invoice data and make a logical choice of whether or not to execute the rule, and an action to perform if the rule in question was triggered. Support for conditional statements included basic logical operators as well as access to a predefined data structure consisting of all of the main elements of an invoice. Actions were a series of functions with specific parameters as defined in an external configuration file. This configuration file defined the names of all supported actions, their parameters, and references to the code that implemented each action. It was therefore relatively simple for the client's professional services department to add custom actions during a product deployment if the default actions did not meet a customer's requirements. In addition, there was a completely separate client application developed for editing business rules in the field. It provided a graphical environment for the Professional Services group to quickly author a series of rules to meet any customer's needs.

An Example Rule. The following is an example of a simple rule that could have been implemented in the invoice management system's rules engine.

```
If

        Invoice.Project.ID == "ACCT-257"

          and

        Invoice.Total > 100000.00

Then

        AddInvoiceWarning "Invoice submitted on " +

          Invoice.SubmitDate + " exceeds the maximum
billable amount

          for Project " + Invoice.Project.ID + "(" +
100000.00 +

          ") and will require special approval!"

End
```

The above rule would have the effect of adding an invoice warning to an incoming invoice if the ID of the related project was "ACCT-257" and the total billed in the invoice exceeded 100,000. An invoice warning is a special message that is attached to an invoice that is prominently visible at the top of the invoice detail screen in the application's web interface. It would be one of the first messages displayed when a user viewed an invoice matching the above condition through the web interface. The message itself contains several variable expressions that are part of the pre-defined data structure mentioned above. They provide access to the various fields and values contained in an invoice and resolve to the appropriate values when the rule executed.

2.2 The Problem

The difficulties in internationalizing a rules engine like the one described above are twofold. First, all existing rules had to function correctly when the application was deployed on a non-English application server. Many non-internationalized applications exhibit problems or cease to function at all when run on a non-English operating system. Even if a non-U.S. customer were to deploy the English version of the application, it is likely that the application would be run on a non-English version of the Windows server platform. Requiring a customer to run an international software product exclusively on an English operating system is not a reasonable option. Second, as evidenced by the example above, this particular rules engine was capable of adding strings to an invoice that were visible in the main application interface. Therefore there had to be some mechanism to translate this text since the application was a web-based system where a single server could support users in multiple languages simultaneously.

Constraints. Although the basic problem is outlined above, there were a number of important additional requirements to consider in the specific situation of the automated invoice management system. These requirements or "constraints" had to be taken into account when designing and implementing an appropriate solution.

Backwards Compatibility. The internationalization improvements were being incorporated in the main version of the application as opposed to an international-specific version. The client had a significant base of existing customers that all had rules configured specifically for their business environments, and there were plans to upgrade a number of these customers to the next major release, which would include the internationalization features. If *any* changes were made that caused existing rules to stop functioning after an upgrade or required changes to existing rules the costs involved would have been unacceptable to current customers.

Multi-language Server. The client confirmed that their first European customer would be hosting the application to run in both English and French simultaneously. There are a number of companies, especially in Europe, that do business in multiple languages, and requiring clients to install a separate server for every desired language would have been unreasonable due to the increased costs of using multiple servers and the lack of an easy way to share data among multiple servers without significant application enhancements. This type of web application has further complications because the user interface locale is variable and does not always match the locale of the server that is running the application. This presented a challenge for the rules engine since it ran in a separate process from the user interface. The rules processor ran using the locale of the server, which could be different from the locale of a particular user session in the web interface. However, the user's locale defined the environment in which a rule's output would be viewed, including examples like the one above.

Dynamic Data. In the example above there are variables inserted into the middle of the invoice warning string. These types of variables are sometimes referred to as "dynamic data" because their value is not determined until run-time and hence may change depending on the specific execution environment. In the example, "Invoice.SubmitDate" would be replaced with the date on which the invoice in question was submitted, and this would change depending on the date on which the rule runs. The rules scripting language supported data insertion for any data field in an invoice, which meant that inserted values could be strings, numeric values, currency values, or dates. These values therefore needed to be rendered according to the user's locale when viewed in the user interface. Deciding upon a locale context to use presented a problem because rules processor executed completely independently of the user interface.

Customization in the Field. The final limiting factor concerned the nature of the rules engine itself. The rules engine was meant as a customization tool, and the client configured it mostly during deployments at customer sites. It was therefore logical that there would need to be a method to create internationalized rules in the field. This spurred the need for a mechanism by which the Professional Services, or even the customer, could create and configure fully internationalized rules and update any necessary translations.

3 The Solution

The final solution to the internationalization problems in the rules engine came down to solving 3 major issues. First, the application had to correctly execute the custom script rules regardless of the language and locale of the server's operating system. Second, dynamic data had to be rendered correctly at runtime depending on the user's locale. Finally, there needed to be some method to translate arbitrary strings utilized in custom business rules without breaking any existing syntax or rules. The following sections outline how each of these problems was solved and how each solution addressed the requirements and constraints listed above.

3.1 Locale Context

When writing code for an internationalized application, it is important to be cognizant of locale. Any piece of code that executes on modern operating systems does so in a particular locale context, and there are many libraries and system functions that will change behavior depending on the locale environment. This is especially true for a language environment like C#.NET where all string-related operations utilize the configured locale context to define their behavior. Many internationalization problems can be traced to code that completely ignores locale or simply assumes behavior based on the rules and conventions of one particular locale.

In the case of the invoice management rules engine, the scripting language processor was largely a string parser and interpreter that assumed the conventions of the U.S. English locale. When this code was executed on a non-English machine there were a number of issues. All string-related functions in the C#.NET libraries automatically picked up the locale of the system, which broke many implicit assumptions in the code. For example, the code assumed a period was always used for the decimal point. However, the French locale uses a comma instead of a period which caused the script language processor to parse many numbers incorrectly.

Two basic solutions to this problem were considered. The first was to make sure the locale was properly detected and then go through the code and eliminate any assumptions based on U.S. conventions. This approach had two major problems. First was that the rules engine was at its core a scripting language interpreter and hence had many lines of code. Combing through this component to find all the potential problems would have been a long process, especially considering project time constraints and the fact that there were few people left at the client that were familiar with the interpreter's inner workings. The second issue was that there was a significant base of default rules that shipped with the product and were used as the basis to customize a client's system. Forcing the interpreter to use the system locale could have potentially required the client to keep different versions of these scripts for each language that differed only in syntax, due mainly to differences in date and numeric literal values.

The second solution, which was the one chosen, was relatively simple. Code was added in a number of places to explicitly set the locale environment of parse operations to use U.S. conventions. This was to ensure consistency such that any rules script running in any language environment would be functionally identical. The rules scripts themselves were never seen by end users and it would have made no sense for the same script to operate differently in two different language contexts or to require rules to be re-written depending on the language environment of the server, as it was assumed that international users would no longer embed literal strings into business rules. This also made sense because the rules script was essentially a programming language, and programming languages tend to follow the U.S. conventions as a standard. Finally, explicitly using the U.S. conventions was a low-risk change because the engine had already been thoroughly tested on an English operating system.

3.2 Lazy Initialization

Lazy initialization is a concept in computer science whereby the creation of an object or the calculation of a value is delayed until such time as it is actually needed versus performing the operation ahead of time and storing the result for later use. The same basic principle was applied to the evaluation of data in the rules engine. Originally, all expressions in a rule were evaluated at the time of the rule's execution. In the example rule above, the invoice warning string would have been completely evaluated and attached to the invoice in its final form, e.g. "Invoice submitted on 4/5/09 exceeds the maximum billable amount for project ACC-257 (100,000.00) and will require special approval!" This was no longer possible in the context of a multi-language server. The locale under which the rule was executed did not necessarily match the locale of the user that logged into the web interface to view that specific invoice. In the case of a user session in French, the date listed above would not match any of the other dates displayed in the internationalized interface and it would therefore be easy for the user to mistake it for May 4, 2009 rather than April 5, 2009. It also would have made translation of the string at run-time for different user sessions extremely difficult.

The output string resulting from rule execution was stored in a table in the application's database. When the corresponding invoice was displayed in the user interface, all of the various comments, warnings and other strings were pulled from the database and displayed directly in the UI. In order to make the system capable of displaying multiple language versions of these strings, there had to be some locale-neutral version of the evaluated string that could be transformed into the correct language form at run-time based on the user's locale. This concept of lazy initialization is the basic idea behind the internationalization of user interface strings for most global software. The differences lie in the exact mechanism used to achieve it.

Several alternatives were considered regarding where and how to store the translations for these user-defined strings. The first idea was to have the rule authors simply place multiple translations of a string in the rule script itself. This was quickly dismissed as a maintenance nightmare, as it would require editing rule scripts every time a language was added and would also require significant modifications to the scripting language itself. It would also not solve the problem of dynamic data. The second idea was to assume users would only ever look at invoices related to specific projects and all users under a specific project were likely to speak one language. If that were the case, there could be a specific language designated for a specific project, and the rules could be segregated by language and project. That again was quickly dismissed, as it assumed too much about the way in which the application would be used. It also did not solve the problem of dynamic data, as there was no way to change the locale of the rule execution and hence the format of numbers and dates at a project level.

Ultimately, the solution was to internationalize the rule code in much the same was as normal application code. Instead of embedding a literal message in rule code, a string identifier would take its place. For example a message like "Invoice exceeds maximum billable amount" would be replaced by an identifier that could be used to look up the actual value when a user viewed the invoice through the web interface. Rule output with any identifiers would be inserted in the database table when the rule executed, just as if it were a typical string. A hook was added to the user interface layer to tell these identifiers apart from normal text when rule output was pulled from the database. When the user interface detected an identifier within rule output, the real value would be pulled from a rules engine resource file according to the user's session locale. Any dynamic data was inserted into the translated string properly formatted for the user's locale before being displayed in the web interface. In this way, final evaluation of rules data could be delayed until the appropriate locale could be obtained. The main problem with this approach was that it required a consistent format to be used for the special string identifiers that for the sake of backwards compatibility could not be confused with normal text data. Otherwise, there was a very real danger of breaking existing scripts. This, and the necessity to support dynamic data, led directly to the final piece of the solution, the introduction of custom syntax into the scripting language processor.

3.3 Custom Syntax

As mentioned above, the introduction of new syntax into the rules scripting language was required to produce a consistent pattern that could be evaluated correctly at the user interface level without changing the behavior of any of the existing syntax.

Originally, following the convention of lazy initialization, it was thought that for dynamic data variables, the simplest solution would be to store the variable name itself and delay evaluation until the user interface layer. For example, store the variable "Invoice.Total" as a string with a marker to identify it as a variable. However, it quickly became clear that delaying evaluation for all variables used in message strings could greatly complicate the code in the user interface layer. It was also realized that there were many situations where the value of the variable could change between the time of the rule's evaluation and when the data was eventually displayed in a web page. For example, if the variable "Invoice.Total" was saved as an identifier and not resolved to its numeric value until displayed to the user, its value might change if any users added discounts or rate adjustments to the invoice after it was posted into the system. In the example rule given above, this would cause a problem if the adjustment lowered the invoice total below the threshold that triggered the rule in the first place since the warning comment would no longer make any sense.

Eventually, the team decided that the dynamic variables would have to be evaluated at the time of rule execution. However, in cases where they were to be used in translatable strings, they had to be evaluated into a locale-neutral format that could be re-interpreted later in order to format them properly for display in the user interface. This forced the creation of a special syntax to avoid impacting the normal evaluation behavior of dynamic data and therefore run the risk of breaking existing rules.

First, a new string concatenation operator (a comma) was added to the language to serve as a companion to the existing string concatenation operator ("+" in the example above). The use of the new operator allowed for the conversion of date and numeric data into a consistent locale-neutral format. Second, a convention was established and documented that any string value in a rules script starting and ending with 2 dollar signs ("$$") would be interpreted as a literal string by the rules processor but would be interpreted as a key to look up a translated value by the user interface lazy initialization hook. Values to be inserted into the string at run-time could simply be concatenated behind the key value using the new concatenation operator.

The example rule given earlier would be rewritten as follows using the new conventions and syntax.

```
If
            Invoice.Project.ID == "ACCT-257"

            and

            Invoice.Total > 100000.00
Then
            AddInvoiceWarning "$$AmountExceededWarning$$",

                Invoice.SubmitDate, Invoice.Matter.ID,
100000.00
End
```

When evaluated by the newly modified rules engine, the above rule would generate the follow warning string to attach to an invoice.

```
"$$AmountExceededWarning$$;2009-4-5;ACCT-257;100000.00"
```

The actual warning text was placed in the rules engine resource file using the given id as follows.

```
AmountExceededWarning = "Invoice submitted on {0:D}

exceeds the

            maximum billable amount for Project {1}
({2:C}) and will

            require special approval!"
```

The "D" and "C" values are format strings defined in C# to indicate date and currency values respectively. In the user interface, the lazy evaluation hook was configured to initiate a re-evaluation based on the presence of the double dollar signs. The translated value was looked up, the dynamic data was parsed according to the established convention, and the final string was constructed using the locale conventions of the current user.

In this way, any rule modified to use the above conventions and syntax could show up correctly in different languages and formats depending on the user locale. At the same time, any rule not adhering to the new syntax or conventions would be evaluated according to the original behavior of the rules engine, therefore ensuring perfect backwards compatibility. There was also discussion of adding support for these conventions and the rules resource file into the rules engine development application, but it was deferred due to time constraints and scheduled for a later release.

4 Conclusion

In the end, the project was completed on time, and neither the client nor their customers were required to modify their existing rules. Two principles proved crucial to accomplishing this. First, the insight of treating rules engine output as an intermediate format to be evaluated further at runtime rather than treating it as final output allowed full internationalization of dynamic data with a minimum of code changes. Second, the deferment of localizable data evaluation as long as possible enabled the evaluation to occur in the correct locale context. Applying these basic principles kept the overall code changes to a minimum in terms of scale and risk while also providing backwards compatibility.

Acknowledgements. The author would like to acknowledge the project team for delivering the project that is the focus of this paper, as well as Brenda Hall and Chris Durand for their many invaluable comments and suggestions during the editing process.

Design of Face-to-Face Multilingual Communication Environment for Illiterate People

Mai Miyabe[1] and Takashi Yoshino[2]

[1] Graduate School of Systems Engineering, Wakayama University,
930 Sakaedani, Wakayama, Japan
s085051@sys.wakayama-u.ac.jp
[2] Faculty of Systems Engineering, Wakayama University,
930 Sakaedani, Wakayama, Japan
yoshino@sys.wakayama-u.ac.jp
http://www.wakayama-u.ac.jp/ yoshino/

Abstract. In the medical field, a serious problem exists with regard to communication between hospital staffs and patients. Currently, although a medical translator accompanies a patient to medical care facilities, round-the-clock or emergency support is difficult to provide due to increasing requests. The medical field has high expectations from information technology. Therefore, we have developed a support system for multilingual medical reception termed M^3. We have installed our system in the Kyoto City Hospital in Japan. However, we found that our system cannot provide support to illiterate people. If an illiterate person and another person speak different languages, it is difficult the other person to communicate face to face with the illiterate person while explaining the meaning of texts shown on the display of the support system. This is one of the problems specific to the multilingual communication. There is a need to solve this problem. Therefore, we have developed a method to provide support to illiterate people engaging in multilingual face-to-face communication. We use a text-to-speech function implemented using a selector switch to provide support to illiterate people in performing operations using a touch screen. We performed an experiment to examine the effect of the proposed method. The results of the experiment are as follows. (1) From the results of the questionnaire, we find that the subjects are able to operate the selector switch easily. Therefore, we conclude that the method using the selector switch has little effect on the operation of the system. (2) Retrieval time using the text-to-speech function is five times that using the normal operation. We need to consider a structure that can retrieve the required information easily if many readings of texts are required.

Keywords: Parallel texts, Multilingual communication, Medical field.

1 Introduction

Opportunities for multilingual communication in Japan have increased due to the increase in the number of foreigners in Japan. When people communicate in their

N. Aykin (Ed.): Internationalization, Design, LNCS 5623, pp. 283–292, 2009.

nonnative language, the differences in languages prevent mutual understanding among communicating individuals. Differences in languages have to be overcome in order for multilingual communication to occur. To overcome the language barrier in communication, machine translation is used for communication using native language. We have conducted research on providing support for multilingual communication in the medical field. Currently, a medical translator accompanies a patient to medical care facilities, and the requests for medical translators to accompany patients are increasing. However, medical translators cannot provide support in cases in which round the clock support is required or in case of emergencies. In the medical field, a system that supports accurate multilingual communication is required. In the medical field, in particular, accurate translations are very important. Medical care directly impacts both human life and health. Despite recent advances in machine translation technology, it is still very difficult to obtain highly accurate translations. Inaccurate translation adversely affects communication, and an incorrect machine translation can cause serious problems.

We have developed a support system for multilingual medical reception termed M^3 [1]. Users operate M^3 using a touch screen and receive text-based support. M^3 provides reliable communication between a hospital staff member and a patient using accurate translations called parallel texts. However, in Japan, there are foreigners that are illiterate in Japanese or natives that are illiterate in their native language [2]. According to statistics, there are many countries worldwide that have a low rate of literacy [3]. In some countries, illiterate people account for more than 70% of the adult population. The actual illiterate population can be estimated to be larger because most countries estimate their illiterate population as being lower than it really is. If an illiterate person and his/her conversational partner speak the same language, the conversational partner can provide support to the illiterate person by a verbal explanation. On the other hand, if they speak different languages, it is difficult for the conversational partner to provide information on texts to the illiterate person by a verbal explanation. Therefore, illiterate people engaging in multilingual communication face problems. It is difficult for M^3 to provide support to illiterate people because it provides text-based support.

In this study, we have developed a method to provide support to illiterate people engaging in multilingual face-to-face communication.

2   Related Work

In order to provide support to illiterate people, it is necessary to read out the text data verbally. Some studies have employed speech synthesis as a text-to-speech technology [4]. Recently, the quality of speech synthesis has improved. Moreover, the text-to-speech technology has been applied for providing support to visually impaired people [5, 6]. An interface that provided support to the illiterate people has been discussed [7]. On the other hand, the interface that supports the illiterate people is not discussed enough. Both visually impaired people and illiterate people require support by voice data. However, illiterate people require a different type of support

(i) Conversation between a hospital staff member and a patient | (ii) Reception support for patients

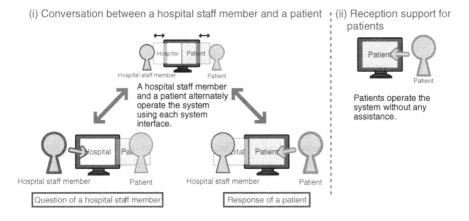

Fig. 1. Image of conversation using M^3

from that required by visually impaired people because the former can look at a display and texts. It is necessary to develop an interface that provides support to illiterate people.

3 M^3: A Support System for Multilingual Medical Reception

1. Summary of M^3

   We have developed a support system for multilingual medical reception termed M^3 [1]. M^3 supports face-to-face communication and the procedure followed at hospital receptions. In order to avoid problems related to translation accuracy, M^3 uses parallel texts that were translated accurately by medical interpreters. M^3 can obtain and share parallel texts using Web services via Language Grid [8]. Users operate M^3 using a touch screen. Figure 1 shows the image of a conversation using M^3. When a hospital staff member and a patient communicate, they alternately operate the system using each system interface. When a patient receives support for following the required procedure at the hospital reception, he/she operates the system without receiving any further assistance. We have installed our system in the Kyoto City Hospital in Japan, and the system has been placed at the reception desk. The system is currently in operation.

2. Problems

   The developed system provides text-based support for conversation and information services. In this system, illiterate people cannot understand the information shown on the display. We received feedback from medical interpreters that the system should provide support to illiterate people. Therefore, we have developed a method for providing support to illiterate people engaging in multilingual face-to-face communication using a touch screen.

4 Text-to-Speech Function in Multilingual Communication Using a Touch Screen

In this study, we have developed a method that provides support to illiterate people when the use the M^3 system (having limitations) that is operated using the touch screen. Although illiterate people cannot understand the meaning of the texts that are shown on the display, they can operate the system by viewing the display. Therefore, illiterate people can use the system if they can understand the meaning of the texts. We provide support to illiterate people by implementing the text-to-speech function. In the system operated by a touch screen, the following problems have to be solved for the realization of the text-to-speech function.

1. Text-to-speech of all texts shown on the display

    We should enable the reading out all texts shown on the display, in order to provide support to illiterate people. Although illiterate people cannot understand the meaning of the texts that are shown on the display, they can operate the system by viewing the display. Therefore, we need to enable a read out of only that text that an illiterate person cannot understand and not all the texts.

2. Screen area

    In the system operated by the touch screen, the sizes of the interfaces operated by users need to be sufficient for the users to touch. The screen area of the system is limited compared to that of a mouse-driven system. Therefore, we require a method in which there is no dependence on the screen area.

We considered that these problems may be solved by the following solutions.

1. Text-to-speech conversion by suitable selections by users.

    If users touch the text shown on a display, only the touched text is read out verbally.

2. Operation of text-to-speech function separate from operation of touch screen.

    The text-to-speech function is not usually used in the system. Therefore, we separate the operation of this function from that of the main functions. The function is physically implemented operated beside the touch screen.

We propose to implement the text-to-speech function using a switch. Texts are displayed on most of the interfaces that are handled by the users of the system. Therefore, we develop two modes of the system: the normal operation mode and the text-to-speech mode. When the text-to-speech mode is in operation, the texts selected by a user are read out verbally. Users can switch between these two modes in order to perform a normal operation or a text-to-speech operation. The selector switch that is placed beside the touch screen is used to switch between the modes. Figure 2 shows the actions by the operation of the selector switch. If users press the selector switch, the clicked text is read out verbally. If users do not press the selector switch, a normal operation is performed.

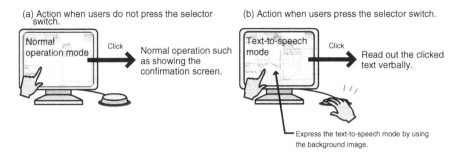

Fig. 2. Actions by the operation of the selector switch

5 Experiment

5.1 Experimental Outline

We performed an information retrieval experiment using the proposed method in order to examine its efficiency and determine the problems encountered in the method. The subjects of the experiment were 12 students from Wakayama University.

In the experiment, the subjects retrieved the answers of five given questions using the Q&A function of M^3. Table 1 shows these five questions.

The subjects performed their tasks under the following experimental conditions.

(a) Texts are readable and subjects retrieve information using the normal operation mode.
(b) Texts are unreadable and subjects retrieve information in both the normal operation mode and the text-to-speech mode.

Each task was performed by six subjects. We compare the results of these experimental conditions.

In the experiment, in order to avoid the influence of the quality of the voice data on the experimental results, we used actual voices that were recorded in advance.

We simulated a situation in which the subjects could not read the text shown on the display, because in reality, the subjects who participated in the experiment were literate. We converted the text shown on the display into unreadable texts in the case of experimental condition (b). Figure 3 shows the screenshots of the experimental tool used for information retrieval. In experimental condition (a), the texts shown on the display are readable. On the other hand, under condition (b), the texts shown on the display are converted into unreadable texts. Under experimental condition (b), if a subject touches an interface with unreadable texts, the texts are converted into readable texts and read out verbally.

After the experiment, we asked the subjects to fill out a questionnaire on the text-to-speech function.

Table 1. Five questions used in the experiment

Question number	Question
1	What is the test/examination charge?
2	How much are parking fees?
3	Where is there a pharmacy?
4	When are medical interpreters available?
5	What are the reception hours and days of the week if you are the previous patient?

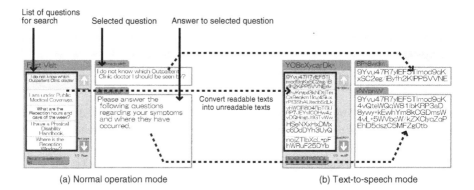

(a) Normal operation mode   (b) Text-to-speech mode

Fig. 3. Screenshots of experimental tool for retrieval

5.2 Results

1. Retrieval time and number of times voice data is played

    Table 2 shows the retrieval time in the experiment. It is the time that the subjects required to search for the answers to the experimental questions. As shown in table 2, the retrieval time using the text-to-speech mode was five times that using the normal operation mode.

    Table 3 shows the number of times voice data of the accurate answers to each question is played. As shown in table 3, the number of times voice data is played was large when the number of letters in the text was large. It is difficult for the subjects to understand the text the first time if the text contains a considerable amount of information. We need to consider this problem in the future.

2. Result of questionnaire

    The evaluation of a five-point scale and a free description of the questionnaire are as follows:

    (a) Evaluation of a five-point scale

    Table 4 shows the results of the questionnaire. We used a five-point Likert scale for the evaluation: 1: strongly disagree, 2: disagree, 3: neutral, 4: agree, and 5: strongly agree.

Table 2. Retrieval time in the experiment

Experimental condition	Subject	Retrieval time (m:s)	Average (m:s)	Standard Deviation (m:s)	Significance probability
Normal operation mode	A	01:18	01:20	00:11	
	B	01:27			
	C	01:18			
	D	01:00			
	E	01:24			
	F	01:33			0.004
Normal operation mode and text-to-speech mode	G	05:07	06:25	01:23	
	H	08:00			
	I	04:23			
	J	07:15			
	K	06:43			
	L	07:04			

Table 3. Number of times voice data of the accurate answers is played

Question number	Number of letters in the answer (letters)	Subject						Average (times)
		G (times)	H (times)	I (times)	J (times)	K (times)	L (times)	
1	36	6	4	4	2	2	2	3.3
2	61	3	5	3	3	6	6	4.3
3	16	1	1	1	2	1	1	1.2
4	45	2	1	1	1	2	2	1.5
5	68	3	5	4	6	8	2	4.7

– Operation of the selector switch

From the results of questions (1), (2), and (3) shown in table 4, we found that the subjects were able to operate the selector switch with ease.

– Support using the selector switch

We proposed the implementation of the text-to-speech function using the selector switch. The selector switch that was placed beside the touch screen was used to switch between the modes. As shown in table 4, the evaluated value of question (4) is 3.5. Therefore, the method using the selector switch has little effect on the operation of the system.

– Effects of using voice data

In the experiment, we used the actual voice data. From the results of questions (5) and (6) shown in table 4, we found that the subjects listened to the actual voice data of a text without any difficulty. However, we received feedback that it was difficult for the subjects to understand all the contents of the text when the text contained a large amount of information. If the text

Table 4. Results of the questionnaire

Questions	Subject						Average
	G	H	I	J	K	L	
(1) I could switch between each mode easily.	5	3	2	4	4	2	3.3
(2) I could play the voice data easily.	5	5	3	2	4	4	3.8
(3) It is difficult for me to touch the screen while pressing the selector switch.	2	1	2	3	2	4	2.3
(4) I think that it is appropriate that the selector switch is used in order to switch between each mode.	5	4	4	4	3	1	3.5
(5) I could understand the contents of the texts by the listening to the voice data.	4	5	4	4	4	5	4.3
(6) I felt that the voice data is hard to catch what it means.	2	1	2	2	1	1	1.5
(7) I think that the voice data helped me when I could not read the text.	4	5	5	2	5	5	4.3

We used a five-point Likert scale for the evaluation: 1: Strongly disagree, 2: Disagree, 3: Neutral, 4: Agree, and 5: Strongly agree.

contains a large amount of information, people need the intelligible voice data that accentuates important information.

– Providing support to illiterate people using voice data

From the result of question (7) shown in table 4, we found that the use of voice data is necessary to provide support to illiterate people.

(b) Free description of the questionnaire

The merits and demerits that were described by the subjects who undertook the questionnaire are as follows:

– Merits

- The switching between the two modes was very easy.
- I could quickly get used to the operation because the behavior of the selector switch was simple.
- The method to play the voice data was easy to understand.

– Demerits

- I was not able to perform the normal operation while using the text-to-speech mode. I think that the users require a structure that enables them to perform a normal operation while using the text-to-speech mode.
- I think that displaying an icon for playing voice data on a display is more understandable than the proposed method.
- It was exhausting to keep pressing the selector switch.

As a merit, the subjects described that the switching between the two modes was very easy and they could get used to the operation. As a demerit, they described that the proposed method had problems regarding the way to use the selector switch. Therefore, we need to improvise the way in which we use the selector switch.

6 Discussion

From the results of the experiment and the questionnaire, we found that it was very easy for users to switch between the two modes by using the selector switch. However, we also found that by the proposed method, the users faced problems in using the selector switch. The problems with the proposed method are as follows:

1. Users cannot perform a normal operation when they use the text-to-speech mode.
2. Users have to keep pressing the selector switch in order to use the text-to-speech mode.

These problems may be solved in the following ways.

1. Using the text-to-speech mode as an additional mode

In our proposed method, the two modes of the system are independent. Users have to return to the normal operation mode in order to perform a normal operation after the use of the text-to-speech mode. If users use the system for a long time, the number of switching modes will increase.

This problem may be solved by the following method: the text-to-speech mode is used as an additional mode with the main mode. In this method, when the mode of the system is changed to the text-to-speech mode, the icons for playing the voice data are shown on the texts in the display. Texts are read out verbally by touching these icons. If users touch anything except these icons, the system deactivates the text-to-speech mode. This will prevent the increase in the number of switching modes.

2. Switching to the other mode every time users press the selector switch

The main mode of the system is the normal operation mode. Therefore, it is necessary to return to the normal operation mode after using the text-to-speech mode.

We propose the following method as a solution to this problem: the system switches to the other mode every time users press the selector switch. Users have to press the selector switch in order to return to the other mode in this method. There is a possibility that users may forget to return to the other mode. Our proposed method was designed to return to the normal operation mode when users released the selector switch. However, we found that the proposed method imposed a burden on the subjects.

If we apply this solution, we also need to devise a method to prevent users from forgetting to press the selector switch. For this purpose, the system has to return to the normal operation mode automatically if users do not operate the system during a given time. This behavior of the system will enable users to perform a normal operation even if they forget to press the selector switch.

7 Conclusion

We have developed a support system for multilingual medical reception termed M^3. M^3 provides reliable communication between a hospital staff member and a foreign patient using accurate translations called parallel texts. Users operate M^3 using a touch screen and receive text-based support. However, there are foreigners that are Japanese illiterate or are their native language illiterate in Japan. It is difficult for M^3 to provide support to illiterate people because it provides text-based support.

In this study, we developed a method to provide support to illiterate people engaging in multilingual face-to-face communication. We performed an experiment to examine the effect of the proposed method. The results of the experiment are as follows.

1. From the results of the questionnaire, we found that the subjects were able to operate the selector switch with ease. Therefore, we concluded that the method using the selector switch had little effect on the operation of the system.
2. The time for the retrieval of information using the text-to-speech mode was five times that using the normal operation mode. We need to consider a structure that can retrieve the required information easily if many readings of texts are required.

The results of this study can be applied to the development of the support system for illiterate people engaging in multilingual face-to-face communication. Moreover, these results can be used as basic data for the design of a speech dialog system. In the future, we intend to improve the method for providing support to illiterate people on the basis of the results of the experiment.

Acknowledgments. This work was supported by the Strategic Information and Communications R&D Promotion Programme (SCOPE) of the Ministry of Internal Affairs and Communications of Japan.

References

1. Miyabe, M., Fujii, K., Shigenobu, T., Yoshino, T.: Parallel-Text Based Support System for Intercultural Communication at Medical Receptions. In: Ishida, T., R. Fussell, S., T. J. M. Vossen, P. (eds.) IWIC 2007. LNCS, vol. 4568, pp. 182–192. Springer, Heidelberg (2007)
2. Kobayashi, Y.: How to Accept Foreign Patients. Elsevier, Japan (2002) (in Japanese)
3. UNDP, Human Development Report 2007/2008, http://www.undp.org/
4. ElAarag, H., Schindler, L.: A speech recognition and synthesis tool. In: Proceedings of the 44th annual Southeast regional conference, pp. 45–49 (2006)
5. Sporka, A.J., Nemec, V., Slavik, P.: Tangible newspaper for the visually impaired users. In: CHI 2005 extended abstracts on Human factors in computing systems, pp. 1809–1812 (2005)
6. Chirathivat, J., Nakdej, J., Punyabukkana, P., Suchato, A.: Internet explorer smart toolbar for the blind. In: Proceedings of the 1st international convention on Rehabilitation engineering & assistive technology: in conjunction with 1st Tan Tock Seng Hospital Neurorehabilitation Meeting, pp. 195–200 (2007)
7. Leporini, B., Andronico, P., Buzzi, M.: Designing search engine user interfaces for the visually impaired. In: ACM SIGCAPH Computers and the Physically Handicapped, pp. 17–18 (2003)
8. Ishida, T.: Language Grid: An Infrastructure for Intercultural Collaboration. In: IEEE/IPSJ Symposium on Applications and the Internet (SAINT 2006), pp. 96–100 (2006)

Internationalization and Localization of Websites: Navigation in English Language and Chinese Language Sites

Helen Petrie, Christopher Power, and Wei Song

Department of Computer Science, University of York
Heslington, York, UK – YO10 5DD
{petrie,cpower}@cs.york.ac.uk

Abstract. Guidelines exist for the internationalization and localization of websites, but these do not mention possible changes in the layout of navigational elements on websites. Two studies were conducted to investigate the importance of navigational layout for Chinese and English language speakers. In the first study it was found that major Chinese and North American/European companies did not significantly adapt the navigation on their websites in relation to the target linguistic/cultural market. In the second study it was found that there were significant difference in the preferences of Chinese and English native speakers for navigational layout on websites. The implications of these studies are discussed.

Keywords: localization of websites, internationalization of websites, navigation in websites, user perceptions of websites.

1 Introduction

Within 20 years of its invention, the World Wide Web has become one of the dominant means of communication of information, commerce, education and entertainment throughout the world. Although the Web is accessible from almost anywhere in the world (apart from certain issues of censorship) and anyone in the world can contribute to it (particularly with the development of Web 2.0 tools), the content of the Web is still predominantly in the English language. Figures from 2002 [1] found that 56.4% of pages were in English, 7.7% in German and 5.6% in French. The most commonly used non-European languages were Japanese with 4.9% and Chinese with 2.9% of pages. However this situation is rapidly changing. Although more up-to-date analyses of languages of pages could not be found, analysis of country code top level domains (ccTLDs) [2] show that in July 2008 China (.cn) had the most registrations (12.36 million domains), surpassing Germany (.de) with 12.15 million domains. Germany (.de) had long been the world's largest ccTLD, but between 2006 and 2008 .cn domain names increased by more than 950 percent. In addition to the country specific ccTLDs, in mid 2008 there were approximately 107 million top level domains (TLDs) which are not country specific (for example, .com, .net, .biz), making approximately 170 TLDs in total.

N. Aykin (Ed.): Internationalization, Design, LNCS 5623, pp. 293–300, 2009.

This makes it clear that creating websites for non-English readers is becoming an increasingly important topic. A number of authors have developed excellent guidelines and principles for the internationalization of websites and other interfaces to digital systems [3 – 5].

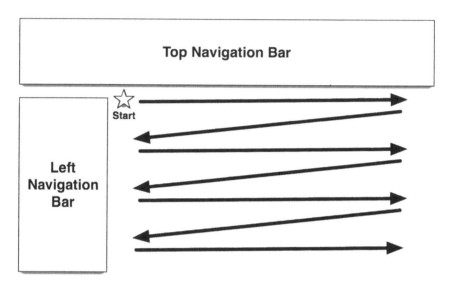

Fig. 1. Typical arrangement of navigational elements on an English language website with the typical scan pattern by a native speaker of English

These guidelines mention the need to align text and graphics appropriately for languages that are written and read from right to left or vertically, but none mention the effects of different writing arrangements on navigational styles in websites. Yet the placement of navigational elements in web pages is clearly important for their effective and efficient use. Many English language websites now use a "top and left" navigation style, with a navigation bar across the top of pages and another down the left hand side of pages (see Fig. 1). This makes sense when one considers that native speakers of English will tend to initially look at the top left of a page and then move down the page in a series of left to right eye movements. Experimental studies [6 - 9] have shown that native English speakers perform best when information for problems is presented in this manner. However readers of languages such as Chinese, Japanese or Hebrew do not traditionally orient themselves this way and often will perform better when information is presented in orientations that match the presentation of their languages. This leads us to hypothesize that the now "default" arrangement of navigation bars will not be optimal for speakers of languages which differ from the left-to-right/horizontal arrangement of English (and other European languages).

2 Study 1: A Comparison of English Language and Chinese Language Commercial Websites

The first study investigated whether major commercial organizations with websites that are originally English language or originally Chinese language alter the navigation when they create a website for the other market. So for example, do major

Table 1. Chinese and European/North American websites used in Study 1

European/North American companies	Chinese companies
British Broadcasting Corporation (BBC) English: www.bbc.co.uk Chinese: www.bbc.co.uk/china	**Air China** Chinese version: www.airchina.com.cn English version: www.airchina.com.cn/en/
Bayerische Motoren Werke (BMW) English: www.bmwusa.com Chinese: www.bmw.com.cn	**Alibaba** Chinese: china.alibaba.com English: www.alibaba.com
Cisco English: www.cisco.com Chinese: www.cisco.com/web/CN/	**Bank of China** Chinese: www.boc.cn English: www.boc.cn/en/
eBay English: www.ebay.com Chinese:www.eachnet.com	**China Mobile** Chinese: www.chinamobile.com English: www.chinamobile.com/en/
Hongkong and Shanghai Banking Corporation (HSBC) English: www.hsbc.com Chinese: www.hsbc.com.cn	**Chinese National Petrochemical Corporation** Chinese: www.cnpc.com.cn English: www.cnpc.com.cn/en/
IBM English: www.ibm.com Chinese: www.ibm.com/cn/	**Haier** Chinese: www.haier.cn English: www.hairereurope.com
Morgan Stanley English: www.morganstanley.com Chinese: www.morganstanleychina.com	**Huawei** Chinese: www.huawei.com/cn English: www.huawei.com/europe/en/
Nestle English: www.nestle.com Chinese: wwww.nestle.com.cn	**Lenovo** Chinese: www.lenovo.com.cn English: www.lenovo.com/uk/en/
Reuters English: www.reuters.com Chinese: cn.reuters.com	**Sina** Chinese: www.sina.com.cn English: English.sina.com
Sun Microsystems English: www.sun.com Chinese: cn.sun.com	**Tsingtao** Chinese: www.tsingtao.com.cn English: www.tsigntao.com.cn/2008/en

European and North American companies change the navigation on their website when they create a version for the Chinese market? Similarly, do major Chinese companies change the navigation on their website when they create a version for the European/North American market?

2.1 Websites

Twenty websites were chosen for analysis: ten from European or North American companies which also have a website in Chinese and ten from Chinese companies which also have a website in English. These are listed in Table 1. In each case, only the home page of each website was analysed.

2.2 Calculation of Navigational Change

A method was needed for calculating the degree of change in the navigational structure, specifically the positioning of navigational elements between the Chinese and English language websites. The navigational elements are the individual items within a navigational structure, usually the words or icons indicating links to other webpages or other parts of the same webpage. For simplicity, a webpage is thought of as a rectangle with four quadrants (see Fig. 2) and changes in position were calculated between these quadrants.

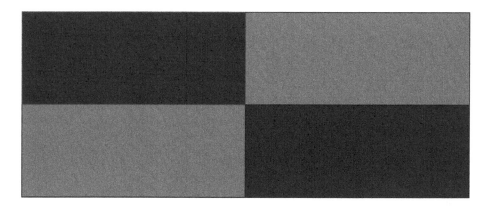

Fig. 2. Quadrants of a webpage for measuring navigational change

The two possibilities for position change are therefore:

- Top/Bottom (T/B): the position of a navigational element changes from either of the top two quadrants to either of the bottom two quadrants of a page or vice versa
- Left/Right (L/R): the position of a navigational element changes from either of the left two quadrants to either of the right two quadrants of a page or vice versa

In addition, the orientation of the navigational element could change from vertical to horizontal (V/H) or vice versa.

If a navigational element changes position or orientation in any of these three manners, it accrues a score of 1. We then take the average change across the three dimensions. For example, if a navigational element changes its from the left to the right of a page and its orientation from horizontal to vertical between the Chinese and English websites, it will accrues two scores of 1 (T/B = 0; L/R = 1; V/H = 1. Average = (0 + 1 + 1)/3 = 0.67.

2.3 Results

Table 2 summarizes the results for navigational changes from English to Chinese and Chinese to English language websites. In each case, the majority of websites did show some change, it can be seen from the figures that the amount of change is very small, and this is true for both the English to Chinese and Chinese to English translation. There were no significant differences in the mean amount of change from English to Chinese and from Chinese English website, regardless of whether we calculate using all 10 websites in the set or only those websites which showed some change.

Table 2. Summary of results for navigational changes in English language to Chinese language and Chinese language to English language websites

	English to Chinese	Chinese to English
Number of websites showing changes	7	6
Mean change per homepage for all 10 websites	0.21	0.28
Mean change per homepage for those websites with change	0.15	0.17

3 Study 2: Preference for Top-Left and Top-Right Navigation by Chinese and English Native Speakers

The second study investigated whether native Chinese and English speakers have different preferences for navigational layouts on websites. To do this, web pages were created with the typical "top and left" navigation and the mirror image of this navigation. Native Chinese and English speakers were asked to assess these pages for their aesthetics and their usability.

3.1 Participants

30 native speakers of Chinese and 25 native speakers of English took part in the study. The Chinese native speakers comprised 20 women and 10 men with ages ranging from 22 to 28 years. 4 were left handed and the remaining 26 were right handed. The English native speakers comprised 9 women and 16 men, with ages ranging from 20 to 56 years. All were right handed.

3.2 Webpages

The homepage for an imaginary university department (the Department of Computer Science at the University of North Yorkshire) was created. Two versions of the page were created, one with the typical top-left navigation (see Fig. 3), the other with the left/right mirror image of that page, with navigation at the top, but right-justified, and down the right hand side of the page (see Fig. 4). Both these versions were created in Chinese and in English.

Fig. 3. Imaginary homepage used in Study 2 (top-left navigation version)

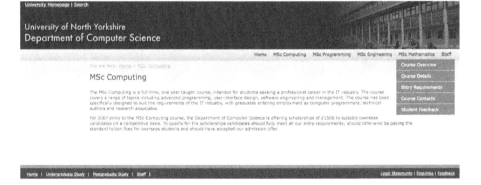

Fig. 4. Imaginary homepage used in Study 2 (top-right navigation version)

3.3 Procedure

Participants were shown the two homepages in their native language. They were allowed to study the two pages briefly, but were not told what the difference between the pages was. Participants were then asked two questions:

(a) which webpage do you find more attractive?
(b) Which webpage do you think would be easier to use?

Participants were asked to make their decisions as quickly as possible, based on initial impressions.

The purpose of the study was then explained and participants were asked whether they had any comments on navigation on websites in different languages. Demographic information was then collected.

3.4 Results

Figure 5 shows the results on the attractiveness question. Figure 6 shows the results on the usability question. Results on both questions were very similar and both showed a significant result (attractiveness: chi-square = 17.5, df = 1, p < 0.000; usability: chi-square = 19.8, df = 1, p < 0.000). For both questions there was an overall preference for the Top-Left navigation, with 78% of participants chosing this option for the attractiveness question and 80% of participants for the usability question. However, there were differences between the Chinese and English speakers. For the attractiveness question, 33% of the Chinese speakers chose the Top-Right navigation page, compared with only 8% of the English speakers. For the usability question, 30% of Chinese speakers chose this option compared with 8% of the English speakers.

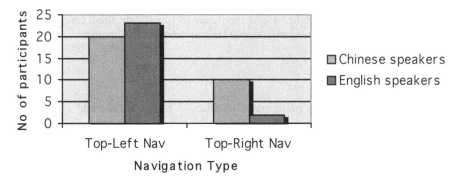

Fig. 5. Results on attractiveness for Top-Left and Top-Right navigation by Chinese and English native speakers

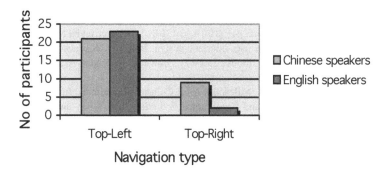

Fig. 6. Results on usability for Top-Left and Top-Right navigation by Chinese and English native speakers

The analysis was repeated with only the right handed participants, but this had no effect on the findings. Unfortunately there were not enough left handed participants to make a comparison between right handed and left handed participants.

4 Conclusions and Future Work

The results of the first study showed that a sample of major Chinese and North American/European companies are not making any adjustments to the navigational layout of their websites when targeting the different linguistic/cultural markets. However, the results of the second study show that there are significant differences between Chinese and English speakers in their perceptions of the navigational layout on webpages, with significantly more Chinese speakers preferring a top-right layout than English speakers.

The results of the second study show that linguistic/cultural differences may well affect navigational layout and this topic warrants further investigation. In particular, a study of whether differences in navigational layout affects the performance of Chinese and English speakers with websites is needed to complement the results of this study which investigated perceptions. In addition, studies of native speakers of other languages such as Arabic, Hebrew and Japanese, to investigate their perceptions of and performance with different navigational layouts would be of interest.

Acknowledgements

We would like to thank the participants in Study 2 for their time and effort. We would also like to thank Roger Wales for useful research leads and discussion, as always.

References

1. Internet Statistics: Distribution of languages on the Internet, http://www.netz.tipp.de (retrieved March 1, 2009)
2. ZookNIC Internet Intelligence, .cn becomes the largest ccTLD (2008), http://www.zooknic.com/pr_2008_08_08.html (retrieved March 1, 2009)
3. Marcus, A.: Global/intercultural user interface design. In: Sears, A., Jacko, J. (eds.) The Human Computer Interaction Handbook, 2nd edn., Lawrence Erlbaum Associates, New York (2003)
4. Aykin, N., Quaet-Faslem, P.H., Milewski, A.E.: Cultural ergonomics. In: Salvendy, G. (ed.) Handbook of Human Factors and Ergonomics, 3rd edn., John Wiley and Son, New Jersey (2006)
5. Zahedi, F., van Pelt, W.V., Song, J.: A conceptual framework for international web design. IEEE Transactions on Professional Communication 44(2), 83–103 (2001)
6. Chen, M.J.: Directional scanning of visual displays: a study with Chinese subjects. Journal of Cross-Cultural Psychology 12(3), 252–271 (1981), doi:10.1177/0022022181123001
7. Nachson, I., Shefler, G.E., Samocha, D.: Directional scanning as a function of stimulus characteristics, reading habits, and directional set. Journal of Cross-Cultural Psychology 8(1), 83–99 (1977)
8. Nachson, I.: Directional scanning of visual stimuli set effects and sex differences among subjects with opposite reading habits. Journal of Cross-Cultural Psychology 10(2), 231–242 (1979)
9. Harsel, Y., Wales, R.: Directional preference in problem solving. International Journal of Psychology 22, 195–206 (1987)

Considerations for Using Eye Trackers during Usability Studies

Anjali Phukan and Margaret Re

UMBC, Baltimore, MD, USA
{anjai2,re}@umbc.edu

Abstract. The purpose of this usability study was to see if eye trackers collect valid data, regardless of the user's method of corrected vision, eye color, or gender. The motivation to explore the idea that these human factors can distort eye trackers is based on marketing claims by several companies that say these factors should not affect results. This study found that the validity of data in usability studies that involved eye trackers in testing can produce biased results based on eyewear and eye color, and that adjustments should be made to control for these variables. The results showed no significant correlations based on gender. As a consideration into developing international signage for mass transportation systems that effectively accommodate global users, this study also explored how first language affects the way in which a user views and organizes a message and hence interprets procedural directions and related imagery. This is within the context of usability testing for a wide variety of users who may not share a first language or have the same method of vision correction.

Keywords: eye trackers, usability testing methodologies, internationalization, eye color, eyewear, gender, and language.

1 Introduction

Some eye tracking hardware manufactures make claims about the validity of their systems in terms of the demographics of the users. However, if these claims are not accurate, then researchers may design studies incorrectly, and hence report incorrect results. This initial study looks at the validity of some of these claims, and attempts to suggest usability methods to account for any unexpected variances in data that may occur as a result of these demographics.

2 Motivation

Several eye tracking hardware and software makers said any eyewear is tolerable. For instance, Tobii says "...Tobii T60 and T120 Eye Trackers track basically everyone, regardless of ethnic origin, age, glasses or contact lenses..."[1] In addition, LC Technologies, makers of Eyegaze systems says "...The system does not get confused by reflections off glasses...or by bright or dark facial features." [2]. This study is focused on seeing if eye tracking systems provide different results for users of different

N. Aykin (Ed.): Internationalization, Design, LNCS 5623, pp. 301–307, 2009.
© Springer-Verlag Berlin Heidelberg 2009

demographics (i.e. eye color, eyewear, gender, and first language), based on these claims. These study also will see if and how the results of the different demographic groups may impact usability studies. This could have implications in many fields, from testing readability of a font [e.g. 3] to user interaction research [e.g. 4]. For more on eye tracking systems, methodologies, and other applications, see [5].

3   Study Design, Assumptions, Definitions

This study used a Tobii T120 and related software Tobii Studio to collect data on html pages with text and jpeg images. There were several Area of Interest (AOI) sections on each web page. In addition to analysis on an AOI, overall analysis on the data looked at general user trends based on various demographics. The analysis includes data gathered from the following:

- Eye movement: eye gaze validity, fixation data, pupil size
- AOI data: count, length, time to each first AOI fixation
- Other user actions: Mouse clicks, Keystrokes, URL starts and stops
- User demographics, gathered at the beginning of the study

The study collected demographic and eye gaze data in a lab setting using predefined web pages of jpeg images and 2 customized directions pages. This was done in two sets of data collection. The first set of data collected was via a pilot study of 9 graduate (Information Systems/Human Centered Computing) students and 1 teacher reviewing 8 jpeg images. The graduate students, who were MA and PhD students, with a variety of undergraduate degrees, viewed informational images specifically designed to show hierarchy of information. The study process was modified so that the survey was administered completely using paper, to remove all possible complications once the user began to use the eye tracking computer. The two studies used the same image viewing directions but the instructions were provided differently, the surveys were completed differently, and the users viewed different images.

The second set of data collected was via a second study of 25 undergraduate students viewing 4 new jpeg images. The undergraduates, senior design students, viewed several visual dictionaries that other classmates had created. The first and last pages of each study session were directions written in H1 and/or H2 on a simple hypertext markup web page. Each visual dictionary was a combination of numerals and letters of a particular typeface (e.g. Gill Sans, Akzidenz-Grotesk) in a jpeg image, where the angle, color, and size of a letter varied based on the intent of the visual dictionary's designer(s). This was a within subjects study, hence all participants viewed all visual dictionaries.

User demographics in this study group, such as gender and eyewear, are shown in Table 1. Second Study User Demographics. Users determined their own 1st alphabet, eyewear, eye color, and gender, although some users asked for advice from other participants or the researchers about the eye color. There were no noted discrepancies from what users picked as their eye color and what the observers felt was their eye color. Eyewear was based on what the user was wearing during the study, whether or not they usually use that type of eyewear, although all participants said they had normal-to-corrected vision with whatever eyewear they were using during the study. All participants in both studies spoke English, but some users in each group used a non-Latin Alphabet as a native language. In the second study group used in this paper, there were 4 participants whose native alphabet were non-Latin, including 3 Korean and 1 Slovak student. All participants who used a Latin based native alphabet learned English as their first language, although their countries of origin varied slightly.

Table 1. Second Study User Demographics

1st Alphabet	Eyewear	Eye Color	Gender
Latin/Other	Contacts/Glasses/None	Blue/Brown/Green/Hazel	Female/Male
21/4	6/6/13	10/7/3/5	17/8

4 Findings and Conclusions

There were findings are based on the second study discussed in the previous section. The results are discussed as follows: eye color, eyewear, gender, and lastly language.

4.1 Eye Color

Larger pupils users have less valid data. Larger pupil sizes are not significantly correlated with a language or eye color, except for hazel eyes that tend to appear to have smaller pupils. In addition, glasses gather the least amount of valid data, followed by contacts, and then no corrective eyewear. Less valid data as a result of these conditions affects correlation tables, and could affect the analysis and interpretations of studies. None of these factors impacted a user's ability to navigate the tasks.

The software used to gather fixation information first verifies a piece of information via a proprietary formula that populates a validity field in a user/session table of data collected. The score ranges from 0 to 4 where 0 is valid and 4 is invalid and are significantly correlated with the pupil size of the eye being validated. The left eye pupil size was correlated to the left eye validity code a rate of .945, and the right eye's pupil size to validity code correlation was .996. When left and right eye data was combined however, the total correlation for pupil size to validity was only .88. This is because, although a piece of eye tracking data can have information on both eyes. There is a tendency for the data to be valid on only one eye at a time, where the pupil size of the left eye was significantly negatively correlated with the pupil size of the right eye. This left/right pupil size correlation and the left/right validity correlation were both valued at -.77. One thing to note is that the validity increases as the data becomes more invalid, so that the positive correlation really means that the smaller pupil tends to be more correlated with more valid data.

Hazel eyes overall did not have significantly different pupil sizes. However, in terms of left eye or right eye, they were clearly different. This perceived pupil size difference impacted the validity of the data collected in regards to left and right eye data, although overall the amount of data gathered was only slightly more than that from other colored eyes. It's interesting to note that hazel eyes are caused by a combination of a moderate amount of melanin in the iris' anterior border layer and

Rayleigh scattering (scattering of light or electromagnetic radiation by particles much smaller than the wavelength of light - can occur when light travels in transparent solids and liquids, such as gases) [6]. This could be the reason for this difference in pupil size during data collection, although there are many other possible reasons. The end result is less data collected for hazel eyes, possibly biasing the data collected, especially the fixations per minute, or even area of interest in a marketing research study, as is shown in Table 2. Average Fixations by Eye Color.

Table 2. Average Fixations by Eye Color

Eye Color	Average Fixation Duration (std)	Average Fixations per minute (std)
Brown	590.15 (132.64)	170.82 (19.87)
Blue	661.85 (84.13)	154.38 (16.48)
Green	661.90 (152.35)	147.93 (13.83)
Hazel	651.19 (101.89)	125.42 (27.69)
All Eyes	639.65 (108.29)	152.42 (24.47)

Table 3. Correlations by Eye Color shows the correlations of color to the validity code of all data gathered from an eye tracker. It is also partially correlated on the colors that had some significant effect on the validity code or average fixations per minute, where '*' indicates statistical significance at .05 and '**' indicates statistical significance at .01. The data gathered did not show an affect of eye color on average fixation duration. The results do not conclude that the eye color plays a role in average fixations or in validity of the data, but do show that there is some correlation, where darker eyes perform better than hazel eyes.

Table 3. Correlations by Eye Color

	Eye Color	Brown	Hazel
Left Eye Validity	(*)-0.449	0.187	(**)-0.548
Right Eye Validity	(**)0.537	-0.248	(**)0.644
Average Fixations per minute	(*)-0.442	(*)0.479	(**)-0.563

4.2 Eyewear

The number of fixations is correlated to a user's eyewear, where glasses include both reading glasses and every day glasses. There were no users of bi-focal glasses in this study. In addition, eyewear in general loosely correlated with 7 of 9 AOIs on the directions page of the study task, where users not wearing contacts or glasses had the higher fixation counts, fixations lengths. On the image pages, users with corrected vision had quicker times to first fixations in general, however on directions page users who did not wear glasses or contacts had faster times to first fixations. Users of glasses had faster first fixation times than contact users on the pages with jpeg images. Table 4. Correlation by Eyewear shows the correlations of validity by eyewear are not significant, however the eyewear is significant when compared to actual data collected. This is an indicator that users who wore no vision correction devices had the longest fixations. However, the opposite order occurred in the number of fixations per minute, calculated by taking the number of fixations in a session, dividing it by the time it took to complete the session.

Table 4. Correlation by Eyewear

	Eyewear	Contacts	None
Left Eye Validity	-0.009	0.118	-0.068
Right Eye Validity	-0.134	0.066	-0.025
Average Fixation Duration	(**)0.641	(**)-0.661	(**)0.465
Average Fixation Per Minute	-0.286	(**)0.525	-0.299

The results in Table 5. Average Fixations by Eyewear show this inverse relationship between average fixation duration and the average fixations per minute count. For example, users of contacts may be perceived to have the most activity due to the fact they have the most fixations, but this is not the case, due to the fact the average duration is substantially less. One hypothesized reason for the breaks in fixations is that it is due to substantial periods of invalid data, caused by glare, reflections, or other light refractions coming off of the lenses of the contacts and/or glasses.

Table 5. Average Fixations by Eyewear

Eyewear	Average Fixation Duration (std)	Average Fixations per minute (std)
Contacts	514.91 (52.95)	174.84 (12.83)
Glasses	661.68 (65.60)	144.90 (26.75)
None	687.05 (100.18)	145.54 (22.37)
All Eyes	639.65 (108.29)	152.42 (24.47)

4.3 Gender

The same analysis was performed on gender, to find no significant findings in terms of pupil size, validity, fixation data, time on task, or task navigational movements.

4.4 Language

There was not enough data to determine significant results regarding language findings, but there are some indications that future research could be warranted. For example, participants with English as their native language took significantly less time to view the images than English-as-a-second-language participants. The average time for English-as-a-second-language participants was 5.98 minutes, where as participants who spoke English as their native language spent only 3.87 minutes on the study. In addition, on 4 AOI fixations both on direction pages and image pages, non-English students had minor significance correlations of 0.408 to 0.840, indicating they spent more time gazing at AOIs, both in terms of number of fixations and fixation lengths. However, these findings were somewhat inconclusive due to a lack of more AOIs with significant or higher correlations. In addition, there was a lack of diversity in the first language of participants, limiting the conclusiveness of the findings even more. However, these preliminary findings will help in preparing future studies on these topics.

5 Summary and Implications for Future Research

In designing usability testing of transportation signs, studies should adjust fixation results for users based on type of eyewear or eye corrective treatment. Specifically, when testing between subjects, the demographics of both sets of subjects may need to have the same eyewear and eye color to yield the most accurate results. Otherwise, sign XYZ could be deemed less effective if testing with users wearing mostly contacts verses sign ABC, which was testing in a group of mostly non-corrective wear users. Hazel eyes and contacts gather the least valid eye tracking data, however there are no other significant differences found between the other eye colors or eyewear.

Implications for international design of usability studies include accounting for eye demographics, which may affect the sensors, and which may vary greatly from one country or locality to the next. Pupil size is of concern, as this was the most significantly correlated item to eye tracker's acceptance of a piece of data. In addition, eye color and eyewear have significant impacts, and can vary greatly from one country to the next. For example, lighter colored iris are most commonly found in Europeans and individuals of European admixture while darker iris colors are more common in the Middle Eastern and Southern Asian populations [7]. Also under consideration is the first language of the user, which can also vary from one part of the world to the next.

One research limitation is that we did not track users who may have had laser eye surgery. In addition, the affect of hazel eyes may be impacting the findings for contact lenses, and vice versa. There was a correlation of only 0.136 between eye color and eyewear, but brown eyes were significantly correlated to eyewear (-.481) and contacts (.484). While no other eye color or eyewear showed a significant relationship, a study with larger, more evenly distributed sample sizes may be needed to remove any impact one factor may have against another.

Future research areas include testing to see if eye validity errors are caused by (rather than just correlating with) eye color and eyewear and if so by how much, as well as to see if the invalid data is the true cause of making one fixation look like multiple fixations may be necessary to validate the need for usability testing where eyewear is controlled. In addition, testing needs to be done to see if this would happen on other eye tracking devices. More research is also needed to find what other fields this is affecting, and if there is a place to report false readings.

In addition, running a study that increased the sample size of the different language groups should provide more data on times to first fixation, fixation durations, etc, and perhaps with other physiological sensors to see if the user reacts in the intended way to the content read. English users take less observation time for English text, although further research is needed into languages that use an alphabet system that is visually more complex. Complex alphabets require more strokes to construct the individually letter forms than simpler alphabets. For example, when comparing Latin and Hindi alphabets, Hindi would be more complex. Future research would look into the time it takes to read simple verses complex alphabets, to see if the adage, "we read best is what we read most true," is really true.

Lastly, we are not sure how the alphabet form/structure effects a user's observation time, verses the orientation of the letters. This is because some of the jpegs had text on an angle and the information was not organized off of a straight horizontal line in neat columns. This could have huge implications when designing messages in a text image, from transportation system signs to computer media images.

Acknowledgments. This material is based upon work supported by the National Science Foundation (NSF) under Grant No. CNS-0619379. Any opinions, findings and conclusions or recommendations expressed in this material are those of the authors and do not necessarily reflect the views of the NSF.

Dr. Andrew Sears provided appreciated guidance and support in this project.

References

1. http://tobii.com/archive/pages/17744/view.aspx
2. http://www.eyegaze.com/content/
   eyetracking-research-tools#reliability
3. Nini, P.: Typography and the Aging Eye: Typeface Legibility for Older Viewers with Vision Problems. January 23, 2006. AIGI online Design Archives (2006)
4. Miniotas, D., Špakov, O., MacKenzie, I.S.: Eye gaze interaction with expanding targets. In: CHI 2004 Extended Abstracts on Human Factors in Computing Systems, Vienna, Austria, April 24-29, 2004, pp. 1255–1258. ACM, New York (2004)
5. Duchowski, A.T.: Eye Tracking Methodology Theory and Practice, 2nd edn. Springer, London (2007)
6. Wang, H., Lin, S., Liu, X., Kang, S.B.: Separating Reflections in Human Iris Images for Illumination Estimation. In: Proc. IEEE International Conference on Computer Vision (2005)
7. Sturm, R.A., Frudakis, T.N.: Eye colour: portals into pigmentation genes and ancestry. Trends in Genetics, vol.20.8 (2004)

The Future of Enterprise Is with the Mobile Workforce: An International Field Study

Lynn Rampoldi-Hnilo, Brent White, Michele Snyder, and Chad Sampanes

Oracle Mobile Applications User Experience, 4001 Discovery Drive Suite 340
Boulder, CO 80303
{lynn.rampoldi-hnilo,brent.white,
michele.snyder,chad.sampanes}@oracle.com

Abstract. To create the most effective mobile applications, Oracle must understand how and in what contexts the mobile workforce is using their mobile devices. Oracle mobile researchers went into the workforce population and conducted an international, ethnographic field study to fully understand the mobile worker's needs, behaviors, and contextually based activities.

Keywords: Ethnography, Field study, International research, Mobile, Enterprise applications.

1 Introduction

Technology experts predict that the next major computing platform will be the mobile device [1]. In the past, enterprise application companies have focused primarily on desktop and laptop software solutions. However, as the workforce becomes increasingly mobile, companies are responding with mobile solutions to complement their desktop applications. A complete enterprise solution that accounts for work context is a growing requirement for maintaining competitive and strategic advantages.

Since the launch of commercial wireless application protocol (WAP) services in 1999, there has been much hope that mobile devices would leverage some of the functionality found in desktop business applications. But the WAP approach failed because of major shortcomings in front-end design and mobile technology [2]. The devices and mobile network technologies of 1999 were too slow to process data, and the design approach of repurposing one design for all platforms resulted in unusable mobile interfaces. However, progressive advances in cellular networks and device capabilities, combined with a new design approach that understands the importance of creating a distinct mobile version, have now taken hold. Developers of consumer mobile applications have been quick to design specifically for mobile devices. A focus on a select set of consumer services and applications designed for specific mobile form factors contributed to the market dominance of Japan's NTT DoCoMo's i-Mode internet service [2]. As of January 2009 there were over 48 million Japanese subscribers comprising 53% of the market for browser-enabled phones [3]. i-Mode has succeeded in offering easy-to-deploy applications in categories such as gaming, multimedia and content creation that mobile subscribers want to use.

N. Aykin (Ed.): Internationalization, Design, LNCS 5623, pp. 308–315, 2009.

That consumer-based applications are driving innovation is not surprising for several reasons. First, although mobile devices were originally targeted for business purposes, it was primarily social usage (such as messaging friends and family) that turned mobile devices into a mass market [4]. Second, consumer mobile applications are widely available and in use by mobile workers. Many of these entertainment and news content services are used during the work day as employees pass time between tasks. Third, enterprise applications have typically been designed to address business processes that may involve multiple steps and high concentrations of data. Both of these characteristics do not fit a work style characterized by working in short spurts while viewing data on a relatively small screen [5].

When mobile, users must quickly access information and immediately take action or pass information on to others. The most successful business applications on the mobile platform match this frequently interrupted and fast-paced work style. The BlackBerry line of devices has dominated the corporate work place and hold more than 40 percent of the U.S. smart phone market [6]. The core service of the Blackberry is a corporate e-mail architecture that provides robust e-mail capabilities refined for mobile users. Other key mobile usage outside of voice calls revolves around messaging, music, games, and single-purpose utilities (such as calculators and alarm clocks). However, the concept of downloading applications onto mobile devices is becoming more common with new distribution models, such as Apple's iTunes Store, which has greatly improved the ease of finding and downloading mobile applications. As of February 2009, there were approximately 15,000 iPhone applications on iTunes. Only 7 percent of these applications are categorized under business [7].

Although mobile workers may not currently be running full-blown business applications, they still complete work tasks with applications that were delivered with or that were downloaded to their mobile devices (such as calendars and note taking). While we know that more sophisticated features (such as using integrated business intelligence when executing transactions) would be useful for mobile workers, we must better understand how users are currently working and meeting these needs through their existing mobile devices. A better understanding of existing usage will enable Oracle to create the most effective mobile applications.

To gain this understanding, Oracle mobile researchers went out into the workforce population and conducted an international, ethnographic field study to fully understand mobile worker needs, behaviors, and their contextually based activities. The study tackled questions, such as "What types of applications do mobile users need to be more successful in their work?" and "Where is the future of mobile devices?"

2 Methodology

Mobile behaviors are not easily self reported because they are opportunistic in nature (that is, mobile tasks are completed when convenient) and are often unexpected or unplanned by the users (for example, users must often urgently respond to spontaneous e-mails or phone calls from managers). Therefore, the issues that we planned to explore in our study were contextual and rooted in behavior.

Ethnography was chosen for our study because it is a process of gaining an understanding of work or activity as it occurs in its natural environment [8]. Using this method enabled us to observe mobile behaviors at the time of occurrence in their authentic work settings. Ethnographic research has been used for many years in fields such as sociology and anthropology, and it has recently become increasingly popular in the field of human computer interaction. Some of the goals of field studies in supporting technology design are to find opportunities, counter assumptions, or support preexisting assumptions [9].

Oracle conducted an international ethnographic research study in the U.S., Singapore, and India to understand users across technologically advanced cultures, diverse mobile workforces, and emerging markets. The goal was to thoroughly understand the mobile work environment by observing where, when, and how mobile workers use their mobile devices. In particular, we wanted to learn about the mobile culture of the participants, including personal versus work usage, percentage of time on their mobile devices, percentage of time spent on work away from their desks, and mobile etiquette. Furthermore, we also wanted to discover the types of content and applications that people expect, need, or want on their mobile devices for both work and personal use.

2.1 Participants

Our study involved interviews of 33 experienced mobile device users residing across the three countries (13 in Singapore, 10 in India, and 10 in the U.S.—a mixture of people from New York and San Francisco). The study was conducted in April and May of 2008.

We recruited three different groups of heavy mobile users for the study:

1. Mobile workers (N = 25): Mobile workers comprised the majority of the participants and were required to use their mobile devices for more than 2 hours a day for work-related tasks. These mobile users also needed to be out in the field at least several days a week. We specifically targeted the following worker roles: field sales representatives, field service technicians, portfolio managers, manufacturing or shipping agents, and retail merchandisers.
2. Everyday mobile users (N= 4): These participants were expected to use their mobile devices for at least 2 hours a day with 25 percent of their mobile usage for work-related tasks. They were not required to fit into any specific work role; however, they were expected to perform some of the following advanced functions on their mobile devices: e-mailing, browsing the Internet, playing games, text messaging, and shopping.
3. Young college age students in their early 20s (Gen Y) (N=4): Although these users do not use their devices for work-related tasks, they are the future mobile workers. In order to participate in the study, these Gen Ys were required to use their mobile devices for 2 hours a day and to perform advanced functions, such as e-mailing, Internet browsing, text messaging, and shopping.

2.2 Method

The field study consisted of us accompanying each of the participants during a day for a 5-hour period. In the 5-hour sessions, there was an introduction interview, a follow-along observation, and a post interview. We used four paired teams of researchers to conduct the research. In Singapore and India, each pair consisted of a mobile researcher from Oracle and a local research counterpart from either Oracle or a research partner. In the U.S., two Oracle mobile researchers conducted the sessions.

The introduction interview lasted approximately 30 minutes and took place at the beginning of each session. The interview began with us introducing ourselves and explaining what would occur throughout the session. Next, the participants were given an opportunity to introduce themselves to us. Once we familiarized ourselves with each other, the participants were asked to describe their typical day and how it involved interacting with their mobile devices. In the final part of the introduction interview, the participants were asked to complete a short questionnaire that contained some demographic information about their mobile usage.

The observation portion of the session lasted for a 3- to 4-hour period, starting directly after the introduction interview. We went along with the participants as they went about their work and day-to-day activities. We remained as unobtrusive as possible during the follow-along period and talked occasionally and briefly only to clarify issues. We photographed, videotaped, and audiotaped participants completing their daily tasks, when appropriate.

The final part of the session was a post interview that occurred after the observation period. During this time, we asked questions based on the observations that we recorded during the follow-along session. This time was also used to prompt discussions regarding other mobile tasks and trends that were not observed during the day. To gain a better understanding of future mobile device and application requirements, the participants were asked the following two questions:

1. What are the coolest new features that you have seen for cell phones or mobile devices?
2. If you could make your cell phone or mobile device do anything, what would it do?

This paper focuses on the results of these questions.

2.3 Analysis

We performed a qualitative analysis on the data to understand mobile trends and requirements for future design. To find trends across multiple users, we grouped data into categories (likes, dislikes, most innovative new features, and desires for future capabilities). We also assessed cultural differences across countries.

3 Results

Fresh designs often are inspired by what users need or want to see in the future. In order to capture forward-thinking ideas, we observed and talked to our participants about what they would like to see in either their current or future devices. What should an application or a device do in the future? This section is a synthesis of the common findings that we found across the U.S., Singapore, and India.

Participants in this study were heavy mobile users. They knew the strengths and weaknesses of their devices. Participants wanted to see improved form factors and functionality, to have their phones better support their work needs, to enhance devices so that they had to carry around only one device instead of many, and to increase the multimedia functionality and services available on their devices.

3.1 Improve Form Factors and Functionality

A top request was for the existing functionality and devices to operate better than they currently do. In other words, don't add more, but make existing functionality better.

Participants wanted their mobile devices to have bigger screens, slimmer designs, increased memory, faster speeds, higher camera resolutions, shortcutting between applications, and better clarity of calls. They also wanted their devices to be water resistant and sturdier.

Participants wanted the features and functionality on their mobile devices to work better with faster speeds, better connectivity, and greater consistency. Participants wanted to receive e-mails consistently, browse the Internet as quickly as they do on their laptops, receive consistently correct GPS coordinates, and receive better Internet website updates of weather, stocks, and traffic.

Participants wanted data entry to be easier, with simplified text messaging programs, predictive text (T9), speech-to-text transformation, voice dialing, business card scanning input, handwriting recognition for contact names, and better data input methods.

Lastly, participants wanted enhanced voice capabilities on their mobile devices. Participants wanted their mobile devices to record what they say and correctly and consistently translate it into text. They also want to leverage "voice commands" to have the devices do what they say (for example, "open e-mail").

3.2 Enable Work

Participants in all three countries generally had their phones with them at all times, especially at work. They identified a number of ways they would like their phones to support them.

Programs and Documents. Participants straddle the mobile and desktop world and always need some way to bridge the two. The mobile workers in this study said that they need VPN to work remotely, to access enterprise programs, to provide real-time answers to their clients, and to retrieve documents from their home computers.

These on-the-move participants need smart phone functionality like MS office to remotely edit documents, e-mail, teleconference, take notes, and access shared document folders.

Immediate Information. Some participants said that they needed access to information that changes frequently or that is central to decisions that they must make while on the go. For example, they wanted access to bank internal deposit rates, exchange rates, stock market data (push and pull), and parts and inventory availability. Information related to current employee performance, budgets, and sales quotas was also identified as "must have" information.

Fig. 1. Participant in Singapore looks to mobile device while driving

Location-based Applications. Participants said that GPS navigation and mash-up applications that leverage GPS would help them identify client sites as they travel from one location to the next.

Sharing Information and Status. Mobile devices are perfectly suited to storing and sharing information with others. Participants want to be able to exchange updates and notes between team members, take pictures of important documents, send text messages to a distribution list of clients or colleagues easily, and bring client presentations with them via their mobiles (not their laptops). Participants also expressed the need to filter calls by time and have a status mode that alerts those trying to contact them when it's a holiday or when the participants do not want to be disturbed.

3.3   Create an All-in-One Device

A number of participants spoke of wanting only one device and making their current devices support a variety of tasks both personal and work related. This theme was most prevalent and articulated in Singapore, but was observed in both the U.S. and in Mumbai. Taking this to the next level, participants suggested the following:

Embedded Identification Chips. Participants want their devices to act as security badges, cash card devices, and credit cards.

Household Management Tools. A hot area of interest was making mobile devices more powerful so that these devices can help participants manage their household appliances. Participants wanted their devices to be able to turn on the air conditioning when they were are 20 minutes from the house, to operate garage doors, to control the television, and so on.

Personal Information Storage. Participants would like their devices to act like an organizer and to take over the functionality of a personal journal, for example to track all policy and insurance numbers.

Record Auto Location. Most Singaporeans need to park in underground parking structures if they drive. These participants said that they wanted their devices to record where they parked so that they did not have to search for their cars in these dark basements.

3.4 Enhance Multimedia

Participants love the notion of using their mobile devices to watch TV, to receive streaming video, to read really simple syndication (RSS) blogs, to teleconference, and to have MP3 capabilities. Participants in all three countries noted that multimedia enhancements such as these are expected in the future for their devices.

Fig. 2. Participant in Singapore teleconferences with a friend

4   Conclusion

Mobile devices and applications provide functionality that support both personal and work tasks. There is no widespread delineation between work and personal use. Mobile users want devices that are robust and help them accomplish a vast array of tasks. It is imperative that mobile devices and functionality continue to improve in form and functionality to make it easier for users to complete their personal and work tasks using their mobile devices. Many of the tasks on mobile devices (for example, sending and receiving e-mails and texts, viewing documents, and getting directions) can serve both personal and professional needs; the only aspects that differ are the content and recipients of the information.

In the past, mobile application development has been focused on creating consumer applications. For this reason, mobile users and mobile subscribers are often using consumer-oriented applications and devices to accomplish business tasks (sometimes creatively so). Therefore, it's imperative that we examine how mobile workers use these consumer applications.

Even though the intent of our study was not to be consumer-focused, requirements that apply both to the consumer and business spaces emerged, making our findings applicable to consumer- and enterprise-oriented mobile application development. Mobile workers want their phones to enable work, such as supporting documents, sharing information, and providing immediate access to data. They also expect applications to account for their location because they are on the go when using their mobile devices. Not only do mobile users want their mobile devices and applications to look good, but also they want these devices to be capable of accomplishing a vast array of tasks for them. Most users are trying not to carry their laptops around. For the same reasons, they most definitely do not want to have to carry two or three mobile devices around to get their jobs done. When mobile workers aren't working, or when they have free time during the work day, they also want their mobile devices to have high media capabilities, such as MP3 or streaming TV.

Following are several key lessons for those designing and developing mobile devices and applications:

1. Consider creating mobile devices and applications that are flexible enough to support work and personal tasks. Many successful products have integrated *both* types of functions into *one* solution or make it easy to integrate and switch between related applications.
2. Consumer needs and applications continue to drive innovation in the mobile domain. To be fresh and creative, enterprise mobile designers and developers should assess the consumer space.
3. Enterprise mobile designers and developers should identify consumer applications that accomplish enterprise-like tasks and should leverage these existing applications as part of the full enterprise mobile solution, rather than trying to recreate these applications.
4. Enterprise mobile designers and developers should leverage the inherent abilities of phone devices, such as the phone's ability to make calls; take photos; navigate (GPS); and list contacts, calendar items, and tasks (personal information management), to enhance mobile solutions and limit the need for additional devices.

Mobile users know the ins and outs of their mobile devices. It is up to designers and developers to know these users and their mobile device habits. This understanding will enable us to enhance the mobile users' experience—to provide smart solutions that improve and expand mobile device capabilities and that blend consumer and enterprise functionality into one innovative device.

References

1. Lessner, I.: Oracle's Ellison Skewers Latest Tech Trends. TheStreet.com (2008),
   http://www.thestreet.com/story/10439433/2/
   oracles-ellison-skewers-latest-tech-trends.html
2. Jones, M., Marsden, G.: Mobile Interaction Design. John Wiley & Sons, Chichester (2006)
3. Telecommunications Carriers Association,
   http://www.tca.or.jp/english/database/2009/01/index.html
4. Matsuda, M.: Personal, Portable, Pedestrian. In: Ito, M., Okabe, D., Matsuda, M. (eds.), MIT Press, MA (2005)
5. White, B., Rampoldi-Hnilo, L.: Designing the Mobile Experience (2008),
   http://usableapps.oracle.com/design/pages/mobile.html
6. Elmer-DeWitt, P.: iPhone grabs 30% of U.S. smartphone market. CNNMoney.com,
   http://apple20.blogs.fortune.cnn.com/2008/12/02/
   iphone-grabs-30-of-us-smartphone-market/
7. Apple.com, http://www.apple.com/iphone/appstore/
8. Martin, D., Sommerville, I.: Patterns of Cooperative Interaction: Linking Ethnomethodology and Design. ACM Trans on Computer-Human Interaction 11(1), 59–85 (2004)
9. Bly, S.: Field Work: Is It Product Work? Interactions (1997)

Part IV

ICT for Global Development

Representation and Reflexivity in ICT for Development (Telecentre) Research

Savita Bailur

London School of Economics
s.bailur@lse.ac.uk

Abstract. The author argues there is insufficient discussion of representation (the problems of showing the realities of the lived experiences of the observed settings) and reflexivity (the relationship between knowledge and the ways whereby knowledge is produced) in ICTD literature, particularly regarding telecentre users and non-users. It first reviews six papers from 2007-8 in *Information Technologies and International Development* and find that the process of research methods and theorizing from findings could be analyzed in more detail. It then shares how deconstructing the research process affected findings in *Our Voices* telecentre, the author's own case study.

Keywords: telecentre, telecentre users, representation, reflexivity, research method.

1 Introduction

In a 2004 paper, Kanungo [1] states that his objective is to discuss barriers to emancipation through a rural telecentre in a neohumanist paradigm. The aim of his research is to discuss the empowerment of those who use the MSSRF village knowledge centres (or telecentres[1]) in Pondicherry, India. His paper praises the approach of the MSSRF project, stating that project staff lived in the setting and understood the issues thoroughly. Yet, the author states that limited direct interaction took place with users. Kanungo does not appear alone in purporting to research themes such as participation, empowerment and the use of telecentres, but not expanding on the research methods used in terms of direct interaction with users and non-users, and how his findings were reached. This paper reviews literature on representation (the problems of showing the realities of the lived experiences of the observed settings) and reflexivity (the relationship between knowledge and the ways whereby knowledge is produced). We then ask if in ICTD literature, especially in telecentre research we pay enough attention to representation and reflexivity by conducting a review of telecentre papers for the past two years in one of the main IT and development journals *Information*

---

[1] Telecentres are usually non-profit physical spaces that provide public access to ICTs, ostensibly for development. This review will also cover papers on for profit cyber cafes in developing countries, as there is growing literature that argues that cyber cafes and as likely to contribute to development as telecentres, as they are potentially more sustainable (***).

N. Aykin (Ed.): Internationalization, Design, LNCS 5623, pp. 319–327, 2009.
© Springer-Verlag Berlin Heidelberg 2009

Technologies and International Development[2], gauging the extent of representation and reflexivity. The paper then offers some practical suggestions, applying these to the case of the *Our Voices* telecentre in India, conducted as part of the author's doctoral research.

2   Literature Review

How do we know what we know? Epistemology is concerned with knowledge and how knowledge is required. In information systems, it is generally accepted that there are at least two epistemological perspectives when conducting research: positivism and interpretivism[3]. Positivism implies that an objective world exists independently of humans [2] and that as this world exists, it can be reached through value free and objective research [3]. Interpretivism argues that distinguishing facts and beliefs/values is subjective in itself and there is no such thing as an objective world, as it is constructed by the researcher's perspective [2]. The American anthropologist Clifford Geertz (1973) puts it simply, saying that what we call our data are really constructions of other people's constructions of what they and their compatriots are up to [4]. Deeper within interpretivism, those concerned with representation and reflexivity argue that in our research, many of us do not question how we represent our subjects, how we have reached that conclusion, essentially how we know what we know.

The issue of *representation* deals with the problems of showing the realities of the lived experiences of the observed settings [5]. Enmeshed with representation is the issue of *voice*, or to what extent it is the research subject's view or the researcher's view that is being portrayed. In researching telecentres, what appears particularly problematic is obtaining the views of telecentre users and non-users, and how this is portrayed by authors. One challenge, according to [6], is that when conducting research, telecentre researchers may inadvertently offer suggestions for the use of the telecentre, which the research subject may simply agree with. Another challenge, given the often remote location of many telecentres, is that several voices may be involved in telecentre research, from the principal researcher, to the research assistant, interpreter, transcriber and so on. The worldview, or *Weltanschauung*, of each of these would be implicated in the research. Finally, the author's voice can also be moulded and perhaps constrained by their research discipline/faculty/publication outlet.

Reflexivity delves deeper into how the problems of representation can be addressed. According to [7] reflexive researchers are interested in assessing the relationship between knowledge and the ways whereby knowledge is produced. Reflexivity acknowledges that research is shaped by various factors, including linguistic, social,

---

[2] Initially, this review covered five years and included the journal *Information Technology for Development* but had to be edited due to space restrictions. [2] Further , there are undoubtedly many other outlets for telecentre papers, including *Information Society, Information Technology and People, New Media and Society, The Electronic Journal of Information Systems in Developing Countries*, as well as conference proceedings such as from *IFIP 9.4, ICTD, HCI,* and *CHI*, but due to space restrictions, the review focuses only on *Information Technologies and International Development*.

[3] Two other perspectives include critical theory and critical realism [2].

political and theoretical elements [7]. The reflexive researcher asks themselves what preconceptions they may be bringing into their research. According to [8], in the social sciences there is only interpretation. Nothing speaks for itself. Reflexivity asks if the findings can be understood in a different way [9, 7]. Alvesson and Kärreman [9] suggest asking can I construct/make sense of this material in another way than suggested by the preferred perspective/vocabulary. Can I let myself be surprised by this material? Can it productively and fairly be constructed in a way that kicks back at my framework and how we-in my research community-typically see and interpret things?

Why should representation and reflexivity matter at all? Firstly, there is the issue of ethics, that we have an obligation to our research subjects to represent them as honestly as they would like to be represented. Secondly, greater discussion of research methods avoids the assumption that data exists and simply reflects reality. Thirdly, it makes the research process and findings more thoughtful and creative, playing with different possibilities and the potential richness of meaning [10]. Fourthly, it questions the authority of the researcher and sees it simply one representation amongst many [7]. Ultimately, findings may be very different if attention is paid to representation and reflexivity. In ICTD research, the issues of representation and reflexivity are particularly important as the world views of the researcher and the research subjects are likely to be very different.

3 Reviewing Representation/Reflexivity in ITID

This brief analysis gives some indication of the extent of representation and reflexivity in telecentre papers in *ITID*. In all the papers, the research question/objective is important as it establishes who should be interviewed. In this sense, it is acceptable not to necessarily interview telecentre users if the research question is something such as the formation of telecentre policy [12], although even here it would have been useful to interview telecentre users and non-users to see if they had been involved in policymaking. This aside, five out of the six papers above deal with issues of sustainability, empowerment, social equity, adoption and trust-all issues which directly relates to users and non-users. Therefore it is critical that both groups are interviewed (representation) and further, the authors discuss how their findings are reached (reflexivity).

In terms of representation, only three of the papers explicitly mention interviews with users [13, 14, 15]. One mentions interviews with users, but with other projects and not with the actual project being researched [16]. Only two mention interviews with non-users [13, 14]. In terms of reflexivity, there is some discussion, such as recognition of author bias [11, 16] although this was either seen positively in terms of

Table 1.

Paper	Research question/aim	Representation		Reflexivity
		Interviews with users	Interviews with non-users	

Table 1. (*Continued*)

[11]	Why were some, but not all of the SARI telecentres in India unsustainable?	No	No	Footnote that this author was a director of the board of the SARI project and participated throughout its lifetime. The research reported here benefited from the access this position afforded. Every attempt has been made to ensure that this paper is evidence-based and free from bias. But does not state how. States that two trained interviewers (whose spoke the local language) were used, but it does not say how they were chosen, who they were trained by, whether they were old, young, male or female and how long they stayed in the field.
[12]	What is the process by which the UNDP-Ministry of Science and Technology telecentre project has been established in rural China?	No	No	States that failure to facilitate such involvement [of villagers] may leave the public unaware of project's potentials and risks and unable to recognize its relevance to their interests but does not appear to have conducted any such interviews with villagers-all interviews with UNDP/Chinese government respondents. Does not appear to have visited any of the telecentres mentioned in the article.
[13]	What is the impact of the Internet through telecentres on social equity in Colombia?	Yes-100 randomly selected telephone interviews, and 28 selected interviews	Yes-102 households from four neighbourhoods	Implies that the authors did not conduct the surveys, in which case who did? How were the surveyors selected? How many were there? Were they from the area /outsiders? Were 100 users truly randomly selected? How were the 102 non-users selected? How did the surveyors report back to the researchers/authors?

Table 1. (*Continued*)

| [14] | How does the Diffusion of Innovations framework explain the adoption of telecentres (communal computing facilities) by the urban poor in South Africa? | Yes-23 at centres A, B and C plus 17 one year later at Centre C | Yes-11 at centres A, B and C | States that authors do not have affiliation with the project initiators. Clarifies that two graduate student groups conducted most of the interviews . Were the research questions for the graduate students different from the questions posed by the authors? What was the interaction between the graduate students and the subjects? Observations were conducted by a research assistant and the lecturer (author). States that to ensure quality information, the research assistant had a meeting with the lecturer for each observation session and was briefed within 24 hours. |
| [15] | How does the Internet lead to female empowerment in Egyptian cybercafes? | Yes-25 | No | 25 interviews conducted in five neighbourhoods, but does not explain breakdown of demographics in those neighbourhoods. Clarifies that the research assistant is Jordanian (but does not expand further on how this may impact), female, Muslim, a former resident of Cairo and questions asked in Arabic. States that ethnographic research has been conducted but only evidence of interviews. How much time did the researcher spend immersing themselves in the phenomenon? 28 questions are asked, but there is no explanation of how these were construed as symbolic of empowerment. |

Table 1. (*Continued*)

[16]	How does trust between citizens and intermediaries affect e-governance through telecentres in India ?	Am-biguous-30 out of 249 total inter-views are conducted with users of Kissan and FRIENDS, but not Akshaya	No	The researcher has had direct association with the project but sees this only in a beneficial light in terms of gaining access. States that the paper is an empirical study of Akshaya but users and non-users of Akshaya itself are not interviewed.

gaining access, or claims that attempts have been made to minimise bias [11]. Simi-larly, in four papers [including 16], there is insufficient discussion of how the users have been chosen, who conducted the actual research, what preconceptions they had and the interactions between them and the research subjects. Some papers are more detailed about the research methods such as [14], which clarifies that graduate stu-dents conducted the research and that the research assistant had a meeting with the lecturer within 24 hours of conducting research, but this still does not enter into de-tails of how findings and theorising were reached -was it a process of negotiation and shared understanding between the assistants and lecturer or did the latter have the final say? What was the process of interaction between the graduate students and the research subjects, who would have been close in age? How could this potentially impact on the findings?

The next section shares some of the challenges of representation and reflexivity when conducting research at the *Our Voices* centre.

4 Representation and Reflexivity in Our Voices

Our Voices is a community radio and telecentre initiative established by a donor agency in 2001 in a village in India. Six months were spent here researching partici-pation in the centre (the thesis discussed the various meanings given to the word par-ticipation). The full findings of the research will be available in this author's PhD thesis. The intent here is not to be prescriptive, but to share some of the challenges in representing and being reflexive in the research design, data collection, analysis and writing up of telecentre research.

Firstly, in terms of research design, [9] recommend an open ended approach to re-search, rather than defining narrow themes. This leaves one open to what they call breakdowns in understanding, which occur when empirical data challenge any theo-retical assumption. This breakdown should be represented *honestly* , as a surprising finding (they give an example of how when investigating gender in an advertising agency, it was the men who emerged with more *feminine* traits, such as being intui-tive, emotional, sensitive to interpersonal relationships, family orientated even at work, but also recognize the irony of such labels). In the case of my research, having read much literature extolling the virtues of *Our Voices*, it was surprising to find that nothing was working. My initial reaction was to find another project to research, but I was encouraged by others to explore the *surprising finding*. My research therefore presents the juxtaposition of how *Our Voices* was portrayed in policy and research literature, and the reality during my fieldwork.

Another element of reflexive research design is allowing for what [7] call polyphony - multiple voices and alternative narratives, rather than the grand *narrative*. In terms of telecentre research, it was imperative for me to research both users and non-users and not just telecentre managers or policymakers. Several findings appeared from researching alternative narratives, such as non users complaining why don't they build a factory here instead of the centre.

Secondly, in terms of data collection, the reflexive researcher can think about how one's own position might be interpreted by the research subject. Drawing upon Goffman, [17] make the point that the interview is a stage, with both the interviewer and interviewee performing. Further, as several authors have stated, the interaction between respondents and researcher is influenced by factors including status, age and gender [18, 19]. An older researcher may be treated with more respect, but they may be greater expectations from the interviewee, particularly of something tangible. A younger researcher may not be treated with so much respect but may therefore have a deeper insight through informal conversations. Female researchers may not be taken seriously, particularly by village headmen [20] but are likely to have greater access to female respondents than male researchers. Further, most telecentre researchers are almost inevitably urban, and may therefore be regarded with skepticism by users of rural telecentres. In my case (a female of Indian origin living in the UK), I did face challenges in interviewing village headmen, and it was easier to talk to women, but the latter also doubted my ability to understand their existence, as I was an urban foreigner. All these factors therefore affected the findings, for example fewer and less satisfactory interviews with village officials.

If the researcher does not speak the language of the respondents, the issue of how the research was conducted would also be discussed by the reflexive researcher. Did the researcher learn the language? Or was an interpreter used? If an interpreter was used, how were they found? Are they from the same area? What preconceptions do they have? How many interpreters were used, as each new interpreter means building a new relationship with interviewees? Is the interpreter older/younger/male/female/ from a different class or religion (or in the case of India, a different caste)? In my case, five interpreters had to be used as one was not available for the entire six-month period. Various complications arose with each-for example two of them were Christian and a mutually distrustful relationship arose between them and interviewees (mainly Hindus), not only affecting findings, but also illustrating the prejudices within Indian society.

Moving on to interviews, reflexivity means awareness of several factors such as: the location of the interview-is it conducted in a public or private space? A private interview might be preferable as sensitive matters such as income can be discussed and interviewees may not be intimidated [18]. For example, a telecentre nonuser may be intimidated by the presence of a telecentre manager. In the early days of my research, the centre management would send an escort with us to interviews, ostensibly to help us. However, this intimidated users and they provided more free answers further on in the research, therefore presenting a large discrepancy between answers in the early part of research and later.

Can the interview be supplemented by observation, allowing for a more natural interaction [19]? [3] states that observation is even helpful when interviewing. That is, the posture and/or tone of the interviewee is important. For example, an interviewee may say that the telecentre is very useful but say it in a bored voice and with a shrug. This particularly emerged later, as respondents revealed they had suffered from interview fatigue from previous researchers.

Finally, in terms of data analysis and writing up, we can think about our own position and how it is likely to influence the research- for example, would the research findings be couched differently if they were analyzed by a black/white/male/female/local/foreign researcher? [20] recommend adopting a reader response strategy, where the researcher reads for himself/herself in the text, trying to understand if and how their response is related to their background/history/culture/experiences. To mitigate this, we can work with other researchers from another cultural background (although there is no guarantee that a researcher from the same country as the research location will have any greater understanding than one who is not from that country, and on the contrary may have greater biases). We can also work with researchers from other disciplines and/or with different theoretical frameworks. This was harder to do in doctoral research but has been attempted subsequently by co-writing with authors from different disciplines, such as economics and anthropology.

5   Conclusion

Why is representation and reflexivity relevant in HCI? I would argue that it is fundamental in understanding the interaction between humans and computers, and how that interaction is interpreted by subjects as well as the researchers, and other voices in between. Suggestions outlined in this paper can be generalized in conducting research for other ICT and development subjects, for example mobile phone and television usage. Inevitably, however, there are several critiques and challenges of representation and reflexivity. Firstly, it is argued that for a subject that aims to deconstruct and diminish the sole voice of the researcher, reflexivity can ironically lead to narcissism in a research paper, where the author focuses extensively on how the research was conducted and what in his/her mind were the breakdowns, and how it may be conducted differently (again, only the author's suggestions) [7]. Secondly, being reflexive can weaken the author's perspective and development of their theory: the more reflexive, the less we know [7]. A more pragmatic challenge is that most research simply does not have the time or space needed for such reflexivity and neither do most publication outlets, given such banalities as funding and word restrictions. Yet, as we conduct telecentre research, if we could think about how we ourselves would like to be represented, or how others might represent us (much harder), it may make us more reflexive researchers.

References

1. Kanungo, S.: On the emancipator role of rural information systems. Information Technology and People 17, 407–422 (2004)
2. Crotty, M.: The foundations of social research: meaning and perspective in the research process. Sage, London (1998)
3. Esterberg, K.G.: Qualitative methods in social research. McGraw-Hill, Boston (2002)
4. Geertz, C.: The interpretation of cultures: selected essays. Basic Books, New York (1973)
5. Altheide, D., Johnson, J.: Criteria for assessing interpretive validity in qualitative research. In: Denzin, N.K., Lincoln, Y.S. (eds.) Handbook of quantitative research, pp. 485–499. Sage, Thousand Oaks (1994)
6. Roman, R., Blattman, C.: Research for Telecenter Development: Obstacles and Opportunities. Journal of Development Communication: Special Issue on Telecenters 12 (2001)
7. Harley, B., Hardy, C., Alvesson, M.: Reflecting on reflexivity. In: Academy of Management Conference Proceedings (2004)
8. Denzin, N.K., Lincoln, Y.S.: The SAGE handbook of qualitative research. Sage, London (1994)
9. Alvesson, M., Kärreman, D.: Constructing mystery: empirical matters in theory development. Academy of Management Review 32, 1265–1281 (2007)
10. Alvesson, M.: Beyond neopositivists, romantics, and localists: a reflexive approach to interviews in organisational research. Academy of Management Review 28, 13–33 (2003)
11. Best, M., Kumar, R.: Sustainability Failures of Rural Telecenters: Challenges from the Sustainable Access in Rural India (SARI) Project. Information Technologies and International Development 4, 31–45 (2008)
12. Zhang, C.: The Institutional Framework of the United Nations Development Programme–Ministry of Science and Technology (UNDP–MoST) Telecenter Project in Rural China. Information Technologies and International Development 7, 39–55 (2008)
13. Parkinson, S., Lauzon, A.: The impact of the Internet on local social equity: a study of a telecentre in Aguablanca, Colombia. Information technologies and international development 4, 21–38 (2008)
14. Chigona, W., Licker, P.: Using Diffusion of Innovations Framework to Explain Communal Computing Facilities Adoption Among the Urban Poor. Information technologies and international development 4, 57–73 (2008)
15. Wheeler, D.: Empowerment Zones? Women, Internet Cafés, and Life Transformations in Egypt. Information technologies and international development 4, 89–104 (2008)
16. Rajalekshmi, K.: E-Governance Services Through Telecenters: The Role of Human Intermediary and Issues of Trust. Information technologies and international development 4, 19–35 (2007)
17. Myers, M., Newman, M.: The qualitative interview in IS research: examining the craft. Information and organisation 17, 2–26 (2007)
18. Devereux, S., Hoddinott, J.: Fieldwork in developing countries. Harvester Wheatsheaf, Hemel Hempstead (1992)
19. Bernard, H.R.: Social research methods: qualitative and quantitative approaches. Sage, London (2000)
20. Mauthner, N., Doucet, A.: Reflexive accounts and accounts of reflexivity in qualitative data analysis. Sociology 37, 413–431 (2003)

Ubiquitous Society – Cultural Factors Driving Mobile Innovations and Adoption in Japan

Henning Breuer

Waseda University Tokyo & Bovacon Berlin
10119 Berlin / Tokyo
henning.breuer@bovacon.com

Abstract. Streets without names, golden silence on the subway, cables installed above-ground, experimental drive of developers and nosy customers prepare the ground for ultimate perfection. This article analyzes and describes culturally embedded usability scenarios, research activities and geographical and political frameworks of developing mobile technologies in Japan. Furthermore, decisive factors contributing to the development of a mobile and ubiquitous scociety in Japan are outlined. This aims at raising awareness for new starting-points of mobile innovation in Europe.

Keywords: Cultural factors, mobile applications, innovation management, intercultural design.

1 Background

In Asia Japan is still leading with regard to economic power and technological innovation. Additionally, it is the second-largest national economy of the world. New technologies are considered to offer a promising way of meeting modern challenges such as globalization and demographic change. Consequently, since the 1990's the investments of Japanese government and private enterprise into research and development exceed those of any other industrial nation. Due to national funding programms, entrepreneurial strategies and customers' needs mobile technologies are omnipresent. Entrepreneurial investments often focused on feasability. However, scepticism against possibly ill-conceived services and products has usually been ruled out by customers' interests. A mobile ecological system which is far apart from the developments of the rest of the world arose out of network effects between heterogenous services. The following data, analyses and thoughts are derived from interviews and discussions with experts as well as literature reviews.

2 Usage and Prevalence of Mobile Applications in Japan

The car phone was introduced in 1979, followed by a shoulder phone in 1985, and an almost not affordable handheld in 1987. The mobile internet service i-mode was introduced in 1999 and shortly afterwards NTT DoCoMo launched FOMA being the first mobile communication service of the 3rd generation worldwide. By now its penetration

N. Aykin (Ed.): Internationalization, Design, LNCS 5623, pp. 328–336, 2009.
© Springer-Verlag Berlin Heidelberg 2009

rate exceeds two thirds and one third of the total ARPU corresponds to the data segment is above. Contactless payment systems are integrated in mobiles and allow for a new range of user services. Leading telecommunication companies such as NTT DoCoMo have entered credit card business. 2D "quick-response" barcodes make targeted online information related to the users' locality available via mobile phones. At public places, products, advertising materials, posters, and journals, even buildings and gravestones barcodes are found pointing to further information or disclosing interaction. Social networks, blogging, games, and even literature is transferred to mobile devices. In contrast to the European market applications such as mobile television, location-based GPS-services and mobile learning are well-established in Japan. Currently, further requirements regarding the infrastructure of mobile communication are derived from remote-control and interaction with auto-mobile robots.

3   Keitai Is "Something You Carry Along"

"Keitai" is not just a phone (denwa) but literally refers to a "snug and intimate technosocial tethering", a personal companion supporting communications that are "constant, lightweight, and mundanely present in everyday life", a new cultural paradigm [1]. In contrast the American term „cellular phone" alludes to the technical infrastructure, while the British expression „mobile" emphasizes the untethering from a fixed location. Keitai cultures arose out of youth street practices and visual cultures and a history of text messaging from early pager [1]. In the 1990's Ketai became (in)famous under the suspicion of NOT serving a particular task to their lead user groups.

Describing these groups Matsuda [2] characterizes Kogyaru and Jibetarian as young urban individuals being eyed suspiciously. Kogyaru refers to young women ready to meeting men for financial rewards. Jibetarian refers to individuals of both sexes spending their time at crowdy crossroads seemingly without reason or obvious goal in life. Both largely relied on Keitai to organize their social relations. Thus, well established ways of social control are jeopardized.

No matter how sceptical the youth culture has been regarded, the youths and the abandonment of task-orientation were crucial for starting mobile applications' triumph in Japan. While the US and Scandinavia lead the deployment and adoption initially NTT DoCoMo launched its i-mode mobile internet service in 1999, driving Japan to the forefront of the mobile revolution. As early as 2001 3G was introduced achieving a subscription rate of 72.3 percent by the end of the year and of 79.2 percent in 2002.

4   Mobile Manga and Literature

In 2007 half of the 10 most sold novels in Japan have not only been read but as well been written on mobile phones [3]. Mobile literature is booming particularly within youth culture. Using pseudonyms like „Mika" or „Yoshi" hobby authors publish on blogs, mobile internet or the Maho i-Land site that provides specialized rankings, editing and searching functions for mobile literature [http://ip.tosp.co.jp]. The main audience consists of young women aged 13 to 18 years [4]. Most novels deal with love, sexuality, drugs and aggression, depicting a fatefully tragic and melodramatical plot. Technical constraints of small display screens and comparably laborious typing resulted in a characteristic style. Thus, typically first person narratives are published predominantly using dialogues and quotes. Furthermore, sentences are concise and syntactically simple, occasionally even in note form. Additionally, abbreviations and emoticons are used. Even though "Keitai"-literature has been criticized for sketchy plots and occasionally primitive linguistic style, some works have been printed or picturized. Mangas for mobile phones delivered by different network providers are very popular as well.

5   Social Network Services

Mobile service usage trends are led by social network services (SNS), blogs, HTML mail, video, gaming and train connection information. Mobile Social Software (Mo-SoSo) adapting web 2.0 applications such as social networking services, blogs and wikis for mobile phones are becoming increasingly popular. They are used to negotiate identity issues, and to find others for social, dating or business networking. Relying on mobile devices MoSoSo makes the trend towards social online software ubiquitous. Mobage-Town [http://www.mbga.jp] has been optimized for mobile phones and provides blogs, forums, games, horoscopes, online-literature and much more. On Mixi [http://www. mixi.jp] mobile page views overpassed PC page views for the first time in August 2007.

6   Navigation Systems

There are rarely more than a dozen of streets carrying individual names in Japanese cities such as Tokyo. Even locals are challenged by finding adresses organized by administrative districts, blocks and years of construction. Roland Barthes refers to Tokyo as a city without categories, "made of rooms without names... To visit a place for the first time requires starting to write it. Since its address has not been written yet an individual signature needs to be created" [5].

Up to now these signatures originate from visitors scetching directions and landmarks on a sheet of paper. Consequently, navigation systems integrating innumerable direction scetches are more popular in Japan than anywhere else. Asian doption rates in exceed those of Europe and the US. Up to 2012 a yearly growth of 8 percent is expected for the Japanese in-vehicle navigation market.

Besides entertainment features, navigation devices are going to integrate more functions, such as voice recognition and driving assistance. "Navigation devices are not just navigation devices any more: The introduction of new technologies will help lower-priced competitors to differentiate themselves," said Wang Tao [6]. Navigation devices in Japan focused on navigation and real-time information originally. But over time, besides infotainment, driver assistance systems, functionality and interactivity will become the major differentiators in the Japanese market. „Device connectivity and the integration of several functions will provide the best penetration as these markets evolve"[6]. Regarding mobile information and communication devices in general terminals with new performance characteristics emerge.

7 Mobile Marketing

The Sony-developed FeliCa standard has been introduced as „Osaifu-Keitai" (money-bag-mobile) and it is available by now on one third of all Ketais. Contactless transactions via RFID enable users to make payments at participating retailers and vending machines, as well as online on mobile shopping sites. Other applications include passing through train gates, using the handset for credit cards transactions, checking into airplanes and redeeming electronic coupons - all of it just by a touch. Furthermore, in 2006 digital terrestrial broadcasting to mobile (called 1seg in Japan) has been introduced and is now available on 41 million devices [7]. A data feed below the TV content window links to programming-related websites and promotional offers. Thereby, it provides an advertising platform to marketers without interrupting the users' media experience. More than 70 major partners have signed up with FeliCa so far. Since revenues from mobile commerce already surpassed mobile content revenues three years ago, the mobile phone is fastly turning into a full-fledged shopping and payment device [8]. NTT DoCoMo has been running trials combining both 1seg and FeliCa technologies: During a baseball game, consumers could participate in a mobile game, betting on the outcome of innings. They received promotional coupons in return, which could be redeemed at McDonalds. A similar concept involved coupons which could be cashed in by simply touching the handset to Coke vending machines.

The prevalence rate of these machines already represents a highly visible difference to Europe. Furthermore, there are many "convenience stores" in Japan within walking distance for everyone beeing open all day. Due to limited space for selling and storing daily deliveries are well calculated and items with low sales volumes are sorted out on a weekly basis. Consequently, products need to be made known within a week. Therefore, mobile advertising provides an effective marketing strategy which is increasingly being combined with traditional techniques like TV-spots and interactive advertising panels. A growth rate of 300 percent by 2007 has already been predicted in 2001 [9]. However, its success depends on the availability of fast 3G access and the prevalence of high-end mobile phones.

8 Research and Developmental Perspectives

Japanese research and developmental departments, specifically NTT DoCoMo and KDDI laboratories are global market leaders with regard to numerous innovations [10]. In particularly, research about robotics and Human-Robot Interaction (HRI) attracts worldwide attention. Following recent advances in locomotions and mechatronics focus has been shifted towards designing HRI. HRI aims at enhancing human and robotic skills by allowing both sides to interact with and to operate on each other. Automobile companies being highly experienced with regard to industrial robots invest in the development for private usage as well. There are numerous projects teaching robots for example how to walk, run, swim, hike, play the flute, or other instruments.

Fig. 1. Asimo at home, Great Robot Exhibition 2008

As an interdisciplinary science HRI promotes innovation in different disciplines. A project at Waseda University explores how humans and robots may live together. Being part of a multi-agent P2P-network, WaBot-House robots are able to react intelligently and dynamically to changing circumstances within households. Nowadays or in the near future robots are supposed to rescue victims of earthquakes, to execute military actions, to sort department stores, to safeguard and clean buildings and above all to entertain and to assist in elderly care.

Partially due to historical reason there is a certain retentiveness in Japan to let workforce from neighboring countries such as China enter Japan in order to care for elderly people. Also in this line of reason one answer to the rapidly aging society is a developmental focus on robots' potentially supporting functions in household and everyday life. In 2008 robots (about 15000) were more frequently sold for caring than for entertaining purposes for the first time [11]. Humanoid ways of communicating and behaving are particularly demanded in everyday surroundings like offices, households, stores or museums.

Anthropomorphic robots operating in corresponding contexts are increasingly presented in an audience appealing way. They are expected to be found in every Japanese household within the next 10 years (similarly to South Korea). There is nothing sinister or uncanny about this vision in Japan. Western dystopias of revolting robots are ignored by Japanese researchers and consumers. In contrast, robots may be cute or „kawaii", which in turn is considered to be cultic. According to the deep-rooted and prevalent Shintoism everything has a soul, trees, rivers, mountains, as well as dolls and stuffed animals. When they are not needed anymore they are considered death and are burned to pay one's last respects. Regularly, useless toys are burned in Shinto shrines. So, we may wonder when (since the first Aibos, Postpets, Tamagocchi already did) outdated robots find their way onto the pet cemeteries. From this point of view, robots

Fig. 2. Therapeutic robot PaRo und announcement of burning toys in a Shinto shrine

are not only extreme cases of formalized interaction and relational maintenance, but postmodern representatives of shintoistic pantheism. Since everything is part of the overall nature humans and robots are not entirely different.

9 Ubiquitous Society

Japan's confidence in the blessings of technological and civilizing progress is still unbroken. What appears to be manageable should be tried out before someone else arrives first.

Following the economic depression of the 1990's Japanese government relied on new technolgies for economic recovery and new affluence. When the national funding program „e-Japan" 2005 expired successfully in 2005 „u-Japan" succeeded in 2006 [12]. Moving from a digital („e") to a ubiquitous („u") society should be accomplished by providing high speed or ultra high speed network access for the whole population. Whereas "e-Japan" [13] mainly aimed at promoting digitalization, "u-Japan" focuses on informational technologies. They are supposed to be the key element of coping with the challenges of the 21st century, such as health care issues due to a rapidly aging society, environment and energy, public safety, etc. By 2010 80 percent of the population is expected to appreciate the problem solving potentials of informational technologies.

10 Contextual Peculiarities

Japan is an island with scarce resources, difficult environmental conditions and a highly spiritual population believing that god is found in every item. Given these circumstances, Akio Morita, founder of Sony, argued that technological development has offered the best way of surviving. Additionally, the meticulousness needed for writing may have been advantageous for technological development requiring precision as well [14]. Japanese design and aesthetics such as the preference for "elegance of simplicity" [15, 16] have nowadays been integrated into user-oriented designs.

Japanese technicians' unique focus on minimizing products has been traced back to spatial narrowness of surroundings [17]. Finally, the unexcelled curiosity of Japanese regarding new technical gadgets is frequently pointed out ("otaku", a nerd thrilled by media, is amongst others characterized by this relation). In contrast, European and German customers tend to wait for the third generation of a product and a seal of quality by Stiftung Warentest (a well respected German customer-oriented trust). Comparably, Japanese customers are an incarnation of curiosity: New products are not suspiciously considered as ill-conceived but are tested immediately. From the author's perspective this curiosity may even partly compensate for the neglect of user research and integration at the onset of product development. Many new products, except for branded ones, are firstly offer in Akihabara in Tokyo, which has been labeled "electrical city" due to the high prevalence of electronic shops. This test market enables companies to estimate sales volumes before large-scale production is started.

It would be quite interesting to analyze cultural differences and similarities and their correspondence with technological developments in detail. Unfortunately, this goes beyond the scope of this article. Therefore, only a few selected observations and perspectives have been discussed. Some aspects have already been mentioned, such as streets without names that may have forstered navigation systems or traditional Shinto beliefs that may have reduced cultural scepticism against robotics.

Commuting has been discussed frequently as a major factor for exceptionally high data transfer rates and the success of mobile services. Compared to traveling time (more than an hour for more than 50 percent of the inhabitants) regulations for Ketai usage on trains and busses are more decisive. As already mentioned, usage of Ketai in public places had a bad reputation for a long time. In particular when Ketais became quite popular among youths in the 1990's their usage on trains was discussed controversly. Towards the end of 1995 inaudible vibrating alerts were introduced and since 1997 travelers were requested to refrain from talking by loudspeaker announcements. Finally, since 2001 talking on the Ketai has been strictly forbidden. Consequently, many travelers exchange text messages via e-mail instead [18]. This social norm made a considerable contribution to the popularity of mobile internet and its variants such as mobile literature and social network services. Furthermore, Japanese companies frequently do not allow navigating websites (especially for private purposes) during working hours. This certainly adds to the popularity of texting on trains.

Fig. 3. Prevalent usage of mobile data transfer in public tansport systems

Additionally, there are geographical particularities. Numerous earthquakes may have contributed to the ingrained knowledge that nothing lasts forever and beauty is most frequently found by looking at the perishable presence. In any case, due to earthquakes cabels have been run above ground. Though it might seem disadvantageous from an aesthetic point of view it is highly convenient for modernizing infrastructures. Regionwide fiberglass was rapidly installed right to the doorstep (FTTH / Fiber-to-the-home) and more than 50 percent of the households (28 million connections) were supplied by 2007. While new broadband services are being introduced, analog TV is to be abandoned by 2011. Last but not least, low costs of running cabels above ground contribute to Japan's ability to adapt so fast.

11 Conclusions

Considering the embedding variety of geographical, cultural and political factors innovation and adoption of new applications and technologies is a complex undertaking [also 19]. Strong connectivity to a unique cultural ground must be given. Mode and structure of usage barriers and beneficial conditions are partly grounded in cultural beliefs (such as Shintoism) and physical infrastructures (such as cables above ground). Therefore, general conclusions regarding other countries may not easily be derived. However, a heightened sensitivity for the geographical, cultural and political characteristics of a market may inspire technical development and sucessful merchandising. Cultural aspects do not only affect acceptance but their analysis may promote innovation as well. In any case, services need to fit aspects whose significance is rarely obvious. Nevertheless, hypotheses about general factors of success and solid methods for designing services may be derived. In the following, two hypotheses are presented to illustrate this point.

The first hypothesis refers to conceptualizing the Ketai as a personal companion. Instead of pointing to the technical features of mobile media ("cellular phone") their personal impact on the user should be analyzed and adressed by merchandizing. This applies particularly to technologies "handled" in such a way as mobile phones.

Lessons learned from the history of the Ketai [1] contrast with the paradigm of task-orientation in designing HRI. The historical experience exemplifies that deficiency of blatant usefulness to accomplish specified tasks or rather openess to interpretation and usage allows answering the mobile medium's purpose. Though the Ketai had been discussed controversely initially it is hypothesized that such openess contributed to its success.

The second hypothesis refers to the emergent features resulting partly unexpected from integrating new and existing services and functions. Network effects (with number of nodes increasing value exponentially) are not only caused by the number of devices and users contributions (as in web 2.0) but by combining known and innovative functions as well. It may be questioned whether a combination of technologies such as mobile television delivering coupons, quick-response barcode readers and Near Field Communicationfor mobile payment, ticketing and email is still akin to a phone. However, the combination of technologies certainly enables new use cases and business models that may increase users' overall value of portable devices for users. When conceptualizing and developing new functions and services network effects should be considered. So, it may be worthwile to simulate possible combinations in advance. Taking in account cultural contrasts robust measures may be derived to formulate guidelines of an intercultural "design-for-all". These include the necessity to meet a variety of preferences, habits, and competencies. Additionally, facilitation of intercultural interaction and communication is considered to be essential in order to provide tourists and business travelers' easy access to information and communication services. Technologies do not only depend on technical feasibilities and infrastructures but on cultural realities, preferences and coincidences as well. These aspects shape, delimit and inspire our technological progress at all times.

References

1. Ito, M., Okabe, D., Matsuda, M.: Personal, Portable, Pedestrian: Mobile Phones in Japanese Life. MIT Press, Cambridge (2005)
2. Matsuda, M.: Discourses of Ketai in Japan. In: Ito, M., Okabe, D., Matsuda, M. (eds.) Personal, Portable, Pedestrian: Mobile Phones in Japanese Life, pp. 205–217. MIT Press, Cambridge (2005)
3. Coulmas, F.: Handy verrückt. In: Die Zeit Internet Spezial, Nr. 21 S.6–7 (May 15, 2008)
4. Mobile Marketing Data Labo,
   `http://mmd.up-date.ne.jp/download/`
   `dl_file.php?item_id=124&SID=5e4fb9f31b196fec8a5d5fd6e1ab870d`
5. Barthes, R.: Empire of Signs. Hill and Wang (1982)
6. Tao, W.: The Asia-Pacific Market for Navigation Devices. Abi Research (2008),
   `http://www.abiresearch.com/products/market_research/`
   `The_Asia-Pacific_Market_For_Navigation_Devices`
7. JEITA - Japan Electronics and Information Industries Association,
   `http://www.jeita.or.jp/japanese/stat/digital/2008/pdf/`
   `200809digital.pdf`
8. Fujita, A.: Mobile Marketing in Japan. The acceleration of integrated marketing communications. Journal of Integrated Marketing Communications. Issue, pages (2008)
9. Dentsu Communication Institute Inc.: 2007-2011 Internet Advertisement Expenditures (2007), `http://dci.dentsu.co.jp/pdf/publication_070416_en_pdf`
10. Breuer, H.: Technology Radar. Interne Publikation der Deutschen Telekom Laboratories, Berlin (2008),
    `http://www.laboratories.telekom.com/ipws/English/`
    `InnovationDevelopment/TechnologyRadar/Pages/default.aspx`
11. Seedplaning, `http://www.seedplanning.co.jp/press/2008/1224.html`
12. Ministry of Internal Affairs and Communications,
    `http://www.soumu.go.jp/menu_02/ict/u-japan_en/index.html`
13. Umino, A.: Japan's New IT Reform Strategy and u-Japan, Präsentation des MIC (2007),
    `http://www.soumu.go.jp/menu_02`
14. Morita, A., Reingold, E.M., Mitsuko, S.: Made in Japan: Akio Morita and SONY. Edward Payson Dutton, New York (1986)
15. Donald, R.: Tractate on Japanese Aesthetics. Stone Bridge Press, Berkeley, California (2007)
16. Tanizaki, J.: Lob des Schattens. Manesse, Zürich 2002 (1933)
17. Bürdek, B.E.: Geschichte, Theorie und Praxis der Produktgestaltung. 3. Auflage. Birkhäuser, Basel (2005)
18. Okabe, D., Ito, M.: Ketai in Public Transportation. In: Ito, M., Okabe, D., Matsuda, M. (eds.) Personal, Portable, Pedestrian: Mobile Phones in Japanese Life, pp. 205–217. MIT Press, Cambridge (2005)
19. Herstatt, C., Stockstrom, C., Tschirky, H., Nagahira, A. (eds.): Management of Technology and Innovation Japan. Springer, Berlin (2006)

A Study of Innovation Design on Taiwan Culture Creative Product – A Case Study of the Facial Mask of Ba Ja Jang

Chi-Hsiung Chen, Being-Chenem Chen, and Cheng-Dar Jan

National Pintung University of Science and Technology, No.1, Shueh Fu Road, Neipu Township, Pintung 91201, Taiwan

Abstract. In the trend of advocating the cultural and creative industry in recent years, Taiwan elevates the people's spiritual satisfaction and the value of cultural products through the mutual impact of art/culture and the creative design. This is just a new-type industry that all nations worldwide pay attention to in recent years. This research studies on Taiwan's local Ja Jang culture transforming in the innovative design of cultural and creative products. Besides actually developing the product design of Ja Jang culture, we emphasize much more the discussion on the essence of cultural products and the construction of designing mode. According to the research result, there are four conclusions: 1. In terms of the development of Taiwan's cultural and creative industry, the focus should be on (1) centering on key industries, (2) cultivating the cultural industries with Taiwan's specialties, (3) introducing international capital, having international communication, making good use of China's resources, and (4) founding a platform of information integration. 2. The designing meanings of cultural products should contain three levels, which are the exterior level (visible and material), the middle level (of using behavior and ritual/customary), and the interior level (ideological and spiritual). 3. Comparing to attributes of general product design, the cultural product design generally changes from use-base to the elevation of symbol value to bring out the product's peculiarity and its differentiation. 4. The design mode of Taiwan's local culture is constructed, and products of global culture are brought from the age of technology to the age of design for "heart" of humanistic culture.

Keywords: Taiwan, cultural and creative industry, innovative design, & Ja Jang.

1 Preface

1.1 Research Background and Motivation

"Design is a kind of expression of culture." Culture is also the base to fire up a designer's creative thinking. Therefore, a design without culture is just one without its root. It cannot vitalize products. Klaus Krippenndorff (1990) proposes that "designing means giving meanings." In the aspect of product design, cultural image can create

N. Aykin (Ed.): Internationalization, Design, LNCS 5623, pp. 337–346, 2009.
© Springer-Verlag Berlin Heidelberg 2009

special product language to bring out characteristics of products and to make products more valuable. Hence, a design has to integrate technology, science, art, culture, and other fields in the future to create more possibilities of future and to impress customers with designed works containing cultural meanings (Holt, 2000; Pilgoim, 2000). In the 21st-century digital and technological age, the design whose spirit is humanity and whose body is culture appears more important. That is called cultural and creative design.

The specialties and types of Taiwan's current cultural and creative industry include the extension of the creative content, which is emphasized by this industry, and the everlasting of art, culture, and life assets. Furthermore, it also includes cultural creative service industry which follows the steps of aesthetic and experiential economy and takes the development of diversified values as a theme to display the aesthetic style and life style in the activities of the industry. Ja Jang culture is the most animate performance group in Taiwan society. On every festivals held by temples to celebrate gods' birthday, many Ba Ja Jang groups will come to participate in the religious ceremony of welcoming gods and the local religious round tour. The facial mask-like makeup of Ja Jang contains strong implication of cultural spirits from its patterns, vivid colors, or exquisite painting skills. Those are attractions of the performance group. This research studies on the creative design of the cultural and creative products through Taiwan's traditional and religious Ja Jang culture. It analyzes the components of Ja Jang's facial mask-like makeup from viewpoints of pictorial symbols, cultural meanings, color meanings, and others to design and develop cultural and creative products and to elevate value of products.

1.2 Research Objectives

Ci-sian Syu (2004) generalizes a conclusion that a cultural product is reflection and review toward the contained cultural factors in the product itself. Designing is used to search a new modern face from the cultural factors and to seek satisfaction of the spiritual level when it is used. Moreover, Leong (2003) claims to study the cultural product design from viewpoints of the concrete, behavior of use, and the cultural space of the invisible spiritual level to formulate a design argument of the cultural integration. Therefore, according to the abovementioned background and motivation, this research made three objectives as the following:

1. Through the development of the relevant policy making and situation for the global cultural and creative industry, this research studies on the differentiation between Taiwan and other countries.
2. This research aims to construct a creative design mode of cultural and creative products for reference for designers to design relevant cultural products in the future.
3. Through the analysis of symbols and patterns on Ja Jang's facial mask-like makeup and the discussion of the cultural meanings, this research transform them into designing elements to develop and design cultural and creative products to give products new value.

2 Literature Review

2.1 Cultural and Creative Industry

In "Challenge 2008 Six-Year National Development Plan" proposed by the Executive Yuan in 2002, the "Development Plan of Cultural and Creative Industry" is especially included in it. In the light of the situation of Taiwan's industry, it gives a definition of the cultural and creative industries, which refer to "those that origin from the accumulation of creativity or culture, that create wealth and potential of working opportunities, and that facilitate the elevation of the entire living environment, through the formulation and operation of the copyright." Fig. 1 shows the relationship among culture, design, and industry in the cultural and creative industry. Gang Pan (2003) mentioned that if an industry only has creative performance and industrial mode, it can only be called a creative industry; if an industry only includes cultural implication with the industrial mode, it can only be called a cultural industry; if there are only cultural implication and creative performance without the implementation of the industrial mode, it will become an overhead development with only culture and creativity.

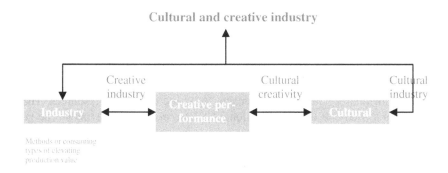

Fig. 1. The relationship among culture, design, and industry

The Current Situation about the Development of Taiwan's Cultural and Creative Industry. According to the statistics gathered by Industrial Development Bureau, Ministry of Economic Affairs, it shows that in terms of the business volume of the entire cultural and creative industry from 2004 to 2006, the total business volume of the cultural and creative industry in 2006 is 586.23 billion dollars and grows 0.89% more than that in the last year. However, the growth range in 2006 is smaller than that in 2005, which is 4.41%. With the investigation of the factors about the deceleration of the entire business volume growth in 2006, we know one of the factors is the assistance and promotion to Taiwan's cultural and creative industry has been supported by the government for five years, so the growth becomes stable. Besides that, according to the individual industry analysis, comparing to the recession range of the growth rate in 2005, the cultural performing facilities industry, musical and performance industry, and the visual art industry has greatest recession. Because most cultural performing facilities operators are operated as non-profit organizations, the estimated total production value should be more than 8.7 billion dollars according to the estimation method for production value of non-profit organization. Therefore, the estimated production value here should belong to the conservatively estimated income.

The Current Situation of the Development of the Global Cultural and Creative Industry. The cultural and creative industry is a newly emerging industry globally developed from various local cultures. It is also a kind of aesthetic economy and a creative industry. It is estimated that the global cultural and creative industry can create 22 billion US dollars of daily production value. In addition to America, Britain, Japan, and other big nations of the cultural and creative industry, Thailand, India, and Singapore emerging in recent years all devote themselves one after another into the relevant promotion and construction of the cultural industry because they realize the enormous commercial profit in the cultural and creative industry.From the analysis, some points can be concluded for reference for the development of Taiwan's cultural and creative industry in the future:

1. Focusing on key industries – Focusing on key industries can centralize resources of cultural and creative development and prevent from the dispersion of the developing focus in order to effectively facilitate the development of Taiwan's cultural and creative industry and to elevate the international visibility.
2. Cultivating cultural industries with Taiwan's specialties – Focusing on and cultivating cultural and creative industries with Taiwan's specialties can not only help the local development but also make Taiwan's culture and creativity differentiated and visible in the international markets.
3. Introducing the international capital, communication with international trend and making good use of China's resources – Taiwan can communicate with China's non-governmental organizations and makes good use of China's resources. These can be seen as outposts to enter the global Chinese market and to extend the visibility of the cultural industry.
4. Establishing a platform of resource integration – In face of industries and the masses, if Taiwan's cultural and creative industry can establish a convergent and integrated communication channel, it is believed that the communication between industries and the government, between industries and consumers can be smoother.

2.2 Cultural and Creative Products

The Relation among Culture, Code, and Design. Culture is a kind of code hidden in these product designs or in the producers (Pei-ling Li, 2002). If relating culture to the design level, it refers to the factors of delivering designing styles. Then, culture contains the following meanings (Ockman, 1993): (1) Culture refers to the designing result from life styles, customs, values, and systems. (2) Culture refers to the thinking level of design, especially those ideas or concepts that can influence designing results. (3) Culture refers to interpretation of reasons about differences of designing products from different races or groups. (4) Culture refers to the designing concepts which take consumers' taste as a center and views these as mobile factors.

From Ockman's viewpoints on the cultural reference to design, we can find that from cultural perspective, many aspects of inner and external meanings presented by design can be analyzed. They can be factors to explain differences, influences, or results. In terms of "de-sign" in English, sign is a cultural code or symbol. It is also a cultural representation. Therefore, design is de-code, re-presentation, or de-culture. In other words, it means through the transformation to interpret the current cultural styles and characteristics, and through meanings of codes, signs, and representation, the relation among design, culture, and code is combined to one.

2.3 Taiwan's Religious and Customary Culture – "Ba Ja Jang"

The Origin of Ja Jang. There are various Taiwan's traditional religions. These lead to the scenery of numerous temples established locally. Among these, "Ja Jang" is the one that can represent the performing groups of religious cultural art in Taiwan's temple fairs. Ja Jang generally refers to god's private guardians. Their job is to guard gods and assist the main god to carry out mission. Because there are different main gods, different guardians will be allocated to different gods according to positions. The religious role of Ja Jang is to assist in arresting ghosts and evils when the main god, Five-blessing Emperor, conducts a royal progress. Ja Jang attack and arrest those ghosts and evils by special footwork and array to protect people and places. From the artistic viewpoint, Ja Jang's facial mask-like makeup, the spirits of patterns, the arrangement of clothes colors, and rhythmic motions are combination of power and beauty.

Ja Jang's Responsibilities and Organization. The sacred guardians played by Ja Jang groups represent different positions according to their roles. Their different looks contain cultural meanings, such as different facial mask-like makeup, clothes, religious objects, and equipments. The detail is illustrated in Table 1.

Table 1. Ja Jang's Responsibilities and Organization

Role	Responsibility
Guardian of punishment implements	The main mission is to "lead the way" for the group and to shoulder the pole of punishment implements.
Civil and military guardians	They are responsible to receive and deliver commands from the main god. They hold edicts and group flats in hands.
Generals Gan and Liou	They and Generals Sie and Fan are organized as a group of four generals to arrest criminals.
General Sie and Fan	They are so-called the "elder and younger master" or the "seventh and eighth master." They stand in the back of the first line. Therefore, they are also called "the second line."
Gods of four seasons	Gods of four seasons assist the back line to arrest criminals and to interrogate the wandering ghosts arrested by the four generals.

3 Research Method and Procedure

3.1 Research Method

1. **Literature Analysis.** Literature analysis is one method used in the history graduate schools. It focuses on the description of the literature content and arranges the literature order chronologically for the convenience of understanding.

2. **Case Study.** Case study is a research to study the subject in order to decide the factors that result in states or behavior of individuals, groups, and institutions and to understand the relationship between these factors.
3. **Morphological Analysis.** Morphological analysis classifies every important part (independent factor) and analyzes them according to each independent and complete data archive system of components. This analysis is provided to the design type and style which is waiting to be completed, and then the final product design will be made.

3.2 Research Procedure

This research aims to study Ja Jang group culture of Taiwan's traditional performance groups and to summarize these cultural implications chronologically and orderly through literature analysis to analyze historical materials and documents. At the same time, this study will adopt case study method to analyze other researches on the development and design of related cultural and creative products based on the analysis of cultural images. These researches may acquire the results from literature collection, analysis, and actual and on-site case study. Through the pattern's styles of Ja Jang's facial mask-like makeup, this study use morphological analysis to classify samples and describe the detail parts to analyze the characteristics and meanings of works in order to obtain the design elements needed by the product design. And then we can further develop and design creative products that represent Taiwan's Ja Jang culture to elevate the value of the products.

4 Results and Discussion

4.1 Case Study of Cultural and Creative Products

In Table 2, cases about cultural and creative products developed from Taiwan's cultural images are listed. Through the analysis of cultural and creative products, we can know the symbolic meanings of the cultural signs, the transformation of the product's functions, the meanings of historical stories, and the design terms.

Table 2. Case Study of Taiwan's Cultural and Creative Products

Title of the Product	The Original Picture before Transformation	Picture of the Cultural Product	Analysis of the Product
Figurine of the Blessing God	Ma Zu, Groundskeeper God, and other gods in Taiwan's religions		These figurines of gods are made by applying Taiwan's religious culture. The products are made with strong religious and cultural stories.

4.2 The Attributes and Implication of Form of Ja Jang's Facial Mask-Like Makeup

The subjects of this research, the innovative design of the cultural and creative products, are General Sie and General Fan of Ba Ja Jang. From their unique and abundant cultural meanings and attributes of difference, morphological analysis will be used to simplify codes and form of the facial mask-like makeup with tracing draft and to understand each code's meaning for the use of application and abstraction of design elements in the future. The analysis is showed in Table 3.

Table 3. The Implied Meanings in Form of Ja Jang's Facial Mask-like Makeup

General Sie	
Implication of Codes	◎ The transformation from the white crane. In the performing array, the action like a white crane stands in a single leg and flaps its wings. (1) In the middle of the forehead writes a transformed word of "loyalty" which is a symbol of combination of Chinese blessing and longevity. There is another saying that some people interpreted the word, center (the pronunciation is the same with loyalty in Chinese), on General Sie's forehead as a code of a weapon. (2) Eyes are painted as black bats. The codes of the painted bats represent blessing (the pronunciation of bat and blessing is the same in Chinese). It is a common metaphor in Chinese culture to express that the blessing should come early or to deliver the meanings of blessing giving or double blessings.
General Fan	
Implication of Codes	◎ It is said that General Fan is transformed from a black monkey whose personality trait is manful and sturdy. Therefore, black is the ground color in most of time. The short and fat body is one of the characteristics. (1) Because he is manful and sturdy, fire patterns will be painted on the forehead, eyebrows, and cheeks. (2) Coin-form patterns are added on the cheeks and represent the meaning of collecting wealth. The ancient coin also symbolizes gathering blessing and wealth. It also has a supreme power to gather blessing and avoiding bad luck.

4.3   The Design of Ja Jang Cultural and Creative Product

This research applies the symbolic codes of the facial mask-like makeup, transforms them into design elements, and introduces them into the design of the cultural and creative product through the analysis of Ja Jang facial form and code meanings. Seven products are designed and developed mainly. The related application of transformation about the cultural and creative product design and code elements is showed in Table 4.

4.4   The Construction of the Cultural and Creative Product Design Mode

According to the concept of "cultural space" proposed by Leong in this article, a culture is formed by time and space. The design meanings of cultural products are extended from this concept. In this cultural space, the culture is divided into three levels. The first level is the exterior level, including those that are tangible and material. The second level is the middle level, including those that are of using behavior and ceremonial. The third level is the interior level of the cultural space, including those that

Table 4. The Analysis of Ja Jang Cultural and Creative Product Design

Figure-form Slippers	Hairpin	USB	Wall Clock
Tableware	Name Card Holder	Furniture	Analysis of Code Transformation

are ideological and invisible spiritual. The three levels are formed as an argument of cultural integration. Yu-fu Yang (2006) utilizes the cultural codes of design to explain the semantic levels of the product design, including the strategic level above the semantic level and the technological level under the semantic level. Rong-tai Lin (2005) proposes a spatial picture about the cultural creativity transforming into product design attributes. The three scholars mentioned above all investigate the changes of cultural implements from three levels of culture. In terms of the transformation of the current traditional implements in the modern cultural context, this research holds the same opinions with these scholars.

Through the analysis of Taiwan's religious Ja Jang culture and through the transformation of the pattern meanings and cultural meanings of the facial mask-like makeup into the design element, this research conducts the design of Taiwan's cultural and creative products. The construction of the cultural and creative product design mode is displayed in Fig. 2.

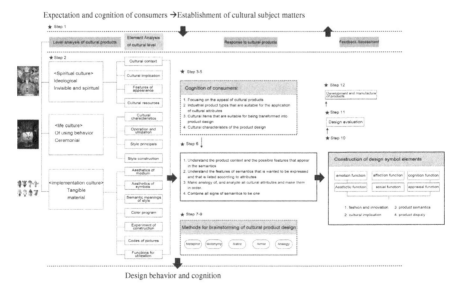

Fig. 2. The construction of the cultural and creative product design mode

5 Conclusion and Suggestion

This research hopes that through transforming Taiwan's traditional Ja Jang culture into the innovative design of cultural and creative products and through the utilization of pictorial symbols, cultural implication, color meanings from aesthetic viewpoint, components of Ja Jang facial mask-like makeup can be analyzed for the design of cultural and creative products in order to elevate the value of products. The result of the study shows the actual design of Ja Jang cultural products and focuses on the studies on the essence of cultural products and the construction of design mode. We hope that the interpretation and analysis of this research can be reference for the researchers, operators, and designers in the future. In sum, this research obtains four conclusions as the following:

1. With the development of the global cultural and creative industries and policy promotion and in terms of the sustainability and the innovative development about Taiwan's cultural and creative industry, Taiwan's cultural and creative industry should focus on in the future (A) centering on key industries, (B) cultivating the cultural industries with Taiwan's specialties, (C) introducing international capital, having international communication, making good use of China's resources, and (D) founding a platform of information integration.
2. The designing meanings of cultural products should contain three levels, which are the exterior level (visible and material), the middle level (of using behavior and ritual/customary), and the interior level (ideological and spiritual).
3. Comparing to attributes of general product design, the cultural product design generally changes from use-base to the elevation of symbol value to bring out the product's peculiarity and its differentiation.
4. Ja Jang culture is the most animate performance group in Taiwan society. This research analyzes the cultural implication and related code creation of the facial mask-like makeup and transforms them into the innovative design research of cultural and creative products. The design mode of Taiwan's local culture is constructed and brings abundant cultural quality and diversified styles. The products of global culture are brought from the age of technology to the age of design for "heart" of humanistic culture.

References

1. Syu, C.-s.: An Application and Case Studies of Taiwanese Aboriginal Material Civilization Confer to Cultural Product Design. M.A. Thesis of Department of Industrial Design, Chang Gung University, p. 20, 50(2004)
2. Dialogue. Design Issues 19, 48–58
3. Pan, G.: The Changed Tune of Cultural Policies and Thinking. China Times on June 3. A4 version (2003)
4. Holt, S.S.: Beauty and the blob: product culture now. In: Albrecht, D., Lupton, E., Holt, S.S. (eds.) Design culture now: national design triennial, Princeton Architecture Press, NY (2000)

5. Industrial Development Bureau, Ministry of Economic Affairs: 2007 Annual Report on the Development of Taiwan Cultural and Creative Industry. Promotion Group Office of Cultural and Creative Industry, pp. 26–37, 170–195 (2008)
6. Klaus, K.: On the Essential Contexts of Artifacts or On the Proposition that Design is Making Sense, The Idea of Design. Massachusetts, pp. 156–184 (1990)
7. Leong, B.D.: Culture-based knowledge towards new design thinking and practice A (2003)
8. Norris, K.W.: The Morphological Approach to Engineering Design. In: Conference on Design Methods, Pergamon Press, Oxford (1963)
9. Ockman, J.: Architecture Culture, Rizzozi, pp. 243–247 (1993)
10. Li, P.-l.: The Initial Study of the Interpretation on Design Signs – A Case Study of Construction and Implication. 2002 China Industrial Designers Association (2002)
11. Pilgrim, D.H.: Foreword. In: Albrecht, D., Lupton, E., Holt, S. (eds.) Design culture now: national design triennial, Princeton Architecture Press, NY (2000)
12. Wang, W.-k.: Research Methods in Education. Wu-nan Cultural Enterprise, pp. 387–390 (2002)
13. Yang, Y.-f.: The Cultural Basis of Design. Asia Pac Books, pp. 123–322 (2006)

The Application of ICTs and Digital Divide in Rural China[*]

Peng Chen[1], Jieping Wang[1], Zuoxian Si[1], Jie Wang[2], and Ying Liu[2]

[1] Tsinghua University, department of sociology, Beijing, 100084, P.R. China
chen-p06@mails.tsinghua.edu.cn, dale0421@gmail.com,
szx04@126.com
[2] Nokia Research Center,Beijing ,100176, P.R. China
{jenny.wang,ying.y.liu}@nokia.com

Abstract. In this article, we explored rural China's digital divide problem from a social structure perspective, especially regarding the practical process and mechanism of the digital divide forming in different village structures. Traditional village and industrialized village represent two types of rural China's social structure, which provide a good case for studying the digital divide between different types of villages. We consider the gap formed in possessing information and communication technologies(ICTs) as the primary divide, and take the gap formed in using ICTs as the secondary divide. Moreover, a "mutual reproduction" effect exists between the divides formed in the course of possessing and using ICTs. Finally we pointed out that cell phones, as a mobile network, may become the first carrier of the integration of the future information technology and an effective agent weapon helps bridging the digital divide.

Keywords: Digital Divide, Social Structure, Traditional Village, Industrialized Village, Mobile Network.

1 Introduction

Since the late 1970s, China's market-oriented reforms have been through a full three decades. This reform originated in the rural areas, then extended to urban areas, and had brought about profound changes in Chinese society. When China was experiencing the reform, the world's economy becomes more globalized and the third wave of information technology revolution is surging. The mankind is embracing a new society——network society, which is not only a new social formation, but also a new social system [2]. It enables information technology network to constitute a basic human survival situation, and greatly influences the people's everyday life. Where will human society develop? Generally speaking, there're two opposite views: the convergence theory argues the development of information technology will ultimately

---

[*] This paper is one of the research results of "Peasants and Information Technology Research Group, Tsinghua University(Department of Sociology)—Nokia research center(Beijing)". Thanks for suggestions of Prof. Yuhua Guo, Prof.Yuan Shen and Prof.Liping Sun. Dr.Jun Jin also contributed essentially to the improvement of this paper.

N. Aykin (Ed.): Internationalization, Design, LNCS 5623, pp. 347–355, 2009.

make the human society into a "one world", the digital divide theory argues that the development of information technology will make a greater gap between the informational rich and the informational poor. The latter point of view is increasingly becoming the focus of people's concern, and the various issues raised by "digital divide" have been widely concerned by countries in the world.

For contemporary China, digital divide is a structure problem in the transformation of Chinese society. For a long time, urban-rural division is a significant feature of Chinese society. After three decades' reform, although this dual structure has been weakened, the duality of Chinese social system fundamentally remains strong. During this course, the "executive-dominated dual structure" in the planned economic system has been changed into "market-dominated dual structure" under market economic system[6].And the existence of this dual structure essentially determines and shapes resource allocations. Thus the most important digital divide problem in China is the digital divide between urban and rural areas. Meanwhile, rural China has its own digital divide between east and west, coastal and inland, namely "regional digital divide". The perspectives above on digital divide in rural China have much influence, but they failed to reflect the internal structural changes in China's rural society caused by the market-oriented reform. So what changes in rural social structure have happened during three decades' reform? A general assessment is that the current rural China has been a highly structure-differentiated areas. Thus exploring the "internal digital divide" of rural China becomes of great significance.

To fully explore the internal digital divide in rural China, we should first develop an alternative paradigm to transcend the conventional dichotomies, such as "coastal and inland", "east and west", "rich and poor", to examine the fundamental transformations in the social structure of Chinese villages. These dichotomies are too superficial to capture some profound structural factors. Traditional villages and industrialized villages represent two types of social structure in rural China. While the traditional villages mainly rely on agricultural industries and remain a relatively simple and traditional rural life, the industrialized villages develop non-agricultural industries and enjoy a semi-urbanized and modern life. To rephrase research topics of rural China's digital divide, this paper will explore the digital divide problem in contemporary rural China from a social structure approach, paying special attention to the practical process and mechanism of digital divide formation under different village structures.

2 Literature Review and Research Framework

The "digital divide" is a widely used and contested concept. Based on different positions and questions, scholars usually give very different definitions [See7, 9,1,12]. But generally speaking, the so-called digital divide mainly refers to the gap between the informational rich and informational poor. From the point of view of research level, the scholarship on digital divide includes both global digital divide and domestic digital divide [11]. The former mainly explores the digital divide among countries and regions in the world , while the latter mainly discusses the digital divide within one country or region. From the point of view of research perspective, the digital divide literature covers economy, gender, technology, education, ethnicity, linguistic, and regional approaches [See 3, 9, 10]. From the point of view of research method, there are quite a few quantitative studies on digital divide, while qualitative studies are neither sufficient nor systematic. The aspects above briefly reflect the achievements and problems in the scholarship on digital divide, and provide important references for exlporing the digital divide in rural China .

At present, while many researches about rural China's digital divides concentrate on urban-rural and regional digital divide, they pay insufficient attention to the internal digital divides among different villages. How to explore this type of rural digital divide? This paper argues that digital divide is not only a technological phenomenon, but also a social phenomenon. From a sociological perspective, purchase and usage of ICTs are socio-economic behaviors, which are always embedded in specific social structures. Thus the problem of embeddedness is the premise basis for exploring how people possess and use ICTs. Meanwhile, we consider the gap formed in possessing ICTs as the primary divide,and take the gap formed in using ICTs as the secondary divide. In this article, "digital divide" refers to a kind of structural relationship formed among different social groups in the practical process of their owning and using ICTs.

Methodologically, we followed the methodology of sociology of practice to employ research methods including ethnographic interviews and participant observation. We selected village Y in Shaanxi Province and village H in Jiangsu Province as field work sites. The comparative significances between the two villages exist in the following four dimensions: Firstly, for geographical position, while village Y is in northwest China, one of the main regions concentrated with traditional villages, village H locates in southeast China, which is one of the main regions concentrated with industrialized villages. Secondly, for historical culture tradition , the area that village Y locates in had a long agriculture cultivation tradition and the peasants were accustomed to be earth-bounded, while the area in which village H locates has been known for its tradition of energetic industrial and commercial activities and the peasants were also quite active. Thirdly, for economy structure , village Y has a typical traditional argriculture production pattern, in which peasants are still self-sufficient, while village H develops a typical industrialized production pattern, in which peasants generally enjoy an urbanized life. Fourthly, for national policies, when village Y follows the green argricultrue policy which pays special attention to ecological environment protection, government encourages village H to advance industry and innovation development. For these two villages, the ICTs we investigated include television, fixed telephone, mobile phone and computer, which are usually used as indicators to measure digital divide by scholars. And television and fixed telephone belong to traditional ICTs, which are the products of Industrial Age; mobile phone and computer belong to new ICTs, which are the products of Information Age.

3   Traditional Village(Y) and Industrialized Village(H): A Comprative Analysis

Firstly we give an introduction of the two villages:

Village Y is located in the northern part of Shaanxi Province and is a typical traditional village. Because Mao zedong had stationed in this village from November 1947 to March 1949, it was named "China's famous historical and cultural village" in September 2005. The village covers an area of 7.8 square kilometers, has 289 households and 1,153 individuals. Nearly 70% of the villagers are migrant workers, who work outside all the year round. They usually earn about 15,000 RMB a year. The peasants who stay in the village still mainly live on agricultural planting. They plant several kinds of grains and potatoes, which are mainly for their own consumption, while only a small amount for sale. The average per capita net income of the villagers in 2007 reached 2,400 RMB. It seems that the living conditions of villagers are getting better consistently, various forms of social security begin to be set up, but still far from sufficient. The villager committee has few village affairs to manage.

Village H is located in the southern part of Jiangsu Province and is a typical industrialized village. This village has won many honors, such as national township enterprises groups, civilization village of Jiangsu Province and Wuxi municipal industrial star village. The village covers an area of 1.64 square kilometers, with 977 households and 3,150 individuals. There'are also about 1,000 non-native outsiders. More than 95% of the native villagers become factory workers. The average per capita net income of the villagers in 2007 reached nearly 20,000 RMB, and the net assets of village amount to 200 million Yuan. At present, the village-run enterprises specialized in textile, sports gears and metal processing. Meanwhile, the village also vigorously developed tertiary industry and achieved remarkable results. Villagers no longer do farming, and they buy their own food from market. Village H also enjoyed running water, electricity, gas and internet at the same time with urban residents of Jiangyin City . It is safe to conclude that the villagers has been enjoying an urbanized life.

Now we will analyse how villagers own and use their ICTs in the two villages.

3.1 Television

As a kind of ICTs, television was once of great significance for Chinese peasants. When prepared for a marriage, peasants always tried their best to purchase a television. Especially in the 1980s, the peasant income was very low, so a television would be very expensive. Thus owning a television was usually regarded as a symbol of achievements. Even today television has been widely available, as a material property, it still has the important cultural significance. As to village Y, nearly every family has a television set, but only a few enjoy the second set. They watch TV programs through "wan zi" (a satellite signal receiver), but channels are still limited. In village H, every family usually has at least 2 television sets, and most families are equipped with advanced rear-projection TVs. Moreover, village H had access to cabled programs relatively early, which were all converted into digital ones in 2007, so villagers can watch even more TV channels. Although there is a wide gap between village Y and H on the number of television sets per family, the quality of TV sets, and the number of program channels, the two villages still have similarities. For example, villagers in both villages like watching weather forecast, which is closely linked with their deep-rooted cultural traditions and customs, because Chinese traditional peasants mainly depended on weather for living. But villagers in H are also accustomed to watch news everyday to learn national policy and international news, which is closely related with their industrial production. The discrepancy of villagers' television quantity in Y and H is gradually developing the discrepancy in the ways of watching TV. While villagers in Y usually watch TV together, villagers in H often watch TV separately in their own rooms. To some extent, the difference in the ways of watching TV also reflects the difference in life styles: the former tends to enjoy a common life, while the latter pursues an individualized living.

3.2 Fixed Phone

Rural China is a society of acquaintances. For villagers, their daily interactions are face-to-face. The emergence of fixed phone makes distant communication possible. However, the penetration of telephone to rural areas was mainly promoted by the coercive state power at first. Under the impetus of National Informationization, nearly all the administrative villages had been equipped with at least a telephone to keep the contact with the outside world. But at that time, the fixed phones were usually located in the office of villager committee, acting as a public authority item. Fixed telephone really going into rural households as private belongings requires at least two basic conditions: 1) the improvement of informational infrastructure; 2) the decrease in installing fee. In Village Y, a three-phase project set up a phone cable in 1999. At present, there are around 30 fixed phones in the village and the installation rate is around 10%. Usually a rural household spends 20 to 30 Yuan each month for a fixed phone (including 20 Yuan compulsive "monthly rent"), as they use telephone answering calls more than making calls. Telephones in Village Y are so scattered that they only communicate villagers under certain "important occasions" and have no substantial influence on villagers' traditional communication and or interaction style. In Village H, when industries began to emerge vigorously in the late 1970s, fixed phones were introduced into factories as an office tool. Industrial economic growth increased incomes, thus in the 1980s many households already had fixed phones as life necessities. Currently, more than 90% of households in Village H install at least one fixed phone. The common demand of telephone is an inevitable result of industrial economic development. With the widespread of telephone, a new network of social interaction was built up among the villagers and to a large extent shaped people's way of communications and interactions. Thus, as a private ICTs product, fixed phones entered the Village Y and Village H not only in different paths, but also led to different impacts and consequences. From the aspect of usage, the two villages' access to fixed phones are basically similar, that is, answering and making telephone calls, and the monthly expenditure are roughly identical as well. Yet, one slightly difference is that fixed phone lines in Village H also provide internet access, which combines the traditional ICTs with the new ones. In this sense, the usage of telephones in village H has more connections to the Information Age.

3.3 Mobile Phone

As a new ICTs product, mobile phone spread to rural areas much faster than fixed phone and its coverage is also broader. According to the data of the National Bureau of Statistics, 4.3 mobile phones were held by every 100 rural households in 2000; by the end of 2004, this number increased to 34.7; and again up to 40 by the end of 2005. An increase of nearly 10 times happened during 5 years. Now mobile phone becoms one of the most important information tools of peasants. Besides the infrastructure construction, the rapid expansion of mobiles mainly bases on two conditions: 1) a sharp drop in mobiles phones price. 2) the decreasing rates. But to the rural China, these two conditions provide only a possibility for mobiles access to local communities. Whether peasants accept mobile phones still needs a social process. After all, for most peasants, mobiles are an unexpected item in their life course and memorial history. After the market-oriented reform, rural areas have undergone profound changes. Holding mobiles gradually becomes a fashion and social trend. In this background senior villagers' possession and use of mobile phones provide a very good analysis case. For Village Y, the whole village population can be divided into two groups: individuals staying in the village, many of whom are the elderly and children, and individuals working outside the village, many of whom are young people and the middle aged. Thus, in essence, the whole social structure of village is in a split state. The person working outside needs to keep in touch with his or her family members to enjoy the common life, and to make "home" a tangible existence. So the "contactability" anytime and anywhere of mobile phones provides the technical possibility for this spatially split home. In Village Y, the usage of the mobiles by the elderly perfectly reflects this. We can see that many senior villagers have mobile phones, which are usually brought by their children working outside of the village. Although probably the only operation they can master is to answer the phone, this simple action itself is of great significance. Knowing their far away children are safe, the elderly are getting a spiritual and psychological consolation, while the younger working outside who are sure that everything is fine at home feel at ease to work and struggle in the competitive outside world. Now we can know that cell phones as a product of information technology not only reconstruct each other's social relations in the physical space, but also help building and maintaining a shared spiritual world. But Village H presents a different picture. After thirty years' market-oriented reforms, Village H has become a fully industrialized village. Villagers were also among the first group of Chinese to try on cell phones. In the late 1980s, the boom of township enterprises made private entrepreneurs the first group to own "shou ji" (literally "the machine in hand", then known as "da ge da", literally "elder brother big" and "elder" "big" pronounces the same, costs 20 to 30 thousand Yuan each set) and become the pioneer of fashion. At that time, possessing a mobile phone showed a highly respected social status, having a strong symbolic significance. When "da ge da" gradually disappeared and new mobiles became more widespread, the peasant entrepreneurs who had used "da ge da" are now using mobiles. However, at this time, mobile phones are no longer a symbol of social status, but an everyday commodity mainly to meet the needs in work.

3.4 Computer and Internet

Computer, as same as mobile phone, is the product of the trend of times. However, there are two major differences between them: 1) a computer usually is far more expensive than a mobile phone, so the purchase of a computer requires considerable economic capacity. 2) the use of computer requires more education and knowledge. No doubt these two conditions cause the difficulty for the diffusion of computer in rural areas. But the potential demand for computer and the internet in rural China should not be underestimated. According to China Internet Network Information Center (CNNIC), data of 2008 shows that the number of netizen in rural areas has reached 52.62 million, with an annual growth rate of 127.7%, much higher than city's 38.2%. The internet in rural areas is in a period of rapid growth. Children are the future of the nation, and computers are considered as the bridge to the future. Therefore, by analyzing the behavior and consequence of children using computers, we can effectively understand people's needs and cognitive of computer and the internet. In Village Y, the computer is truly a rare item. The villagers hardly have private computers. Schools have no computer courses for kids. Kids who want to use computers have no choice but to go to "net bar". In the opinion of adults, kids are "playing" computers in net bar only for fun. Indulging in playing internet games could seriously influence children's school performances. Several crimes in the net bars of the town made parents even more anxious. Local government shut down the only two net bars in the town. Hence according to villagers, "going to net bar" means delinquent. While villagers see the internet as a real monster, they also recognize that it is very important for the future development of their children. There is a completely different picture in village H. In H, nearly half of the households have a computer, and even primary schools provide various computer programs. Consequently, the possibility of children going to net bars is much lower. Although children using computers at home may also be indulged in games and affect their school performances, the negative impact of internet will be much less under the instruction of parents. Moreover, computer courses in school may teach children how to tell useful information from the useless ones, how to set up a blog to display themselves and make friends, and how to not waste time and energy on it. All of the above greatly develop and enrich the inner world of children. Meanwhile, it should be noted that, although the computers have been relatively widely penetrated into households and enterprises in Village H, on the whole, the role of computer for villagers is still entertainment-oriented, such as listening music, watching movies and operas, playing games, reading news, online shopping,etc.Their functions in industrial production are still limited.

4 Conclusion and Discussion

In this paper, we have discussed the digital divide formed in the practice of occupying and using ICTs between the traditional village Y and industrialized village H by case-comparison method. We also analyzed the practical patterns and socio-cultural significance of the digital divide under different social structures.

As we can see from above, the villagers not only show a vast divide upon the occupying and using televisions, fixed phones, mobile phones, and computers, but also display a great diversity in their cognition and notion of these ICTs. Moreover, the divide formed in the process of occupying and using demonstrates a "mutual reproduction" effect. The earlier one owns these ICTs, the deeper these ICTs will penetrate his or her life. And the deeper these ICTs penetrate one's life, the stronger demand of these ICTs this individual will develop. The traditional ICTs, such as TV and fixed phones, are the results of the Second Industrial Revolution, and the new ICTs, including mobile phones and computers, are the products of the Third Information Technology Revolution. Before the Reform, TV and fixed phones had been more or less introduced into rural areas. At that time, TV played an important role in peasant life as one of personal belongings, while fixed phones mainly existed as one of public authority items, so we can see the earliest telephones were usually located in the offices of villager committees in Village Y and H. After the market-oriented reforms village Y still maintains the original, but gradually hollowed social structure of a traditional rural community; Village H turns the farmland into industrial use, forming a modern industrial structure. The great transformation of social structure will inevitably reshape peasants' production and consumption needs. Following globalization, mobiles and computers entered China and then penetrate in and expand to rural areas by the government-led and market-assisted impetus of "National Informationization Project". In Village Y and H we can see that mobiles entered rural areas through different ways and played different social and cultural roles. In Village Y, there is hardly any demand of computer, while in village H its "quasi-urbanization" life style creates most demand of computer. Therefore, when entering and penetrating the specific society, the ICTs must be redefined and reconstructed by local culture.

Also we should see, in essence, the digital divide which Village Y and H demonstrated reflects a basic feature of the social structure of contemporary China, namely, the cleavage of social structure. As a well-known sociologist Sun Liping said: from the 1990s, China began to step into a "cleavage society" [5]. The substance of a cleavage society is the co-existence of structural components from pre-industrial, industrialized, and post-industrial societies which lack functioning connections between each other at the same time. And one of the major components of the "cleavage" is the divide in the urban-rural dual structure. From our study on the digital divide in rural areas, we can see this characteristic of cleavage also exists within rural China. In a sense, traditional and industrialized villages represent two sharply different social structures, namely traditional and modern social structure, so the digital divide between them substantially illustrates the significances of traditional-modern dichotomy. However, this traditional-modern relationship is not the diametrical divide, but mutually entangled closely.

At last, what can we do to bridge this digital divide between the two villages? From the state of occupying and using of the four kinds of ICTs, no doubt that mobile phone hold the most important position in both villages, being most closely integrated into their everyday life and production. More importantly, compared to other three types of ICTs, villagers are interested in and receptive to cell phones regardless of their education, knowledge, or conception, and cognition. In addition, as the mobile phone has had a widespread coverage, speedy infiltration, and high recognition in rural areas, together with its networking functions, it may become the first carrier of the integration of the future information technology and an effective agent weapon helps bridging the digital divide.

References

1. Angang, H.: Zhongguo ruhe yingdui riyi kuoda de shuzi honggou (How does China deal with the expanding digital divide?). zhongguo gongye jingji (Chinese Industry Economy) 3 (2002)
2. Castells, M.: The Information Age. In: The Rise of the Network Society, vol. I, p. 469. Blackwell, Oxford (1996)
3. Harwit, E.: Spreading telecommunications to developing areas in China. The China Quarterly 180, 1010–1030 (2004)
4. Granonetter, M.: Economic Action and Social Structure: the problem of embeddedness. American Journal of Sociology 91, 481–510 (1985)

5. Liping, S.: Duanlie: 20 shiji 90 niandai yilai de zhongguo shehui (Cleavage: the Chinese society since 1990s), p. 1. Social science academic press (P.R.China), Beijing (2003)
6. Liping, S.: Zhuanxing yu duanlie: gaige yilai zhongguo shehui jiegou de bianqian (transition and cleavage: the changes of Chinese social structure since reform), p. 362. Tsinghua University Press (P.R.China), Beijing (2004)
7. NTIA: Falling through the net: new data on the digital divide, US Department of Commerce NUA Internet Surveys (1999)
8. Rongxiang, C. (ed.): Jiedu shuzi honggou: jishu zhimin yu shehui fenhua (expain digital divide: the technology colonizing and social differentiation). Sanlian bookstore, Shanghai (2003)
9. Rongxiang, C.: Shuzi honggou yinlun: xinxi bu pingdeng yu shuzi jiyu (Introduction to digitial divide: informational inequality and digital opportunity). Makesi zhuyi yu xianshi (Marxism and realities) 6 (2001)
10. Xinhong, Z.: zhongguo shuzi honggou baogao 2008 (The 2008 report of China's digital divide). Dianzi zhengwu (Electronic government) 11 (2008)
11. Yanhong, C.: Shuzi honggou wenti yanjiu shuping (a review of ditital divide researches). Qingbao zazhi (Journal of Information) 2 (2005)
12. Yanping, H. (ed.): Kuayue shuzi honggou——miandui dierci xiandaihua de weiji yu tiaozhan (bridge ditital divide: the crisis and challenge for facing second modernization), vol. 1. Social science academic press (P.R.China), Beijing (2002)

Perceptions on Interaction Design in Malaysia

Idyawati Hussein[1], Esmadi Abu Abu Seman[1], and Murni Mahmud[2]

[1] Universiti Malaysia Sabah
{idyawati,esmadi}@ums.edu.my
[2] International Islamic University of Malaysia
murni@iiu.edu.my

Abstract. Even though researchers have introduced Human Computer Interaction (HCI) methodologies, since 1980's, Malaysia's user interface is still considered inadequate. Despite being aware of the importance of usable design, several non-technical issues have more significant influence towards poorly designed user interfaces in Malaysia. This paper reports the findings of a study of interaction design and/or any HCI methodologies in practice among Malaysian companies for software design and computer-related design development. The research involved senior Information Communication Technology (ICT) managers and focused on the application developers, whose job descriptions and responsibilities vary. The study used semi-structured interviews and a focus group study to uncover the current perceptions of people involved in ICT project development. The findings serve as a pointer to the Malaysian government and stakeholders towards the improvement of user interface design.

Keywords: HCI, usable design, interaction design, practices, Malaysia.

1 Introduction

The term *interaction design* is widely used in Human Computer Interaction (HCI); however, the definition varies [4]. Among many other areas, HCI aims to identify and understand usability problems in task-oriented computer systems [1]. Usability is the key to HCI [5][8] but many researchers in HCI have explored more advanced features; for instance, emotional design [13]. Emotional design is an important dimension in interaction design, in addition to usability, ease-of-use and fitness-for-purpose. Interaction design, HCI and usability design have pragmatically been the focus of researchers and practitioners in developed countries. However, there have been few studies on design of interaction between human and computer in developing countries [7].

Since 1996, Malaysia has been among developing countries with the highest ICT investment [2] as Malaysians are widely exposed to information technology, from the entertainment arcade to wireless connection available in shopping malls and restaurants. The need for appropriate usability and correct interaction design are critically important to ensure excellent information usability. Unfortunately, there is no clear distinction between software design or computer-related design and the adoption of interaction design in Malaysia. This study is among the first attempt to learn about the current status of interface or interaction design among practitioners in Malaysia. In

N. Aykin (Ed.): Internationalization, Design, LNCS 5623, pp. 356–365, 2009.
© Springer-Verlag Berlin Heidelberg 2009

this paper, we will report the results of two data collection procedures: semi-structured interviews and focus groups. Most of the participants described themselves as application developers.

2 Related Work

The literature indicates that designing interfaces has been studied for more than twenty years [5]. The fact that there is lack of such studies in the Malaysian context may suggest opportunities for more attention to be paid to the subject in Malaysia. Understanding interaction design in developing countries may have a significant impact on the usage of computer interfaces.

Most designers in developed countries are trying to support and address the needs of users by nurturing, serving and caring for them [4]. In contrary, designers in developing countries are competing with users, struggling to fulfill their project's due date [12], trying to satisfy clients [19], project leaders and/or system analysts and finding the best words to describe their design [14].

Design practices may cover graphics design, product design, artistic design, industrial design and the film industry [12]. How to create a useful design, to meet the diversity of users' needs and requirements, must be clearly understood by designers [7][16]. However, designers' perception and behavior will be influenced by the design community and organizational culture in which they are working [21]. Organizational cultures are patterns of basic assumptions that are considered valid and that are taught to new members as the way to perceive, think, and feel in an organization [4]. In software project development, risks were not often from the designing team but from the other issues such as the organization's policy [20].

In Malaysia, designing usable interfaces has been applied, although few studies and results have been published or made accessible to the public [2]. On the whole, these user interface designs have rarely been studied, and few comparisons have been made. As suggested, lessons learned in one project are not transmitted to others. Additionally, appropriate technologies are rarely evaluated; and financial sustainability, scalability and cost recovery are seldom addressed [6]. Such situations create many possibilities to learn from the diverse issues of human and computer interaction design in Malaysian design experience.

2.1 Proposed Framework

The study aims to find out the general perceptions of the application developers involved in interaction design processes. The study were conducted directly with the people involved in the design; i.e. a few organized groups of practitioners in Malaysia. Our primary aims are to (i) learn about the status of interaction design and HCI methodologies used in IT and IT-related projects among practitioners in Malaysia; and (ii) identify the influencing factors that contribute to design decisions.

Figure 1 shows the proposed framework of the relationship between applications developers and their final product. The products that are designed by application developers are influenced by several factors which include user requirements, functionality, decision making and creativity.

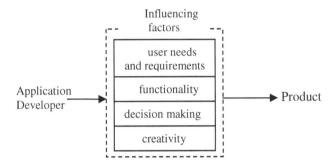

Fig. 1. Non-technical issues that influence design amongst application developers

Application developers, especially those who are involved in the design phase, will design according to users' goals [18], motivation [12], and task domain [5]. As the designers interact with their designed product (including software, systems and services), they form interpretations that influence how they think, feel and behave. Such interpretations are based on forms and functionalities [3]. At the same time the interpretations are actually more complex responses which may include assessment of the values of the products. The judgment may be associated with cultural values [7]. Crilly [3] asserted that people attach such meanings to products; designers may form intentions that the products they design will be interpreted in particular ways, and these intentions shape the product's result.

3 Methodology

This study used two methods of data collection. First, eight semi-structured interviews were conducted with application developers in four different companies based in Kuala Lumpur, Malaysia. These companies are located in urban areas where software and computer-related projects are actively conducted and managed. Secondly, one focus group was held among selected application developers to study perceptions and collaboration among different task practitioners in design reasoning, methods and values of design development.

3.1 Participants

The study's participants were IT Manager, Information Architect, Head of Creative Design, Head of Enterprise Portal, Assistant Manager, Graphic Designer, Application Developer and Programmer. The participants did not receive any compensation. They were willing to share their experience and concerns in interaction design which are part of their daily work and practices. Table 1 shows the list of participants' type of work and their previous job title.

Table 1. Participants' current and previous job titles

Participant	Current Job Title	Previous Job Title
P1	IT Manager	System Analyst, Programmer
P2	Assistant Manager	Application Developer
P3	Head Creative Designer	Website, Courseware Development
P4	Head Enterprise Portal	Lecturer, Broadcasting, Director, Scriptwriter
P5	Information Architect	Application Developer
P6	Graphic Designer	Artist
P7	Application Developer	Programmer
P8	Programmer	-

3.2 Questionnaire

The main aim of this study was to collect data on the perception of participants towards design in system development (i.e. interfaces that they have designed and developed). The questionnaire consisted of demographic information and questions about interaction design. Closed-ended questions were to find out ethnic group and level of design experience, which is part of their work responsibilities. Participants were also asked to describe their job responsibilities, people or users that they dealt with during design development and how they acquire design knowledge and learn about different design methods. The latter part was asked in open-ended format.

We explored participants' perceptions and beliefs with open-ended questions which aimed to engage the participants' perception of the importance of design, description of design, sensitive issues in designing for different ethnic groups, and what they think important in design. The participants were also asked to give a rating on a 1 to 5 scale on each perception question (1 for the Least Important and 5 for the Most Important influence or factor to consider in design). Each reply has been categorised into common terminology which includes perceptions, training in design, cultural element perceptions and design guidelines used in the development process.

3.3 Focus Group

Focus groups brought together the SKALI [15] design team who shared interests in the design of software and computer-related development. The focus group provided opportunities to explore shared beliefs and experiences with respect to SKALI's culture and way of work (i.e. design process and procedure). Table 2 summarises demographic information of the focus group participants. During the focus group session, the participants were given a questionnaire about their design practices according to its importance (Likert scale 1 to 5).

Table 2. Focus Group Participants' current job title and years of experiences

Current Job title	Years of Experience
Project Manager	More than 3 years
Assistant Manager	4 years
Creative Designer	8 years
Information Architecture	More than 3 years

4   Results

4.1   Demographic

The results are divided into three main sections: demographics, perceptions and focus group. Four male and four female subjects participated in the interview sessions. Their ages ranged from 25 to 34 years. All participants had a bachelor's degree or higher. Of the eight application developers participating in the study, four judged themselves proficient with design interface or interaction and four somewhat intermediate. Questions regarding ethnicity were asked and there was one anomaly to the standard replies:

Q1: Which ethnic group you belong to?
P8: Mixed Chinese and Malay

4.2   Perceptions

Generally the perceptions are identified by three terminologies: HCI, usability and interaction design. These perspectives directly reflect the importance of HCI by the participants.

Table 3. Awareness of common HCI terminologies

Users were asked questions on	Yes	No
1) Terminology		
• HCI	6	2
• Usability	7	1
• Interaction Design	3	5
2) Have had training in design	4	4
3) Is there any ethnic issue regarding design	5	3

Table 3 shows the perception of participants of HCI terminology. Most were aware of the important terminology and had heard about HCI and usability. However, five participants never heard of interaction design. Half had attended formal training in design. Five participants indicated that they were aware of the sensitivity of ethnic issues, for example use of colour.

Participants were also asked about important factors or issues in design for interaction. Their feedback varied, and included creativity, design feedback (e.g. graphics, text, colour), grabbing people's attention [18], usability [8], impression [13] and brand, passion [6], functionality and getting it right the first time [14]. As for application developers, the participants perceived their design as satisfactory but need more information to ensure their users' satisfaction. Participants also described their design output as based on experience and the users' needs and requirements. They also reflected on the meaningfulness of design, which must be relevant to its usage.

Considering the different ethnicity and religions in Malaysia, the implementation of design should be according to ethnic groups. Although all the participants have different job functionality, they all agreed on the usefulness of design guidelines.

They normally referred to their project leader, systems analyst, senior colleagues and the decision maker. Additionally, they mentioned website that has common design guidelines or government authority, such as MAMPU [10]. MAMPU is a government agency that handles the functions of administrative modernisation and human resource planning.

During the interview and focus group sessions, participants were asked which they considered the most important perceived factors in design development. The result, adjusted by Net Positive Value (NPV) [17] has proven that the highest rank of perceived importance in design is the user's requirements. The lowest rank is the superior's or manager's satisfaction on design.

Table 4. Net Positive Value (NPV) of perceived importance in design development

	NPV
Aesthetic design	+1
Functional design	+3
User requirements	+7
Due date of Completion	-1
Superior's or Manager's satisfaction	-5
User's satisfaction	+5

The results in Table 4 indicate that participants (i.e. application developers or practitioners) do not always agree with their managers (NPV=-5) because they are not necessarily the person who will interact most with the user interfaces. Due date completion (NPV=-1) is the second lower rank in perceived importance in the interview results. This research suggests that the application developers think that they must meet end users' requirements of the system rather than management's requirements. Aesthetic design (NPV=+1) occupies the third lowest rank. Most application developers believed that no matter how aesthetic the application is, failure to achieve users' needs and requirements will cause users to abandon the product. Functional design therefore scores +3 in the NPV ranking.

When it comes to a project where the client is both the decision maker and the user, application developers may have to agree to certain design issues against the basic principles, for example, the client's desire for animated unrealistic graphics and/or dynamic text for important messages on the website. According to ISO 14915 [9] still images and text should be used for all important information other than time critical warnings. However, not many decision makers were aware of or understood this standard. Practitioners also did not know of the ISO details, so many of the principles were ignored. The result of the NPV analysis shows that user satisfaction (+5) is considered more important than aesthetic design or even the function of the application. Application developers perceived that the user's requirement (NPV=+7) is the most important phase in design development.

4.3   Focus Group

Four of the subjects who answered the questionnaire and participated in the in-depth interviews were also involved in the focus group discussion. The outcomes of the focus group highlight several issues and influencing factors in interface design.

Data Requirements Gathering from the Right Users. The results of the NPV analysis showed that user requirements is the most important consideration in design. The focus group, however, identified user requirements as the most difficult phase in the design process. The waterfall model [2] is one of the common system development methodologies used by Malaysian practices, and it is also used for website development. Since data requirements are always identified by the information architect and systems analyst, the designer has no first-hand contact with the potential users. Unfortunately, the information gathering does not always cover all stakeholders, which should include end users and decision makers. Difficulties arise when the end users and decision makers cannot agree on a single solution for the application developers. For example, end users require items which would help them perform better in their jobs. On the other hand, decision makers will always consider the costs involved to provide such requirements.

All application developers agreed that the decision makers always get what they want throughout design decision. However, in the case of the SKALI (the only company in this study which has a usability team), project managers will meet the decision makers of the project and educate those decision makers in the design consequences, based on their own experience and scientific principles underlying their decisions.

> *P8 [translated]: There was the time that an elderly client complained that the font was too small. We could not do anything because the space was limited. However, because of his authority, we had to change the font size even though many people disagreed.*
>
> *P5: The most difficult part is to get agreement on who is the user, and who is the decision maker. We had many experiences where the people we interviewed happened to be the end user but not the decision maker. Decision makers decide on cost, timeline and context. Most of the time, these people do not use the system or interface.*

According to Zhang [21], it is time to focus on making top management realize and incorporate the HCI perspective into corporate strategic planning and management. HCI issues and concerns in the business, managerial and organizational context should be integrated. It is assumed that in this structure, the designer's role is isolated from the organization or from the development team itself [14][19]. For example, in the user requirement information gathering, in most projects, the role will be done by an Information Architect (IA) [2] and/or systems analyst [8][17].

Importance of HCI Studies. A knowledge of HCI can be used to justify design, for example in convincing the users of the selection of certain design elements, for instance using certain colors is not appropriate because of how our eye processes the information.

P6: I do design for web but I never heard of the term usability... [laugh]...What is it actually?

The research discovered that 25% of the participants had never heard of HCI. This is a critical issue since these participants were the IT Manager who had been working for more than 5 years, and a graphic designer who has been designing for more than 2 years.

Designers are rarely involved in fieldwork; they are the people who usually sit in front of the computer monitor with pencils, colours and blank paper in their hands. However, Stolterman [16] has argued that designers, even in the most demanding situations, are able to deliver a design that is practical and has good design outcomes. He also named several researchers who have provided fundamental understanding of design, which is a unique human activity deserving its own intellectual treatment.

These research findings have supported those of Stolterman [16]; an in-depth approach has showed that, due to the lack of knowledge of psychological studies related to design, designers are unable to justify their own inventive designs during presentation. When clients disagree about a proposed design, the designers will more often than not justify their creation based on comparison with competitors' products. Therefore, the intention is to give designers a tool which is based on the understanding that designers should be supported by a "being prepared-for-action" tool [14]; another tool for "guided-in action" is required to support communication between designers and stakeholders.

All of these methodologies and theories will only be found in an HCI curriculum [1]. Therefore, HCI must be introduced to the practitioners through short courses or other educational approaches.

Design Guidelines for Interface. The result of this focus group has uncovered the fact that practitioners in Malaysia have their own guidelines, compile guidelines from websites, refer to their own experience and to MAMPU [10]. There is no current in-depth study to compare the guidelines used by practitioners in this region and current research into design guidelines produced by specialists. This research contributes to a promising and challenging future in research for design guidelines used in practice by Malaysian industries.

Although designers' inventive designs are usually based on their personal intuitions and motivations [16], they sometimes ignore the fact that users do not possess the same cognition, levels of expertise or intention of use [3]. Furthermore, with only a little time allocated for user testing, designers often grab the most convenient users available – themselves – to test their own design [12].

Multiracial Influences. According to the research results, use of colour is a recurring issue in design. Government websites normally avoid using green because the opposition's official colour is green. However, critical websites like the Ministry of Natural Resources and Environment [11] used a different green colour.

> P1: [translated]: If the clients are Chinese, the application focuses more on business; Malay will be more on information display, organisation chart and so on.
> P2: Government websites must have an organisation chart. Certain colours should not be used because they may reflect personal belief...
> P3: Cultural differences could have different aspects; they want the product to be delivered, for example, must be sharp on time for Chinese clients. Malays have a lot of bureaucracy. A lot of people need to sign the paper work. I don't know why they cannot use the electronic medium to communicate efficiently. Colour, yes, government projects normally avoid using green. Well, just in case..

5 Discussions

This study has been significant as it is perhaps the first to investigate the issues of interaction design among website and systems programmers in Malaysia. Many programmer-designers are working in the industry, and interaction design has received insufficient attention. Our work on the effectiveness and importance of HCI should be followed–up, and re-look. Some work has been done in this area but the results are yet to be published [6]. While the Malaysian government portal has received awards and recognition, the issue of updated information needs to be addressed [10][11], and maintenance of the portal has been a concern. Human factors have been discussed in many conferences, but the specific issue of interaction design has not received full attention by the designers. Few local companies focus on interaction design [6][7], and more seminars, workshops and awareness programmes have to be established in order to increase knowledge of the importance of applying interaction design skills.

This research has revealed that design failures in Malaysia are not mainly because of technical issues, but rather because non-technical managers [20] have a significant impact on design as a whole. Such non-technical issues include decision making in design teams, organisational policy towards design issues, and lack of awareness of cognitive psychology related to design among designers themselves [18].

Finally, the main factor contributing to the design delay and failures in Malaysia is that designers do not have authority in decision making. Organisational policy may aim to impress the client company in general, rather than the specific user [20], and the designer's creativity will be wasted. In the Malaysian context, too little information is being addressed to the designer's dilemma in ICT project developments. This study is urgently needed as Malaysia is aiming to engage seriously in the knowledge-based economy.

Acknowledgments. The authors are grateful to SKALI (Malaysia) Company for their co-operation in the focus group session.

References

1. ACM SIGCHI: Curriculum for Human-Computer Interaction,
   http://sigchi.org/cdg/
2. Alvin, W.Y.: Are Usability Assessment Technique Reliable in Non-Western Cultures?. The Electronic Journal on Information Systems in Developing Country (2000),
   http://www.ejisdc.org

3. Crilly, N.: Product Aesthetics Represents Designer Intent and Consumer Response, Doctoral of Philosophy theses, University of Cambridge (2006)
4. Fallman, D.: The Pragmatics of Design Studio Culture: Our Story. In: Proceeding CHI 2007 (2007)
5. Gould, J.D., Lewis, C.: Designing for Usability: Key Principles and What Designers Think. ACM 28(3), 300–311 (1985)
6. Khalid, H.M.: Human Factor Engineering for Malaysia and Singapore, http://www.damai-services.com
7. Halimahtun, M.K., Helander, M.G., Alvin, W.Y.: Work With Computing Systems. In Work With Computing Systems, Royal Institute of Technology (2004)
8. Hammond, N., Jorgensen, A., MacLea, A., Barnard, P., Long, J.: Design Practice and Interface Usability: Evidence from Interviews with Designers. In: Proceedings CHI 1983, pp. 40–44. ACM, New York (1983)
9. ISO: ISO 14915 Multimedia User Interface Design Software Ergonomics Requirements, Part 1: Introduction and Framework; Part 3: Media Combination and Selection in International Standard Organization (2000)
10. MAMPU: Electronic Government Information Technology Policy and Standards (EGIT), http://www.mampu.gov.my/mampu/
11. Ministry of Natural Resources and Environment, http://www.nre.gov.my
12. Mueller, J.: Getting Personal with Universal. In: Innovation Spring, IDSA (2004)
13. Norman, D.A.: Emotional Design: Why We Love (or Hate) Everyday Things. Basic Books, New York (2004)
14. Schön, D.A.: The Reflective Practitioner. Basic Books, New York (1983)
15. SKALI Official Website, http://www.skali.net/
16. Stolterman, E.: The Nature of Design Practice and Implications for Interaction Design Research. International Journal of Design, 55–65 (2008)
17. Sutcliffe, A.G.: Scenario-based Requirements Analysis. Requirements Engineering Journal 3(1), 48–65 (1998)
18. Sutcliffe, A.G., Kurniawan, S., Shin, J.: A Method and Advisor tool for Multimedia User Interface Design. International Journal of Human-Computer Studies, 375–392 (2007)
19. Weiss, A.: The Web Designer's Dilemma: When Standards and Practice Diverge. ACM, New York (2006)
20. Zaitun, A.B., Mashkuri, Y., Wood-Harper, A.T.: Systems Integration for a Developing Country: Failure or Success? A Malaysian Case Study. e-Journal of Informations Systems in Developing Countries 3(1), 1–10 (2000)
21. Zhang, P., Galletta, D.: Human-Computer Interaction and Management Information Systems: Foundations, pp. 1–18. Sharpe, Armonk, New York (2006)

The Cultural Creative of Product Design for Pingtung County in Taiwan

Yen-Yu Kang[1], Ming-Shean Wang[2], Wei-Shiang Hung[1], and Han-Yu Lin[1]

[1] Dept. Industrial Design, National Kaohsiung Normal University.
No.62, Shenzhong Rd., Yanchao Shiang, Kaohsiung County 824, Taiwan
yenyu@nknu.edu.tw
2 Department of Fashion Imaging,
Mingdao University
No.369, Wen Hwa Road, Pee-Tow 52345
Chang-Hwa, Taiwan

Abstract. Research results relies on the cooperation of National Kaohsiung Normal University Industrial Design and Cultural Affairs Department of Pingtung County. Method of Cultural Creative Design shows Pingtung County cultural connotation will display in the Pingtung County villages and towns characteristic commodity design, is helpful to the designer regarding the villages and towns discussion and the understanding. Entrusts with the new annotation and the creation using the design Taiwan multi-dimensional tribal grouping tribal group culture characteristic, expected that achievement of this research will be helpful to design on the cultural commodity in the future reference.

Keywords: Cultural Creative Design, Product Design, Creative Industries.

1 The Advance of "Creativity Taiwan"

In this globalized time, society's cultural structure and the various countries' economical state are having the fierce change.

In June, 2002 the government proposed that "challenges 2008 national prioritize project", and "the cultural creativity industrial development project" which composed of different department. This will be our first time regard abstract "the cultural software" as important national construction project. "Creative Taiwan" will plan for the future administration goal and the prospect. Not only creates the economic efficiency by the culture, but also has included the invisible value added. The cultural creativity industry's goal is conformity with place wisdom and the cultural art vitality, applies it in the industrial development by challenge in accordance to the globalized

Content including three directions: 1. cultural art core industry, 2. design industry, 3. creativity support and peripheral creativity industry. "The creativity support and the peripheral creativity industry" is one projects of cultural creativity industry; how to add "creativity" in the culture is the key point in the project of cultural creativity

N. Aykin (Ed.): Internationalization, Design, LNCS 5623, pp. 366–375, 2009.

industry. And assists each villages and towns development in the place culture creativity industry, promotes the place industry creativity economy the value.

2 Meaning of Culture Creativity Industry

In 1996 UNESCO declared that culture is the foundation of our progress. Culture represents a country art and accumulate characteristic of life's experience. Culture unifies into new inspiration and creation. By the creativity culture resources is representing connotation and characteristic of country culture. Definition UNESCO gives to cultural industries the union creation, the production and the commercial content. Based on this content essentially, have the intangible asset and the cultural concept characteristic, and obtains the protection of intellectual property rights, but presents by the product perhaps the service form. From the content, cultural industry may regard as the creative industries; or in the economic domain, named it future oriented industries; Or in the technology domain, named it content industries.

UNESCO mainly divides cultural creativity industry into three items: the cultural product, the cultural service and the intellectual property rights. Cultural product refers to books, magazine, multimedia products, software, CDs, movie, videotape, acousto-optic entertainment, craft and the fashion design. Cultural service included the performance (theater, opera house and circus troupe), publication, news newspaper, media and the construction service. They also include the seeing and hearing service (the movie to retail, the television/radio program and the home video; Production all stratification plane for example duplication and photographic printing; the movie displays, wired / satellite, with broadcasts the facility or the movie theater property rights and the operation and so on), library service, file, museum and other services.

In the new century cultural creativity industry is must strive. Across culture exchange and establishes a cultural creativity product though the communication. Become a kind of exchange that might be person to person, or person to thing. Takes advantage of this promotes Taiwan's industry, from OEM to ODM and finally, achieves OBM the goal. Enhances design can value up the price of product. By the culture adds the value design industry, homemade brand, promotion product value added, that is OBM as Figure 1 [2].

After modern global environment highly information, the invisible distance is smaller, the country and country's demarcation line gradual fuzziness, between the region the difference concept also receives gazes, people started to pay attention on the characteristic region culture. Creates the new style art of local, lets the residents approve the local culture, and promotes the competitive power, facing the globalized competition, keeps pace with the international culture. The world various countries also develop design style stressed that oneself culture characteristic, the cultural characteristic can strengthen the product difference, displays the local culture connotation. The creation product distinctive quality conforms to the modern design guidance expense environment.

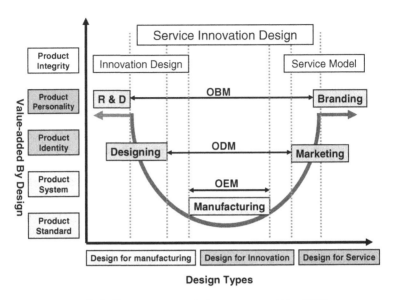

Fig. 1. Smile curve economical concept map (Lin, 2008)

3 Villages and Towns Designer's Impetus

Taiwan itself has the bright indigenous people culture, experienced, the Qing Dynasty Han nationality in the historical path to immigrate for the first time clearly. According to the time Japanese-style ideological trend style influence, the Kuomintang and Communist Parties war latter two Han nationality immigrants. In recent years has 'the foreign bride' to invest this land to pour into the new cultural element for Taiwan. Each time's fusion rendezvous, lets Taiwan have the rich historical culture connotation. Surrounding in many foreign culture exchanges in the historical evolutionary process, also lets Taiwan's cultural multi-dimensional diversification.

In 2006, Ministry of Economic Affairs sets at variance with again the structure way, the series connected national 319 villages' and towns' local characteristics industries, by most close to the daily life, arouses the people approval with yearned to Taiwan villages and towns characteristic product OTOP (One Town One Product). Various counties city are pondered in the literary arts activity's promotion, stressed on the local characteristic or custom festival celebration. Under "OTOP" background, promotes the expanded culture field of vision or the literary arts exchange international art festival; perhaps sightseeing of historical construction culture. Also by local folk custom culture art festival's characteristic and lively; or promotes in accordance to the season on behalf of the place industry culture characteristic agricultural special products takes the promotion.

Besides the seasonal agricultural product, should promote represents culture of commodity the local characteristics. From the cultural product's angle, the villages and towns may relate the place story to the client by Characteristic commodity. Lets the clients feel or the thorough experience understood that tradition of local, its history, manners and customs, and all related cultural event. For villages and towns, may condense the place the centripetal force, establishes to the cultural approval. May assist the place development, and attract people come to have sightseeing not only make economic developing, also brings the rich exterior resources. The resident can gain the sense of achievement and proud of this, and establishes the long-term marketing opportunity.

4 Culture and Design

By traditional culture's analysis, transforms its cultural connotation the creativity product

4.1 Cultural Commodity Design

Design is to all around, one kind of concise words which explodes not without reason to the world. The cultural product is the cultural element which contains in view of the cultural utensil or the cultural state itself, performs to carefully examine with examines thinks. The utilization design will have the cultural element, by conforms to present's new form development, and seeks the cultural depth energetic stratification plane satisfying.

Take historical cultural element to deduce carefully, might observe cultural characteristics then and so on life background, use way, and thought humanities. When commodity design joins the space and time background factor, lets the life have the exchange, the consumer approve the external life style to have the Trans-Culture study. The products contain the culture and using the design improves the life quality, promotes another kind of subconscious economy, and produces design way that we call "cultural design".

Leong [1] elaboration of visible product starts in the basic life, takes the connection by the social knowledge, finally is the energetic promotion, or material's localization and demand, after using product function values. This design itself gives the culture to produce into the valuable system, by a simple construction inspected the cultural utensil contains the cultural factor is for the discussion culture by the time and the spatial perspective drawing. In the different level and process which will mutually respond to cultural attribute.

Integration the above elaboration, its culture space division for the external level, the middle tones and the intrinsic level is approved gradually. Lin(2007) identified product attribute in three levels. By the local culture's symbolic significance and the life shape, are passing through the different level to transform become the different creativity style the cultural product.

Three cultural space levels, when product design must consider the factor, differentiate for the cultural product design attribute, like right side Figure 2 shows. Three attributes are:

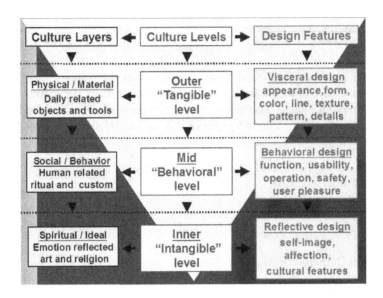

Fig. 2. Three layers and levels of cultural objects and design features (Lin, 2007)

1 External level: Including color, sense of reality, shape, superficial decorative design in a utensil, line, detail processing, component composition and so on.

2 Middle level: Covering function, operational, attributes, use convenience, security, associative relation and so on;

3 Internal level: product has special meaning, story. It has sentiment and cultural special characteristic and so on. Figure 2 cultural level, the cultural space and the culture product design attribute comparison, may take the culture product design the reference.

The cultural commodity is the cultural element which contains in view of the utensil itself performs to carefully examine thinks with the province. Utilization of design, seeks its cultural element the new modern appearance, and seeks energetic stratification plane satisfying which the utensil uses. This is the difference between cultural commodity and general commodity, lay in its culture identity function.

The cultural product's design should also have its design pattern and procedure. The designer must investigates to the cultural representation and meaning, then aims at its visible, cultural attributes and so on material, use behavior, ceremony custom, consciousness state, invisible spirit, carries on design preparatory works and acquisition of information, analysis, synthesis such stuff. When the design enters sends thinks stage, utilizes each kind method to inspire the idea and design technique, by design appropriate cultural news expression on product, achieves the consumer depth expectation, triggers its use demand. Finally, by interpretation of cultural cognition, designer projects own experience emotion on the product, arouses user's sympathy, but achieves the satisfied emotion demand.

5 Pingtung County Villages and Towns Designer Designs Model

Pingtung County chief advocated with all strength the Pingtung characteristic culture and sightseeing industry, also promote community overall building, development tribe, community's characteristic industry. Cultural Affairs director takes administration goal from chief magistrate's policy that is culture place expansion development to the community overall building development, and place cultural building, industry and industrial culture, the cultural voluntary worker and each literary arts activity promotes. By the cultural design's method, hoped that the Pingtung County villages' and towns' cultural connotation will display in the Pingtung County villages and towns characteristic commodity design, this part of students' instruction creates by work together and introduction will as following figures:

5.1 Safety Key Holder (Fig. 3.)

Share and build safe fun for the family, pray for blessings with the image of supporting each other, with kind phoenix being palace letter all to send heart donate mercy shielded and sustained to fail as take place, think, combine tile and special of temple, design one group have, pray for blessings key shelf that purpose call, utilize tile keyring movement of furnishing with shelf take in, representatives utilize the tiles, the ones that built and built up are safe. And while sticking by transparent major parts of kinsfolks, choose oneself the role at home sticks the paper, stick it on the tile, represent traditional united strength of family of Taiwan, and Mazu's blessing.

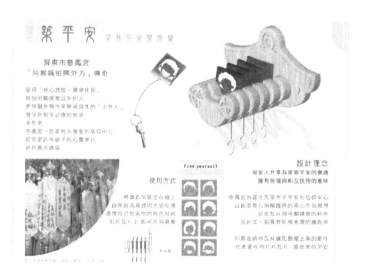

Fig. 3. Safety Key holder

5.2 Safety Water Bottle (Fig. 4.)

The east grand palace cook Wang Ye ship well-known whole Taiwan, ship Taiwan's Wang Ye to hold a memorial ceremony for allusion quotation, undertake the mission of praying for blessings, subduing the calamity, solving strategic point, by sending the ship ceremony ceremoniously, ask gods to assist and bless, sees the strategic point of the calamity off as gods will leave, make the people receive better life. In the conversion of cultural meaning, borrowed by the metaphor and the tactics of analogizing display the model of the kettle and inherent cultural meaning, make image their interesting to transform ' quench one's thirst ' from function of a original one ' solve strategic point ' bicycle with kettle it. The image transforms to the city street at the same time, gallop speeds in the wind with the bicycle, kettle like the Taiwan's Wang Ye ship form like throw, move all all worried sorrow of people with fair wind on the sea. Respond the long bicycle activity popularized of Cao County at the same time, save the earth resource.

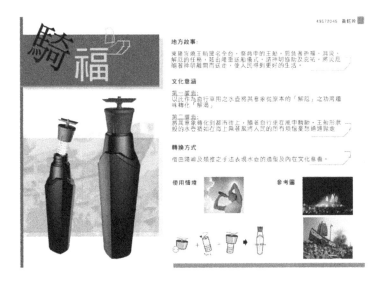

Fig. 4. Safety water bottle

5.3 Rice Field Plate (Fig. 5.)

Writer teach in " whether car pass square-column small house ", fertile meaning of capital of fruit image on behalf of poem of the over light, regard " tired " conceptual design of word as the fruit ware, incorporate poesy in the products, let people who call on the square-column small house take poesy home! This cultural image is changed and changed by a spiritual level image, the technique of expression, in order to reproduce the poem scene on the fruit ware, by using the fruit ware, let users experience poem justice. Propose sugarcane conversion of image, can put into the toothpick, it is convenient to use.

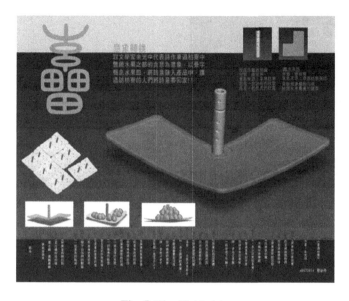

Fig. 5. Rice Field plate

5.4 Parachute Hunger (Fig. 6.)

Because the parachute of the normality trains the number of times intensively, often the people stop and view and admire, and pay attention to a paratrooper and become the most special sign in road safety of Taiwan. Around fish, sesame oil woods stand, let, drop from the air, train challenging, hang with parachute jumping fault of interest upside down tree Italy picture of hair change; And the paratrooper is for attacking the front of defending of country's army, generally enter the first outpost of the tax office

Fig. 6. Parachute hunger

Fig. 7. Tea cup

on the door like the stores pylon hanging on the door. Works this " hang almost " combine stores pylon with hang upside down tree paratrooper Italy picture of head come, change a door with interest stores pylon goods.

5.5   Tea Cup (Fig. 7.)

1. Teacup: Hope not to forget the culture of the hometown in the drink tea.
2. Rub: Study and receive a training, all need to temper and grow up from us constantly.
3. Black: Archaism say ' one stomach ink ' say this people dark rich intension, have much literature attainments.

Fig. 8. Wang Ye ship

4. Poem: Good at neglecting delineating such one ' family property outside inside hardworkingly playing, it is destroyed in and up to that a deed is accomplished through taking thought. ' verse that Han Yu burns.

5.6 Wang Ye Ship (Fig. 8.)

The design turn into pray for activity to set up decreasing amplitude gradually already now, but still there is thick pestilence god's color. Utilize, cook ship Taiwan's Wang Ye take away image of pestilence come getting to display line spices flat perfume sent out, take the bad smell in the environment away by this; Or the brightness brought of candle stand ' burns ', it is dark to take away. Appearance develop, can display, cook global image of ship Taiwan's Wang Ye event more by appearance of ship Taiwan's Wang Ye directly.

References

1. Leong, B.D.: Culture-Based Knowledge Towards New Design Thinkingand Practice – A Dialogue. Design Issues 19, 48–58 (2003)
2. Lin, R.T.: Service Innovation Design for Cultural and Creative Industries – A Case Study of the Cultural and Creative Industry Park at NTUA. In: International Service Innovation Design Conference 2008, Dongseo University, Korea, October 20-22, 2008, pp. 14–25 (2008) (keynote speech)
3. Lin, R.T.: Transforming Taiwan Aboriginal Cultural Features Into Modern Product Design: A Case Study of Cross Cultural Product Design Model. International Journal of Design 1(2), 45–53 (2007)

A Study of Service Innovation Design in Cultural and Creative Industry

Yu-Yuan Ko[1], Po-Hsien Lin[2], and Rungtai Lin[2]

[1] Department of Industrial Education and Technology,
National Changua University of Education
N0 516, Chung Shan Rd, Sec 2, Huatan Village,Changhua county, 503, Taiwan
service@jaguarcar.com.tw
[2] Crafts and Design Department, National Taiwan University of Art
Ban Ciao City, Taipei, 220, Taiwan
rtlin@mail.ntua.edu.tw

Abstract. Service design is considered to be one of the pivotal components in cultural and creative design industries which has a significant impact on consumer perception of innovation. Despite service design's recognized importance, cultural and creative industries lack a systematic approach to it. Therefore, based on the "Taiwan experience", this paper proposes a service innovation design model and provides examples illustrating how to transfer cultural features into service design, and design these cultural features into modern products to reinforce their design value. Results presented herein create an interface for looking at the way service innovation design crosses over cultures, as well as illustrating the interwoven experience of service design and cultural creativity in the innovation design process.

Keywords: service innovation design, creative industries, experiencing culture.

1 Introduction

There has been a recent shift from technological innovation to service innovation based on discovering new opportunities in the marketplace. Companies are more focused on adapting new technologies and combining them in ways that create new experiences and value for customers. With the development of industrial tendency, most companies gradually realize that the keys to product innovation are not only market and technology aspects but also service innovation design [2,4,12]. Ulrich and Pearson [25] point out that service design has received increased attention in the academic and business communities over the past decade. Both academics and practitioners emphasized that the role of service design in innovative product development relates not only to aesthetics, but also to aspects such as ergonomics, user-friendliness, efficient use of materials, functional performance [8].

However, we now live in a small world with a large global market. While the market heads toward "globalization", design tends toward "localization." So we must "think globally" for the market, but "act locally" for design. In the global market - local design era, connections between culture and design have become increasingly close. For

N. Aykin (Ed.): Internationalization, Design, LNCS 5623, pp. 376–385, 2009.
© Springer-Verlag Berlin Heidelberg 2009

service design, cultural value-adding creates the core of product value. It's the same for culture; service design is the motivation for pushing cultural and creative industries development forward [17, 18, 19]. While service innovation design is under tough competitive pressure from the developing global market, it seems that the local design should be focused on "service" to adapt "innovation" to product "design."

The importance of studying service innovation design is shown repeatedly in several studies in all areas of the design field. Despite the recognized importance of service design in cultural and creative design industries, they lack a systematic approach to it. Therefore, the main purpose of this paper is to study factors affecting service innovation design. These factors are discussed in order to understand the change of service innovation design in cultural and creative design industries [28].

A service innovation design approach is proposed which integrates the difference between products and services of cultural and creative design industries into the service innovation design activities of current service development practice. A model is then provided illustrating how the National Taiwan University of Arts (NTUA) has established the link between service innovation design and cultural and creative industries through Our Museum, Our Studio and Our Factory respectively. It is the service innovation design approach that joins design, culture, creativities and economy, and further illustrates some implications through the cultural perspective.

2 The Change of Service Innovation Design

A literature review summary on innovation and service design is presented. From a design point of view, we examined previous studies on innovation design and the concepts used. There is no widely agreed definition of service design in the literature [1, 5, 6, 7, 13, 14, 20, 26, 27]. Through the review, it was noted that no matter what the interpretations for service design were, it was agreed to be crucial to the overall service development process [28]. However, we will discuss the change of service innovation design from the design point of view as follows.

2.1 From "Function" to "Feeling" in Design History

In the early 20th century, when users thought about "design", "form follows function" often came to mind. Today, the technology progress has shifted dramatically and provides platforms for completely new forms of "design" and "service" delivery. Now, we communicate with our friends using a cell phone (design) or plan and buy a trip around the world using the internet (service). From a design point of view, we could use five "Fs" to describe the change from designing "function" for the user's need to servicing "feeling" for the user's pleasure as shown in Figure 1. These five F's include: (1) 1930's – design for "Function", (2) 1950's - design for "Friendly", (3) 1970's - design for "Fun", (4) 1990's - design for "Fancy", and (50) 2001's - design for "Feeling", respectively [17,18].

Along with the technology progress, if we examine the design history of the last century, we find "form follows function" to be the motto to design for function, and dominated design conceptualization. After world war II, the new discipline of human factors was introduced and the concept of "design for human use" applied to product design. The concept of "user friendly" become common sense with the popularity of the PC in the commercial market. In the 1970's, talking too much about "function" and "friendly" in designing products became boring, and some designers tried designing "Fun" into the product. The application of post-modernism in the design field is a typical example of designing for fun. Then, in the 1990s, designers tried designing "fancy" into their design based on advance technology such as concurrent engineering or RPT (Rapid Prototyping Technology).and the concept of product personality became a tool for differentiating the market.

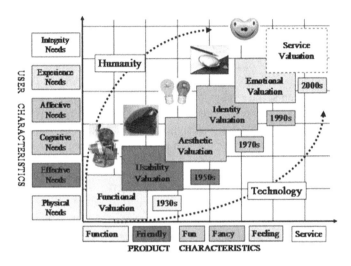

Fig. 1. The change of innovation design from "function" to "feeling"

Finally, designing "Feeling" into products to present the emotional communication of user experiences become a design trend in the 21st century. As a result, "design for feeling" became the key factor for innovative products. In other words, the product must be endowed with an immediate attraction and this therefore renders user perception of innovative product form an important issue for "pleasure" [9, 10, 11]. In Figure 1, we use a pencil sharpener as an example to demonstrate the change from "design for function" to "design for feeling".

This change of service in innovation design has also created even more complex organizations and systems of service delivery to satisfy user needs. The users not only need the 5 Fs but also innovation service for their integrity needs. The only way to deal with this complexity is to keep user needs and desires central to any design development. Indeed, service innovation design is part of the solution to this challenge, with deep user involvement throughout the creative process and a keen view of the functional and emotional details that enable people to enjoy the services that are important in their lives [26, 27].

2.2   From OEM to OBM in Taiwan Design Development

Taiwan's industrial design is developing along with its economic development. The design development could be represented as a smile face, proposed by the former ACER president Shi, from OEM (Original Equipment Manufacture), ODM (Original Design Manufacture), to OBM (Original Brand Manufacture) as shown in Figure 2. Before 1980, OEM vendors in Taiwan reduced costs to produce "cheap and fine" products to be successful in the global manufacturing industry. With the OEM style of having "cost" but without a concept of " price" in mind, or just by knowing " cost down" but not knowing " value up", these vendors created Taiwan's economic miracle by earning a low profit from manufacturing. Those dependent upon hard-working patterns from the OEM pattern became obstacles in developing their own design. These vendors were extremely busy producing products to meet manufacturing deadlines; there was no time to develop design capabilities, so that environment could not nurture design talents [17, 19].

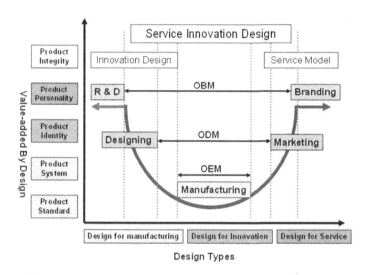

Fig. 2. From OEM to OBM in Taiwan design development

After 1980, Taiwan enterprises began to develop ODM (Original Design Manufacture) patterns to extend their advantages in OEM manufacturing. Taiwan's government addressed a series of measures to stimulate the nation's economic growth, including the "Production Automation Skill Guidance Plan", and the "Assisting Domestic Traditional Industrial Skill Plan". These plans were to guide vendors to make production improvements, to lower costs and to increase competition. Especially starting from 1989, the industry Bureau pushed the "Plan for total Upgrading of industrial Design Capability" within three consecutive five-year plans to build up working models of experienced design scholars from universities and their students to work on designs. The design students worked with the enterprises on specific projects to set up a working pattern of industrial design based on enterprises' real needs [17, 18, 19].

Recently, product design in Taiwan has stepped into the OBM (Original Brand Manufacture) era. In addition, cultural and creative industries have already been incorporated into the "National Development Grand Plan", demonstrating the government's eagerness to transform Taiwan's economic development by "Branding Taiwan" using "Taiwan Design" based on Taiwanese culture [17, 18, 19]. Designing "culture" into modern products will be a design trend in the global market. Obviously, we need a better understanding of service innovation design in cultural and creative design industries not only for the global market but also for local design. While cross-cultural factors become important issues for product design in the global economy, the intersection of service innovation design and culture becomes a key issue making both local design and the global market worthy of further in-depth study as shown in Figure 2.

2.3   From" 3Cs" to" 4Cs" in Taiwan Industry Development

In the past, Taiwan developed information technology to produce hi-tech 3Cs products as "Computer", "Communication", and "Consumer" electronic products and many related accessories. As mentioned above, Taiwan's economic miracle was promoted by small enterprises through the hard working spirit and cheap labor of the people. But all these advantages have been replaced by China in recent years. If Taiwan still wants to play a role in the global economy, it should establish a Taiwanese cultural brand. Besides its skill leverage, it has to cover both ODM and OBM, which is the purpose of promoting cultural and creative industries from the service innovation design point of view. Therefore, the required change in Taiwan's design industry structure is to maintain its cost down advantage, to reinforce design value up and to seek service innovation design in cultural and creative design industries [17, 18].

Cultural and creative design industries are the "4Cs" industries: "Cultural", "Collective", "Cheerful" and "Creative". The 4Cs will be a design evaluation key point in the future. Many countries that are major in design popularity are promoting service as design as part of cultural and creative design industries. Taking England as an example, service design has been the second highest output value of their creativity industry. The potential market is quite large. In the knowledge economy era, the connections between culture and industry have been increasingly close.

Designing local features into a product appears to be more and more important in the global market where products are losing their identity because of the similarity in their function and form. Cultural features then are considered to be a unique character to embed into a product both for the enhancement of product identity in the global market and for the fulfillment of the individual consumer's experiences [15, 16]. The increasing emphasis on localized cultural development in Taiwan demonstrates an ambition to promote the Taiwanese style in the global economic market. However, in order to reach this purpose, some changes need to be made in Taiwan's industry structure. If we can mix cultural concepts with diverse service innovation design to make art livable, then we can create a new design model of cultural and creative design industries and become culturally industrialized to highlight Taiwan's international image.

3 Conceptual Framework

National Taiwan University of Arts (NTUA) established an art museum, known as "Our Museum", in 2007 for the purpose of linking professional teaching with the museum's research, education, and display functions while presenting cultural and aesthetic ideas about art and artifacts to the public. Developing craftsmanship and creativity as well as competences related to the arts are of strategic importance to NTUA. For turning "Art" to "Business", we need "Creativity" and "Design" [24]. Therefore, a design studio, known as "Our Studio", was set up at the college of design in NTUA following the "Our Museum" for providing innovative products. NTUA is located in the Taipei metropolitan area, one of the most competitive regions in Taiwan. This area contains a significant concentration of craftsmanship and research establishments, linked by various formal and informal networks. Due to the challenging nature of cultural and creative industries, NTUA is devoted to developing its regional and international networks by operating a cultural and creative industry park, known as "Our Factory." NTUA has established the link between "Art" and "Business" and combined "Creativity" and "Design" through Our Museum, Our Studio and Our Factory respectively. It is a new approach that integrates design, culture, artistic craftsmanship, creativities and service innovation design in cultural and creative design industries [23].

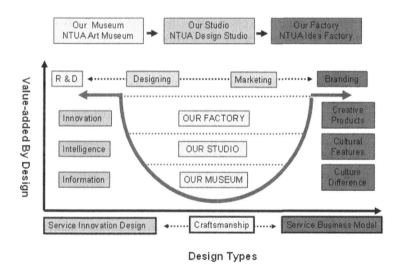

Fig. 3. A conceptual framework for service innovation design

With increasing globalization of the economy, rapidly developing information technology, rapidly growing market competition, shortening life cycles of products and services, and increasing customer demands, companies and public sector actors will find it increasingly difficult to survive just on their past operating models. Therefore, based on the previous review of service design change, we propose a conceptual framework to innovation service design of cultural and creative design industries by using the smile paradigm as shown in Figure 3.

According to the smile paradigm, craftsmanship is a part of Cultural creativity, and like the mouth in the smile face, it must still go up through innovation deign and branding before it can become a "business". However, craftsmanship is not the entirety of culture, nor is creativity the whole of business; good craftsmanship at best earns outsourcing money, like an OEM vendor. The key to innovation design is to blend craftsmanship, creativity and service design, and "branding" is the key to any business [21].

In general, craftsmanship is the use of local materials to develop localized skills; localization is an important force behind the globalization of any international conglomerate, especially in the employment of cultural creativity. Crafted products produced in small volume seek to represent the spirit of "attention to details", and are a demand on the person, a representation of the person, an expression by the person, and a story from the person. Craftsmanship plumbs the depth of skills, while creativity seeks the height of impression, and branding asks for the width of acceptance. Only through culture and creativity, by allowing craftsmanship and creativity to facilitate branding, can one makes one's way in this field [22].

The goal of the cultural and creative park is to combine artistic craftsmanship and economy with service design, and ultimately establish NTUA as a distinctive trademark of the park. To accomplish this goal, NTUA aims to combine artistic craftsmanship from "Our Museum" with cultural creativities from "Our Studio" in order to result in aesthetics in business for "Our Factory". Creativity and business are the elements for reaching an aesthetic economy. It is the concept of "Think Globally - Act Locally" to process the "Digital Archive" of Our Museum through the cultural creativities of Our Studio, producing cultural products in Our Factory in order to establish a local industry making aesthetic and economical products.

The current development of the Cultural Creative Park at NTUA is based on using creative knowledge of crafts elements and materials from Our Museum and, through Our Studio to transform this cultural information into creative industry. In the near future, we will further practice this exclusive mode of cultural creative production to promote the "Savoring Culture", forming "Taiwan industry concept". We are encouraging more and more creative products which contain colorful Taiwanese culture and styles. By supporting the development of cultural creative industry of NTUA, we can enjoy the fruitful success of an aesthetic culture in creative industry.

4   Experiential Journey to the NTUA Cultural and Creative Park

To accomplish this goal, NTUA has taken public education as a commitment since its beginning. One example is the establishment of the *Taiwanese UFO* Cultural Creative Park, known as "Our Factory", with the cooperation of Taipei County providing an innovation service by the *Holiday Cultural Bus Tour*. The *Holiday Cultural Bus Tour* is operated between NTUA main campus, the *Taiwanese UFO Cultural Creative Park,* and t*he Lin Family Mansion and Garden*. The major purpose is to prompt the cultural creative development of Banciao City where the University is located. The tour journeys first to The Lin Family Mansion and Garden for experiencing cultural aesthetics. Then, based on the structure of *Our Museum, Our Studio* and *Our Factory* of NTUA, the tour customer can appreciate arts in *Our Museum,* experience crafts in *Our Studio,* and also purchase creative products from *Our Factory*. The purpose of this customer journey is to fulfill the aesthetic experience by connecting design and culture through which to synthesize technology, humanity, cultural creativities, and thus achieve the aim of service design promotion in public.

The *Taiwanese UFO Cultural Creative Park* is established by NTUA in the Fu-Jhou suburb of Banciao City, only ten minutes walk from the main campus. UFO is an abbreviation for "high quality Fu-Jhou suburb" in Chinese and it also describes the *Taiwanese UFO Cultural Creative Park*. There are four crafts companies which are incorporated with the Innovation and Incubation Center of NTUA. Within additional ceramic and metal studios, each studio provides hands-on workshops in different craft materials. The public can physically understand and experience fascinating crafts of ceramic, glass, metal, and fabric.

NTUA has taken the commitment of improving Taiwanese cultural qualities. The *Taiwanese UFO Cultural Creative Park* is a significant step to benefit the surrounding area. Many exclusive projects are under construction by NTUA. We are expecting a fulfilling aesthetic environment in the near future.

5 Conclusion

With increasing global competition, service innovation design is not merely desirable for a company; rather, it is mandatory. The importance of studying service innovation design is shown repeatedly in several studies in all design areas. However, there is a lack of a systematic approach that covers service design in cultural and creative design industries. Therefore, a new approach was proposed by applying service innovation design to the domain of cultural and creative design industries. The service innovation design model is presented herein to provide designers with a valuable reference for designing "service" into a successful cross-cultural product. The purpose of this paper is to fulfill the aesthetic experience by connecting design and culture, through which to synthesize technology, humanity, cultural creativities, and then, achieve the aim of service design promotion in public.

For future studies, we need a better understanding of the acculturation process not only for the service design, but also for innovative product design. While cultural features become important issues in the interactive experiences of users, the acculturation process between human and culture becomes a key issue in cultural product design and worthy of further in-depth study. However, the effectiveness of using service innovation design in cultural and creative industries can be further enhanced. This can be done by incorporating more information of the best practices in service industries into the service innovation design in cultural and creative design industries.

Acknowledgments. The authors gratefully acknowledge the support for this research provided by the National Science Council under Grants No. NSC-97-2410-H-144-005. The authors wish to thank the various students who have contributed to this study over the years. Especially, the authors would like to thank Dr. J. G. Kreifeldt for his valuable comments.

References

1. Berkley, B.J.: Designing services with function analysis. Hospitality Research Journal 20(1), 73–100 (1996)
2. Baxter, M.: Product design: a practical guide to systematic methods of new product development. Chapman & Hall, London (1995)
3. Chuang, M.C., Ma, Y.C.: Expressing the expected product images in product design of mirco-electronic products. International Journal of Industrial Ergonomics 27, 233–245 (2001)
4. Crawford, C.M., Benedetto, C.A.D.: New Product Management, 6th edn., pp. 10–11. Irwin, McGraw-Hill (2000)
5. Edvardsson, B., Thomasson, B., Øvretveit, J.: Quality of service: Making it really work. McGraw-Hill Book Company, London (1994)
6. Gummesson, E.: Nine lessons on service quality. The Total Quality Management Magazine 1(2), 82–90 (1989)
7. Gummesson, E.: Qualitative methods in management research. Sage Publications, Newbury Park (1991)
8. Gemser, G., Leenders, M.: How integrating industrial design in the product development process impacts on company performance. The Journal of Product Innovation Management 18, 28–38 (2001)
9. Hekkert, P., Leder, H.: Product aesthetics. In: Schifferstein, H.N.J., Hekkert, P. (eds.) Product experience, pp. 259–286. Elsevier, San Diego (2008)
10. Hekkert, P., Snelders, D., van Wieringen, P.C.W.: Most advanced, yet acceptable: Typicality and novelty as joint predictors of aesthetic preference in industrial design. British Journal of Psychology 94(1), 111–124 (2003)
11. Helander, M.G., Tham, M.P.: Hedonomics-Affective human factors design. Ergonomics 46(13/14), 1269–1272 (2003)
12. Johnson, S.P., Menor, L.J., Roth, A.V., Chase, R.B.: A critical evaluation of the new service development process: Integrating service innovation and service design. In: Fitzsimmons, J.A., Fitzsimmons, M.J. (eds.) New Service Development: Creating memorable experiences, Sage Publications, Thousand Oaks (2000)
13. Langeard, E., Reffiat, P., Eiglier, P.: Developing new services. In: VenKantesan, M., Schmalensee, D.M., Marshall, C. (eds.) Creativity in services marketing: What's new what works, what's developing, American Marketing Association, Chicago (1986)
14. Laurea University of Applied Sciences: Service innovation and design. Laurea Communications (2007),
http://www.laurea.fi, http://servicedesign.laurea.fi/
15. Lee, K.P.: Design methods for cross-cultural collaborative design project. In: Redmond, J., Durling, D., De Bono, A. (eds.) Proceedings of Design Research Society International Conference, Paper #135, DRS Futureground, Monash University, Australia (2004)
16. Leong, D., Clark, H.: Culture -based knowledge towards new design thinking and practice - A dialogue. Design Issues 19(3), 48–58 (2003)
17. Lin, R.T.: Transforming Taiwan Aboriginal Cultural Features Into Modern Product Design – A Case Study of Cross Cultural Product Design Model. International Journal of Design 1(2), 45–53 (2007)
18. Lin, R., Cheng, R., Sun, M.-X.: Digital Archive Database for Cultural Product Design. In: Aykin, N. (ed.) HCII 2007. LNCS, vol. 4559, pp. 154–163. Springer, Heidelberg (2007)

19. Lin, R., Sun, M.-X., Chang, Y.-P., Chan, Y.-C., Hsieh, Y.-C., Huang, Y.-C.: Designing "Culture" into Modern Product: A Case Study of Cultural Product Design. In: Aykin, N. (ed.) HCII 2007. LNCS, vol. 4559, pp. 146–153. Springer, Heidelberg (2007)
20. Martin, C.R., Horne, D.A.: Services innovation: Successful versus unsuccessful firms. International Journal of Service Industry Management 4(1), 49–65 (1993)
21. Ravasi, D., Lojacono, G.: Managing design and designers for strategic renewal. Long range planning 38, 51–77 (2005)
22. Robertson, T.S.: The process of innovation and the diffusion of innovation. Journal of Marketing 31, 14–19 (1976)
23. Roy, R., Riedel, J.: Design and innovation in successful product competition. Technovation 17, 537–548 (1997)
24. Stevens, G., Burley, J., Divine, R.: Creativity + business disciplines = higher profits faster from new product development. Journal of Product Innovation Management 16, 455–468 (1999)
25. Ulrich, K.T., Pearson, S.: Assessing the importance of design through product archaeology. Management Science 44, 352–369 (1998)
26. Veryzer, R.W.: Discontinuous innovation and the new product development process. Journal of Product Innovation Management 15, 304–321 (1998)
27. Voss, C., Zomerdijk, L.: Innovation in Experiential Services – An Empirical View. In: DTI (ed.) Innovation in Services, pp. 97–134. DTI, London (2007)
28. Zhang, J., Tan, K.C., Chai, K.H.: Systematic Innovation in Service Design Through TRIZ. In: The Proceedings of the EurOMA-POMS 2003 Annual Conference, Cernobbio, Lake Como, Italy, June 16-18, 2003, vol. 1, pp. 1013–1022 (2003)

The Impact of Culture on the Design of Arabic Websites

Aaron Marcus[1] and Sundus Hamoodi[2]

[1] Aaron Marcus and Associates, Inc., 1196 Euclid Avenue, Suite 1F, Berkeley,
CA 94708 USA
Aaron.Marcus@AMandA.com
www.AMandA.com
[2] Arab Academy for Banking and Financial Science,
Faculty of Information Systems and Technology
P.O. Box 13190, Amman 11942, Jordan
SundusHamodi@Yahoo.com

Abstract. This paper discusses issues regarding the influence of culture on Arabic Websites. Arabic Websites from three countries serve as an initial sample for this study. Do the Websites of Arabian countries reflect their culture? How specifically? Do they share attitudes about design? Can an Arabian designer achieve what users in other cultures need and want? What are differences reflected in the differences between Arabic countries in the Eastern world and Western countries? This paper discusses these and other issues.

Keywords: Arabic, culture, design, interface, user, Website.

1 Introduction

In this study, we analyze selected Websites from different Arabic countries that may provide fundamental concepts for analyzing most other Arabic Websites. There is a little ambiguity among the terms Arab, Arabic, and Arabian. We shall generally use the term Arabic, pertaining to the language, but also the culture. We start with three Arabic countries (Jordan, Egypt, and the United Arab Emirates, or UAE). We plan to expand our research in the future to include other Arabic countries.

We consider different educational Websites and analyze them according to a combination of Geert Hofstede's theory of culture dimensions with one of the author's (Aaron Marcus') theory of user-interface components [3]. We follow the assumptions about culture markers that Marcus introduced in previous studies [4, 5].

1.1 Hofstede's Model of Culture

One of the culture models more widely used by researchers and Web designers is Hofstede's model [2]. Hofstede formulated his model of culture dimensions based on surveys and interviews with several hundred IBM employees, originally in 53 countries during (1978-1983), since expanded to 74 countries in the second edition of his book describing his theory. Using his survey, augmented by later studies, Hofstede determined

N. Aykin (Ed.): Internationalization, Design, LNCS 5623, pp. 386–394, 2009.

pattern of similarities and differences in how signs, rituals, heroes/heroines, and values are expressed by group members. Hofstede's culture dimensions, or indices, are the following:

Power Distance: high *vs.* low.
Individuality: high *vs.* low (i. e., Collectivist).
Uncertainty Avoidace: high *vs.* low.
Gender Role Differences: masculinity *vs.* femininity.
Time Orientation: long-term *vs.* short-term.

1.2 Marcus' Model of User Interfaces

Human-computer interface designers try to determine the most usable (effective, efficient, and satisfying, according to the definition of the International Standards Organization in Geneva) means to communicate the functions and data, or tools and content, of computer-based media. Every phase of development must consider users' needs, wants, requirements, and expectations. The development tasks (essentially verbs modeled on software development tasks) include planning, researching, analyzing, designing, implementing, evaluating, documenting, training, and maintaining. Ultimately, these tasks must account for the cultural attributes of the target market of users. Marcus developed five essential components (or nouns) of user-centered, user-interface development. Those components are useful in all stages of development:

Metaphors: Essential concepts conveyed through images, words, sounds, touches, and even smells.

Mental model: Organization of data, functions, content, tools, tasks, roles, and people.

Navigation: Techniques of moving through the mental model, such as links, buttons, dialogue boxes, panels, and windows.

Interaction: Techniques of input, output, and the overall behavior of systems.

Presentation: Visual appearance characteristics, such as typography, color, layout, sequencing; verbal characteristics, tactile characteristics, sonic characteristics, and aromatic characteristics.

1.3 Objectives of the Study

This paper has several objectives:

Analyze Arabic Websites in three different Arabic countries in order to determine whether or not the Websites reflect Arabic culture.

Stimulate discussion and the sharing of ideas among Arabic designers.

Help designers to design for users and to compare these designs with others from different countries, including non-Arabic.

Formulate guidelines that help not only Arabic Website developers, but also non-Arabic Website developers, if they need to localize their Websites for Arabic users.

2   Arabic Websites

The following examples show Arabic Websites and comment on the culture factors that seem to have influenced their design. Following the discussion of individual sites, comparisons of the sites elaborate on similarities and differences.

Fig. 1. Egypt: Cairo University, http://www.cu.edu.eg

The Websites of Figures 1 and 2, which are similar in design to most Arabic educational Websites, seem to have simple user-interface components. The primary images, located prominently on the Website, show official buildings, and the official seal of the university, which represents the university's history and importance. These two components are typical elements of university Websites.

There are many notable characteristics. The Website of Figure 1 seems to emphasize team management, not individuals, with less authentication and password apparatus. The site also contains much detailed information that seems to meet the needs of high-uncertainty-avoidance users, who may need more information resources to be comfortable. The site distinguishes itself as a goal-oriented Web site, because it focuses on employee and student skills-development. The Website helps the user to obtain all information he/she needs. The official university logo reflects the historical background of the country and the civilization. This connotation may satisfy those who which wish to emphasize high-power orientation and perhaps to emphasize a long-term time orientation. The colors of the Website are dark, and the Website seems to reflect a strong masculine orientation.

Many links and menus can found in this Website. The orientation of the site towards tasks and roles may reveal a masculine Website. Full information, easy navigation, and easy access to information all help to clarify the user's understanding of the site and provide a strong incentive to remain at the Website.

Fig. 2. Jordan: Al-Zaytoonah University, http://www.alzaytoonah.edu.jo

Fig. 3. Jordan: Applied Science University: http://aspu.edu.jo

Like many similar university Websites, the images of this university architecture and a logo in Figure 3 represent the university's history and importance. The metaphorical references to the university are simple and clear: university monuments and laboratories. The Website does not provide a challenge to the user; rather it reflects a calm experience, through its color and relative simplicity. Throughout the Website, there are many pictures of the university's leaders, but these do not appear in the Home page. There also seem to be many distinct passwords mentioned, but they do not interfere with rapidly exploring the content. Passwords generally indicate a high power-distance value, with some moderation in this site.

The mental model seems clear, and the content is classified, organized, and distributed effectively throughout the Website. For example, a section offers answers to frequently asked questions. Menus presented in a clear way help the user to keep in control and navigate effectively. This Website seems to emphasize concern with social issues and culture, satisfying people with high uncertainty-avoidance.

The site could be classified as a long-term time-orientation Website, because it maintains its relation with students who have graduated. In addition, the site allows users to deliver their questions and opinions through E-mail in different ways. This feature emphasizes the Website as more interactive. The Web served the individualism for both students and other users, and it could be considered as a task-oriented Website.

Fig. 4. Jordan: Al Isra University: http://www.Isra.edu.jo

The Website of Fig. 4 displays a logo that represents the university's importance at the top right side. The mental model has is richly categorized and deeply structured. Many links and menus appear in the Home page to help with navigation. There are issues of security, as indicated by offering the option of restricting access (for university students and employees) in this Website.

Fig. 5. United Arab Emirates (UAE): Zayed University: http://www.zu.ac.ae

This site appears masculine in design because of its orientation towards tasks and roles. The primary colors used for this website are white and blue.

The Home page in Figure 5 shows an image of leaders along with multimedia animation effects. What makes this site different is that the university specializes in female students; therefore, images of female students appear on the Home page.

The well-designed site in Figure 5 is accessed with fewer authentication and password rituals, unless they are necessary, making it seem less high power-distance oriented. The links to internal and external Websites seem easily found and selected, making navigation easy. The links or menus provide a clear hierarchy and complete information, making the site suitable for high-uncertainty- avoidance users. Visitors can reach any information and functions they require. Multimedia effects found at the site seem suitable for a wide range of visitors. The primary colors of the Website are red and white. The only language used in the Website is English, which may be a barrier to some Arabic-speaking students.

3 Comparisons of the Websites

3.1 General Observations

Some general observations about these Websites are the following:

According to [1], Callahan's study of university Website design, most university Websites have a banner with the name of the university, a university logo and/or university seal, and images of university buildings and people. Most of the universities treat the Website as a visible representation of their values, and of their "products", namely, students and education. Therefore, Callahan found strong similarities in Website design across countries within this single genre. The authors found educational Arabic Websites shared these characteristics with most university Websites.

Most Arabic Websites also shared the characteristic of reflecting high power- distance through the pictures, the structure or organization of the design, and access to information. The authors also found similarities in the way the sites offer navigation through links and menus to reach different internal pages and external sites.

In terms of individualism or collectivism, it appears that most of the Arabic Websites studied gave more attentions to individuals than to groups, which is somewhat atypical, perhaps arising from the educated community of users.

Arabic university Websites may use different languages (Arabic and/or English). The English-language usage raises the question of whether the language presents a barrier to local Arabic visitors or not, especially if the design is only in English.

Graphics (images) appear in most of these Arabic university Web sites. They are not purely text-oriented.

3.2 Use of Color

Color is an essential characteristic of appearance that is influenced by culture. According to Callahan [1] in the study "Cultural Similarities and Differences in the Design of University Websites," Callahan made the following observations:

In Malaysian sites, a white background was commonly chosen in (17 sites), but in three other cases, the background was purple or blue.

Swedish sites displayed a strong preference, also, for a white background (18 sites). Colors were used carefully as a background for links. Blue and yellow, the Swedish national colors are a frequent theme, in addition to grey, purple, pink, and dark red.

In Greek university Websites, two color schemes are often used. Nine Websites were designed in various shades of blue. 11 Websites used various shades of brown and yellow, and many of those sites used ancient Greek art as a central visual theme of the page design. Only two sites displayed brighter, livelier colors.

In the present study of Arabic university Websites, two color schemes seem to dominate, the use of blue and green, which is a frequent theme of Arabic visual communication. A white background was also commonly chosen for Arabic Web sites.

3.3 Mental Model or Information Architecture

In regard to the mental model, or the structure of content, Callahan [1] found that two of the most important criteria of Web design are page orientation (horizontal *vs.* vertical) and the number of links existing within the pages. Regarding orientation, Austria and Denmark have a preference for horizontal page design, while Japan and Malaysia have a preference for a vertical layout. The current study shows that most of Arabic university Website pages use a horizontal orientation and a large number of links within the Website.

4 Conclusions and Future Directions

As stated in the objectives above, this initial study seeks to discover what differences and similarities in design are apparent within Arabic Websites and whether these differences and similarities correspond to characteristics predicted by culture models. The examples shown do seem to exhibit patterns that correspond to those described in discussions of culture dimensions based on culture models.

From this initial study, the authors found that Arabic Websites exhibit certain characteristics and may need to consider changes:

Most pictures focus on university buildings. Arabic Websites may wish to consider more representative pictures.

Most do not feature multimedia. They may wish to consider more multimedia content.

Most do not invite student activities and input. They may wish to consider more sharing and student activity.

Most offer limited external links. They may wish to add more links to external Websites.

Most offer less Help and documentation. They may wish to add more to their Website designs.

They may wish to consider adding more multilingual content. Designing an Arabic Website in English-only may be considered a barrier to access for Arabic users.

Based on a small number of interviews with students who use the Websites for doing tasks, the following comments were collected:

Students want/need more pictures of university buildings and students in different areas of the university.

Students want/need more frequently updated information and more specific content that can answer frequently asked question by both new and experienced students.

Most users would like to see blue and gray colors in the Websites.

Websites need more interactive design features.

Based on the analysis thus far, the study of Arabic Websites needs to be expanded to cover different types of Websites, other Arabic countries, and more extensive interviews with students and faculty to gather usage data.

In future analysis, the authors plan to examine university Websites in greater detail and to expand the analysis to other Website genres (*e.g.*, e-commerce sites, government sites, travel sites, *etc.*) and to other Arabic countries not covered in the present study.

References

1. Callahan, E.: Cultural Similarities and Differences in the Design of University Websites. Journal of Computer-Mediated Communication 11(1), article 12 (2005), http://jcmc.indiana.edu/vol11/issue1/callahan.html
2. Hofstede, G., Hofstede, G.J.: Cultures and Organizations: Software of the Mind. McGraw-Hill, New York (2005); http://www.geert-hofstede.com
3. Marcus, A.: Globalization of User-Interface Design for the Web. In: Probhu, G., Delgaldo, E.M. (eds.) Proceedings of 1st International Conference on Internationalization of Products and Systems (IWIPS), May 22-22, 1999, pp. 165–172. Backhouse Press, Rochester (1999); ISBN. 0-965091-2-2

4. Marcus, A., Baumgartner, V.J.: Mapping User-Interface Design Components vs. Culture Dimensions in Corporate Websites. Visible Language 38(1), 1–65 (2004)
5. Marcus, A., Gould, E.W.: Crosscurrents: Cultural Dimensions and Global Web User-Interface Design. Interactions 7(4), 32–46 (2000), http://www.acm.org

Supplementary Relateed References

1. Evers, V.: Cross-Cultural Understanding of Graphical Elements on the DirectED Website. In: Proceedings of Annual Workshop on Cultural Issues on HCI, December 5, 2001, pp. 3–8 (2001)
2. Fitzgerald, W.: Models for Cross-Cultural Communications for Cross-Cultural Website Design. National Research Council of Canada, NRC-CNRC, pp. 3–8 (2004)
3. Hamoodi, S., Sheikh, A.E.: The Impact of Culture on Design and Usability International. In: Proceedings of International Conference on Information and Knowledge Engineering, Las Vegas, June 25-28, 2007, pp. 285–288 (2007)
4. Khaslavsky, J.: Integrating Culture into Interface Design. In: CHI 1998 Conference Summary on Human Factors in Computing Systems, Los Angeles, pp. 365–366. ACM Press, New York (1998)
5. Komlodi, A., Carlin, M.: Identifying Cultural Variables in Information-Seeking. In: Proceedings of the Tenth Americans Conference on Information Systems, New York, August 2004, pp. 3–5 (2004)
6. Lo, B.W.N., Gong, P.: Cultural Impact on the Design of e-Commerce Websites, Part 1: Site Format and Layout. Issues in Information Systems 6(2), 182–189 (2005)
7. Simon, S.J.: The Impact of Culture and Gender on Web Sites: An Empirical Study. The Data Base for Advances in Information Systems 32(1), 21–27 (2001)
8. Zahedi, F.M., Van Pelt, W.V., Song, H.: A Conceptual Framework for International Web Design. IEEE Transaction on Professional Communication 44(2), 83–86 (2001)

Personalizing the Shared Mobile Phone

Nimmi Rangaswamy[1] and Supriya Singh[2]

[1] Microsoft Research Bangalore 560080, India
nimmir@microsoft.com
[2] RMIT University, GPO Box 2476V, Melbourne 3001, Australia
supriya.singh@rmit.edu.au

Abstract. Sharing mobile phones, an enduring practice in developing nations, finds insufficient empirical effort or theoretical scrutiny as a sociological phenomena. Predominant conceptions of design for a mobile phone are aimed at independent and private behaviour as the device is perceived and designed to be a private object for personal use. In this paper we draw attention to the need for designing personalized spaces within the shared or familial culture around the mobile phone. We report on a qualitative case-study of shared mobile phones in low-middle income families in Mumbai city and Dharamshala, reframing personal communication devices as shared objects.

Keywords: Mobile Phone, Shared phones, India, Middle-class, Ethnographic Design.

1 Introduction

Sharing mobile phones, a common practice in developing nations, finds insufficient empirical effort or theoretical scrutiny as a sociological phenomenon. Predominant conceptions of design for a mobile phone are aimed at independent and private use.. In this paper we draw attention to the need for designing personalized spaces within the shared or familial culture around the mobile phone. This approach to design could transform an individually owned mobile phone to a family device or may lead to a family device that is personalized for each family member. The design will involve personalizing a public object. Therefore, even if the mobile phone is individually owned, it can be personalized and customized to suit the needs of multiple-users.

Mobile remittances in Asia and Africa need to contend with shared mobile phones but money that is often private within the household. In India among urban patrilineal middle income households, money is predominantly controlled by men. In joint families, information about money travels more easily between father and son than between husband and wife. Even when the husband and wife have a joint account, the wife may not have information about money in the account. She may never have deposited or withdrawn money from the joint account [19]. The issue of a woman's personal spending money is especially fraught, particularly in patrilineal joint families.

While shared mobile phones may be a transitional stage [4] money management and control in families will continue to include some measure of jointness and privacy. Hence design that takes into account the need for flexible boundaries between shared and private spaces will continue to have wide currency.

N. Aykin (Ed.): Internationalization, Design, LNCS 5623, pp. 395–403, 2009.
© Springer-Verlag Berlin Heidelberg 2009

We report on a qualitative study of shared mobile phones in low-middle income families in Mumbai city and middle income families in the small town of Dharamshala. Our family ethnographies of shared mobile phone usage reflect family dynamics; that material resources are often shared at the level of the family rather than the individual. Communication technologies enable family interaction and co-ordination. Our research findings in middle class Indian homes challenge received notions of mobile phones as necessarily personal, private, individually owned and used.

We draw attention to two arguments in this paper. The first addresses the design of personalized spaces within the shared or public space. We found in the middle class Indian families we studied, the personal mobile phone can be shared while an individual may own the family phone. In the Indian context there is significant sharing at the level of family or community or neighborhood and the desire for privacy articulates as personalization of space that is otherwise public. We also see tensions, especially coming out of youth behavioral practices that seek individual identity through ownership of mobile phones and simultaneously desire to share the phone with family as socialized members of a shared culture [3].

The second argument deconstructs a dominant perception that the sharing of personal communication objects thrives only when there is economic constraint. In our data, this idea is questioned when we find multiple phones in Indian households, being shared.

2 Methodology

We conducted a qualitative study of 49 lower middle income households in Mumbai and 11 households in Dharamshala between May 2005 and June 2006. Mumbai is India's largest metropolitan city with 17.7 million people [15] and Dharamshala, a Himalayan town with a population of 19,034 [5]. We defined the lower middle income households as those that had a monthly household income of between INR 9,000 and INR 30,000 (1 US Dollar = 49 Indian Rupees Feb 2009).

In Mumbai, we used multiple ways of collecting data through focus groups, open ended interviews, family case studies and participant observation. We draw on the focus groups for a general understanding of the use and consumption of mobile phone against the background of the household and family. For the detailed discussion of mobile phone usage we draw on the richer open-ended interviews, family studies and participant observation. As this data was collected in the households, the household and family context was immediately at the fore, with the individual elaborating on personal use.

In the small town of Dharamshala, the research drew upon participant observation with a particular focus on mobile phone ownership and usage. Participant observation in Dharamshala was based on an 11 year relationship with friendship and neighborhood groups.

The focus group data in Mumbai were taped and fully transcribed. For the interviews and participant observation, only one interview was taped and transcribed. The taping of family interviews became socially problematic in Mumbai and Dharamshala. So we depended on detailed field notes and field journals.

3 The Mobile Phone in the Literature

The mobile phone has been at the centre of media research in developed nations viz Europe and Japan, for its varied usage as a personal device [12, 13, 14, 18]. Mobile phones are also seen as status markers and fashion items [10, 16, 17]. The mobile phone is a tool for community development, sometimes the first family communication device, the small business enhancer and identity marker for youth. Specific studies speak about mobile technology shaping social relations. Research has emphasized the mobile phone, as a means of cementing, sustaining, and managing relationships. Youth and friendship have received considerable notice [4] identifying texting and social networking, chatting and friendships via the mobile phone, and the new agendas to which they give rise.. Importantly, interactions of a more romantic or flirtatious kind found ease of existence through mobile dialogues and communication. All of these studies, interesting as they are, follow the life and times of the mobile phone in either a western or hyper-modern contexts.

Our focus is on the use of mobile phones primarily in the context of the family and in cultural settings that lay emphasis on the collective and shared use of media. Previous researchers have focused on particular elements of mobile use within families predominantly in western contexts. Some have looked at how mobile use and family rules and norms dictate appropriate mobile use [8] and the ways in which families manage and allocate money and finance for personal communication devices [11].

There is an emerging body of work on the use of the mobile phone in developing countries from diverse perspectives [8]. Sharing of mobile phones is acknowledged as a common practice in developing nations. As noted in the Information Economy Report [20].

> ...in developing countries a single mobile phone is frequently shared by several people, particularly in poor, rural communities, and people at all income levels are able to access mobile services either through owning a phone or using someone else's (p. 12).

The leasing of mobile phones in the villages of Bangladesh by *Grameen Bank* is based on shared use [1]. A 2004 study of rural municipalities in the Philippines found that fifteen per cent of the cell phones were family owned but 62 per cent allowed others in the household to receive and respond to messages [17].

The sharing of mobile phones is common in Africa (Vodafone, 2005). In Rwanda as Donner notes [6].

> ...handsets often pull double-duty, used by multiple family members, shared among friends (perhaps by swapping SIM [Subscriber Identity Module] cards in and out), or perhaps by a whole set of users in a village or neighborhood. Across the region, many people make their living by selling individual calls on handsets. (p. 2).

Shared mobile phones in Asia are used within a culture of sharing in Asian homes. As Bell says [2], firstly material resources are often shared at the level of the household and neighborhood . Secondly, the middle class Indian home is the hub of family life even if the family is nuclear in nature. Domestic communication technologies are seen not only as enablers but support devices for family interaction and co-ordination. Thirdly, Asian cultures privilege the family over the individual. Though there are several social units competing as identity markers, the individual is not seen as the primary unit of social organization.

We must note that the picture is nuanced and not always uniform. Yu notes [21] the mobile phone in China

> ...allows privatized and mobile communications based on personal choices and individual pleasures. As such, the mobile phone has become the technology of privatized and individualized networking of our age, par *excellence* (p. 33).

4 Findings and Discussion

The mobile phone, in our sample of low-middle income families, is largely perceived as a functional and affordable family communication device. The image of the (immobile) land line in the drawing room as the family phone informs the usage of the family mobile phone in the lower middle-income households. In eight per cent of the households the mobile was the only telephone and functioned as the family phone. As Akshata,[1] 32, in Mumbai says 'The mobile in our home is the walking landline.' She not only shares her husband's mobile but also uses her neighbor's as a contact number for emergencies.

Savio Miranda, 36, has not taken up a land line connection at all. His mobile works as the common phone number for both him and his wife. 'Most of our calls are long distance and are all calls to our home towns. Besides, STD (Subscriber Trunk Dialing to call long distance within the country) is cheaper on the mobile.'

The mobile phone in lower income households in Mumbai is still male and often a business communication device. Women are given less priority when it comes to owning a personal phone though men often share the phone with their wives or mothers. In our Mumbai sample, of the 19 single mobile phone households, 17 belonged to the men. In Mumbai and Dharamshala, both men and women feel that housewives do not need mobile phones as long as they can make and receive calls at home. When women own a mobile phone it is often shared and attains the status of a family phone.

The gender divide for mobile phones disappears for young men and women. Young people's use of the mobile phone shares many of the characteristics of youth in other parts of the world [7, 16]. They talked of the mobile phone as personal and an identity marker, used to communicate with friends or listen to music. Mobile phones were personally owned, often bought with their own earnings. The mobile phone is a status marker, and important for maintaining their friendship networks. Music and the camera functions are important for their status and functionality. In the absence of home PCs, the phones became a social networking device, the affordable iPod and an identity enhancer to absorb and transmit the look and feel of their owner.

---

[1] All the names from the qualitative studies are pseudonyms.

4.1 Multiple Mobile Phones in a Household Are Shared

Sharing of mobile phones draws on a tradition of shared, public access to communication in developing countries. Universal access as opposed to universal service is seen in terms of providing a public shared communication device for a designated area.

Mobiles were shared across a range of household incomes in our sample. Around 40 per cent of mobile phones in our Mumbai sample (Table 1) were shared. In Dharamshala, the mobile phone was shared in all the four households that had a mobile phone. In Mumbai, mobile phones were shared when there were one, two, or three phones in the household. Many single phones in a household were not shared while twin and triple phones were shared amongst members of the household. Sharing was not restricted to households where there was only one phone per household.

4.2 Patterns of Sharing

The phone was shared in multiple ways. Individual ownership of the mobile phone does not preclude sharing. Of the 52 mobile phones (out of a total of 81 mobile phones in 49 homes in the Mumbai sample) attached to their owners, a third of them were being shared in the household.

The sharing can be partial. Some women use the mobile only to receive calls, rather than for making calls. With low mobile rates, the mobile phone is often cheaper than the landline and so is also used to speak to extended family outside Mumbai. The shared phone can also be earmarked to receive calls from family members overseas.

In Dharamshala one phone could be shared but with two SIMs or two phones with one SIM; or the appropriation of the phone without paying. The disaggregation of the phone from the SIM [13] is an important element of sharing. Below we give some vignettes from our data in Dharamshala. The sharing was between siblings, between father and daughter, and between extended kin.

Charan in Dharamshala has completed his BA and has a GPRS (General Packet Radio Service) enabled mobile which cost him INR 9,000. He lends it to his younger brother, Chetan, .who is still in school. Chetan does not have a mobile because schools in Dharamshala do not allow their students to use the mobile phone during school times. When Chetan goes to a party, he borrows his brother's phone. 'I just put in my own pre-paid SIM, and it becomes my phone,' Chetan says. 'My brother manages without it for that time.'

Table 1. Sharing of mobile phones in Mumbai homes n=49

Households and mobile phones	Number of Households	Not shared	Shared
No mobiles	4	NA	NA
Single mobiles	19	14	5
Two mobiles	16	5	11
Three mobiles	10	6	4

Anita, 20, in Dharamshala does not yet have her own SIM so borrows her father's SIM. 'If there are messages for Papa,' Anita says, 'I ring him up and tell him this or that Uncle wants him to call.' Amar, 15, Anita's brother who is still in school also uses the same phone. If Anita's friends ring up while he has the phone, Amar asks 'Sowhat?' Anita agrees. 'No,' she says, 'there is nothing personal about my mobile phone.'

Dharam (in his 40s) in Dharamshala is in trade and sees his mobile phone as an essential business tool. He says tradesmen do not borrow from each other, and if they do, it would only be for a local call. His wife Dheera (in her 30s) interjects that her husband lends his mobile to anyone who asks. She says,

> We were going to a wedding and his cousin who was in the other car asked him for his mobile. The idea was that they could be in touch if the cars lost sight of each other, as another person in my husband's car had a mobile. But then his cousin kept the mobile for five days and spent all the INR 500 that was on the recharge card. What can one say?

Dharam says, 'Now I don't set it to Roaming when I go away to the village. ...So I neither receive calls, nor have other people make calls.'

4.3 Not Sharing Phones

Phones were not shared for three reasons Firstly, the household or the owners had more than one phone. One was shared with family and the other was for business communication. There are instances where in one household, one phone is used only by one individual, whereas the other one is shared. In the Solan Lal household in Mumbai, Rakshita (22) sees her mobile as her own. She says, 'I need to keep it with me all the time. Also, clients may want to call up anytime, so I have to make sure that the phone is not engaged.' But her father, Kishna's mobile functions as the *de facto* landline for the whole family.

Secondly, mobiles are not shared when they are used primarily for business. This is particularly true for men as they are more likely to have mobiles for business. Where a father shared a business mobile with his daughter, it was because the daughter helped him with his business. Where the woman has the mobile for work, she too does not share the mobile. Chandan, a trader in his 50s in Dharamshala cannot contemplate offering his mobile to anybody because all his business calls come on the mobile.

The exceptions are when the businessman is not very mobile as with Anita's father who can rely on his fixed line phone or Dharam who was caught in a difficult social situation. Men spoke about their business phones as being personal but often shared them with their children, wives or mothers when they got home from work. Children used it to play games. Some of the women respondents in Mumbai gave the husband's mobile as their contact number.

Sometimes fathers stored their address books on their children's phone. One of them said "My 13 year old son insisted on getting a fancy mobile with large storage and features.... I compensated buying a cheap phone for myself. I store my address book on his device." Children shared mobiles of fathers when the device was brought home from work. The radio, camera and text messaging were features used largely by children (12 years or above) on owned or borrowed phones.

Thirdly, for young people there is tension between the emotion invested in the mobile phone, contribution to purchase and the norm of sharing. Youth in our sample perceived the mobile as a personal and life-style device in contrast to the more functional mobile of their parents. Hence not every young person is comfortable sharing the mobile.

In the Mumbai data, nine young persons shared the mobile phone, whereas ten did not. In Dharamshala sharing the phone was the norm, particularly between siblings. It is interesting to note that daughters are more likely to share than the sons. Of the nine who shared in Mumbai, six were female and three male. The position reversed itself among the ten who did not share – three female and seven male.

The phone was shared when it was bought by the parents or older sibling (6 instances) or from the young person's own income (3 instances). Of the 10 who did not share, three belonged to the same family and the father had bought all of them a mobile phone. Two work late, but the other five do not want to share. Sudarshan, 19, says, 'It is my mobile, and nobody uses it. My parents do not even know how to…'

Rakshita's story in Mumbai illustrates the strength of these norms of sharing, even when there is much emotion and status associated with the mobile phone. Rakshita, 22, saved up for ten months to buy her first mobile phone in 2002 while she was still in college. She took the phone with her wherever she went. It became the family phone when she was at home. Everyone could receive calls and messages but she was the only one who made outgoing calls from it. The others used a Public Call Office except in the case of an emergency.

When Rakshita's father got a mobile in 2004, his phone became the default family phone, but Rakshita's brother used her phone for messaging and receiving calls. He felt he could chat for a longer time with friends on his sister's phone. Rakshita then upgraded her phone to a *Nokia* phone with a radio. Now her brother uses the radio when she is at home. It is the only radio in the house. Rakshita is now saving up to buy a camera phone. Rakshita says her family is entitled to the benefits and convenience the phone affords. She adds, 'They are family'.

5 Concluding Remarks

Our research on middle class Indian families challenges received notions of mobile phones as private, personal and individual. In many cases the mobile phone was shared, even when there were multiple phones in the household. Young people especially felt the tension between individual ownership, the emotion invested in the phone and norms of sharing. Yet, even young people shared the phone, particularly with siblings. Even when older persons used the phone for business, this phone at times became shared after work. There were many different patterns of sharing, ranging from no sharing to partial and more complete sharing. .

Ethnography informs technology design by incorporating awareness of cultural contexts and social meanings [2]. Our research establishes the importance of culture in shaping the use of technology, especially the seemingly personal communication device, the mobile phone. The social/cultural approach is important for the design of a shared private mobile as this sharing is in the context of several other realms of being and living in an Indian family.

There are precedents for shared access to information and communication technologies in multi-user PCs and telecentres, which could usefully be used for shared mobile phones. Personalization of the mobile phone would allow shared access and absorb diverse sharing behavior. With close-knit family sharing of a mobile phone, we might locate the personal and private within the public family device.

The paucity of empirical studies of the sharing of the mobile phone means there are many unaddressed issues. What does the sharing of the mobile phone say about family connectedness, youth culture and privacy? Is this sharing a temporary phenomenon that will disappear once every person in the household has a functioning mobile phone? Does the sharing of the mobile phone question the individualization of new media?

New media research could usefully take three directions. Firstly, research on new media needs to probe whether media outside Europe, Japan and the United States – given time – will follow the same trajectory of individualization, multiplication, and personalization. Or will there be a different kind of connected individualism, which tries to bridge individual ownership with the norms of a shared family life? Secondly, these questions may well lead to a re-examination of the use of new media in its traditional markets, to see how individuals manage to share personal media.

The third area is the ethnographic study of diverse constructions of privacy and trust in families across cultures [2]. The broad issue is the ways in which people negotiate the competing demands of individualism on the one hand and connectedness of the household and the community on the other. With greater empirical research, we could reveal the varieties of ways in which people use new media to negotiate their need for individual privacy, trust and connectedness. We could then begin to bridge the gap between social and cultural practice on the one hand and regulatory policy and design on the other.

References

1. Bayes, A., Braun, J.V., Akhter, R.: Village Pay Phones and Poverty Reduction: Insights from a Grameen Bank Initiative in Bangladesh. ZEF Bonn, Zentrum für Entwicklungsforschung, Center for Development Research, Universität Bonn,
   http://ww.telecommons.com/villagephone/bayes99.pdf2
2. Bell, G.: Other homes: Alternate visions of culturally situated technologies for the home. In: CHI 2003. ACM Press, New York (2003), 1-58113-630-7/03/0004
3. Chavan, L.A.: A dramatic day in the life of a shared mobile phone in India. In: 12th International conference on. Human Computer Interaction, Beijing, P.R. China, July 2-27 (2007)
4. Chipchase, J., Tulusan, I.: Shared Phone Use,
   http://www.janchipchase.com/sharedphoneuse
5. Dharamshala Himachal Pradesh,
   http://www.indianetzone.com/8/
   dharamsala_himachal_pradesh.htm
6. Donner, J.: User-Led Innovations in Mobile Use in Sub-Saharan Africa' Receiver Newsletter#14,
   http://www.vodafone.com/flash/receiver/14/articles/
   index02.html
7. Donner, J.: Research Approaches to Mobile Use. The Developing World: A Review of the Literature, The Information Society 24(3), 140–159 (2008b)

8. Donner, J., Rangaswamy, N., Steenson, M.W., Wei, C.: "Express yourself" and "Stay together": The middle-class Indian family. In: Katz, J. (ed.) The handbook of mobile communication studies, pp. 325–338. MIT Press, Cambridge (2008a)

9. Ellwood-Clayton, B.: All we need is love—and a mobile phone: Texting in the Philippines. In: The International Conference on Cultural Space and the Public Sphere in Asia, Seoul, Korea (2006)

10. Haddon, L.: Information and Communication Technologies in Everyday Life: A Concise Introduction and Research Guide, Berg, New York (2004)

11. Haddon, L., Vincent, J.: Making the most of the communications repertoire: choosing between the mobile and fixed-line. In: Nyiri, K. (ed.) A sense of place: The global and the local in mobile communication, Passagen Verlag, Vienna (2005)

12. Ito, M., Okabe, D., Matsuda, M. (eds.): Personal, Portable, Pedestrian: Mobile Phones in Japanese Life. MIT Press, Cambridge (2005)

13. Lacohee, H., Wakeford, N., Pearson, I.: A Social History of the Mobile Telephone with a View of its Future. BT Technology Journal 21(3), 203–211 (2003)

14. Livingstone, S.: Young People and New Media. Sage Publications, London (2002)

15. Mumbai municipality and suburban population since 1981,
    http://www.demographia.com/db-mumbai1981.htm

16. Özcan, Y.Z., Koçak, A.: Research Note: A Need or a Status Symbol? Use of Cellular Telephones in Turkey. European Journal of Communication 18(2), 241–254 (2003)

17. Pertierra, R.: Mobile Phones, Identity and Discursive Intimacy. Human Technology 1(1), 23–44 (2005)

18. Plant, S.: On the Mobile. The Effects of Mobile Telephones on Social and Individual Life,
    http://www.motorola.com/mot/doc/0/234_MotDoc.pdf

19. Singh, S.: Balancing separateness and jointness of money in relationships: The design of bank accounts in Australia and India. In: 13th International conference on. Human Computer Interaction, San Diego, USA, July 19-24 (2009)

20. United Nations Conference on Trade and Development: Information economy report,
    http://www.unctad.org/en/docs/sdteedc20051_en.pdf

21. Yu, H.: The Power of Thumbs: The Politics of SMS in Urban China. Graduate Journal of Asia-Pacific Studies 2(2), 30–43 (2004),
    http://www.arts.auckland.ac.nz/sites/index.cfm?P=7328

Affordable Wireless Connectivity Linking Poor Latin American Communities Binding Their Schools by Sharing ICT Training for "Maestros" of Primary Schools

C. Osvaldo Rodriguez

INIFTA, Universidad Nacional de La Plata,
Diagonal 113 y 64,
La Plata 1900, Argentina
cor_ar@yahoo.com

Abstract. A very poor neighborhood in Argentina that has many features of lower middle class is called "barrio carenciado". Many heads of the families are unemployed and although children have access to schools it is common that they do not finish their basic instruction. In many cases NGOs play a fundamental role in changing this reality. In this presentation we detail the implementation of a test bed where 14 families and a school were provided with computers, Internet access and were educated out of digital illiteracy. Connectivity was provided by Wireless Mesh Networking (WMN). The research project, was carried out by a group of researchers from the Universidad de La Plata with different backgrounds in collaboration with the NGO Barrios del Plata (a chapter of Muhammad Yunus´s Grameen Bank). The study monitored the changes in families' life (in particularly children education and parents opportunities related to obtaining work). The deployment of WMN in a such a broad area, aimed to define the possible lowest cost implementation, and conforms an important part of the research activities. The school #502, originally a node of the WMN, has become a "Laboratory for the use of innovative methodologies in ICT training of primary school teachers". The project was financed through an award given in a public competition by Microsoft research and CentralTech, a leading Argentinean educational center.

Keywords: Digital Inclusion, Wireless Mesh Networking, ICT Teachers Education.

1 Introduction

If true what Thomas Friedman states in his best seller "The World is Flat" [1], then underdeveloped countries have a great opportunity, meaning, an opportunity for the promotion of new businesses and changes in areas such as education, R&D, health and many others.

The facts that Friedman stated made the world to become flat go from Ethernet's invention, the Personal Computer, Internet, the dot com bubble (that filled the earth with optical fiber), Netscape, XML, SOAP (which gives the possibility of connecting very varied applications), free access to information (search engines such as Google,

N. Aykin (Ed.): Internationalization, Design, LNCS 5623, pp. 404–412, 2009.

Yahoo and MSN) to the most recent advances such as mobiles, wireless, virtualization and quadruple-play. It was the sum of these factors which happened in conjunction with some very particular political events.

In resume, a more planar world has been generated, where information is a click away. Some underdeveloped countries are somehow better prepared than others after the technological changes of the last years. And these countries could obtain immediate benefits from the use of ICTs. They have acquired the necessary physical infrastructure (as optical fiber) and possess the human capital required to operate the associated systems. Its use cannot bring any other consequence than economical growth and improved standards of living.

When PCs still did not interconnect, the challenge to break the "digital divide" was enormous for underdeveloped economies. The panorama was dull since those societies with access to computers and the applications running on top of them would become more and more apart from those that needed first to come out of digital illiteracy to just then start benefiting from the so called "Information Society".

"Those rich in information would become richer and those in need would be still poorer". With this phrase, Nicholas Negroponte expressed in his article "One-Room Rural Schools" which appeared in Wired Magazine (of which he was founder), in September 1998, his concern for the increasing separation of those who had access to computers and those who didn't.

But access to internet and the many ingredients that made the earth flat modified this situation, transforming a problem into a challenge. The same tools of IT and advances in telecommunication (today nearly convergent) gave the tools to solve the problem.

There is no doubt that the opportunity is there, the important issue is to know how to take advantage of it. Some countries like India are already immersed in big changes. In Africa the problem is still more complex since huge investments in physical infrastructure are needed. Many Latin-American countries that have the necessary physical infrastructure are still "deciding" what to do.

But, the fact that the earth is flat, the free access to libraries and their content offered by Internet, thousands of developers willing to help in open-source projects, the multiplicative effects for education and many other areas makes it possible to perform a radical change in poor countries. Simple: start tackling problems.

From our perspective two of the most urgent and key actions are: Internet connectivity and enhancing teacher's digital literacy.

2 ICT4D-AR, UNLP

ICT4D-AR is a project that gathers researchers from different backgrounds, mostly from the Universidad Nacional de La Plata and that belong to the most prestigious research institutions in Argentina: CONICET and CIC. Its main objective is to investigate the design and implementation of new technologies that favour underdeveloped regions.

The purpose of ICT4D-AR is to focus on the challenges posed by the ICT revolution to those that live in countries where great parts of their population are below the poverty line. The great majority of this type of projects use technologies developed in countries with intellectual, economical and educational wealth. The sheer implementation of many of them simply fails since no questioning is made on costs, feasibility of implementation, energy problems or the need to orchestrate the appropriate educational support and study these technologies within the local eco-systems. What's the value of giving away laptops to primary school children if their teachers never used a word processor nor sent an e-mail?

ICT4D-AR tackles problems related to hardware, software, connectivity and its influence in education and work opportunities. The project, finally, pretends to give a diagnosis, promote the proper technologies that eventually might be adopted by governments and corporations.

Today ICT4D-AR is focused on two projects: wireless connectivity using WMN and innovative methodologies for ICT training of primary school teachers. The project's participants come from different backgrounds and include technologists, scientists from the hard sciences, engineering and social areas. One of the pre requisites of any new project is that it should be carried out in real environments (pilot tests, testbeds). This is vital, since it provides the answer to its feasibility and gives a diagnosis for scalability.

3 Project Wireless Mesh Networking (WMN)

In 2004 Tom Krag and Sebastian Buettrich [3] proposed, during the Emerging Technology Conference organized by Tim O'Reilly that took place in San Diego, CA., how WMN could become an important technology for the promotion of wireless and internet access in underdeveloped regions. They addressed the question of how one could give access to internet and connectivity to those places not included in the commercial plans of telecom companies or if the connectivity was there, how it could be provided at a low cost.

One of their main arguments in their analysis was the need to have a decentralized connectivity infrastructure. In this manner one avoided a single point of failure. Another, that the technology would be sufficiently simple and low cost so that it could be maintained and expanded by local participants with very little technological experience.

It basically proposed the use of low cost hardware, home constructed antennas and ubiquitous technologies simple to implement. Wi-fi (802.11b/g) prompted as a candidate technology and connectivity in mesh architecture a promising ingredient.

In the last years the group of Dr. Victor Bahl, from Microsoft Research implemented mesh technology as part of Windows XP [4]. Krag´s and Buettrich´s proposal made us interested in the idea. In 2006 the project won a RFP made by Microsoft Research for the implementation of the test bed described in this paper using the technologies developed by Dr. Bahl´s group.

3.1 Definition of Mesh Networking

"A mesh network is a network that employs one of two connection arrangements, full mesh topology or partial mesh topology. In the full mesh topology, each node is connected directly to each of the others. In the partial mesh topology, nodes are connected to only some, not all, of the other nodes" [3].

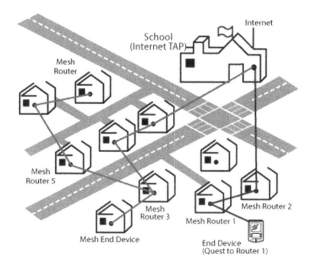

Fig. 1. Diagram of "Barrio Carenciado" and Mesh Nodes

When we speak of mesh networking, we understand a network that has connections many to many and capable of dynamically updating an optimizing these connections. The nodes can be mobile or not. In our case they are not mobile since their position as a function of time does not change. Fig. 1. shows a diagram of a possible mesh implementation. The biggest challenge for any mesh configuration is the administration of the complex information from the routing tables since they must include external networks and the internet gateways.

Mesh network technologies have matured and have found a place together to other possible wireless technologies. Some of the outstanding issues, adapted to our scenario, as pointed by Krag and Buettrich [3], are:

- **Price:** 802.11 radios have become relatively inexpensive, although they are still among the most expensive elements of such a network. It's the fact that each mesh node runs both as a client and as a repeater, which permits saving on the number of radios needed and thus the total cost.
- **Ease and simplicity:** In our case each node is a PC running Windows XP with wireless mesh software and uses standard wireless protocols such as 802.11b/g and the setup is extremely simple.
- **Organization and business models:** The decentralized nature of mesh networks.
- **Network robustness:** Mesh topology and ad-hoc routing should provide more stability in the face of changing conditions or failure at single nodes.
- Today a mesh infrastructure can be built with hardware from CISCO or Motorola but they are very expensive. The challenge is a low cost implementation.

4 Barrio Carenciado, NGO "Barrios del Plata" and Testbed

The WMN project started in September 2006 and ended in december 2007. The test bed linked 14 homes (with children in primary school age and unemployed parents)

Fig. 2. El Obrador

and had its gateway to the Internet in a local community meeting place ("El Obrador, Fig. 2.). Another selected node was the primary "Special School #502" for children with learning disabilities. Each of the families used Internet for different purposes but, the study concentrated on educational issues of primary school children and if it could provide possible means for reverting the parent's situation of unemployment.

The idea of Grameen Bank started by Muhammad Yunus, has helped improve millions of peoples life worldwide. In Argentina Grameen Bank exists since 1999 as "Aldeas Argentinas". Our project rested on the NGO as the way for selecting the families that received the computers, give them support in education and guiding the participants as a community. "El Obrador", normally the meeting place of the ONG, was practically converted in a training centre. For months the families received courses and several very interesting experiences and positive returns emerged.

The project put up the whole infrastructure, serviced the antennas and connectivity and provided funds for IT education.

5   WMN: Reality versus Laboratory

In 2004 in the Freifunk Summer Convention in Berlin, Krag and Buettrich [3], demonstrated the feasibility of a mesh network using a few laptops connected using the protocol Mobile Mesh on top of the GNU/Linux kernel 2.2 in the streets of Berlin surrounding a park.

Could it be possible to implement this at a very low cost in a real environment and not as an experimental laboratory? This was basically the question that made us implement the project.

Our 15 nodes were distributed as shown in Fig. 3.: two groups of 5-6 nodes and 4 nodes at the border.

In parallel to the study of connectivity and as already stated each family assisted to training in basic informatics tools (Word, Excel, PowerPoint). All the training was done in the node called "El Obrador" that also served as the gateway for Internet using an ADSL connection of 512Kbps.

Two advanced engineering students from the Facultad de Telecommunications of the UNLP made the appropriate deployment. They had special contracts through university fellowships, a legal figure called "pasantes". They were in charge of deployment and monitoring of the network.

Each node consisted of a PC running windows XP, a wireless network card 802.11g and an external antenna 5m high placed on the roofs of the precarious housing of each family. In the implementation we made use of the "Mesh Networking Academic Resource Toolkit 2005" offered by Microsoft Research. The protocol used is called Link Quality Source Routing (LQSR) based on Dynamic Source Routing. The MCL (Mesh Connectivity Layer) driver was installed in each wireless card. Linksys WMP54G cards were used on each node, connected to an 8Bdi antenna. A coaxial RG8 cable of little loss was used for connecting the antenna and the PC. The antenna was held together with the TV antenna of each home. Although not optimal due to losses in the cable, this solution was decided due to cost. Use of a bi-directional amplifier or LNA would have increased total cost. It was always in the spirit of the project a search for lowest cost implementation. Although commercial antennas were used, the final aim was to replace them by home made ones.

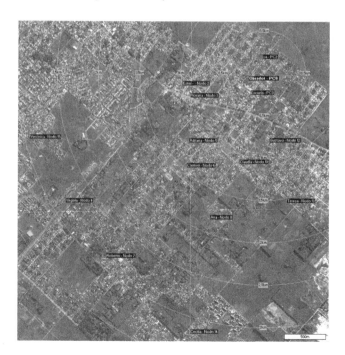

Fig. 3. Map of Villa Elvira and Nodes

5.2 Implementation #1

The first implementation was a full mesh topology where all the nodes participated meshing and a single gateway was located at the node called "El Obrador". Omini directional antennas of 8Dbi were installed at a cost of U$50 each.

Connectivity was achieved between all 15 nodes but several factors attempted against the stability of the network. The Mesh protocol was installed in "zero configuration". This brought many problems. If a node needed to be reset, it would modify some parameters and technical personal needed to be called to reconfigure.

Given the small number of nodes, the disappearance of one of them would leave several others without connectivity. Zero configuration was finally eliminated in the installation scripts. This made that many of the problems described when resetting disappear.

5.2 Implementation #2

As a possible solution to the instability observed in implementation #1 the antennas of some nodes were changed for directional ones of 24 dBi. This hybrid model then had mesh in the two more dense areas and the rest in infrastructure mode and provided a much more stable network.

6   Project Escuela # 502: ICT Training for Teachers

The "Laboratory for the use of innovative methodologies in ICT training of primary school teachers" was implemented in the Escuela Especial #502 (see Fig. 4.), Villa Elvira, La Plata at the end of the WMN project. The school, caters for children with learning disabilities is a public school and belongs to the Provincia de Buenos Aires. The laboratory´s formal inauguration was November 2007 although already many actions had been made as pilot tests using a reduced infrastructure.

Fig. 4. Front image of Escuela#502

The neighbourhood, the school's infrastructure and the children's families are poor. Within the project researchers and university professors from the Universidad Nacional de La Plata, CONICET and CIC were in charge for the training of primary school teachers. The theoretical propositions made for the Masters Degree projects in Tecnologias Educativas are used the laboratory as a test bed. As examples we mention work carried out with professors from the School of Music of Facultad de Bellas artes from the UNLP and the use of classmate PCs in the classroom with children with learning disabilities.

The teachers find an environment of great academic level for their training immersed in original and creative projects. This is later reflected in the projects proposed by the teachers to carry out with their students.

The year 2008 was fundamentally used for training for those that teach in the school and will continue expanding to teachers from other establishments. Several teachers have already been detected with great interest in the project and will become trainers in future cycles. Part of the projects objective is this multiplicative factor.

The coordination is made by the Instituto de Investigación en Informática (LIDI), Facultad de Informática, UNLP together with the Cátedra de Postgrado de la UNLP one Tecnologías educativas (http://www.info.unlp.edu.ar/externas/postgrado/).

7 Results and Conclusions

The WMN project was carried out by a multidisciplinary research group from the Universidad Nacional de La Plata in conjunction with the NGO Barrios del Plata. Funding was provided until December 2007. Conclusions related to this project are detailed below:

- The implementation of the wireless mesh was far more complicated than originally assumed. Laboratory test beds are described in the literature but many complications as antennas, selection of wireless NICs, and other details made the deployment far more difficult.
- Dealing with the paperwork due to regulations from CNC (Comision Nacional de Comunicaciones) for sharing an Internet connection through a broad area was also a hurdle that took energy and was originally not foreseen as a problem.
- One main conclusion after the experience is the importance of having an NGO involved. They have been many years in the neighbourhood, know the families and are there for the daily issues. A Test bed deployment without such a support would surely end in failure.
- One family that received a computer with access to Internet was selected independently from the NGO. The idea was to monitor changes in their life as compared to the rest. They, of course were free to pursue actions without constrains. The mother of the family found a small mosaic factory that offered her part-time work using her computer in processing daily excel editing.
- The "Special School #502" was originally incorporated as a node that provided Internet to the establishment. A few months later, a teaching/research laboratory was planned. Some pilot educational projects were carried out and at present a complete learning laboratory has been implemented.

- After the end of our involvement, the mesh could not be maintained and the shared connection at the "Obrador" discontinued.
- Four families have established a small enterprise based on the computer and internet connection. Other four use it as a tool for their small businesses. They are mostly run by the woman in the house.
- All families except one, keep their CPUs working. Most use free dial-up connectivity to internet and 60% bought a printer. All of the children use the computers for school work. The only case where the CPU is not active was due to a falling of a ceiling.
- Although the costs of sharing an internet connexion are far less per household, keeping an infrastructure like WMN is complex. The scale of our project was most probably too small.

Acknowledgments. The project has been funded by an award from Microsoft Research (RFP 2006 on Digital Inclusion) and CentralTech, a leading educational center in Argentina.

References

1. Friedman, T.L.: The World is Flat. Farrar, Straus, Giroux (eds.) (2006)
2. Rodriguez, C.O.: La tierra es plana, una oportunidad única para Latinoamérica. NEX IT Specialist 27, 62 (2006); Revista AHCIET # 109 (2007) (Winner of the II Edición del Premio Periodístico AHCIET-CISCO "Pepe Cela" Competition)
3. Krag, T.: Buettrich,
   http://www.oreillynet.com/pub/a/wireless/2004/01/22/wirelessmesh.html
4. Bahl, P.: Workshop Keynote, Opportunities and Challenges of Community Mesh Networking. In: MICS Workshop ETH Zurich (June 2004); this talk was also presented at the Annual MSR Faculty Summit in Redmond, Washington (August 3, 2004)

Testing of a Novel Web Browser Interface for the Chinese Market

Siu-Tsen Shen[1], Stephen D. Prior[2], and Kuen-Meau Chen[3]

[1] Department of Multimedia Design, National Formosa University,
64 Wen-Hua Rd, Hu-Wei 63208, Taiwan
[2] Department of Product Design and Engineering, Middlesex University,
London N14 4YZ, United Kingdom
[3] Department of Industrial Design, National United University,
1 Lien Da, Kung-Ching Li, Maioli 36003, Taiwan
shen31@hotmail.com, s.prior@mdx.ac.uk, tancred_0721@hotmail.com

Abstract. This paper compares the perspicacity, appropriateness and preference of web browser icons from leading software providers with those of a culture-specific design. This online study was conducted in Taiwan and involved 103 participants, who were given three sets of web browser icons to review, namely Microsoft Internet Explorer, Macintosh Safari, and culturally specific icons created using the Culture-Centred Design methodology. The findings of the study show that all three sets have generally high recognition rates, but that some icon functions (e.g. Go/Visit and Favourite) in all three sets have poor recognition rates and are considered inappropriate.

Keywords: web browser icons, icons, perspicacity, Chinese, culturalisation, user interface design.

1 Introduction of the Growth of the Chinese Market

The recently published 22nd statistical survey report – 'Internet Development in China' (July 2008), states that there are approximately 84.7 million computer hosts and 253 million Internet users in China. This only amounts to a penetration rate of 19.1% of the population [6]. Even with this low rate, China has now overtaken the USA (230 million) in terms of the number of Internet users. The number of Internet users in China has grown by 347% during the period (2000-2006) [11], and if as predicted, China continues to grow at a conservative estimate of 40% per annum (note that Chinese Internet users grew by 43 million in the first half of 2008), it will approach saturation (≈70% penetration) by 2012 (see Fig 1).

The average weekly surfing time of Chinese internet users is currently 19 hrs, with the largest professional sector within the Chinese internet market being Students with 76 million users (30%). It is therefore no surprise that the 18-24 age group has the highest number of internet users. However, only 3.9% of people over 50 yrs use the internet, the biggest reason for not using the internet is stated as 'Not having the necessary skill' (43.3%). China clearly needs to reach out to this underutilized market.

N. Aykin (Ed.): Internationalization, Design, LNCS 5623, pp. 413–418, 2009.
© Springer-Verlag Berlin Heidelberg 2009

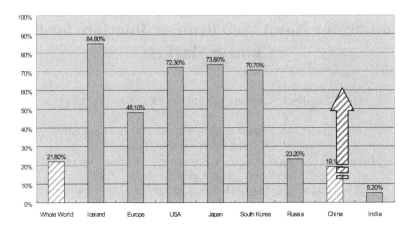

Fig. 1. Internet Penetration Rates [11]

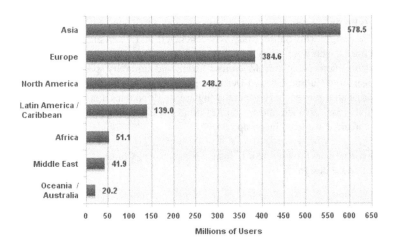

Fig. 2. Internet users by world region [10]

As of September 2008, 164 million people have downloaded the Maxthon browser since its launch in 2003. It has been reported that 14% of Chinese users have used the browser and 17% employ it for web searching through Baidu (the largest search engine in China) [12]. The reasons for its success are its customizable and innovative icon features, fast speed and the fact that it is built on top of the IE engine.

According to the August 2008 report from the Taiwanese Foreseeing Innovative New Digi-services (FIND) organisation, there were approximately 15.4 million Internet users (67.2% penetration rate) in Taiwan, the most frequent use was for web browsing (71%) [15].

Brandon [2] has suggested that a majority of internet users primarily speak languages other than English; Sun [14] has suggested that this could be as high as 70%. It has also been reported that 75% of users in China and Korea prefer content in their own languages [9]. This mismatch highlights the need for more research and shows possible commercial potential.

1.1 Cultural Aspect of Chinese Users

It has been stated that Chinese users have better cognitive ability in terms of visual perception. Chinese characters are two-dimensional graphic symbols, which are made up of lexical and morphological elements, by comparison with one-dimensional, linear, alphabetical systems of Indo-European languages [5].

Choong and Salvendy [4] examined the impact of cultural differences on the cognitive abilities of American and Chinese users in terms of their performance time and errors with three different icon displays. Their results indicated that American subjects had better verbal ability with alphanumeric icon displays, whereas Chinese subjects had better visual distinction ability with pictorial icon displays, if both of subjects are not provided with combined modes.

Fang and Rau [8] reported that "The Chinese way of thinking tends to be synthetic, concrete and remains on the periphery of the visible world. The US way of thinking tends to be analytic, abstract and imaginative or beyond the realm of the immediately apprehended."

The purpose of this study was to investigate users' perspicacity, appropriateness and preference of web browser icons, and to compare the influence of gender, educational level and computer experience on these findings.

2   Research Questions

- How will the rapid growth in non-English speaking internet users affect the balance of power in terms of the development of the internet?
- How well can Chinese users associate IE 7.0 and Safari 3.0 web browser icons with their intended functions?
- Do Chinese users think that these representations are appropriate?
- Is it possible to design culturalised web browser icons for Chinese users?
- What form would these culturalised web browser icons take?
- Will Chinese users prefer to use culturalised web browser icons over the industry leading offerings from Microsoft Internet Explorer and Macintosh Safari?

Does the gender, educational level, level of computer experience or computer platform of the user play a role in determining any of the above factors?

3   Research Methods

The web browser icons chosen for this study were taken from Internet Explorer 7.0 and Safari 3.0, since Microsoft IE and Macintosh Safari are the two most frequently used PC and Mac web browser platforms. We then compared these with Culture-Centred Design (CCD) (culturally specific) icons that aim to differentiate from standardised ones, and have been designed specifically for Chinese users [13]. Eight basic

Fig. 3. Selection of IE 7.0, Safari 3.0, and CCD web browser icons

icon functions were selected from each of the latest IE, Safari, and CCD web browsers, i.e. Forward, Backward, My Favourite, Go/Visit, Home, Refresh, Search, and Stop. The order of these when presented to participants was deliberately mixed up to prevent guessing by test subjects.

The experiment was conducted online in Jan/Feb 2008 at the College of Art and Humanities, National Formosa University (NFU). The duration of the experiment was approximately 20 minutes which included tests for iconic perspicacity, appropriateness, and preference. Participants had to complete each page in order to continue to the following experimental page. No feedback or results were presented to the participant at the end of the test. There were a total of 103 undergraduate students (52 male, 51 female) involved in this online experiment through a website hosted by the department.

There were four categories as independent variables: (a) gender: *males vs. females*; (b) educational background: *high school vs. college vs. university vs. graduate school*; (c) level of computer experience: *<2 yrs vs. 3-4 yrs vs. 5-6 yrs vs. 7-8 yrs vs. >9 yrs*; and (d) the participants' regular computer platform: *PC vs. Mac*. These four variables were tested independently to evaluate overall usability. The dependent variables were the usability measured by icon perspicacity, icon appropriateness, and icon user preference. Other relevant knowledge of the participants was shown by the use of the mean and standard deviation for qualitative analysis of icon perspicacity, appropriateness, and preference.

4   Discussion of the Results

Within this study a comparative experimental evaluation with 103 participants has been conducted using an online resource. The results of this study support the theory that Microsoft's Internet Explorer has successfully globalised non-English speaking internet users within Taiwan.

In terms of perspicacity, most users could easily associate the web browser icons with their intended functions. However, there were several usability problems reported with the IE 7.0 Go/Visit and Search icons. The Apple Safari web browser icons also caused several problems for users, of particular note being the Favourite, Go/Visit and Refresh icons.

In terms of appropriateness, the participants felt that several of the IE icons were either highly inappropriate or inappropriate; in order of severity these were: Go/Visit (38%), Favourite (30%), Stop (27%), and Forward (25%). For the Apple Safari icons, participants felt that several icons fell into the categories of either highly inappropriate or inappropriate; in order of severity these were: Go/Visit (62%), Favourite (52%), Forward (27%), Backward (25%), and Refresh (25%).

In order to gauge the level of support amongst Chinese computer users for a web browser containing specifically designed culturalised icons, we compared icons developed using the Culture-Centred Design methodology with those of IE 7.0 and Safari 3.0. Analysis of our results shows that the CCD icons had perspicacity rates, which were almost equivalent to those of IE 7.0 and Safari 3.0, however, when we analysed the data on appropriateness, it was clear that several of these icons had high levels of either highly inappropriate or inappropriate: Go/Visit (69%), Refresh (65%), Favourite (62%), Forward (48%), Backward (48%), Stop (44%), Search (40%), and Home (38%). To some extent, this is comprehensible due to the high levels of PC users (98%) amongst the participants. However, we intend to further develop these to lower these levels in line with those of IE.

5 Conclusions

The Chinese netizen community is expanding rapidly and has recently overtaken the USA to become the largest Internet user base in the world. By 2012, we estimate that there could be over 900 million Internet users in China alone. However, having conducted a thorough literature review, we have found very few citations with regards to web browser icon developments specifically for Chinese users.

Of course it is true that Chinese culture is somewhat different between mainland China, Hong Kong Chinese and Taiwan Chinese, etc. However, in so far as they all communicate using a common ideographic language and share a similar cultural hegemony, we can consider them as a common group with shared cultural markers.

Web browser icons should be intuitive, associative and easy to navigate, in supporting the comprehensibility of Chinese web users. With the rapid growth of usage of computers and the Internet, designers need to be culturally-sensitive to specific users needs [1, 3, 7, 16].

The CCD icons used in this testing have been developed over several years, using Taiwanese participants, we believe that these show promise as alternative browser icons to both IE 7.0 and Safari 3.0. We fully accept that several of these require further enhancements to increase their perspicacity and appropriateness.

The market for web browsers is highly competitive and with the recent introduction of Google's Chrome it is getting ever more crowded. The level of acceptability and preference for Chinese users to use culturalised web browser icons over the traditional offerings from Internet Explorer and Safari remains challenging.

Icon preference testing results clearly show that the vast majority of participants prefer IE 7.0 icons over Safari 3.0 icons; and Safari 3.0 icons over CCD icons. These results are irrespective of gender and educational level. Again, to some extent, this is predictable given the high level of PC (IE) users.

The results of this study provide a solid foundation for future development of all web browser icons. We believe that even the most successful browser, i.e. Internet Explorer can be improved by remodelling their Go/Visit and Favourite icons.

The strength of an iconic representation lies in the user's ability to recognise and interpret its functionality when taken out of context. Further issues that we would like to explore include a 2D versus 3D comparison, use of size, colour. In future we would also seek to balance user groups in terms of PC/Mac users, Experience Levels and Educational Levels.

References

1. Barber, W., Badre, A.: Culturability: The Merging of Culture and Usability. In: Proceedings of the 4th Human Factors and the Web Conference (1998)
2. Brandon, D.: Localization of web content. Journal of Computing in Small Colleges 17(2), 345–358 (2001)
3. Bourges-Waldegg, P., Scrivener, S.: Meaning, the Central Issue in Cross-Cultural HCI Design. Shared values and shared interfaces: The role of culture in the globalisation of human-computer systems. Interacting with Computers: the interdisciplinary journal of human-computer interaction 9(3), 287–309 (1998)
4. Choong, Y.Y., Salvendy, G.: Design of Icons for use by Chinese in Mainland China. Interacting with Computers 9(4), 417–430 (1998)
5. Chu, K.: The Cognitive Aspects of Chinese Character Processing. In: Chang, T.S.I., Ligomenides, P.A. (eds.) Visual Language, pp. 349–392. Plenum Press, New York (1986)
6. CNNIC. Statistical Survey Report on the Internet Development of China (2008), http://www.cnnic.net.cn/en/index/00/index.htm (cited September 7, 2008)
7. Every, D.K.: Innovation: Desktop Metaphor (Netscape 4.7) (1999), http://www.mackido.com/Innovation/Desktop.html (cited November 13, 2001)
8. Fang, X., Rau, P.: Cultural differences in design of portal sites. Ergonomics 46(1-3), 242–254 (2003)
9. Ferranti, M.: From Global to Local. In: Infoworld (1999)
10. Miniwatts. Internet Users by World Region (www) (2008), http://www.internetworldstats.com/stats.htm (cited September 7, 2008)
11. Miniwatts: Internet World Stats (August 14, 2008), http://www.internetworldstats.com/ (cited August 14)
12. Olsen, S.: Maxthon: China's hip browser (June 22, 2006), http://news.com.com/ (cited August 13, 2006)
13. Shen, S.T., Woolley, M., Prior, S.D.: Towards culture-centred design. Interacting with Computers 18(4), 820–852 (2006)
14. Sun, H.: Building a culturally-competent corporate web site: An exploratory study of cultural markers in multilingual web design. In: SIGDOC 2001, ACM, Santa Fe, New Mexico, USA (2001)
15. TWNIC: The report of the use of broadband networking in Taiwan (July 2008), http://www.twnic.net/NEWS/1085.bin (cited September 7, 2008)
16. Yeo, A.W.: Are usability assessment techniques reliable in non- western cultures? (August 23, 2000), http://www.cityu.edu.hk/is/ejisdc/vol3/v3r1.pdf (cited 2001)

Looking for the Image of Modernization:
The Story of Made in Taiwan (MIT)

Ju-Joan Wong

Dept. of Industrial Design, Chang Gung University
259 Wen-Hwa, 1st Road, Kwei San, Tao-Yuan 333, Taiwan, R.O.C.
wtosons@gmail.com

Abstract. Beginning in the 1980s, Taiwan's most vigorous global economic activity trade department faced several difficult issues in succession. Reversing this unfavorable situation by improving the MIT product image in international markets was seen as the solution to these issues. This paper analyzes the cultural contents of those economic and trade policies, and reveals how Taiwan, a marginal state forced by the wave of globalization, constructed a national identity by improving the product image of MIT. Furthermore, this process demonstrates Taiwan's desire to be a 'modern' nation among the developing countries. Based on the above, this paper argues that 'Taiwan's modern design movement' was promoted by MIT discourses through a succession of economic and trade policies. Besides declaring an aesthetic form, this movement also was one of nationalism. However, whether modern design or nationalism movement, both are transcended by the reasonable manipulation of capitalism, and become ideological bubbles.

Keywords: Made in Taiwan (MIT), modernization, economic development, industrial design, national identity.

1 Introduction — Taiwan's Oxymoronic Situation in the International Political Economy of the 1980's

In the globalization era, the production of commodities, expansion of markets, and introduction of technologies, etc. often crosses international boundaries as transport and communication technologies eliminate spatial barriers. More and more corporations are dividing production lines several segments, and then relocate the segments to different countries or regions under manufacturing cost considerations, according to places of origin of products or parts. The dynamic organization of the 'global commodity chain' (GCC) [1] is not regarded as an intact production unit, and thus, investigation of a 'true' production country has become meaningless. Therefore, traditional delimitation of boundaries by country or national identification, have gradually become fuzzy under trans-border operations of global capital. The concept of the nation state of the 19th century was challenged further as political boundaries were gradually blurred as economic globalization weakened fanaticism of nation state, and thus, multi-national enterprises flourished. The face-off of country and capitalism forced government to pass institutional regulations that redefine regions [2], which created tense dialect between

N. Aykin (Ed.): Internationalization, Design, LNCS 5623, pp. 419–428, 2009.

state identification and capital flow. In the 1980s, Taiwan broke off diplomatic relations with several countries following its withdrawal from the United Nations, and then immediately lost its reputation in the international arena. At the same time, Taiwan was included in the post World War II reconstruction of 'new international divisions of labor' (NIDL). The 'Economic Miracle' of the 1960s and 1970s established Taiwan as a developing paradigm of the Non- Communism world. As a result, Taiwan became famous for its enormous industrial productivity, and earned a reputation of the 'shoe-making kingdom', 'the umbrella kingdom', 'the bicycle kingdom', etc, while the Republic of China was gradually removed from the global market. Under this politically incompatible situation of economy, products for export, stamped with Made In Taiwan (MIT), were distributed to world markets, and thus, toys, umbrellas, shoes, hats, and bicycles became the main source for the global image of Taiwan.

As mentioned previously, world trade department in the economic activity of Taiwan faced many great difficult problems: U.S.A. imitation of Taiwan's industries, raised the pressure progressively, 'Chinese and U.S protecting the intelligence proprietary meeting' regularly every year after 1984. American can take 'special 301' as a reprisal measures in case of necessity. Taiwan's increasing trade deficit with Japan in 1991 Taiwan foreign trade gap appeared. MIT products secondary product lacked the competition advantage in the international market. Under abroad buyers cutting prices, a succession of international trade disputes implied that MIT products had flooded the international market and were repelled by various countries. Even Hollywood films have ridiculed MIT products in movie scenes as a kind label of shame. In the 1980s there were many economic and trade officers filled with anxieties regarding the poor image of products made in Taiwan, and thus, called upon Taiwanese manufacturers to devote their energies to improving the MIT image.

The origins of the MIT label began according to Regulations Governing Export Commodities, as issued by the Ministry of Economic Affairs of Taiwan, 'Commodities for export manufactured in the Republic of China shall be marked with "Made in Republic of China", "Made in Taiwan, Republic of China", and "Made in Taiwan", or the equivalent in a foreign language.' In practice, in order to ensure consumers' rights and interests in overseas markets, the Taiwanese government stipulated that commodities transported to countries in diplomatic relations with Taiwan had to be labeled with "Made in Republic of China" or "Made in Taiwan, Republic of China", and for countries without diplomatic relations with Taiwan, the commodities should be labeled "Made in Taiwan", and because there were few countries with formal diplomatic relations with Taiwan at that time, MIT became the general sign used by most manufacturers of Taiwan.

After World War I, the Allies forced German manufacturers to mark the origin country of production, to educate consumers of other countries to resist German goods during economic sanctions on Germany [3], and thus, the mark of 'Made in' for commodities was begun. However, because of excellent product quality, German goods were in great demand on the market. By the 1960s, correspondence between the successful sale of products in international markets and the mark of 'Made in' on products became the norm. Academia, specializing in marketing, focused on probing into this phenomenon as well [4].

Nagashima defined country of origin image as the picture, reputation and stereotype of products from specific countries in consumers' mind. Such stereotype comes from the economic, political, cultural, science and technological development and representative products. The faith generated by consumers about the message of the country of origin is the 'country of origin effect' [5]. Most of follow-up studies analyze the constituent elements of product country of origin, image identification, and discussions about the attitudes of different consumer groups, assessment and willingness to buy [6], [7]. Meanwhile, thanks to the global division of labor of multinational enterprises, the differences between country of brand and country of manufacture are distinguished carefully in details [8]. Product country of origin can be categorized into state labels of different stages such as "made in", "assembled in" and "designed in" [9]. These studies normally hypothesize: 1) country image has been associated with product image; and country image will become a major element of consumer perception if the product information is not significant; 2) although the country image reflected in the product has been associated with economic development and cultural level, it is basically a given fact. These marketing-oriented papers seemed to believe that consumer stereotypes cannot be changed and did not process the construction process of the cultural meaning of product image. In late days, the academic circle started to question the point, basically having reservations. Scholars of marketing such as Koltler and Gertner believed that country image could be managed and influenced although it was not easy to do so [10]. Unless false information is against their own interests, they (consumers) are extremely reluctant to modify their views and knowledge. The above-said studies mean that country image can be a "brand" and affects the international market price according to the position in the market structure. Thus, Shimp, Saeed & Madden proposed the concept of "country equity" to illustrate the interactive influence of country image and the domestic enterprise "brand equity" [11]. In this way, country and product image are linked with each other through international trade on the level of symbolism: In addition to the representation of quality of products made in Taiwan, MIT has become an indicator of the international image of Taiwan, even a vehicle to assess the moral level of "national dignity".

However, how the invisible force of the hierarchical structure of the international market constructs the objective reality and further affects the product values? Is this objective reality is an established structure that cannot be shaken? The author believes that the focus of discussion of these issues does not lie in the validity of the conceptual analysis, but rather to explore how the cultural meanings of MIT to come into being in the pulling and consultation of the globe and the local, the capital and the state, the government and the governed? Moreover, if the market price MIT represents also includes the national identity in addition to production and circulation cost factors, then what are the goals of the national plan reflected by such a dominating structure? The question raised from the perspective of the study of design history actually involves in the dramatic changes of modernization and is related to discussions of product image and national identity.

2 Methodology Retrospect and beyond — Modern Design Movement and National Construction

The history of design has been around the designers and works of the modern design movement as the core, and does not necessarily take any nation as a unit in writing design development. However, many works still regard nation-state as an independent area of research. These writings about design history reflected that the "modern design movement" as described by Peversner as a universal "*Zeitgeist*" (the sprite of age) [12], [13] was not certain. In fact, differences do exist in between different nations and the superiority of nation-state has not been superseded by the modern design movement. Design historian Heskett [14] pointed out that people would use object and environment to build identity to express personal, collective or national special significance. The formation of national identity has often been regarded in many writings of the recent times as a design developmental theme at the turn of the twentieth century. For example, Sparke described that countries in Europe and American had already developed their unique design styles before World War I. Then, in between two world wars, advanced industrial nations hosted large-scale fairs and expositions one after another such as the 1925 Paris Exhibition of Decorative Arts and the 1939 New York World's Fair. It can be seen from there that enterprises also followed the states to integrate design to bring about the commercial publicity and ideological transformational effects [15]. Therefore, design was not only for economic purposes, but also has its political motives, being misappropriated by the power group for political repression or as a means of symbolism. Woodham further illustrated how Britain, Germany, Italy, and the U. S. faced with difficulties of declining national strength and broken economy used by turn the traditional and modern means to shape their new country images to call on identity of the people from aspects including science and technology, industry, household and recreation during the complex international political turmoil of the time period in between two world wars [16].

Regarding the understanding of this period in history, rather than the ideological differences affected the rise and fall of specific design styles; it reflected that the design development had been inseparable from national construction. Heskett directly pointed out that arms race of nations stimulated and accelerated science and technology development and acceleration. In design, functionalism was subject to the military aesthetics [17]. Through the foregoing analysis, firstly, we can find that apart from aesthetics and economics, modern design also includes the political aspect; namely, design development actually relates to modernism and/or national construction. Secondly, the so-called "modern design movement" was created and shaped by a few European and American industrialized nations at the turn of the twentieth century. This also means that modern design movement had well established by the start of the World War II. And the design development in area other than Europe and America after the war has become a forgotten history.

In different historical periods, contemporary design always responded to the commotions of all times to represent national identity by forms of nostalgia and innovation while reflected the reality contractions of economic interests and ideology. This study on the series of movements of Taiwan to create the MIT product image in the 1980s and 1990s reviews Taiwan as an emerging industrialized nation after World War II about its aspiration for modernization and the role design played in the process, expecting to break the myth containing the design history and the Europe and US centered theory to make up the research in design history. And the paper furthermore establishes the multiple perspectives for the study of contemporary design history and gain reflective self-understanding through the design development experience of different areas and countries.

3 From ROC to MIT — Counterfeiting and Creating Brand

Following the pullout of ROC from the UN in 1971 and the break-off diplomatic relations with the US, Taiwan was recognized by the world in names of "fake empire", "piracy kingdom", "counterfeit paradise" and so on. Internally well-known magazines such as *Newsweek*, *Fortune* and *Life* published special reports on piracy in Taiwan one after the other. Back in the early 1970s, relevant administrators had been crying out to eliminate the problem of counterfeiting. However, the efforts seemed to be at the level of moral persuasion only. Except for from time to time investigations, there were no further relevant laws and measures. In the early 1980s, the government prohibited the electronic gaming industry to correct the recreational life of teenagers, forcing the electronic industry originally making microprocessors to imitate Apple II. By 1983, 11 computer makers in Taiwan were charged with counterfeiting. The trading authority and the factories in Taiwan for the first time were taught a hard lesson. Ever since then, the counterfeiting issue of Taiwan has gradually become an issue of particular concern for the rising protectionism in the US.

The important result of this event was that calls to correct product image and criticism on counterfeiting emerged in Taiwan in response to the rising protectionism in the United States. Former minister of Ministry of Economic Affairs, Yao-tung Chao, clearly pointed out in a speech, 'To establish new image for products made in Taiwan', to China Engineers Association in 1983: "*...to present the industrial revolution new achievements by the quality of products made in Taiwan...was the mission of the association.*" Afterwards, director of the Foreign Trade Bureau, Wan-chang Hsiao, delivered a strongly worded open speech entitled 'Counterfeiting is our public enemy'. The speech can be regarded as the further explanation of the meaning of "counterfeiting" by economic and trade officials in Taiwan, see Fig. 1.

It is worth noting that, in the same report, Hsiao also pointed out the need to help manufacturers to build brands, cultivate industrial design talents, and implement new type log system to eliminate copycatting. It can be seen that the government has started to think about applying industrial design resources to help Taiwanese manufactures to promote the quality of MIT products.

In fact, authorities in Taiwan have been encouraging manufacturers to create their own brands to solve this intractable problem. As early as 1970, the official of Ministry of Economic Affairs did call on industries in Taiwan to create and use brands of their own as possible. However, it was to arouse people's self-confidence and self-esteem, expecting that self-created brands could win national dignity and was not related to the elimination of counterfeiting.

Although the government expected to improve MIT product image by helping manufacturers to create their own brands, manufacturers have a lot of misgivings before the MIT international image is improved. It was a great irony that "MIT" label was instead regarded as the greatest burden to the manufacturers to create their own brands. The Brand International Promotion Association (BIPA), a Taiwanese association devoted to promoting manufactures' fame, deliberately stayed away from MIT product image. The director of the Association at that time, Mr. Stan Shih admitted: "*the common ground of members of the association is to avoid being linked with MIT to be adversely affected by the stereotype of poor quality in the world.*" Even Hong Song International Group claiming to build a world brand owned by Chinese used advertisement filled up with sexual appeal for lines of casual shoes in its own brand Travel Fox (see Fig. 2). The naked western male and female models in the backdrop of the product background often make people mistakenly believe that travel fox was a foreign brand. Prof. Hsia, the director of Graduate Institute of Building and Plan of Taiwan University, said bluntly: "*'Made in Taiwan' has never an opportunity to design in accordance with their own images... the so-called Made in Taiwan means the products should look like being made in Japan or the US, instead of Taiwan.*"

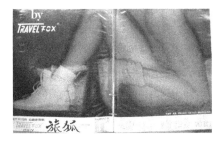

Fig. 1. By institutionalized publicity, counterfeiting was painted not only as a legal problem; it was also related to honor and morals

Fig. 2. In the Travel Fox casual shoes series of advertisements, the naked western male and female models often made people mistakenly believe it was a foreign brand

As for the brand counterfeiting, although it was interpreted as an issue of certain type of commercial ethics, it was actually supported by capitalist economic structure. David Harvey had extended the concept of "monopoly rent" to explain that brand had become new monopoly tool for capitalists to claim for the uniqueness of their commodities which had lost monopoly due to homogenous quality in the global capitalism competition. The aesthetic values and qualities had been converted into the monopoly prices, and thus created a new type of rent [18].

MIT products "borrowing" world-renowned brands wavered in the legal/illegal border areas and shuttled in between European and American well-known brands. Through identifying and pursuing of genuine merchandises, Taiwan was in pace with the global market in taste while the factories filled up with fake products, and become a "consumer society" full of symbols [19].

4 From MIT to ROC — Image Enhancement Plan (IEP)

The US Special 301 Report threatened and confined Taiwan to further expand the exportation to the United States. The given policies of entering for GATT/WTO forced MIT products to compete in both home and abroad markets with products from other countries. After ups and downs, the root to all these problems finally emerged--- how to reshape Taiwan's product image. And this was the beginning of the Image Enhancement Plan (IEP). The father of the plan, former President of the Taiwan External Trade Development Council (TAITRA), Ting-chu Liu, understood fully well in many international trade scenarios the bias and embarrassment of MIT products.

Speaking from the Japanese experience, "...*products made in Japan will benefit even they are not well-known*". Moreover, the Korean Goldstar advertised heavily in American media, closing in on MIT products. As far as an export-oriented country is concerned, such awareness of crisis convinced the relevant governmental departments to reach consensus from top to bottom and was well supported by the Economic Ministry. Under the economic and trade policies led by Chiang Pin-Kung, the IEP was started in 1990. The purpose of IEP, oriented as international marketing, was to promote Taiwan's world standard products and disseminate information of high quality, exquisite and valuable products to the international community. As for the plan implementation, IEP was commissioned by the Foreign Trade Bureau in 1990 to the IEP Team of the TAITRA. The Phase I five-year program was funded in a total of 1.027 billion NT. In the second year of the IEP, Taiwan Excellence Award was granted and used along with the slogan "It's Very Well Made in Taiwan" by the award winning enterprises to symbolize the highest honor of products made in Taiwan. Advertisement started to be published in foreign media such as Business Week, Forbes, Times, NEWSWEEK and The Economist.

The theme of the advertisement sub-plan under the 1992 Image Plan was "Made in Wall Street, Taiwan" (Fig. 3), cleverly connecting Taiwan with the world financial center and confirming the contributions Taiwan made as "Kingdom of Computer" to the economic achievements of the United States.

Fig. 3. The 1992 IEP with the topic of "Made in Wall Street, Taiwan" cleverly married Taiwan with the world financial center and recognized the contributions Taiwan made as "Kingdom of Computer" to the economic achievements of the United States

The implementation of Phase one was agreed by all walks of life including the government, the business and the academics. Therefore, the second phase five-year plan was carried on consecutively with "Innovalue" as the topic, presenting the depth and meaning of MIT products. The budget was increased to 330 million NT, and 62 million of which were set aside as subsidies for joint advertising. The US, the west Europe, Japan as well as the global media were the top priority areas for advertising.

The building of MIT product image at this stage was originated in the publicity activities taken by Taiwan due to the trading pressure and discrimination of MIT products in the international market. It was aimed at making distinction in favor of MIT products in terms of product image and improving the competitiveness of MIT products in the international market. If product prices can be raised and trading partners increased, the trade deficit with Japan could be ironed out while the impact of the US Article 301 on restricting the export of MIT products could be reduced. However, with the apparent economic considerations to get more trading benefits, IEP in fact had more political meanings. On one hand, the government selected excellent products and granted them the honorable titles. On the other hand, the award winners were treated preferentially in taxation and were encouraged to create their own brands. In addition, they were funded to carry out publicity in international media.

The state endorsed MIT products, and in turn, the achievements of enterprises affirmed the legitimacy of the state. Therefore, the more import in-depth meaning of improving MIT image is: with screening, awarding, and exhibiting, the state/government endorsed the products, by issuing the so-called Taiwan Excellence Award in exchange for the loyalty of these enterprises to the government. Also, the government shared the glory and confidence brought about by the industrial achievements to establish a new nation state in the world community "in reality" by products of good image. These can be seen in internationally broadcast ads (Fig. 3). Taiwan voices itself through the excellence products in the ambiguous background; and the products become the mouthpiece of the nation. The state lies behind the awarded businesses and the product-state becomes a one entity with two faces, which are equal and interchangeable. By 2006, the IEP was expanded into the program of "Branding Taiwan" to support Taiwan's own enterprise brands. Enterprise has already become synonymous with Taiwan.

5 Conclusion: Design Movement and Pursuing Modernization

When we retrace history, we see the series of economic and trade policies, anti-counterfeiting and creating on own brand to improve the economic structure of export promotions since the 1970s and enhancing the MIT image of the 1990s, that were initiated by government and organizations overwhelmed by the turbulent international market. Through promotion of the MIT image among featureless products of the worldwide market, Taiwan manufactures could attain competitive advantage. Meanwhile, the Taiwan government could promote its national reputation as well. However, what is the national image that Taiwan wants to create?

After World War II, Taiwan became the sanctuary of Kuomintang (KMT) which lost its authority in Mainland China. The KMT was thoroughly aware that the only way to establish a power base in Taiwan was to pursue economic prosperity. Therefore, the KMT was devoted to molding Taiwan into a notable model of the Three Principles of the People to announce to Chinese of the world, and further challenge China's Communist Party. Teng-hui Lee succeeded the presidency, after Ching-kuo Chiang passed away, and still followed this belief: "*to reform the quality of products and not merely contribute to improve the image of Taiwan, also it can attract people of Mainland China by contrast, spurn Communism, and participate in unification, based on the Three Principles of the People.*" Therefore, anything that diminished the nation's popularity would be monitored closely.

As one of the Newly Industrialized Countries (NICs), emerging in East Asian, Taiwan had an ardent ambition to establish a new national identity, which compared with European and North American countries, promoting novel technical products to distinguish from each other in the major fairs after the Industrial Revolution of 19th century. Sparke argued that design had the political function to communicate national identity, therefore products became part of a country's ideological super-structure, conveying and molding the aspirations and values of the nation [20].

In discussion and examination of the qualities of products/objects, the people/subjects accepted one kind of new value, and simultaneously transformed into 'modern style'. The movement to shape the image of MIT products was the process of a nation to seeking the 'modernized' appearance through design. Thus, design intervened in the construction of national identity, and sophisticated products became symbols of modernity. If products identities, corporate identities, and national identities became the trinity, and enlarged the total effect of promotions to each other, would it be the victorious strategy in international competition, or a beautiful vision of various identities that could be exhibited in Olympiad? Aldersey-Williams, an American design critic argued that nationalism would not be ruined in the powerful current of globalism; design can manipulate national characters to invent new cultural identities [21].

However, facing the globalization of commodities, we should regard new global cultural economy as one numerous, jumbled, overlapped, and disjunctive order, and it can no longer be understood with centre/periphery models [22]. During the globalization era, production and business activities mostly came from multinational corporations' operations and logistics. It was ridiculous to build national identities on products because these activities had crossed political disciplines. In the struggle between 'flow of space' and 'construction of subject', identities gradually became ambiguous; can 'modern' 'state' absorb projections from national enthusiasm?

Marshall Berman reflected on aesthetic consequences of capitalism, and described the contradiction of modernism: "our desire to be rooted in a stable and coherent personal and social past, and our insatiable desire for growth — not merely for economic growth, but for growth in experience, in pleasure, in knowledge, in sensibility,…our desperate allegiances to ethnic, national, class, and sexual groups, which we hope will give us a firm "identity", and the internationalization of everyday life — of our clothes and household goods, our books and music, our ideas and fantasies — that spreads all our identities all over the map…" [23].

People sought permanent and solid national identity in order to obtain a sense of safety, but product images manufacturers cared about were floating and unconfirmed. This aesthetic conflict had reflected the inherent contradiction between state and capitalist. Design, as one kind of professional means to accelerate the circulation of products in capitalism. Even out of political purpose, design would never go against the sophisticated calculations of manufacturer' economic reasoning, just as BIPA meant to keep duplicitous relationships with state. The sharpened political perception relieved them of the dilemma of having to choose one national identity, thus facilitating passing in and out in global markets, especially in Mainland China.

This paper concludes with how those area or countries, whose positions in the spectrum of the modern design movement, were ambiguously connected to design history. To relocate them, modernization would be the critical process; i.e. how design parasitized political and economic activities, and mediated institutional powers of modernity. It also presented submergence behind the modern design movement: the modern design movement was not only one kind of stylistic announcement, but also a political claim of promotion by state. The modern illusions were realized by manufacturers at first; however, capitalism would finally destroy the myth of nationalism hiding behind the modern design movement.

References

1. Gereffi, G.: The Organization of Buyer-driven Global Gommodity. In: Gereffi, G., Korzeniewicz, M. (eds.) Commodity Chains and Global Capitalism, pp. 95–111. Greenwood Press, Westport, Conn. (1994)
2. Scott, A.J.: Regions and the World Economy. Oxford University Press, Oxford (1998)
3. Morello, G.: The 'Made-In' Issue — A Comparative Research on the Image of Domestic and Foreign Products. European Research, pp. 95–100 (July 1984)
4. Schooler, R.D.: Product Bias in the Central American Common Market. Journal of Marketing Research, 394–397 (February 1965)
5. Nagashima, A.: A Comparison of Japanese and U.S. Attitudes Toward Foreign Products. Journal of marketing 34, 68–74 (1970)
6. Johanson, J.K., Douglas, S.P., Nonaka, I.: Assessing the Impact of Country of Origin on Product Evaluation: A New Methodological Perspectives. Journal of Marketing Research 22, 388–396 (1985)
7. Han, M.C.: Country Image: Halo Or Summary Construct? Journal of Marketing Research 26, 222–229 (1989)
8. Han, M.C., Tepstra, V.: Country-of-Origin Effects for Uni-Natiolnal and Bi-National Products. Journal of International Business Studies 19(2), 235–255 (1988)
9. Chao, P.: Partitioning Country of Origin Effects: Consumer Evaluations of a Hybrid Product. Journal of International Business Studies, Second quarter, 291–306 (1993)
10. Kolter, P., Gertner, D.: Country as Brand, Product, and Beyond: a Place Marketing and Brand Management Perspective. Journal of Brand Management 9(4/5), 249–261 (2002)
11. Shimp, T.A., Saeed, S., Madden, T.J.: Countries and Their Products: a Cognitive Structure Perspective? Journal of Academy of Marketing Science 21(4), 323–330 (1993)
12. Pevsner, N.: Pioneers of Modern Design: from William Morris to Walter Gropius. Penguin Books, Harmondsworth, Middlesex (1975) (reprinted with revisions)
13. Pevsner, N.: The Sources of Modern Architecture & Design. Thames & Hudson, London (1968)
14. Heskett, J.: Toothpicks & Logos: Design in Everyday Life. Oxford Univ., New York (2002)
15. Sparke, P.: An Introduction to Design & Culture: 1900 to the Present. Routledge, London (2004)
16. Woodham, J.M.: Twentieth- Century Design. Oxford, New York (1997)
17. Heskett, J.: Industrial Design. Thames and Hudson, London (1980)
18. Harvey, D.: Space of Capital: Toward a Critical Geography. Routledge, New York (2001)
19. Baudrillard, J.: Consumer Society. In: Poster, M. (ed.) Jean Baudrillard: Selected Writings. Stanford University, California (1988)
20. Sparke, P.: Design in Context. Bloomsbury, London (1987)
21. Aldersey-Williams, H.: World Design: Nationalism and Globalism in Design. Rizzoli, New York (1992)
22. Appadurai, A.: Disjuncture and Difference in Global Culture Economy. Theory, Culture & Society 7, 295–310 (1997)
23. Berman, M.: All That is Solid Melts into Air: the Experience of Modernity. Simon and Schuster, New York (1982)

Innovation through Customers' Eyes

Yanxia Yang and Mayuresh Ektare

Trend Micro, Incorporated,
10101 N. De Anza Blvd., Cupertino, California, USA

Abstract. The User Centered Design (UCD) process is well established and used extensively in the industry, except with varying results. Upon engaging the customers in the iterative design process why it is that in some cases the UCD process results in a less than stellar outcome needs to be discussed. A thorough analysis of one scenario reveals that the design innovation means different things to various stakeholders. This paper is a case study illustrating ways of enhancing the UCD process while providing insight into varying viewpoints on the product innovation.

Keywords: Innovation, User-Centered Design process, and Unified messaging.

1 Introduction

Innovation means a new way of doing something. It may refer to incremental, radical, and revolutionary changes in thinking, products, processes, or organizations. The change must increase value, customer value, or producer value. The goal of innovation is positive change, to make someone or something better. Innovation leading to increased productivity is the fundamental source of increasing wealth in an economy [1]. The innovation related to customer experience could be generated through the User-Centered Design (UCD) process.

The UCD process is well established and used extensively in the industry, except with varying results. Upon engaging the customers in the iterative design process why it is that in some cases the UCD process results in a less than stellar outcome needs to be discussed. A thorough analysis of one scenario reveals that the design innovation means different things to various stakeholders. Customer's expectations are established long before they actually use the product. Many different functions of an organization, namely marketing, sales, product development and support interface with the customers, establish these expectations. To a customer, innovation is the best solution that aligns with their expectations. The UCD process does an excellent job of involving customers in the design cycle, but falls short in aligning the various organizational functions that set the correct customer expectations.

During the design phase, a product feature could appear innovative to the customers and development team, but may not deliver the desired satisfaction when viewed as a part of a comprehensive offering and measured against the broader customer expectation. In today's competitive marketplace, it is essential to distinguish your product from others. How a product is distinguished reflects the highlighted organizational value that establishes a certain image in the eyes of the customers. Companies wanting

N. Aykin (Ed.): Internationalization, Design, LNCS 5623, pp. 429–434, 2009.
© Springer-Verlag Berlin Heidelberg 2009

to distinguish themselves on the basis of 'operational excellence' will end up designing a product differently than companies that emphasize on 'product innovation'. Such products have very different marketing strategies, sales cycles, and customer support. The products are considered successful and innovative when the marketing highlights the distinguishing value, the sales team reflects the same with pricing, the product itself shines in those areas, and the support team instills the same value through its interactions with the customers. Together, and cohesively, these various functions in an organization demonstrate value to the customers.

2 Case Study

A newer version of security product was in production to accommodate key customer requirements and replaced the older version. The product aimed to prevent email messages from carrying viruses and other security threats, as well as necessary enhancements towards the way security policies were managed within the product. At Trend Micro Inc. the UCD process is utilized appropriately to execute such product development.

2.1 The UCD Process at Trend Micro Inc.

The user experience group at Trend Micro Inc. has a well-defined user centered design process that aligns with the company strategy of a customer-centric innovation process. The user experience group delivers user interface designs and closely works with the development team to support superior product development. To ensure timely deliverables and the quality of the user-centered designs, the different roles within the user experience group, such as the user researcher, the UI designer, the visual designer, and the usability engineer closely communicate and collaborate during the design and development process. Detailed information about the different roles, their responsibilities and ownerships at different design and development stages is described in [2].The following diagram helps to understand the general user centered design process at Trend Micro.

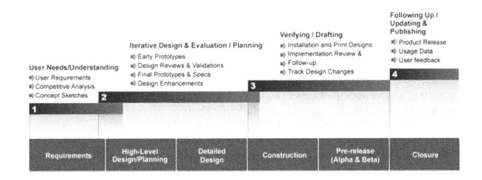

Fig. 1. User Centered Design Process (Copyright @ HIE department, Trend Micro, Inc.)

The user experience group initiates the design project by gathering the user needs. The group receives and absorbs the detailed project roadmaps and raw requirements from in-house domain experts. Customer visits are then conducted to better understand the user behavior and their needs for certain features. Detailed user and task analysis offers design insight to support different user types. Such information is leveraged to design a detailed UI for the product, the design concepts are demonstrated by using a high fidelity prototype. This, being an iterative process, requires efficient communication between the UI designer, the user researcher, and the product manager in order to deliver an innovative design. Formal usability testing is conducted and the technical limitations, if any, are assessed at this time. The user experience team offers continued assistance to address issues that surface during the development cycle.

2.2 UCD Process: As Applied to This Project

The users of existing product offered detailed requirements for the policy management function of the security product. To understand the needs of a broader set of customers, the user researchers visited a few customers during the requirement gathering stage. Some of the key characteristics of the target users were thus identified.

Target User's Key Characteristics:

- Busy, hardworking administrators who could lose their jobs if the enterprise went down or if sensitive information from or to certain company divisions was lost or leaked.
- Phones ringing all the time, used to late-night calls, mailboxes filling with hundreds or thousands of mails almost constantly
- No cards or titles-- military backgrounds and terms like "DMZ"- many of whom worked their way up from the entry level
- Security conscious but used to constant change
  The real needs of target users for policy management were also identified.
  Customer Quotes:
- "They need the modularity and global exceptions for the rules"
- "The current UI is too hard to use, it must have been designed by UNIX administrators"
- "Want to scan everything for viruses-Mandatory"
- "The program should execute policies in whatever order the user specifies."
- "Need for global policies with exceptions for executives, legal, HR, and so on."

Based on the user research data and human behavior, the UI designer came up with a design for security policy management. Using policy rule creation as an example, with people describing a thing, who, when, and what; a rule is created with three parts:

- **User(s)**: who the rule applies to
- **The condition(s)** to evaluate
- **The action(s)** to perform
  That maps in the rule setting UI as:
- For messages **To:** HIE-US,
- If the message is > 10MB,
- Then strip the attachment

The new policy/rule structure had gone through the usability testing for both exist-ing and new customers. The feedback for this design was well-accepted by seven testing participants. In the seven-scale survey (with 1 being very difficult and 7 being very easy), participants rated the tasks related to rule management as:

- How easy or difficult was it for you <u>use the Rules section</u> in the user interface today? (**Average Rating = 5.0**)
- How easy or difficult was it for you to <u>add a rule</u>? (**Average rating = 6.5**)
- How easy or difficult was it for you to <u>update an existing rule</u>? (**average rating = 6.0**)

From the design perspective, the user-centered design process was followed and aligned with the customer-centric innovation process; and the new policy or rule management system was considered intuitive and easy to use.

2.3   Shortcomings of the UCD Process

A year after the product was released, a few follow-up customer visits revealed issues relating to the customers that were using the older version. Some existing customers chose not to migrate to the newer version. Why was the product not as successful as expected? The follow-up customer visits conducted by the support and engineering team revealed certain feedback from existing customers.

What are their current situations?

- "The existing customers had used the older version for about seven years, and they had invested heavily in creating hundreds of policies by using the older generation policy management."
- "They had extensive email traffic and were very concerned about the product sta-bility."

What existing customers expected for the new release?

- "They expected a smooth transition that worked the same after migrating, with previous features kept intact and new features satisfied. Regardless of what changed inside the product, it should run efficiently and remain easy to use."

What is the reality?

- All the existing rules in the older version had to be migrated to a newer version by tuning and merging the existing policies. It was painful and time-consuming for the existing users in the beginning of using the newer version.
- Because the existing customers were used to the older version, there was a learning curve to get accustomed to the new way of defining policies.

While designing the policy management feature for the newer version, we fol-lowed the UCD process. The new product was expected to be easier to use and better than the older version. During the iterative product development process, the team did identify the migration issues, but decided to leap ahead and go with the new policy architecture because it had the potential of bringing customers more benefits such as accommodating their new feature requests by using a well-designed and innovative UI.

2.4   Recommendations to Overcome These Shortcomings

In an enterprise, the system administrators are very risk-averse, especially security administrators. Any changes that require extra effort or involve risk are often pushed back.

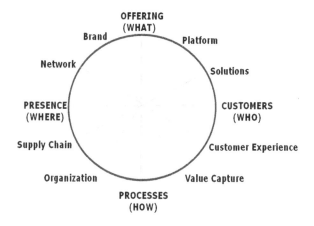

Fig. 2. Innovation full spectrum (adapted from [3])

Innovation is a full spectrum as shown in the previous figure. It requires different functional teams working together, in order to make the innovative product release successfully. What if we did not only market the benefits, but also set up the correct expectation for the existing customers and communicated the cost associated with such migration? A possibility worth exploring was to maintain existing customers on the older version, and target the new release to new customers. For example, when a consumer switches from an old phone to a new one, like an iPhone, they understand that they might have to redo their contacts, but the advanced features and ease-of-use offered in the iPhone balance out the initial migration inconvenience.

3   Conclusion

There are benefits and costs associated with adopting the next generation of innovative products. In the case we discussed, the customers were required to redefine the process of creating policies rendering the methods they were used to in the past versions obsolete. Such disruptive innovation would have been well-accepted if the customer's expectations has been set accordingly. A unified marketing message to justify the cost of adopting the innovation was essential. The messages did highlight the benefits but ignored the associated costs. Because customers were not expecting such a change, their initial impression was an "out-of-balance innovation." Regardless of how well the customer is engaged in the design process, it is essential to remember that a customer providing the feedback is a representative of a broader user base that might not have a realistic insight into the design rationale. They certainly would not understand the benefits of disruptive innovation if all customer facing functions within an organization did not accurately communicate the costs and benefits, as illustrated below.

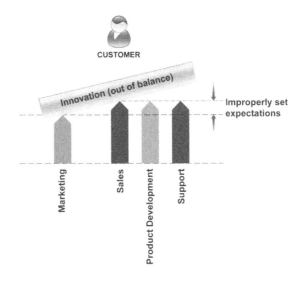

Fig. 3. Innovation through customers' eyes

Innovation is not only about a great design, but also about finesse in execution, management, and fulfillment of customer's expectations. For an organization, each of these different internal functions are tools that, when effectively used in a synchronized manner, can deliver products that do not simply meet expectations but can exceed them.

Acknowledgments. The full support of Trend Micro Incorporated helped to make this article possible. We would like to express our gratitude to our management and colleagues at Trend Micro. We appreciate their support and involvement with this study.

References

1. http://en.wikipedia.org/wiki/Innovation
2. Ektare, M., et al.: User Experience and Design Team: Efficient Handshake between Different Roles. In: Proceeding of Asia Pacific Computer Human Interaction 2006, Taipei, TW (2006)
3. Sawhney, M., et al.: The 12 Different Ways for Companies to Innovate. MIT Sloan Management Review 47(3), 75–81 (2006)
4. Collins, J.: Good to Great: Why Some Companies Make the Leap.. and Others Don't. In: Collins Business, 1st edn. (2001)
5. Kelly, T.: The Art of Innovation. Doubleday Business (2001)

Part V

Designing for E-Commerce, E-Business and E-Banking

The Effect of E-Learning on Business Organizations: A UAE Case Study

Osama Alshara[1] and Mohamad AlSharo[2]

[1] Information Technology Department- HCT, UAE
[2] Computer Science Departement, JUST, Jordan
osama.al-shara@hct.ac.ae, mshare@spirawn.com

Abstract. A major problem that most researchers in developing countries face is that of data availability. The UAE is experiencing advances in many areas; however, availability of raw data is not one of those areas. We are interested in measuring the level of response and adaptation as well as the correctness of the practice of e-learning in non-educational organizations in the UAE. We reviewed the literature to learn about the state-of the art of global practices and experiences of e-learning in non-educational organizations. Unfortunately, we were unable to find any reference to similar work that was done for the UAE market. This paper presents factors of implementing E-learning in non-educational organizations and how does that apply to the UAE culture. UAE based survey with a thorough analysis of the results are presented too.

1 Introduction

Competitive organizations can not over look the critical role of training. It is well known that training increases employee productivity, builds stronger more effective relationships with business partners and allows for better customer service, just to list few. However, training does not come without the usual obstacles of cost, accessibility, time allocation, etc., obstacles that are prohibitive in some cases.

This research has many benefits such as depicting the status of e-learning adaptation by non-educational organizations in the UAE, which has the following advantages:

- It encourages organizations that are not adapting e-learning to do so when they recognize the benefits of such technology.
- It highlights the best practices to be followed by these organization and the problems to be avoided and or solved from the start.
- Allows researchers to study, analyze and give feedback to these organizations.
- It enables the technology providers to understand the UAE market requirements and better serve it.

We have short listed the direct effects of such studies and why it is important for local researchers to put the effort in conducting this type of research. However, we are not touching on the economical, human resources, regional and global competitiveness benefits and factors.

It is important to identify technological, pedagogical, and organizational factors that impact the introduction of e-learning in an organization and not just the technology

N. Aykin (Ed.): Internationalization, Design, LNCS 5623, pp. 437–446, 2009.

part [4]. Unfortunately, and based on our observation of the UAE, e-learning perceived mainly from a technological prospective only. New inventions in high-speed network technology, multimedia delivery, knowledge management (KM) and learning management systems (LMS) represent technological factors [3, 16]. Pedagogy in an e-learning context is about company-specific teaching programs, theories of workplace learning, and conceptual frameworks for evaluating individual and organizational learning [13, 25]. Organization is about company-wide initiatives of sharing knowledge, designing new ways of working and learning, as well as encouraging participation from multiple levels in an organization when decisions about e-learning are made [8, 9, 20].

The complexity of introducing e-learning is to a large extent a result of the complexity of the interdependencies among these three dimensions [19]. Our survey did not cover the above points fully. It did however, cover few major issues but with various details.

2 Factors in E-Learning Implementation

In this section we present six main points organizations should review closely when implementing e-learning. There are questions to answer, initiatives to be taken, challenges to be expected and factors to consider.

2.1 Reasons

Many organizations have implemented e-learning for several reasons. In this subsection we will sight couple studies and its results, which demonstrate some of these reasons. Cost is a major reason as indicated by Dow Chemical whose global e-learning programs saved the company $34 million a year. Before e-learning, the company used to pay $95 per student per course, but now it just pays $11 per student per course [2].

According to a study by Delphi Group on e-learning practices in international business on more than 700 companies, the major reasons why companies invested in e-learning was as follows: 1) that 628 of the companies stated that they needed to have their employees develop additional skills. 2) the need to retain existing employees. 3) 494 companies indicated that lack of training and investment in employees is a reason for leaving the job. 4) lack of qualified employees was indicated by 309 companies [24].

2.3 Marketing E-Learning

To insure the success of e-learning initiatives, organizations must market those initiatives to its employees. The Internal Marketing of an e-learning initiative has four stages:-

a. Planning stage: it is in this stage that you should get the support of the management and the involvement of the users. Users involvement should reflect on content, methods of delivery, users' requirements, etc [17, 18, 30, 32].

b. The launch stage: it introduces employees and managers to the new e-learning program. It is recommended for the organization to have a major launch promotion campaign.

c. Internal Marketing stage: there are various techniques and initiatives to promote an e-learning program internally. Following is a list of the most used approaches:

1. Integrate the e-learning into employees' development and performance improvement programs.
2. Integrate it into the employees' orientation program.
3. Prepare short seminars for managers, trainers, and supervisors. Use mail, email, telephone messages, brochures and bulletin boards to promote.
4. Recognize and reward accomplishments.
5. Provide online courses for family members of employees.

d. Maintenance stage: by developing ways to maintain and increase usage over time. You need to update your offerings and its content by getting users feedback, and discussing the needed changes in your program to tailor for new initiatives by other departments in the organization

2.4 Measuring the Cost

In order to measure the true cost of e-learning, organizations must not only calculate the direct costs of design and development of the program, but also the indirect costs involved in the delivery, and maintenance. Moreover, it is beneficial if the organization conducts a comparison between an Instructor-Led Training (ILT) and the Technology-based Training (TBL) used by the organization. We will not elaborate further on this issue aside from pointing out that TBL would only be cheaper than ILT if there is high number of trainees. .

2.5 Critical Success Factors

There are five critical success factors that make e-learning successful. These factors help companies with e-learning decisions and in avoiding some training failures. These factors or "Cs" consist of culture, content, capability, cost and clients [5]. It is critical for companies to look closely at each of these factors to insure the success of its implementation of e-learning. We will not further discuss these success factors and how they affect or influence the e-learning implementation in this paper.

3 UAE Survey

A major problem that most researchers in developing countries face is that of availability of data. Yet a more problematic issue is the issue of communication, where the data needed by the researcher is available but not published nor communicated properly in order to found. To solve the first problem, we had to implement our own information gathering of data to be analyzed, compared and contrasted. Only then we gain the knowledge of the culture of the problem on hand and reach a set of findings and recommendations.

The problem on hand is the status of e-learning in non-educational organizations in the UAE. We are not aware of any available data on this subject and where to find it if it was available.

The purpose of this survey is to collect data on the awareness, adoption and utilization of e-learning in non-educational organizations (ENO) in the UAE. The survey focused on the cost, tools and success of implementing e-learning initiatives characteristics of such initiatives.

3.1 Survey Analysis

We will present a goal driven analysis of our results. Our analysis will reflect the set the following goals:

- Training programs: if the company promotes training and personal development and which ways.
- E-learning awareness and initiatives: if the company has or is considering E-learning as a method of training.
- Cost and gain: How much is the company influenced by the cost and ROI of e-learning.
- Tools and methods: to find out the tools and methods used in e-learning initiatives.

3.2 Training Programs

All the surveyed organizations showed interest in the personal development of their staff and for various reasons. Chart 1 depicts the reasons for providing training by UAE organizations. If we are to group these reasons based on the number of organizations, we could divide them into four categories;

1. Category 1: Improving job performance and productivity fall into this category. Almost all the surveyed organizations indicated that they perceive training as a major factor in improving employees' skills and compliance with best practices.
2. Category 2: Skills transfer, Maximize profit and achieve total quality management (TQM) fall into this category. 50% - 65% of the organizations reflected that they aim to increase their profit through training; they put more emphasis on best practices in terms of Skills transfer and TQM. Such results demonstrate the organizations' awareness of the highly competitive market of the UAE and thrive for enhancement.
3. Category 3: Compliance issues and Health safety fall into this category. 38% percent of the organizations conduct regulatory based training. This type of training can be perceived as mandatory.
4. Category 4: Short term business problems and Minimizing training cost fall into this category. Only 29% of the surveyed organizations indicated that training cost or contingency problems are a factor in their training initiatives. We would like to believe that most organizations have training as a strategic goal and not a contingency matter.

UAE organizations varied in the type of training programs used for that purpose. Chart 2 shows the ratio of usage of different types of training by UAE organizations. It is clear that more organizations are still using the more traditional approaches of On the job and Classroom based training.

Table1 presents different categorizations and percentages of the used training type by the surveyed organizations. Two figures give us strong indications of the status of

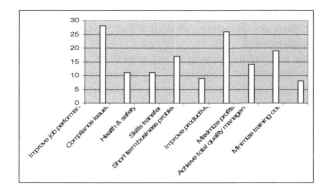

Fig. 1. Reasons for providing training by UAE organizations

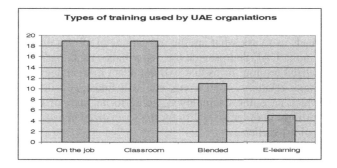

Fig. 2. The ratio of usage of different types of training by UAE organizations

Table 1. Further categorization of the used types of training

Category	Number of Organizations	Percentage
Classroom only	3	10.3 %
Use 1 method only	14	48.3 %
Use all 4 methods	1	3.4 %
Blended or e-learning	6	20.7 %
E-learning only	1	6.9 %

training type adapted by these organizations. Almost half (48.3%) of the surveyed organizations single out one training type and use it, where there is only one company that uses all four methods.

3.4 E-Learning Awareness and Initiatives

The results of this category are very encouraging for the future utilization of technology in cooperate UAE training. When asked if they are considering updating their e-learning initiatives, 70% of the companies said Yes, 10% said No and 20% were undecided. Yet, these numbers reflect strong move towards the future use of technology for training purposes. However, we realize that we failed to ask about a potential time frame for such plans.

The size of the training department in any organization has different indications. It could reflect the interest and emphasis of the organization in personal development. However, it could reflect the ratio of internal versus external training. The results of the survey show that almost 72% of the UAE organizations have 10 or fewer staff members in their training department. From personal experience and the results of this survey, all the organizations deliver training to their employees regardless of the method, which means that there is interest and realization to the benefit of personal development through staff training. This leads us to believe that outsourcing is widely used in the UAE, more than internal training.

Based on these results we foresee two major reflections on the training market: 1) the need for specialized training human resources who are qualified in the setup of technology based training centers to replace the large dependency on the outsourcing of training. 2) the need for digital content for training material. Therefore, content development companies should witness a major increase in business in the near future. All this leads us to ask what are the indications of all this on the more than 500 training firms in the UAE that provide the major bulk of training? It is our prediction that non specialized training firms that will not adapt new strategies, be it in content, delivery, customer relations, contracting, etc, will find major difficulties staying in business. In which case, the unemployed, going to be, staff of these firms need to develop their skill set in order to qualify for the specialized human resources positions referred to in point 1 earlier.

3.5 Investments and Gain

The numbers in this category highlight a major problem in the UAE organizational culture. It is the problem of information confidentiality. 41% of surveyed organizations did not answer this question. This is a problem that we faced in our research that we conducted in the UAE. Organizations are not welling to share financial figures, failures, reasons for swift change of policies, etc.

Based on the results shown in table 2, we can say that about 7 % of the UAE organizations have established a meaningful e and blended learning centers. The rest, which is at least 50%, have not. This is ignoring completely the 41% that did not answer this question.

Through vertical analysis of the questionnaire, we found that more than half the organizations that did not answer this question are organizations that does not use technology based learning.

Table 2. The amount of money invested on e-learning initiatives by UAE organizations

Investment on e-learning initiatives	percentages
- $1000	3.4%
$1000 - $10000	24.1%
$10000 - $25000	3.4%
$25000 - $50000	20.7%
$50000 - $100000	6.9%
$100000 +	0.0%

We can conclude that about 93% of the UAE organizations have not spent that much money on the e and blended learning initiatives. This is a strong indication on the size of this market.

When asked about direct benefits, two thirds of the surveyed organizations believe that e-leaning saves training costs (65.5%), saves travel costs (69%), and allows for better accessibility for the learners (72.4%). Chart 3 depicts the overall results of e-learning benefits from the UAE organizations' point of view.

3.6 Tools and Methods

The top three option for the used e-learning tools were, Learning Management System (LMS), Simulation Tools, and None, as shown in table 3. Less than five organizations use virtual classrooms and authoring tools. LMS is the most commonly used tools as fifteen companies use it, and eight companies use simulation tools. Ten clients do not use any of the mentioned tools.

Table 3. Usage of E-learning tools in the UAE organizations

E-learning tool	Usage
LMS	51.7 %
Virtual Classroom	6.9 %
Authoring tools	13.8 %
Simulation tools	27.6 %
None	34.5 %

Table 4. The percentage of importance of options to the training objectives

Options	1	2	3	4	5
Interactive learning environment	0	7	17	35	38
Variety of media	0	14	27.6	27.6	27.6
Meaningful communication (S-S)[1]	0	7	20.7	31	38
Meaningful communication (S-I)[2]	0	7	10	17	55
Ability of retention measurement new users acquired knowledge	0	7	17	17	52

The results of the used e-learning tools, as reported in table 3, are within expectations, in the most part. Half of the companies are using the LMS, which shows strong administrative requirements by the training departments. The 27.6% reported for the use of Simulation Tools is not a small percentage as it might seem. This is simply the specialized nature of these tools and the need for them in the type of surveyed organizations. Our survey did not cover the industrial sector of the UAE cooperate, which would require such tool more than the type of organizations that we surveyed.

Statistics of the other questions in the survey showed that Better than 70% of the organizations need a tool that manages and administers the training process in their

---

[1] Student-to- Student Communication.
[2] Student-to-Instructor Communication.

organization. Moreover, 50% of the organizations are looking for e-learning tools that allow for content authoring. If we link these results with the analysis in the e-learning and awareness and initiatives section earlier, we can conclude that companies are moving toward expanding the internal training department choice. Hence the content authoring demands new specialized personal to be hired in order to perform this task. These results should send alarming signals to training firms in the UAE market.

The overall results of this question show the bios of the company representatives who filled these questionnaires where most of them were from the HR or training admin staff. They seem to stress the need for the tools that ease up and reflect on the nature of their work. We believe and based on our experience that trainees would have put more emphasis on the synchronous nature of the tool.

Almost 50% of UAE organizations use the Intranet as the delivery method to disseminate online training. The use of CD technology is about 38% and the World Wide Web at about 24%. These figures indicate an overlap in the use of delivery methods, where some organizations use more if not all three methods. However, it is important to know that 24% use none.

The surveyed organizations were asked to indicate, on a scale of 1-5 (5 being the best), how important to their training objectives are different options that are listed in table 4. It is clear that all the organizations did not fully ignore any of the listed options. That is clear from the 0% across the 1 column in the table. To the contrary, the last two options namely "meaningful communication between the student and the instructor" and the "Ability of retention measurement new users acquired knowledge" were of high importance to these organizations at 55% and 52% respectively.

If we add the above average importance, we find that the "variety of media" option and the "meaningful communication between students" are almost of equal importance with 38% scale 5 for both and 31% and 35% scale 4 respectively.

4   Conclusion and Future Work

This paper shows that a good percentage of UAE organizations are aware of the advances in e-learning technology. Furthermore, they recognize the importance and the benefits gained from implementing such technology. It is however, clear that the investment, in the most part, is not sufficient enough to result in serious initiatives.
The survey showed a need for qualified e-learning specialists to be hired and reflected alarming signals to traditional non-specialized training firms in the country to restructure and review its training methods.

This paper does not present the full results of the survey. Hence, further analysis of the survey is needed. Possibly new studies of the market would be conducted based on the result of the analysis.

References

1. Ackerman, M.S., Pipek, V., Wulf, V.: Sharing Expertise: Beyond Knowledge Management. The MIT Press, Cambridge (2003)
2. AILIA Inc.: The Canadian Language Training Industry, Technology Roadmap (2004)
3. Alavi, M.: Knowledge Management Systems: Issues, Challenges, and Benefits. Communication of the AIS 1(7), 1–37 (1999)

4. Anders, I.M., Bård, K.E., Hege-René, H.Å.: Cases and experiences: The workplace as a learning laboratory: the winding road to E-learning in a Norwegian service company. In: Proceedings of the eighth conference on Participatory design: Artful integration: inter-weaving media, materials and practices, vol. 1, pp. 142–151 (2004)
5. Anderson, T.: Is E-Learning Right for Your Organization? the five Cs (2002),
   http://www.learningcircuits.org/2002/jan2002/anderson.html
6. Åsand, H.-R.H., Mørch, A., Ludvigsen, S.: Super Users: A Strategy for Introducing New Technology in the Workplace. In: Kanstrup, A.M. (ed.) eLæring på arbejde (Elearning at work), pp. 131–147. Roskilde University Press, Copenhagen (2004)
7. Bernstein, L.: Biggest e-Learning Challenges, A White Paper, MindIQ (2003),
   http://www.tpic.org/Conference03/TPIC-eChallenges.pdf#search='Biggest%20eLearning%20Challenges'
8. Bjerknes, G., Bratteteig, T.: User participation and democracy: a discussion of Scandina-vian research on systems development. Scandinavian Journal of Information Systems 7(1), 73–98 (1995)
9. Bjerrum, E., Bødker, S.: Learning and Living in the 'New Office'. In: Proceedings of the Eighth European Conference on Computer Supported Cooperative Work (ECSW 2003), pp. 199–218. Kluwer Academic, Dordrecht (2003)
10. Blythe, M., Overbeeke, K., Monk, A., Wright, P.: Funology:From Usability to Enjoyment. Kluwer Academic, Dordrecht (2003)
11. Brandt, E., Grunnet, C.: Evoking the Future: Drama and Props in User Centered Design. In: Proceedings of Participatory Design Conference (PDC 2000), pp. 11–20. ACM Press, New York (2000)
12. Brynhildsen, B.: User Participation in the Early Development of a System to Support Learning at Work, Master's Thesis, Department of Informatics, University of Oslo, Norway (2004)
13. Burton, R., Brown, J.S., Fischer, G.: Analysis of Skiing as a Success Model of Instruction: Manipulating the Learning Environment to Enhance Skill Acquisition. In: Rogoff, B., Lave, J. (eds.) Everyday Cognition and Its Development in Social Context, pp. 139–150. Harvard University Press, Cambridge (1984)
14. Chen, Y.: Corporate e-learning ROI scoreboard: Early leaders emerge. Eduventures Con-sulting, Boston, MA (2001)
15. DigitalThink: The Corporate E-Learning Solution (2000),
   http://www.infotoday.com/KMWorld2000/presentations/WhitePaper.pdf#search='DigitalThink'
16. Elementk: Learning Management Systems in the Work Environments: Practical Consid-erations for the Selection and Implementation of an E-learning Platform. White Paper. Elementk, Rochester, NY (2003)
17. Fischer, G.: Supporting Learning on Demand with Design Environments. In: Proceedings of the International Conference on the Learning Sciences, pp. 165–172 (1991)
18. Fischer, G.: Putting the Owners of Problems in Charge with Domain-Oriented Design En-vironments. In: Gilmore, D., Winder, R., Detienne, F. (eds.) User-Centered Requirements for Software Engineering Environments, pp. 297–306. Springer, Heidelberg (1994)
19. Fjuk, A., Sorensen, E.K., Wasson, B.: Incorporating Collaborative Learning, Networked Computers and Organizational Issues into Theoretical Frameworks. In: Proceedings of the 19th ICDE World Conference on Open Learning and Distance Education, Austria (1999)
20. Grudin, J., Palen, L.: Why Groupware Succeeds: Discretion or Mandate? In: Proceedings of the Fourth European Conference on Computer Supported Cooperative Work (ECSCW-1995), pp. 263–278. Kluwer Academic, Dordrecht (1995)

21. Horton, W.: Designing Web-based training, Industry Report 2000. Training, pp. 45–95. John Wiley & Sons, New York (2000)
22. http://www.ailia.ca/documentVault/Rpts/
    Canadian_Language_Training_Industry.pdf#search=
    %22%20Dow%20Chemical%20whose%20global%20e-
    learning%20programs%20%22
23. ISOPH: E-Learning In Nonprofits And Associations 2004 Nonprofit And Association E-Learning Survey Results (2004),
    http://www.isoph.com/pdfs/
    2004_Nonprofit_E-learning_Survey.pdf
24. Kutilek, L., Conklin, N., Gunderson, G.: Investing in the Future: Addressing Work/Life Issues of Employees. Journal of Extension 40(1) (2002)
25. Lloyd, R.: Survey Tracks Trends in E-Learning. Knowledge Management Magazine (2001),
    http://www.destinationkm.com/articles/
    default.asp?ArticleID=394
26. Ludvigsen, S.R., Havnes, A., Lahn, L.C.: Workplace Learning Across Activity Systems: A Case Study of Sales Engineers. In: Tuomi-Gröhn, T., Engeström, Y. (eds.) Between School and Work: New Perspectives on Transfer and Boundary-crossing, pp. 292–310. Elsevier Science, Amsterdam (2001)
27. Driscoll, M.: Web-Based Training: Creating e-Learning Experiences, 2nd edn., pp. 5–19. Wiley Inc., Chichester (2002)
28. Mørch, A.I., Engen, B.K., Åsand, H.-R.H.: The Workplace as a Learning Laboratory: The Winding Road to E-learning in a Norwegian Service Company. In: Proceedings of the 8th Conf. on Participatory Design (PDC 2004), pp. 142–151. ACM Press, New York (2004)
29. Nielsen, K., Kvale, S.: Current Issues of Apprenticeship. Nordisk Pedagogik 17(3), 130–139 (1997)
30. Rosenberg, M.J.: E-Learning: Strategies for Delivering Knowledge in the Digital Age. McGraw-Hill, New York (2001)
31. Tødenes, A.: From Mock-up to Pilot: User Participation in Evolutionary Prototyping of an E-learning System, Master's Thesis, Department of Information Science and Media Studies, University of Bergen, Norway (forthcoming, 2004)
32. Watson, J.B., Rossett, A.: Guiding the independent learner in Web-based training. Educational Technology 39(3), 27–36 (1999)
33. Wenger, E.: Communities of Practice and Social Learning Systems. Organization 7(2), 225–246 (2000)
34. Wetzel, M.: Stuck in the middle. Online Learning Magazine 34, 30–32 (2001)

txteagle: Mobile Crowdsourcing

Nathan Eagle

MIT Media Laboratory, E-15 383, Cambridge, MA 02139, USA
nathan@mit.edua
and
The Santa Fe Institute, 1399 Hyde Park Rd., Santa Fe, NM 87501, USA
nathan@santafe.edu

Abstract. We present txteagle, a system that enables people to earn small amounts of money by completing simple tasks on their mobile phone for corporations who pay them in either airtime or MPESA (mobile money). The system is currently being launched in Kenya and Rwanda in collaboration with the mobile phone service providers Safaricom and MTN Rwanda. Tasks include translation, transcription, and surveys. User studies in Nairobi involving high school students, taxi drivers, and local security guards have been completed and the service has recently launched in Kenya nationwide.

Keywords: crowdsourcing, mobile phones, appropriate technology, reputation systems.

1 Introduction

The impact of mobile phones throughout the world has been widely documented. These devices now function as fundamental tools instrumental to billions of economic livelihoods. The transformative impact of what is now the fastest technology adoption in human history has had the most dramatic ramifications within some of our most underserved societies. Indeed, while mobile phones were originally designed for Western business executives, the vast majority of mobile phone subscribers today live in the developing world. Africa, with East Africa at the forefront, is currently the fastest growing mobile phone market in the world.

As the price of unlocked GSM phones (complete with sim card and airtime) falls below US$20 in many of these markets, the mobile phone has become many people's single technology purchase. As such, the expectations for this technology far exceed simply two-way communication. In East Africa, where over 90% of the population live in an area with GSM reception, mobile phones are also expected to serve as flashlights, as music players, and now, even as digital wallets.

The reduction in the price of handsets has allowed a dramatic increase in the number of individuals relying on this technology to do their jobs. Day laborers repairing roads throughout Nairobi no longer need to congregate in the morning in central areas throughout the city waiting for prospective employers to collect them for the day's work. Instead, in many of these regions, daily labor is now organized via text message.

N. Aykin (Ed.): Internationalization, Design, LNCS 5623, pp. 447–456, 2009.

However, with unemployment levels rising to almost fifty percent in countries such as Kenya, there are still hundreds of millions of mobile phone subscribers who are unable to find consistent work. Given high rates of unemployment and marginal income sources, many of the more than 2 billion mobile phone subscribers currently living in the developing world would greatly benefit from even an extra dollar per day. Amazon's Mechanical Turk[1] has successfully introduced "human intelligence tasks" that can be completed by individuals with a personal computer connected to the internet for small amounts of money. We apply the same principle to "txteagle", a mobile phone-based system that untethers these tasks from the PC and offers them to the world's billions of mobile phone users - providing an additional source of supplementary income to rural and low income populations.

2 Related Work

SMS Bloodbank. The idea for txteagle originated in the Kilifi local district hospital on the coast of Kenya, where the author worked for the two years between 2006 and 2007. The village of Kilifi is located on one of Kenya's major thoroughfares between the cities of Mombasa and Malindi – a road that hosts a significant number of serious traffic accidents. The Kilifi local district hospital provides emergency support to the victims of these vehicular accidents, which causes the relatively small hospital's blood supplies to be regularly depleted. Messages periodically circulate around the hospital asking for volunteer donors of a specific blood type, and hospital staff become emergency blood donors far more often than is preferable. This situation is at least partially due the lack of direct communication between the rural hospitals and the officials in Kenya's central blood banks.

Together with University of Nairobi research assistant Eric Magutu, we developed a SMS server application that enabled nurses in the local district hospital to directly provide current blood supply levels directly to officials in the centralized blood bank via text message. The information in the text was incorporated in a visual representation of blood levels at the local hospitals. This would have allowed officials to recognize an upcoming shortage before the rural blood supplies were fully depleted. However, the original SMS Bloodbank system was a total failure. While the officials at the centralized blood repositories could regularly check the website to view the rural blood supply levels, the levels were almost never updated by the nurses in the rural hospitals. While virtually all of the nurses owned a mobile phone, they were very reluctant to use their own airtime to regularly pay for the text message necessary to update the system.

In the summer of 2007, we made a slight modification to the SMS Bloodbank system such that it would automatically transfer a small amount of airtime to each nurse after they sent an appropriately formatted SMS with the day's blood supplies. With the simple additional feature, we changed our failed system into an information gathering system that is now being considered for national deployment. Our experience with this initial automatic compensation system led us to consider other types of work that can be completed on (extremely) low-end phones.

---

[1] http://mturk.com

Mobile Airtime & Money Transfers in East Africa. Originally developed to enable subscribers to transfer small amounts of airtime to others, transfer protocols like Safaricom's Sambaza[2] or MTN Rwanda's me2u[3] systems became quickly popular throughout East Africa. It was common practice in many rural areas for mobile phone subscribers to accept an airtime transfer to their phones *in lieu* of a cash payment.

The popularity of airtime transfer systems in East Africa and the use of airtime as a surrogate for currency in rural regions led local mobile phone service providers to allow subscribers to transfer currency as well as airtime. MPESA[4], the first of such a system, was originally developed by Safaricom in Kenya to enable any mobile phone subscriber to send or receive Kenyan Shillings from another mobile phone subscriber. A recipient can withdraw money at any Kenyan post office or one of the thousand MPESA agents throughout the country. Virtually overnight Safaricom became the largest bank in East Africa, and MPESA is rapidly scaling to neighboring countries.

Crowdsourcing on the Web. Enabling the public to earn small amounts of money as compensation for completing simple tasks is not a novel idea. Crowdsourcing, a term coined in 2006 [8], has taken off in a wide range of application domains (see Table 1). Amazon's Mechanical Turk (AMT) is a web service that enables anyone to post 'human intelligence tasks' (HITs) to the AMT's users ('turkers'), as well as be paid for completed tasks. Typical HITs include tasks that are easy for humans but typically extremely difficult for computers such as image tagging, natural language processing, and even survey responses. Most tasks require little time to complete and payments are generally on the order of cents.

Table 1. Types of crowdsourcing applications

Application	Example
Image Tagging	Google, Flickr, ESP Game
Natural Language Processing	OpenMind.org
Photo Sales	iStockPhoto
Coding	Rent-a-Coder, Innocentive

Inferring 'Accuracy' from Noisy User Responses. Inferring the correct answer from the responses of multiple error-prone respondents has been a problem addressed in detail throughout a variety of academic literature. Dawid and Skeene approached the problem in 1979 when attempting to infer a patient's history based on potentially biased reports from different clinicians [2]. They introduce an expectation-maximization (EM) model that simultaneously estimates the bias of these different clinicians as well as the underlying latent variable, in this case the patent's medical record. Variants of this approach have been used for a variety of other applications including linguistic annotations [7], image categorization [5], and biostatistics [1]. While these methods generally assume that all respondents complete all of the available tasks, it is fairly trivial to adjust these models to a crowdsourcing scenario. Snow et al. employ a similar

---

[2] http://www.safaricom.co.ke/index.php?id=244
[3] http://www.mtn.co.rw/me2u.htm
[4] http://www.safaricom.co.ke/index.php?id=745

EM model to infer respondent bias in categorical data [6], while Sheng et al. discuss the problem of response uncertainty and methods to estimate the number of samples required to achieve a given confidence of a correct response [3].

3 Tasks

Humans can outperform computers in many types of simple tasks. Below are some examples of potential tasks using only text and voice communication channels that can be completed on every one of the 4 billion GSM phones in the world today [9].

Transcription. The global transcription market is expected to grow to 18 billion dollars by 2010. With currently over $12B in annual revenue, standard rates in the medical transcription industry are $100 for every 1,000 lines of text, or approximately 10 cents per 65 character line, with a 98% average accuracy rate [10]. Using SMS concatenation, we have shown that 5 lines of audio text can be written down by hand and then copied into an SMS in less than 2 minutes. Paying proficient users $3/hour to do this work on their mobile phone drops the cost to 2 cents per line. Even collecting 100% overhead to cover payments to the operator and our other partners, this still results in a price reduction of over 60% from today's transcription rates, corresponding to an annual savings within the medical transcription industry of over 7 billion dollars.

Software Localization. There are over 60 distinct languages in Kenya alone. It is impossible for software companies to incorporate these languages into their interfaces because no translation service exists currently. We are generating a 'phrase book' of relevant words in every Kenyan language and to date, txteagle users in Kenya have translated these words into more than 15 local languages.

Citizen Journalism. While the idea of citizen journalism is not new, it has yet to have significant penetration within the developing world due to low connectivity and literacy rates. Furthermore, the need for compensation is critical to aspiring journalists in the developing world. By leveraging our existing mobile payment system we enable anyone with a phone to submit a story for free and have compensation directly transmitted back to the handset.

Search Relevancy. The major players in the multi-billion dollar internet search industry all have similar approaches to generating search results and as a result, all perform fairly similarly. By augmenting the machine learning search algorithms with human input, it may become possible to make dramatic improvements in relevancy for specific queries.

Blog / News Translation & Sentiment. Major products get mentioned online thousands of times every day in many different languages. Gauging the sentiment of what is being written about a particular product is critical information for branding and marketing departments, yet extremely difficult to quantify in an automated way using traditional natural language processing techniques. We will ask users if a section of web-scraped text expresses a positive, negative, or neutral sentiment about a particular product or brand.

Fig. 1. There are particular words or phrases that are necessary to adequately localize software, such as the interface of a mobile phone. The photos above shows a phone receiving a translation task targeted at users who speak Giriama, the local language of coastal Kenya and the user being compensated after the successful completion of a set of translation tasks.

Surveys & Market Research. Conducting large demographic surveys in remote areas of the developing world is a challenging and costly endeavor. However in countries such as Kenya, where even the most isolated areas generally have GSM reception, it becomes possible to remotely administer surveys using text messaging. Phone-based surveys are an efficient and economical method of collecting a wide variety of information including market research, census, health, activity, and commerce data. While there is no 'correct' answer when assessing personal opinions, we are also asking users to estimate what the opinion is of the average person in her area. With enough respondents in the area, we will learn if these responses converge.

Beyond txt. We are also developing voice tasks for use during off-peak hours when network usage is significantly below capacity. Our first voice tasks will be rating radio commercials; these ratings will be incorporated into our collaborative filtering algorithms to provide subscribers with targeted advertisements. Additionally, we are working with Nokia to develop tasks for use in training speech recognition engine. Lastly, we are hoping txteagle tasks will soon be able to be completed online, taking advantage of the dramatic growth of the mobile web in many parts of the developing world. Whether it is auditory information for local language transcription, image recognition tasks for video security camera monitoring, or simply more extensive text analysis, we are currently working with operators to offer bandwidth rich services during times when their network bandwidth is underutilized.

4 System Design

txteagle is an active service in contrast to most crowdsourcing services, such as Mechanical Turk, services that are passive. We are building our system to actively select the most appropriate tasks for a txteagle user. By customizing the task difficulty for a given user, we have created a more efficient system to generate high-confidence task responses in the shortest amount of time. The more a user responds to tasks, the more the system learns about the user's areas of expertise and improves the task assignments.

Improving Accuracy through Task Repetition

To ensure tasks have been completed correctly, we send out the same task repeatedly and verify that we are getting the same response across multiple, independent users. Formally, we note that each response y_{ij} comes from an error-prone user j that has an accuracy p_j drawn from a known distribution of accuracies shown in Figure 2a. We initially assume that p_j is independent of a particular task x_i and true answer y_{Ti}, such that $Pr(y_{ij} = y_{Ti} \mid x_i) = Pr(y_{ij} = y_{Ti}) = p_j$.

A simple way to assess the validity of a response is through majority voting. Following a notation similar to Sheng et. al [3], we infer a single integrated response, $\hat{y}$ that is simply the most popular response from a set of users. The probability this response is correct is noted as $q_i = Pr(\hat{y}_i = y_{Ti})$ and is referred to as the integrated quality of the most popular response. Assuming there are an odd number of users $(2N+1)$ to avoid the potential of a tied vote, integrated quality q is defined as a sum of probabilities,

$$q = \Pr(\hat{y} = y_T) = \sum_{w=0}^{N} \binom{2N+1}{w} \cdot p^{2N+1-w} \cdot (1-p)^{w} \tag{1}$$

where w is the number of potential incorrect labels. Figure 2b represents how integrated quality increases as a function of the number of independent respondents who have an accuracy shown in Figure 2a.

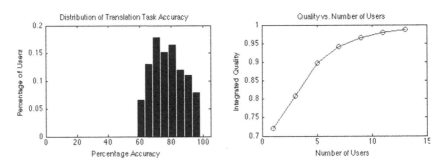

Fig. 2a/b. Figure 2a represents the distribution of initial accuracies of 20 txteagle users for a given set of translation tasks. Figure 2b. depicts how integrated quality q increases as a function of the number of independent users responding to the same task.

Maximum Likelihood Estimates for Task and User Evaluation. While the majority voting technique described above is adequate for simple task completion, we would like to be able to assess the accuracy of an individual user while simultaneously inferring the correct answer to a given task. Dawid and Skene [2] have demonstrated that maximum likelihood estimates of user error rates can be calculated with expectation-maximization (EM) with noisy responses from a set of error-prone individuals (in their case, clinicians collecting a patient record). This technique was similarly used for image classification [5] and Mechanical Turk data [6]. We have developed a similar model infer correct answers, estimate txteagle users' accuracy levels, and infer their expertise (individual accuracy conditioned on task type) based on their response history.

Following a similar notation as above, let T be the total number of tasks and n_{yi} be the number of times x_i is labeled y_i. We define C_{yi} as a binary variable with a corresponding value of 1 if y_i is the true label (out of a total of L possible labels) of x_i and 0 otherwise. If we initially assume that we know the true label y_i, then

$$p\left(y_{i1},...,y_{iW},\mid y_{Ti},x_i\right) \propto \prod_{y=1}^{L} p\left(y \mid y_{Ti}\right)^{n_{iy}} \tag{2}$$

and assuming the user responses are independent, the joint can be described as

$$p\left(y_{i1},...,y_{iW},y_{Ti}\right) \propto \prod_{i=1}^{T}\prod_{y=1}^{L}\left(p(y)\prod_{y=1}^{L} p\left(y \mid y_{Ti}\right)^{n_{iy}} \right)^{C_{yi}} \tag{3}$$

Following from Equation 3, the maximum likelihood estimators of $p(y|y_T)$ and $p(y_T)$ can be simply written as

$$\hat{p}\left(y_i \mid y_{Ti}\right) = \frac{\sum_i C_{yi} n_{yi}}{\sum_1^L \sum_i C_{yi} n_{yi}} \tag{4}$$

$$\hat{p}\left(y_{Ti}\right) = \frac{1}{T}\sum_i C_{yi} \tag{5}$$

Equation 4 enables us to get an estimate of each users' accuracy and with the application of Bayes' rule we can find the posterior

$$p\left(C_{yi}=1 \mid y_{i1},...,y_{iW}\right) = \frac{1}{K}\prod_{y=1}^{L} p\left(y \mid y_{Ti}\right)^{n_{yi}} p\left(y_{Ti}\right) \tag{6}$$

where K is a normalization constant

However, for the development above, we need to know C_{yi} to be able to infer the probability of the prior and the probability of the label conditioned on the prior. If we do not know the true answers, we can use expectation-maximization (EM) to find a local maximum of the likelihood function, treating C_{yi} as a hidden variable, obtaining an initial estimate of the its expected value

$$E\left[C_{yi}\right] = \frac{n_{yi}}{\sum_y n_{yi}} \tag{7}$$

and subsequently selecting values of $p(y|y_T)$ and $p(y_T)$ to maximize the Equation 7. Given these new estimates, we recalculate the conditional expectation of C_{yi} and repeat until the estimates converge.

5   Interaction Scenarios

The following example user scenarios are intended to illustrate how txteagle facilitates financial earnings in rural settings.

Ruth & Betty, Home-Maker / Village Phone Operator, Butare, Rwanda. Ruth is the mother of four and while she reads and writes English fluently, she hasn't been able to find much work in her local village. She'd like to own a phone, but hasn't been able to save up the money. Betty operates a village phone in Ruth's village. By 'renting' the phone to Ruth for 50 cents/hour during off-peak times when Betty has no other customers, Ruth is able to complete 3 hours of transcription tasks – accumulating $7.50 into her savings account and $1.50 into Betty's account. A couple of more sessions like that and Ruth will be able to afford her own phone!

David, Maasai Herdsman, Kisumu, Kenya. While David had been unable to complete formalized education, he, along with many of his Maasi peers, does own a mobile phone. David completes voice-tasks, helping Nokia train a speech recognition engine on his native Maasai dialect. When David wishes to complete a task, he 'flashes' the txteagle Asterisk box that calls him back, asking him to repeat specific key words and phrases. After 30 minutes of work, David has earned enough airtime to last him a week (assuming he doesn't trade it again for another necklace to give to his new wife).

Sophie, Unemployed School Teacher, Kilifi, Kenya. Sophie is an active member of her local woman's microfinance institute and understands the importance of savings. However, she rarely is able to make ends meet for her growing family and has no money to open a traditional savings account. Occasionally she is able to borrow her husband's phone and uses it to begin earning small amounts of money by completing translation tasks for Nokia; texting back the correct translation to words such as "Address Book" in her mother-tongue, Giryama, she soon is on the road to accumulating her own savings.

Emmanuel, Recent high-school graduate (age 14), Mtwapa, Kenya. Emmanuel has just finished secondary school, but is unsure what to do next. He has a lot of time on his hands but he could really use money of his own. Emmanuel begins experimenting with the txteagle transcription tasks and finds that he gets fairly high accuracy scores. Now instead of spending his time loitering around the village with his peers, he's riding a new bike he purchased with his savings.

6   Deployment

As of February 2009, the txteagle service is currently deployed in Kenya on the Mobile Planet shortcode 3007 and will be soon launching in Rwanda. We have studied usage of the service at local high schools, taxi drivers, and with a group of security guards (askaris) in Nairobi. While the groups successfully completed the translation tasks with similar accuracy (~75%), we found the high-school students were able to complete almost twice as many tasks as the drivers and security guards, presumably due to their proficiency with text entry on numeric keypads.

Fig. 3. Two txteagle users completing tasks in Nairobi. During this particular session, they both completed 20 translation tasks in their native languages (Kikuyu and Luo, respectively) and earned 100 Ksh (US$1.25) of airtime.

Porting to USSD. Unstructured Supplementary Service Data (USSD) is a common protocol common to all GSM phones that enables services such as checking an airtime balance (dialing *144#) or topping up with an airtime scratch card (*141#12345678912#). Because over 95% the Kenyan and Rwandan mobile phone markets are prepaid, subscribers are extremely familiar with USSD applications and, unlike SMS, there is no fee associated with its usage. (In Kenya, this has meant that balance enquiry events occur more often than actual phone calls!) USSD is also sessions based, as opposed to SMS which is store-and-forward, which means there is very little latency with interactive USSD-based services, making it an ideal platform for menu-driven applications such as surveys. In collaboration with MTN Rwanda and Safaricom, we are developing a USSD txteagle service that is scheduled to launch in both countries during the summer of 2009.

7 Conclusions

Mobile phones are not only empowering most humans on the planet to connect with each other in real-time communication, but soon phones will enable anyone to conduct real-time, peer-to-peer financial transactions. Although the ability for a Western company to remotely 'hire' a local Kenyan for the completion of simple tasks may be troubling for some [11], it is the author's view that providing additional sources of income to remote and impoverished areas of the world has the potential to have a profound and transformative positive impact on the lives of billions. While this project has demonstrated that it is possible to do work and earn money through a phone, we envision txteagle being the first of many such services that help transform billions of mobile phone subscribers into a powerful knowledge workforce.

Acknowledgements. The author would like to acknowledge the following organizations instrumental in txteagle's initial development and deployment: Mobile Planet (Kenya), Safaricom (Kenya), MTN Rwanda (Rwanda), and Nokia (Finland).

References

1. Albert, P.S., Dodd, L.E.: A Cautionary Note on the Robustness of Latent Class Models for Estimating Diagnostic Error without a Gold Standard. Biometrics 60, 427–435 (2004)
2. Dawid, A.P., Skene, A.M.: Maximum Likelihood Estimation of Observer Error-Rates Using the EM Algorithm. Applied Statistics 28(1), 20–28 (1979)
3. Sheng, V., Provost, F., Ipeirotis, P.G.: Get Another Label? Improving Data Quality and Data Mining Using Multiple, Noisy Labelers. In: Proc KDD (2008)
4. Singh, P.: The public acquisition of commonsense knowledge. In: Proc. Of AAAI Spring Symposium on Acquiring (and Using) Linguistic (and Wold) Knowledge for Information Access (2002)
5. Smyth, P., Burl, M.C., Fayyad, U.M., Perona, P.: Knowledge Inferring ground truth from subjective labeling of Venus images. In: NIPS, pp. 1085–1092 (1994)
6. Snow, R., O'Connor, B., Jurafsky, D., Ng, A.: Cheap and Fast – But is it Good? Evaluation Non-Expert Annotations for Natural Language Tasks. In: Proc. of the Empirical Methods in Natural Language Processing, Honolulu, pp. 254–263 (2008)
7. Wiebe, J.M., Bruce, R.F., O'Hara, T.P.: Development and use of a gold-standard data set for subjectivity classifications. In: Proc. of ACL (1999)
8. http://www.wired.com/wired/archive/14.06/crowds.html
9. http://www.gsmworld.com/newsroom/press-releases/2009/2521.htm
10. Official Newsletter of the Medical Transcription Industry Association of the Philippines (January 2008)
11. Exploitation or globalization, http://news.bbc.co.uk/2/hi/technology/7881931.stm

User Experience Research and Management of Online Advertising and Merchandising

Frank Y. Guo

405 Howard St, San Francisco, CA 94105, USA
frank.guo@barclaysglobal.com

Abstract. Managing user experience of advertising on eCommerce sites poses unique challenges due to the need of balancing profiting and optimizing user experience. Merchandising on eCommerce sites is similar to online advertising, because users oftentimes do not perceive and interact with them differently due to their similar look and feel. This paper proposes a framework of user experience management, an approach towards user research, and a number of design recommendations for online advertising and merchandising.

Keywords: eCommerce, advertising, merchandising, eye tracking, user experience, usability.

1 A Framework of User Experience Management of Online Advertising and Merchandising

Having conducted extensive user research and provided user experience consulting around online advertising and merchandising when working at eBay Inc., I have found that managing user experience of advertising on eCommerce sites poses unique challenges. Defined broadly, user experience management in a corporate setting goes beyond just enhancing the user experience (e.g., usability and desirability of the product). It should also address how to leverage user experience to effect the ultimate business objective – profiting. In most cases these two objectives are in line with each other. For instance, improving the usability of software is likely to increase the sales of the software and bring in more profits. However, with regard to online advertising, conflicts arise between generating profits and improving user experience. The primary goal of having ads on an eCommerce site is to generate advertising revenue. Few would think having ads is an efficient way to improve user experience. Actually, because users typically visit eCommerce sites to buy items directly from those sites, their experience is likely to turn negative by seeing 3rd-party ads. Based on such dilemma, I will describe a framework of managing user experience around advertising, which can easily extend to merchandising.

1.1 Balance between User Experience and Profits – The Big Picture

Based on the above discussion, when managing user experience around online ads, we have to strike a balance between the business objective of increasing ads revenues

N. Aykin (Ed.): Internationalization, Design, LNCS 5623, pp. 457–466, 2009.

and the user experience objective of having better usability, findability, and user satisfaction. That means we need to improve the noticeability and/or click through of ads, while introducing as little harm to user experience as possible. See Figure 1 for illustration. Ideally, well designed ads should have minimal negative impact on user experience, while attracting a decent amount of user attention, indicated by Ideal Ads in Figure 1. Too much attention to ads would distract shoppers from paying attention to the inventory of the site per se. Take one study I conducted as an example. Five ads designs were evaluated, illustrated by Ads version 1 through 5 in Figure 1. Based on the findings I *qualitatively* rated these five versions using this framework. Some of the ads were good at attracting user attention but caused negative user experience (e.g., version 3), and some were ineffective in attracting user attention while causing little negative user experience (e.g., version 4 and 5). In this hypothetical situation, among all these designs, Version 1 was the all-around best design, because it attracted a significant amount of user attention while avoiding too much negative experience. Version 2 and 3 fared worse than Version 1 because they led to more negative experience. Version 4 and 5 led to negligible negative experience, but unfortunately they attracted almost no attention, and thereby defeating the purpose of having ads on the web pages. We can further improve Version 1 by attracting a little less user attention (e.g., making the positioning less salient on the page) so that it does not take too much user attention away from the items that belong to the site itself and decreasing negative impact on user experience (e.g., making the ads sound more functional and less promotional). Using Figure 1 as an example, this means moving Ads version 1 towards the position of Ideal Ads. I will describe specific ways of improving ads design later in the paper.

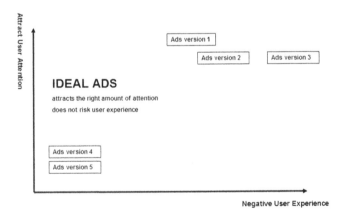

Fig. 1. A proposed model of evaluating advertising. Two factors, attracting user attention and avoiding negative user experience, should be considered together when evaluating user experience success around advertising.

Relative to advertising, there is less controversy around merchandising (e.g., featured items on eBay.com) on eCommerce sites. It is ok for merchandising to attract more user attention, because by promoting items on the same site to the shoppers, it is not "stealing" attention away from the site and undermining the core monetization model of the site, that is, to profit from selling its own merchandise.

The above framework needs revisions based on the context. For instance, it is ok to attract a lot of user attention when a search query does not return any results. In this case, having ads on the page is not competing with the inventory of the site as much as when there are many items found. It also depends on the monetization model of the ads and merchandising. If the monetization model is based on pay per click, then attracting user attention is not good enough for generating profits – click through is a better way of measuring ads effectiveness. Use case also matters. When a user comes to Amazon to perform research, he will be less likely to be annoyed by seeing ads than if he comes here to only shop for Amazon items.

1.2 User Experience Management Objectives

Consistent with the framework outlined above, based on my research and consulting experience, I developed a list of user experience management objectives that are uniquely suitable for online advertising and user research questions that we need to answer in order to help achieve these objectives:

- *Increasing ads effectiveness.* As user experience professionals, we should leverage our knowledge of user behavior to make ads more effective, by making users spontaneously notice and click the ads in their natural way of using the site. In terms of user research, we need to understand if users click the ads intentionally or by mistake, and whether they will re-visit the ads or avoid the ads after clicking them the first time.
- *Avoiding confusion around ads.* We should make sure that we do not introduce confusion to users by presenting ads on the site. In terms of user research, we need to understand whether users understand the nature of the ads, before and after clicking into the ads, and whether users mistake ads for merchandising given their apparent similarity.
- *Avoiding negative attitude.* We should decrease the amount of negative attitude towards ads, or even introduce positive experience towards ads if possible. In terms of research, we should assess user attitude throughout the entire process, including before and after they click into ads.
- *Enhancing usefulness.* We should design ads so that they are useful to the users. For instance, the ads might supplement the inventory when users cannot find what they are looking for within the inventory. In terms of research, we can probe users about use cases in which ads could be useful as well as observing if users spontaneously leverage ads when doing shopping.
- *Avoiding interference with user tasks.* Whereas there is little usability value in having ads per se, the presence of ads might hurt the usability of the rest of the site. In terms of research, we should investigate if ads interfere with users' completion of their intended tasks, such as looking at product reviews, checking out an item, etc.
- *Preventing leaving the site.* For pay per click ads, we would like users to click the ads. On the other hand, we would like users to return to the site after clicking into the ads. In terms of research, this requires us to observe user behavior after clicking into the ads.

Most of the above objectives and research questions also apply to merchandising because of the apparent similarity between advertising and merchandising. On the other hand, we should be less concerned with avoiding negative attitude and preventing leaving the site when it comes to merchandising, because merchandising contains content or inventory that belongs to the site itself instead of a 3rd party.

2   User Research Approach around Online Advertising and Merchandising

As mentioned above, in order to achieve the aforementioned user experience management objectives, we need to conduct research about how users interact with ads and merchandising first. User research around online advertising is rather different from typical user research such as inspecting software usability and evaluating the comprehensibility of web content, due to three reasons. First of all, there is *no clear use case* for ads per se – users do not come to an eCommerce site in order to see ads. Also, ads research generally *does not focus on usability*. Ads are not designed to accomplish particular tasks that users would typically perform, and therefore usability is not a main concern. So unlike when investigating software usability, we cannot ask users to perform a task that is intentional with regard to ads, such as "please find out the price of a camera that is NOT coming from an eBay seller", because this kind of task is not part of users' actual use cases on an eCommerce site. Another related point is that users probably *do not spontaneously notice ads*, so if we ask about their experience around ads, we will bias participant response by pointing their attention to something that they might not spontaneously notice. Given the unique nature of ads research, in this section I will introduce a recommended research approach and a set of common research questions. I will also highlight eye tracking as an optional research approach.

2.1   Research Approach

The above discussion points to the importance of studying *spontaneous* behavior in *realistic* contexts when conducting ads research. Whereas there are many research paradigms that could potentially accomplish the research goal, I would like to focus on in-lab user evaluation in this paper, because this approach provides the most in-depth exploration into user behavior relative to non-interactive techniques such as surveys and quantitative remote user sessions. Below is a list of key techniques to employ when conducting in-lab ads research:

- *Have participants do spontaneous shopping tasks.* In order to understand real user behavior, we should use tasks that ask participants to do whatever that they would typically do on a site, such as "please do some online shopping at your own pace", without further specifications. Spontaneous shopping task allows participants to engage the eCommerce site in a natural manner and see realistic ads served by actual ads algorithms. In addition, relevance of ads might be an important factor in ads experience. If we force users to do a task that they do not care about, we lose the opportunity to see how relevance plays a role in their experience. Take shopping on eBay for an example, a participant might be a collector and would look for a rare antique clock on eBay. It is unlikely that any crafted task that the researcher can think of would match this participant's main use case when shopping on eBay, and will not get the participant engaged and exhibit natural shopping behavior.

- *Use realistic testing environment.* Unlike conventional user experience studies that heavily leverage low-fidelity prototypes, because we want to observe users' natural behavior, we should use a live site or high-fidelity testing environment, which allows users to search and browse as they wish and which will serve ads intelligently based on ads algorithms.

- *Mask true intention during moderation.* When moderating the sessions, please keep in mind that noticing ads is a low frequency behavior, and if we force participants to comment on ads or do things specifically related to ads, we will get findings that do not reflect their natural behavior. Therefore, when interviewing participants, it is important to reveal our intention of investigating about ads as late as possible. Even when probing about ads, we should avoid only focusing on the ads and let the participants talk about other things on the screen as well.

- *Observe first, probe later.* This technique is in line with the masking true intention point. As soon as we start probing, we start loosing the chance of understanding users' spontaneous behavior. Observing without asking questions is a great way to understand unbiased user behavior around ads. I would suggest not probe participants about the ads during the tasks, except when they mentioned the ads spontaneously. Only probe about ads *after* all tasks, to avoid biasing participants for later tasks.

- *Avoid referencing to the ads as" ads" during moderation.* This makes it possible to understand how participants naturally interpret the ads – they might not realize that these are ads at all.

- *Have users perform similar shopping tasks multiple times.* Because noticing ads is a low-frequency behavior and user behavior towards ads is dependent upon the context (e.g., what kind of information they are looking for on the site), asking users to do a variety of tasks will give us more chances of observing how users interact with ads in various contexts and when looking for various items to shop. For instance, we can ask users to shop for several items instead of just one item and observe how they behave around ads when shopping for them.

- *Investigate how search results impact ads experience.* For search-related tasks, user behavior around ads might be affected by the quantity and quality of the search results. For instance, when a user searches for an item on the site, if there is no item found, the user will be more likely to notice the ads than if there are many items found. The researcher should design a few tasks, some of which yield many search results and some of which yield few search results.

- *Be cognizant of how context affects ads experience.* Finally, the researcher needs to be cognizant of how context might affect user experience around ads, and design tasks and interpreting findings accordingly. For instance, users might be less tolerant about ads when doing transaction than when exploring shopping options. It is advisable to design tasks addressing different contexts separately and avoid making generalizations across contexts when interpreting research results.

2.2 Eye Tracking as an Optional Research Approach

Visual attention is an important component to understanding user experience around ads and merchandising. For instance, is the user simply ignoring the ad or is paying attention to the ad without clicking on it? Such question can only be answered by a direct assessment of visual attention. Visual attention is rather spontaneous in nature, so oftentimes participants are not cognizant of where they looked at. This makes think aloud protocol less useful when investigating visual attention. Eye tracking, by tracing where the eyes fixate on the screen momentarily, is the most suitable research tool. I applied eye tracking to some advertising and merchandising studies that I conducted to complement the conventional evaluative techniques I used in those studies. Beware that eye tracking data alone are hard to interpret. For instance, users fixating at one area of the screen can either be interpreted as this area works well or this area confuses users – both possibilities lead to lots of visual attention. Therefore in order to help interpret eye tracking data and yield a comprehensive understanding of user behavior, eye tracking data should be cross referenced with think aloud protocol, interview, and observation of behavior. This does not mean that eye tracking session should be run at the same time when thinking aloud is elicited – talking while doing the tasks will affect eye movement and thus make the eye tracking data less valid. Typically, instead of running a stand alone eye tracking session, I use eye tracking to supplement the conventional user evaluation method that leverages think aloud protocol, probing, and observing of behavior in order to get additional information not collected by the conventional methods. To avoid bias and collect clean eye tracking data without the influence of moderation and learning, eye tracking session should precede conventional usability session. When running the eye tracking session, spontaneity is the key. Moderation, lack of interactivity in the prototype, think aloud protocol, and any kind of study-induced artificiality would make the eye tracking data less reflective of users' natural visual attention pattern.

There are various ways to interpret eye tracking information. Conventionally eye tracking data are analyzed quantitatively by aggregating data across a large sample of participants for each task [1]. The "heat map" that we saw from many eye tracking studies is an example of the quantitative data. The quantitative data can help us understand how much attention various screen regions attract user attention, but do not let us know about the process of how users discover information on the page. On the other hand, eye tracking data can be analyzed qualitatively one participant at a time on a task by task basis, much like how we analyze data for ethnographic research and one-to-one interviews. The qualitative data, when cross-referenced with think aloud protocol and observation of behavior, can provide rich insight into the process of information discovery. Both types of eye tracking data are rather valuable to advertising and merchandising research.

3 Recommendations for Managing Online Advertising and Merchandising Experience

Based on observation, interview, and eye tracking data collected around numerous websites from the many user evaluations I have conducted, I was able to derive consistent insights around advertising and merchandising experience. Many of these insights were also validated against findings from research conducted by others, which includes analytics, A/B tests, and market research studies conducted around same or similar websites about same or similar advertising and merchandising designs. I break down the insights in details below:

- *Looking like ads leads to negative user experience and attracts less user attention.* This might sound counterintuitive to many advertising professionals. After all, professional achievement by default should be measured by how crafted an ad design is. And the notion of "advertising campaign" is based on the idea that ads should be explicitly promoted to consumers in order to effect its marketing goals. However, at least in the eCommerce context, in order to attract user attention and avoid negative user experience, ads that look promotional (e.g., using polished graphs, containing generic motivational texts like "come and get one!") frequently annoyed the participants I interviewed when they did online shopping on the sites. By contrast, ads that were similar to the rest of the page attracted much more attention and produced much less negative experience. This is consistent with the well documented "banner blindness" phenomenon [2], according to which online users consciously or unconsciously ignore any thing that looks like a banner. In cognitive psychology, there is also such well-documented behavior called inattentional blindness, according to which people tend to ignore information that they are not actively attending to, even when the information is presented in a rather salient manner [3, 4]. It is noteworthy that making ads look like the rest of the page might sound deceptive, but as long as the ads did feature actionable inventory, my participants exhibited negligible negative attitude, despite the fact that they realized they were misled into believing the ads were featured items on the site.
- *Graphics might hurt, if too promotional or without pictures of the items.* We often talk about graphic ads versus text ads, without realizing the distinction within graphic ads: graphic ads with pictures of specific items and graphic ads without pictures of specific items. Pictures of the specific items for sale attract user attention and do not give users the impression of being ads-like. By contrast, graphic ads without item pictures or with artistically rendered item pictures feel like too promotional and ads like, and attract less user attention and lead to negative user experience.
- *Ads experience on eCommerce sites are different from that on search engines.* Users are less annoyed by ads on search engines such as Google than on eCommerce sites, because the former is not a shopping destination. Users go to search engines in order to get to specific shopping sites. Advertising on search engines is consistent with this user goal. In contrast, eCommerce sites are shopping destinations – users visit these sites because the sites have unique values to their shopping and do not want to go elsewhere.
- *Concrete items lead to better user experience and more user attention.* Ads that feature concrete items with specific information such as price (e.g., "a 30G iPod at $200") and pictures of the item are more likely to attract user attention than ads that feature a generic store (e.g., "click here to check out our store, which has a large selection of iPods.") User attention always gravitates towards concrete and

easy to understand information that forms the "don't make me think" experience, consistent with some previous research [5, 6].

- *Habituation alleviates negative user experience.* Multiple rounds of user evaluation of ads on the same sites showed that negative experience towards ads subdued as time passes. This finding is corroborated by direct comments made by participants, who explicitly mentioned that they were getting used to seeing ads on the sites. The overall internet experience also matters. Many participants mentioned that as more eCommerce sites feature ads, they began to feel less hostility towards seeing ads.
- *Context-dependent advertising.* Users are more annoyed by advertising on pages where they engage in targeted tasks (e.g., search results page, transaction page), and are more tolerant of ads on pages where users explore the content (e.g., homepage).
- *Interfering with user tasks leads to negative user experience.* Ads that interfere with user tasks (e.g., ads placed at top of search results) lead to worse user experience than ads that do not interfere with users tasks (e.g., ads placed at bottom of search results).
- *Relevance helps improve user experience and attract user attention.* Conventional wisdom tells us that relevance might be a key factor in the success of online advertising. My research corroborates this idea. In particular, both think aloud protocol and eye tracking revealed that ads relevant to users' tasks led to better user experience and attracted more user attention.

It is noteworthy that these insights are related to eCommerce sites that serve as a shopping destination such as eBay and Amazon, rather than comparison shopping sites such as shopping.com. Because users do not buy directly from comparative shopping sites, without conducting user research on them personally, I would hypothesize that they are more tolerant to 3rd-party ads on these sites.

Whereas these insights were derived primarily from my experience with eCommerce platform, they should also apply to other types of websites because they are related to some basic psychological mechanisms of online behavior. For instance, we can hypothesize that the reason that text ads work great on Google is because they look rather similar to the rest of Google content. This is consistent with the idea that ads should not stand out as ads on the page, and should blend well into the rest of the page.

4   Discussion

Proposals and recommendations presented in this paper are based on a basic premise – online advertising is more or less detrimental to user experience, and it is user experience professionals' job to balance profit making and user experience concerns. Some might argue that ads might actually improve user experience by providing more abundance to shopping experience. For instance, if a user cannot find an item on Amazon.com, 3rd-party ads can provide the user with alternatives. However, this is a risky way of enhancing shopping experience, as it undermines users' perception of the inventory quality of the site itself and might turn the user away from the site in the long run. Improving inventory and findability of the site itself is a much better approach than leveraging ads. So I would advise never to treat online ads as a means of improving user experience – it is always just a means to make profits. And if the business does not make significantly more money with online ads than without them, then just do not have them on the site. On the other hand, well designed merchandising is a safe way of enhancing users' shopping experience, as it features items from the site itself.

This paper offers many recommendations around improving online advertising. These recommendations are based on many rounds of user evaluations rather than an outcome of intuition, and are cross referenced with extensive quantitative research findings and analytics data. These recommendations are also the outcomes of cross-referencing between what participants said and what they did, rather than just listening to what they said. Some recommendations are rather counterintuitive. To summarize, the most important take-home message is that optimizing online advertising is not just about addressing the *what*, (i.e., what items the ads feature) – it has a lot to do with the *how* (i.e., the presentation and implementation of ads). Many ads professionals spend much time thinking about what message the ads should deliver. For instance, they might debate about whether to convey winning the bid or getting a cheap price when determining what messages an ad that features an auction item should deliver on eBay.com. But they tend not to pay an equal amount of attention to how the ads are substantively presented, such as visual treatment, page layout, the look and feel of the ads in relation to the rest of the page, length of the ads text, the quality of graphics, and so on, which also greatly impacts how well ads work. Another important piece of advice is that we should stop presenting ads like ads, that is, artsy and polished, and start making ads look like the rest of the eCommerce site, that is, showcasing concrete pictures and concrete item information and being functional, not flashy, in visual treatment. When making ads look similar to the rest of the page (e.g., featured items), so long as the ads feature concrete and actionable merchandise, users will not be upset by being misled, as indicated by my interviews with online shoppers. We also need to be clearly aware of the distinction between how users interact with ads online and how users interact with ads on other types of media, such as TV commercials – It is relatively much easier for users to neglect online ads. For instance, they do not even have to use the remote control to change the channel. Participants of my studies almost unconsciously filtered out ads from their attention. So in order to attract user attention to online ads, the ads experience should be designed in such way that makes users attend to ads without them even thinking about it. These recommendations also generally apply to merchandising, an area that is very similar to advertising in users' mind.

Disclaimer. The views expressed herein are those of the author and do not necessarily reflect those of Barclays Global Investors or its subsidiaries, management, or employees.

References

1. Jacob, R.J.K., Karn, K.S.: Eye Tracking in Human-Computer Interaction and Usability Research: Ready to Deliver the Promises. In: Radach, R., Hyona, J., Deubel, H. (eds.) The mind's eye: cognitive and applied aspects of eye movement research, pp. 573–605. North-Holland, Elsevier, Boston (2003)

2. Norman, D.A.: Commentary: Banner Blindness, Human Cognition and Web Design, Internet Technical Group (1999)
3. Simons, D.J., Chabris, C.F.: Gorillas in our midst: Sustained inattentional blindness for dynamic events. Perception 28, 1059–1074 (1999)
4. Benway, J.P.: Banner blindness: The irony of attention grabbing on the World Wide Web. In: Proceedings of the Human Factors and Ergonomics Society 42nd Annual Meeting, vol. 1, pp. 463–467 (1998)
5. Krug, S.: Don't Make Me Think: A Common Sense Approach to Web Usability. New Riders Press, Indianapolis (2005)
6. Gladwell, M.: The Tipping Point: How Little Things Can Make a Big Difference. Back Bay Books, New York (2002)

Supportive Web Design for Users from Different Culture Origins in E-Commerce

Kyeong Kang

Faculty of Engineering and Information technology, School of Systems, Management and Leadership, P.O. Box 123, Broadway, NSW 2007, Australia
Kyeong@it.uts.edu.au

Abstract. This paper presents an investigation of supportive design features for users from different cultural origins in global e-commerce sites applying the principles of human computer interaction to web interface design. This investigation was necessitated from a need to establish an understanding of the barriers in the implementation of e-business on a global level. The paper begins with an overview of current business-to-user (B2C) e-commerce implementation on the web, and then describes cultural issues in the global e-commerce.

Keywords: culture, e-commerce, web design.

1 Introduction

In a global context, a good web design for attracting international users in BtoC e-commerce is a challenging issue. A good web design supports effective business activities and user satisfaction. Therefore a supportive web interface is the essential concern in a competitive global market. Business developers are stepping up the use of new technology to achieve their goals but there is little concern in expanding their markets beyond their home countries expect for English speaking users. It is expected that such an expansion in e-commerce will support the economy of several nations and create new opportunities in and around their physical locations. Cultural differences may also be reflected in user-service provider relationships, communication channels and user expectation levels of information service functions. So a good web design enables support opportunities for increasingly diverse culture users' involvement by reducing cultural and language barriers that may exist for being part of a global market through the Internet.

2 Background

In Human Computer Interaction (HCI), there is substantial literature suggesting that supporting user trust and response to a web design are far more important than just entertaining users though fancy features [1-4]. There are many different approaches for designing web sites, supporting users, and in designing web sites to help users

N. Aykin (Ed.): Internationalization, Design, LNCS 5623, pp. 467–474, 2009.

efficiently achieve their goals [4-10]. Certainly several design approaches are continuously evolving. Though, general design guidelines in the Human Computer Interaction are always relevant. Literature suggests that the elements of the quality of navigation and information presentation are essential [8, 11-15]. Particularly, the literature relating to user trust in HCI puts an emphasis on user motivation and satisfaction, relating to quality of navigation and information presentation [16-18]. However, most of the time international e-commerce sites are directly translated into different languages at most and distributed to different country origin users. In an international context, the image features employed in interface development makes a somewhat lesser impact on the variety of contexts it is concerned with, although it will be very clear to a minor proportion of the population [19]. This provides an indication that consideration of human factors in the design of web for an international user base is an important factor in promoting effective usage of information systems. However most web interfaces do not support effective usage due to use of unsuitable images in a global context. Most of the information is presented on the web by icons, metaphors, shapes, colors of text and background, frame and text locations on screen, etc. These may be relevant to their culture of origin but may not be understood by the global audience.

Another general principle for designing interfaces is minimisation of memorising, optimisation of operations and engineering for error [20]. Also the use of attractive multimedia features in a page should not interfere with the speed of the web site download (maximum download time 10 seconds) [21]. The user should be able to interrupt any multimedia display if it takes to display more than 20 seconds. Generally, customers are seeking information with some expectations. So the effective display of information on the web site is an important issue when designing a usable e-commerce site. Some recent literature has discussed about localised design issues in language, context and user performance, and design of localised interfaces needs to be based in local culture [22-24]. However the key issue of how designers are influenced by their culture and incompatibilities with users' cultures has been ignored and not been investigated so far. Design of web sites for effective use is a highly innovative process involving intuition, experience and resolving various technical issues.

3   Aim and Approach

3.1   Aim

The study's aim was to find supportive design features by identifying web design characteristics in different countries. This was achieved through examination of users' experiences in global e-commerce sites, focusing on favorite site features and preferences for Australians and Korean users.

Australia is a recognised multi-cultural society, based on migration from many different countries established over the past two hundred years. The population adapts many cultural features from different countries and incorporates it into an evolving Australian culture. The population spread is about 78.5 % English only spoken at home, and the balance with Italian, Greek, Cantonese, Arabic and other minority cultures [25]. The majority of the population show a distinct European outlook towards business practices and cultural interpretations. There is however, a substantial proportion of the Australian population who navigate between the main cultural sphere and their ethnic subculture simultaneously. Hence, they are influenced by their cultural backgrounds in negotiating everyday transactions of life, including surfing of web sites and purchasing goods and services online. For improving e-commerce usage in different e-commerce sites and web design issues, this paper discusses issues which should be addressed it to suit international customers on a global level. This paper addresses issues relating to users' experiences and preferences on e-commerce sites in two different countries.

3.2 Approach

The research methodology used in this study was survey based, with participants from Australian and Korean participants residing in Australia. The research method combined quantitative and qualitative research methods as described in references [26, 27]. The process involved data collection through questionnaires, and interviewing participants. This approach enabled confirmation of generalizations and testing the impact of cultural differences on users' preferences.

According to Hofstede's dimensions [28] and Galdo and Nielson's [29] findings, the collectivist-type users have common behavior as a group, and under individualism, users want to have control over their surrounding environment. Hence these characteristics can be reflected in typical attitudes used in web based e-commerce. Korea is an example of collectivist society as identified by Hofstede [28], while Australia has an individualistic culture. Difference in users' country of origin is the most important factor for the site implementation. However current e-commerce practices take minor account of cultural issues while design technologies continuously attempt to introduce more attractive and convenient tools for local users. Table 1 describes different nature of individualism and collectivism based on Hofstede's study [28]. From Hofstede's study [28], there are different cultural aspects in Australia and Korea (South), which are comparably opposite. From this view, different cultural aspects will impact on e-commerce differently.

From the point of view of developing a good e-commerce web site, there are always issues about lack of collaboration in design, layout and information presentation that need to be resolved successfully to achieve a satisfactory outcomes [8, 30]. Also user's culture has a strong influence on the customers' (or users') responses, feeling, trust and/or satisfaction [31, 32]. Users feel and act on web sites within the culture. Users' negative or positive reaction to e-commerce web sites needs to be understood and identified in e-commerce practice.

In Chau et al's (2002) study on user behaviour in relation to culture in e-commerce, it was argued that e-commerce users are different in nature as they are surrounded by different cultures, and the emphasis should be on local user preferences. This is the key issue in supporting e-commerce practices. Even though the Chau et al's study has not fully investigated users' responses from the same e-commerce web site in different cultures, it shows user responses in e-commerce sites and has important implications in improving user responses. Rose et al (2003) also emphasised that culture has a major impact on user responses to e-commerce sites. Rose et al's (2003) study shows that, users understanding of information on the web will be different to users from different

Table 1. Differences in individualism and collectivism based on Hofstede's study [28]

Nature	Individualism	Collectivism
Attention	Everyone grows up to look after him/herself and his/her immediate family only	People are born into extended families or in other groups which continue to protect them in exchange for loyalty
Identity	Identity is based in the individual	Identity is based in the social network to which one belongs
Communication	Low-context communication	High-context communication
Employee-employer relationship	Employee-employer relationship is a contract supposed to be based on mutual advantage	Employee-employer relationship is perceived in moral term, like a family link
Management	Management of individuals	Management of groups

cultures. Therefore presenting information on e-commerce sites can be an essential issue for users and providers. Barber and Badre's (2000) study about merging culture and usability work is a helpful guideline for attracting potential international users.

We targeted two user groups from Australia and Korea (South) and the survey responses were analysed, comparing user experiences. The researcher approached the users individually in several social group settings. Then the researcher conducted surveys followed by a short semi-structured interview within the social group. Each user completed the questionnaire, with 62 Australian and 100 Korean (South) respondents. Amongst the Australian participants, 53 were born in Australia, and rest of the respondents were not born in Australia (6 from UK, 1 each from China, Ireland and Sri Lanka). Korean (South) respondents were all born in Korea (South).

The questionnaire was formulated separately for Australian and Korean (South) groups in English and Korean languages respectively. The questionnaire contained four categories of information: user background, favourite site and services, reasons for using Australian based sites, user feelings about the sites and whether they found sites from their home country useful.

4 Findings and Comparison

4.1 Findings

The most favourite sites in the two groups were "ebay.com.au" for Australian respondents and "daum.net" for Korean (South) respondents respectively. The two groups were found to have distinctly different interests in e-commerce sites, Australians used the e-commerce sites for purchasing various types of goods from global and local e-commerce sites, while Koreans (South) were interested in using multiple services in a single e-commerce portal especially focussed on local sites and the most favourite item for the Korean (South) respondents were fashion items.

Australian and Korean participants responded that the most popular site for searching products was an auction site. They were browsing for clothes, tickets and other products as listed in Table2. On the other hand, Koreans seem to have a strong motivation in use of the e-commerce site for checking email, searching for fashion goods, reading news, downloading games, downloading songs, searching for electronic goods, etc.

Table 2. Survey responses-user favourite goods and services

Favourite goods/services			
Australian	count	Korean	count
auction items	20	email	14
clothes	4	fashion goods	12
entertainment tickets	2	news	6
browsing	1	game	4
computer (hardware/software)	1	computer (hardware/software) and download songs	5
flight tickets	1	checking price for digital cameras	4
horse gear	1	comparing prices (looking for discount or a cheap price)	4
electronic goods	1	gym equipments	3
no answer	30	electronic goods	1
		no answer	47
Total	62		100

No Australian respondents had experienced the use of a Korean (South) site prior to this study. In contrast, most of Korean (South) respondents were familiar with or had experienced an Australian site. The reason for this is because most Korean (South) respondents who participated in this survey were visiting Australia or residing for a period of time in Australia. However, Korean (South) respondents preferred to use sites based in Korea (South) first, and then went on to global sites if they wished to make purchases. The language barrier was the most stated reason in both the groups. However there are other possible reasons including differing attitudes that influences their preferences for making purchases on global sites for both the survey groups.

Korean (South) respondents also commented that they felt different about Australian sites in the aspect of having a different reason for finding information (15%), delivery methods (10%), payment methods (9%), language (10%), speed (3%) and other unspecified reasons. It implies that perhaps users not only depend on language but also on sensitive characteristics of product information on e-commerce sites and other services for making decision to make purchases or usage of services.

4.2 Comparison – Two Culture Groups

The study shows that majority of the Korean (South) users prefer to use same popular communication tools, and looked for similar types of products, and wanted to be connected to a popular site, all characteristics of collectivism. In the Australian group, users looked for similar sites but were more focused on personal interests. In a way, Australian users were found to have a combination of characteristics from both the collectivist and the individualist traits. It perhaps provides an indication that the characteristic traits in the Australian group probably relate to the factor of the diverse countries of origin of respondents within in the Australian group.

Australian and Korean (South) groups also demonstrated different preferences in local (Korean (South)) and global e-commerce sites. The Australian group had no boundaries in visiting local and global sites, while the Korean (South) group had a distinct interest in visiting only local sites. Australians were more likely to find products from local and global sites while Koreans (South) preferring to find information in the local (Korean (South)) sites and then the global sites as an alternate choice. This shows that the 'e-mall' type of e-commerce model has popular names as 'portal site' and seems to work for Koreans but not for Australians.

According to Hofstede's (1980 and 1991) cultural dimensions, comparing Australian and Korean populace, Australians have a high score in individualism and masculinity in comparison to high scores for Koreans in power distance, uncertainty avoidance and long-term dimensions. However from this study, the results show the cultural dimension of individualism was different from the Hofstede's study (1980 and 1991) in this instance. Other dimensions could not be applied because they were not prominent from the interview data. Though in the current study Hofstede's dimensions of individualism vs. collectivist were not numerically measured, these were interpreted from the study through participants' comments during the interviews. From the interviews, the cultural dimension of individualism was found to be higher for the Australian culture and collectivism higher for the Korean culture confirming Hofstede's outcomes (1980 and 1991).

5 Conclusion

The result shows that the characteristics of design features in different countries were identified in BtoC e-commerce on the global level. Overall, the design of favourite sites for Australians look relatively simple compared to Koreans' favourite sites. The global site based in USA provided similar design features to the Australian site except display of local products and images. The Koreans' favourite sites looked very different from Australian preferred site. Features such as use of multiple menus and contents contained various types of information, products promoted for shopping and community communication tools. This study with Australian and Korean (South) group of respondents provides an understanding of what customers need to support e-commerce in different cultural settings. Also, this concept can be extended to help in creating supportive web design for users from different cultural origins in e-commerce, especially for users positioned in both collective and individual cultures simultaneously.

References

1. Gefen, D.: Reflections on the dimensions of trust and trustworthiness among online consumers. ACM SIGMIS Database 33 (August 2002)
2. Kules, B., Shneiderman, B.: Users can change their web search tactics: Design guidelines for categorized overviews. Information Processing & Management 44, 463–484 (2008)
3. Smart, K.L., Rice, J.C., Wood, L.E.: Meeting the needs of users: towards a semiotics of the web. In: IPCC/SIGDOC 2000: Proceedings of IEEE professional communication society international professional communication conference and Proceedings of the 18th annual ACM international conference on Computer documentation: technology & teamwork (2000)
4. Spool, J., Scanlon, T., Snyder, C., Schroeder, W.: Measuring Website Useability. In: CHI 1998, Los Angeles, April 18-23 (1998)
5. Dormann, C., Chisalita, C.: Cultural Values in web site design. Vrije University, Amsterdam (2002)
6. Elnahrawy, E.: Accommodating Users from Different Cultures: Guidelines for Web Developers. HCI Journal of Information Development, Third Quarter (2003)
7. Head, A.: Design Wise: A guide for evaluating the interface design of information resources. Information Today, Medford, NJ (1999)
8. Nielsen, J.: Designing Web Usability. New Riders Press, USA (2000)
9. Simpson, A.: Business and IT together. Software Management 29, 16–17 (1992)
10. Smith, A.: Human Computer Factors: A Study of Users and Information Systems. The McGraw-Hill Companies, London (1997)
11. Anders, G.: Better, faster, pretties. The Wall Street Journal 22, 12–20 (1999)
12. Instone, K., Chan, L., Lund, A., Arble, F.: Practicing Information Architecture. In: Special Interest Group meeting at CHI 2001, April 3, Seattle, Washington, March 31 (2001)
13. Norman, D.A.: Emotional design: why we love (or hate) everyday things. Basic Books, New York (2004)
14. Preece, J.: A Guide to Usability: Human Factors in Computing. Addison-Wesley, Wokingham (1993)
15. Shneiderman, G.B.: Designing information-abundant web sites: issues and recommendations. International Journal of Society 47, 5–29 (1997)
16. Fogg, B.J., Marchall, J., Laraki, O., Osipovich, A., Varma, C., Feng, N.G., Paul, J., Rangnekar, A., Shon, J., Swani, P., Treinen, M.: What makes Web Sites Credible? A report on a large quantitative study. In: CHI 2001, Seattle, Washington, March 31-April 5, vol. 3, pp. 61–68 (2001)
17. Cyr, D., Bonanni, C., Ilsever, J.: Design and E-loyalty Across Cultures in Electronic Commerce. In: Sixth International Conference on Electronic Commerce, pp. 350–360 (2004)
18. Zang, P., Dran, G.: User Expectations and Rankings of Usability Factors in Different Web Site Domains. International Journal of Electronic Commerce 6, 9–33 (2002)

19. Kang, K.S., Corbitt, B.: Effectiveness of Graphical Components in Web Site E-commerce Application-A Cultural Perspective. Electronic Journal of Information Systems in Developing Countries 7 (January 2002)
20. Hansen, W.J.: User engineering principles for interactive systems. In: The Fall Joint Computer Conference, Montvale, NJ, pp. 523–532 (1971)
21. IDC, Internet Market Commerce Model: the Industry Standard (2006),
    http://www.idc.com
22. Onibere, E.A., Morgan, S., Busang, E.M., Mpoeleng, D.: Human-computer interface design issues for a multi-cultural and multi-lingual English speaking country-Botswana. Interaction with Computers 13, 497–512 (2001)
23. Starr, J.: Design considerations for multilingual web sites. Information Technology and Libraries 24, 107–116 (2005)
24. Sun, H.: Building a culturally-competent corporate web-site: An exploratory study of cultural makers in multilingual web design. In: SIGDOC 2001, Santafe, New, Mexico, USA (2001)
25. A.B.O. Statistics: 2006 Census QuickStats, Australia, Canberra (2007),
    http://www.abs.gov.au/Ausstats
26. Mason, R.D., Lind, D.A.: Statistic techniques in business and economics. Irwin, Chicago (1990)
27. Yin, R.K.: Case study research: Design and methods. Sage, Thousand Oaks (1994)
28. Hofstede, G.: Cultural Consequences: International Differences in Work Related Values. Sage, Bevery Hills (1980)
29. del Galdo, E., Nielsen, J.: International User Interface. Katherine Schowalter, USA (1996)
30. Norman, D.: The Invisible Computer. MIT Press, Cambridge (1998)
31. Rose, G., Evaristo, R., Straub, D.: Culture and consumer responses to web download time: a four-continent study of mono and polychronism. IEEE Transaction on Engineering Management 50, 31–44 (2003)
32. Chau, P., Cole, M., Massey, A., Montoya-Weiss, M., O'Keefe, R.M.: Cultural Differences in the online behavior consumers. Communications of the ACM 45, 138–143 (2002)

How Mobile Money Can Drive Financial Inclusion for Women at the Bottom of the Pyramid (BOP) in Indian Urban Centers

Apala Lahiri Chavan, Sarit Arora, Anand Kumar, and Praneet Koppula

Human Factors International, USA
apala@humanfactors.com

Abstract. This paper looks at challenges and opportunities on how mobile money can drive financial inclusion for women at the BOP (Bottom of the Pyramid) in urban Indian centers. We explore the current ecosystem of financial transactions and the role of women in a BOP household. Specifically we look at how this ecosystem differs based on how long ago they migrated from rural India and how that impacts their financial transactions. By understanding the gaps and the barriers, we outline specific challenges and opportunities for driving financial inclusion for women, through mobile money. We also posit that the success of mobile money depends on whether the 'solution' moves away from the paradigms used for designing mobile money solutions for those at the top of pyramid.

Keywords: Financial inclusion, mobile money, women, bottom of the pyramid (BOP), microfinance, loans, credit, payments.

1 Introduction

Women have the responsibility of looking after the household and they may control some of the inflow of money in the urban BOP household, but the outflow of money is still very much controlled by men. In this scenario, women are very resourceful in managing the limited amount of money, by having secret savings and they optimize on the consumption of household resources, mostly without the knowledge of men. They fear that men may unnecessarily spend if they are aware of the existence of this money in the household.

1.1 Financial Transactions

Access to credits and repayments is a very important aspect of their financial ecosystem. Since income within the household is very limited, even with both the man and woman working, borrowing of money is key to their existence and survival. The two major reasons for 50% of the borrowings from non-banking sources are financial emergency and medical expenses [1]. Loan repayments (mostly informal lenders) form a large part of the financial transactions, for the women, on a daily basis.

N. Aykin (Ed.): Internationalization, Design, LNCS 5623, pp. 475–484, 2009.
© Springer-Verlag Berlin Heidelberg 2009

Access to formal loans or even banks, is a challenge [1] due to various factors: Illiteracy; Lack of collaterals (no identity proof, lack of fixed assets); No permanent occupation.

They have to resort to informal money lenders. The access to this informal loan system again depends largely on how long they have been staying in the urban centre and the connections with the local community. The choice of the informal money lender depends on many factors: Ease of repayments; Trust - money lender being from the same community; Amount of money to be borrowed; How quickly they need the money, i.e., criticality of the situation (financial crises, medical emergency, etc.)

Women face yet another challenge – from a gender perspective. If they are borrowing money for the first time, they usually have to be accompanied by men to the money lender's place, even if they are the ones who will repay the money.

Women are mainly responsible for medical and healthcare of the children in the household. In the time of a medical crisis, women have to take quick decisions including borrowing of money or taking the sick to a doctor. At such times, they are in need of quick ready finances. All the transactions are purely cash based. They usually carry cash along with them as they do not feel safe to keep their money in their house.

These are some of the issues which largely influence their financial ecosystem.

Since the women in BOP in urban areas do have better access to technology as compared to women in rural India, they are more likely to adopt technology solutions that directly enhance their livelihood and financial inclusion. For example the penetration and the use of cell phones in urban India is higher than in rural India.

Can mobile money be a solution to address these gaps and barriers?

Case studies and pilots [2, 3, 4] of M-banking and M-payments in many parts of Africa, the Philippines and Bangladesh have shown positive impact on how mobile phones may alter patterns of money sharing within families by giving women greater autonomy and control over household savings.

We will look at specific design challenges pertaining to security, infrastructure and cultural issues, through two user stories, that will be fundamental to initiate adoption of mobile money and drive financial inclusion for women in the Indian ecosystem.

2 Research

We did primary dip stick research (6 participants) with women in the lower socio economic segment (Socio Economic Classification, SEC D). The research was done in urban and semi-urban centers in Bangalore.

All of the women were employed. The women who have been in the urban centers for more than 5 years were self employed and the others were daily wage earners. (This was also a finding of the research – that more the time they spend in the urban centre, more they try and move towards independence through self employment.)

Half of them were using mobile phones (either as a shared device or individual usage). Mostly they used mobile phones to make or receive calls. One of them was specifically using the mobile phone for her business (flower vendor, taking orders). The impact the phone has on their lives is that it increases their efficiency in their daily activity and reduces costs that they could have incurred without the phone [5].

For example: One of the participants, who needs to take public transport, gets a status call from her father when the bus is only two stops away. This helps her maximise the time with her family, otherwise she would need to wait at the bus stop for a long time.

To complement the primary research we also did an existing literature research which included: Impact and adoption of mobile phone [6] across the world in development initiatives; Existing mobile money initiatives and its impact [7, 8, 9]; General structures of the informal credit suppliers in India [1]; Role of women in micro lending and payments in rural and BOP [2]

2.1 Stories of Mallamma and Manjula

We highlight the challenges and the opportunities for mobile money through two user stories. Mallamma and Manjula are representative users where Manjula represents a more sophisticated user in terms of her financial transactions.

2.2 Mallamma

Migrated to Bangalore 5 years ago.
Occupation: Construction worker (without a permanent contract).
Family: Widow, mother of five children (2 children staying in the village).
Sister's family lives in the adjoining shack.
Household income: ~ Rs 3,700 ($ 74) per month.

Mallamma lives in a kaccha house (shack) with no electricity or sanitation. She works as a construction worker without any permanent contract with her employer. This means, she has to look for work on a weekly basis. She lost her husband a year back and most of his financial liability has been passed onto her, even though she was not aware of most of her husband's borrowings. She has five children, two of whom have stayed behind in the village with their grand parents where they go to school. The children, who are with her in the city, have recently started working as house maids to help augment their mother's income.

From her construction work, Mallama earns Rs 500 – 600 ($12) a week, if she is able to find continuous work. She receives her wage on a weekly basis on a Saturday evening. She also has the flexibility of getting an advance on a Wednesday, in case of an emergency. Two of her daughters are able to earn Rs 600 a month each while working as house maids. So the total earnings in her household could be about Rs 2000 – 3700 ($ 74).

Mallamma's expenses
She plans her expenses on a weekly basis, after receiving her wages on Saturday. This includes:

- Repayment of short term credit (which needs to be paid back in a couple of days, like credit from the grocery shop, people within the community).
- Small savings in form of a chit fund to pay long term credit. This chit fund is very specific to her community from her village, who have moved to the city

- Grocery buying for the coming week.
- She also does very small savings, which she keeps with her always, as she does not have any safe place to store them. She does not trust the men at home (specifically her brother-in-law). This small money is to take care of any unplanned expenses.

Once in every couple of months, she sends money (Rs. 300, $ 6) back home to her parents for her children. She visits her village at least once every 3 months. This is usually an unplanned expense. She still has a very strong connection with her village.

Since she does not have regular employment and there is no assured source of income, she invariably ends up borrowing to make her ends meet. She has a credit of Rs. 5000 ($ 100), borrowed from the village money lender, to pay for her daughter's medical expenses. Even though it was an emergency situation, they were not able to generate enough money locally in the city and they had to travel for three days, and spend more than Rs 300 ($ 6), to go back to the village to borrow Rs. 5000 ($ 100).

Over and above that there is a huge credit of Rs, 20,000 ($ 400) passed on to her after her husband's demise. She was not even aware that her husband had borrowed this much amount of money from the village money lender. After her husband expired, the village money lender showed her some documents claiming that her husband had borrowed this money and now she is liable to pay. Typically, in her village, the village elders are involved as witness whenever money is lent. This also forces the person to repay in case there are any disputes.

Interestingly, in her village, women are not encouraged to appear before the money lender for loans. Only the men in the household go to the money lender. She recollects that her husband had said that Rs. 5000 had been borrowed for their daughter's treatment, but she had not been taken along as it was understood she would not be the one repaying the loan. Now, ironically enough, she is the one who has to repay all loans.

She feels more comfortable in borrowing money from the village money lenders as compared to the ones in the city. There are a few reasons for that: They know her and so the trust factor comes in -she has no social interaction outside her community; The rate of interest is lower as compared to the city; She can repay the loan depending on her convenience.

The ties with the village are very strong. Even in the scenario that she receives a large amount of money, say through chit funds, the first thing she does is to carry the money personally to the village for safe keeping, again spending that Rs. 300 and three days of travel. She does not trust that the money will be safe with her in the city, especially since she goes out everyday for work.

Opportunities for Mallamma

- *Mobile money to aid efficiency and access.* Malamma still has very strong ties with her village. She travels every couple of months back to the village mainly to: Repay loans; Borrow money; Give money to her children and her parents. She can save a lot of time, effort and money if she can use some form of mobile money. The key challenges will be to bring in some form of social validation while these transactions are done, specifically repayment and borrowing of money.

- *Mobile money for savings and safety.* Malamma does not trust the men at home. Moreover, she does not have any secure place to store money in the house. She feels most comfortable when she carries the money with her. Mobile money can be a secure alternative for her.
- *Mallamma may not use mobile money by herself.* Mallama is illiterate and does not even understand fully how to use a mobile device. She may not be too comfortable using mobile money by herself; for her a proposed solution should address the challenges of accessibility and affordability [9] more than that of convenience.

She might need assistance. There is an opportunity where trusted people from her community [7] can provide the mobile money service, while it can be monitored through established financial institutions.

For example, the neighborhood grocery shop owner (who could be from the same community as Mallamma) can be a provider of financial services through mobile money. This will help Mallama to transfer money back to the village for planned expenses as well as in case of emergencies. She can also get credit from her village where the money lender can send in the money directly or through the services of a local grocery store in the village. This will help Mallamma save cost of travelling every time there is a financial crisis. Since there is an overall monitoring by a financial institution Mallamma will feel very comfortable and secure while making the transactions. It's important to have a physical proof, like a receipt [6], every time a transaction is done, until they are comfortable with the concept of virtual money. Though the details of the transaction can always be available from where ever the financial institution operates from, it's essential that she have a proof of each and every transaction in case any dispute arises in the future.

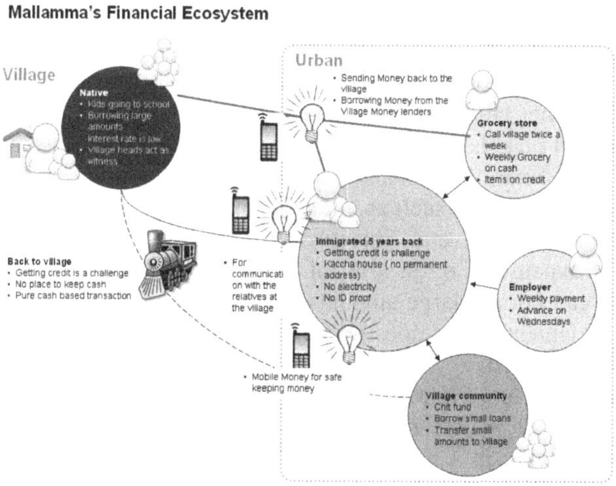

Fig. 1. Mallama's Financial Ecosystem & Opportunities

2.3 Manjula

Migrated to the city 13 years ago.
Occupation: Flower vendor.
Family: Mother of 2-year-old girl and 8 year old son, living with her father and mother
Income: Rs 7000 ($ 140) per month, contract flower supplier for temples

Manjula lives in a rented house with her parents. She used to have a flower stall near the temple. She had to close down the stall to take care of her family emergency (sister's child birth). Currently, she only takes care of the contract orders of three temples. Earlier her mother used to run the house, now she is bedridden with diabetes. With the reduced income she now has to borrow money to meet her expenses. She plans to open her flower stall in the next few weeks. This would give her substantial income to meet her expenses.

Manjula's expenses
She manages her expenses on a day-to-day basis, but some of her finances are on a monthly basis, based on the contract payments from the temples.
    Daily expenses: Capital for the flowers; Payment of loans and small savings (This is through PIGMY, PIGMY is a form of saving fund, which also doubles up as a source of loan in times of need.); Medical expenses for her mother (last year she had to spend more than 30,000 rupees)
    Monthly expenses: House rent; Interest for the loans; Payment of chits (This is also done on a weekly basis or whenever she gets money.)

Savings & loans
Along with PIGMY, Manjula also saves money for some emergency expenses as well as planned expenses like festivals and other rituals. This money is with her all the time. She visits her village once in a year or whenever there are some religious rituals. Last time she visited her village was for the ear piercing ceremony of her daughter.
    She prefers PIGMY as the mode of saving and borrowing because: Can save on a daily basis to repay some of the loans incurred from money lenders, etc; Source of money for planned purchases (such as a television), family events (ear piercing ceremony of the child at home), etc; This system also prevents her from withdrawing money for frugal expenses, i.e., in a lot of ways their money is "locked in."; Once trust is built, she can borrow large amounts (Rs 25,000 – 30,000); Flexibility in payment (lenders are lenient if she does no pay for one day, they do not insist on two days payment on the next day).
    Even though she prefers PIGMY for both her savings and loans, she feels it is a huge liability to maintain the records of her savings.
    She has started saving in a nationalized bank to build some financial credibility. But she still prefers PIGMY as they come to collect from her doorstep. She is planning to take a loan from the bank but is not sure if she would be eligible.
    During emergencies, she either borrows from the informal money lenders on an interest or from a pawn broker. In both cases, the money borrowed has to be paid back

in one go. The interest rates, from the informal money lenders, is very high (60 – 120% per annum). She prefers taking loan from the pawn broker because there is no harassment to repay, which generally happens with other money lenders (very often they use abusive language and harass her to pay up in front of the neighbors).

Even though Manjula runs her own business and takes care of all the household financial transactions, the lenders take reference of her father, the first time they lend the money. Now she has built enough trust and in fact, they prefer giving loan to her than to her father, as everyone knows that she is the one who will repay the loans. There have been couple of instances when her father had borrowed from the money lenders, at very high interest rate, and she had to repay. Whenever she has to collect the money (loans or savings) from PIGMY, she either takes her sister or her father (this is purely for safety purposes) as she has to go in the evening to collect the money from the lender's office.

Whenever she receives large sums of money, she either deposits in a bank or gives it to her relatives so that they can pay off their high interest loans. She has to inform them 2-3 months in advance whenever she wants her money back (the relatives sometimes take another low interest loan to pay her back).

Manjula owns a mobile phone. Earlier they had only one phone, which was used by her father and there have been instances when her clients have called her father and she has missed the orders. Her brother-in-law had given her his mobile for few days, and she found it very useful. Now she has purchased a mobile for herself. This has eased a lot of her work and also helped her in business.

Opportunities for Manjula

Most of the opportunities for Mallamma will hold true for Manjula. However, there can be some additional opportunities for Manjula.

- *Empowering Manjula through a personal finance tool.* Manjula handles various financial transactions and instruments – Some on a day-to day-basis and some of which are on a monthly basis. Most of the time she is not aware of the rate of interest that she is paying for the loan. She gravitates towards those loan instruments which are simpler to understand and easy to pay, though she may end up paying higher rate of interest. Mobile phone can empower her to manage her finances. Nokia in India has introduced a concept of Nokia Life Tools [10] – a range of agriculture, education and entertainment services designed specially for the consumers in small towns and rural areas of the emerging markets. Such services can be extended to the financial services with tie-ups between the hardware manufacturer and the financial institutions. This would help her to not only understand her earnings and the various loans but also plan for her future to fulfill her aspirations.
- *Mobile Phone as an information dissemination tool.* A mobile phone can be used as an information dissemination tool by the government and private initiatives to help women like Manjula understand how she can be part of more formal financial systems. And she can also receive daily updates on market prices as well. This information can be used to persuade people like Manjula to accept mobile phone as more than just a communication tool.
- *Mobile money for transactions.* Mobile money can be seen as a way through which regular monetary transactions can be expedited. The financial ecosystem around

Manjula is pretty much stabilized in terms of the people she interacts with finan-cially. She has her customers who pay her back on a monthly basis and she still has to buy from the wholesale dealer on a daily basis. Her savings and loan repayments happen on a regular basis. She personally handles these transactions and more than often these are delayed, if she cannot travel on that day. An automatic payment system through mobile money can help her save time taken to travel and wait for the person involved (for example: PIGMY collector). Mobile money can help her to be more efficient in her daily activities and maintain a good work-home balance.

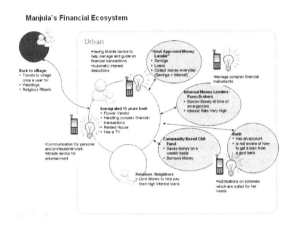

Fig. 2. Manjula's Financial Ecosystem & Opportunities

2.4   Key Challenge for Mobile Money for Malamma and Manjula

We envision that there should be an ecosystem level adoption of such a mobile money initiative for maximum acceptance and convenience of handling the transactions.

To help solve this, it's important to understand community dynamics.

- People, when they migrate from rural to urban regions, have close contacts with those people in the city who belong to the same village or the surrounding villages.
- These community members help carry money or goods back to the village if peo-ple are unable to travel.
- There is availability of multiple loan options from different people within the community.
- Trust, reputation and credit histories of individuals are well known within commu-nities and most often they may not need a collateral to avail of loans.

If mobile money can be initiated as a community model rather than an individual model, it will lead to widespread adoption. Ultimately, through these opportunities, mobile money will empower women and drive financial inclusion by providing better access to funds and decision making, safety and security of their savings, making them efficient and helping them plan their financial future.

3 Conclusion

For the women in the lowest socio economic class, as in the case with Mallamma and Manjula, there is an interesting new paradigm for a successful mobile money solution. This new paradigm is that this socio economic class being so deprived of conveniences /gadgets/devices and living life on the edge that a solution that simply looks at the question of enabling women to be able to "deal with money" via a device like the mobile phone misses the point! All other socio economic segments have more resources/money that makes it possible for them to own and use multiple devices where each device does specific tasks. In other words, if we look at the hierarchy of needs as stated by Maslow and map these to different Socio Economic Segments (SECs), we find that the higher one climbs the more the variety and number of devices and channels to help individuals achieve their everyday tasks and objectives.

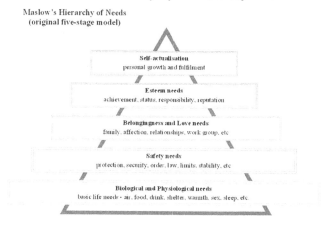

However, for the lower SECs, no solution that assumes that one device will be designed for a few primary tasks is likely to succeed. Individuals who belong to the lower SECs live a much more complicated life than those who belong to the higher

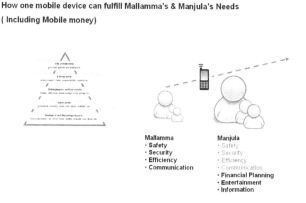

Fig. 3. The needs (including mobile money) of Mallamma and Manjula, that can be catered by through a device

SECs. They traverse all the levels of the hierarchy of needs all the time (example from Mallamma and Manjula's life) and hence advanced technology is even more important for the lower SECs to provide a flexible yet all encompassing solution.

Hence, for high adoption of any mobile money solution and its consequent driving of financial inclusion for women, the device must also provide solutions for all other levels of needs in a smooth and seamless manner.

You can see that for Mallamma, the needs are less and basic, like safety and security and having efficiency through mobile money. But for Manjula her needs are more sophisticated and just one mobile device, along with fulfilling mobile money needs, will fulfill other needs as well.

Further studies can inform how many or what range of needs are to be fulfilled through a mobile device for women in lower socio economic segments, for the tipping point to be reached, which will drive them to adopt mobile money.

Since a mobile device will be capable of fulfilling many needs including mobile money, it will be the vehicle through which women in the lower socio economic segments can move up the levels of hierarchy of needs thereby empowering them to fulfill all needs ranging from basic needs to financial inclusion to self actualization.

Acknowledgments. The authors would like to thank Rasika Wadodkar for help with the paper.

References

1. Informal lenders are giving banks a run for their loans (retrieved March 26, 2009),
   http://economictimes.indiatimes.com/News/
   News_By_Industry/Informal_lenders_are_giving_banks_a_run_
   for_their_loans/articleshow/2554678.cms
2. Moni, M., Uddin, M.: Cellular Phones for Women's Empowerment in Rural Bangladesh, Asian Center for Women's Studies. Ewha Womans University Press (2004)
3. Ivatury, G., Mas, I.: The early experience with branchless banking. CGAP, Washington, DC (2008)
4. von Reijswoud, V.: Mobile banking - an African perspective (retrieved February 2, 2009) http://www.regulateonline.org/content/view/948/63/
5. de Silva, H., Zainudeen, A., Ratnadiwakara, D.: Perceived economic benefits of telecom access at the Bottom of the Pyramid in emerging Asia, LIRNEasia (2008),
   http://www.lirneasia.net
6. Donner, J., Tellez, C.: Mobile banking and economic development: Linking adoption, impact, and use. Asian Journal of Communication 18(4), 318–322 (2008)
7. Morawczynski, O., Miscione, G.: Exploring trust in mobile banking transactions: The case of M-Pesa in Kenya (2008)
8. Bassey, C.: Digital Money in a Digitally Divided World: Nature, Challenges and Prospects of ePayment Systems in Africa. In: Workshop on Everyday Digital Money: Innovation in Money Cultures and Technologies, University of California, Irvine (2008)
9. Cracknell, D.: Electronic banking for the poor—panacea, potential and pitfalls. Small Enterprise Development 15(4), 8–24 (2004)
10. Nokia LifeTools (retrieved March 26, 2009),
    http://www.nokia.co.in/A41427315

Mobile-Banking Adoption and Usage by Low-Literate, Low-Income Users in the Developing World

Indrani Medhi, Aishwarya Ratan, and Kentaro Toyama

Microsoft Research India, Scientia, 196/36, Sadashivnagar
Bangalore-560080, India
{indranim,aratan,kentoy}@microsoft.com

Abstract. Due to the increasing penetration of mobile phones even in poor communities, mobile-phone-enabled banking (m-banking) services are being increasingly targeted at the "unbanked" to bring formal financial services to the poor. Research in understanding actual usage and adoption by this target population, though, is sparse. There appear to be a number of issues which prevent low-income, low-literate populations from meaningfully adopting and using existing m-banking services. This paper examines variations across countries in adoption and usage of existing m-banking services by low-literate, low-income individuals and possible factors responsible for the same. It is observed that variations are along several parameters: household type, services adopted, pace of uptake, frequency of usage, and ease of use. Each of these observations is followed by a set of explanatory factors that mediate adoption and usage.

Keywords: m-banking, mobile UX, financial inclusion, economic development.

1 Introduction

Across the developing world, there are more people with mobile phones than with bank accounts [23]. In 2007, there were over 3.3 billion phone users [6], and close to 60% of the subscribers lived in the developing world [26]. Thus, many entities with a global development focus have turned to the mobile phone as a potential platform for delivering financial services to the "unbanked". The unbanked are people without formal bank accounts who operate in a cash economy; they are limited in their ability to take out loans, maintain savings, or make remote payments, and these constraints can inhibit their economic opportunities. It is anticipated that these obstacles could be partially overcome if financial services were delivered over mobile phones.

Mobile phone-enabled banking (m-banking) services are already available in some countries and are increasingly being targeted at unbanked populations that are largely low-income and low-literate. However, there seem to be a number of issues which prevent this population from meaningfully adopting and using existing services [15, 22]. Research in understanding actual usage of existing m-banking services by low-income, low-literate populations in developing countries, though, is sparse [28].

In this paper, we present a preliminary study that discusses the variations across countries in adoption and usage of existing m-banking services by low-income, low-literate

N. Aykin (Ed.): Internationalization, Design, LNCS 5623, pp. 485–494, 2009.

populations and sheds some light on the possible factors that mediate adoption and usage by this target population. Through an ethnographic exploration involving interviews and qualitative observations with 90 subjects and 100 hours spent in the field in India, Kenya, the Philippines and South Africa we observe how low-income, low-literate subjects currently use (or don't use) existing m-banking services.

2 Related Work

2.1 Mobile Banking User Experience in the Developing World

There is a fair amount of literature beginning to emerge in m-banking user experiences in the developing world. One study notes that since physically wrapping digital money is difficult, gift-giving rituals may not translate to mobile money transfers [25]. A group from Nokia cautions against the metaphor of the cell phone as a digital wallet or purse, because owners have different mental associations and behaviors for mobiles [12]. One emerging issue, with important implications for our discussion on adoption and usage, is that of trust and trustworthiness. This is a complex concept, as people can trust (or distrust) various interrelated parts of the m-banking system; including themselves to execute a transaction effectively [9, 14, 18]. Another study in user interfaces for mobile money-transfers explores whether electronic access to complex financial services is enough to bring formal financial services to the unbanked, and, if so what sort of user interface is best [19].

Other works focus on broader issues of regulatory choices and business models which affect adoption and usage of these services [8, 15, 22, 23, 26,].

2.2 Mobile Phone User Experiences for Low-Literacy Users

There is some amount of research that looks specifically at mobile phone user interfaces for low-literacy users. Much of this work makes design recommendations - voice feedback [20, 21], speech interfaces [10, 21, 24], fewer menus and dedicated buttons [17], which make sense for low-literate users. Others have questioned the suitability of menu-based navigation for novice users [16].

Again there is work that looks beyond the user interface at coping mechanisms of illiterate and semi-literate users when confronted with traditional mobile phone interfaces [11, 13].

2.3 Mobile Phones for Poor Communities

The phenomenal market penetration of the mobile phone extends even into some of the world's most impoverished regions. Although it would be a mistake to overestimate its penetration in poor communities, in those areas that have mobile phone service, it's safe to say that many of the (comparatively) wealthier households own mobiles. As a result, there has been an explosion of interest in mobile phones and how they can contribute to socio-economic development, and we point readers to the twenty articles recently selected by the GSMA Development Fund [5]. Among the papers cited are those that highlight direct economic benefits to microentrepreneurs, methods of remote money transfer, and entire businesses based on selling talk time directly to neighbors.

The work presented in this paper occurs at the unexplored intersection of these three streams of research. The domain of m-banking being targeted towards low-literate, low-income populations in the developing country context give rise to new questions about how effectively these users are able to adopt and use existing services. This paper contributes novel insights about the determinants that affect the adoption and usage of mobile-banking services by this population.

3 Study Context and Methods

We studied five m-banking services – Globe Telecom's GCash in the Philippines, Safaricom's M-PESA and Equity Bank's Eazzy 24x7 in Kenya, WIZZIT in South Africa, and Eko in India. Each of the services had a different paradigm for mobile banking both in terms of the service design as well as the UI [1,2,3,4,7]

We conducted a total of 90 interviews and qualitative user studies: 26 in New Delhi and Bangalore, India, 11 in Nairobi, Kenya, 30 in Bohol, Philippines, and 23 in Cape Town and Globersdale, South Africa. (Variations in number are due in part to the complexity of identifying customers with the characteristics we were seeking.) Our hope was that by investigating most of the developing geographies with active mobile payment schemes, we could get a better overall sense for the recurring issues.

We looked for varying degrees of experience with using existing m-banking services: (a) those that did not use or own a mobile phone; (b) those that owned or used mobile phones but did not use any kind of m-banking systems; and (c) those that used m-banking systems. 40 of our subjects were in the first category, 34 in the second and 16 in the third. These traits make them an ideal user population with which to explore issues mediating adoption and usage of these services.

Our subjects had three common background traits: (1) functional illiteracy or semi-literacy but partial numeracy; (2) low levels of formal education (highest education attained being schooling up to the eighth grade of the K-12 education system or its equivalent across the four countries); (3) zero experience with personal computers.

To identify subjects with these characteristics, we worked with intermediary organizations. In order to reduce sampling biases based on the nature of the organization, we worked with for-profit corporations running the m-banking services, as well as with non-profit organizations working with poor populations. This is still far from having randomized samples at an individual level, and the appropriate cautions about generalizing from our results apply.

Our subjects were typically domestic workers and daily wage laborers like plumbers, carpenters, construction workers, mechanics, vegetable vendors, weavers, farm hands, fishermen, drivers, etc. Household income ranged from USD 20 – USD 200 per month. Some of our subjects had television sets, music players and gas burners, but these were not owned by all households. A few had seen computers in person (but again, none had ever used them). Naturally, differences also exist across geographies. The subjects' primary languages were Kannada, Hindi and Tamil in India, Tagalog in Philippines, Afrikaans, Xhosa and Zulu in South Africa and Kiswahili in Kenya.

The interviews were one-on-one, open-ended conversations that lasted for at least an hour. Questions and discussion themes included basic demographic information, access and use of financial services, and access and use of mobile phones. The study involved over 100 hours spent in the field. We visited individuals at their homes in order to talk to our subjects in a comfortable environment, and to observe their living environments. We also conducted interviews at m-banking agent locations where transactions took place. We conducted qualitative user studies with our subjects for the locally available m-banking service in which they were given a set of usability tasks to perform both on their own handsets and on mobile phones provided by us (in order to determine how much of their usage was by rote memorization).

All users were compensated for their time, at the end of the study. We consulted the intermediary organizations to establish the right mode and amount. Participants without mobile phones were given gift cards for local stores and those with mobile phones were given talk-time cards roughly equivalent to half a day's wage.

4 Observations

Across the locations and providers studied, we observed substantial variation in the adoption and usage of m-banking services by low-income low-literate individuals. The variations were along a number of parameters: household type, key service adopted, pace of uptake, frequency of usage, and ease of use. Some of the key variations noted are described in this section, with each observation followed by a set of likely explanatory factors.

4.1 Household Characteristics

It did not seem to be the case that only rural or only urban households in any given country had adopted the m-banking service. Instead, we found that among our respondents, certain types of rural and urban households had adopted the m-banking service. Some sections of the poor seemed to be active users, others infrequent users, while others did not adopt the service at all.

Why?

Location of family members. In Kenya, certain subjects' families had a young male member working in the city, while the rest of the family continued to farm in the village. This specific form of rural-urban migration that involved a geographically 'split' family corresponded with a pre-existing need to frequently send money from urban to rural locations. As a result, such families saw high adoption of M-PESA [see 28, 29]. Similarly, urban residents with immediate or distant family members in rural areas used M-PESA to send money transfers to their relatives. In the other direction, rural households with a child in an urban school or college periodically used the service to transfer fees to a person at their child's educational institution and/or send their children pocket money. Conversely, entirely rural households had not adopted the M-PESA service in Kenya. Their relatives and family were all co-located, and so all transactions were local. As a result, they had no need for a long-distance money transfer service, the key offering of M-PESA. [29]

Employment. The uptake of m-banking services in a location seemed to also depend on whether adoption was forced or optional depending on the kind of employment of the household's wage earners. All the 7 users of WIZZIT in South Africa we spoke with were farmhands at farms (with 50-70 employees) that were signed on by WIZ-ZIT for salary accounts for the farms' employees. The monthly wages were remitted to the WIZZIT salary accounts of each of these employees by the farms. None of the farmhands we spoke with had adopted the service on their own.

4.2 Services Adopted

While a broad range of financial transaction services were offered through the m-banking platform in certain cases (GCash and M-PESA), the service that saw aggressive adoption by our respondents varied. In Kenya, for instance, though information services (bank balance check, transaction history, etc.) were offered through Equity Bank's SMS banking service, and money transfers and airtime top-up services were offered by M-PESA, it was only the domestic money transfer service that had seen widespread uptake. GCash in the Philippines was used primarily for international remittance transfers, and much less for domestic money transfers.

Why?

Match between offerings and need. In the case of South Africa, we did not observe as strong a need for domestic remittances. Instead we saw that 5 out of 7 Wizzit users, were migrant workers from Zimbabwe, who expressed a strong need for international remittances. However at the time this study was conducted, WIZZIT in South Africa was only offering domestic remittances. In Kenya, while airtime purchase was offered via M-PESA, none of our respondents, even those who actively used M-PESA for money transfers had begun buying airtime through the m-payment channel [29]. When asked why, they said the 'bamba' prepaid talktime cards were so easy to get and use. For them, that was "enough".

Pricing vis-à-vis alternate channels. The pricing of the m-banking service with respect to other formal and informal remittance channels available in a location, was a determinant of how our subjects adopted and used the m-banking service. In Kenya, one of the reasons for some users to shift to M-PESA for remittance transfers was because it was half the price of the formal alternative, i.e. the postal money order that they were currently using. For transacting with or between the unbanked, compared to the nearest formal, secure alternatives, M-PESA was lower cost, though it remains more expensive than using informal channels like family or friends [29]. On the other hand in the Philippines, 9 out of 30 subjects mentioned that they would prefer to use the local bus line because it costs less. They could simply hand over cash in an envelope to the driver traveling in the direction of the recipient's location. In the case of 7 out of the 9 subjects, this transfer had no explicit cost given that the driver was a friend or a family member of the sender or the recipient.

Reliability with respect to informal channels. Our subjects in South Africa and Kenya would use WIZZIT and M-PESA respectively because of the reliability these m-banking services provided compared to informal channels. 8 out of 34 subjects described sending money through friends and relatives had no explicit cost, but sometimes the money never reached the intended recipient. Instead, with m-banking, doing the transfer directly to the recipient's phone and receiving confirmation for the same did not leave any uncertainty on whether the money had reached the intended recipient or not.

Service paradigm. The m-banking service paradigm seemed to affect the way our subjects were using these channels for financial transactions. As mentioned earlier, for GCash, Eko and M-PESA, the service allowed for cash transactions to be done at cash-in/cash-out corner shops, and for WIZZIT and Equity, bank branches were used for cash deposits and ATMs used for cash withdrawals. We observed that 7 out of 9 clients of Equity had debit cards and used them primarily to withdraw money at ATMs. However, none of the subjects had ever made a deposit at an ATM, with some not knowing how it worked or if it was even possible. Instead they would visit the bank branch for making a deposit [29]. In the case of M-PESA and Eko, however, the corner shop paradigm seemed to encourage both deposits and withdrawals as frequently as 5 times per week.

4.3 Pace of Uptake

The pace at which various m-banking services have spread in the low-income segment has differed substantially from country to country, and even between service providers. The overall pace of adoption has varied from 2 million M-PESA customers signed up in the first year in Kenya, to just over 50,000 WIZZIT customers signed up in South Africa over 2 years. There has been rapid uptake of the M-PESA service by low-income, low-literate customers in Kenya, vs. virtually no uptake by the target segment in the Philippines. In both India and South Africa, the uptake of the offered m-banking services by low-income households has been slow.

Why?

Level of awareness. The level of awareness about availability and features of m-banking services affects the way in which our respondents were adopting (or not adopting) these services. 21 out of 30 subjects in the Philippines, 11 out of 23 in South Africa and 22 out of 26 in India had never heard of m-banking channels. Among the subjects who were aware, the perception was that the service would be expensive because it involves the use of technology.

Trust. Among our subjects, there were issues of trust which seemed to mediate the adoption of m-banking channels for remittances. 7 out of 30 subjects in the Philippines and 6 out of 23 subjects in South Africa were concerned about the money transfer not reaching the recipient's phone and were wary about whether it would be possible to retrace lost money in case the recipient did not receive a remittance that was initiated. In contrast, adopters of M-PESA in Kenya had acquired a great deal of trust in the new channel, primarily due to the clear marketing by the provider Safaricom and the strong pre-existing ties with the local prepaid talktime agents, who 'sold' the new service as a trustworthy channel to their low-income customers.

4.4 Frequency of Usage

In places like Kenya, M-PESA is used by those who have an active need as frequently as 2-3 times a month, whereas in the Philippines, the m-banking channel is hardly used with any frequency. In South Africa, despite having accounts, low-income customers did not conduct banking transactions on their mobile phone.
Why?

Agent proximity and ubiquity. The proximity and ubiquity of m-banking agent locations (cash-in/cash-out stores for GCash, Eko, and M-PESA, and bank branches and ATMs for WIZZIT and Equity) seemed to be an important determinant affecting the motivation for adoption and frequency of usage by our subjects. In Kenya for most of our respondents, getting to the nearest M-PESA agent was in many cases faster than getting to the nearest Post Office or bank branch, given the number of Safaricom agents in different locations who offered this service especially in low-income residential areas. The proximity to the nearest agent location/ATM also seemed to affect users' frequency of withdrawal. [29]. Similarly in India, for 3 out of 4 users, the proximity of the Eko agents which resulted in bringing down travel cost to minimal was a key attraction. Whereas in the Philippines, for 19 out of 30 subjects the absence of GCash agent locations especially in rural areas seemed the deterrent in adoption of m-banking services.

Transaction time at agent stores. The time saved by transacting at an m-banking agent store location (cash-in/cash-out stores for Eko, GCash and M-PESA), where there was likely to be lower customer traffic, was important in raising the convenience of these services. Subjects across these three locations, whether banked or not, associated banks with long queues. It was important that the agents were open later in the evenings (unlike banks operating only during banking hours from 9am-5pm). Another feature that impressed users was the speed with which the transaction was completed. Even in cases where there were delays in receiving the confirmation SMS, it was a matter of minutes or hours.

4.5 Ability to Transact on the Application

There was significant variation in users' ability to conduct the m-banking transaction on their mobile phones themselves. Despite having their own M-PESA accounts, for instance, 3 of 8 M-PESA users transacted on their account only through peers or their local agents. They did not access the application on their own device, instead handing over their money and sometimes their phone to a peer or agent, and having them perform the transaction.
Why?

Interaction Design. There were a number of challenges encountered by our subjects in interacting with the m-banking services and navigating through mobile phones in general which mediated their ability to use these services effectively. Of the total 90 subjects, 56 (40 non-users of mobile phones + 16 existing mobile phone users) were initially unable to understand or navigate hierarchical menus as they currently exist. Usability tasks showed that few had an abstract hierarchical model in mind. Furthermore, functions buried in deep hierarchies were less discoverable to them, especially when functions were categorized under seemingly un-related functions. Again out of the total 90 subjects, 48 (40 non-users of mobile phones + 8 voice-only users) did not initially understand vertical scrollbars. These subjects did not realize that there were functions "beneath" what was displayed. As many as 45 users had difficulty with soft keys - associating the numerical index with the function in an enumerated list of functions and/or building mental models when buttons located alongside the display resulted in different functions dependent on the application. Again out of the total 27 voice-only users, 24 subjects were unable to type even a single word, much less an entire text message. For constructing a USSD syntax comprising of digits and symbols ("*" and "#"), our subjects were comfortable typing the digits, but could not locate the symbols. Again subjects, most of whom were not fluent in English, had difficulty reading the text portions of the receipts which were entirely in English (except in the case of M-PESA where they were in English and Kiswahili). But almost all could identify the numbers and what they meant. However, subjects still had difficulty with receipts indicating multiple transactions. Finally, since most of our subjects were unbanked, they were not familiar with the vocabulary of banking. "View last transaction," "Get balance", "Change PIN", and so forth, were all alien concepts, in the absence of detailed explanation.

Degree of human mediation. The degree of mediation by m-banking agents is an important determinant affecting how these services are adopted and used especially by low-literate users. In the current state, registration and trouble-shooting for the m-banking services are done by human intermediaries (agent locations for GCash, Eko, M-PESA, Wizzkids for WIZZIT and ATM lobby assistants for Equity). All of the services provide instruction manuals and information brochures for assisting users. Most of these manuals are overloaded with textual information, mostly in English. For low-literate users, these are all but useless, since the accompanying visuals often are not self-explanatory. Some of the services offer local-language manuals, but these too are complex and laden with banking jargon. For the most part, our subjects did not even attempt to read these manuals, and human mediation was critical for successful transactions.

5 Conclusion

In this paper, we explored a number of factors that mediate the ability of low-income, low-literate users in developing country contexts to adopt and use existing m-banking systems. We studied five existing m-banking services across India, Kenya, the Philippines and South Africa and conducted interviews and qualitative user-studies with 90 subjects in these four countries. Our observations were around variations in adoption and usage across locations and potential factors responsible for the same. The variations were along a number of parameters: household type, key service adopted, pace of uptake, frequency of usage, and ease of use. We followed each observation by a set of likely explanatory factors that mediate adoption and usage.

While preliminary, this study points to the set of variables that together influence the adoption and intensity of usage of m-banking services by low-income, low-literate users. Understanding these variations in m-banking usage is imperative to evolving accurate understandings of impact. In future work, we expect to explore improvements in UI/UX for specific m-banking services targeted at low-literate clients, understand the optimal role of mediators in driving usage, as well as arrive at rigorous estimates of welfare impact by varying usage profiles.

References

1. EKO, `http://www.eko.co.in/pilot.html`
2. Equity Bank, `http://www.equitybank.co.ke/`
3. M-PESA, `http://www.safaricom.co.ke/index.php?id=228`
4. GCASH, `http://www.GCash.com.ph/`
5. GSMA Development Fund,
   `http://www.gsmworld.com/developmentfund/`
   `report_top20_form.shtml`
6. ITU ICT Eye,
   `http://www.itu.int/`
   `ITU- D/icteye/Reporting/ShowReportFrame.aspx?ReportName=/`
   `WTI/CellularSubscribersPub-`
   `lic&RP_intYear=2007&RP_intLanguageID=1`
7. WIZZIT, `http://www.WIZZIT.co.za/`
8. infoDEV: Micro-payment systems and their application to mobile networks. Micro (2006),
   `http://infodev.org/files/`
   `3014_file_infoDev.Report_m_Commerce_January.2006.pdf`
9. Benamati, J.S., Serva, M.A.: Trust and distrust in online banking: Their role in developing countries. Information Technology for Development 13(2), 161–175 (2007)
10. Boyera, S.: The Mobile Web to Bridge the Digital Divide? In: The IST-Africa Conference 2007, Maputo, Mozambique (2007)
11. Chipchase, J.: Literacy, Communication, and Design. In: UIAH (2006)
12. Chipchase, J., Persson, P., Piippo, P., Aarras, M., Yamamoto, T.: Mobile essentials: field study and concepting. In: Proc. Designing for User eXperience Conference, San Francisco, USA (2005)
13. Chipchase, J.: Understanding Non-Literacy as a Barrier to Mobile Phone Communication (2005),
    `http://research.nokia.com/bluesky/`
    `non-literacy-001-2005/index.html` (retrieved September 16, 2008)
14. Donner, J.: M-Banking and M-Payments Services in the Developing World: New channel, same ties? In: The panel on living and livelihoods at HOIT 2007: Home/community oriented ICT for the next billion, IIT Madras, Chennai, India, August 23 (2007)
15. Ivatury, G., Pickens, M.: Mobile phone banking and low-income customers: evidence from South Africa. Consultative group to assist the poor (CGAP) and the United Nations Foundation, Washington (2006)
16. Jones, M., Buchanan, G., Thimbleby, H., Marsden, G.: User interfaces for mobile web devices www9 mobile workshop position paper. In: Proc. 9th International World Wide Web Conference (2000)
17. Lehrman, S.: Dialing in. Mobile phones target the world's nonreading poor. Scientific American 296(5), 30–31 (2007)
18. Morawczynski, O., Miscione, G.: Examining Trust in Mobile Banking Transactions in Kenya: The Case of Value-Ex. In: Draft Submission for HCC8 Conference (2007)

19. Medhi, I., Nagasena, G.S.N., Toyama, K.: A Comparison of Mobile Money-Transfer UIs for Non-Literate and Semi-Literate Users. In: Proc. ACM Conference on Computer Human Interaction, Boston, USA (2009)
20. Parikh, T., Javid, P., Sasikumar, K., Ghosh, K., Toyama, K.: Mobile Phones and Paper Documents: Evaluating a New Approach for Capturing Microfinance Data in Rural India. In: ACM Conference on Computer-Human Interaction (CHI), Montreal, Canada (2006)
21. Plauche, M., Prabaker, M.: Text-Free User Interfaces. In: ACM Conference on Computer Human Interaction, Montreal, Canada (2006) (working papers)
22. Porteous, D.: Just how transformational is m-banking? (2007),
    http://www.finmarktrust.org.za/accessfrontier/Documents/
    transformational_mbanking.pdf (retrieved November 1, 2007)
23. Porteous, D.: The enabling environment for mobile banking in Africa. DFID, London (2006)
24. Sherwani, J., Ali, N., Mirza, S., Fatma, A., Memon, Y., Karim, M., Tongia, R., Rosenfeld, R.: HealthLine: Speech-based Access to Health Information by Low-literate Users. In: Proc. IEEE/ACM Int'l Conference on Information and Communication Technologies and Development, Bangalore, India (2007)
25. Singh, S.: The Digital Packaging of Electronic Money. In: Aykin, N. (ed.) Usability and Internationalization. Global and Local User Interfaces, pp. 469–475. Springer, New York (2007)
26. UNCTAD, Information Economy Report 2007-2008: Science and Technology for Development - The New Paradigm of ICT, Geneva: United Nations Conference on Trade and Development (2008)
27. Vaughan, P.: Early lessons from the deployment of M-PESA, Vodafone's own mobile transactions service. In: Coyle, D. (ed.) The Transformational Potential of M-Transactions, vol. 6, pp. 6–9. Vodafone Group, London (2007)
28. Morawczynski, O.: Surviving in the "dual system": How M-PESA is fostering urban-to-rural remittances in a Kenyan Slum. Working paper, Social Studies Unit, University of Edinburgh (January 2008)
29. Ratan, A.L.: Using technology to deliver financial services to low-income households: a preliminary study of Equity Bank and M-PESA customers in Kenya, Microsoft Research Technical Report (June 2008)

Examining the Usage and Impact of Transformational M-Banking in Kenya

Olga Morawczynski[*]

Science Studies Unit, University of Edinburgh,
Chrystal Macmillan Building, 15a George Square, Edinburgh, EH8 9LD, UK
o.morawczynski@sms.ed.ac.uk

Abstract. Since its introduction in March of 2007, the M-PESA application has acquired a user base of over five million, and an agent network of over five thousand. Because of its rapid growth, the application has received a significant amount of attention. There have been assertions that it can engender transformational benefits by providing the unbanked with new opportunities to access financial services. There is, however, very little discussion of what these transformational benefits are and how they are engendered. This paper will contribute to filling this gap in the literature. It will draw from ethnographic fieldwork that was deployed over a period of fourteen months in two locations—an informal settlement near Nairobi and a farming village in Western Kenya. It will show that the M-PESA application was utilized for the cultivation of livelihood strategies. Such strategies helped residents to cope with (temporarily adjust) and recover from (longer term shifts in livelihood strategies) stresses and shocks. The outcomes of these strategies will also be discussed.

Keywords: M-PESA, m-banking, livelihoods, impact, transformational technologies, migration.

1 Introduction

In March of 2007 a mobile-banking application was introduced into the Kenyan market by Safaricom, Kenya's largest mobile service provider. The application, called M-PESA, facilitates a variety of financial transactions through the mobile phone. Users can check their account balance, make deposits and withdrawals, pay bills, purchase mobile phone credit, and transfer such credit to other users. The growth of the user base has been impressive. Over five million customers have registered with the

---

* I would like to extend my gratitude to Microsoft Research and the University of Edinburgh for providing the funding for the research, to the African Centre of Technology Studies (ACTS) for providing institutional support in Kenya, to Safaricom for facilitating access to the M-PESA agents, to the numerous informants in the research sites, and to my research assistant in Kibera. A special thanks to my Supervisor, Dr. James Smith, for providing valuable feedback on the numerous drafts of the paper.

N. Aykin (Ed.): Internationalization, Design, LNCS 5623, pp. 495–504, 2009.

service.[1] The agent network has also grown rapidly. Over five thousand retail outlets have signed up as agents [20].

The rapid uptake and extensive reach of the application has led some to assert that M-PESA has the potential to become "transformational"[44]. That is, it can extend financial access to a sufficient segment of the unbanked population.[2] The literature further notes the developmental impacts of these transformational applications. There have been assertions that such applications can help the poor to increase their household income, build their asset base and improve their resilience to shocks [13], [44]. Similar assertions regarding transformational benefits have also been made about information communication technologies (ICTs) in general, and the mobile phone in particular [1, 3, 4, 33]. However, questions still remain regarding the impact of mobile phone use on the livelihoods of the poor.[3] This is because the evidence of such impact, particularly at the micro-level, remains scarce.[4] Furthermore, most of the literature has examined impact of the mobile phone as it used for communication. Very little is said on this subject when it is used to access financial services.

This paper will contribute to filling this gap in the literature. It will draw from ethnographic fieldwork that took place over a period of fourteen months in two locations—an informal settlement near Nairobi and a farming village in Western Kenya.[5] There was an emphasis on tracking urban-rural 'money trails' throughout the course of the fieldwork. Urban migrants who used M-PESA to send money home were interviewed along with their rural relatives who were the recipients of these transfers. The paper will show that the M-PESA application was utilized for the cultivation of livelihood strategies by both the urban migrants and their rural relatives. Such strategies helped residents to cope with (temporarily adjust) and recover from (longer term shifts in livelihood strategies) stresses and shocks. It will also explain the outcomes that were engendered from these strategies. In particular, it will show how M-PESA was utilized for the solicitation and accumulation of financial assets and the maintenance of social networks. Attention will also be given to some of the negative outcomes, or unintended consequences, that were generated through usage.

2 Following the Money Trail: Introducing the Research Sites

As was mentioned in the introduction, the two sites were chosen after the "money trail" was followed. The research began in Kibera, an informal settlement outside

---

[1] This is in a country of 38 million. It is estimated that Safaricom has over 80% of the market share. See [34].

[2] In Kenya, this segment is large. It is estimated that only 19% of the adult population can access formal financial services through the banks. Another 8% are served by microfinance institutions (MFIs) and savings and credit cooperatives (SACCOs). This is low in comparison to mobile phone penetration. It is estimated that 55% of Kenyans own or have access to a mobile phone [18].

[3] For a summary of the livelihoods literature see [6], [11], [12], [14], [17], [39].

[4] This point was made by Jonathan Donner in a review of the literature on mobile phones. See [15].

[5] During this period, over three hundred interviews (semi-structured and unstructured) and twenty three focus groups were conducted with M-PESA users and non-users.

Nairobi with a population of over 1 million. Most of the residents migrate from villages in Western Kenya where it is difficult to find work.[6] Whilst residing in Kibera, they usually find employment as casual labourers or in the informal sector. Only 10% are reported to be formally employed [26]. These informal, or casual jobs, provide migrants with little job security. As such, it is common for them to move between Kibera and their rural home—returning when they can no longer afford to live in the city [27].

Many of the urban migrants interviewed confirmed that they came to Kibera from Western Kenya. After a visit to this area, a village called Bukura was chosen as the second site. The majority of the residents are subsistence farmers holding one to five acres of land. On this land they usually grow food crops for domestic consumption. There are very few opportunities for employment within and around Bukura. Many of the households depend on remittances sent by friends and family in urban areas such as Kibera. According to many of the interviewees, these remittances make up a substantial part of the household income. Some even asserted that 50-100% of such income was derived from remittances.

Time was also spent in other sites, both urban and rural, in Western Kenya. These sites were visited during the post-election crises. Kibera was not accessible during this period because of the ongoing violence within the informal settlement [36].

3 Money through the Mobile: Explaining Usage

Throughout the course of the fieldwork, there were several factors and events that affected the nature of usage. One such event, which had a tremendous impact, was the post-election violence. This was instigated by the disputed presidential elections of December 2007. During this two month period, over 1500 people died. Another 300,000 were displaced from their homes [28]. The movement of goods and people was also constrained. Many of the main roads were blocked by rioting youths. Parts of the railway were dismantled. This had a significant impact on money flows within Kenya. It was difficult, and sometimes impossible, to physically move money across the country. Financial services were also affected. Many banks and MFIs remained closed because of the constant insecurity. This was problematic for many Kenyans. There was a great demand for cash during this period. Some needed to escape the threat of ethnic violence. Others needed to purchase basic commodities such as food and water.

Some M-PESA agents were operational throughout the clashes. The urban agents in particular asserted that the demand for services had increased drastically during this period. Some even claimed that their customer base had doubled, or tripled. Many agents further saw a fundamental change in the nature of transactions—urban customers were making withdrawals rather than deposits. An agent interviewed in Eldoret explained:

> *I was serving over 600 customers per day. Guys had no other way of getting money. After they finished the transaction they ran out of here and looked for transport. They wanted to go home.*

---

[6] The majority of interviewees asserted that they came from Western Kenya. The finding that Kibera is dominated by the Luo and Luhya has also been noted by Ishihara. See [27].

Several M-PESA users in urban areas like Eldoret and Kibera asserted that the application was vitally important during the clashes. It became one of the only means through which they could access cash, especially during periods of escalated violence. A single mother of two in Eldoret asserted that she lost her savings when a group of young men looted and burned her house. She called her sister, who lived in central province, to ask for help. Her sister responded to the request, and sent her money through M-PESA. This money was used to purchase "daily bread" for the entire family. It was also used to pay for transport back to their rural home. The urbanites were also receiving airtime from their rural relatives. Because of the road blockages, the supply of scratch cards was limited. In some instances, these cards were being sold at twice their value. An elderly man in Kisumu said that he was receiving airtime from his brother during the clashes. He was using the airtime to text other relatives, and friends, and make additional requests for money and airtime.

Seasonality also influenced how the application was used. In Bukura, farming cycles determined the financial requirements of the household. For example, the M-PESA agent in Bukura asserted that the shop was busiest during the harvest and planting season. He explained that the financial demands on the farm increased during this period. Farm inputs such as seed and fertilizer needed to be purchased. Additional "farm hands", who helped with the planting, also needed to be paid. The agent further explained that the traffic in the shop also increased during the "hunger season" or "hunger months", which usually occurred between March and June. During this period the food stocks from the previous harvest had depleted. Subsistence farmers thus required additional income to replenish these stocks. Many of the farmers asserted that they would use M-PESA for the solicitation of funds during these periods. They claimed that with M-PESA they could access a larger network of potential remitters or lenders. This increased the chance that they would receive the required funds.

Seasonal pricing also had an impact on usage. In Bukura, some of the shop keepers would raise their prices at month end. The demand for products was high during this period as many of the villagers received their remittances. To avoid the inflated cost of commodities, some of the recipients asked their urban relatives to send the money "in bits". They wanted to receive the money on a bi-weekly or weekly basis. This would allow them to purchase essential items during other periods of the month when the shops had more stock and when the prices were lower. Several farmers asserted that by spacing out their spending, they decreased the total amount spent on household consumption during the month. Many of the urban migrants confirmed that they increased the frequency, while decreasing the value of the money transfers. Many of the respondents claimed that they would send at month-end with the other money transfer channels. With M-PESA, they would make these transfers on a weekly, or bi-weekly basis. They asserted that they did this because it helped their rural relatives to organize the finances in the house. They also claimed that they did this because it helped them to organize their own finances.

This phenomenon of sending money "in bits" instigated another interesting outcome. On average, there was an increase in the total amount of money that was remitted back to the rural home. Both the senders and the recipients noted this change. The senders asserted that they were able to send more money because they saved on the act of making the transfer. A shoemaker working in Kibera described this change:

Shoemaker: Before M-PESA, I would give money to my friend. He would go home every two months...I usually gave him 2000 [KES] for my wife and parents. I also contributed 300 [KES] for his transport, and another 200 [KES] to say thank you.
Interviewer: So, you sent about 1000 per month.
S: [Nods].
I: And now?
S: Now I am sending every two weeks. But I send a smaller amount. Usually 700-800 [KES]. I can send her more because I save on the transport cost. I also don't pay my friend.
I: Now you are sending about 1400-1500 per month? Your wife must be happy.
S: Yes. [laughs]. But my friend is not.

The wife of the shoemaker, who stayed in Bukura, confirmed this increase. She also asserted that since her husband started using M-PESA, the inflows of money were more regular. He no longer needed to depend on his friend to transfer the cash. In most cases, it was found that this increase was between 20-40%. The urban migrants claimed that they would include the amount saved on making the transfer into the amount sent back home. In most cases, the amount saved was from 50 KES-400 KES. The recipients also noted that they saved money because they no longer needed to pay transport fees to collect the money.

A focus group in Kibera composed of female M-PESA users, asserted that they frequently used the application to store their "secret savings". These savings were used to purchase household items, to address "illness", to pay for school fees and to invest in business. The women explained that they preferred to store money outside of the home because it decreased the risk of it being found, and stolen, by their husbands. They further explained that they preferred M-PESA to the bank because it was accessible. They did not need to travel into town to deposit or withdraw their money. They could also check their account balances from home, via their mobile phone, without their husbands knowing what they were doing. Jenifer, one of the group members, asserted that:

Having something small in my secret savings is important. I can make decisions and not ask my husband. I want to save money and then start some business. Maybe I can sell some onions around Kibera...I know that he [my husband] won't give me the money. So, I will put a small amount of money into M-PESA every week...I will soon have enough to start business...

These secret savings thus provided these women with some financial autonomy. By having an accumulation of funds they were able to make decisions without asking their husbands.

This section has shown that the M-PESA application was appropriated for the cultivation of livelihood strategies. It must be noted, however, that individuals also mobilize an array of other assets. They utilize these assets and adjust their strategies according to their circumstances and the changing context in which they live. As such, even though M-PESA was vitally important for individuals in both communities, alone it was not sufficient for the reduction of vulnerability.

4 Soliciting Capital and Maintaining Networks: Explaining Impact

The most significant of the outcomes generated by M-PESA usage, was a reduction in vulnerability. This was done in two ways—by the solicitation of financial capital, and the maintenance of social networks.

M-PESA was one of the only available channels for the transfer of money and airtime during the post-election period. As such, the application became fundamentally important for urban migrants who were trying to escape from, and cope with, the threat of ethnic violence. It provided these migrants with new opportunities for the reduction of vulnerability through the mobilization of financial assets. This was also the case during the "hunger months". Subsistence farmers used M-PESA to expand networks of potential remitters and lenders. This increased the chance that they would receive the necessary funds to secure their "daily bread". M-PESA was also used for the cultivation of strategies during other shocks, such as illness. It provided a platform through which funds could be instantly sent to address an urgent situation. The recipients did not need to wait for the money to physically travel from the city.

M-PESA also helped the urban migrants to maintain their social networks. It did this by fostering money transfers between urban centres and rural areas. Most of the interviewees in Kibera confirmed that they would send money home "regularly". For some, this meant that they would send several times per month. For others, it meant once per year. The act of sending money home had not only a practical but also symbolic function. With each transfer, the migrant was sending an important message—that they had not forgotten their obligation to the village whilst residing in the city. With each transfer, the migrant was also maintaining relations with their rural relatives. According to the literature, such relations are vitally important for the urban migrants [23, 41]. They provide them with a safety net whilst residing in the city. As was shown here, urban migrants looked to the village for support and received both money and airtime from their rural relatives. This helped them to purchase basic commodities such as food and water. It also allowed them to escape the threat of ethnic violence.

It must be noted, however, that in some instances M-PESA usage engendered the opposite outcome—it weakened relations between urban migrants and their rural relatives. As the fieldwork progressed an interesting discovery was made. Urban migrants were making fewer visits back to the village. Before M-PESA was introduced, many of these migrants would deliver the money home by hand and spend some time at their rural homes. Since adopting the application, however, they claimed that they no longer needed to make these home visits. In the village, the recipients confirmed that their urban relations were visiting home less often. They further claimed that this arrangement caused some problems. The wife of the carpenter voiced her concern. She explained that her husband had not come home since he started using M-PESA. This was four months ago. This made her life "more difficult". She now had to take care of the farm by herself. Some of the women were also concerned that if their husband decreased the number of home visits they would become "lonely" and find a "city wife". The outcome of this, the woman explained, could be the reduction or elimination of money sent back home.

The application also helped to reduce the vulnerability of women by providing them with a safe place to keep their money. As was mentioned above, many women claimed that they preferred to save with M-PESA because it decreased the risk of the money being stolen by their husbands. This savings base was vitally important for several reasons. It could be used by to smooth consumption, cushion shocks and for investments in other vital assets. This allowed the women to have more financial autonomy. They had an accumulation of savings that could be used to cultivate livelihood strategies.

Besides the reduction of vulnerability, the M-PESA application also facilitated another important outcome. It helped users to generate additional income. This happened in several ways. It was mentioned above that M-PESA users were changing the way in which they sent money home. Rather than sending at month-end, they would send the money "in bits", making transfers weekly or bi-weekly. The result was an increase in the total amount that was remitted back home. As was mentioned above, the amount remitted back home usually increased between 20-40%. The recipients also saved money on the transfer. They no longer needed to pay travel expenses when retrieving their cash. It would be interesting to examine whether this trend will continue, and if remittance patterns will continue to change with increased usage.

Finally, the application extended the network of potential remitters and lenders. This was beneficial for subsistence farmers during the hunger months. It made it easier for them to acquire small amounts of money from a larger base of contacts. This also resulted in an increase in the gross remittance inflows. Some farmers even stated that such inflows had doubled since they started using M-PESA. However, the extension of potential remitter and lender networks resulted in new problems for urban migrants. These migrants were receiving more demands for their limited income. In some cases, this resulted in new tensions between the urban migrants and their rural relatives.

5 Conclusion: Substantiating the Transformational Debate

What does this all mean for the transformational literature? How can these findings be used to substantiate this emerging debate [16, 30, 31, 38]? The first thing that must be considered is how the term transformational has been defined. In most of the literature, the term has not been defined at all. Only Porteous has made explicit what this term means in the context of the m-banking debate [38]. According to his definition, an m-banking application is transformational when it targets the unbanked sector, and provides this sector with new opportunities to access financial services. If this definition is to be appropriated as is then it can be argued that M-PESA is already transformational—at least in the two contexts in which this research was deployed. It has provided individuals in these contexts with new opportunities to save, transfer money, and purchase airtime. What has not been made clear, however, is what happens *after* an m-banking application becomes transformational.

Within the debate, there is very little said about how the technology is being used and why it is being used in these ways. In the two research sites, a divergent set of usage patterns were noted. This divergence was explained by the vulnerability context. It was argued that M-PESA was used for the cultivation of livelihood strategies that helped residents to cope with, and adjust to, shocks and trends within their communities. More research is needed, however, to determine how the application is being used for the reduction of vulnerability in other contexts. It would further be useful to identify the aspects of the application that generate impacts. One of the success factors of M-PESA is its impressive outreach. The substantial customer base has generated a network effect.[7] That is, the usefulness and value of the service has increased as the customer base has expanded. This is because each user is a potential recipient, lender and remitter. As was shown here, many rural farmers realized the benefits of the extended M-PESA network as they acquired small amounts of money from a larger base of contacts. The impact was an increase in the total amount received by these farmers. This is one of the most significant benefits offered by these so-called transformational applications. It is not just about providing individuals with access to a technology. It is also about tapping them into an extensive financial network.

Finally, this study challenges an argument that is frequently made in the literature on mobile phones—that these technologies amplify existing relations [21, 22]. As was shown here, increased usage resulted in a decrease in the number of home visits made by the urban migrants. This caused some of rural wives to worry that their husbands would stray. It is not yet known whether these migrants will continue to decrease their visits and just how this will affect urban-rural relations. Such a finding, however, supports the statement made earlier in the paper—the impacts of usage are different when the phone is used as a tool for communication than when it is used to access financial services.

References

1. Abraham, R.: Mobile Phones and Economic Development: Evidence From the Fishing Industry in India. Information Technologies & International Development 4, 5–17 (2007)
2. Agesa, R.U.: One Family, Two Households: Rural to Urban Migration in Kenya. Review of Economics of the Household 2, 161–178 (2004)
3. Aker, J.: Does Digital Divide or Provide? The Impact of Cell Phones on Grain Markets in Niger, working paper, University of California, Berkeley (2008),
   http://www.cgdev.org/doc/events/2.12.08/
   Aker_Job_Market_Paper_15jan08_2.pdf
4. Aminuzzaman, S., Baldersheim, H., Jamil, I.: Talking back! Empowerment and Mobile Phones in Rural Bangladesh: A Study of the Village Phone Scheme of Grameen Bank. Contemporary South Asia 12, 327–348 (2003)
5. Anderson, S., Baland, J.M., Moene, K.: Sustainability and Organizational Design in Roscas: Some Evidence from Kenya, University of Namur (manuscript, 2002),
   http://www.fundp.ac.be/eco/recherche/cred/papers/
   enforce811.pdf (accessed December 12, 2008)
6. Arun, S., Heeks, R., Morgan, S.: Researching ICT-Based Enterprise for Women in Developing Countries: A Livelihoods Perspective, IDPM, University of Manchester (2004),
   http://www.womenictenterprise.org/LivelihoodsResearch.doc (accessed December 12, 2008)
7. Baker, J.: Rural-Urban Links and Economic Differentiation in Northwest Tanzania. African Rural and Urban Studies 3, 25–48 (2004)
8. Besley, T., Coate, S., Loury, G.: Rotating Savings and Credit Associations, Credit Markets and Efficiency. Review of Economic Studies 61, 701–710 (1994)

---

[7] For a description of the network effect see [29, 43].

9. Bigsten, A.: The Circular Migration of Small-Holders in Kenya. Journal of African Economies 5, 1–20 (1996)
10. Africa Calling: The Economist (June 15, 2008), http://www.economist.com/people/displaystory.cfm?story_id=11488505 (accessed July 18, 2008)
11. Chapman, R., Slaymaker, T., Young, J.: Livelihoods Approaches to Information and Communication in Support of Rural Poverty Elimination and Food Security. Overseas Development Institute, http://www.odi.org.uk/rapid/publications/Documents/SPISSL_WP_Complete.pdf (accessed March 12, 2008)
12. Chambers, R., Conway, G.R.: Sustainable Rural Livelihoods: Practical Concepts for the 21st Century, discussion paper 296, Institute for Development Studies, University of Sussex (1992)
13. Clark, M.: Unserved by Banks, Poor Kenyans Now Just Use a Cell Phone. The Christian Monitor, October 12 (2007), http://www.csmonitor.com/2007/1012/p01s03-woaf.html?page=1 (accessed December 12, 2008)
14. DFID. Sustainable Livelihood Guidance Sheets, http://www.livelihoods.org/info/guidance_sheets_pdfs/section1.pdf (accessed November 15, 2008)
15. Donner, J.: Research Approaches to Mobile Use in the Developing World: A Review of the Literature. The Information Society 24, 140–159 (2008)
16. Donner, J., Tellez, C.: Mobile Banking and Economic Development: Linking Adoption, Impact, and Use. Asian Journal of Communication 18, 318–322 (2008)
17. Duncombe, R.: Using the Livelihoods Framework to Analyze ICT Applications for Poverty Reduction through Microenterprise. Information Technologies and International Development 3, 81–100 (2006)
18. FSD Kenya. Financial Access in Kenya: Results of a 2006 National Survey, http://www.finscope.co.za/documents/2007/FSAC07_003.pdf (accessed October 1, 2008)
19. Geschiere, P., Gugler, J.: The Urban-Rural Connection: Changing Issues of Belonging and Identification. Africa: Journal of the International African Institute 68, 308–319 (1998)
20. Gikunju, W., Mark, O.: Minister Orders Audit of Safaricom's M-Pesa Service. Business Daily, December 10 (2008), http://www.bdafrica.com/index.php?option=com_content&task=view&id=11685&Itemid=5812 (accessed December 10, 2008)
21. Goodman, J.: Linking Mobile Phone Ownership and Use to Social Capital in Rural South Africa and Tanzania. Policy Paper Series, No. 2. Vodafone Group Plc., London (2005)
22. Goodman, J., Walia, V.: Airtime Transfer Services in Egypt. In: Coyle, D. (ed.) The Transformational Potential of m-transactions, vol. 6, pp. 30–35. Vodafone Group, London
23. Gugler, J.: The Son of the Hawk Does Not Remain Abroad: The Urban-Rural Connection in Africa. African Studies Review 45, 21–41 (2002)
24. Hoddinott, J.: A Model of Migration and Remittances Applied to Western Kenya. Oxford Economic Paper 46, 459–476 (1994)
25. Hughes, N., Lonie, S.: M-PESA: Mobile Money for the "Unbanked" Turning Cell phones into 24-Hour Tellers in Kenya. Innovations: Technology, Governance, Globalization 2, 63–81 (2007)
26. Ilako, F., Kimura, M.: Provision of ARVs in a Resource-Poor Setting: Kibera Slum. In: The International Conference on AIDS, Bangkok, Thailand (2004)

27. Ishihara, S.: The Informal Economy of Kibera Slums. PhD Dissertation, SOAS, University of London (2003)
28. Kenyan Police Defend Crackdown. BBC News (July 6, 2008), http://news.bbc.co.uk/2/hi/africa/7497554.stm (accessed August 1, 2008)
29. Liebowitz, S.J., Margolis, S.E.: Network Externality: An Uncommon Tragedy. Journal of Economic Perspectives 8, 133–150 (1994)
30. Lyman, T., Pickens, M., Porteous, D.: Regulating Transformational Branchless Banking: Mobile Phones and Other Technology to Increase Access to Finance. CGAP, http://www.cgap.org/gm/document-1.9.2583/FocusNote_43.pdf (accessed June 7, 2008)
31. Mas, I., Kumar, K.: Banking on Mobiles: Why, How, for Whom? CGAP, http://www.cgap.org/gm/document-1.9.4400/ FN_48%20ENG_9-10-08.pdf (accessed June 7, 2008)
32. Mbugua, J.: Kenya: Big Banks in Plot to Kill M-PESA. The Nairobi Star (December 23, 2008), http://allafrica.com/stories/200812230962.html (accessed January 9, 2009)
33. Molony, T.: The Role of Mobile Phones in Tanzania's Informal Construction Sector: The Case of Dar es Salaam. Urban Forum 19, 175–186 (2008)
34. Okoth, J.: Rival Networks Cut Safaricom's Market Share. The Standard (November 11, 2008), http://www.eastandard.net/InsidePage.php?id=1143999671&cid=1 4&j=&m=&d= (accessed November 11, 2008)
35. Oucho, J.O.: Migration and Regional Development in Kenya. Development 50, 88–93 (2007)
36. Osborn, M.: Fuelling the Flames: Rumour and Politics in Kibera. Journal of Eastern African Studies, 315–327 (2008)
37. Owuor, S.: Urban Households Ruralising their Livelihoods: The Changing Nature of Urban-Rural Linkages in an East African Town. African Studies Centre Seminar Series. Leiden (December 2005)
38. Porteous, D.: The Enabling Environment for Mobile Banking in Africa. DFID, http://www.bankablefrontier.com/assets/ ee.mobil.banking.report.v3.1.pdf (accessed December 10, 2008)
39. Radoki, C.: A Livelihoods Approach: Conceptual Issues and Definitions. In: Radoki, C., Lloyd-Jones, T. (eds.) Urban Livelihoods: A People Centred Approach to Reducing Poverty, Earthscan, London (2002)
40. Rice, X.: Kenya Sets World First with Money Transfers by Mobile. The Guardian (March 20, 2007), http://www.guardian.co.uk/money/2007/mar/20/ kenya.mobilephones (accessed December 10, 2009)
41. Ross, M.H., Weisner, T.S.: The Rural-Urban Migrant Network in Kenya: Some General Implications. American Ethnologist 4, 359–375 (1977)
42. Safaricom. Results for the Six Month Period Ended (September 2008), http://www.safaricom.co.ke/fileadmin/financials/Press%20Relea se.pdf (accessed October 1, 2008)
43. Sidorenko, A., Findlay, C.: The Digital Divide in East Asia. Asian-Pacific Economic Literature 2, 18–30 (2002)
44. Vodafone. The Transformational Potential of M-Transactions, http://www.vodafone.com/etc/medialib/attachments/ cr_downloads.Par.3477.File.tmp/VOD833%20Policy%20Paper% 20Series%20FINAL.pdf (accessed October 1, 2008)

Balancing Separateness and Jointness of Money in Relationships: The Design of Bank Accounts in Australia and India

Supriya Singh

RMIT University, GPO Box 2476V, Melbourne 3001, Australia
supriya.singh@rmit.edu.au

Abstract. Personal bank accounts are an important way of signaling the separation, ownership, control and management of money. They are however a blunt instrument for balancing the separateness and jointness of money in relationships. This paper draws on the author's research on money and banking in Australia and India to describe the ways in which middle-income urban families in Australia and India use bank accounts in personal relationships. The paper points to ways that bank account holders can retain control by setting the limits to which information and money in the account can be shared with a designated person for a set time limit. It is submitted that having this partial shared account, together with existing personal accounts, will fit social practice, and help reflect the changing balance of separateness and jointness of money across a person's life stage.

Keywords: joint accounts; India; Australia: separateness; jointness.

1 Introduction

Bank accounts are an important mechanism for separating different kinds of money according to source, use and ownership. Money from consultancies, tax refunds, bonuses or occasional activities like umpiring is kept apart from wages. Money from inheritance is put in a different account, so that it does not get spent on groceries. Money for personal spending is separate from joint expenses. Money to be remitted to parents overseas also does not mix with family expenses in Australia. Money from an investment property or a retirement package is parked in a separate account for taxation purposes. Loan accounts are separated from savings accounts. At times, the money is separated by the ways in which it is paid out, withdrawn or transferred - via the passbook, the check account or via the Internet.

The importance of earmarking is in tune with Zelizer's [1] argument that there are multiple monies which are 'routinely differentiated' by meaning and use. As Zelizer (1989) says, 'Not all dollars are equal' (p. 343). One kind of money cannot necessarily substitute for another kind of money for each kind of money is qualitatively distinct.

This paper draws on two qualitative studies on money in the household in Australia and India. These studies yielded important data on bank accounts for they are the basic

N. Aykin (Ed.): Internationalization, Design, LNCS 5623, pp. 505–514, 2009.

building blocks of the way people perceive and separate money in the household. The paper also draws on the Australia-wide quantitative data set from the Household, Income and Labour Dynamics in Australia (HILDA) for 2006 (N = 12,905).

The Australian qualitative study conducted between April 2005 and July 2006, focused on money and intimate relationships within the context of an online banking environment with a particular emphasis on issues of security, trust, identity and privacy[1]. It covered 108 persons in Melbourne, rural Victoria and Brisbane. It included married, de facto (cohabiting) and single people. It had a diverse sample in terms of age, household income an educational background. Data collection was via open-ended interviews, group interviews and focus groups.

The Indian study conducted in late 2007 on the privacy of money in urban middle-income households in India covered 40 persons in 27 households in metropolitan Delhi (25 persons), peri-urban areas around Delhi (seven persons) and the regional town of Dharamshala in Himachal Pradesh (eight persons)[2]. These three sites were chosen to prevent focusing only on the metropolitan experience of the management and control of money. The sample included joint and nuclear family households. Data collection was via open-ended interviews conducted in English, Hindi and Punjabi and participant observation of money relationships among the authors' kin, neighbors, and friends in India. Questions about family money were asked in a roundabout way in a culturally appropriate manner (See [2, 3]).

Both studies had a convenience sample drawn from the personal and professional networks of the research team. Both studies were 'grounded' in that the aim was to move from data to middle-range theories, rather than a testing of hypotheses [4]. There was a palpable recognition that the interviews were jointly constructed, shaped by the social positioning of the researcher and the way the participant chose to represent matters of money, banking and marriage to himself or herself as well as the researcher (See [5]).

The interviews and focus group sessions were transcribed so that it was possible to repeatedly go back to the participants' voices. N6 and NVivo7, computer programs for the analysis of qualitative data were used, to ensure transparency as to the how theory emerged from the data. Following Glaser and Strauss [6], coding and analysis went alongside the collection of data. The data were broadly coded, then organized into matrices to check emerging themes in a transparent manner. These codes were accompanied by memos reflecting on the way data were shaped, and how connections and variations were recognised and theories began to emerge [7].

Section 2 examines the incidence and symbolic significance of the joint account for marriage in Australia. Section 3 considers the joint account in India and how it protects the interests of the survivors. Section 4 proposes ways to design joint accounts to balance jointness and separateness of money in a relationship. The concluding section summarises the findings and draws out the implications for design.

---

[1] I am grateful to Jenine Beekhuyzen, Anuja Cabraal, Gabriele Hermansson, Margaret Jackson, Lesa Beel and Doug Lorman who helped conduct the qualitative study.

[2] I am grateful to Dr Mala Bhandari who helped conduct the qualitative study.

2 The Australian Joint Account Symbolizes Togetherness in Marriage

Joint accounts became popular for married couples from the 1950s and 1960s. A move towards joint accounts was influenced by changes towards a partnership model of marriage, married women's increased employment and greater joint homeownership. It was also propelled forward by the Privacy Act 1988 which meant that bankers could no longer check a wife's creditworthiness by looking at the husband's file alone. Separate files for husbands and wives led bankers to prefer joint accounts and joint loans.

It is widely expected that money in the joint account will go to the survivor. Keith[3] and his wife who are both retired have two joint accounts for this reason. Keith says, '....if one of us goes, then the accounts are at least 50 per cent accessible. Otherwise you may need to wait for three months or longer for the access to the accounts.' The first account holder is seen as the primary account holder. This becomes most clear in jointly held credit cards, for only the first named person can change the contact details. The legal status of the rights of joint account holders in case of death is however unclear, for there are also known instances when the joint account is frozen to protect the interests of the estate[4].

2.1 Incidence of the Joint Account

In Australia, 83 per cent of married men and women in 2006-07 had a joint account, with or without a separate account (See Table 1). The joint account is seldom held between siblings or between parents and adult children. This is because money is private to the married couple. The opening of a joint account is symbolic of the commitment and jointness of marriage. The joint account is a secular ritual which

Table 1. Financial Institution Accounts for Married Men and Women 2006-2007

Accounts	Married		De facto	
	Male N = 3085	Female N = 3213	Male N = 570	Female N = 596
Joint accounts only	56%	45%	14%	13%
Separate accounts only	16%	16%	57%	58%
Joint and separate accounts	27%	38%	27%	27%
No bank account	1%	1%	1%	1%

Source: HILDA (The Household, Income and Labour Dynamics in Australia survey) Wave 6 [5]

helps focus on the togetherness of marriage, by theoretically converting separate and individual earnings to joint ownership of money. It masks questions of power and financial inequality [8]. As Celia, 45-54, in her second marriage, says, 'I think for both of us a joint account would signify a joint relationship.'

---

[3] All the names from the qualitative studies are pseudonyms.

[4] Personal communication, Rhys Bollen, Senior Manager, Strategic Policy, Australian Securities and Investments Commission.

[5] I am grateful to Prof Clive Morley for the analysis of the HILDA data.

The joint account is one of the factors that distinguishes money in marriage from money in de facto (cohabiting) relationships, where separate accounts are the norm (See Table 1). The joint account is part of the transition from the de facto relationship to marriage. Shane, 25-34, had only separate accounts when he and his partner were in a de facto relationship. When they got married, Shane pushed for having only joint accounts, mainly because his parents had joint accounts. He says, 'I wanted to have joint accounts because I saw that as being ... almost a symbol or a practical application of our functioning as a team.'

The joint account in Australia most often yields joint information and access to money for the couple. Joint access and information about earnings, expenditure and money in the joint account has been aided by the computerisation of banks, for a person is no longer limited to the use of one branch. The direct crediting of wages, benefits and pensions when accompanied by a joint home loan, also means that the bulk of the money comes into the joint account. Access to the money and information also increased with the Automated Teller Machines (ATMs), Electronic Funds Transfer at Point of Sales (EFTPOS), telephone and Internet banking.

2.2 Bank Accounts Are a Blunt Instrument

Bank accounts are a blunt instrument for signaling the jointness or separateness of money. The qualitative study shows there is only a limited relationship between financial accounts, money management and control. Joint or separate accounts do not necessarily translate to joint or independent ways of managing and controlling money. It is important only in that having joint accounts only, excludes independent management and control. Having separate accounts only, excludes joint money management and control.

The form of the account, whether it be joint or individual, remains important in terms of meaning [8]. The Australian qualitative study shows that some married couples use joint accounts as if they were separate accounts. This allows for the control of separate money streams while allowing for the portrayal of jointness and emergency access to money.

David, 45-54 with an annual household income of more than $100,000 with two adult step children. He has a joint account with his wife. His wife also has a separate account for her part time salary and housekeeping expenditure. David says,

> *I put my pay into our joint account and I budget from that joint account. And I wouldn't expect my wife to spend money out of that joint account without me knowing....It's effectively my account that she has access to in case ... for any reason she'd need to have access to it.*

Others use separate accounts as joint accounts. In traditional branch based banking only the person named on the separate account could withdraw money or gain information about the account. The exception to this rule had to be negotiated with the bank in the form of third party signatories or a power of attorney. With electronic banking – that is the use of the ATM, EFTPOS, phone and Internet banking – if a couple choose to share their banking passwords, then money in the separate accounts can be accessed and managed as if they were joint accounts.

People routinely share banking passwords and Personal Identification Numbers (PINs). Roy Morgan Research for the Smart Internet Technology Cooperative Research Centre and RMIT University in September 2007 found that nearly half (43%) of a random representative sample of 669 Australians over 18 and with a bank account had shared their banking passwords and PINs. The Australian qualitative study shows that when one person in a couple relationship manages the money – that is paying the bills, and monitoring Internet banking – it is not unusual for that person to manage the joint accounts as well as all the individual accounts, including the accounts of the partner. The Internet in that sense is breaking down the traditional boundaries limiting access to money and information in the separate account [9, 10].

Benjamin, 34, a farmer, and his wife know each other's log-ins. Sometimes his wife logs in as him to pay for the bills. "Now that she is at home (on maternity leave) it is easier for her to do this" Benjamin says, he has also logged in as her a few times to conduct some transactions.

3 The Joint Account in India Protects the Survivor

In India in middle income urban families, the joint account is predominantly a way of ensuring that money in the account goes to the surviving account holder. It is an inheritance device. The account may be Joint (Either or Survivor); Joint (Former or Survivor) or Joint (Latter or Survivor) [11]. In this aspect, the joint account is similar to placing a nomination on the single account. However, the nominee cannot operate the account unlike the either/or survivor clause in a joint account. [12].

These characteristics of the deposit account in India go some way towards making for a less stressful transfer of funds to the survivor in the joint account or the nominee in the separate account.

3.1 The Nominal Joint Account

It has been difficult to find nationally representative data about the relative incidence of separate and joint accounts in India.

The Indian qualitative study shows that nearly three-fifths (61%) of the married persons in the sample have joint accounts, with or without separate accounts (See table 2). The Indian joint account may only nominally be a joint account for the sake of protection rather than transaction. Often it works as if it were a separate account.

In the sample less than half (11 of the 24 married persons with joint accounts) could transact on these accounts. This is because the joint account often substitutes for the separate account because it offers superior legal protection to the survivor and convenience of emergency access.

Table 2. Deposit Accounts of Married Persons (n=39)

Joint Account/s only	15
Separate account/s only	12
Joint and separate accounts	9
No bank account	2
Did not ask	1

Balu, 45-54 says he has a joint account for the sake of convenience. Since he travels a lot, he wants his wife, Beatrice to conveniently withdraw money as and when required. Beatrice too has her own joint account for her professional fees and inheritance. She says, 'It is totally my account. I withdraw. I deposit.'

Different streams of money go into these joint accounts. Mahesh, a retired professional says all their accounts are joint in name but managed separately. He says,

> *In India the salaries go into separate salary accounts for...the income tax lawyer wants separate streams of money coming in and going out. ... The joint account is a matter of contingency, either or survivor. But the income tax rules are that the owner of the account is the first name on the account.*

In the above cases, the married couple has information about each other's joint accounts. The money is meant for common use. In the sample, however, there are four cases where there is no information or transactional access to the joint account. Neera, a businesswoman in Delhi has a joint account with her husband and a separate business account. She does not access the joint account even when her husband is away. She also has no information about money in the account. She says,

> *He has never said 'I don't want to tell you.' ... I myself have not taken the initiative. Many times he tells me 'You should know. You should take more interest.' I feel he is better at it than I would be. He knows better what to do.*

The other three women are virtually unbanked for they have only this one joint account. Amar, a widow over 65, living with her son in a three generational joint family in Dharamshala knew she had a joint account but until her husband's death did not know how much was in the account. Now that the same account is joint with her son, she does not ask him either. Her daughter-in-law Amrit, 45-54 and a graduate, also does not know what is in her joint account with her husband. She says, 'I don't go to the bank. He does everything. I don't have any knowledge about it.' Santokh, over 65, also in Dharamshala says his wife has never withdrawn money from the joint account. This is partly because she lives in another town.

Though more than three-fifths of the sample has a joint account, the joint account does not necessarily lead to the joint management and control of money. The overwhelming pattern in the qualitative study is that of male control (21 of 40) and female management (28 of 40) in a variety of combinations. However, having a joint account excludes male management and control on the one hand and independent management and control on the other.

3.2 Wider Boundaries of Family Money

The joint account in Indian urban middle income families may also be held with unmarried adult children, parents, siblings and the undivided joint family. A distinctive aspect of personal banking in India is the bank account in the name of the Hindu Undivided Family (HUF) [12]. The HUF can invest and be assessed for tax as a distinct unit [13].

In the Indian qualitative study there are no cases of joint accounts with the Undivided Joint Family. There are however five cases where a person has a joint account with his or her children and one case of a woman having a joint account with her mother who is ill. Accounts with the children are because of protection and convenience. Gauri, 45-54, has joint accounts with her two working sons so that she can deposit and withdraw money for them. Tara, also 45-54 has a joint account with her husband and a child, and another joint account with another child. These joint accounts enable the children, who are studying away from home, to withdraw money from an ATM.

Urmilla, 55-64, does not have a joint account with her working son, but he has given her an ATM card, so that she can withdraw money from his account. These accounts are all with unmarried adult children. Asha and Avinash in Delhi used to have joint accounts with their unmarried daughters. These accounts have ceased now that they are married. However participant observation suggests that the joint account may continue to be used for married children, if the only reason is that of ensuring inheritance by the 'either/or survivor' clause.

4 A Design for Balancing Separateness and Jointness

The design challenges are different in India and Australia. In Australia, the lack of an account which is partially joint and partially separate leads to the use of joint accounts as if they were separate, and separate accounts as if they were joint. There is thus a need for an in-between Joint/Separate Account which acknowledges that money in personal relationships comes in different shades of jointness and separateness across cultures and life stages. In India, the nominal joint bank account, in the absence of a separate account can lead to the person (usually a woman) becoming unbanked.

4.1 The In-between Joint/Separate Account

Enabling a person to choose the level of control he or she wants to exercise will lead to an in-between joint/separate account. This account will be separate in terms of control and joint in some measure in terms of information, transactions and ownership of money after the death of the account holder.

The in-between joint/separate account can be useful in four different contexts. Firstly, it will be useful for couples who want to separate different kinds of money and yet share information and money to some extent with the partner. Secondly it will better fit the needs of fluid relationships, as people will have the ability to designate a partner for a particular time limit. This will prevent the need to set up new accounts and direct debits when a relationship ends. Thirdly, it will help older parents who would like some help with the management of finances, without ceding total control. And fourthly, it will enable accounts to be set up solely for the purpose of internal and international remittances.

There are four essential elements for a personal bank account that can balance the changing mix of jointness and separateness in relationships. These are:

1. Control of the account by setting limits to sharing
2. Enable sharing of information about money in the account
3. Enable shared transactions to the financial limits and time period set by the account holders
4. Ability to ensure that at the death of one of the joint account holders, money will go to the survivor.

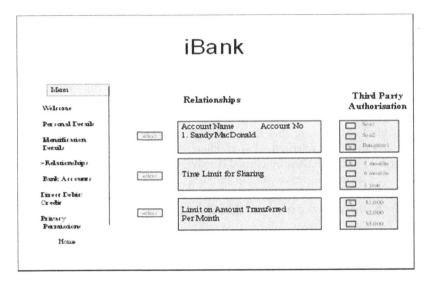

Fig. 1. Personalized iBank options

Personalization is central to the design of the in-between joint/separate account. The starting point for the design interface is a personal profile that would set out a person's preferences and would work across the bank. Some of these preferences have been set out in the model called iBank [14]. It would allow customers to choose between bank defaults, while continuing a trustful (though a more protected) financial relationship with family or professionals. These options would of course need to be usability tested across diverse cohorts and cultures.

Technologically, banks are used to setting limits to the amount of money a person may withdraw from an ATM, transfer to another account, or use for personal credit on a credit card. The challenge will be to enable legacy systems to recognize the customer across the bank and the limits he or she has placed on the use of bank accounts. Banks will also want to derive a revenue stream from this change in the account structure, until it becomes a staple of bank offerings.

4.2   The Unbanked Joint Account

The joint account in India protects the financial interests of the surviving spouse. But if this account is only nominally joint in name – without access to the money or the information – and if that is their only account, it can lead to a person being unbanked. This has immense policy implications in countries like India for the unbanked may be substantially larger than estimated.

A design solution that works in the counseling field may be appropriate. When a couple comes for counseling, it is common practice to interview them together as well as alone[6]. Hence, when a joint bank account is opened, separate accounts for all parties to the joint account could also be opened, unless they already have separate accounts.

---

[6] I am indebted to Anita Anand for this suggestion.

These separate accounts will not solve the issue of information and access to the joint account, but it will offer a separate account to the secondary account holder/s. The advantage of this proposal is that the unbanked person will get a bank account without having to ask for one and without being seen to intrude into the male financial domain. This aspect is particularly important in traditional joint family households where information about money is more likely to flow between the father and the son, rather than husband and wife. It is also important overall for the traditional pattern is one of male control of money.

5 Conclusion

The joint bank account among middle-income married couples has different social meanings and uses in Australia and India. In Australia the account is most often joint with a spouse. The joint account is an instrument of payment for a joint home, shared expenses and information on the one hand and a symbol of the togetherness of the marriage on the other. The new information and communication technologies have increased the potential for sharing information and access to money in the joint account.

In India, joint accounts reflect the broader boundary of domestic money and may be held by married couples, parents and adult children, siblings and the Undivided Joint Family. In India the joint account is primarily used as a way of ensuring that money in the account goes to the survivor when the first named account holder dies. The togetherness of marriage is not signified by a joint account. Both account holders do not necessarily use the joint account for transaction or information.

In India and Australia, the joint account is a blunt instrument for balancing separateness and jointness. It does not necessarily translate to joint management and control. In both countries the joint account may only be nominally joint in name, while being managed separately. In India, the joint account is established for the protection of the survivor, but is most often used as if it were a separate account, with only one person transacting and managing it. In Australia, unlike India, a separate electronic banking account may be used as if it were joint.

This paper demonstrates that bank accounts are culturally and socially shaped as they exist within different legal, banking and family frameworks. Hence user-centered design needs to take into account social practices and cultural values. This approach becomes particularly important with the greater use of mobile remittances and other transfers across borders. The starting point of effective design needs to take into account the different ways people manage money in the household and in banking.

Acknowledgments. I am indebted to the Smart Internet Technology Cooperative Research Centre and the RMIT Global Cities Institute for support for the two qualitative studies on money.

References

1. Zelizer, V.A.: The social meaning of money: "Special monies". American Journal of Sociology 95, 342–377 (1989)
2. Firth, L., Mellor, D., Pang, J.: Data quality issues in practice and theory: A cross-cultural example. Qualitative Research Journal 5, 5–14 (2005)

3. Ho, D.Y.F.: Indigenous Psychologies: Asian Perspectives. Journal of Cross-Cultural Psychology 29, 88–103 (1998)
4. Charmaz, C.: Grounded theory: Objectivist and Constructivist Methods. In: Denzin, N.K., Lincoln, Y.S. (eds.) Handbook of Qualitative Research, pp. 509–535. Sage Publications, London (2000)
5. Mishler, E.G.: Research Interviewing: Context and Narrative. Harvard University Press, Cambridge (1986)
6. Glaser, B.G., Strauss, A.L.: The Discovery of Grounded Theory: Strategies for Qualitative Research. Aldine, Chicago (1967)
7. Clarke, A.E.: Situational Analysis: Grounded Theory after the Postmodern Turn. Sage Publications, Thousand Oaks (2005)
8. Singh, S.: Marriage Money: The Social Shaping of Money in Marriage and Banking. Allen & Unwin, St. Leonards, NSW (1997)
9. Singh, S., Cabraal, A., Demosthenous, C., Astbrink, G., Furlong, M.: Password Sharing: Implications for Security Design Based on Social Practice. In: SIGCHI conference on Human factors in computing systems CHI 2007, San Jose, pp. 895–904. ACM, New York (2007)
10. Singh, S., Cabraal, A., Demosthenous, C., Astbrink, G., Furlong, M.: Security Design Based on Social and Cultural Practice: Sharing of Passwords. In: Aykin, N. (ed.) HCII 2007. LNCS, vol. 4560, pp. 476–485. Springer, Heidelberg (2007)
11. The Banking Codes and Standards Board of India. Code of Bank's Commitments to Customers, http://www.bcsbi.org.in/Code_of_Banks.html
12. Reserve Bank of India. Report on Banking Operations (May 7, 2008), http://rbi.org.in/scripts/PublicationReportDetails.aspx?ID=379
13. The constitution of a Hindu undivided family. Indian Express (March 2, 1998)
14. Singh, S.: Secure shared passwords: The social and cultural centered design of banking. The Journal of Financial Transformation (2008)

Mobile Remittances: Design for Financial Inclusion

Supriya Singh

RMIT University, GPO Box 2476V, Melbourne 3001
Supriya.singh@rmit.edu.au

Abstract. This paper investigates the design requirements for international mobile remittances in the context of users' money management and control in the
household and the family. Through scenarios that draw on remittance literature,
the paper suggests five design principles for mobile remittances that could be a
US$ 41 billion market while empowering women, varying patterns of money
management and control in transnational families and aiding financial inclusion.

Keywords: mobile remittances; money management; money control; empowering women; privacy, financial inclusion.

1 Introduction

*I use(d) to send money home by taxi. It wasn't secure, it was expensive
and it took a long time. Now that I use Wing, it has become convenient
for me. It is secure with low cost ...*
Som Mony, 22 years old, Garment Factory Worker in Cambodia, eld-
est of 10 children[1]

WING is a new business wholly owned by the Australia and New Zealand Banking
Group (ANZ). It launched its controlled pilot with garment workers in November
2008. The company is trying to capture the main remittance corridors from Phnom
Penh to the six closest provinces. This is where over 90 per cent of garment workers
come from today. The workers have been using informal methods of money transfer
including mobile scratch cards, taxis/couriers or taking the money home themselves.
It costs Som Mony 10 per cent to send an average payment of $US 20-30. Now it
costs approximately US$0.50, that is US$0.10 for the person to person transfer, and
then US$0.40 for the cash out

WING's project in Cambodia is one of several projects in the developing countries.
Mobile money transfer projects started from 2003 in the Philippines, Kenya and South
Africa. In most countries the take-up has been encouraging, though the technological
and regulatory infrastructure varies.

The literature on money being transferred by mobile phones is reminiscent of electronic money and e-commerce in the 1990s. There is an overall lack of user studies,
though there are some early exceptions (See [13, 19, 20]). The business excitement
now as then, centers round the lower cost of transactions, the growth of mobile
phones in developing countries, their greater availability and convenience compared

---

[1] Personal communication, Brad Jones, CEO, WING, 13 February 2009.

N. Aykin (Ed.): Internationalization, Design, LNCS 5623, pp. 515–524, 2009.

with bank branches and ATMs. An important difference is that innovation and take-up is happening in the developing countries rather than the developed world.

The picture on the ground is more mixed. Despite the growth of mobile phones in developing countries approximately two billion people, particularly in low income rural areas do not have a mobile phone. This is not counting the estimated 500 million users who may be using shared phones [14].

We know about the successes of mobile money projects in the Philippines, Kenya and South Africa. However, as Mas and Kumar [18] say 'With a few exceptions, the road to implementing mobile banking is littered with discontinued mobile banking projects, failed new technology vendors, and shelved deployment plans' (p. 1).

Security of the technology may be adequate, particularly with SIM-based solutions, but it remains challenging to ensure that the dispensers of cash in the recipient areas have the required liquidity and reliability. There are reports from the Philippines that sometimes the agents do not give the whole amount remitted [6]. In Kenya, a study of the use of M-Pesa, a form of mobile money, found that consumers trust the mobile service provider Safaricom, but do not trust the agents [19].

At present consumer protection measures for the most part remain undefined. Regulators are trying to regulate mobile banking and its agents [18] , but also have to be conscious of 'enablement'[25]. They need to manage 'the delicate balance between sufficient openness and sufficient certainty' (p. 50) to enable new models and markets to emerge but at the same time protect customers who must entrust their money to new mobile money providers.

1.1 The Mobile Remittance Market

Remittances are a large market for mobile money transfers. Formally recorded international remittances to developing countries are estimated at $283 billion in 2008 [27]. In addition, there is an estimated 45 per cent in international remittances that go through informal channels. Figures vary from 15-80 per cent in Asia, 28-46 per cent in Mexico, [3], 53 per cent in Zambia [12].

Building on the experience of the use of electronic money, we know that people will use a mix of channels that match their needs for their varied activities in different social and cultural contexts [30]. Even if mobile remittances can capture only 10 per cent of the US$410 billion in formal and informal remittances to developing countries, it would be a US$41 billion market.

Mobile money transfers can particularly address some of the impediments that encourage informal remittances from the senders' and receivers' perspectives. Senders move to the informal channels because of high cost particularly for smaller amounts, inconvenient access to banks and their inability to prove identity for the formal financial system. Hence mobile remittances will attract senders who are unskilled, unauthorized or in shift work. Mobile remittances will particularly suit receivers in rural unbanked area lack of access to bank accounts, and those who lack financial literacy among poor, rural users or women – the dominant components among the unbanked. Formal transfer mechanisms have seldom been able to serve this segment [3, 17, 23].

Governments are enthusiastic about the conversion of informal remittances to the formal transparent channel. This change will make a larger amount available for securitization of loans. This greater transparency is also seen to reduce the threat of money laundering and aiding terrorism [6].

In order to tap this lucrative mobile remittance market, it is important to understand the characteristics of remittances and the social and cultural context of the users [7]. At present, there are few bridges between the macro picture of the scale of remittances and the anthropological study of the effect of remittances on money management and control in the recipient household. There are no connections at present between mobile use and the dynamics of remittances.

1.2 Empowering Women to Aid Financial Inclusion

Mobile money transfers can potentially increase the percentage of the banked by offering connections between the mobile channel and the more formal financial system. The best estimates of the unbanked, based on the number of accounts per 1000 adults, range from 98.1 per cent in Afghanistan, 83.1% in Kenya, 43.4% in the Philippines; 44.8% in South Africa and 34.3% in India [33]. Hence the enthusiasm around mobile money transfers extends from the business and technological communities to governments, non-government and international organizations.

To date however, the dimensions of the increase in financial inclusion are unclear. The advantages have as yet been tracked mainly to existing customers [33]. Real-time person-to-person transfers have yet to become commonplace [24]. Costs are lower for mobile transactions when compared with banking transactions, but the poor may not always be able to afford them [28].

If the large market for mobile remittances is to aid financial inclusion, it has to help women for they routinely figure as an important group among the unbanked [34]. Hence it is important to ask: Is mobile money helping women have a greater role in the management and control of money in the household? Is it giving women a greater sense of control over their lives?

In section 2, the paper draws on remittance literature to discuss the impact of remittances on the management and control of money in the household and family. Section 3 paints four scenarios of the use of mobile money transfers as they amplify and modify the control and management of money in the household. Based on these scenarios, it outlines user-centered design principles for mobile remittances. The concluding section summarizes the paper and poses questions for further research.

2 Management and Control of Remittances

Domestic and international remittances are important flows of money. They are also an expression of caring for the family and community, and are one of the ways the migrant expresses a continued sense of belonging to both [38]. The migration of a person or a component unit of the extended family leads to changes in the way money is managed and controlled by the migrant/migrant family and in the family left behind.

The mobile phone has already had the effect of encouraging more regular communication within the transnational family, and the micromanaging of remittances [10, 11]. There is however scant literature on the way remittances influence the management and control of money at both ends. As with other domestic technologies it is expected that mobile money will at first re-affirm traditional patterns, but after a series of small changes, may in the end transform them [11, 29].

The literature on money in the household distinguishes between the everyday management of money, that is organising money to make ends meet, and money control, that is the power to make major financial decisions or prevent discussion about them [16, 22, 35-37]. The research focuses on Europe and North America leading to a 'unitary model of household finances' [21]. Relatively little work has been done on money in the family in developing countries. We know little of how money is managed and controlled across gender and generation in the extended families which are common in developing countries. Issues of the privacy of money within the nuclear and extended family still have to be addressed in detail. It thus becomes essential not to transfer the assumptions of the jointness of marital money – common in middle-income Anglo-Celtic households – across cultures and different household structures [31].

Management and control of money has been a tangential issue in literature on transnational families and remittances. Ethnographic studies however give some insights. Kurien [15] and Gulati [9] in their different stories of remittances to Kerala – a state in India with a high percentage of migration particularly to the Middle East - tell stories of women who were empowered because of the remittances. They are the ones who received the money, opened bank accounts for the first time and learnt to manage money and make financial decisions, thus altering the traditional male control of money. In other cases where the woman and children were staying with the husband's family, and the money was sent to the father-in-law, mother-in-law or brother-in-law, the woman became even more dependent.

Kurien's study [15] shows there are important differences between the Muslim, Hindu and Syrian Christian communities in Kerala. She argues that religion, gender, and status shape migration and remittance patterns and are in turn transformed by migration. In the patrilineal Mapilla Muslim community, the wife has no control over household money as the remittances are sent via informal channels to the male relatives. In the matrilineal Ezhava Hindu community, the remittance comes via postal orders to the wife's father or to her, leading to a greater emphasis on girls' education and the matrilineal traditions. Among the Syrian Christians, it is often the wife who is the primary earner and migrant. But if only the husband migrates, the money comes semi-annually via bank drafts to the wife. She manages the investments and the construction of the house.

There is also considerable pressure on the migrants, when they migrate singly or as a family. There can be an overwhelming demand for money and goods from family at home who assume that money is easy to earn overseas. This money-tree syndrome comes at the same time that the migrant family is trying to establish itself [2]. Greater access to telephones in the home country can make this pressure so overwhelming that the migrant family is at times pushed to temporarily disconnect their phone, despite the moral frameworks supporting remittances [1].

In other cases, the author's continuing work on remittances from Australia reveals that the tension results from husbands wanting to show care for the natal family, while the wife is managing a difficult budget. Lack of overt recognition from the family left behind worsens the tension. At times, this leads to the husband trying to keep secret the money he sends home.

A common theme when women migrants send money home is that they lose control over the use of these remittances. Some Sri Lankan women working overseas send money home to find that their husbands, losing the breadwinner role, spend the money on drink without looking after the home or the children.[8].

3 Four Scenarios of Mobile Money Transfers

This section presents personas and scenarios drawing on insights from the ethnographic literature on remittances, money management and control across cultures and the known characteristics of mobile phone usage in developing countries. As Carroll (2000) [4] says scenario-based design can help focus human-computer interaction on the person and activity within a particular context. The detail can evoke reflection, help manage the 'fluidity of design situations' give 'multiple views of an interaction', while at the same time capturing abstractions (p. 43). Personas embedded in the scenarios help further focus attention on the person at the center of design [5].

These scenarios and personas are derived from the lessons learnt from electronic money and the literature on remittances. If mobile remittances are to aid financial inclusion, an essential aspect of the design of mobile remittances is to use the lower cost and convenience of this technology to direct at least a small part of the remittances to the women in the non-migrant household.

3.1 Sending Money to His Mother Privately so She Has Some Personal Money

Amit, 36, works as a doctor in Philadelphia. He comes from a well to do family in Dharamshala, a small town in India. There is enough money available for the family's needs. Amit is single at present and wants his mother to enjoy some of the benefits of his earnings. She has always been a housewife. She gets a housekeeping allowance from her husband. She and her husband have a joint account but he alone manages it. Though she has much influence in the family, this money is directly or indirectly, accountable to her husband.

Amit's issue is: How does he send money to his mother so that she can control this money? He thought of opening a joint account in India in his name and his mother's name. He can freely move money online from his account in Philadelphia to this joint account in India. He could have an arrangement with his mother that she could take out INR 4000 every 2nd of the month. But, at the time he was thinking of it, Dharamshala had only two ATMs, and one often did not work. He also suspected his mother would not be comfortable going alone to the bank which was in the center of the market place.

Sending a postal money order was more expensive. It would also be more public as the postal order would arrive home, leaving his mother to explain.

When Amit went home last year, he bought his mother her own mobile phone. Previously she would use the phones belonging to her husband or daughter. Now he is able to go to his bank and do a mobile transfer. An SMS arrives on his mother's phone giving her a PIN number. She can collect the money from a post office, the offices of the self help groups of a microfinance financial organisation (which acts as an agent for the bank) or the ATM, if it is working.

When the first lot of money arrived, Amit's mother went to the temple to make an offering of gratitude that she had a filial son. Then she posted some money to her niece for her birthday via a postal money order. She also bought a present for Amit, waiting for his visit home.

3.2 Sending Money to His Wife While Leaving Control with His Father

Maryam, 24, lives with her parents-in-law and her children in Kerala, while her husband, Abdullah, 29, works as a carpenter in the Middle East. Though her own parents live in the next village, Maryam's husband wants her to live with his parents.

In the first year of working in the Middle East, Abdullah sent money back every month through 'the tube' – an illegal channel which exchanged money at 1.3 to 1.5 times the exchange rate. He also sent money, gifts and letters with friends who were returning home. These remittances were sent to his father, for he was the head of the household and controlled the money. His letters were also addressed to his parents. One of his gifts to his wife was a mobile phone, so that it was easier to talk to her. Maryam was not a fluent reader.

In one of these phone conversations, Maryam told Abdullah she was worried about the education of their five year old daughter. He sent INR 1000 to his wife via the mobile phone. He rang her up to find out if she had received the SMS for he was unsure what he would do if the money did not reach her. He explained how she could cash it at the nearest ATM. He continued to send money to his father via 'the tube' because of the better exchange rates. He also continued to send money and presents home via his friends.

When Maryam received the SMS, she went with her mother-in-law and brother-in-law to the bank. The bank officer helped her open her first bank account and showed her how to get money out of the ATM and get a receipt. Maryam bought a small present for her mother-in-law, gave a small sum to charity and they began inquiring about tutors in the neighbourhood.

3.3 A Man Cares for His Mother without Telling His Wife

An IT professional, Ibrahim, in Melbourne from the Middle East sends money regularly to his mother. She is well looked after, as she lives with her daughter. Her other son, a doctor, remains in the Middle East. So his mother does not go without. Ibrahim, however feels guilty that he is not contributing to the care of his mother.

He does not share these feelings with his wife, for he knows she will say that his mother does not need the money, and that she will most likely hand it to her daughter.

His solution to this quandary is to open a separate account that his wife does not know about and send money from that account to his mother. Every time he sends money to his mother, he feels good for it allows him to show he cares. However, he worries that one of these days this secret account will get revealed, bringing into question their avowed jointness in the management of money. He moves to mobile remittances to ensure the privacy he seeks.

Ibrahim begins sending his mother mobile money transfers. When she receives the money, she asks her daughter to go to the ATM and get the money. As predicted, she hands over most of the money to her daughter, but also has the pleasure of giving ceremonial packets of money to her two grand daughters.

3.4 Targeting Remittances and Keeping Control

Anna, 32, is from the Philippines and works in Hong Kong as a maid. She has left her two children, 8 and 10 years old in her mother's care. Her husband has been unable to get regular work, and is expected to help in the household.

Anna does not know how her money is being spent. She hears from the other maids about husbands who feeling they lack the provider role, use the money for drinks and gambling. Anna tries to hedge her bets by sending money one month to her mother, and another month to her husband. And through all of this, she worries whether her children are getting the care and education they need.

On their Sunday gatherings in the square, Anna hears from other maids that sending money via the mobile is cheap and reliable. She goes with one of her friends to a participating dealer and sends $50 to her mother. She rings up her mother telling her what is happening and how she should go to a participating dealer in their neighbourhood, show him her electronic money card and he would give her the money. She also tells her mother to make sure she receives the full sum of money for some agents try and keep back a bit for themselves without permission. The mother rings her daughter to confirm receipt.

Anna then begins to use mobile money transfers with more confidence. Now she herself pays the school fees, the tuition fees, money to her mother, and money to her husband for the utility bills and some for his personal expenditure. This way she also gets to keep some of the money as savings for a home she wants to buy once this work contract is over.

3.5 Design Principles for Mobile Remittances

The scenarios above show the importance of placing the design within the social and cultural context of the user, so as to give control to the sender and receiver of remittances. The designers of mobile remittances need to keep in mind cross-cultural differences in the management and control of money across different types of households and families. Privacy of money in the household in the developing countries remains to be studied, but it is often at the center of the management and control of money in the household. It is important to recognize that small changes in the handling of money may over time lead to empowerment. The scenarios illustrate the importance of the following design principles for mobile remittances:

- The starting point should be to design for everybody, including users who lack print and financial literacy. This approach is particularly important when the recipient has little financial literacy and numeracy. Universal design [26] has to be a starting point of the design of mobile remittances, particularly if women are to become banked and financially included as a result of this technology.
- Give a choice of cash-in and cash-out points to make the mobile a preferred channel. The greater choice will widen the options so that the characteristics of the channel meet the needs of the senders and recipients for different kinds of remittances;
- Use the ability of mobile remittances to target multiple recipients. This will enable the remittance to empower women, without directly confronting traditional patterns of money management and control;

- Ensure the privacy of the information of money transfers, keeping in mind the boundaries of information sharing within the family. Issues of fit, privacy and trust are particularly important as they differ across cultures; and
- Engender trust in the transaction, the provider and the agent by clarifying ways of gaining redress.

4 Conclusion

This paper connects the discussion of mobile money transfers with the macro data on international remittances, and anthropological studies of money management and control. Part of the excitement about mobile remittances is that they will tap into a large, growing market. If mobile remittances were to capture only 10 per cent of the estimated US$410 billion in remittances to developing countries in 2008, it would mean a US$ 41 billion market. Governments are encouraging of this development for moving international remittances to formal channels will give them greater options for securitization. Given the large percentages of the unbanked in developing countries, it is hoped that this technology will also aid financial inclusion.

Keeping the user at the center, this paper connects the business and technological literature around mobile transfers with the remittance literature, focusing on insights into money management and control. Through scenarios and personas, it emphasizes the importance of placing the user at the centre of his or her social and cultural context. This is particularly important because money management and control differs across cultures. Universal design also has to be an important starting point to ensure financial inclusion. The social and cultural approach to user centered design can increase the likelihood of getting a slice of the possible US$41 billion market.

This paper in dealing with mobile remittances, money management and control has dealt with one of the large social issues relating to the use of mobile money. Many questions warrant further study. It is important to ask: Is mobile money used differently from other kinds of money? Will mobile money change cash dominated societies? How will people use mobile money on shared phones? Will remittances be divided up and targeted more than they have been? Will credit be available via mobile phones?

These questions will need to be considered if mobile transfers are to continue to grow and keep their promise of empowerment and inclusion.

Acknowledgments. I am indebted to the RMIT Global Cities Institute for support for the study of remittances. I would also like to acknowledge the valuable comments of Chris Law and Brad Jones.

References

1. Akuei, S.R.: Remittances as unforeseen burdens: the livelihoods and social obligations of Sudanese refugees. In: Global Migration Perspectives. Global Commission on International Migration, Geneva, p. 17 (2005)
2. Baldassar, L., Baldock, C.V., Wilding, R.: Families Caring Across Borders: Migration, Ageing and Transnational Caregiving. Palgrave Macmillan, New York (2007)

3. Buencamino, L., Gorbunov, S.: Informal Money Transfer Systems: Opportunities and Challenges for Development Finance, vol. 2005. United Nations, DESA Discussion Paper No. 26 (2002)
4. Carroll, J.M.: Five reasons for scenario-based design. Interacting with computers 13, 43–60 (2000)
5. Cooper, A.: The inmates are running the asylum. SAMS, Indianapolis (1999)
6. Development Prospects Group: Migration and Development Brief 3, vol. 2008. World Bank (2007)
7. Donner, J.: Research Approaches to Mobile Use in the Developing World: A Review of the Literature. The Information Society 24, 140–159 (2008)
8. Gamburd, M.: Breadwinner no more. In: Ehrenreich, B., Hochschild, A.R. (eds.) Global Woman: Nannies, Maids, and Sex Workers in the New Economy, pp. 190–206. Metropolitan Books, New York (2002)
9. Gulati, L.: In the Absence of their Men. Sage Publications, New Delhi (1993)
10. Horst, H.A.: The blessings and burdens of communication:cell phones in Jamaican transnational social fields. Global Networks 6, 143–159 (2006)
11. Horst, H.A., Miller, D.: The Cell Phone: An Anthropology of Communication. Berg, New York (2006)
12. Hougaard, C.: The landscape of remittances in Zambia. FinMark Trust Zambia (2008)
13. Ivatury, G., Pickens, M.: Mobile Phone Banking and Low-Income Customers: Evidence from South Africa, vol. 2009. Consultative Group to Assist the Poor/The World Bank and United Nations Foundation, Washington, DC (2006)
14. Kalba, K.: The Global Adoption and Diffusion of Mobile Phones. Program on Information Resources Policy, Harvard University (2008)
15. Kurien, P.A.: Kaleidoscopic Ethnicity: Internation Migration and the Reconstruction of Community Identities in India. Oxford University Press, New Delhi (2002)
16. Lukes, S.: Power: A Radical View. Macmillan, London (1974)
17. Maimbo, S.M., Adams, R.H., Aggarwal, R., Passas, N.: Migrant Labor Remittances in South Asia. The World Bank, Washington (2005)
18. Mas, I., Kumar, K.: Banking on Mobiles: Why, How, for Whom? In: Focus Note, Washington, vol. CGAP, p. 28 (2008)
19. Morawczynski, O., Miscione, G.: Examining trust in mobile banking transactions: The case of M-Pesa in Kenya. In: Avgerou, C., Smith, M.L., Besselaar, P.v.d. (eds.) Social Dimensions of Information and Communication Technology Policy, pp. 287–298. Springer, Boston (2008)
20. Morawczynski, O.: Surviving in the 'dual system': How M-PESA is fostering urban-to-rural remittances in a Kenyan slum (2008)
21. Pahl, J.: Family finances, individualisation, spending patterns and access to credit. In: The ESRC seminar: University of Exeter, vol. 2008 (2006)
22. Pahl, J.: Money and marriage. Macmillan, London (1989)
23. Passas, N.: Formalizing the Informal? Problems in the national and International Regulation of Hawala Regulatory Frameworks for Hawala and Other Remittance Systems. In: International Monetary Fund, Monetary and Financial Systems Department, Washington, pp. 7–16 (2005)
24. Porteous, D.: Just how transformational is m-banking? FinMark Trust (2007)
25. Porteous, D.: The enabling environment for mobile banking in Africa. Department for International Development, London (2006)
26. Preiser, W.F.E., Ostroff, E. (eds.): Universal Design Handbook. McGraw-Hill Professional, New York (2001)

27. Ratha, D., Mohapatra, S., Xu, Z.: Migration and Development Brief 8, vol. 2008. Migration and Remittances Team
28. Rosenberg, J.: How do you price a mobile banking service?, vol. 2009 (2008)
29. Silverstone, R., Haddon, L.: Design and domestication of information and communication technologies: Technical change and everyday life. In: Mansell, R., Silverston, R. (eds.) Communication by design: The politics of information and communication technologies, pp. 44–74. Oxford University Press, Oxford (1996)
30. Singh, S.: Electronic money: Understanding its use to increase the effectiveness of policy. Telecommunications Policy 23, 753–773 (1999)
31. Singh, S.: Marriage Money: The Social Shaping of Money in Marriage and Banking. Allen & Unwin, St. Leonards, NSW (1997)
32. Soriano, E.: Mobile Remittances from Canada to the Philippines, vol. 2009 (2007); Development Prospects Group, The World Bank Washington (2008)
33. The World Bank Group: Banking the Poor: Measuring Banking Access in 54 Economies. The World Bank, Washington (2009)
34. Thorat, U.: Financial Inclusion – The Indian Experience. In: HMT-DFID Financial Inclusion Conference 2007, Whitehall Place, London, UK (2007)
35. Vogler, C.: Money in the household: some underlying issues of power. The Sociological Review 46, 687–713 (1998)
36. Vogler, C., Lyonette, C., Wiggins, R.D.: Money, power and spending decisions in intimate relationships. The Sociological Review 56, 117–143 (2008)
37. Vogler, C., Pahl, J.: Social and economic change and the organisation of money within marriage. Work, Employment and Society 7, 71–95 (1993)
38. Zelizer, V.A.: The Purchase of Intimacy. Princeton University Press, Princeton, New Jersey (2005)

Author Index

Printed in the United States
By Bookmasters